UNDERSTANDING
Canadian Business

THIRD EDITION

William G. Nickels
University of Maryland

James M. McHugh
St. Louis Community College at Forest Park

Susan M. McHugh
Learning Specialist

Paul D. Berman
McGill University and John Abbott College

McGraw-Hill Ryerson

Toronto Montréal New York Burr Ridge Bangkok Bogatá Caracas Lisbon London Madrid
Mexico City Milan New Delhi Seoul Singapore Sydney Taipei

McGraw-Hill
Ryerson Limited
A Subsidiary of The McGraw·Hill Companies

Understanding Canadian Business
Third Edition

ISBN: 0-07-560767-0

1 2 3 4 5 6 7 8 9 0   VH   0 9 8 7 6 5 4 3 2 1 0

Printed and bound in the United States.

Care has been taken to trace ownership of copyright material contained in this text. The publishers will gladly take any information that will enable them to rectify any reference or credit in subsequent editions.

Editorial Director and Publisher: Evelyn Veitch
Sponsoring Editor: Susan Calvert
Developmental Editor: Karina TenVeldhuis
Supervising Editor: Alissa Messner
Copy Editor: Dawn Hunter
Senior Marketing Manager: Jeff MacLean
Marketing Manager: Bill Todd
Production Co-ordinator: Brad Madill
Cover Designer: Dianna Little
Cover Image: © CP Picture Archive (Phill Snel)
Typesetter: Bookman Typesetting Co.
Printer: Von Hoffmann Press, Inc.

Canadian Cataloguing in Publication Data

Main entry under title:

Understanding Canadian Business

3rd ed.
Includes bibliographical references and index.
ISBN 0-07-560767-0

1. Business.   2. Canada—Commerce.   I. Nickels, William G.

HD31.U5135   2000   650   C99-932822-0

Dedication

To my students—who taught me so much.

Paul D. Berman

About the Authors

Dr. William G. Nickels is an associate professor of business at The University of Maryland, College Park. With more than 30 years of teaching experience, Bill teaches an introduction to business in large sections (250 students) and marketing principles (500 students) each semester. Bill has won the Outstanding Teacher on Campus Award three times, including two out of the past three years. Bill received his M.B.A. degree from Western Reserve University and his Ph.D. from The Ohio State University. He has written a principles of marketing text and a marketing communications text in addition to many articles in business publications. Bill is a marketing consultant and a lecturer on many business topics.

Jim McHugh is an associate professor of business at St. Louis Community College/Forest Park. Jim holds an M.B.A. and has broad experience in both education and business. In addition to teaching several sections of introduction to business each semester for 18 years, Jim maintains an adjunct professorships at Lindenwood University, teaching in the marketing and management areas at both the undergraduate and graduate levels. Jim has conducted numerous seminars in business and maintains several consulting positions with small and large business enterprises in the St. Louis area. He is also involved in a consulting capacity in the public sector.

Susan McHugh is an educational learning specialist with extensive training and experience in adult learning and curriculum development. She holds an M.Ed. degree and has completed her course work for a Ph.D. in education administration with a specialty in adult learning theory. As a professional curriculum developer she has directed numerous curriculum projects and educator training programs. She has worked in the public and private sector as a consultant in training and employee development. In addition to her role as co-author of the text, Susan designed the instructor's manual, test bank, student assessment and learning guide, and the telecourse guide.

Paul D. Berman founded a firm of chartered accountants and was actively engaged in the fields of management consulting, auditing, and taxation for 35 years. These activities involved considerable time overseas. He then went on to John Abbott College near Montreal, where he taught a variety of business courses for more than two decades. Since 1988 he has been teaching an international business policy course at McGill University.

Paul's academic work has also taken him overseas. He has taken students to Denmark and the former East Germany to study these countries' education systems and how they do business. In the late 1980s Paul spent considerable time in China, under a CIDA program, teaching, lecturing, and doing management consulting. This led to a special award from China's highest economic body, the State Economic Commission. Paul has also spent time in Japan, where he engaged in a joint research project with Japanese colleagues and he has conducted seminars in several countries. Paul has also written a book on small business and entrepreneurship.

Brief Contents

Contents

Chapter 4

The Role of Government in Business 92

Chapter 5

Ethical Behaviour, the Environment, and Social Responsibility 126

Chapter 10
Providing World-Class Products and Services 296

Chapter 11
Information Technology: A Vital Component of Management 332

Part 4
Management of Human Resources 359

Chapter 12
Motivating Employees and Building Self-Managed Teams 360

Preface

As we enter the twenty-first century, we are witnessing a high degree of doubt and uncertainty, as well as many difficult problems, in Canada and around the world. A new and complex world is slowly and painfully taking shape. Change dominates the global economic environment—rapid and significant political and technological developments are changing the nature of how we live, prepare for careers, and do business with each other. New challenges present new opportunities.

Understanding Canadian Business had been designed to help students understand and cope with the sometimes bewildering array of information they face in learning about business. It also provides insight into career choices and opportunities, as well as a look at the ethical dilemmas businesses and managers face.

This book marks the third Canadian edition of one of the most popular introductory business texts in Canada and the United States, where it is in its fifth edition. Hundreds of colleges and universities in both countries have adopted this text. *Understanding Canadian Business* is a complete revision with substantial changes in every chapter to properly reflect the Canadian scene. Chapter 11 is new. Chapters 1 to 6 and 14 have been completely rewritten. Nearly all the examples cited are Canadian companies or transnational companies operating in Canada, as are the cases and statistics. The number of chapters, 19, was decided on after careful thought and discussion. This number takes into consideration the limitations of the 13- to 15-week semester or term (commonly found in Canada) and student capacity to absorb information.

MAJOR THEMES

There are four major themes in the book, exemplified by the boxes that appear in each chapter: Spotlight on Small Business, Reaching Beyond Our Borders, Spotlight on Big Business, and the Ethical Dilemma and Ethical Dilemma Review. This structure stresses the vital importance of these factors in the Canadian economy and society.

Small businesses have been the major creators of new jobs for more than two decades; they provide numerous goods and services for both big business and consumers. They create livelihoods for almost two million Canadian men and women who run their own businesses. Many of these entrepreneurs operate businesses out of their own homes, which is a rapidly growing phenomenon. Small business is responsible for a great deal of computer software development and other technological innovations. In addition, a large and growing number of women are setting up small businesses and achieving great success. *Spotlight on Small Business* focuses on this important sector of the Canadian economy.

Reaching Beyond Our Borders underlines the importance of international business in today's world. Major pacts, such as the North American Free Trade Agreement and the European Union, have emerged. These pacts have had a major impact on Canada; the need to be internationally competitive has permeated every aspect of Canadian business. This is particularly important since more than one-third of our economy is dependent on exports. This need has led to an unprecedented restructuring of companies and has stimulated major technological developments. On the downside, these developments have triggered massive layoffs and unemployment.

Spotlight on Big Business highlights the crucial role big businesses play in Canada. They produce most of the products we consume or export and they employ many people. Big businesses are essential in many industries, such as automobile and airplane manufacturing, pulp and paper mills, telecommunications, and pharmaceuticals, where large amounts of capital are required to start up and operate.

Business ethics have received a great deal of attention in both the media and in academic research. Canadian society's expectations about the standards of behaviour of managers of business, government, and other organizations has changed significantly in recent years. Managers, executives, and businesses in general are now expected to be concerned with the effect of their decisions and actions on society. In addition, they are expected to apply ethical standards in decision making and in dealing with employees, minorities, and other countries. The environment has become a major concern and businesses are expected to do their utmost to protect the environment, and in some cases, to bear the costs of cleaning up past misuses. Most large companies have set up departments to ensure that ethical and environmental standards are set and maintained. The sections on Ethical Dilemmas and Ethical Dilemma Reviews provide scenarios in which students must think about ethical standards in decision making.

REAL WORLD EMPHASIS

The Canadian author has applied his extensive practical experience to ensure that the book portrays the real business world. Thus, most chapters contain new material not usually found in other texts. The impact of technological change is clearly noted in every aspect of business—accounting, marketing, information systems, finance, production, human resources, and management in general. In accounting, computers have forever changed the traditional sequential nature of recording transactions and producing reports and financial statements. Production and operations have been revolutionized by computers. In addition, the emphasis on quality and employee participation in management has changed the nature of how we manage.

Many of these chapters contain text, figures, and illustrations that highlight information in a way not previously seen. In Chapter 6, a comparison of the pros and cons of each form of ownership is an example. A comparison of the different modes of financing in Chapter 19 is another example. Realistic guidelines for increasing chances of success when starting and operating a small business are illustrated in Chapter 7. A great deal of new and empirically based material is introduced in this important chapter.

The ever-increasing importance of the Internet in the real world of business is demonstrated in many chapters, especially in Chapter 11 on using technology to manage information and in those on marketing—Chapters 15, 16, and 17. The Internet Challenges at the end of each chapter highlight the importance of this technological tool. Margin web addresses and short descriptions, researched by the Canadian author and by Ray Klapstein of Dalhousie University, provide sites relevant to chapter material.

···· ▬▬ ····

HISTORICAL PERSPECTIVE

A historical perspective has been provided in many chapters to help illustrate the source of certain developments so they can be projected into the future. This applies to the first chapter on trends affecting business: how technology is a prime mover of change, the rapid growth of home-based businesses, the growing importance of environmental issues and sustainable development, and so forth. It also applies to Chapter 14 on labour–management issues, where a knowledge of the history of the union movement is important in understanding the difficulties in that relationship today. Current conditions require a major change in attitudes of both labour and management; cooperation between management and labour is critical for the future. Similarly, the role of government (Chapter 4) and ethical issues (Chapter 5) can be best understood if we know where we are coming from so we can more readily move into the future.

It is the Canadian author's belief, based on his business and teaching experience and on the reviews of the second edition and the manuscript for the third edition, that students and instructors will find *Understanding Canadian Business* informative, thought provoking, and challenging.

···· ▬▬ ····

STRUCTURAL CHANGES FROM
THE SECOND EDITION

In response to suggestions from adopters of the second edition and reviewers of drafts of the third edition, a number of important changes have been made.

1. The appendix *Using Technology to Manage Information* has been made into Chapter 11, which covers this important topic more comprehensively.
2. The role of the Internet is given important prominence throughout the text and especially in the Internet Challenges at the end of each chapters.
3. The chapter boxes entitled *Making Ethical Decisions* have been transformed into the more useful opening sections in each chapter called *Ethical Dilemma*.
4. Responses to these ethical dilemmas are given at the end of each chapter by two important Canadian executives. The two executives are Mr. Normand Bédard, vice-president, human resources, Cambior Inc., and Mr. Dennis Reilley, general manager, Pratt & Whitney Canada International Inc. It should be noted that both Mr. Bédard and Mr. Reilley have given their personal opinions on these ethical dilemmas and these opinions do not necessarily reflect those of their companies.

···· ▬▬ ····

IMPORTANT CURRENT ISSUES AND TRENDS

The two major trends affecting economies and business are **technology** and **globalization**. A third major trend is the need for the **ethical behaviour and social responsibility** of businesses. As all three trends continue their rapid development, they are given prominence throughout the book. In addition, the following are some of the important current issues and developments that are given attention:

- economic problems of East and South Asia
- ISO 14,0000 and 9000 certification
- explosive growth and impact of the Internet
- marketing issues and trends
  - pleasing the customer
  - integrated communication
  - infomercials and interactive television
  - relationship marketing
- mass communication
- self-managed teams and employee empowerment
- cross-functional cooperation between departments
- competitive benchmarking
- trade treaties and common markets
- outsourcing
- privatization and deregulation
- small-business networking
- home-based work and businesses
- changing nature of work
- quality-driven operations

···· ▬▬ ····
PEDAGOGICAL FEATURES

Here are the major pedagogical devices used in the text.

- **Learning goals.** Tied directly to the chapter summaries and questions, these learning goals help students preview what they are supposed to know after reading each chapter. Students then test that knowledge by answering the questions in the summaries. The Study Guide is also closely linked to the learning goals as part of the total integrated teaching, learning, and testing system.
- **Opening profiles.** Each chapter begins with a profile of a person whose career illustrates an important point covered in the chapter. Not all the personalities are famous since many of them work in small businesses or nonprofit organizations. These profiles provide a transition between chapters and a good introduction to the text material.
- **Ethical dilemmas.** Each chapter contains an Ethical Dilemma that business people of today may face. Students are asked to consider the dilemma as they make their way through the chapter. At the end of the chapter, the dilemma is revisited, with commentary from two real business executives.
- **Progress checks.** Throughout the chapters there are Progress Checks that ask students to remember what they have just read. If students are not understanding and retaining the material, the Progress Checks will stop them and show them that they need to review before proceeding. We have all experienced times when we were studying and

our minds wandered. Progress Checks are a great tool to prevent that from happening for more than a few pages.

- **Critical thinking questions.** These new and unique inserts, found throughout each chapter, ask students to pause and think about how the material they are reading applies to their own lives. This device is an excellent tool for linking the text material to the students' past experience to enhance retention. It greatly increases student involvement in the text and course.

- **Boxes.** Each chapter includes boxed inserts that apply the chapter concepts to particular themes, including *small business, big business,* and *global business.* Although examples of such topics are integrated throughout the text, these boxes highlight the application in a particular area.

- **Key terms.** Key terms are developed and reinforced through a four-tiered system. They are introduced in boldface, repeated and defined in the margin, listed at the end of each chapter with page references, and defined in a glossary at the end of the text.

- **Photo and illustration legends.** Each photo and illustration in the text is accompanied by a short paragraph that shows the relevance of the visual to the material in the text. The accompanying descriptions help students understand what is being shown in the graphic and how it applies to the text. To enhance their pedagogical value, many of these photos were commissioned specifically for use in this edition.

- **Interactive summaries.** The end-of-chapter summaries are directly tied with the learning goals and are written in a unique question-and-answer format. Answering the questions and getting immediate feedback helps prepare students for quizzes and exams. Students have been extremely positive about this format.

- **Developing workplace skills.** Developing Workplace Skills activities are designed to increase student involvement in the learning process. Some of these miniprojects require library work, but many of them involve talking with people to obtain their reactions and advice on certain subjects. Students then come to class better prepared to discuss the topics at hand. These assignments can be divided among groups of students so they can learn a great deal from outside sources and about teamwork without any one student having to do too much work.

- **Practising management decisions.** Each chapter concludes with two short cases to allow students to practise managerial decision making. They are intentionally brief and meant to be discussion starters rather than to take up an entire class period. The answers to the cases are in the instructor's manual.

···· ▬▬▬▬ ····

SUPPLEMENTS: AN INTEGRATED TEACHING AND TESTING SYSTEM

The resource package for instructors is a very comprehensive set of tools that gives instructors a wide choice. No other introductory business text package is as easy to use and as fully integrated. To accomplish this integration, the authors of the text prepared the *Instructor's Manual,* the *Test Bank, Computest,* and the *Transparency Masters.*

INSTRUCTOR'S MANUAL   This detailed manual gives close guidance for each chapter lesson. It provides a topic outline, key terms, lecture outline, a detailed planning table, application exercises, answers to case questions, lecture enhancers, and other helpful material.

COMPUTERIZED TEST BANK   Brownstone's Diploma Testing is the most flexible, powerful, and easy-to-use computerized testing system available in higher education. The Diploma system allows the test maker to create a test as a print version, as an online version (to be delivered in a computer lab), and as an Internet version. Diploma includes a built-in Gradebook for instructors. The test bank contains some 4000 questions, including multiple-choice questions, true or false questions, and essay questions.

POWERPOINT® PRESENTATIONS   The PowerPoint® presentation package includes a series of slides for each chapter of the textbook.

ONLINE LEARNING CENTRE   <www.mcgrawhill.ca/college/nickels> contains instructor and student resource material linked to *Understanding Canadian Business*.

VIDEO   A complementary video is available in VHS format to accompany the text.

STUDY GUIDE   The Study Guide reinforces what is learned in the text. It is not merely a synopsis of the text nor a collection of multiple-choice questions. The exercises contain various forms of questions that require students to write their answers so that the material becomes part of them. It is not an easy study guide; it is an effective one that demands active participation. If your students use this guide, they will be fully prepared for class discussions and exams. The Study Guide also contains a new feature entitled *Driver's Ed for the Information Superhighway*, designed to aid students in manoeuvring on the Web.

···· ▬▬ ····

ACKNOWLEDGMENTS

Many friends, colleagues, academics, entrepreneurs, and managers have made important contributions, in different ways, to *Understanding Canadian Business*. There are too many to be able to thank them all individually. I would like to single out the reviewers from across the country, who on several occasions took the time to review different versions of the manuscript for the second or third edition. They made invaluable suggestions to improve the quality and coverage and also noted any inaccuracies or weaknesses. I would like to extend my deepest thanks to all of these people, whose names are listed below:

Jim Alsop—Seneca College

Barry E. C. Boothman—University of New Brunswick

Nina Cole—Brock University

Brad Davis—Brock University

Dorothy Derksen—Red River College

Jane Doyle—Sheridan College

Stephen Drew—McMaster University

David Fleming—George Brown College

Chris Gadsby—British Columbia Institute of Technology

Sean Hennessey—University of Prince Edward Island

Geraldine Joosee—Lethbridge Community College

Ray Klapstein—Dalhousie University

George Knight—Grant MacEwan Community College

Lionel Lustgarten—Vanier College

Don Mask—Dawson College

Mike Manjuris—Ryerson Polytechnical University

Blane McIntosh—Camosun College

Richard C. Powers—University of Toronto

Adele Stirpe—Seneca College

Gerry Stephenson—Okanagan College

Jim Tehranian—Kwantlen College

Keith Willoughby—University of Saskatchewan

I would like to give special thanks to the two executives, Mr. Normand Bédard and Mr. Dennis Reilley, who took time out of their busy schedules to peruse the Ethical Dilemmas posed at the beginning of each chapter and to come up with suggested responses. Their many years of practical experience in the real world of Canadian business, which lend important weight to their opinions, will be greatly appreciated by students.

Thanks are also due to the following McGraw-Hill Ryerson staff who worked hard to make this book a reality: editorial director and publisher, Evelyn Veitch; sponsoring editor, Susan Calvert; supervising editor, Alissa Messner. Also thanks to copy editor, Dawn Hunter, and photo researcher, Elke Price. Special thanks to developmental editor, Karina TenVeldhuis, who, often under considerable time pressures, bore the brunt of my endless queries, delays, and stubbornness and with whom it was a pleasure to work.

Finally, many thanks to my children, Victor, David, Joanne, Judith, and Rae. I owe them a great deal for their patience and cooperation as I plied them with questions and requests relating to their various fields of expertise. Finally, I would like to express my deep appreciation to my wife, Esther Berman, whose patience, direct and indirect assistance in so many ways, and critical comments over an extended period of time really made this book possible.

PAUL D. BERMAN

Secrets to Your Success (Confidential for Students Using This Text)

Prologue

This is an exciting and challenging time to be studying business. Never before have there been more opportunities to become a successful business person anywhere in the world. And never before have there been more challenges. Understanding basic principles and learning to apply those principles effectively is an important aid to success. There are some secrets to success that can make the task easier and give you an edge over the competition. One of the purposes of this prologue and of the entire text is to help you learn these principles and some of the secrets of success that will help you not only in this course but in your entire career.

Experts say it is likely that today's college and university graduates will hold seven or eight different jobs in their lifetime. That means you will have to be flexible and adjust your strengths and talents to new opportunities as they become available. Many of the best jobs of the future don't even exist today. Learning has become a lifelong job. You will have to constantly update your skills.

This book and this course together will be an important learning experience. They're meant to help you understand business so that you can use business principles throughout your life. But you don't have to be in business to use business principles. You can use marketing principles to get a job and to sell your ideas to others. Similarly, you'll be able to use management skills and general business knowledge wherever you go and in whatever career you pursue in business, government, or not-for-profit organizations. What you learn now could help you be a success for the rest of your life.

···· ▬▬▬ ····

YOU ALREADY KNOW ONE SECRET: THE VALUE OF A COLLEGE OR UNIVERSITY EDUCATION

The gap between the earnings of high-school graduates and college and university graduates is growing every year. It now ranges from 60 to 70 percent. That is, college and university graduates may make 70 percent more than high-school graduates. Thus, what you invest in your education is likely to pay you back many times. That doesn't mean there aren't good careers available to non–college or university graduates. It just means that those with an education are more likely to have higher earnings over their lifetime.

To get the most out of your education, we encourage you to take any opportunity that arises to use the computer and to learn the latest computer applications, including spreadsheets, databases, word processing, desktop publishing, and e-mail, as well as using the Internet. The investment you make now in developing computer skills will likely be quite rewarding. It will be even more valuable if you study your text carefully and make the effort to complete all the exercises in the Study Guide.

···· ▬▬▬ ····

THE SECRET TO STARTING A SUCCESSFUL CAREER

Almost all of us want to find a rewarding career and to be successful and happy. We just find it hard to decide what that career should be. Even many of those who have relatively successful careers continue to look for something more fulfilling, more challenging, and more interesting. If you're typical of many students, you may not have any idea what career you'd like to pursue. That isn't necessarily a big disadvantage in today's fast-changing job market. There are no perfect or certain ways to prepare for the most interesting and challenging jobs of tomorrow, many of which have yet to be created. Rather, you should continue your education, develop strong computer skills, improve your verbal and written communication skills, learn other languages, and remain flexible while you explore the job market.

One purpose of this text is to introduce you to the wide variety of careers available in business and management. You'll learn about production, marketing, finance, accounting, management, economics, and more. At the end of the course, you should have a much better idea about what careers would be best for you and what careers you would *not* enjoy. Not only that, you'll be prepared to use basic business terms and concepts that are necessary for achieving success in any organization—including government agencies, charities, cultural institutions, and social causes—or in your own small business.

••• GETTING STARTED •••

A great place to start in your career search is with a course like this one. Each chapter in this book will begin with a profile of someone in the business world who exemplifies what the chapter is about. Many of the people you'll meet in the profiles learned the hard way that it's easy to fail in business if you don't know what you're doing. Reading these stories is a good way to learn from the experiences of others.

••• ASSESSING YOUR SKILLS AND PERSONALITY •••

The earlier you can do a personal assessment of your interests, skills, and values, the better it will be for you in finding some career direction. In recognition of this need, many schools offer self-assessment programs. Many schools use a software exercise that creates personalized lists of occupations based on your interests and skills, and provides information about different careers and the preparation each requires. The Strong-Campbell Interest Inventory and the Meyers-Briggs Personality Indicator can be used to reinforce the results. Visit your school's placement centre, career lab, or library and learn what programs are available to you.

It would be helpful to use one or more self-assessment programs early in this course so you can determine, while you're learning about the different business fields, which ones most closely fit your interests and skills. Self-assessment will help you determine the kind of work environment you'd prefer (for example, technical, social service, or business); what values you seek to fulfill in a career (for example, security, variety, or independence); what abilities you have (for example, creative/artistic, numerical, or sales); and what important job characteristics you stress most (for example, income, travel, or amount of job pressure).

Even if you're more than 25 years old, an assessment of your skills will help you choose the right courses and career path to follow. Many others have taken such tests because they are not satisfied with what they're doing and are seeking a more rewarding occupation. Armed with the results of your self-assessment, you, too, are more likely to make a career choice that will be personally fulfilling.

••• LEARNING PROFESSIONAL BUSINESS STRATEGIES •••

Business professionals have learned the importance of networking and of keeping files on subjects that are important to them. These are two secrets to success that students should begin practising now. One thing that links all students is the need to retain what they learn in business courses. While it's important for you to learn about various careers and businesses, you may tend to forget such data. You need a strategy to help you remember what you've learned. It's also extremely important to keep the names of contact people at various organizations. In addition, you may want to keep facts and figures of all kinds about the economy and business-related subjects. These are all reasons why you should develop resource files.

An effective way to become an expert on almost any business subject is to set up your own information system. Periodically you should store this data on computer disks for retrieval on your personal computer and to access professional databases as business people do. Meanwhile, it's effective to establish a comprehensive paper filing system.

If you start now, you'll soon have at your fingertips information that will prove invaluable for use in term papers and throughout your career. Few students do this filing, and, as a consequence, most lose much of the information they read in college or university or thereafter. *Developing this habit is one of the most effective ways of educating yourself and having the information available when you need it.* The only space you'll need to start is a small corner of your room to hold a portable file box. In these files you might put your course notes, with the names of your professors and the books you used, and so on. You may need this information later for employment references. Also, be sure to keep all the notes you make when talking with people about careers, including salary information, courses needed, and contacts.

Each time you read a story about a firm that interests you, either cut it out of the publication or photocopy it and then place it in an appropriate file. You might begin with files labelled Careers, Small Business, Economics, Management, and Resource People. You might summarize the article briefly on a self-sticking note and stick this summary on the front for later reference.

You definitely want to have a personal data file titled Credentials for My Résumé or something similar. In that file, you'll place all reference letters and other information about jobs you have held. Soon you'll have a tremendous amount of information available to you. You can add to these initial files until you have your own comprehensive information system.

Business people are constantly seeking ways to increase their knowledge of the business world and to increase their investment returns. One way they do so is by watching U.S. television shows such as *Wall $treet Week*, and the *Nightly Business Reports*, or in Canada, *Newsworld's Business News*. Watching such programs is like getting a free graduate education in business. Try viewing some of these shows or listening to similar shows on the radio, and see which ones you like best. Take notes and put them in your files. Another way, one of the best, to increase your business knowledge is to read your local newspaper and *The Globe and Mail* or the *National Post*. The monthly *Canadian Business* magazine is also a good source of business news. Keep up with the business news in your local area so you know what jobs are available and where.

···· ▬▬▬ ····

ANOTHER SECRET WEAPON: GOOD MANNERS

Good manners are back and for a good reason. As the world becomes increasingly competitive, the gold goes to the person who shows an extra bit of polish. The person who makes a good impression opens the door to jobs and promotions, or clinches the deal.

Too often professionals spend their energies becoming experts in their particular field, often neglecting other concerns. They look great on paper and many even get through the interview, then they get to the workplace and may not fit in. They have reached their destination and their behaviour becomes critical, but they haven't learned how to get along with people.

One source of irritability and rude behaviour within a company may result from downsizing and the extra work and stress it produces. Even under stressful conditions, however, it is important to maintain your composure at work and not lose your cool.

The lesson is this: You can have good credentials, but a good presentation is just as important. You can't neglect etiquette, or somewhere in your career you will be at a competitive disadvantage because of your inability to use good manners or to maintain your composure in tense situations.

··· LEARNING TO ACT LIKE A PROFESSIONAL ···

You can probably think of contrasting examples of sports stars who have earned a bad reputation by not acting professionally (e.g., swearing, hitting, criticizing teammates in front of others, and so on). People in professional sports are fined if they are late to meetings or refuse to follow the rules established by the team and coach. Business professionals also must follow set rules; many of these rules are not formally written anywhere, but every successful business person learns them through experience.

You can begin the habits now that will make for great success when you start your career. Those habits include the following:

1. *Making a good first impression.* "You have seven seconds to make an impression. People see your clothes before you even open your mouth. And make no mistake, everything you say following those first few moments will be weighed by how you look," says image consultant Aleysha Proctor. You don't get a second chance to make a good first impression. Skip the fads and invest in high-quality, classic clothes. Remember, "high-quality" is not necessarily the same as "expensive." Take a clue as to what is appropriate at any specific company by studying the people there who are most successful. What do they wear? How do they act?

2. *Focusing on good grooming.* Be aware of your appearance and its impact on those around you. Consistency is essential. You can't project a good image by dressing up a few times a week and then show up looking like you're getting ready to mow a lawn. Wear appropriate, clean clothing and accessories. It is not appropriate to wear wrinkled shirts or to have shirttails hanging out of your pants.

3. *Being on time.* When you don't come to class or to work on time, you're sending a message to your teacher or boss. You're saying, "My time is more important than your time. I have more important things to do than be here." In addition to the lack of respect tardiness shows to your teacher or boss, it rudely disrupts the work of your colleagues. Promptness may not be a priority in some circles, but in the workplace promptness is essential. But being punctual doesn't always mean just being on time. Executive recruiter Juan Menefec recalls a time he arrived at 7:40 A.M. for an 8:00 A.M. meeting only to discover he was the last one there. "You have to look around, pay attention to the corporate culture and corporate clock," says Menefec. To develop good work habits, it is important to get to class on time and not to leave early.

4. *Practising considerate behaviour.* Considerate behaviour includes listening when others are talking and not reading the newspaper or eating in class. Don't interrupt others when they are speaking. Wait for your turn to present your views in classroom discussions. Of course,

eliminate all words of profanity from your vocabulary. Use appropriate body language by sitting up attentively and not slouching. Sitting up has the added bonus of helping you stay awake! Professors and managers get a favourable impression from those who look and act alert. That may help your grades in school and your advancement at work.

5. *Being prepared.* A business person would never show up for a meeting without having read the materials assigned for that meeting and being prepared to discuss the topics of the day. To become a professional, one must practise acting like a professional. For students, that means reading assigned materials before class, asking questions and responding to questions in class, and discussing the material with fellow students.

From the minute you enter your first job interview until the day you retire, people will notice whether you follow the proper business etiquette. Just as traffic laws enable people to drive more safely, business etiquette allows people to conduct business with the appropriate amount of dignity. How you talk, how you eat, and how you dress all create an impression on others.

Business etiquette may have a different meaning in different countries. It is important, therefore, to learn the proper business etiquette for each country you visit. Areas that require proper etiquette include greeting people (shaking hands is not always appropriate); eating; giving gifts; handling business cards; and conducting business. Honesty, high ethical standards, and good character (e.g., reliability and trustworthiness) are important ingredients to success in any country. Ethics is so important to success that we include ethics discussions throughout the text and in a separate chapter.

···· ▬▬▬ ····

THE SECRET OF THE RESOURCES FOR THIS COURSE

College and university courses are best at teaching you concepts and ways of thinking about business. However, to learn firsthand about real-world applications, you will need to explore and interact with actual businesses. Textbooks are like comprehensive tour guides in that they tell you what to look for and where to look, but they can never replace experience.

This text, then, isn't meant to be the only resource for this class. In fact, it's not even the primary resource. Your professor will be much better than the text at responding to your specific questions and needs. This book is just one of the resources your instructor can use to help you understand what the business world is all about. There are six basic resources for the class including the text and study guide:

1. *The professor.* One of the most valuable facets of college or university is the chance to study with experienced professors. Your instructor is more than a teacher of facts and concepts. As mentioned above, an instructor is a resource who's there to answer questions and guide you to the answers for others. It's important for you to develop a friendly relationship with all of your professors. One reason for doing so is that many professors get job leads they can pass on to you. Professors are also excellent references for future jobs. By being a serious student and following the rules of etiquette outlined above, you can create a good impression, which will be valuable should you ask a professor to write a letter of recommendation for you. Finally, your professor is

4. *Boxes*. Each chapter contains a number of boxes that offer extended examples or discussions of concepts in the text. This material is designed to highlight key concepts and to make the book more interesting to read. One of the questions most frequently asked by our students is: "Will the stuff in the boxes be on the test?" Make sure you read the boxes whether your instructor tests you on them or not—they're often the most interesting parts! The boxes cover major themes of the book: (1) small business (Spotlight on Small Business); (2) big business (Spotlight on Big Business); and (3) global business (Reaching Beyond Our Borders).

5. *End-of-chapter summaries*. The summaries are not mere reviews of what has been said in the text. Rather, they're written in question-and-answer form, much like a classroom dialogue. This format makes the material more lively and should help you remember it better. The summaries are directly tied to the Learning Goals so that you can see whether you've accomplished the chapter's objectives.

6. *Developing Workplace Skills exercises*. Regardless of how hard textbook writers and professors try to make learning easier, the truth is that students tend to forget most of what they read and hear. To really remember something, it's best to do it. That's why there are Developing Workplace Skills sections at the end of each chapter. The purpose of Developing Workplace Skills questions is to suggest small projects that reinforce what you've read and help you develop the skills you need to succeed in the workplace. These activities will help you develop skill in using resources, interpersonal skills, skills in managing information, skills in understanding systems, and computer skills.

7. *Internet Challenges*. The Internet exercises serve two purpose: to enhance your understanding of the concepts presented in the chapter and to build your Internet skills. Many of these exercises involve interactive activities that help you apply the chapter's concepts. It is important to remember that the Internet is constantly evolving and that Internet addresses (known as uniform resource locators, or URLs) are subject to constant and frequent change. If an address in an exercise is no longer available, you can impress your instructor by finding a Web site with similar information and completing the exercise there.

8. *Practising Management Decisions*. The management decision cases give you another chance to think about the material and apply it in real-life situations. Don't skip the cases even if they're not reviewed in class. They're an integral part of the learning process because they enable you to think about and apply what you've studied.

If you use all of these learning aids plus the Study Guide, you will not simply take a course in business. Instead, you will have actively participated in a learning experience that will help you greatly in your chosen career. The most important secret to success may be to enjoy what you are doing and to do your best in everything. You can't do your best without taking advantage of all the learning aids that are available to you.

Now you know the secrets to succeeding in this course and in your career. Begin applying these secrets now to gain an edge on the competition. Good luck.

Part 1

Business Trends: Cultivating a Business in Diverse Global Environments

Major Trends Affecting Canadian Business

Chapter 1

LEARNING GOALS

After you have read and studied this chapter, you should be able to

1 explain the importance and impact of technological developments.

2 describe what is meant by the *information age* and what its implications are.

3 discuss the globalization of business and why it is so important for Canadian companies.

4 identify how big business is becoming more competitive and the pressures to do so.

5 explain why small and home-based businesses have become so popular.

6 show how the service sector has replaced manufacturing as the principal provider of jobs, but why manufacturing remains vital for Canada.

7 explain current population trends and their major impact on business.

8 describe how environmental and other ethical issues play a major role in all business planning and actions.

9 show how jobs and careers are affected by the trends discussed in the chapter.

Back in 1979 Robin King had a wild idea: he wanted to establish a computer-animation program at Sheridan College in Oakville, Ontario. At that time very few people had even heard of computers much less computer animation. Yet here was this visionary pushing to develop a program that probably seemed like science fiction.

Today, as chairman of media and communications at Sheridan, Robin King is receiving accolades for having developed a program that is turning out the leading computer animators in North America. Every year, top animation companies from the United States, including leading Hollywood production companies, head for Sheridan College to interview graduating students for employment. Starting salaries are in the US$45,000 range.

Other educational institutions that have developed similar programs are Algonquin College in the Ottawa area, and three in the Vancouver area: Capilano College, The Emily Carr Institute of Art and Design, and The Vancouver Film Institute. Today there is a proliferation of public and private organizations offering such programs. This proliferation of institutions with expert computer animation programs, combined with the success of the 1996 film *Toy Story*, which was entirely computer generated, led the Disney Company to establish two Canadian locations, one in Toronto and one in Vancouver. Disney wanted to be near the source of the talent necessary to facilitate production of other computer-animated films. Graduates of Sheridan and other colleges have animated many other films including *Men in Black* and *Antz*.

For Sheridan this success has caused such an increase in enrollment in the program that King reports they are limiting the size of classes to control quality. Sheridan is now erecting a $35 million Centre for Animation and Emerging Technologies. The college also has received two research grants, each for $1.5 million, from the Ontario government and private sources for a visual design project.

Robin King is an example of how technologically oriented forward thinking creates significant competitive advantages for institutions, companies, and countries and thereby significant employment opportunities for Canadians. King is one of the pioneers who have given Canada its global reputation in the computer-animation field. King also heads his own consulting firm, Imagina Corp., which specializes in new technologies. Imagina is currently advising a new school being built in Tokyo for computer animation. Other projects are also in progress.

PROFILE

Robin King—A Canadian with Advanced Technological Vision

Sources: Interview with Robin King, February 15, 1996, and October 26, 1998; Janet McFarland and Gayle MacDonald, "Sheridan's a Draw for Film Makers," *Globe and Mail, Report on Business*, December 4, 1995, p. B6.

Ethical Dilemma

FACING THE ISSUES

As you work your way through the chapter, you will see that, in their ceaseless quest for competitive advantage and growth, companies are constantly searching for the lowest-cost countries to manufacture their products and services. For the same reason, companies are also driven to adopt the latest manufacturing and information technologies. These twin trends often cause hardship for company employees and towns where operations are located when plants and offices are closed and employ- ees are terminated. At the same time the vast expansion of the economies of many countries has put enormous pressure on our fragile environment, causing problems for the people who inhabit this globe, including Canadians. You will read about these issues in many chapters in this book. The question is, how do we go about solving these difficult problems? Toward the end of the chapter you will see an attempt to come to grips with these difficult issues.

<www.sheridanc.on.ca>

For more information about Sheridan's computer-anima-tion program, visit its Web site. Click on the icons avail-able to see what Sheridan's program does and discover its impressive achievements. Pay particular attention to its *media releases*.

business
An organization that manufactures or sells goods or services in an attempt to generate a profit.

TRENDS

In this chapter we will explore some of the significant trends (many of which nourish each other) that are revolutionizing the nature of the business world. It is this new world in which you will find yourself when you graduate.

Before proceeding let us define what a *business* is. A **business** is an orga-nization that manufactures or sells goods or services in an attempt to gener-ate a profit. A business may be an Internet service provider selling its service to individuals, companies, educational institutions, libraries, hospitals, or governments, or it may be part of a complex chain of providers of goods. An example is a chemical company that sells raw materials to a pharmaceutical company, which manufactures drugs that it sells to wholesalers, that in turn sell to pharmacies, which sell to consumers.

Trends have a profound impact on the kind of jobs and careers that will be available to you after you graduate from college. Specifically, what should you be planning and doing to take advantage of the opportunities that will be there? The last section in this chapter will help to provide answers to this ques-tion. These trends also raise significant environmental and other ethical issues. (See the Ethical Dilemma box above.)

••• TWO MAIN TRENDS: TECHNOLOGY AND GLOBALIZATION •••

The two most important universal trends for business are the extremely rapid developments in technology—the *technological revolution*—and the *globaliza-tion* of business, which has become totally international in nature. Computers, robots, lasers, fibre optics, satellites, and many other significant advances in technology have radically altered the way we produce and what we produce, the way we buy and sell things, the way people and businesses communicate, the manner and speed with which goods and information are sent and received, the way funds are obtained, and just about everything else in the busi-ness world. The Profile of Robin King and the world of computer animation are good examples of such radical changes. Advances in communication and transportation technologies have made the planet into a very small place and have made it possible for business to operate globally. Uptown and downtown may now be, and often are, thousands of kilometres away without causing any great inconvenience. When you phone Air Canada or American Airlines or any large company, you do not know where the person answering you is located. Just try asking an airline what the weather is like and you may find out that the call centre is in Calgary or Denver, Colorado, or Saint John, N.B.

These two dominant trends have meant a drastic shake-up for business around the globe: giant companies merging into still larger entities; employees and managers laid off by the millions; long-term job security replaced by short-term or temporary jobs; high and persistent unemployment rates, especially among the young; new technologies sprouting weekly; barriers to world trade dropping steadily; fierce competition for consumers' money; the economic awakening of East Asia; companies scouring the world for low-cost production areas.

Competition is so intense that many companies and governments have stepped up efforts to find out what competitors and *their* countries' governments are doing. These efforts have led to a sharp increase in what is called industrial or economic espionage.

These major developments are creating a new economic world order. In the process, tens of millions of people's lives are being turned upside down—some for the better and some for the worse. How these enormous changes are affecting Canada will be the essence of this book as they are the essence of the world of business today.

In this chapter we will examine briefly these and other trends that interact with, and are mainly the result of, technological change and the globalization of business. Topics include how companies compete; the drastic reductions in company workforce size; the mushrooming of small-business start-ups, including home-based businesses; the service sector as the main job creator and the continuing importance of the manufacturing sector; changes in demographics; ethical and environmental issues; and higher educational requirements for jobs.

···· ▬▬▬ ····

THE TECHNOLOGICAL REVOLUTION

Human history is characterized by a steady flow of improvements in how work gets done, how products are made, and how life is made easier for people. Every time somebody finds a new way of doing something by using a better or new tool, device, or machine, we have an advance in technology. Sometimes the advance is a revolution. The first animal-drawn plow was such a revolution. Figure 1.1 lists some other important inventions. All these advances made significant changes to how we lived, worked, and produced.

Prior to 1700	The wheel, writing, bronze, iron, the arch, printing, gunpowder, clocks
Late 1700s	Steam power
1800s	Railways, telegraphy, photography, telephones, phonographs, steel-making, typewriters, oil and gasoline, rubber, automobiles, electricity, light bulbs, X-rays, a vast array of machinery for agriculture and industry
1900s	Motion-picture cameras, radios, refrigeration, airplanes, computers, plastics, rocketry and space exploration, satellites, television, photocopiers, atomic energy, robots, telefaxes, cellular phones, fibre optics

FIGURE **1.1**
····
REVOLUTIONARY TECHNOLOGICAL ADVANCES

These inventions radically altered how societies functioned.

Reaching Beyond
Our Borders

<www.telespace.org>

Small Canadian Firm Has Big International Clout

Starting from his home office in Toronto, consultant Uriel Domb played a role in more than half the world's satellite projects launched in the 1980s and the early 1990s. Now in a small Toronto office, with field offices in Los Angeles and London, England, Domb, an Israeli-born, U.S.-educated aerospace engineer, first worked at NASA in Washington, DC, from 1967 to 1970. In 1970 he was recruited by Telesat Canada, then establishing its satellite-communications program, to direct ground-control systems. He spent a year at Bell-Northern Research Ltd., Toronto, then left to start Telespace Ltd. He built a team of 25 independent consultants for his company.

The firm has an enviable track record for complicated international communications contracts specializing in satellite-technology consulting. Telespace has helped launch satellites on all continents and for many companies and space agencies. It operates without the sophisticated marketing efforts, office bureaucracy, and centralized operations of large satellite consulting firms.

"My basic philosophy is, it's important to serve our clients where they are," Domb says. And since Canada's satellite-communications market is already mature, Telespace has pursued contracts around the world. Telespace has an international reputation for excellent work, says Keith Rowe, ground-control manager of Inmarsat in London, who has worked with the firm on several projects. "Domb's strength is overall knowledge of satellite operations. But we have used their systems and people in every area."

Most clients learn of Telespace by word of mouth, Domb says. Certainly that was the case with Thailand, which choose Telespace over at least four bigger competitors for a large consulting project in 1991. The first THAICOM satellite was successfully launched only 25 months after contract signature.

Telespace is cost effective, partly because it doesn't spend money on expensive marketing efforts, Domb says. Its resources have instead gone into hiring the right people. Thailand needed a consultant who could provide expertise in all areas of satellite communications, but the Thais wanted to develop their own expertise so they wouldn't remain reliant on consultants. "We found this through our work with Brazil," Domb says. "Developing countries put a high priority on transferring technology and training people."

Domb helped Norway and Israel prepare to launch their own satellites in 1996 and 1997.

Telespace is now concentrating on telecommunications and on direct-broadcasting satellites in Europe, the Middle East, and North America. In Europe Telespace is working with EUTELSAT, which is a consortium of European countries, based in Paris. In North America Domb is working with various companies, including Shaw Communications. Telespace is also involved in developing new satellites for mobile telephones as well as the next generation of satellites for Israel.

Sources: Interview with Uriel Domb, February 16, 1996, and October 26, 1998; company publications; Susan Noakes, *Financial Post*, May 1, 1992, p. 1.

If you look carefully at the list of technological advances in Figure 1.1, which is far from complete, you will note that many inventions took place within the past two centuries. Since then the pace of technological advance has been increasing, especially in the past two decades. Most commentators on technology expect that the rate of change will accelerate even more in the next few decades.

The most significant change in our era has been the advent of the computer. The computer and other electronic marvels—CD-ROMs, communication satellites, faxes, modems, cellular phones—as well as fibre optics, have had three major effects on business:

The "chunnel" train is a technological advance that has made life easier. Developed by Bombardier, the train transports commuters from London to Paris much more rapidly than previously possible. The train uses the tunnel under the English Channel called the "chunnel."

1. Operations have been revolutionized.
2. The information age has been ushered in.
3. Our large planet has been made into a small globe.

Throughout this book we examine each of these three phenomena and their spinoffs. These developments have such sweeping ramifications that the operation of modern business cannot be understood unless they are taken into account. Chapters 10 and 11 are devoted to a detailed examination of the impact of technology on production and operations.

THE INFORMATION AGE

Toward the end of the eighteenth century, the invention of steam power in England led to the Industrial Revolution, which started in Europe and quickly spread across the Atlantic Ocean. For the first time in history, it became possible to set up factories employing many people under one roof to produce large quantities of a given product. Prior to that time only limited amounts of consumer and other goods were produced, by hand, at home or in small workshops by craftspeople. Trade was slow and very limited.

Continual inventions expanded production until we reached the almost limitless capabilities we now have. Vast improvements in transportation facilitated trade and increased distribution of the now much greater supply of goods. The nineteenth century into the early twentieth century was the era of production—trying to produce enough of everything from food to cars to meet people's needs. It is obvious that today, at least in Canada and the rest of the developed world, there is no longer a shortage of goods and services. Many individuals may be unable to afford them, but they are certainly available.

••• INFORMATION AS A VITAL COMPETITIVE TOOL •••

Today, producers of goods and services compete fiercely for buyers. Any edge gained by a company gives it a competitive advantage. Information has

information age
An era in which information is a crucial factor in the operation of organizations.

become a very important edge. That is why our time is called the **information age**, an era in which information is a crucial factor in the successful operation of organizations. (Perhaps inaccurately, we are often said to be living in a postindustrial information society.)

Computers and the whole range of electronic gadgets—laptop computers, modems, cellular phones, and more—have made the information age possible. One key to competitiveness is access to information about your own operations. You require a similar information flow about your competitors, your markets, government activities, and technological developments that may affect your business. To achieve this, businesses require good communication systems, especially the giant corporations with operations and facilities around the world. This area is where computers and information systems play a critical role.

Information technology has revolutionized businesses of all kinds. Farmers now use computers to keep track of all kinds of information, from organizing animal vaccination schedules to figuring out which animal is ready to breed.

Information has become a crucial element for competitiveness, and competition has become fiercer as it has become global. How can the CNR or CPR know exactly where each of their tens of thousands of railcars is located, loaded or empty, anywhere in Canada or the United States? How can a courier

service like Federal Express promise next-day delivery to any major city in the world from almost any other city? A computerized information system makes it possible. Every Federal Express unit, truck, and plane has a computer that is tied to the main computer system, so at any given moment the system knows where any parcel is.

This trend has reached a point where new terminology is required to describe the whole range of communication activities. Now we refer to the *information highway* and *electronic data interchange (EDI)*. Attempts are being made to define just what the information highway means or will encompass. (Chapter 11 at the end of Part 3 examines the importance of these technologies in some detail.)

The electronically fed information age also makes possible home-based businesses and home-based employees (discussed later in the chapter). How could they function without the whole battery of modern gadgetry? Information technology also allows companies to operate on a global basis, which is our next topic.

<www.fedex.ca>

Explore Federal Express's Web site for more information on the company.

THE GLOBALIZATION OF BUSINESS

From the earliest days, countries have traded with each other. Sailing vessels and other boats crisscrossed many of the oceans, seas, lakes, and rivers of the world. In Canada aboriginal peoples and Europeans travelled by canoe through the Great Lakes and the thousands of rivers and lakes that span North America. What is different about the new globalized world of business, an expression that has become almost a cliché? There is no comparison between doing business today and yesterday.

••• A GLOBALLY INTEGRATED SYSTEM OF OPERATING •••

globalization
A globally integrated system of production, marketing, finance, and management.

When we refer to the **globalization** of business, we are talking about a globally integrated system of production, marketing, finance, and management. All of these functions are carried out with little regard for borders or distances. Companies that operate globally are often called *transnational companies (TNCs)*. Some large Canadian TNCs are Nortel Networks (formerly Northern Telecom), Nova Corp., Bombardier, Magna International, International Nickel (INCO), and Power Corp. These companies have operations scattered around the world. They may raise funds in Toronto, New York, London, or Tokyo. Some of these funds may be provided by the Royal Bank of Canada, which has agencies and branches around the world to service Canadian and other TNCs.

A telephone or switching equipment, a computer, a plane, or a train may have components from a dozen different countries. Nortel and Bombardier do far more business outside Canada than in their home market, and both have international boards of directors. A so-called Canadian, American, or Japanese car may be designed, engineered, and tested in various countries. It certainly has components made on every continent. That is what globalization means.

Companies scour the world for the most reliable, lowest-cost, highest-quality sources to produce all or part of their products. Management personnel are sought from all over the world. That means that all countries are in a globally competitive market. Tokyo vies with New York for financing, Mexico and Brazil with China and Indonesia for production, and Canada with the United States or Germany to provide computer software. Toyota and Honda both produce cars in Ontario. This trend toward companies investing and producing in countries outside their home base is a basic aspect of globalization.

ALLIANCES WITH COMPETITORS   A logical extension of this trend includes telecommunication companies worldwide combining to form networks, and General Motors getting together with Toyota to manufacture cars in the United States. GM has a joint venture with Suzuki to produce cars in Ontario and truck engines in California. Ford and Volkswagen have also combined their efforts to produce their cars in the same assembly plant in South America. These are **strategic alliances** or **joint ventures**, arrangements whereby two or more companies cooperate for a special or limited purpose.

Peter Drucker, a world-famous management consultant, expects the trend to international investment in manufacturing and financial services to continue to grow in importance.[1] (Chapter 3 is devoted to this global phenome-

strategic alliances or joint ventures
Arrangements whereby two or more companies cooperate for a special or limited purpose.

<www.pfdf.org/portal>

To learn more about Peter Drucker and his prolific career, visit the Drucker Foundation Web site. Read his brief biography at <www.drucker.net/people/pfdrucker.shtml>.

A new strategic global alliance called "oneworld" was formed by various airlines. The executives from American Airlines, British Airways, Canadian Airlines, Cathay Pacific, and Qantas say the alliance will coordinate their flight schedules and cooperate on their frequent flier programs to better serve customers.

non.) This means that Canadian, American, Japanese, or Korean firms are losing their clear-cut identities as pure companies of one national origin. As one Harvard economist put it, it is getting increasingly harder to answer the question (in the industrial sense): Who is us?[2]

Critical Thinking

Some people are concerned that technology is "taking over." Do you see it as a threat or as an opportunity? What about the job market?

Can you suggest what any particular business should be doing to make it more competitive globally? How do you feel about the prospect of working in a global environment?

••• THE TREND TOWARD THE PACIFIC RIM: ••• B.C. TAKES THE LEAD

Globalization also means that the differences in time zones around the world has been removed. Although half the world is sleeping while the other half is awake, stock exchanges are moving to 24-hour operations and some businesses are operating outside regular hours. The end of the business day in Canada is the start of the next business day in the Pacific Rim countries of the Far East.

The Pacific Rim contains some of the most dynamic economies in the world. Led by Japan, the *Four Tigers*—South Korea, Taiwan, Singapore, and Hong Kong—and the *Three Mini-Tigers*—Indonesia, Thailand, and Malaysia—offer tremendous opportunities for investment and trade. China, with one-fifth of the world's population, is a rapidly developing country with endless similar opportunities, and vast India is not far behind.

British Columbia leads the country in trade and investment with the Pacific Rim countries (see Figure 1.2). Nationwide, slightly less than 84 percent of our exports in 1998 went to the U.S.,[3] while for B.C. the amount was 63 percent. But the Pacific Rim accounted for 27 percent of B.C.'s exports. Over the previous six years, B.C.'s average annual exports to the U.S. was 53 percent of total exports, while the average to the Pacific Rim was 35 percent.[4] (The shift in 1998 reflects the serious recession that gripped Pacific Rim countries in 1998 and is discussed on the next page.) The different profile of B.C. exports compared to the Canadian profile is not due simply to the province being on the Pacific Ocean; it is also because of the vast influx of immigrants from Hong Kong and Taiwan.

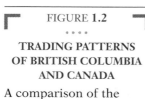

FIGURE **1.2**
• • • •
TRADING PATTERNS OF BRITISH COLUMBIA AND CANADA

A comparison of the trading patterns of B.C. and the rest of Canada shows B.C. is much less reliant on the United States. B.C. is strongly turned toward the Pacific Rim.

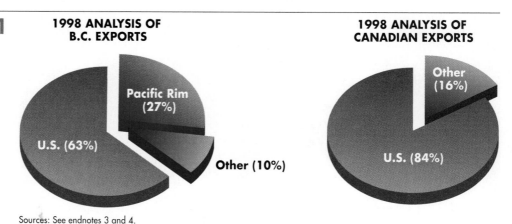

1998 ANALYSIS OF B.C. EXPORTS

Pacific Rim (27%)
U.S. (63%)
Other (10%)

1998 ANALYSIS OF CANADIAN EXPORTS

Other (16%)
U.S. (84%)

Sources: See endnotes 3 and 4.

EFFECT OF EAST-ASIAN IMMIGRATION ON B.C. BUSINESS[5]   Consider what is happening to Vancouver and the lower mainland: "Thousands of new-comers, led by affluent Hong Kong and Taiwanese immigrants, are injecting new vitality and a sharper edge into the city's once parochial business culture." Twenty-five percent of Vancouver's population is of Asian descent, which makes it "the most Asian-flavoured municipality on the continent."

At first, most of the investments were in real estate developments, led by Li Ka-shing, Hong Kong's wealthiest industrialist, who bought one-sixth of downtown Vancouver and is creating a $3 billion minicity on the site of Expo '86. Later, entrepreneurial money began to flow into start-up ventures in electronics, apparel, and other industries. Canada's thriving West Coast jewel was being powered by entrepreneurial Asians who were building the economy one small business at a time. Asian investments worth upward of $1.5 billion a year were helping British Columbia set the pace for economic growth in Canada.

The people and investments coming to British Columbia and developing significant trade with the Pacific Rim is a good example of one aspect of the globalization of business. The rest of Canada is well behind B.C. in exporting to Asia. Canada's outlook is still dominated by the free trade agreement with its largest trading partner, the United States. According to Wendy Dobson, director of the Centre for International Business of the University of Toronto and former associate deputy-minister of finance, our trade policy focuses on North America because Asian markets are seen as unprofitable. The large immigrant population in B.C. obviously does not hold those beliefs.

The Korean coal carrier *Bluebell* comes alongside at Westshore Terminals Berth Two. Korea is the second largest customer for Canadian export coal and has an ownership interest in Greenhills, an Elk Valley Mine in southeastern British Columbia.

In the late 1990s the Canadian government and important businesses, recognizing this problem, organized some large, high-profile trade missions to East-Asian countries. The Prime Minister, senior trade officials, and representatives from a variety of businesses met their counterparts in China, Indonesia, and so on. The media gave great prominence to these events. These missions helped to raise Canadian business consciousness about the major opportunities that exist in a region that contains almost half of the world's population and that experienced rapid and major economic growth for three decades. Unfortunately, in mid-1998, this rosy picture changed. Most of the economies seemed to collapse overnight. Suddenly there were widespread currency- and asset-value declines, followed by inflation, bankruptcies, and unemployment.

In late 1999 there were signs that these Asian countries had begun to recover. Economic, trade, financial, and government experts who were all concerned about the profound effect that this *Asian flu* and uncertainty were having in Asia, and indeed in the entire world, were expressing cautious optimism. This important change will be examined at greater length in Chapter 3.

We turn next to what Canadian big business is doing to compete in the tough global marketplace.

Progress Check

- Why does technology have such an impact on business today? Give some examples. What advance has single-handedly revolutionized how business operates? How?
- What is meant by the *information age*? How is it connected to technology? Why is information so important to business?
- What is meant by the *globalization of business*? How is it different from what came before? Can you give some Canadian examples of globalization?

BIG BUSINESS SHARPENS ITS COMPETITIVE POSITION

A major trend of the last decade involves Canadian companies becoming very cost-conscious, which has led to the severe process of cutting all possible costs of operations. This was part of a greater global trend whereby companies sought to become more competitive by reducing costs. Management, office, and factory personnel all felt the weight of the axe. The recession at the beginning of the 1980s gave strong impetus to this movement. The deepening of the recession into the early 1990s, as global competition heated up, extended the trend into that decade.

restructuring
The process of reorganizing the structure of companies to make them more efficient.

decentralized
Decision making is spread downward from the top of an organization.

••• COMPUTERS PAVE THE WAY •••

It is not an exaggeration to say that without computers it would have been impossible to engage in such wholesale cutbacks in staffing, usually referred to as *downsizing*. Senior managers use computers instead of middle managers to get information and to keep on top of operations. Factory personnel, secretaries, and assistants have been let go as the ubiquitous computer takes up a lot of the slack. Technology has paved the way for these massive changes, called **restructuring**. This is the process of reorganizing the structure of companies to make them more efficient.

As a result of these policies, and despite growth in production and sales during the decades, there was no increase in the number of people working for large companies from 1980 to 1999. Yet the total number employed in Canada rose by three million in that period (see Figure 1.3). Who employed them? While governments and nonprofit organizations increased their employment rolls, small business took up the lion's share (see Chapter 7).

In late 1999 many companies continued to announce significant layoffs and cutbacks. However, other steps were also taken to improve competitiveness. One of these ties in with the reduction in personnel because it leads to a significantly different managerial style.

The booming software industry has simplified the implementation of many business tasks. Corel Corporation is a software company based in the Ottawa area that has enjoyed worldwide success.

My office. My choice.

The ability to work *your* way. Introducing WordPerfect® Office 2000, powerful business software that lets you stay in touch with your favorite word processor and in tune with the latest technology. Better-than-ever WordPerfect. Innovative spreadsheets and presentations. Advanced Web and speech-recognition technology. And compatibility that makes file sharing a breeze.

Who says you can't have it all?

www.wordperfect.com

WordPerfect® OFFICE 2000
Today's Office. Undeniably WordPerfect.™

••• TOWARD MORE EFFECTIVE ••• MANAGEMENT

As companies trim the numbers of managers and reduce the size of the workforce, those employees and managers who remain are given more responsibility. This delegation of power downward from the top of the hierarchy is a complex process that simultaneously achieves many desirable effects.

One aid to greater effectiveness is a more rapid response to the demands of the market and to challenges from competitors. The more decision making is **decentralized** (spread downward from the top), the quicker the reaction time to these demands and challenges, improving the company's ability to compete.

FIGURE **1.3**

• • • •

NUMBER OF PEOPLE WORKING IN CANADA FROM 1950 TO 1999

This figure shows the rise in employment over half a century.

YEAR	PEOPLE WORKING (000S)
1950	5,163
1955	5,610
1960	6,411
1965	7,141
1970	8,395
1975	9,974
1980	11,573
1985	12,532
1990	13,681
1995	13,600
April '99	14,650

Source: *Daily* Archives, Statistics Canada, <www.statcan.ca>, May 1999.

A second advantage is that employees and lower-level managers feel a greater sense of participation in decision making, which makes their work more meaningful and fulfilling. This, in turn, boosts morale and, therefore, performance. There is a growing trend toward the empowerment of employees. **Empowerment** means that the leaders of organizations give their workers the freedom, incentives, and training to be decision makers and creative contributors to the organization.

empowerment
The leaders of organizations give their workers the freedom, incentives, and training to be decision makers and creative contributors to the organization.

A third advantage complements this point: employees who are involved in making decisions carry them out more enthusiastically. This *participative management* leads to more suggestions for improvement of procedures and thus to greater efficiency. All of these advantages are illustrated in the Chrysler story in the next section on quality.

The combined result of these developments is companies that are more customer-focused or **customer-driven**—customer satisfaction becomes the driving force of the company.

customer-driven
Customer satisfaction becomes the driving force of the company.

Finally, many surveys have shown that a more satisfied workforce means fewer accidents, less absenteeism, and lower turnover of personnel, substantially reducing costs of operations. Parts 3 and 4 of this book present a more detailed discussion of these important issues.

These advantages were normal features of large Japanese companies and were some of the reasons that Japan occupied the top rungs of international competitiveness for so long. Another major feature of Japanese (and German) competitive strength is the high quality of their products.

••• QUALITY: A NEW INTEREST IN AN OLD VALUE •••

An old concept has recently gotten a lot of attention in Canadian (and American) business circles—*quality*. Why is this? Hasn't quality always been a normal way of doing things? Unfortunately, that has not been true since the 1960s. Before that, things were made to last. It didn't matter whether it was a pot, a chair, a car, or a house.

Then a strange new scenario took over. The throwaway philosophy of management gradually became the norm. Perhaps it was meant to boost sales and profits by ensuring a steady flow of replacement purchases. The philosophy was also partly based on the belief that quality work costs more, so no more quality would be provided than was necessary to keep the customers buying.

At about the same time, the Japanese (and the Germans) were going in the opposite direction. Led by an American, Edwards Deming, who was ignored in his own country, the Japanese proved that quality is not more costly; it provides a wonderful competitive edge, which the Japanese exploit. That edge is the reason their autos and electronic products made such headway in North America and all over the world.

We finally got the message, almost too late for the electronics industry, but not too late for the important auto industry. Deming, who died in 1993 at age 92, and a few others, were avidly courted in the United States beginning in the mid-1980s. Their quality message swept through North America, but companies are finding that it is a lot easier to talk about it than to put it into practice.

CHRYSLER SETS AN EXAMPLE   Chrysler is one company that has gotten into quality seriously. In June 1992 its then chairman, Lee Iacocca, was in Ontario at the Chrysler plant in Bramalea. Talking about why Canadians are buying so many imported cars, he said to workers and guests at the official launch of production of the new LH models:

> *The only question in the mind of the import buyer is quality. Is our quality going to be first class? You bet it is. But we're going to get it right from the start. That's why we've got a slow launch ... quality will drive the daily schedule.*

Iacocca noted that there is a normal temptation to ease standards and crank up output, but "we've had that in the past and it doesn't work." That statement represented a significant shift of philosophy and showed that the quality message had finally gotten through to Chrysler. The movement to quality production requires that the workforce become more involved in the whole process, which ties in with the trend to greater empowerment and decentralization of management.

Previously, cars were handed over to the plant only 22 weeks before production, but this time workers were involved in assembly nearly a year and a half before start day. At the one-year mark, all pre-production vehicles were being built by the employees. "Decision making at Bramalea has been moved to the lowest levels," said plant manager Jim Franciosi. "So far [workers] have identified many improvements in the product and production processes—and they have been encouraged to continue to do so."[6]

Chrysler Canada official Walter McCall stated that by 1996 the process had reached the point where this plant became involved 24 months prior to production. He noted that with the LH model in the American auto industry, Chrysler pioneered this process of early input by assembly workers

<deming.org>

You can visit the W. Edwards Deming Institute Web site. Find out about Edwards Deming and "the Deming system of profound knowledge."

Chrysler is one company that has demonstrated its commitment to quality by having the plant's workforce participate in the decision-making process throughout the production of its vehicles.

into final product and production.[7] This process has proven so successful that Chrysler is investing $500 million to overhaul the Bramalea plant to make it the sole producer of the LH model, which it began to do in 1998.[8]

Now that we have seen what big business is doing, it is time to focus on the important small-business sector.

Progress Check

- Why is there so much pressure on business, especially big business, to be more competitive? Can you name three things business is doing to meet that challenge?
- Why is so much importance attached to quality? What demands are being placed on the new workforce?

···· ▬▬▬ ····

SMALL BUSINESS: A GROWING IMPACT ON THE CANADIAN ECONOMY[9]

Entrepreneurship—the ability and undertaking to form and operate a business—is flourishing. About 150,000 new businesses are started annually in Canada; most of these new companies are small businesses. There are some one-million small businesses in Canada (and another million self-employed people). Although 50 percent do not survive the first five years, the number of active small businesses continues to increase and their impact on the economy is very significant.

What exactly is a small business? A *small business*

- is independently operated.
- is not dominant in its field.
- meets certain size limits in terms of number of employees and annual sales. Various organizations, laws, and regulations use different size limits. The number of employees can range from zero to 100, sales up to $10 million, and profits up to $200,000 (or higher) annually.

Statistics Canada reports that such businesses contribute 60 percent of our gross domestic product (GDP) and account for two-thirds of our private-sector employment. Industry Canada's Entrepreneurship and Small Business Office states that some 80,000 small and medium-sized enterprises are exporting.

Small companies frequently provide services such as computer consulting, software development, or auto repairs. Some are restaurants or bars, retail stores such as clothing shops, or construction firms. Many are also manufacturing companies. More recently, a growing number of these start-ups are home based. They usually offer a variety of consulting and professional services.

The majority of new small businesses are in the service sector (discussed in more detail later in this chapter). Small business created most of the jobs for the additional three million people working in Canada in 1999 (compared to 1980). Industry Canada notes that in recent years small business "has been responsible for almost all net job creation." Many people regard the small-business sector as vital for the continuing success of big business. These entrepreneurs are adventurous and innovative and play "a dynamic role in [our] new [global] economy" by providing essential services to big business. (See the Spotlight on Small Business box on the next page.)

Spotlight on Small Business

<www.platform.com>

Small Business's Dynamic Role

Songnian Zhou, president and CEO of Platform Computing Corp., based in Markham, Ontario, offers a simple reason for his company's success: it created a software product needed by businesses around the world. As Babe Ruth said, "It ain't bragging if you can do it."

Since it was founded in 1992 to provide Fortune 500 firms with "workload management" systems—software that essentially manages your computer network's complex functions—Platform has doubled in size each year. In 1998, sales soared to $19.2 million, up from just $273,000 in 1993, a five-year gain of 6964 percent, good for seventh spot on *Profit's* 100 fastest-growing companies.

An associate professor of computer science at the University of Toronto, Zhou pioneered Platform's LSF (load-sharing facility) software while doing his PhD dissertation in 1987. After developing a prototype that was adopted at Northern Telecom, Zhou and two partners launched Platform commercially. Zhou calls LSF "a suite of systems software for managing workload across heterogeneous computers." Translation: LSF acts as "a virtual manager," ensuring computers on a network carry out their duties in a seamless fashion.

"In a human environment, the manager is not there actually doing the work himself. He's there to coordinate the resources, know who all the people are, and know which skill sets are needed," says Zhou, 42. "It's the

same principle for computer systems: our software determines which computers and servers are needed, and then manages all the different application resources across the whole network."

Platform's technology is applicable to a variety of industries and runs on any platform, says Zhou. Available customized or off the shelf, the company exports to many countries but its chief market so far is in the U.S. Customers include Boeing, Shell, and Pacific Data Images (PDI), the California-based animation studio that created *Antz*, the computer-animated box-office hit. PDI used Platform's LSF software to track its myriad computers churning out armies of animated ants. "We made sure that no usable machine would stay idle when there was work to do," says Zhou. "If a machine crashed in the middle of the night, we would recover the job" to run on another computer. *Antz* thus enjoyed faster product development and generated higher profits. Still, Zhou is not resting on his laurels.

Last year Platform invested 30 percent of its profit in R&D. It is constantly developing new products as it operates in a very competitive high-tech field. *Antz* aside, staying on top is no picnic. The company is exploring the desirability of going public.

Sources: David Menzies, *Profit*, June 1999, p. 55; interview with CFO Gordon Booth, June 1, 1999.

••• HOME-BASED BUSINESSES •••

Already considered the fastest-growing small-business trend in Canada, the home-based business movement is expected to expand even more rapidly in the future. The latest estimates are that 53 percent of all self-employed Canadians are home-based, which accounts for more than one million Canadians or about 9 percent of our workforce. Canadian futurists Frank Ogden, Frank Feather, and John Kettle, who operate out of their own home-based offices, predict that telecommuting from home and freelancers working from home will become very common.[10]

Why do people start such businesses? Some disliked their jobs or found them unfulfilling, some had jobs that disappeared or were threatened, others had a dream or strong passion, some want to be their own boss, and still others wanted a change in lifestyle. Many women welcome this opportunity because they find their career path blocked because they *are* women. Or they are single mothers and find that a home-based business is a good way of earning income, being their own boss, and being home to look after their children. The common threads are:

- Workers are prepared for a major shift from employment to self-employment for reasons noted above.
- The new technology of low-cost computers, modems, and faxes makes home-based business more feasible.
- Home-based businesses require less capital to start and operate.
- There is a growing market for services to fill big business needs.

A good example is Judith Aston, who, after completing the professional translation program at McGill University started a French–English translation service working out of her home. She emphasized high quality and fast service. At first she supplemented her income with a part-time job at a translation service, but as her billings grew, she was able to devote all her time to her own business. Working at home kept the overhead low and made it easier for Judith to raise her son, who was 10 when she started. Now, with the help of her husband, John, she runs a very profitable operation, and has moved out of Montreal into a country home in the Laurentians. State-of-the-art equipment enables her to operate from her new home location while enjoying country life.[11]

Here are some other examples from *The Globe and Mail*.[12]

One of the current trends in business is allowing employees to work from home. They maintain contact with the office and with customers through telephone, e-mail, and fax. This telecommuting frees up office space and eliminates commuting time for employees.

- Terry and Nancy Belgue, aged 53 and 40, "dropped out of the Toronto corporate rat race to move to Victoria and set up an advertising agency in the basement of their home" in the Oak Bay area. They "wanted a slower pace of life and to spend more time with their young boys."
- Louis Garneau, "a former national cycling champion, started his successful sportswear company bearing his name, in St. Augustin, Quebec, by making cycling shorts in his parents' garage."
- Elizabeth and Don Purser transferred the office of their freelance film company, Beulah Films Inc., from a downtown Toronto location to their home in Hamilton. The move cut their costs, gave them more time with their daughters ("I didn't want to see our kids go home with a key."), and allowed for flexible home and business duties, but it also lengthened their work week.

Home Inc.: The Canadian Home-Based Business Guide (McGraw-Hill Ryerson, 1994), the National Home Business Institute, and the Canadian Federation of Independent Business are resources to help home entrepreneurs start and operate their own businesses. The major Canadian banks all provide information and help.

EMPLOYEES WORKING AT HOME (TELECOMMUTING) Working at home is not confined to the self-employed. Many large companies are experimenting with having employees in certain departments work out of their homes. The idea is to cut down on expensive office space, employees' time, and the costs of travelling to and from work, without sacrificing efficiency. Tests have shown that employees who arrive at work after a frustrating commute do not function at their best for about an hour, until they settle down.

For example, American Express, Digital Equipment, and Du Pont all have work-at-home (telework) programs for some Canadian and American personnel and all report excellent results. They also supply varying types and amounts of equipment for home use.[13]

It is clear that the work-at-home trend is well established and growing in importance. Later we will look at the broader question of the rapid growth of the number of small businesses, especially in services, in Canada, and at other developments that are nourishing small business and its home-based aspect. (Also see Chapter 7.)

We now turn to the service sector, where small business plays an important role.

···· ▬ ····

THE SERVICE SECTOR[14]

goods-producing sector
The sector that produces tangible products, things than can be seen or touched.

service sector
The sector that produces services, not goods. Examples are banking, insurance, communications, and transportation.

The service sector of society is distinct from the goods-producing sector. The **goods-producing sector** produces tangible products that can be seen or touched, like clothes, oil, food, machines, or automobiles. The **service sector** produces services rather than **goods**, like banking, insurance, communications, transportation, tourism, computer servicing, programming, and consulting, health, recreational, or repair services. In the past 25 years the service sector in Canada and around the world has grown dramatically.

The shift in Canada's employment makeup away from goods-producing industries began slowly, early in the century, and has accelerated rapidly since the 1950s. The trend is expected to continue, although perhaps at a reduced rate. In the year 2000, the service sector will account for 78 percent of all jobs in Canada. This growth is due to a complex series of factors.

First, technological improvements have enabled businesses to reduce their payrolls while increasing their output. This accounts for the fact that despite the huge increase in gross domestic product (GDP) between 1960 and 1999, manufacturing still accounts for 18 percent of GDP (Figure 1.4), while its *percentage* of total workforce has been cut in half—from 30 to 15 percent—in the same period. At the same time, because staffing has been sharply pruned and business has become more complex and specialized, companies rely more heavily on outside service firms.

In a study of the service sector for the Institute for Research on Public Policy, economist William Empey showed that the service component of Canadian products has been growing steadily since 1971. He argued that "competitiveness in manufacturing depends critically on access to efficient producer services." He mentioned banking, insurance, transportation, and communication as such important services.

··· CONTRACTING OUT ···

As large manufacturing companies seek to become more efficient, they contract out an increasing number of services, which has led to the proliferation of service specialists. Canada has a large number of high-quality software specialist companies scattered across the country from Halifax, Nova Scotia, to Burnaby, British Columbia, whose products are in demand in Canada as well as Hollywood, Europe, and Japan. These companies produce everything from computer games to movie special effects. For example, Alias Wavefront software was used by George Lucas's Industrial Light and Magic Company for most of the computer-generated animals in the Robin Williams movie *Jumanji*. Softimage of Montreal created the software that was used to animate

	1960	1999
Total employed in Canada	6,400,000	14,650,000
Number employed in manufacturing	1,920,000	2,222,000
Percentage	30%	15%
Manufacturing share of GDP	19%	18%

Source: *Daily* Archives, Statistics Canada, <www.statcan.ca>, May 1999.

FIGURE 1.4

· · · ·

ROLE OF MANUFACTURING IN THE ECONOMY

Manufacturing had only a slightly lower percentage of GDP in 1999 than in 1960, despite the fact that it employs only 15 percent of the workforce now, compared to 30 percent in 1960, and that GDP has grown enormously. This means a huge increase in manufacturing productivity.

the dinosaurs in *Jurassic Park*. Computer animation has played an important role in movie-making from the first *Star Wars* all the way down to *Independence Day, Starship Troopers, Godzilla*, and *Antz*. George Lucas's hit in 1999, *Star Wars: The Prequel, Episode 1—The Phantom Menace*, uses the most advanced computer-animation techniques. The Profile at the beginning of this chapter indicates how this led the Disney company to locate branches in Canada to tap into our valuable high-tech animation specialists.

Other service firms have risen or expanded rapidly to provide traditional or personal services that used to be done by women at home. So many women have entered the workforce that there is a greater demand for food preparation, child care, and household maintenance. An additional boost for this type of service was the rise in wages that occurred in the 1950s, 1960s, and 1970s, providing more disposable income for families to pay for such services.

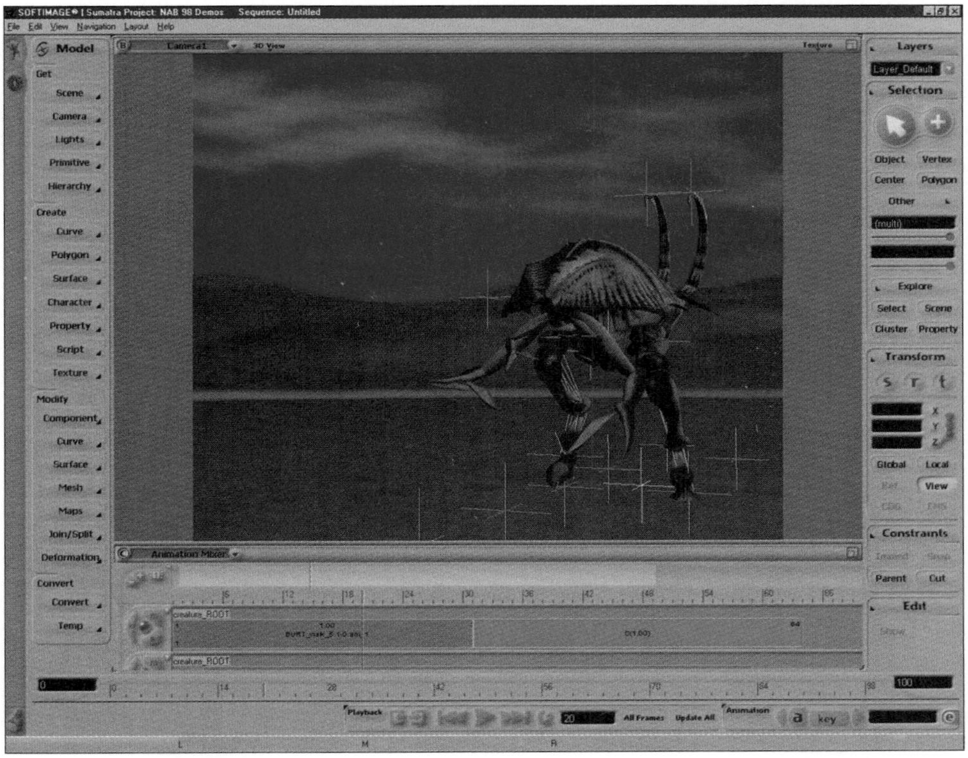

Canada is a leader in the production of computer graphics software. Softimage, Inc., a Montreal-based company, provides software used in the motion picture industry.

Critical Thinking

Can you see yourself setting up your own business? In the service sector? Does a home-based business attract you? Why or why not?

Do you think the trend to home-based business improves the quality of life? Why? How about the reduction in interaction with people?

A third area that has contributed to the rise in service-sector jobs is the government or quasi-government area, which includes public administration (federal, provincial, and municipal), health, and education. The postwar baby boom, the installation of Medicare in 1970, and the large growth in immigration to Canada all stimulated the demand for such services. This demand has now gone into reverse as governments are cutting back spending, reducing staffing, and privatizing many services.

Given the large growth in service industries, the question may be asked, what is happening to manufacturing? We look at this next.

Progress Check

- Why is big business no longer a creator of new jobs? Why is small business creating so many jobs? In what sector of the economy are these new companies and jobs to be found?

- How does small business stimulate big business? How does it complement big business?

- Why are home-based businesses so popular? What conditions favour this trend?

- What exactly is the service sector? Why is it so essential to the Canadian economy?

- What role has technology played in stimulating the growth of the service sector? What other factors have contributed to its growth?

···· ▬ ····

HOW IMPORTANT IS MANUFACTURING TO CANADA?[15]

Given all the changes in the global economy, is manufacturing still important to a modern economy? One person who has strong opinions is Akio Morita, the world-famous founder and retired chief executive of Sony Corp. He spoke in Ottawa in May 1989, warning Canada and the United States about the danger of a shrinking manufacturing sector and reliance on the service sector for growth and stability. Morita continued:

> *If Canadians ignore manufacturing, while thinking of themselves as information technicians in a service-based economy, they might find themselves on the sidelines of international business. It is only manufacturing that creates something new, which takes raw materials and fashions them into products which are of more value than the raw materials they are made from.*

Sony is a giant transnational corporation with plants, subsidiaries, and operations on all continents, and Morita has been the guiding light in its very successful history. Perhaps we should pay close attention to what he says. He may be biased toward manufacturing, but he should not be ignored.

Various opinions and data on this important question were examined in a detailed article in *The Globe and Mail*. Michael Walker, director of an ultra-conservative think tank, the Fraser Institute, stated that "the service sector could account for 99.9 percent of economic output without damaging the economy."

The opposite opinion was voiced by Jayson Myers, now senior vice-president and chief economist of the Alliance of Manufacturers and Exporters, Canada. He maintained that it was "ridiculous" not to realize the importance of the manufacturing sector. He pointed out that Canada runs an annual deficit of approximately $25 billion in all its dealings with the U.S. If not for the contribution of exports of manufactured goods, this deficit would be a lot greater. A *Globe and Mail* article emphasized the importance of manufacturing to a healthy economy. The headline read: "Manufacturing keeps economy on growth track," and the article noted that manufacturing played an important role in helping the Canadian economy achieve 15 consecutive quarters of growth to March 31, 1999.

··· MANUFACTURING AND SERVICE ··· SECTORS FEED EACH OTHER

Economist Gordon Betcherman suggested that "too much emphasis on one sector at the expense of the other is bad." He pointed out that a study, based on a model of the Canadian economy, determined that

> *When you stimulate the goods sector, the whole economy does well. If you stimulate the services sector, there's basically no payoff. Both goods and services are extremely important to a healthy economy.*

Echoing Morita's ideas, Betcherman said:

> *Japan is the only major industrialized country where employment in manufacturing increased before, during, and after the 1981–82 recession. In both Japan and West Germany manufacturing output and employment is higher as a proportion of the overall economy than in the other industrialized countries. Could there be a link between the size of their manufacturing sector and their continued economic success?*

Finally, Statistics Canada believes that some aspects of what manufacturing companies used to do have shifted to service companies. Tasks such as accounting, payroll, legal work, and advertising are commonly contracted out to service companies specializing in these fields. This accounts for some of the shift in jobs from manufacturing companies, although they were really service jobs all along.

Jayson Myers confirmed this, noting that every dollar of manufacturing output adds three dollars of value to the Canadian economy, so that while, directly, manufacturing constitutes only 18 percent of the economy, indirectly it creates an additional 37 percent of economic activity.

Another voice downgrading the importance of manufacturing is that of Canadian economist Nuala Beck, who argues:

> *A new knowledge economy is rapidly replacing the old mass-manufacturing economy. "Knowledge workers" now make up 30 percent of North America's workforce while only 10 percent are actually involved in production. What's more, knowledge-intensive new industries are creating most of the jobs and driving the economy.*[16]

<www.speakers.ca/ beck.html>

This Web site introduces several well-known Canadians who frequently appear as public speakers. It includes biographical information and highlights their achievements, topics they speak on, and examples of comments from audiences. You can visit this Web site to learn more about Nuala Beck.

If we look at the significant international competitors (in addition to Japan and Germany) such as South Korea, Taiwan, Singapore, and Hong Kong, their strength was and continues to be manufacturing. In these countries that sector directly contributes much more than 18 percent of GDP and employs much more than 15 percent of the workforce as is the case in Canada (see Figure 1.4).

Are there any lessons here for us? Should we be paying more attention to the importance of manufacturing to our continuing economic health? Or are these the success stories of yesterday, as Nuala Beck and many others claim? The answers to these questions will influence the kind of economy that you will be living in during the decades to come and the kind of jobs that will be generated.

POPULATION TRENDS[17]

Demographic (population) trends have a significant effect on business planning and activities. For example, in the 20 years following World War II (1946 to 1966), Canada witnessed on unusual phenomenon. Large numbers of war veterans, aided by government grants, got married and acquired housing for their families. In addition, the hundreds of thousands of immigrants who were entering Canada annually also needed housing. Four children per family was the norm. These children were eventually called the *baby boomers*. This explosive growth in population and family formation led to a 20-year boom in many industries.

••• THE POPULATION-LED POSTWAR BOOM •••

As the population grows, the construction industry must keep pace to provide accommodation for more people. This, in turn, leads to an expansion in other industries, such as retail.

Construction of houses, cottages, apartments, and other dwellings—as well as schools, colleges, CEGEPs, and universities for the hundreds of thousands of children—took off. Home furnishings and appliances, children's clothing, and sports and school supplies industries also flourished. To accommodate this vast growth in retail business, new stores, malls, and shopping centres sprang into being. Companies expanded rapidly and new firms mushroomed, and all required additional space; office towers and factories began appearing everywhere. These offices in turn needed furniture, equipment, and supplies.

The explosion of the construction industries fuelled tremendous growth in all the allied industries and services that feed on new construction: banks, trust, and insurance companies; lawyers and notaries; lumber, concrete, brick, electrical, paving, plumbing, landscaping, carpentry, painting, and roofing; and telephone, hydro, and heating. All these businesses and many more experienced great expansion in employment, sales, and profits. As suburbs developed to accommodate all this population and business growth, cars and buses were needed for transportation and new roads were built.

Those businesses that analyzed what was happening and prepared for the effect of these demographic trends became very profitable. Today, other important demographic trends have emerged that will have a great impact on the next few decades. Those individuals and companies that correctly analyze these trends and their impact on future business obviously

Spotlight on Big Business

<www.canon.ca>
<www.westport.com>

A Constructive Approach to Environmental Problems

Companies around the world have taken major steps to make their operations less harmful to the environment. A typical, and important, case concerns Canada's forest companies, many of which have been on the receiving end of severe criticism for a long time. Major forest companies began marketing "eco-certified wood and paper products" in 1996. These products carry the stamp of the Canadian Standards Association "affirming that they come from substainable forest operations." This is the Canadian version of a worldwide effort by the International Forest Stewardship Council to accredit independent local auditors.

Canon ran a full-page ad publicizing its toner cartridge recycling program. It thanked "the four biggest participants ... Ontario Lottery Corp., SHL Systemhouse, Commonwealth Insurance Co., and Hong Kong Bank of Canada," for making possible the recycling of thousands of cartridges. Canon donates $1 per unit to the ▲

World Wildlife Fund and The Nature Conservancy of Canada.

These are but two examples of a heightened awareness by corporations of the need to incorporate environmentally responsible policies in their normal operations. Some critics believe that they are merely responding to societal pressures to behave properly and that these are mere marketing ploys. Nevertheless, regardless of motivation, the result will be a cleaner and safer environment.

Finally, Wesport Innovations of Vancouver has produced a clean diesel engine—an elusive goal of engineers for years—based on natural gas. This is another case of a Canadian technology advance that will help to produce a cleaner environment.

Sources: Paula Kaihla, "Wesport's Green Machine," *Canadian Business*, June 25/July 9, 1999, p. 31; *Globe and Mail, Report on Business*, December 19, 1995, p. B4; Patricia Lush, *Globe and Mail, ROB*, December 28, 1995, p. B4.

will do very well. What are these current population trends? You may already be familiar with some of them.

··· THE POPULATION IS AGING ···

The population in Canada has been aging for several decades. More people are living longer due to better medical knowledge and technology; better health habits, proper nutrition, and more exercise; a reduction in number of people smoking; and other reasons. Figure 1.5's data of past and future population trends over a 40-year period shows that the two youngest age groups decline steadily from 40 percent to 24 percent, while the two oldest age groups increase steadily from 38 to 56 percent. The middle age group of 20 to 34 shows only a 10 percent drop.

At the same time, the portion of the population that is very young continues to decrease because of declining birthrates since the mid-1960s. Although the rate is low, the actual number of children being born is still large because of the *echo-boom*. The echo-boom is the result of the large number of baby boomers, born in the 1946–66 period, starting families. In addition, we have had steady immigration into Canada. In the 1980s more than one-million immigrants entered Canada. More than half of these were under 30, so many are likely to have children. The 1990s saw some two-million immigrants enter Canada.

What does all this add up to regarding the needs of the population? Businesses that cater to older people should prosper, in everything from health care to recreation, from education to travel. Smaller apartments should be in

FIGURE **1.5**

. . . .

**POPULATION
DISTRIBUTION
BY AGE GROUP**

Percentages for 2001, 2006, and 2011 are projected, and the earlier years are actual percentages. If you compare 1971 and 2011 you will note a pronounced shift to a heavier weighting of older persons.

YEAR	UNDER 4	4-19	20-34	35-64	65 AND OVER
2011	6%	18%	20%	42%	14%
2006	6	19	20	42	13
2001	6	20	21	41	13
1996	7	20	23	38	12
1991	7	21	26	34	12
1981	7	25	27	31	10
1971	9	31	22	30	8

Sources: Statistics Canada, *Population Projections for Canada, Provinces and Territories, 1984–2006*, Cat. No. 91-520 (Ottawa, Ministry of Supply and Services), May 1985; *Daily* Archives, Statistics Canada, <www.statcan.ca>, CANSIM Matrix 6367, May 1999.

greater demand. More grandparents with more money in their pockets will be buying more gifts for more grandchildren. The continuing large number of births assures prosperity for those businesses supplying children's needs. There should be many opportunities for existing and new businesses to explore.

<www.climatechange.
nrcan.gc.ca>

This Natural Resources Canada Web site provides considerable information about the nature and impacts of climate change and how they can be addressed. It also provides feature reports on the topic and links to many other topical items on the World Wide Web.

. . . . ▬▬▬▬ . . . .

ENVIRONMENTAL AND OTHER ETHICAL ISSUES

One of the most important ethical and social issues of our times is the serious deterioration of the physical environment of our planet. The unlimited expansion of population and industry has so altered the air, water, forest, insect and plant life, and soil that we face grave threats to our very existence. We are all familiar with the problems of too much waste—much of it highly toxic—and how it pollutes our air, rivers, lakes, oceans, and soil. We have learned about the emission of vast quantities of gases that are heating up the atmosphere and what this greenhouse effect will do to our climate, agriculture, and ocean levels. We have become aware of the chemicals we put on the food we grow and the indiscriminate destruction of tropical forests leading to soil erosion and silting up of rivers. Many more problems will not be solved unless we begin to live and think in a new, more socially responsible way.

In Canada we are confronted by many of these problems and are seriously affected by acid rain. Thousands of our lakes are completely dead, with no plant or fish life remaining. Our maple trees are dying off, paint is peeling from houses, and bricks are disintegrating. The polluted rain and snow from factory chimneys thousands of kilometres away continue to cause hundreds of millions of dollars in damage to Canada each year. The whole world, from the Arctic to the Antarctic, is affected by this problem. Dr. David Schindler, a biologist at the University of Alberta, reported that a complex interaction between acid precipitation, climate warming, and ultraviolet radiation from the sun is having a serious impact on the deterioration of all life forms in lakes.[18]

Companies can no longer make decisions based only on their immediate economic interests. This new input into the planning and thinking of management involves a major shift and will continue to grow in importance. The Spotlight on Big Business on the previous page gives some examples of this.

Governments have passed many new laws requiring industries to observe ever more stringent environmental standards. This often involves greater costs, which inevitably find their way into the prices consumers have to pay. Are these costs any higher than the damages caused to people and property by unrestricted operations?

New industries and professions are being spawned from the new awareness of environmental issues. Recycling and waste management companies have sprung up, and alternative materials and processes are being explored. This has led to new discoveries, jobs, and investment opportunities. The movement toward conservation has had the same effect. Businesses have discovered ways to reduce costs, making them more competitive.

The concept of **sustainable development** was promoted in 1988 at a major international conference on the environment in Toronto. Sustainable economic development meets the needs of the present without endangering the external environment of future generations. In the Brundtland report, the Prime Minister of Norway made it clear that, in her committee's opinion, the only way for the world to survive is to abandon unlimited development for the socially responsible alternative.

Although threats to the environment are obviously an important problem, they are not the only ethical issue that business faces. Doing the *right* thing does not mean only obeying the laws of Canada and the countries in which you do business. A host of issues such as bribery and corruption, price fixing, bid rigging, clear-cutting of forests, product safety, arms sales especially to dictators, and other ethical questions are occupying an increasingly important position in the corporate agenda. Because of their importance Chapter 5 is devoted exclusively to a review of ethical and environmental issues. In addition, each chapter makes reference to ethical problems relevant to that chapter.

sustainable development
Economic development that meets the needs of the present without endangering the external environment of future generations.

Recycling has resulted from an increasing awareness of the environmental damage caused by waste. This has spawned the development of a new industry dedicated to waste management.

···· ▬▬▬ ····

CAREERS AND JOBS FOR THE FUTURE[19]

What is the effect of all of the trends discussed in this chapter on jobs and careers into the next century? To date the most striking result of these developments is what up to the mid-1990s was called *jobless recovery*. (A good example is the case of Chrysler noted in Chapter 10. Chrysler was investing $600 million in a new plant in Ontario that would not create a single new job.) Perhaps a more accurate description would have been a *slow jobless recovery*.

The seriousness of this problem was highlighted by the spate of commentaries in all media about the jobless recovery. For example over a period of four days there were articles in the *Toronto Star* and the *Los Angeles Times*, an editorial in the *Montreal Gazette*, and a long interview with Harvard professor and former U.S. Secretary of Labor Robert Reich on the CBC *National News Magazine* (February 29, 1996). In addition, Prime Minister Jean Chrétien and President Clinton of the United States appealed to businesses to seriously consider ways of providing jobs, especially to young people.[20]

··· **THE BAD NEWS**[21] ···

The official unemployment rate in Canada all through the 1990s hovered in the 8 to 10 percent range, finally declining below 8 percent by the end of the decade as the earlier recession moved into a recovery phase. Although the gross domestic product (GDP) continued to rise from 1993 onward, the net increase in the number of people working from 1990 to 1998 was approximately 400,000 or a little below 3 percent. Our country, as well as most European countries, were bedevilled by this problem despite many studies and attempts by governments and experts to *do* something about it. Of all developed countries only the United States was able to decrease its unemployment rate to below 5 percent. In late 1998 the threat of global economic recession, and perhaps worse, was once again a serious concern for governments, financial and other large business corporations, and for the media and people in all countries. This problem is discussed in greater detail in the next chapter.

Two major effects on the job market of the trends discussed in this chapter are evident, one positive and the other negative. Let's look at the bad news first. The technological and globalization revolutions have been relentlessly reducing the number of jobs in Canada. Significant job losses occurred steadily due to many plant closings, record bankruptcy levels, automation, and downsizing by companies and governments. There have also been plant closings and layoffs due to mergers or plants moving to the United States, Mexico, or elsewhere. For most of the 1990s we heard mostly bad news on the job front.

In the past, as the population increased, the number of people working in Canada increased every five years despite recessions. But given the very heavy job losses in the early 1990s, the total workforce in Canada remained stuck in the 13,600,000 to 13,700,000 range from 1990 to 1996. The workforce then began to increase and by mid-1999 the figure had climbed to 14,650,000 (see Figure 1.4). Between April 1998 and April 1999, 371,900 new jobs were created.[22] In addition, an Asian recovery seemed likely. This began to engender some hopeful forecasts for the health of the global economy and added to the signs of good Canadian economic growth. This was good news, but there are other positive signs for the job market.

••• THE GOOD NEWS •••

Canada has a booming software development industry. Some examples were noted earlier in this chapter. There are many large and small software companies scattered across Canada, and they are having great difficulty finding suitable employees. Paul Swinwood, who heads up the Software Human Resource Council in Ottawa, reported that as of February 1996 there were 20,000 job vacancies across Canada in this mushrooming industry. He noted that the software industry is expanding at a 25 to 30 percent annual rate, so it will continue to generate large numbers of jobs. The number of job vacancies was unchanged by 1999.[23]

The problem is that change is so rapid and constant in this field that universities and other educational institutions have difficulty keeping up. Some companies are so desperate for help, said Swinwood, that they have to hire people from Sweden and the United States.

Another bit of good news is that there are more high-paying jobs in the service sector than in the goods-producing sector. Since the mid-1980s the service industry has generated almost all of the increases in employment. Although this growth has slowed, it still remains the largest area of job growth. Chances are very high that you will work in this sector at some point in your career. Do not overlook the retail area; any time a large chain such as Wal-Mart or Loblaw's opens a new store, many managerial jobs are created for college graduates. High-paying service-sector jobs can be found in marketing, accounting and auditing, finance, management consulting, telecommunications, transportation, and in many sectors that are related to computers including programming, animation, servicing, and consulting.

Another positive development is in the manufacturing sector, which has been responsible for a continuing boom in exports. This is expected to continue and to prevent further job losses in that sector, which directly employs two million people and has a major ripple effect on the service sector. A Canadian Manufacturers' Association survey reported that companies are just about through downsizing and that the emphasis now is on increasing efficiency in other areas.[24]

··· THE IMPORTANCE OF EDUCATION ···

One thing is certain: if you examine Figure 1.6 carefully, you will see that the more education you have, the less likelihood of your being unemployed. Most of the new jobs being created require college or university education. A good example is Gallatin Steel Co., which operates a steel mill in Kentucky, United States. This is a joint venture of two Canadian steel companies, Dofasco and Co-Steel. Gallatin is a perfect example of the many-sided effects of the technological revolution.

In today's workplace, higher education is becoming more valuable. Forty percent of Gallatin Steel's employees have degrees, many of them in mechanical engineering or metallurgy.

It used to take 5000 people to produce as much steel as Gallatin's 300-person workforce can produce. Furthermore, 40 percent of them have college degrees, many in mechanical engineering or metallurgy.[25]

These developments require managers and employees who have more advanced education. They must be able to grasp mathematical concepts and reason logically. They need university degrees. This preparation develops a person's confidence to be a modern knowledge worker or manager, to make decisions as authority is decentralized and the entire workforce adapts to the quick response time required in today's fast-moving, highly competitive world.

	PERCENTAGE UNEMPLOYED IN 1998
Average for total workforce	8.3
Age bracket 25 and over	7.0
Age bracket 15–24	15.0
High-school dropouts	14.7
High-school graduates	8.3
Technical/college graduates	6.6
University graduates	4.3

FIGURE **1.6**
····
UNEMPLOYMENT RATE IN CANADA FOR VARIOUS CATEGORIES OF THE WORKFORCE IN 1998

Note how the unemployment rate decreases as the years of schooling increase.

Source: *Daily* Archives, Statistics Canada, <www.statcan.ca>, May 1999.

Ethical Dilemma

REVIEW

At the beginning of the chapter we noted the ethical dilemmas that companies face as they try to be more competitive by moving production to low-cost developing countries, and as they continually update their technology. These changes often mean job cuts, relocations, or plant closings in Canada, causing hardships for employees and for small communities. The issue of negative environmental impacts in loosely regulated developing countries also arises. We present here the responses of two business executives (see Preface) to these issues.

When companies lower their costs, they are more competitive and can expand their businesses. This expansion ultimately creates more jobs. As developing countries raise their standards of living, as we have seen in South Korea, Singapore, Poland, Brazil, and China, they also become consumers of these products, giving the companies a competitive edge there and providing additional jobs at home as the business grows. As for environmental problems, Normand Bédard, vice-president, human resources, of Cambior Inc., believes that "the vast majority of companies are sensitive to the social and environmental impacts that any human activity will entail."

Bédard states that, "only naive CEOs think that they can go to countries with less organized environment legislation and carry out activities that they would not carry out in their own country. This practice, if it existed in the past, is no longer acceptable [or] tolerated. Companies must have the same respect for the environment in host countries and they must also consider the impact of their presence on society as a whole."

Dennis Reilley, general manager, Pratt & Whitney Canada International, says that in his experience, "most Canadian high-tech companies operate in this fashion," and that it is possible that "Canadian *industrial age* or commodity-based companies aren't nearly so concerned about their employees or the environment." These companies have to strike while the iron is hot — commodity market prices are very volatile, so they must take profits quickly.

As for developing countries, Reilley agrees with Prime Minister Chrétien that Canadians need jobs first and clean up afterwards, "not the other way around." Canadian executives of international firms and host governments need to be educated about the IMF and UN protocols.

Being ethically and environmentally conscious pays large dividends in the long run.

In the meantime, because we are in the transition period from the old industrial economy to the new information age, finding a job, especially a full-time, permanent job, is a very challenging process.

···· ▬▬ ····

YOUR FUTURE IN THE GLOBAL ECONOMY

It's exciting to think about what role you will play in the new global economy. You may be a leader, one of the people who will implement the changes and accept the challenges that the new information-based economy offers. This book will introduce you to some of the concepts that will make such leadership possible. Are you preparing yourself for this challenging new job market? (The Appendix after Chapter 12, will help you get the job you want.)

Critical Thinking

Should Canadians strengthen the manufacturing sector? What can they do? Is there a role for government in this effort?

How do you feel about the challenge of a safer environment? Do you see it as an opportunity or a threat to Canadian business?

Do you think we can develop environmental expertise that will create new industries? What, specifically, needs doing?

Can you think of any type of service or product not currently on the market that would appeal to the growing number of seniors? Would you be interested in trying to develop that item? Why or why not?

Have any of the trends discussed in the chapter given you any ideas for a career? Explain. Are you thinking about whether the rest of your education should be broader or more specialized? Review the pros and cons of each choice.

Progress Check

- Why are environmental issues so important now? What effect does this have on business plans and actions? What opportunities does it open up for business?

- Why are population trends significant? What are some major current trends that are important to business? Why are they important?

- What is the effect on careers and jobs of current business trends? What should students be doing to meet these requirements?

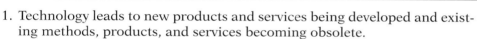

SUMMARY
• • • • • •

1. Technology leads to new products and services being developed and existing methods, products, and services becoming obsolete.
   - **How does this affect business?**
   Technological developments—including more efficient and automated equipment, networks, computers, and robots—lead to a reduction in the number of employees and managers, thus reducing costs. Employees must be trained to cope with the new technology. Companies and individuals that do not keep up with these developments cannot compete in the job and business market.

1. Explain the importance and impact of technological developments.

2. The *information age* refers to the fact that rapid, reliable, and relevant information has become a vital component of effective competition.
   - **Why has this development taken place?**
   Computers and ever-improving communication technology have developed information to a high level. They have shrunk the planet into a small world. Information has become as important a component of operations as finance, materials, and labour. It enables management to plan better and to react more quickly to favourable or unfavourable developments.

2. Describe what is meant by the *information age* and what its implications are.

3. Big business now operates on a global basis.
   - **What accounts for this development and what are its implications?**
   The technological revolution in transportation and communication has made possible buying, selling, borrowing, staffing, investing, and manufacturing as if the world were one country. Canadian companies search for the lowest costs and markets and opportunities wherever they exist.

3. Discuss the globalization of business and why it is important for Canadian companies.

4. Canadian companies must participate in the globalized world of business and meet world competitive standards.
   - **How do companies improve their competitiveness?**
   Becoming more competitive means adopting the latest and most efficient means of production, financing, distribution, and management information systems as technology and experience make available. This search is done internationally, as are investment decisions. Alliances and joint ven-

4. Identify how big business is becoming more competitive and the pressures to do so.

tures are sought on a global basis. The pressures arise from competitors who are engaged in a similar process.

5. Explain why small and home-based business have become so popular.

5. There has been an explosion in the number of small businesses in Canada. A growing number of these are home based.
   - ***What factors led to these developments?***
   Some of the factors are new technology (computers, faxes, modems); the rise in the number of women and single parents in business who find working at home easier and less costly; women finding their career paths blocked due to sexism; the rising number of professionals and managers who find themselves laid off with poor prospects for re-employment; and people opting out of the rat race or seeking more control over their lives.

6. Show how the service sector has replaced manufacturing as the principal provider of jobs, but why manufacturing remains vital for Canada.

6. The manufacturing component of the Canadian economy has remained unchanged in the last decade at about 19 percent of GDP.
   - ***Despite this, why has the service sector become much more important?***
   The manufacturing sector employs fewer people and its labour force is a much smaller percentage of the total labour force as the service sector has grown enormously, employing some 75 percent of the workforce. Manufacturers contract out many service aspects of their business and also require new services in the information age. Nevertheless, many people believe that an efficient competitive manufacturing sector is the motivator of the entire economy.

7. Explain current population trends and their major impact on business.

7. Shifts in the makeup of the population of Canada have been a constant feature. We have had the baby boom and now the composition of our population is shifting again.
   - ***What is the significance of the latest demographic trend for business?***
   Demographic changes create new markets as old markets diminish. They also determine whether there will be an adequate supply of labour. Current trends are for a gradually aging population and a declining percentage of younger people. Businesses must look for opportunities in the new markets being created by the large number of older people.

8. Describe how environmental ad other ethical issues play a major role in all business planning and actions.

8. People are increasingly concerned by the actions of business that affect society. This applies to a wide range of activities, including ethical behaviour in general and the environment in particular.
   - ***Why have these questions come to the fore recently?***
   A series of scandals in different industries has drawn attention to the need for ethical procedures and ethical behaviour by managers. The serious deterioration of the environment has forced business and government to examine closely every element of operations to ensure that these problems are not being aggravated.

9. Show how jobs and careers are affected by the trends discussed in the chapter.

9. So many trends are changing the way business operates that jobs and careers are being greatly affected.
   - ***How is the nature of jobs and careers moving in new directions?***
   Technology now requires better educated, more skilled employees. Decentralization means that managers and employees must be prepared to undertake more responsibility. Everyone has to have wider horizons to encompass global business, which means a broader education. More young people have to think seriously about working for small businesses or starting their own business, perhaps at home.

business 4
customer-driven 13
decentralized 13
empowerment 13
globalization 8

goods-producing
   sector 18
information age 8
joint ventures 9
restructuring 12

service sector 18
strategic alliances 9
sustainable
   development 25

**DEVELOPING
WORKPLACE
SKILLS**

1. Use a word-processing program to write a one-page report on how technology will change society in the next 10 years. Consider not only computers but the whole rage of technological developments discussed in the chapter.

2. The text describes the growth trend in the number of businesses in the service sector. Look through your local Yellow Pages phone book and list five businesses that provide services in your area. The text also describes how certain demographic and social changes affect businesses. Look at your list of local service businesses and consider how these trends affect them—positively or negatively.

3. The stress on quality is having a big impact on business operations. Do you think your education is preparing you to function in a quality-conscious business atmosphere? Where is it succeeding? Where is it failing? How can it be improved?

4. Go to the library and see what small-business magazines you can find. Scan through back issues for some stories of successes and failures. See if you can get a few ideas that might inspire you to consider a small-business venture. Make sure you examine the possibility of a home-based business.

5. Find out which nonprofit organizations in your community might offer you the opportunity to learn the skills that will help you find a job in the field you are interested in. Write a letter inquiring about their programs and the opportunities for volunteering.

**INTERNET
CHALLENGES**

1. Using the key term "business trends" (you may have to use quotation marks for the whole phase) search the Canadian Yahoo Web site at <www.ca.yahoo.com> to see what new trends are emerging and affecting business. If your search is not successful try <www.yahoo.com>, which is Yahoo's U.S. site. See if there are any chat groups you can join to discuss this important topic.

2. Try the same sites to answer the question: What are the fastest growing occupations in Canada and the U.S.? See if you find some that interest you as potential careers. Try the Nortel Networks Web site at <www.nortel. com> to see what job opportunities there may be there in the fast growing information technology (IT) field.

Practising Management Decisions

One of the oldest, largest, and most prestigious companies in Canada has announced a total transformation in what it produces and how it will operate in the future. Northern Telecom had previously changed its name to *Nortel Networks* to better reflect the real nature of the company today. In May 1999 Nortel fleshed out the significance of that name change by announcing that it was getting out of manufacturing its traditional lines of telecommunication equipment. It was doing so to better concentrate its resources on high-end software development necessary for modern networking facilities.

One-hundred-year-old Nortel, based in Brampton, Ontario, has a global workforce of 73,000 employees, of whom only one-third are in Canada. Two-thousand Canadian employees in various provinces would be affected by this change in operations. Nortel's aim is to get rid of most of its manufacturing facilities "as it transforms itself into a so-called systems house with a heavy reliance on outside contractors."

Analysts note that similar transformations are occurring in other manufacturing industries, including the auto-parts sector. American competitors of Nortel have also moved to outsourcing or are disposing of their manufacturing facilities altogether. Nortel decided that if it wants to stay in the big league of global competitiveness, it would have do the same thing. A report on the same page where Nortel's announcement is carried, notes that the world's largest long-distance phone network company, AT&T, has adopted Nortel's network products to handle its network expansion.

CASE 1

A REVOLUTION IN A MAJOR CANADIAN COMPANY

The previous month a senior officer generated some controversy when he said that like other companies, Nortel "owed no allegiance to Canada." A spokesperson for the Canadian Autoworkers Union said this indicated that Nortel was preparing Canadians to accept Nortel's departure from Canada. He criticized the company because he maintained that it had been the largest beneficiary of Canadian tax incentives for research and development.

Decision Questions

1. Can you see how Nortel's actions relate to important trends discussed in the chapter? What specific trends do you think Nortel's changeover highlights?

2. Do you see any connection between what Nortel is doing, or may be preparing to do, and ethical issues raised in the chapter? What are the issues that are relevant here?

3. Did Nortel have any options other than what it chose to do? What options can you suggest? What is the significance of the AT&T decision?

4. Does the fact that only one third of its employees are in Canada mean that Nortel is no longer a Canadian company? What does it mean when we say a *Canadian company*? What does such a term mean in the twenty-first century? Does it have any significance for your future career?

Sources: Michael MacDonald, "Nortel's Changing the Way It Does Business," *Montreal Gazette*, May 15, 1999, C 11; interview with Alain Bourget, manager public relations, Nortel Networks, May 17, 1999.

Every year *Profit* magazine publishes a list of Canada's 100 fastest-growing companies. The June 1999 issue reports in detail on the latest selection. The importance of many of the major trends discussed in the chapter is quite clear. However, some other interesting facts emerge from the detailed data. For example, the leading 100 are split almost evenly between what the magazine calls *high-tech* and *non-tech* firms. Furthermore, the non-tech companies are growing faster than the high-tech ones.

Another interesting fact is that while manufacturing firms constituted 35 percent of the lead-

CASE 2

CANADA'S 100 FASTEST-GROWING COMPANIES

ing 100 in the previous year, the percentage fell to 28 in 1999. Then the issue of just what constitutes *manufacturing* enters into the analysis. If companies producing software are added to the manufacturing category the percentage jumps to 44, making it again the largest category. Only some of the software creators consider themselves to be manufacturers so that muddies the water.

Another set of informative facts shows that 61 percent of companies report that the Internet had a major impact on their business in 1999, compared to 28 percent in 1997. Other data show that

96 percent of CEOs use cellphones and 74 percent use laptops. The number of the 100 companies that export has climbed to 76 from 42 in 1993, and the importance of exports has almost doubled since 1993. In 1998 exports were 43 percent of sales against 23 percent in 1993 and actual dollar volume was 44 times greater, jumping from $49.5 million to $2.2 billion.

The 1999 report also shows that a record six women were the leaders of the top 100 companies. New technology industries have made an important impact in the last five years: desktop publishing, machine vision, and software all contributed to new companies and fast-paced growth. Nevertheless, companies in traditional industries were growing at a faster clip than the high-tech group: the five-year growth was an average of 2927 percent compared to 2383 percent.

Decision Questions

1. Which of these data support the trends shown in the chapter and which do not? Show the trends in both cases and explain your answers.

2. Can you see how the lines between service and manufacturing companies are getting blurred? Is there a clear distinction between a product and a service?

3. What does all this mean for your career choices? Do you concentrate on high-tech or traditional industries? Is there a clear distinction between the two? Do you look for companies that are globally oriented?

4. What overall conclusions can you draw from these statistics pertaining to the fastest-growing companies in Canada? Is it safe to arrive at any general conclusions based on this information?

How Economic Issues Affect Business

Chapter

2

LEARNING GOALS

*After you have read and studied this chapter,
you should be able to*

1 describe how free markets work using the terms *supply*, *demand*, and *prices*.

2 discuss some limitations of the free market system and what countries do to offset these limitations.

3 understand the mixed economy of Canada.

4 explain how inflation, recession, and other economic developments affect business.

5 discuss the issues surrounding the national debt and its effect on business.

J. M. Keynes (pronounced *canes*), an economist from Cambridge University in England, became famous in the 1930s when Canada, England, the U.S., and most of the world were in the midst of a severe economic depression. His theories became known as *Keynesian economics* and exerted an important global influence for almost 50 years. Keynes suggested ways that governments could get their countries out of the Depression. The basic concepts were that governments should borrow and use the money to stimulate the economy. Complementing that, was Keynes's insistence that these loans should be repaid when the economies were flourishing again and governments were collecting enough taxes to make these repayments. Since economic depressions and recoveries have an enormous effect on businesses, employment, and all forms of economic activity, Keynesian ideas attracted a lot of support and were followed by many governments, but there was much dis-

agreement among economists, politicians, business, and labour leaders. The main opposition came from those who continued to support the concepts set forth by Adam Smith, often called the father of modern economics, whose ideas will be discussed in this chapter.

Keynes fell into disfavour in the 1980s as various economists and political leaders in the U.S., England, and Canada strongly urged governments to reverse their Keynesian actions and reduce their involvement in the economy as much as possible. These proponents argued that such involvement only disrupted and distorted the free market's ability to function most efficiently, as Adam Smith proposed in 1776. However, in the late 1990s when the world was facing its most serious economic crisis in 70 years and the free market seemed unable to solve the grave problems, calls were once again being heard for governments to do something and to come to the rescue. Is Keynes being resuscitated?

PROFILE

John Maynard Keynes

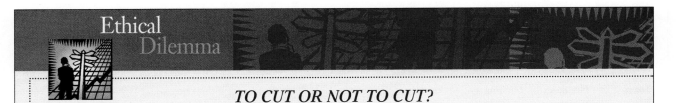

Ethical Dilemma

TO CUT OR NOT TO CUT?

When you study this chapter you will see that an important problem for the Canadian government was how to help keep the Canadian economy in good shape when our national debt had, perhaps, played a big role in dragging the economy down. All our governments embarked on a program of reducing expenditures to avoid incurring annual deficits and adding to the national debt burden. The aim was to start generating annual surpluses to be used to reduce our enormous national debt.

To achieve this goal many civil servants were let go and many programs such as employment insurance, funds for education and health, welfare, and so on were reduced, causing great hardship to many people. Many organizations and individuals were strongly opposed to what governments were doing because of the serious adverse effects on so many people of all ages across Canada. Child poverty levels rose, food banks reported a big jump in the number of people applying for food, and so on. Supporters of the governments' actions, as well as governments themselves, argued that there was no choice. If this was not done, they said, economic and social conditions would deteriorate further and everyone would be worse off.

Think about this difference of opinion as you read the chapter and see how you feel about it. At the end of chapter we will try to answer these questions: Did the government go too far in cutting expenditures in its deficit battle? Did it have any alternatives that might have produced fewer harsh side effects?

THE ECONOMIC AND POLITICAL BASIS OF BUSINESS OPERATIONS

If you want to understand the underlying situation and conditions in which Canadian business operates, it is essential that you (1) have some grasp of economics, (2) be aware of the impact of the global environment, and (3) understand the role of the federal and provincial governments in Canada. You should pay close attention to these three factors because they strongly influence the kind of careers and jobs that will be available to you. This chapter will deal with the first point and the other two will be reviewed in the next two chapters.

••• ECONOMIC FLOWS •••

The Canadian economy is an integral part of the world economy. Business firms use labour from other countries, buy land in other countries for their facilities, and receive money from foreign investors. To understand events in the Canadian economy, therefore, one has to understand the world economy.

For various reasons, companies find it advantageous to expand outside their home country. Many Canadian assets are cheaper for foreigners to buy because their currency is high in relation to our dollar and because prices for these assets are much higher in their own countries. For example, the famous Chateau Whistler Resort in British Columbia was bought by a Japanese company, Yamanouchi Pharmaceuticals. A French company bought the very successful Connaught Laboratories in Toronto.

When Canadians buy Japanese cars, VCRs, and other products, money flows out of the country. It flows back in when Japanese business people buy property such as the Chateau Whistler Resort. Such international flow of money shows the importance of international economics.

Another reason that foreign investors like Canada is because we have a stable economic and political environment. Investing is risky enough without having to worry about unpredictable dictorial regimes, massive corruption, and a weak rule of law. The country with the largest investment in Canada by far is the United States. British, Dutch, Japanese, and French companies are also significant investors in Canada. At the same time, billions of dollars are invested outside Canada by Canadian companies.

···· ━━━━ ····

WHAT IS ECONOMICS?

Economics is the study of how society chooses to employ resources to produce goods and services and distribute them for consumption among various competing groups and individuals. An important contribution of businesses to an economic system is the constant expansion of available resources. This expansion is achieved by discovering new ways of increasing the variety and production of energy, food, and a wide range of products and services.

economics
The study of how society chooses to employ resources to produce goods and services and distribute them for consumption among various competing groups and individuals.

···· ━━━━ ····

A BRIEF HISTORY OF BUSINESS AND ECONOMICS

capitalism
An economic system with free markets and private ownership of companies operated for profit.

In 1776 Adam Smith wrote the now-famous book *An Inquiry into the Nature and Causes of the Wealth of Nations*, later considered the foundation of the study and understanding of the newly developing capitalist industrial society. Smith's ideas held sway for about one-hundred fifty years because many of his ideas and predictions have been proven true. He developed a theory about the (then) new developing industrial economy, **capitalism**, an economic system with free markets and private ownership of companies operated for profit. Smith said that all companies would function best with little government involvement. His most-quoted comment concerns the so-called *invisible hand* that made everything work well in the economy. Individuals take the risk of investing money to build factories to produce what people want, creating profits for the investors and jobs for people. Because more people have jobs and can buy all the new products being produced, their standard of living improves and the factory owners make profits that they can reinvest to build new factories to produce more goods, and so on. In the end, said

Adam Smith developed a theory of wealth creation more than 200 years ago. His theory relied on entrepreneurs working to improve their lives. To make money, they would provide goods and services, as well as jobs, for others.

<www.adamsmith
institute.com>

This is the Web site of
the British Adam Smith
Institute. The site includes
information on Adam
Smith himself and on the
work of the Institute.
Check it out to learn more
about this man, whose
ideas spawned much of
modern thought about
how capitalism works.

mixed economies
Economies with varying degrees
of state ownership or control of
the means of production or both.

<www.marxists.org>

The writings of Karl Marx
and his colleague Friedrich
Engels are, indeed, diamet-
rically opposed to the capitalist views of writers like
Adam Smith, John Maynard
Keynes, and Ayn Rand. Visit
this Web site to learn more
about Marx and his teach-
ings and the work of others
who shared his views.

Smith, individual producers and buyers make for a prosperous and happy society. As the first person to develop a theory about capitalism, Smith is called the father of economics.

Unfortunately, the normal operations of our capitalist economy, while producing the benefits noted previously and as envisaged by Adam Smith, also produces many unpleasant side effects. There is much poverty, unemployment, and homelessness. How can rich countries like Canada allow children to be hungry and homeless? Furthermore, there are up-and-down cycles that are unpredictable and cause a great deal of hardship in and disruption of people's lives. The search for solutions to these and other problems gave rise to attempts to improve or replace capitalism.

•••• ▬▬▬ ••••

DIFFERENT ECONOMIC SYSTEMS

By the twentieth century different countries had developed various forms of capitalism, as well as communist and socialist systems. These systems arose as countries attempted to overcome the weaknesses of the capitalist system. The differences involved greater or lesser degrees of government regulation, control, and ownership of the means of production—the various ways of creating wealth and providing goods and services for their people. The United States is the strongest and most important capitalist country. The Soviet Union and China were once the most important communist countries. In between were various countries with a variety of systems, often referred to as **mixed economies**, that is, economies with degrees of state ownership or control of the means of production. At one end of the spectrum, no country, including the United States and Canada, is an example of pure or 100 percent capitalism. Similarly no country was a pure example of socialism or communism.

••• KARL MARX AND ALTERNATIVES TO CAPITALISM •••

One person who gave a lot of thought to this problem in the middle of the nineteenth century was a German economist called Karl Marx. He eventually wrote a massive multi-volume book called *Das Kapital*, which contained a detailed analysis of capitalism and its contradictions. Marx also laid out a vision for a radically different economic structure, calling it a *socialist* society. He envisioned no private ownership of factories and companies. The state, representing the people, would own all the means of production. Marx believed that this would eventually make it possible for every person to have all their needs provided for, at which time the society would then become a communist system.

This system of Marxian beliefs attracted a lot of support. In the twentieth century Marxism resulted in several revolutions in European countries in the attempt to set up communist states. These revolutions were unsuccessful in Hungary and Germany, but in the huge Russian Empire, a new communist state, the Soviet Union, was established in 1917. By 1949 there were eight communist countries in Eastern Europe and four in east Asia, including China, the most populous country in the world. Finally, North America saw the addition of Cuba in 1960 to the communist family of countries.

All of these countries had repressive, dictatorial governments, but they did achieve some economic growth and avoided the cycles that bedevilled capitalist countries. Everyone was guaranteed a job and free educational and health services; however, the accumulation of a variety of serious problems, both external and internal, led to the collapse of the communist systems in all these states with a few exceptions. By the end of the twentieth century only China, Viet Nam, Cuba, and North Korea still made formal claims to espousing Marxian ideology. In reality all these countries, with the exception of North Korea, have adopted important capitalist practices and goals and are moving toward becoming capitalist mixed economies. We will look shortly at mixed economies.

It is now clear that the capitalist economic system has become the only viable system in the world. That does not mean that there are no problems with it. On the contrary, as we entered the new millennium, there were very serious problems in many countries and in the world's economy. *Time* magazine, for example, referred to "how close the world came to economic meltdown" in 1998.[1] We look at some of these problems in this chapter. In the next chapter we look at how the capitalist system works in Canada. In the rest of this chapter we examine how that system woks and how it affects Canada and your future, in terms of what career opportunities are likely to be growing or declining. We start by looking at how free markets work.

Even though people in Cuba are suffering from the lack of goods and services available in many other countries because of the American embargo on trade, loans, and investments, Cuban leader Fidel Castro declared that Cuba would remain communist. Castro has been Cuba's leader since his revolution triumphed in 1959.

···· ▬▬ ····

HOW FREE MARKETS WORK

The free market system is one in which decisions about what goods to produce or services to provide in what quantities and at what prices, are made by buyers and sellers making free choices. The buyers may be companies or individual consumers. In Canada and all over the world buyers are constantly sending signals to sellers about what they what and at what prices. They send such signals by buying a lot, not very much, or nothing at all. The terms economists use for these activities are *supply* and *demand*. **Supply** is the quantity of particular products or services that suppliers are willing to sell at certain prices and at certain locations. **Demand** is the quantity of those products or services that buyers are willing to buy at those prices and at those locations. Where supply and demand meet or intersect is called the *equilibrium point* and becomes the actual price at which the transaction takes place (see Figure 2.1). That's what the theory says, but let's see how the free market and supply and demand actually play out on a global scale.

supply
The quantity of particular products or servcies that suppliers are willing to sell at certain prices and at certain locations.

demand
The quantity of particular products or services that buyers are willing to buy at certain prices and at certain locations.

··· WORLD MARKETS: SUPPLY AND DEMAND ···

Every day billions of consumers throughout the world are sending signals to millions of producers throughout the world, telling them what they want. The

					Equilibrium Point					
Price	$11	$10	$9	$8	$7	$6	$5	$4	$3	$2	$ 1
Number willing to buy a steak at this price	0	1	2	3	4	5	6	7	8	9	10
Number willing to sell a steak at this price	10	9	8	7	6	5	4	3	2	1	0

FIGURE **2.1**

····

BUYERS AND SELLERS AT DIFFERENT PRICES

Five people are willing to buy or sell a steak for $6.

signals are sent through the amount of goods and services being bought. The signals are sent very quickly, so there should be little delay in ending surpluses and shortages. In the real world, however, there are many interferences to the free exchange of goods and services among countries. Consequently, some countries have surpluses (for example, Canada has a surplus of many crops) and others suffer from scarcity (many countries do not have sufficient food). A free market system would seem to be the best system for improving the world's economic condition, yet there are many limitations and impediments to the free market system.

••• LIMITATIONS OF THE FREE MARKET SYSTEM •••

The free market system, with its freedom and incentives, was a major factor in creating the wealth that advanced countries now enjoy. Some experts even speak of the free market system as a true economic miracle. But certain inequities seem to be inherent in the system. As capitalism developed, business people in England, Europe, United States, Canada, and other countries began to create wealth. They set up factories and hired people, and the countries began to prosper. Soon these business people became the wealthiest class in each country. Although this new system created jobs and wealth, the benefits did not flow evenly to everybody. Factory owners built large homes, had fancy carriages, and enjoyed luxurious lifestyles. Workers lived in poverty and had no security.

Thus, we have the situation today in which many people cannot afford enough food or adequate housing. The same thing is true of dental care, clothing, and other goods and services: the wealthy seem to get all they need, and the poor gets less than they need.

MIXED ECONOMIES

A different and more common path to reduction of the unpleasant side effects of capitalism took the form of government intervention to restrict and regulate the totally free market. Starting in the nineteenth century, governments in the newly industrialized countries in Europe, Japan, and North America began to play a larger role in exerting some control over the rapidly growing capitalist economies. Canada, like the U.S. and other countries, passed laws and regulations and established agencies in the attempt to smooth out the worst features and inequities of the expanding economy mentioned previously in this chapter. These attempts created the category of a *mixed economy*. In the next chapter we will examine in detail how and why Canadian governments began to influence the operation of the free market in Canada.

<www.wam.umd.edu/
~mglondon/London/
Keynes/keynes.htm>

A visit to this Web site will give you the flavour of Keynes's work and the impact that he has had on modern economic thought.

In the 1930s the whole world, except for the Soviet Union, which had a socialist and communist economy, was plunged into a very serious economic decline called the *Great Depression*. This was a terrible period of vast unemployment, hunger, and homelessness. Businesses were going bankrupt and economies were shrinking. For several years nothing governments tried seemed to reverse the conditions. Then, economist John Maynard Keynes, profiled at the beginning of the chapter, came up with his proposals to lift the world out of the seemingly endless Depression.

As the Profile notes, Keynesian economics were applied by the U.S., Canada, and many European governments and they seemed to work. A half-century later the world economy was in relatively good shape and a movement developed, led by the English and U.S. governments (which the Canadian government supported), to reduce the role of government. This movement led to a wave of deregulation and privatization (governments selling off companies they owned). The general push was to have freer uncontrolled markets in a back-to-Adam-Smith movement. This movement was led by the giant corporations seeking the ability to operate more freely across borders in the quickly growing globalization of business.

However, as the end of the twentieth century approached, serious cracks in the economy of various countries began to threaten the whole global economy. In country after country that had formerly enjoyed strong growth, currency values were crashing, foreign investors were withdrawing their money, and bankruptcy and unemployment rates were rising sharply. Countries like South Korea, Thailand, Indonesia, Mexico and Brazil were affected. Russia was a particularly bad case and concern was widespread that it faced total collapse of its financial institutions and its economy. Mighty Japan had been unable to pull itself out of a decade-long slump. The combination of these problems had many world leaders seriously worried about the possibility of a major global recession and about how to avoid one.

Again, many voices were heard suggesting or demanding that governments should *do something*. A good example comes from an editorial in the prestigious U.S. weekly, *Business Week*:

> *Without government playing a major role, international capital flows can lead to corruption, overcapacity, currency devaluations, recessions, and even a backlash against capitalism itself…. Free markets need government action to work best.*[2]

This editorial also shows how the global economy is quite different from what it was in the 1930s. The entire globe is closely linked and all countries are dependent on each other for investment, employment, technology, and exports. In the next chapter we will look at the global effect of the serious Asian economic problems nicknamed the *Asian flu*. These problems are like a disease that can spread, and in 1998 they started spreading rapidly around the world. Problems such as these affect all Canadians and in particular your job prospects.

••• THE MIXED ECONOMY OF CANADA •••

As mentioned earlier, Canada is not a purely capitalist national. Rather, it has a mixed economy, a combination of free markets and government allocation of resources. As a mixed economy, Canada falls somewhere between a pure capitalist state and a socialist state. This is probably the most common economic system in the world today. The degree of government involvement in the economy is a matter of some debate.

Several features have played a major role in Canada's becoming an independent economic entity with a high percentage of government involvement in the economy.

First, we are one of the largest countries in the world geographically, but we have a small population (30 million in 1999). We have one of the lowest population densities in the world.

Most important, our neighbour to the south has nine times our population and an economy even greater than that proportion, speaks our language, is very aggressive economically, and is the most powerful country in the world. The United States exerts a very powerful influence on Canada. To control our destiny, Canadian governments have passed many laws and regulations to make sure significant economic and cultural institutions, such as banks,

Reaching Beyond Our Borders

<www.standardandpoors.com>
<www.dbrs.com>
<www.cbrs.com>

How Two U.S. Companies Affect the Canadian Economy

There are two companies in New York whose decisions have a significant effect on Canadian governments, businesses, and consumers. Both Moody's Investors Services Inc. and Standard & Poor's Corp. (S&P) are important and famous credit-rating agencies. They evaluate the degree of risk that investors would be exposed to if they bought the bonds of governments or companies around the world. They then give each bond a specific rating, such as AA or B+, and that rating has a major effect on the interest rate that must be set for that bond.

When a Canadian government or company needs to borrow on a long-term basis, which they do regularly, the interest cost for the life of that bond—5, 15, or 25 years—is determined by an American company that has established an excellent international reputation for reliable credit ratings. Each rating level leads to a particular interest rate. The higher the level (meaning lower degree of risk), the lower the interest rate. Conversely, the lower the rating (meaning higher degree of risk), the higher the interest rate investors will demand.

When the Canadian (or a provincial) government issues a 30-year bond and the rating requires a higher interest rate than planned, it could cost that government hundreds of millions of dollars over the 30-year period. That cost could lead to higher taxes and have a ripple effect on the entire economy.

Further, since the level of interest rates for Canadian government bonds affects general interest levels in Canada, the impact on the economy is very significant, affecting the rates businesses and consumers have to pay when they take loans from banks or other financial institutions. It also affects mortgage rates and the rates financial institutions pay to depositors who invest their money with them. Large businesses that normally borrow by issuing bonds are also directly affected by the ratings of their own bonds by Moody's or S&P. These ratings also determine how much interest they must pay.

There are two Canadian bond-rating companies: the Dominion Bond Rating Service and the Canadian Bond Rating Service. Their ratings are important, but do not carry the international weight that Moody's and S&P do with the international lenders who buy Canadian bonds. In effect, the actions of two foreign companies can have major repercussions in the Canadian economy. Of course, this applies to many countries, not only to Canada.

On March 20, 1996, Premier Bouchard of Quebec, after a three-day meeting with major provincial groups to get consensus on a budget-balancing program, announced he would personally go to New York to convince Moody's and S&P that the plan was sound and that they should maintain their ratings of Quebec bonds.

Sources: Interviews with various stockbrokers, March 1999, *Globe and Mail, Report on Business,* March 1996, p. B24ff; CBC news, March 21, 1996.

<www.moodys.com>
<wallstreetdirectory.com>

These are additional Web sites you can visit to see what services Moody's and Standard & Poors provide.

insurance companies, and radio and TV stations, remain under Canadian control. (Even powerful countries like the United States and Japan have similar regulations.)

All of these factors led to the Canadian capitalist system taking on many characteristics of a mixed economy. Massive government support was necessary to build ou first national rail line, the CPR, in the 1880s. When air transport was beginning in the 1930s, no company wanted to risk investing in it in such a large country with only 10 million people spread thinly across the land. So the government set up Air Canada (then called Trans Canada Airlines) to transport mail, people, and freight. There are many such examples of government action to protect the national interest.

In the 1980s many countries, including Canada, began to reduce government involvement in, and regulation of, the economy. This trend toward deregulation was widespread. In Canada, airlines, banks, and the trucking industry have all seen a marked reduction in regulatory control. Even in communist China there have been significant movements in this direction.

The former communist countries of Europe, namely Hungary, Poland, and the Czech Republic, and the republics of the former Soviet Union are moving rapidly in this direction as well. It may not be an exaggeration to say that communism is disappearing as it moves toward mixed economies, socialist countries move toward mixed economies, and mixed economies move toward purer capitalist systems.

···· ▬▬ ····

ECONOMICS AND BUSINESS

The strength of the economy has a tremendous effect on business. When the economy is strong and growing, most businesses prosper and almost everyone benefits through plentiful jobs, reasonably good wages, and sufficient revenues for the government to provide needed goods and services. When the economy is weak, however, businesses are weakened as well, employment and wages fall, and government revenues decline as a result.

Because business and the economy are so closely linked, business newspapers and magazines are full of economic terms and concepts. It is virtually impossible to read such business reports with much understanding unless you are familiar with the economic concepts and terms being used. One purpose of this chapter is to help you learn additional economic concepts, terms, and issues—the kinds that you will be seeing daily if you read the business press, as we encourage you to do.

··· GROSS DOMESTIC PRODUCT ···

Almost every discussion about a nation's economy is based on **gross domestic product (GDP)**, the total value of a country's output of goods and services in a given year. It is good for GDP to grow, but not too fast or too slowly.

Here's how Canada's GDP grew, in annual percentage rates, in the last few decades:[3]

gross domestic product (GDP)
The total value of a country's output of goods and services in a given year.

1960s	5.2
1970s	4.3
1980s	3.2
1991 to 1998	3.1

The indications for 1999 were even better as, based on first-quarter figures, the Bank of Canada says GDP grew at an annual rate of 4.0 percent.[4] One way to increase GDP is to be more productive, to increase productivity. This important subject is discussed in more detail in Chapter 10, but as a brief preview is relevant at this point, we will look at productivity shortly.

DISTRIBUTION OF GDP   The money that is earned from producing goods and services goes to the employees who produce them, to the people who own the businesses, and to governments in the form of taxes. The size of the share that goes to governments has a major impact on the economy as a whole. The general trend worldwide is for governments to reduce their share of GDP. A constant debate rages in Canada (and other countries) as to what percentage of the GDP pie should go to governments to most favourably affect the economy.

It is difficult to make comparisons between countries, because the right percentage depends on what services each government provides. For example, in Canada our national health-care system is financed by taxes. In the United States there is no such universal plan, so taxes are lower, but individuals and companies must pay these very substantial costs themselves.

··· PRODUCTIVITY AND LABOUR COST ···

productivity
The total output of goods and services in a given period divided by the total hours of labour required to provide them.

Productivity is measured by dividing the total output of goods and services of a given period by the total hours of labour required to produce them. A similar calculation is done for countries to compare their rates of productivity. An increase in productivity is achieved by (1) producing a *greater* quantity of a certain quality for a *given* amount of work hours or (2) producing the *same* quantity with *fewer* work hours.

Labour cost measures the same equation in dollars. The dollar value of the output is divided by the dollar value of the work hours to arrive at the labour cost per unit. Anything that increases productivity or reduces labour cost makes a business, and a country, more competitive. The great gains in productivity that have occurred during the past century, especially in the past few decades, are due mainly to the introduction of increasingly efficient machinery, equipment, and processes. The past 15 years in particular saw computers and robots play a major role in this development.

It's a very difficult thing a measure a country's productivity or the rate at which it is improving. In mid-1999 a fierce dispute raged about how much Canada's productivity had improved in the past decade or two. A good exam-

In the service sector, workers are becoming more productive as the use of robots, computers, and other machinery increases. It is becoming increasingly important to measure service quality as well as quantity.

ple of this argument was an article in the *Montreal Gazette* in which Statistics Canada states that its revised figures show we have been performing as well as, if not better than, the U.S. since at least 1985. However, Industry Canada, another government ministry, maintains that its figures show that Canada is slipping farther behind the U.S. Then we have the prestigious Paris-based Organization for Economic Co-operation and Development (OECD) saying it erred in rating Canada too low and it was now in the process of revising these figures upward. The OECD blames Statistics Canada for the confusion because the latter revised previously issued statistics.[5]

Further, in the next chapter you will see (from the same *Montreal Gazette* article) that the OECD continues to rate Canada's standard of living as being 10 percent above the average of industrial countries and the powerful World Economic Forum puts Canada fifth in international competitiveness in 1998, only 10 percent behind the U.S. The whole issue of assessing international competitiveness is complex and open to varying opinions, and is discussed in more detail in the next chapter.

Any country that does not keep up with the international level of technological improvements falls behind in the fierce global competitive battle. In Canada this is a major problem, because our businesses are spending less on research and development than many advanced countries.

Of course, technological advances usually lead to people being replaced by machines, often contributing to unemployment. We will now examine this important issue.

Progress Check

- What is a mixed economy? What are its advantages over a free market economy?
- What does deregulation mean and how is it affecting the economy of Canada?
- Can you define gross domestic product? Productivity? Labour cost?
- How can productivity be improved and labour cost decreased?
- Why is productivity so important to a country's ability to compete?

THE ISSUE OF UNEMPLOYMENT

For a decade, Canada's official unemployment rate has ranged from 7.5 to 11.3 percent (see Figure 2.2). This means that officially 1 million to 1.5 million people were constantly reported as being out of work. The real rate is much higher because Statistics Canada does not include people who have given up looking for jobs, those who are working at part-time or temporary jobs or who stay in or return to school because they cannot find full-time work, and various other categories of people. If you work only one hour per week, you are classified as employed.

People are unemployed in Canada for various reasons. Perhaps their employer goes out of business or their company cuts staff. Young persons enter the job market looking for their first job and other employees quit their jobs but have trouble finding new ones. Companies merge and jobs are consolidated or trimmed. Companies transfer their operations to another country or a branch of a foreign company is closed down.

Of course, in a period of economic recession, such as in the early 1980s or 1990s, unemployment increases. Different categories of unemployment are discussed next. However, one of the important causes of unemployment in the

Source: Statistics Canada, CANSIM, Matrix 3451.

past decade has been relentless downsizing by many large companies. Every
few weeks a major company announced layoffs of thousands of employees.
These layoffs were driven by intense global competition (discussed later in the
chapter) and technological advances. The former drove companies to relentlessly reduce costs, while the latter enabled them to operate with fewer
employees. In Chapter 8 we will see that some management experts believe
that the downsizing trend has been overdone and may have consequences for
companies that have made significant reductions in their workforces.

An important cause of unemployment is technological advances. When a
company acquires a new machine that replaces five existing machines, each
tended by one person, then four of the employees may no longer be required.
When computer terminals are installed at the desks of senior managers, they
may need fewer middle managers and secretaries. They can now access and
send information directly. This situation creates *technological unemployment*.

This art student tries
to earn tuition fees
during a jobless summer
by creating street art.
Finding innovative ways
to earn money can be
especially important
during difficult
economic times.

Technology can lower costs for companies, making them more competitive and able to expand and hire more people. Although we are now more automated than ever, we also have more people working then ever before. So while people are constantly being displaced by machines, eventually new jobs are created—and somebody has to make and service those new machines.

From the economic point of view, unemployment is a great waste of resources. It means that people who could be producing goods or services are producing nothing—and receiving unemployment benefits or welfare. This reduces GDP. The terrible human cost of continued unemployment—the lack of funds and the demoralization that can destroy individuals and families—must also be considered. Retraining our unemployed citizens to become more skilled and thus help the country become more competitive is a necessity.

··· CATEGORIES OF UNEMPLOYMENT ···

Cyclical unemployment is caused by a recession or similar downturn in the business cycle. Unemployment fluctuates with the economic cycles of boom and recession that occur regularly in capitalist economies.

Seasonal unemployment arises in industries in which the demand for labour varies with the season. For example, ski hills employ very few people in summer. Summer resorts and some children's camps to not employ anyone in winter. The Christmas season sees an increase in retail jobs. Summer is a much bigger tourist season in Canada than winter.

Structural unemployment results from changes in the structure of the economy that phase out certain industries or jobs. Employees of fish plants in the Atlantic provinces are laid off when fish catches are reduced or fishing banned to rebuild cod stocks. Our shift from a manufacturing-based economy to a service-dominated one is a major structural cause of unemployment. This situation is further aggravated as manufacturers restructure to meet strong international competition. Canada is moving from a resource-based to a knowledge-based economy.

Employees laid off in a tire plant in Ontario do not have the skills to be employed by a forestry company in B.C. that is trying to hire more staff. There is an unfilled demand for knowledge workers in computer software and other aspects of information technology. Retraining programs may help unemployed people to acquire the necessary new skills.

REGIONAL DIFFERENCES   Finally, since Canada is such a large country with regional economies, there are always major regional differences. For example, when the auto and related businesses were booming in Ontario in the mid-1980s, the Atlantic provinces were enduring unemployment rates in the 15 percent and higher range. When B.C. was booming in the early 1990s, Quebec and Ontario underwent a serious decline and had high unemployment rates. Saskatchewan suffered a decade-long problem of unfair foreign competition in the grain market due to massive government subsidies of competing countries' farmers. The regional unemployment picture can be seen in Figure 2.3.

cyclical unemployment
Unemployment caused by a recession or similar downturn in the business cycle.

seasonal unemployment
Unemployment that occurs when the demand for labour varies over the year.

structural unemployment
Unemployment that results from changes in the structure of the economy that phase out certain industries or jobs.

Critical Thinking

Would Canada be better off today if we had not introduced modern farm machinery? More people would be employed on the farm if we had not. Would the world be better off in the future if we did not introduce new computers, robots, and machinery? They do take away jobs in the short run. What happened to the farmers who were displaced by machines? What will happen to today's workers who are being replaced by machines?

FIGURE **2.3**
· · · ·

**ANNUAL PROVINCIAL
UNEMPLOYMENT RATES**

You can see how
provincial rates of
unemployment vary
widely.

	Actual	Estimated	
	1998 (%)	1991 (%)	2000 (%)
Newfoundland	17.9	17.4	16.3
Prince Edward Island	13.9	14.5	14.1
Nova Scotia	10.7	10.4	10.6
New Brunswick	12.1	11.5	11.4
Quebec	10.4	9.8	9.8
Ontario	7.2	6.8	6.7
Manitoba	5.7	5.6	5.4
Saskatchewan	5.9	6.1	6.1
Alberta	5.7	5.9	5.9
British Columbia	8.9	8.9	8.8
Canada	8.3	7.9	7.9

Source: *Canadian Regional Outlook*, Bank of Montreal, February 1999.

Progress
Check

- Can you explain the differences between seasonal, structural, and cyclical unemployment? Which is causing the largest unemployment today?
- What are regional differences in unemployment? Why do they exist?

· · · · ▬▬▬ · · · ·

INFLATION AND THE CONSUMER PRICE INDEX[2]

Inflation
A general rise in the prices of
goods and services over time.

One of the measures of how an economy is doing is its ability to control inflation. **Inflation** refers to a general rise in the price level of goods and services over time. For 20 years from the early 1970s, Canada's inflation rate was substantially above 3 percent. The rate peaked in 1981 at 12.5 percent, and hovered between 4 and 6 percent until 1992, when it dropped below 2 percent, where it has remained. The question of inflation was a central issue in Canada for almost 20 years. Economists do not agree about the causes of inflation, the specific cures, or whether the cures might be worse than the disease.

Inflation increases the cost of doing business. When a company borrows money, interest costs are higher; employees demand increases to keep up with the rise in cost of living; suppliers raise their prices; and as a result the company is forced to raise its prices. If other countries succeed in keeping their inflation rates down, then Canadian companies will become less competitive on the world market.

One popular measure of price changes over time (inflation indicators) is the **consumer price index (CPI)**. The consumer price index measures monthly changes in the price of a basket of goods and services for an average family. Such an index gives a vivid picture of the effects of inflation on consumer prices. If the cost of the market basket is $1000 one month and goes up to $1006 the next, the inflation rate was 0.6 percent for the month, or roughly 7.2 percent annually. At that rate, the cost of consumer goods would double in about 10 years. Figure 2.4 shows the whole CPI picture from 1981 to 1998.

Because the inflation rate in Canada and in most countries recently has been low and fairly stable and because there is a growing concern about a serious global economic recession, attention has now shifted to the possibility of deflation, which is the opposite of inflation. **Deflation** is a general decline in the price level of goods and services. Deflation may bring new problems to the fore, problems the world has not seen since the Great Depression of the 1930s.

consumer price index (CPI)
Measures monthly changes in the price of a basket of goods and services that an average family would buy.

deflation
A general decline in the price level of goods and services.

•••• ▬▬▬ ••••

THE NATIONAL DEBT[6]

Canadian government policies for many years followed only one of Keynes's suggestions. The government borrowed heavily for many years, but it forgot to reduce spending when times were good to pay back these loans. The result is a large **national debt**, the accumulated amount owed by the Canadian government from its past borrowings. This debt totals approximately $600 billion, and the interest alone amounts to approximately $100 million every day. Twenty percent of the total revenues the government receives go to pay interest on the national debt.

Governments must borrow when they spend more in a year than they receive from taxes and other sources. An excess of expenditures over revenues is called a **deficit**. In Canada 25 years of annual deficits, starting in the mid-1970s, has resulted in a huge national debt. The United States and many other countries also have serious debt loads that limit efforts by governments to help their economies out of a recession. However, in relation to the size of its economy—its GDP—Canada's debt problem is one of the biggest among developed countries.

national debt
The accumulated amount owed by the Canadian government from its past borrowings.

deficit
An excess of expenditures over revenues.

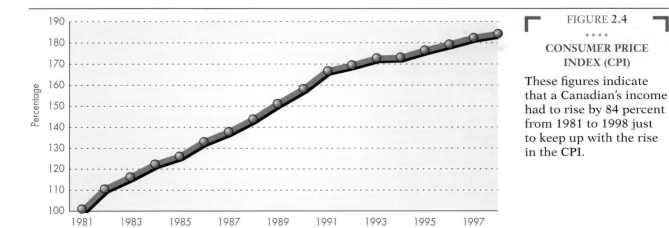

FIGURE **2.4**
••••
CONSUMER PRICE INDEX (CPI)

These figures indicate that a Canadian's income had to rise by 84 percent from 1981 to 1998 just to keep up with the rise in the CPI.

Source: Statistics Canada, CANSIM, Matrix 9957.

Spotlight on Small Business

Internet Tax Fairness Coalition
<www.stopnettax.org>

Selling in Cyberspace

The impact of the Internet is discussed in several chapters in this book. Every day millions of World Wide Web users are browsing, shopping, ordering, and paying online for all kinds of products and services for individual and commercial usage. Many people also use this medium to search for jobs because they can quickly access a wide range of job possibilities in more than one country. The Internet has totally changed many factors and conditions relating not only to businesses, but to governments as well.

Consider this fictional situation: software developer, Virinder Assad, lives in India and has no office. Assad operates out of his van where he has a fax, laptop, printer, and a cellphone. He is an employee of a small software company located in the home of the owner, Tom Lee, in Halifax, Nova Scotia. The company sells software products exclusively via the Internet to buyers all over Canada and the U.S., and is beginning to get nibbles from some European countries. If a customer in Germany ▲ downloads software and pays for it by credit card, where was the sale made? Which country is entitled to charge the taxes? In Canada we have the GST and provincial sales taxes (except for Alberta) and Germany has a value added tax (VAT). What about Mr. Assad? He never comes to Canada, but is he subject to any Canadian employee taxes or benefits? How about Tom Lee's company: can it be deemed to be operating in provinces and U.S. states where buyers are located? If so will it be subject to taxes and other legislation affecting businesses operating in those jurisdictions?

Because of the explosive growth of Internet developments, the issues of who is entitled to collect taxes or has responsibility for product warranty or employee-related issues are becoming increasingly complex. Determining just where an Internet transaction was made can be difficult. The huge growth in the number of such transactions has significant implications for the economies and tax revenues of countries, provinces, and states.

A large debt load means that when tough times hit our economy, such as in the early 1990s, our government is unable to follow Keynes's recipe—reduce taxes and borrow to spend more—to help the economy out of a recession. Consequently, taxes remain high just when businesses need to reduce the cost of operations to stay afloat. Individuals also have less take-home pay to put back into the economy through spending. These factors deepen and prolong a recession in Canada.

Government cutbacks have resulted in reduced payments to better-off seniors. Spending cuts have been implemented to reduce the deficit.

••• WIPING OUT ANNUAL DEFICITS: •••
PROCESS AND RESULTS

After relentless pressure from business organizations and right-wing political groups, the Canadian government decided in 1996 that the only way out of that recession was to eliminate annual deficits and stop the debt from growing. This plan meant cutting expenses and cash outlays as much as possible, including reducing transfers to provinces to pay for health care, education, and welfare. the government also reduced employment insurance (EI) payments by raising eligibility standards, paying for shorter periods, and paying smaller amounts. The government also laid off thousands of people and reduced pension payment to wealthier senior citizens.

These reductions in spending contributed to Canada's slow recovery from the recession. Increased government borrowing and spending stimulates an economy, while cuts in spending have the opposite effect—they slow down the economy.

By 1998 the government was able to announce that, for the first time in 25 years, government operations had resulted in a surplus of $3.5 billion rather than a deficit. Another surplus followed in 1999. Minister of Finance Paul Martin announced that this surplus would be used to reduce the national debt and that future surpluses would also be applied to the debt. As the debt comes down, the annual interest costs are reduced. Every billion-dollar reduction in the debt reduces annual interest costs by about $50 million. A cumulative $10 billion reduction leads to a $500 million annual savings in interest. Reducing government spending will allow the government to reduce taxes, which in turn will stimulate the economy as companies and individuals will have more disposable income.

Members of the Poverty Action Network stage a demonstration to demand more welfare money for a longer time.

The drastic slashing of government spending was strongly opposed by left-wing political groups and many organizations such as churches, unions, welfare groups, food banks, and many other community-centred groups because of the hardship these cuts inflicted on many people. Reduced EI and welfare payments, a reduction in hospital funding, the closing of hospitals, and so on affected many poor and sick people. Cuts to higher education funding resulted in fewer staff members and more students per class, higher fees, increased costs of some services and a reduction of other services. Food banks across Canada reported a jump in the number of people seeking food. When economic problems become severe, attempts to remedy them can be difficult and painful.

The outlook for the Canadian economy in the next few years affects your future because the economy will determine your prospects for a good job. We look next at how the Canadian economy is likely to perform.

···· ▬▬▬ ····

THE OUTLOOK FOR THE CANADIAN ECONOMY

With the health of the world's economy uncertain as we enter the twenty-first century, the Canadian economy's performance in the next few years is also uncertain. We are living in a very closely connected and interdependent global economy. Economic problems in Asia and South America can quickly spread to Europe and North America. Canada, as a major exporter, immediately feels the impact of economic weakness elsewhere. If the countries who import our products reduce their buying or if world prices of lumber, newsprint, coal, oil, nickel, wheat, canola, or other commodities drop, we feel the pinch very quickly.

At the end of the 1990s the state of the global economy was discussed using words like *turmoil, crisis, collapse, depression*. The economy moved from the business pages to the front pages and conflicting analyses were made by economic and business journals, Nobel Laureate economists, financial experts, and governments around the world.

Given this level of confusion, what is reasonable to expect from the Canadian economy in the next few years? Canada emerged from a recession at the beginning of the 1990s and our economy has been expanding, as measured by growth in GDP. Unemployment has dropped from more than 11 percent to less than 8 percent (see Figure 2.2), leaving Canada's unemployment rate in the middle versus other industrialized countries. The finance minister warns of future difficulties but is cautiously optimistic that GDP growth will continue, but at a slower rate than in 1997 and 1998. The Bank of Canada has lowered interest rates, following the lead of the Federal Reserve Board in the U.S.

The interest rate cuts were designed to give companies the confidence to continue investing in capital expansion because lower interest rates mean lower costs of borrowing. Lower interest rates also mean lower mortgage rates, encouraging families to buy homes and stimulating the construction industry. Growth in the construction industry then has a spillover effect on many feeder industries. Consumers are also encouraged to spend more as the costs of carrying credit card debt also declines with lower interest rates. Overall, the cuts should stimulate the entire economy, providing more jobs for Canadians.

Encouraging reports have been issued by Gordon Thiessen, governor of the Bank of Canada, and by the senior vice-president and chief economist of the Bank of Nova Scotia, Warren Jestin. Thiessen said that "Canada has shaken off the effects of the Asian crisis and is on course for much stronger economic growth than previously expected." Jestin commented that "the Canadian economy has weathered two years of global economic turbulence remarkably well." He did see some "storm clouds" ahead, but believed that the "prospects are relatively bright into the new millennium."[7]

···· ▬▬▬ ····

PROSPECTS FOR CAREERS AND JOBS

What does all this mean as far as your future is concerned? The Canadian and the world economic pictures looked much rosier at the end of 1999 than they

Ethical Dilemma

REVIEW

Remember the question about the huge impact on Canadian life of governments slashing expenditures to reduce and wipe out annual budgetary deficits? Our executives answer that difficult as it was, with many people losing jobs and government aid, there was no choice. The method used may leave room for argument, but not the need to do it. Reilley notes that "the national debt grew because Canadian governments at all levels kept piling on new and expensive programs without taking stock of either the utility or cost. Also, outdated and inefficient programs remained on the books." He concludes that "the current adjustment in Canada is painful

to many. Yet without this adjustment, our standard of living and productivity as a country would erode."

Bédard comments that "what most people demanded of government was not necessarily to slash all social programs; many of these programs are what makes Canada unique. [But] the bureaucracies surrounding many programs are much too heavy and complex. By reducing inefficiencies and waste, many of the objectives could have been attained." He concludes that "Canada can no longer afford to be as generous as it has been, [which is why there was] the need to reduce certain programs to balance the budget."

had looked at the start of the year. The new millennium will offer young people a good choice of jobs and careers, and young people with the most years of education will continue to have a lower unemployment rate. Many jobs will be available in our continually globalizing and technologically driven world. In respect to job prospects, your future looks a lot more promising than it did a few years ago.

Progress Check

- What is a recession? What is deflation?
- What is the size of the national debt? Why is it so important?
- According to Keynes, how should the government use fiscal policy to manage the economy?

SUMMARY

1. A free market system is one in which decisions about what to produce and in what quantities are decided by the market.
   - ***How do supply and demand affect what kind and in what quantity products are produced in a free market system?***
   The price of a product tells producers to make more or less of a product. The more money producers make from higher prices, the more product they are likely to produce. Price is determined by supply and demand. The higher the quantity of demand, the higher the price. In turn, the higher the supply, the lower the price.

1. Describe how free markets work using the terms *supply, demand,* and *prices*.

2. In spite of the wealth that countries with a free market system enjoy, the system suffers from certain inequities.
   - ***What are some limitations of the free market system?***
   In countries with free market systems, the rich can buy almost everything, and the poor often cannot buy what they need. There may be a high crime rate and tolerance of negative social behaviour; economic freedoms and social freedoms often go hand in hand.

2. Discuss some limitations of the free market system and what countries are doing to offset those limitations.

3. Canada does not operate under a pure capitalist system but is a mixed economic system.
   - ***What does it mean to say Canada has a mixed economy?***
   Canada falls somewhere between a pure capitalist state and a socialist state. Its economy is a combination of free markets and government allocation of resources.

3. Understand the mixed economy of Canada.

4. Inflation is the rise in the cost of living and a recession is a decline in the overall economy.
   - ***How do these and other economic developments affect business?***
   When the economy is healthy, companies expand, buy new equipment, and hire more employees, which further stimulates the economy. In a recession the reverse happens, deepening the recession. Inflation leads to demands for higher wages as employees try to maintain their standard of living. This raises prices, boosting inflation, and making companies less competitive internationally.

4. Explain how inflation, recession, and other economic developments affect business.

5. When the government is spending more than it is receiving, the national debt increases.
   - ***What is the national debt and how did it get so high?***
   The national debt is the sum of money the government has borrowed and has not paid back. It is the accumulation of annual deficits.

5. Discuss the issues surrounding the national debt and its effect on business.

• *How does the large national debt affect Canadian companies?*
Companies pay higher taxes due to the large annual interest payments, reducing their ability to compete with companies in countries where taxes are lower.

KEY TERMS
• • • • • •

capitalism 37
consumer price
   index (CPI) 49
cyclical
   unemployment 47
deficit 49
deflation 49

demand 39
economics 37
gross domestic
   product (GDP) 43
inflation 48
mixed economies 38
national debt 49

productivity 44
seasonal
   unemployment 47
structural
   unemployment 47
supply 39

DEVELOPING WORKPLACE SKILLS

1. What are some of the disadvantages of living in a free society? How could such disadvantages be minimized? What are the advantages? How could Canada broaden the base of the free market system? Write a short essay describing why a poor person in India might reject capitalism and prefer a socialist state. You could debate capitalist versus socialist societies with a classmate to further reveal the issues.

2. Identify one of the most widely debated economic issues and discuss the various viewpoints with your classmates and instructor. Choose a position and be ready to defend it by researching facts and figures to support it. Have you set up a filing system yet to maintain such information?

3. The text discusses three major indicators of an economy's health: gross domestic product (GDP), unemployment rate, and consumer price index (CPI). The text also describes the close relationship of productivity to GDP. Each of these indicators rises and falls during periods of recession and periods of growth. Devise two charts to illustrate whether each economic indicator goes up, down, or remains the same during a condition of (1) economic recession and (2) growth.

4. Most of the world's nations are moving toward some variation of a mixed economy that could be labelled welfare capitalism. What do you see as the primary differences between the emergence of welfare capitalism and pure capitalism? Which would you favour and recommend? Why?

INTERNET CHALLENGES

1. Analyses of the constantly moving economy are made regularly by various experts and government departments. See if you can find some forecasts, using the keywords *Canadian economic forecasts*, of the current outlook for the Canadian economy by searching Web sites such as *The Globe and Mail* <www.theglobeandmail.com>, the *National Post* <www.nationalpost.com>, and *Canadian Business* magazine <www.canbus.com>. Also try a search engine.

2. Can you see, or do any of the articles mention, the possible impact of this information on specific Canadian companies or industries? Perhaps you are considering a career in one of these industries or a job possibility with one of these companies. See if you can find any reports or statements on the Internet from these companies.

Practising Management Decisions

Canada is a very large country, rich in minerals and metals. Finding and exploiting these important natural resources have always been important activities that have given a great boost to our economy. Canada is known throughout the world for its natural riches and its ability to develop them into important national assets. Many thousands of enterprising individuals explored Canada searching for deposits of nickel, copper, silver, gold, and other metals. Many companies were created and so were a large number of jobs.

This is a good illustration of the relevance of the theories of Adam Smith mentioned in the chapter. These entrepreneurs were driven by the incentive for profit and wealth. In the process, the economy was developed, jobs were provided, communities were established, and the country as a whole benefitted. People usually worked under very difficult conditions of climate and terrain, and put in long, hard hours, often without success. Eventually some giant companies—Noranda, International Nickel (INCO), Falconbridge—emerged.

In 1995 and 1996, Canadian newspapers were full of stories about a tremendous nickel discovery in a remote area of Labrador. The Voisey's Bay deposit is said to be the largest nickel ore body in the world. Originally, Al Chislett and Chris Verbiski persuaded Diamond Fields Resources to risk almost a half-million dollars to back their search for diamonds and gold. Although no diamonds and no gold were found, they did discover the huge nickel ore body, and both Chislett and Verbiski, as well as Diamond Fields, have become very wealthy by later selling the company to INCO. Their discovery will spawn a huge development and provide many jobs in a province that badly needs jobs. In addition, some 285,000 mineral claims have been staked in that area. This story is an excellent example of what entrepreneurial Canada does well.

However, a serious issue was raised by the 6500 Innu and Innuit aboriginal peoples who inhabit, trap, fish, and hunt in that area. They have been trying unsuccessfully for more than 25 years to get their land claims in that area settled with the federal government. Now they want their share of

CASE 1

......

A GIANT LABRADOR PROJECT FACES SOME DILEMMAS

......

the newfound riches to be negotiated before work commences. They are also concerned about damage to the environment, which is always a major issue in such developments.

In 1998 a series of developments combined to confuse and delay this giant project. Disputes involving INCO, the Newfoundland and Labrador provincial government, the aboriginal peoples, the federal government, and environmental organizations led to court actions, hearings, and many meetings involving these parties. In addition, the international price of nickel dropped sharply and stayed there. By late 1999 many of these issues remained unresolved.

The provincial government wanted INCO to process all the ore on-site to provide badly needed jobs, thus adding to the local economy and generating revenues for the government. INCO argued that the high price it paid to acquire the location, $3.5 billion, and the low price of nickel meant that the lowest possible cost of production was its prime consideration. The Innu and Innuit wanted jobs, but were concerned about possible environmental impact of the operation, as were environmental groups. The Innu and Innuit also wanted settlement by the federal government of their long-outstanding land claims.

Decision Questions

1. Think carefully about the economic issues in this case. How many such issues can you list? What is the effect of each one on the project?
2. How does this case relate to Adam Smith's theory about capitalism that was reviewed in the chapter? Why is this a good example of his beliefs?
3. Can you see this case as an example of the role of government in the economy? Do you think this case is an example of the positive or negative impact of government? Explain.
4. How much importance do you attach to the environmental issue in this case? What about the ethical issue of aboriginal rights? Do you think that these questions are important enough to delay this giant project?

Ogre Mills is a typical factory in Latvia, formerly part of the communist system that existed in the now-defunct Soviet Union. As the world opens to free competition, these factories have to compete with world-class factories in countries such as Canada, the United States, Germany, and Japan. Are they ready for such competition?

Under the previous system, the factory submitted a budget to the government. The government then set quotas for the factory, decided who would supply the factory with raw materials, distributed final goods, and set the price. The government also decided how much workers would be paid. Management's pay was based on whether or not quotas were met and whether the budget was followed.

Now that the mill faces a market economy, things will be very different. The firm must acquire materials in global markets, pay for those goods in hard currency, and price the goods competitively. In most advanced countries, businesses rely on information systems to provide the information needed to set global prices, track inventory and shipping, and track profits. Because the Latvian information systems are not world-class, Ogre Mills will have trouble competing.

CASE 2

OGRE FACES A MARKET ECONOMY

The firm has been able to find enough hard currency to buy raw materials overseas. It has also joined the International Wool Society to make sure that its products meet the world's quality standards. Nonetheless, the company still has obsolete production equipment and information systems.

Decision Questions

1. Explain how prices are determined in free markets. How does such a system result in few surpluses or shortages? Contrast that system with the communist economy to which Ogre once belonged.
2. What are some of the advantages and disadvantages that people in Latvia will experience as the country moves toward a free market? How would a mixed economy alleviate some of the problems?
3. What advantages do Latvian firms have over firms in the United States and Germany, if any?
4. If you were a counsellor to the Latvian people, what kind of economic system would you recommend: socialism, capitalism, or a mixed economy? Explain your reasons.

Competing in Global Environments

Chapter 3

LEARNING GOALS

After you have read and studied this chapter, you should be able to

1 discuss the critical importance of the international market and the role of comparative advantage in international trade.

2 understand the status of Canada in international business.

3 illustrate the strategies used in reaching global markets.

4 discuss the hurdles to trading in world markets.

5 review what trade protectionism is and how and why it is practised.

6 discuss the future of international trade and investment.

Francesco Bellini is CEO of BioChem Pharma Inc., a pharmaceutical company near Montreal that is making a name for itself internationally. Bellini has been the driving force in pushing the company from its small beginnings to its present international stature. Bellini took the company public to get additional financing to develop two major drugs: 3TC, which is important in the treatment of AIDS, and Zeffir, which was the first oral treatment for hepatitis B. The company was helped in the necessary research by another injection of capital, this time from the giant British pharmaceutical firm Glaxco Wellcome Inc., which received a 12 percent share in BioChem Pharma. In return for its financing, Glaxco also received the licence to market both of these drugs internationally and the royalties that Glaxco pays for the licence provides BioChem with substantial cash flow. BioChem expects to receive about $1.5 billion in the five years from 2000 to 2004.

In 1999 Bellini arranged for BioChem to buy back about half of Glaxco's shares in BioChem for US$160 million, half payable immediately and the balance 18 months later. Bellini believes that this action, combined with the cash flow from the royalties, will enable BioChem to achieve a number of important goals. BioChem will be able "to develop and retain total control of the rights to future drugs and vaccines" and to set up its own marketing system. The company will also retain a greater share of the profits because it will be paying out less to Glaxco.

Bellini expects that the company's profits will continue to grow as it brings new drugs to market. BioChem currently has two new drugs undergoing clinical trials: dOTC is designed as a powerful treatment for AIDS in combination with 3TC, and Troxacitabine is aimed at several kinds of cancer. For BioChem, setting up its own marketing system to handle these and other products will mean adding 10 marketing people in Canada and between 100 and 200 sales reps in a new U.S. office.

Francesco Bellini at BioChem is an excellent example of much of the material in this book and in this chapter. A dedicated entrepreneur starts a small company, goes public, then makes connections with a giant firm to further help develop the company. Bellini used licensing as a way to expand internationally, but maintained control of his company. Now, BioChem is strong enough to finance its own research, to set up its own marketing division, and to retain a larger share of the profits.

Source: Sheila McGovern, "BioChem Strikes Out on Own," *Montreal Gazette*, June 12, 1999, C1.

PROFILE

BioChem: From Local Firm to International Success

Ethical Dilemma

A QUESTION OF HOT NIGHTGOWNS

As a top manager of Nightie Nite, a maker of children's sleepwear, you are required to be aware of all the new government regulations that affect your industry. A recently passed safety regulation prohibits the use of the fabric that you have been using for girl's nightgowns for the past 15 years. Apparently the fabric does not have sufficient flame retardant capabilities to meet government standards. Last week Nightie Nite lost a lawsuit brought against it by the parents of a young child severely burned because the nightgown she was wearing burst into flames when she ventured too close to a gas stove. Not only did you lose the lawsuit, but you may lose your nightshirt if you don't find another market for the warehouse full of nightgowns you have in inventory. You realize that there are other countries that do not have such restrictive laws concerning products sold within their borders. You are considering exporting your products to these countries. What are your alternatives? What are the consequences of each alternative? What will you do? Ponder these questions as you go through the chapter and we will try to find some answers at the end.

THE GLOBALIZATION OF BUSINESS

If you want to get some idea of how business has become a global affair you have only to look at Canada. According to Statistics Canada, *every day* they "process documents containing over *twenty million* import/export transactions obtained when goods cross the Canadian border, going to or coming from over *200 countries*."[1] [Given such a huge amount of data to store and analyze, you may wonder how reliable Statistics Canada (StatCan) reports are, especially since these transactions are only part of a much larger number of varied economic activities in Canada. The answer is that the internationally prestigious magazine *The Economist* rated StatCan the number one statistical agency in the world in 1994 and 1995.][2]

Because of developments in communications and transportation, our planet has become a small place. Products and services are marketed to, and provided from, the whole world. The Reaching Beyond Our Borders box on page 61, is a good example of how closely enmeshed the Canadian economy has become with the rest of the world. All significant business activity involves international aspects.

THE IMPACT OF THE GLOBAL ECONOMY ON CANADA

Why should we in Canada be so concerned about deflation and recession in South Korea or Russia or Brazil? We actually export only a small percentage of our products to them and our companies invest relatively little there. So why should we pay careful attention to what's happening to the economy of these distant countries? Will their problems affect your career and job opportunities? To better appreciate the extent to which the economies of all coun-

Reaching Beyond Our Borders

Canadian Companies Spread Their Wings

The extent of Canadian companies' involvement in the globalization of business can be grasped by looking at news reports. Our mining companies—large and small—are busy exploring in Indonesia, Chile, Kazakhstan, China, Africa, and elsewhere. Bombardier is selling planes and is in joint ventures to supply railcars and set up rail transportation systems around the globe. Roy Thomson, Conrad Black, and Pierre Peladeau are buying up newspapers and printing companies in Europe and North America. Nortel Networks is heavily involved in major deals in China and has a major contract with AT&T in the United States. Viceroy Homes is supplying Japan with manufactured homes. The architectural firm of Robbie, Young & Wright, who designed the Toronto Skydome, won the contract for a stadium and sports complex in Frankfurt, Germany.

The Bank of Montreal and the Bank of Nova Scotia acquired stakes in Mexican and Central American banks. Softkey International acquired The Learning Co. to create the world's biggest educational software company. Dreco Energy Services of Edmonton is selling rigs to Siberia. Suncor teamed up with Australian companies for a huge shale oil project there. Vancouver-based QLT Phototherapeutics is selling its new light-activated cancer drug in Europe and the United States. Toronto pharmaceutical firm Biovail Corp. acquired an important Puerto Rican drug company. Hydro-Quebec is part of a joint venture in Japan to manufacture tiny batteries the size of postage stamps. Manulife Insurance beat out 80 major international insurers to win the right to operate in China. Unican Security Systems acquired control of an Italian and a Swiss security system firm. CEO Ross Dembo of the Vancouver company, Algorithmics, reports that their software models have been sold to 70 banks worldwide.

The list goes on and on. It is almost impossible to find any field of business in which Canadian companies are not involved in significant international investment, trade, or manufacturing.

Sources: *Globe and Mail, Report on Business; Montreal Gazette; Financial Post;* the Internet—all 1995, 1996; interview October 18, 1995; *Newsworld Business News,* November 2, 1998.

---

tries are interlocked and interdependent, we turn next to an examination of the globalization of business.

Anyone who reads Canadian newspapers or magazines, uses the Internet, or watches TV business programs can find numerous examples of the ceaseless expansion of Canadian companies into global markets, deals, joint ventures, and so forth. World barriers to trade and investment have been dropping steadily.

If we look at some facts about this world market, we will see why this trade is so important:

- There are 30 million customers in Canada but over *six billion* potential customers worldwide.
- Every year, the world's population increases by some 90 million people. That's more than three times the total Canadian population.
- Combined world trade exceeds *$6 trillion* each year (a trillion is a million million.)

Nortel Networks has become a world player in a big way. This type of globalized, or transnational (TNC), company is very different from the old-style multinational (MNC) company that has been engaged in world trade for a long time. Both **TNC** and **MNC** are often used interchangeably to refer to an

TNC or MNC
An organization that has investments, plants, and sales in many different countries; it has international stock ownership and multinational management.

Nortel Networks is a world player in the telecommunications field and an excellent example of a Canadian-based company that has transformed itself into a transnational company.

organization that has investments, plants, and sales in many different countries and has international stock ownership and multinational management.

MNCs did business in various countries and had plants in a number of countries. TNCs have gone from that stage to organizing management, investment, production, and distribution as if the world were one country or even one city. Goods can be designed in one country, raw material shipped to or from a second country, partially or completely manufactured in a third country, and then shipped to the ultimate customer. The company thus makes maximum use of the competitive advantage (discussed in the next section) of each country to be the most efficient producer. Top management and boards of directors now have an international component to reflect the new nature of operations.

Nortel Networks is a good example of a Canadian company that has been completely transformed by this globalization. The company has employees and plants all over the world specializing in various aspects of production, and also has an international board of directors. Some of the technological advances that Nortel Networks pioneered helped produce the revolutionary changes in communications that, in turn, facilitated the globalization of business.

•••• ▬▬▬ ••••

WHY COUNTRIES TRADE WITH EACH OTHER

There are several reasons why a country trades with other countries. First, no country, no matter how advanced, can produce all the products its people need or want. In Canada, we must import those products that our climate does not allow us to grow, including tropical fruits, citrus fruits, and all fruits and vegetables during the winter season. We also cannot grow cotton.

Second, some nations have an abundance of natural resources and lack technological know-how. Others, like Japan, have very few natural resources but may be world leaders in technology.

EXPORTS	(BILLIONS)	IMPORTS	(BILLIONS)
Autos, trucks, and parts	$ 79	Auto, trucks, and parts	$ 67
Industrial goods	57	Industrial goods	60
Machines and equipment	79	Machines and equipment	102
Forest products	36	Forest products	3
Energy products	23	Energy products	9
Agricultural and fish products	25	Agricultural and fish products	17
Consumer goods	13	Consumer goods	34
Special transactions trade	5	Special transactions trade	6
Unallocated adjustments	6	Unallocated adjustments	6
Total	323	Total	304

Source: *Daily* Archives, Statistics Canada, <www.statcan.ca>, May 1999.

FIGURE 3.1
····
CANADIAN EXPORTS AND IMPORTS
Analysis of Canadian exports and imports of merchandise for 1998.

comparative advantage theory
The theory that a country should produce and sell to other countries those products that it produces most efficiently and effectively and should buy from other countries those products it cannot produce as effectively or efficiently.

Third, some countries produce a lot more of certain products than they can consume, so they must export these surpluses. Canada has a small population but produces vast quantities of grains, autos, auto parts, lumber, manufactured goods, newsprint, metals, minerals, and other products. Thus we rank very high among nations that export. In fact, we depend on exports to maintain a substantial segment of our standard of living, around 35 percent. Figure 3.1 shows that in 1998 Canada exported $323 billion, ranking Canada seventh amongst exporting nations of the world.

··· THE THEORY OF COMPARATIVE ADVANTAGE ···

Some countries are better than others at producing certain products in terms of quality or price, so they have what is called a *comparative advantage*. Japan has shown this ability with cars and electronic items. Canada has such an advantage with certain forestry products, aluminum, and various minerals. The guiding principle behind international economic exchanges is supposed to be the economic **comparative advantage theory**. This theory states that a country should produce and sell to other countries those products that it produces most effectively and efficiently and should buy from other countries those products it cannot produce as effectively or efficiently.

In practice, this theory does not work so neatly. For various reasons, many countries decide to produce certain agricultural, industrial, or consumer products despite a lack of comparative advantage. To facilitate this plan, they restrict imports of competing products from countries that can produce them at lower costs. For example, Japan and South Korea ban all imports of rice. The U.S. makes it difficult to import sugar or cotton and insists that ships carrying cargo between American ports must be U.S. owned.

The theory of comparative advantage dictates that a country should specialize in producing those products it can produce most efficiently and effectively and import those it cannot produce as well. Most Western countries import rice, as this is more economical than trying to produce it domestically.

balance of trade
The relationship of exports to imports.

Farmers in Europe are subsidized so that their grains can compete with the less expensive ones from countries such as Canada and the U.S. Canada has done the same with cars, textiles, and shoes at different times. The net result of such restraints is that the free movement of goods and services is restricted. We will return to the topic of trade protectionism later in the chapter. It will be useful to examine some of the terminology relating to international trade first.

··· **TERMINOLOGY OF INTERNATIONAL TRADE** ···

When you read business periodicals or listen to news reports, you will see and hear terms relating to international business. Many of these terms may be familiar to you, but it will be helpful to review them before we discuss international business in more detail.

In measuring the effectiveness of global trade, nations carefully follow two key indicators: balance of trade and balance of payments. The **balance of trade** is the relationship of exports to imports. A *favourable balance of trade*,

FIGURE **3.2**
· · · ·
EXPORTS, IMPORTS, AND TRADE BALANCE

These graphs from Statistics Canada show how our exports continue to exceed our imports, resulting in a favourable trade balance. The results are tracked monthly.

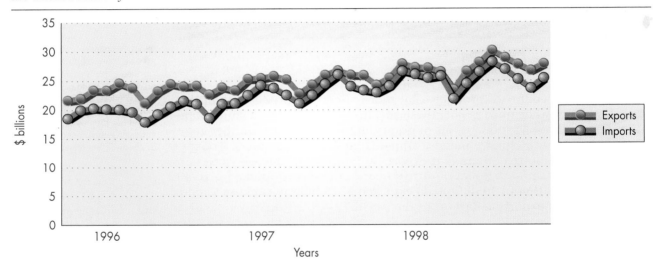

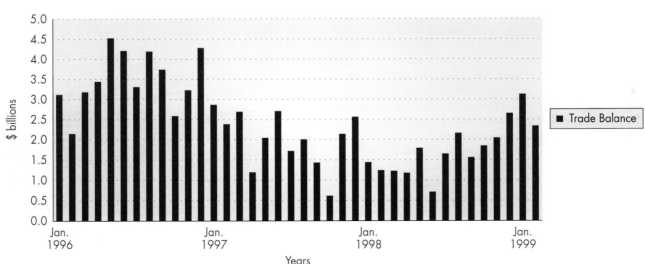

Sources: (Imports) Statistics Canada, CANSIM, Matrix 3651, Series D397768, May 1999.
     (Exports) Statistics Canada, CANSIM, Matrix 3685, Series D399224, May 1999.

or trade surplus, occurs when the value of exports exceeds imports. An *unfavourable balance of trade*, or **trade deficit**, occurs when the value of imports exceeds exports. It's easy to understand why countries prefer to export more than they import. If I sell you $200 worth of goods and buy only $100 worth, I have an extra $100 available to buy other things. However, I'm in an unfavourable position if I buy $200 worth of goods and sell only $100. For the 18 years from 1981 to 1999, Canada has usually had a favourable balance of trade (see Figure 3.2).

Countries often use trade protectionism measures to protect their industries against the dumping and foreign competition that hurt domestic industry. **Trade protectionism** is the use of government regulations to limit the import of goods and services. Protectionism is based on the theory that such practices will help protect domestic producers from foreign competition, allowing them to survive and grow, producing more jobs. We shall discuss trade protectionism in more detail later in this chapter.

The **exchange rate** is the value of one currency relative to the currencies of other countries. A *rising value of the dollar* means that a dollar will buy more foreign goods (or will be traded for more foreign currency) than normal. A *falling value of the dollar* means that a dollar buys less than it once did, making foreign goods more expensive because it takes more dollars to buy them. It also makes Canadian goods cheaper to foreign buyers because it takes less foreign currency to buy them. The net effect is to export more and buy fewer foreign products, improving the balance of trade but increasing inflation as imported goods now cost more (see Figure 3.3).

For many years the U.S. dollar has played the role of the international currency, so most international transactions are quoted in U.S. dollars. The constant movements in the exchange rate of this dollar relative to other currencies affect nearly all international trade and investments. This role is particularly important for Canada, because more than 80 percent of all our imports and exports are with the United States. Since 1980, the value of the U.S. dollar has fluctuated greatly, creating ups and downs for many trading nations. In addition, as the U.S. dollar fluctuates against other currencies, it affects Canada's competitiveness with other countries, because it makes our exports more or less expensive.

In mid-1998 the Canadian dollar fell to 63 cents, an all-time low against the U.S. dollar. This record low made it cheaper for American companies to buy Canadian goods and services while it made it more expensive for Canadian companies and consumers to buy these from Americans. By mid-

trade deficit
Occurs when the value of imports exceeds exports.

trade protectionism
The use of government regulations to limit the import of goods and services, based on the theory that domestic producers should be protected from competition so that they can survive and grow, producing more jobs.

exchange rate
The value of one currency relative to the currencies of other countries.

<www.consumersinternational.org/campaigns>

This consumers' organization is very concerned about the impact of protectionism on the agricultural industry and on consumers in all parts of the world. Visit this site and click on *food* to learn more about its views.

	Importer Pays	Exporter Gets
Import of VCRs from Japan		
72 yen per dollar	$200	¥14,400
90 yen per dollar	160	14,400
Export of potash to Japan		
72 yen per dollar	¥14,400	$200
90 yen per dollar	18,000	200

Note: Prices quoted in the exporter's currency.

FIGURE 3.3
• • • •
EFFECT OF FLUCTUATIONS IN CURRENCY EXCHANGE RATES ON PRICES OF IMPORTS AND EXPORTS

As the dollar rises in relation to the yen (it takes 90 yen to buy a dollar instead of 72, or one dollar buys 90 yen instead of 72 yen), a Canadian importer now pays less but the Japanese importer pays more.

<www.elcompanies.com/brands/mac.html>

A Small Cosmetics Firm Hits the Big Time

In the mid-1980s, Toronto hairdresser Frank Angelo and photographer Frank Toskan had an idea. They were trying to solve the problem their fashion models encountered with makeup when working constantly under hot lights. Experimenting with homemade lipsticks and eye makeup, they came up with a line of densely pigmented cosmetics that did the trick. Not only did professionals start using this new line of products, but all women were attracted to it. The company, Make-up Art Cosmetics Ltd., better known as MAC, was soon growing rapidly.

Since the two Franks were young and daring and wanted to have a little fun in the process, they broke many of the conventional traditions in the cosmetics industry. First, they selected as a model for their products "RuPaul, a seven-foot-tall African-American drag queen." Second, they did no advertising in an industry that is known for extensive advertising in all media. Neither of these breaks with tradition seemed to hurt MAC as sales continued to leap ahead. Instead of ▲

advertising, word-of-mouth was a powerful stimulator of sales with some famous mouths such as Madonna and Princess Diana praising the products.

By the end of 1994 MAC had sales of more than $100 million. They had already expanded into the U.S. and England and now wanted to expand into Europe and Asia. This required large amounts of capital, as did satisfying the mushrooming demand that copycat companies were rushing to meet.

At that point, Toskan and Angelo made a deal with Estée Lauder, who had been pursuing them for three years. They sold half the company and a controlling interest for $38 million. Not bad for a couple of young Canadians who a decade earlier were rank amateurs in business.

Sources: Various issues of *The Globe and Mail, Report on Business,* 1995; Jennifer Low, "Will Success Spoil MAC?" *Profit,* April–May 1996, pp. 43–44; C. A. Bartlett and S. Ghoshal, *Transnational Management,* 2nd ed. (New York: Times Mirror, 1995), p. 58ff.

1999 our dollar was back up to 68 cents American. Nevertheless we continued to have a favourable balance of trade for the first quarter of 1999.

Now that you understand some terms, we can begin discussing international trade in more depth. The first question to address is how Canada is doing in world trade. First let's check your progress.

Progress Check

- Can you cite statistics to show why international trade is so vital for Canadian business (population, size of market, growth of market)?
- What is comparative advantage?
- Can you explain how changes in the value of the dollar affect imports and exports?

TRADING IN WORLD MARKETS: THE CANADIAN EXPERIENCE

Statistics must be examined very closely to make sense of them. This is especially true in the case of Canada's foreign trade statistics. At first glance, they are impressive. For a country with only 30 million people we usually rank seventh or eighth in volume of world trade.[3] However, if we look carefully at the figures, we see that more than 80 percent of this exporting and importing is

	EXPORTS $ MILLIONS	%	IMPORTS $ MILLIONS	%
U.S.	270,561	83.7	234,177	77.0
Japan	9,636	3.0	9,657	3.2
European Union	17,837	5.5	25,424	8.4
Other OECD countries	7,487	2.3	11,377	3.7
All other countries	17,880	5.5	23,348	7.7
Total	323,400	100.0	303,984	100.0

Source: (Imports) Statistics Canada, CANSIM, Matrix 3651, Series D397984-D397989, May 1999.
   (Exports) Statistics Canada, CANSIM, Matrix 3685, Series D399443-D399448, May 1999.

FIGURE **3.4**

· · · ·

EXPORTS AND IMPORTS IN 1998

The United States is by far our main trading partner, and we had a $36 billion trade surplus with them in 1999. Overall there was a $19.5 billion surplus.

with one country, the United States (see Figure 3.4). No other modern industrialized country is so dependent on one country for trade and investments. The controversial Canada–U.S. Free Trade Agreement that came into effect in 1989 is designed to facilitate and further increase trade and investment between the two countries. The 1993 North American Free Trade Agreement (NAFTA) added Mexico to the deal, discussed later in this chapter.

An even closer look at what we export to the United States shows that the largest single item—some 25 to 30 percent—is autos, trucks, and parts and has been so for some time. This is offset by a somewhat smaller amount that we import. All of this stems from the Canada–U.S. Auto Pact signed in the mid-1960s, which was designed to stimulate the auto industry in both countries. This trade is subject to the vagaries of the demand for autos of the Big Three (Chrysler, Ford, and General Motors) in Canada and the United States. The growing success of Japanese cars severely reduced demand for Big Three cars in 1990 and 1991. The reduced demand had a serious impact on business and employment in Canada, especially in Ontario, which relies heavily on auto parts and auto manufacturing. By 1995, the situation had turned around.

A traditional major area for Canadian exports is natural resources, which are abundant across the country. Pulp and paper products and lumber from our forests and forest industries, combined with agricultural products, fish products, energy (natural gas, coal, and electricity from water power), minerals, and metals constitute almost half our exports. Developing countries are now giving Canada stiff competition in the natural resource area.

Although Canada is still weak in the high-tech "glamour" industries, biogenetics, telecommunications, computers, air and rail transport, and materials technology are some of the areas where high-skilled jobs and exports are expected to be important. There are some Canadian stars that have a strong international posture in some of these areas. For example, Nortel Networks and Bombardier are making substantial gains in exports—but there are not enough of these stars.

A number of smaller but successful firms have made an impact globally: SPAR Aerospace, maker of the robotic Canadarm on the U.S. space shuttle; CAE Electronics Ltd., one of the few makers of flight simulators in the world; Rolls Royce (Canada) Ltd., a leader in aircraft and industrial engine repair and maintenance; and Phoenix International Life Sciences Inc., one of the top drug-testing labs in North America, are but a few of dozens of small companies with excellent records outside of Canada. We also have some excellent software companies that compete well internationally, such as Softimage, Corel Corporation, Alias, and Delrina.

Critical Thinking

You have read that there are six billion people in the world, but only a small percentage of Canadian companies engage in world trade. Why is that? What do such figures indicate about the future potential for increasing Canadian exports? What do they say about future careers in international business?

In thinking about other countries, you should be asking yourself: What languages do they speak? What are the trade possibilities? Am I missing out on an opportunity by failing to take other languages in school and courses in international business?

STRATEGIES FOR REACHING GLOBAL MARKETS

An organization may participate in international trade in many ways, including exporting, licensing, creating subsidiaries, franchising, joint venturing, and countertrading. These topics relate to careers that will be both challenging and rewarding for the future graduate.

••• EXPORTING •••

<www.dfait-maeci.gc.ca>

Visit the Department of Foreign Affairs and International Trade Web site. You will learn how DFAIT gets involved in exporting and the services it provides to encourage the export-trade business.

The simplest way of going international is to export your products. As you will see in the chapters on marketing, many decisions have to be made when a company markets a new product or goes into new markets with existing products. Often the first export sales occur as a result of unsolicited orders received. Regardless of how a company starts exporting, it must develop some goals and strategies for achieving those goals.

Other decisions include what distribution channels are appropriate: direct sales, sales to wholesalers, or an exporting or importing agency. Each route has its pluses and minuses. Important decisions about pricing policy must also be made. In the next chapter you will see how the Canadian government helps companies that want to export.

Success in exporting often leads to licensing a foreign company to produce the product locally to better serve the local market.

••• LICENSING •••

licensing
An agreement in which a producer allows a foreign company to manufacture its products or use its trademark in exchange for royalties.

A firm may decide to compete in a growing global market by **licensing** to a foreign company the right to manufacture its product or use its trademark on a fee (royalty) basis. The company generally sends representatives to the foreign producer to help set up the production process and may also assist in such areas as distribution and promotion.

A licensing agreement can be beneficial to a firm in several different ways. Through licensing, an organization can gain additional revenues from a product that it would not have normally generated. In addition, foreign licensees often must purchase start-up supplies, component materials, and consulting services from the licensing firm. Coke licenses the right to sell merchandise with the Coke name, but not the drink itself. Even the Royal Canadian Mounted Police had a licensing agreement with the Walt Disney Company to market products bearing Mounties images, which ended in 1999.[4] One final advantage of licensing worth noting is that licensors spend little or no money to produce and market their products. These costs come from the licensees' pockets. Therefore, licensees generally work very hard to see that the product succeeds in their market.

However, as you may suspect, licensing agreements may have some disadvantages for a company. One major problem is that often a firm must grant licensing rights to its product for an extended period, maybe as long as 20 years. If a product experiences remarkable growth in the foreign market, the bulk of the revenues goes to the licensee. Perhaps even more threatening is that a licensing firm is actually selling its expertise in a product area. If a foreign licensee learns that technology, it may break the agreement and begin to produce a similar product on its own. If legal remedies are not available, the licensing firm may lose its trade secrets, not to mention the agreed-upon royalties.

••• CREATING SUBSIDIARIES •••

As the size of a foreign market expands, a firm may want to establish a foreign subsidiary. A **foreign subsidiary** is a company that is owned by another company (parent company) in a foreign country. Such a subsidiary would operate much like a domestic firm with production, distribution, promotion, pricing, and other business functions under the control of the foreign subsidiary's management. Of course, the legal requirements of the home and host country would have to be observed. The primary advantage of a subsidiary is that the company maintains complete control over any technology or expertise it may possess.

Canadian subsidiaries of American companies played a major role in developing the Canadian economy. More and more countries are welcoming such investments as a way of developing their economies. The main concern for Canada and these other countries is that decisions made by the parent company are not primarily based on the needs of the country where the subsidiary is located. For example, if an American company decides to reduce its workforce or close a plant, it may more readily do that to a subsidiary in Canada than in its home base in the U.S.

Millions of times a day, things do go better with Coke. Coca-Cola Ltd. is just one example of a company that licenses the right to sell merchandise with its corporate name.

foreign subsidiary
A company owned by another company (parent company) in a foreign country.

Franchising is popular in both domestic and international markets. McDonald's operates in a number of countries around the world. This tray liner is from a McDonald's restaurant in Russia.

••• FRANCHISING •••

Franchising is popular both domestically and in international markets. Firms such as McDonald's, Ramada Inc, Avis, Hertz, and Dunkin' Donuts have many overseas units operated by franchises. In Canada there are thousands of franchise units, such as Harvey's, Speedy Muffler, and Delta Hotels, in many categories of business. This topic will be discussed in detail in Chapter 6.

Franchisers have to be careful to adapt to the countries they serve. For example, Kentucky Fried Chicken's first 11 Hong Kong outlets failed within two years. Apparently, the chicken was too greasy and messy to be eaten with fingers by the fastidious people of Hong Kong. McDonald's also made a mistake when entering the Amsterdam market. It originally set up operations in the suburbs, as it does in North America, but soon learned that Europeans mostly live in the cities. McDonald's began to open outlets downtown and thousands of franchises are now operating internationally. McDonald's franchises serve beer in Germany and wine France.

••• INTERNATIONAL JOINT VENTURES •••

international joint venture (JV)
A partnership in which companies from two or more countries join to undertake a major project or to form a new company.

An **international joint venture (JV)** is a partnership in which companies from two or more countries join to undertake a major project or to form a new company. This has become a very popular avenue for companies that want to go into business in foreign countries. There are obvious advantages to having a partner that shares in the financial investment and risk, knows the local market, understands local ways of thinking, has good government connections and access to local skilled labour or supplies, and is acquainted with the laws and regulations affecting business in the country. The Canadian or other foreign company brings additional assets to the joint venture. These usually include the technology, management skills, specialized equipment and material, and financing necessary to commence and continue operations.

consortium
A temporary association of two or more companies to bid jointly on a large project.

Sometimes companies, including competitors, form a **consortium**, a temporary association, to submit a joint bid on a very large or complex construction project such as a dam, bridge, tunnel, or large building. This may make it easier for the government or company that asked for bids, since it deals with only one entity instead of many different groups. If the consortium gets the contract, the work is divided up according to the specialties of each member company.

Sometimes two or more competitors make a joint bid. For example, Bombardier teamed up with Alsthom of France to bid successfully for the subway car contract for New York City.

Thousands of joint ventures of different types exist around the world and are constantly being formed. General Motors and Toyota combined to set up CAAMI in Ingersoll, Ontario. Many such deals are being set up in the former communist countries of eastern Europe and in the independent countries of the former Soviet Union. For example, McDonald's of Canada teamed up with Russian partners to set up the largest franchise unit in the world in Moscow; and Nortel Networks formed a large joint venture with Chinese associates in Shanghai to produce advanced telecommunication products for the Chinese market.

••• FOREIGN DIRECT INVESTMENT •••

Regardless of how a company invests in another country—joint venture, subsidiary, franchise—the total of these *foreign direct investments* has become a significant proportion of any country's economic activity. As Figure 3.5 indicates, the United States is an attractive country for such investments. Canadian

	1996	1997
United Kingdom	$121 billion	$130 billion
Japan	115 billion	124 billion
Netherlands	74 billion	84 billion
Canada	55 billion	64 billion

FIGURE **3.5**

• • • •

FOREIGN DIRECT INVESTMENT

Countries with the highest foreign direct investment in the United States.

Source: <www.stat.usa.gov/Online.nsf/vwFileLookup/INT-INV.BEA/$File/INT-BEA?OpenElement>.

Spotlight on Big Business   <www.bombardier.com>

Bombardier: From Snowmobiles to Airplanes and Trains

As CEO of Bombardier Inc. for more than three decades, 60-year-old chartered accountant Laurent Beaudoin was responsible for the transformation of the company from a local manufacturer of snowmobiles into a giant transnational producing trains, planes, and the famous Ski-Doos and Sea-Doos. From 1985 to 1995 sales increased tenfold to $6 billion. For the year ended January 31, 1999, when Beaudoin stepped down as CEO and was replaced by Robert Brown, gross revenues were almost $12 billion. For the quarter ended April 30, 1999, the company reported a 25 percent increase in sales over the same quarter the previous year.

Bombardier has a workforce of 40,000 in facilities in nine countries. The company is a leading contender for aerospace and mass transit contracts all over the world. Bombardier's rail units operate in the Chunnel between France and England, in Disneyland, in Montreal, in New York, and in Asian countries. Its regional jets are everywhere. The company has alliances and joint ventures with dozens of companies around the world. Some are technology-sharing agreements, others are production-sharing agreements, and still others involve operating luxury corporate jet services. Bombardier is a classic example of a true transnational corporation whose domain is the entire world.

J. Armand Bombardier, founder of the company and inventor of the snowmobile, died in 1964. Within 10 years, the company went public, experienced higher gasoline prices due to the energy crisis, and saw sales drop by 70 percent. Beaudoin then led the company through a very imaginative, difficult, and risky but successful transformation. In 1982 the company landed a billion-dollar contract to supply the New York Transit Authority with 825 subway cars. Within the next 10 years Bombardier acquired four aircraft companies—Canadair in Montreal, Learjet in Kansas, Shorts of Northern Ireland, and de Havilland in Toronto. In each case Bombardier bought companies in difficulty and in three cases it got substantial local government aid to expedite the takeover.

Business leaders greatly admire Laurent Beaudoin's brilliant acquisition program and transformation of these money-losing companies into profitable operations. He is no less admired for his ability to create a successful mass transit operation, one of the very few in the world. Hardly a month passes without some reference in the media to Bombardier having landed more orders for its regional jets or its railway and subway cars. At April 30, 1999, the order backlog was a record $25.5 billion. This track record led Canada's chief executives in 1996 to select Bombardier as the most respected company in Canada. Bombardier exemplifies what this chapter is all about—the globalization of business.

Sources: Company reports and documents 1998 and 1999; Raymond Boyer, president and COO, Bombardier, speech at McGill University, March 1, 1996; Kenneth Kidd, "The Bombardier Express," *Globe and Mail, Report on Business*, April 1996, p. 48ff.

bartering
The exchange of goods or services for goods or services.

countertrading
Bartering among several countries.

<www.bxicanada.com>

BXI Trade Exchange assists companies in reducing costs by helping them to make barter arrangements instead of purchasing needed items for cash. Their Web site includes a description of how barter works and the range of goods and services that BXI offers.

companies rank fourth in countries investing in the United States, having invested some $64 billion U.S. dollars there. This includes large companies previously mentioned and others such as Bank of Montreal and Seagram's.

··· COUNTERTRADING ···

One of the oldest forms of trade is called **bartering**, the exchange of merchandise for merchandise, service for service, or service for merchandise with no money involved. **Countertrading** is more complex than bartering in that several countries may be involved, each trading goods or services for other goods or services. It has been estimated that countertrading accounts for 25 percent of all international exchanges.

Examples of countertrade and bartering agreements abound. Chrysler traded its vehicles in Jamaica for bauxite. McDonnell Douglas traded jets in the former Yugoslavia for canned hams. General Motors traded vehicles with China for industrial gloves and cutting tools.

Barter is especially important to poor countries that have little cash available for trade. Such countries may barter with all kinds of raw materials, food, or whatever resources they have. Colombia has traded coffee for buses. Romania traded cement for steam engines. The Sudan pays for Pepsi concentrate with sesame seeds. Tanzania uses sisal and Nicaragua uses sesame seeds and molasses for barter.

With many emerging economies still in a state of flux, countertrading may continue to grow in importance. Trading products for products helps avoid some problems and hurdles experienced in global markets.

Progress Check

- Can you name four ways to enter foreign markets?
- What are the major benefits a firm may gain from licensing its products in foreign markets? What are the primary drawbacks?
- What are the major benefits of a joint venture in global markets?
- How does countertrading work?

HURDLES TO DOING BUSINESS IN WORLD MARKETS

Succeeding in *any* business takes work and effort because of the many hurdles encountered. Unfortunately, the hurdles get higher and more complex in world markets. This is particularly true in dealing with differences in cultural perspectives, societies and economies, laws and regulations, and fluctuations in currencies (see Figure 3.3). Let's take a look at each of these hurdles.

··· CULTURAL DIFFERENCES ···

Anyone who travels to different countries cannot help noticing peculiarities of life in each country that are different from how we live in Canada. Every company that engages in international trade or investment must take these cultural differences into account if it wants to succeed in these operations.

In Canada and the United States, we like to do things quickly. We tend to call each other by our first names and try to get friendly even on the first encounter. In Japan, China, and other countries these actions would be considered surprising and even rude. Canadian negotiators will say *no* if they mean *no*, but Japanese usually say *maybe* when they mean *no*.

Religion is an important part of any society's culture and can have a significant impact on business operations. For example, in Islamic countries, dawn-to-dusk fasting during the month of Ramadan causes workers' output to drop considerably. Also, the requirement to pray five times daily can affect output.

Cultural differences can also have an impact on such important business factors as human resource management. In Latin American countries, managers are looked on by workers as authoritarian figures responsible for their well-being. Consider what happened to one North American manager who neglected this important cultural characteristic. This manager was convinced he could motivate his workers in Peru to higher levels of productivity by instituting a more democratic decision-making style. He brought in trainers from North America to teach his supervisors to solicit suggestions and feedback from workers. Shortly after his new style was put in place, workers began quitting their jobs in droves. When asked why, Peruvian workers said the new production manager and supervisors did not know their jobs and were asking the workers what to do. All stated they wanted to quit and find new jobs, since obviously this company was doomed because of incompetent managers.

Without question, culture presents a significant hurdle for global managers. Learning about important cultural perspectives toward time, change, competition, natural resources, achievement, and even work itself can be of great assistance. Today, firms often provide classes and training for managers and their families on how to adapt to different cultures and avoid culture shock. Your involvement in courses in cultural variations and anthropology can assist you in your career in global business.

••• SOCIETAL AND ECONOMIC DIFFERENCES •••

Certain social and economic realities are often overlooked by North American businesses. General Foods once squandered millions of dollars in a fruitless effort to introduce Japanese consumers to the joys of packaged cake mixed. The company failed to note, among other factors, that only 3 percent of Japanese homes were then equipped with ovens. Similarly, American auto makers tried to sell their cars in Japan without providing right-hand-drive vehicles for a country that drives on the left side of the road. Since Japan is such an important trading partner, you would think that business people would know such important information about the Japanese market, but often that is not so.

It's hard for us to imagine buying chewing gum by the stick instead of the package. However, in economically depressed nations like the Philippines, this buying behaviour is commonplace because consumers have only enough money to buy small quantities. Factors such as disposable and discretionary income can be critical in evaluating the potential of a market. What might seem like an opportunity of a lifetime may in fact be unreachable due to economic conditions.

Technological constraints may also make it difficult or impossible to carry on effective trade. For example, some less developed countries have primitive transportation and storage systems. International food exchanges are ineffective because the food is spoiled by the time it reaches those in need.

Exporters must also be aware that certain technological differences affect the nature of exportable products. For example, how would the differences in electricity available (110 versus 220 volts) affect an appliance manufacturer wanting to export?

A good example of how disaster can strike a company that does not fully appreciate that countries have different cultural and social customs is shown in Chapter 15. After more than 25 years in Canada, nearly all loss years, the famous British retail clothing chain Marks & Spencer was forced to cease operations here. The company closed all its stores across Canada in 1999.

••• LEGAL AND REGULATORY DIFFERENCES •••

In any economy, the conduct and direction of business are firmly tied to the legal and regulatory environment. Business operations in Canada are heavily affected by various federal, provincial, and local laws and regulations. In global markets, there is naturally a wider variation in such laws and regulations, making the task of conducting world business even tougher.

What business people find in global markets are myriad laws and regulations that are often inconsistent. Important legal questions related to antitrust, labour relations, patents, copyrights, trade practices, taxes, product liability, and other issues are written and interpreted differently country by country. In many countries, bribery is acceptable and perhaps the only way to secure a lucrative contract. How do you think Canadian business and government leaders should handle this ethical dilemma?

To be a successful trader in foreign countries, you might choose to begin by contacting local business people and gaining their cooperation and sponsorship. The problem is that foreign bureaucracies are often stumbling blocks to successful foreign trade; to penetrate those barriers, often you must find a local sponsor who can pay the necessary fees to gain government permission.

TRADE PROTECTIONISM

As noted previously in this chapter, cultural differences, societal and economic factors, legal and regulatory requirements, and currency exchange rate shifts are all hurdles to those wanting to trade globally. What is often a much greater barrier to international trade is the overall political atmosphere between nations.

Business, economics, and politics have always been closely linked. In fact, economics was once referred to as "political economy," indicating the close ties between politics (government) and economics. For centuries, business people have tried to influence economists and government officials. Back in the sixteenth, seventeenth, and eighteenth centuries when nations were trading goods with one another, business people advocated an economic principle called **mercantilism**. Basically, the idea of mercantilism was to sell more goods to other nations than you bought from them; that is, to have a favourable balance of trade. This results in a flow of money to the country that sells the most. Governments assisted in this process by charging a tariff (tax) on imports, making it more expensive to import goods.

mercantilism
The economic principle advocating the selling of more goods to other nations than was bought from them.

Today, there is still much debate about the degree of protectionism a government should practise. For example, when the government was concerned about protecting domestic auto producers and workers from Japanese producers, it convinced Japanese producers to voluntarily limit the number of Japanese cars sold here (see "Protectionism Backfiring" on page 76). The term that describes limiting the number or value of products in certain categories that can be imported is **import quota**.

import quota
A limit on the number or value of products in certain categories that can be imported.

••• NONTARIFF BARRIERS •••

James Thwaits, former president of international operations of the 3M Co., said that as much as half of all trade is limited by *nontariff barriers*. In other

Farmers demanded millions of dollars in emergency relief when faced with a collapse in pork markets and low wheat prices. Pig farmers have experienced drastic price drops in the past few years.

words, countries have established many strategies that go beyond tariffs to prevent foreign competition. For example, Japan tried to keep out French skis by claiming that Japanese snow was different from French snow; the French retaliated by saying that French rain was different from Japanese rain, which made Japanese motorcycles too dangerous.

France tried to protect its VCR industry by requiring that all imported VCRs be sent through an understaffed customs post that was 100 miles from the nearest port. Denmark required that beverages be sold in returnable bottles; this effectively cut off French mineral water producers, who found the cost of returning bottles prohibitive. Margarine must be sold in cubes in Belgium, closing the market to countries that sell margarine in tubs.

Other nontariff barriers include safety, health, and labelling standards. The United States stopped some Canadian goods from entering because it said the information on the labels was too small. Canada has stopped American cattle or beef from entering because of hormone and antibiotic injections that violate our health standards. Canadian electrical standards have prevented certain appliances from being imported because they are not safe.

Sometimes, as in the Japanese and French cases, the intent is clearly to put difficulties in the way of imports. Other times it is not so clear whether the barriers are deliberate or are a normal part of a reasonable set of standards. Of course, when a country is in a protectionist mode, it will exploit these standards or use any excuse to try to reduce imports. The 1996 U.S. election triggered a wave of protectionist statements and attitudes.

The same thing seems to have happened before the Congressional election in the fall of 1998. South Dakota and other mid-West states started blocking Canadian exports of wheat and pork, claiming that they didn't meet U.S. health requirements. It was widely believed that farmers in these states were having trouble selling similar products because world prices were depressed and the U.S. dollar was high in value in relation to the Canadian dollar and to other currencies. Feeling this pressure, the farmers used the health excuse to block Canadian exports. As explained previously in the chapter, major currency shifts have an important effect on international trade.

••• PROTECTIONISM BACKFIRING •••

Sometimes attempts to keep out foreign goods or restrict their entry into a country lead to strange results. A good example of this occurred in the 1980s with Japanese cars, which had become very popular in Canada and the United States. The cars were of better quality, offered better warranties, used less gas, had better trade-in values, and cost less than the Big Three North American products. Instead of competing on value, the Big Three pressured the Canadian and U.S governments to restrict the entry of Japanese autos. Both governments negotiated deals with the Japanese government and their automakers to "voluntarily" not increase the number of vehicles they would export to Canada and the United States for three years. These quotas were based on the number of units, not total dollar value.

The Big Three, feeling less pressure, raised their prices. The Japanese carmakers proceeded to do the same so that their prices were still competitive. They wound up exporting fewer cars but making more profit. They used this excess profit to build auto plants in Canada and the United States, which ultimately led to Japanese cars capturing an even greater share of the North American market (about 35 percent).

••• OTHER RESTRICTIONS ON INTERNATIONAL TRADE •••

embargo
A complete ban on all trade with or investment in a country.

Sometimes countries restrict trade for purely political or military reasons. For example, for some years Canada and many other countries had an embargo on doing business with South Africa because of its racist laws and policies at that time. An **embargo** is a complete ban on all trade with or investment in a country. The United States has restrictions or embargoes on exporting what it classifies as secret or very high-tech parts or equipment that could be used for military purposes by its enemies. The United States also restricts trade with Cuba because of Cuba's communist government. All these restrictions are of a purely political or military nature and should not be confused with trade protectionism, which is of an economic nature.

••• CONSEQUENCES OF PROTECTIONISM •••

Today, nations throughout the world are debating how much protectionism they should use to keep foreign competition from driving their firms out of business. You can read about this trend in current business periodicals. As you do, keep in mind that the severity of the Great Depression of the 1930s was attributed by some people to the passage of the highly protectionist Smooth-Hawley Tariff Act of 1930 in the United States. Economists were almost unanimous in opposing the bill. Nonetheless, believing it would protect American business, the government put tariffs on goods from England, France, and other nations. The result was that other countries raised tariffs in return. This hurt business in all countries badly as world trade dropped sharply.

By 1932 U.S. exports to England were at one-third the 1929 level, exports to France were only one-fourth those of 1929, and exports to Australia were one-fifth. Wheat exports fell from $200 million to $5 million, and auto exports fell from $541 million to $76 million. In short, some economic theorists contend that protectionist policies of governments (based on old mercantilist thinking) helped create the greatest depression in the history of modern capitalism. Unemployment soared in Canada and most countries, with serious economic consequences.

Having learned a very costly lesson from various attempts at trade protectionism, the major countries began to plan how to avoid such problems in the future. They started thinking about international agreements that would be useful to all countries. We look at this in the next section.

- What are the major hurdles to successful international trade?
- Identify at least two cultural and societal differences that can affect global trade efforts.
- What are the advantages and disadvantages of trade protectionism?
- What is an embargo? Can it be applied for noneconomic reasons?

INTERNATIONAL TRADE ORGANIZATIONS

<www.wto.org>
<www.imf.org>

The World Trade Organization and International Monetary Fund Web sites provide descriptions of these organizations, their membership, their objectives, and their activities. See, for example, the description "What is the International Monetary Fund?" at the IMF Web site.

The major trading nations learned an important lesson from the terrible effects of trade protectionism. In 1948 the nations got together and formed the **General Agreement on Tariffs and Trade (GATT)**, an agreement among trading countries that provides a forum for negotiating mutual reductions in trade restrictions. For almost half a century it has succeeded in getting all nations to agree on a gradual reduction in tariffs and nontariff barriers to international trade. The road has not been smooth and there are still serious obstacles, but the trend and goals are clearly established and agreed to by all countries involved. On January 1, 1995, the World Trade Organization (WTO) assumed the task of supervising GATT.

Even before GATT, the **International Monetary Fund (IMF)** was signed into existence by 44 nations at Bretton Woods, New Hampshire, in 1944. The IMF is an international bank supported by its members that usually makes *short-term* loans to countries experiencing problems with their balance of trade. The IMF's basic objectives are to promote exchange stability, maintain orderly exchange arrangements, avoid competitive currency depreciation, establish a multilateral system of payments, eliminate exchange restrictions, and create standby reserves. The IMF makes *long-term* loans at interest rates of just 0.5 percent to the world's most destitute nations to help them strengthen their economies. The function of the IMF is very similar to that of the World Bank.

The **World Bank** (the International Bank for Reconstruction and Development), an autonomous United Nations agency, is concerned with developing the infrastructure (roads, schools, hospitals, power plants) in less-developed countries. The World Bank borrows from the more prosperous countries and lends at favourable rates to less developed countries.

Some countries believed that their economies would be strengthened if they established formal trade agreements with other countries. Some of these agreements involve forming producers' cartels and common markets, to be discussed next.

••• PRODUCERS' CARTELS •••

Producers' cartels are organizations of commodity-producing countries. They are formed to stabilize or increase prices, optimizing overall profits in the long run. The most obvious example today is OPEC (the Organization of Petroleum Exporting Countries). Similar attempts have been made to manage prices for cooper, iron ore, bauxite, bananas, tungsten, rubber, and other important commodities. These cartels are all contradictions to unrestricted free trade and letting the market set prices.

General Agreement on Tariffs and Trade (GATT)
Agreement among trading countries that provides a forum for negotiating mutual reductions in trade restrictions.

International Monetary Fund (IMF)
An international bank that makes short-term loans to countries experiencing problems with their balance of trade.

World Bank
An autonomous United Nations agency that borrows money from the more prosperous countries and lends it to less-developed countries to develop their infrastructure.

producers' cartels
Organizations of commodity-producing countries that are formed to stabilize or increase prices to optimize overall profits in the long run. (An example is OPEC, the Organization of Petroleum Exporting Countries.)

COMMON MARKETS

A **common market** consists of a regional group of countries whose aim is to remove all internal tariff and nontariff barriers to trade, investment, and employment. To achieve this the countries try to harmonize all their laws and regulations so that money, goods, services, and people can move freely between all the members of the group. Some notable examples are the Association of Southeast Asian Nations (ASEAN), the Central American Common Market (CACM), the Caribbean Common Market (CCM), Mercosur in South America, the European Union (EU), and the North American Free Trade Agreement (NAFTA). The last two are particularly important for Canada, so we look at them in the next two sections.

••• THE CANADA–U.S. FREE TRADE AGREEMENT[5] •••

An important common market was established between Canada and the United States when the Free Trade Agreement (FTA) came into effect on January 1, 1989. The agreement affected nearly all goods and services traded between Canada and the United States, as well as intercountry investments. These two countries are each other's largest trading partners. More than 80 percent of Canada's imports and exports are with the United States. The Canada–U.S. trading bloc has the largest two-country trade in the world, about $1.4 billion daily.

The formal purpose was to phase out most tariffs and other restrictions to free trade between the two countries over a period of 10 years. The FTA made it easier for cross-country investments and buyouts to take place and guaranteed the United States access to our energy resources. The movement of professionals and certain other categories of people across the border was also eased. For various reasons, each side kept certain items outside the FTA. For example, Canada insisted that beer and cultural industries and products be excluded. The United States insisted that shipping be excluded.

One major goal of the Canadian negotiating team was to provide relief from unilateral U.S. trade restrictions. A binational panel would adjudicate on disputes between the two countries. Unfortunately, this has not stopped the United States from continuing what many Canadians feel is harassment of our exporters (three examples are B.C. lumber, wheat, and steel from Ontario). Some cases were so frivolous (for instance, uranium from Saskatchewan) that they were easily won. But the process involves Canadian exporters in heavy legal costs and draws executives' time away from productive efforts. It also makes foreign companies wary of investing in Canada.

Both Simon Reisman, who was our chief negotiator of the FTA, and his deputy, Gordon Ritchie, were extensively quoted in the media in early 1992, criticizing the United States for continuing actions they deemed not to be in keeping with either the spirit or letter of the agreement.

The second aim of the FTA was to expose Canadian companies to greater competition from American companies to force them to become more competitive. This competition was deemed essential for Canada to compete in the tough, globalized business world. The thinking was that, since the world has now become one market, only the best can survive in that fiercely competitive global marketplace. The problem was that the Canadian government gave no aid to help certain industries through what it admitted would be a very difficult transition period, despite promises to do so.

Other countries, such as Japan, Singapore, and Korea, that wanted to raise certain industries to world-class competitiveness followed a different path. They gave their companies three years to shape up while protecting them from foreign competition. The governments aided the companies and monitored them closely to see that they were moving forward, and helped to retrain workers whose jobs were disappearing.

The third aim of the FTA was to give better access to the vast American market for Canadian goods and services. This goal was closely related to forcing Canadian companies to become more competitive, since they would have to compete with American companies.

••• THE NORTH AMERICAN FREE TRADE AGREEMENT •••

On January 1, 1993, the North American Free Trade Agreement (NAFTA) between the United States, Canada, and Mexico came into effect. This replaced the previous FTA between Canada and the United States. Why another free trade agreement? What impact did it have on Canada?

The movitators for NAFTA are to be found basically in the needs of the United States and Mexico. Mexico's population continues to explode, and its economy cannot provide jobs for large numbers of its people. For many years they have been pouring across the long U.S. boarder, mostly illegally. These uncounted millions of Mexicans are having a major, rapid impact on American society that is disturbing many Americans. The U.S. government seeks to stop this flow by helping the Mexican economy growing fast enough to provide jobs in Mexico. The Mexican government is, of course, interested in developing its economy and sees access to the vast American market as the way to spur growth, provide jobs for its people, and raise the low standard of living in Mexico.

Canada is really a minor player in this deal. It was concerned that it would be left out or penalized indirectly unless it sat at the table. We do have something to gain by having freer access to the growing Mexican market, but it is still a minor customer for Canada. The United States sought to modify the FTA in its favour as the price for letting Canada be a part of NAFTA. We did not have many bargaining chips and it is unclear if the United States succeeded.

There is a continuing concern in Canada, which is even greater in the United States, that many manufacturing jobs will be lost to Mexico because of NAFTA. Wages and general conditions are much lower in Mexico. This time around (unlike with the FTA), many Canadian business people were opposed because they did not like many of the details. In addition, Mexico has a poor policy on environmental problems, bad working conditions, and a bad record on human rights and political freedom. The country has repeatedly been condemned by many organizations in North America and abroad for serious flaws on all of these counts. Others believe that NAFTA will force Mexico to gradually improve these conditions. This has been happening, but at a very slow pace.

The United States and Canada announced a broad strategy of creating one vast free trade area of the entire western hemisphere. The U.S. sees itself as dominating this bloc, which will give it important leverage in trading with the rest of the world. With Europe moving to a single market and Japan becoming the linch-pin of a huge East Asian bloc, the United States wants to be sure it has the strength to compete with these major trading blocs. However, while

<www-tech.mit.edu/Bulletins/NAFTA.htm>

This Web site presents the actual terms of the NAFTA Act.

One result of NAFTA is that many manufacturing jobs have been moved to Mexico. It is much cheaper to produce goods in Mexico due to lower wages and lower costs in general.

protectionist sentiment in the United States is holding back accepting Chile into NAFTA, Canada signed its own free trade deal with Chile. Chile has also become the fifth member of the Mercosur common market, joining Brazil, Argentina, Uruguay, and Paraguay.

Progress Check

* What is the primary purpose of the International Monetary Fund (IMF) and the General Agreement on Tariffs and Trade (GATT)?
* How does a common market work? Why do countries enter into common market agreements?
* What were the objectives of Canada that led it to sign the FTA and NAFTA?

<www.europa.eu.int>

See this Web site about the European Union.

••• THE EUROPEAN UNION •••

On December 31, 1992, after 40 years of preparatory organizational structures, 12 nations of Europe, organized into a common market called the European Union (EU), effectively dissolving their economic borders. In 1994 three more countries were added. (See Figure 3.6 for a detailed list.) Most of the advanced part of Europe is now one vast market of some 370 million inhabitants with the free movement of people, goods, services, and capital. Centuries-old regional characteristics will remain a strong force for many years, but economic, political, and social differences are beginning to narrow. Many EU structures now in place are helping the movement in that direction, including a European parliament.

There were two major goals the EU hoped to achieve by the end of the century: monetary and political union. That means one currency—the *euro* unit—and an EU government. You can see how having a single currency avoids all the trade problems of currency fluctuations discussed earlier. One government will also make a common trade policy much easier to fashion for the 15 countries. This union is a historic movement toward countries giving up their sovereignty, which is a major reversal of the past few hundred years' evolution toward the modern independent nation-state.

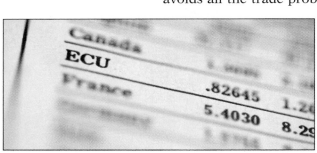

In 1999 it was clear that there were still serious obstacles preventing the achievement of complete monetary and political union. Most of the countries were suffering from economic decline and massive unemployment, possibly the worst crisis since the end of the war in 1945. Other issues were also delaying progress. It is not the first time in the 45-year history of this movement that major problems have arisen. In the past these were overcome, so there is hope that the current difficulties will also be overcome.

The eurodollar came into effect in January 1999. Since that time, prices in the participating countries have been shown in both the national and euro currency.

Despite all the difficulties 11 of the 15 members of the European Union agreed to phase out their own currencies and to use the *euro* as the common currency effective January 1, 1999. This process is complex and is being phased in over a two-year period. Since January 1999 all prices in these 11 countries have been shown in both the euro and the national currency.

The complex and very difficult process of uniting Europe began with six countries in 1957 led by some farsighted politicians in France and Germany. They felt that the only way to avoid even more devastating wars in Europe than the two terrible world wars of the twentieth century was to unite in a common destiny. Gradually, other reasons emerged for strengthening this unity movement. More people began to see such integration as the only way to raise their standard of living while improving their ability to compete with Japan and the United States in European and world markets.

Austria	Germany	Luxembourg
Belgium	Greece	Portugal
Denmark	Holland	Spain
Finland	Ireland	Sweden
France	Italy	United Kingdom

FIGURE 3.6

• • • •

THE EUROPEAN UNION

The 15 countries that were members of the European Union in 1999.

The free movement of people, money, goods and services, and shared social programs, new tax systems, and shared professional standards are extremely difficult to achieve. This movement is now seen by the rest of Europe as the wave of the future, and many of the countries that are not in the EU are eager to join. The EU will eventually be the largest unified market in the world, packing a powerful economic punch.

One advantage for Canadians is that English is the common business language of the EU. This should help Canadian companies compete in this giant market, as it will be one less barrier to international trade and investment. Figure 3.4 shows that the EU is one of our important trading partners. Some observers fear that a European protectionist superstate, "Fortress Europe," may emerge, but others see no danger of this happening. One of the most significant international developments of the next decade will be the progress of this newly united Europe.

Critical Thinking

Many countries in the world are called less-developed countries. Whey are they less developed? Is it the lack of natural resources? Then how do you explain the success of Japan, which has few natural resources?

Does lack of free markets keep countries from developing? Why would a government restrict free trade?

What could happen to the world's standard of living and quality of life if all countries engaged in free trade? What is keeping that from happening? What would it take to eliminate all barriers?

•••• ▬▬▬ ••••

A GLOBAL INDUSTRY RUNS INTO ETHICAL PROBLEMS[6]

Many transnational businesses are constantly searching for countries in which labour costs are low to reduce their manufacturing costs and make them more competitive. Makers of sneakers have practised this international sourcing, particularly in East Asian countries, and as a result ran into substantial criticism in the early 1990s for their weak ethical values. The criticism was mainly directed at the two largest companies in this field, Nike and Reebok. Specifically, the Indonesian Institut Teknology Bandung (ITB) and the Asian-American Free Labor Institute (AAFLI) alleged that "Nike's system of procuring shoes in Indonesia was rife with exploitation." They accused Nike's South Korean contractors of "forcing employees to work overtime, violating child-labor laws, and not respecting special work rules for women," and other violations.

At first Nike said that these factories were owned and operated by independent contractors who produced the running shoes for them. There was similar criticism of Reebok from the International Labor Rights Education and Research Fund (ILRERF) and an initial response from Reebok that aped

Nike. Eventually, both companies issued formal documents specifying principles and procedures that all their subcontractors were required to follow to ensure that human rights and local laws were respected. Reebok's program seemed to have more teeth in it than Nike's. Senior Reebok officials were quoted as saying, "I think corporations are increasingly finding that you need to be more than good business people. You have to be responsible business citizens," and "consumers today hold companies accountable for the way products are made, not just the quality of the product itself."

<www.gbn.org/Book Club/Competitive.html>

Visit this Web site to read about Michael Porter's views on a number of the controversial issues regarding NAFTA as part of a review of his most recent book.

···· ▬▬▬ ····

HOW DOES CANADA SHAPE UP AS AN INTERNATIONAL COMPETITOR?

The 1990s saw a torrent of complaints in Canada that our competitiveness has been sliding steadily. One of the most influential sources assessing Canada's competitiveness is the Porter report, commissioned by the Canadian government. It is called *Canada at the Crossroads: The Reality of a New Competitive Environment*. This year-long study by a team headed by Michael E. Porter, the guru of competition from the Harvard University Business School, was released in January 1992. It is a very comprehensive analysis; the summary is 101 pages long. The report is based on concepts and techniques elaborated in Porter's influential book *The Competitive Advantage of Nations*.

What are Porter's conclusions? According to the analysis by Professor Donald N. Thompson of York University, "Drastic and immediate action ... [is] required by Canada." He continues:

> *It is hard to overstate the urgency of the problem highlighted by Porter. Canada is behind in the technology race, and has shown almost no productivity growth in a decade. Its 30 percent high-school dropout rate is the highest in the western world. In training effectiveness Canada ranks 20th of 24 [developed] countries rated by the OECD (Organization for Economic Co-operation and Development). A government that should be taking the lead in research, technology, and training has spent almost two terms pursuing noninterventionist policies such as deregulation, privatization, and free trade. Reversing that policy and finding initiatives that are affordable is difficult.*

Porter "is unrelenting in ... [his] criticism of government, business, and labour for Canada's failure to abandon old ways of thinking and to embrace a new economic order of continual productivity growth and innovation."

Porter believes governments should concentrate on education, employee training, developing "closer links between government, universities, and industry research bodies," and specialized regional development policies. Business must "treat labour as a partner and act in a less authoritarian way," be "innovative-driven," spend more on training, "transform foreign subsidiaries into home bases," "rely more on advanced technologies and methods," and "focus on products, markets, and businesses that provide a lasting competitive advantage." Labour's "priorities must become encouragement of technological change and skills upgrading, and more cooperative labour-management relations" as "the best guarantee of good wages" and jobs in the long term.

Porter, an American, notes that "one of Canada's competitive problems is the high concentration of foreign-owned firms that perform little sophisticated production or R&D." Not mentioned by Porter is that these are nearly all subsidiaries of U.S. firms. Nearly half (45 percent) of Canada's manufacturing sector is foreign owned. Thompson points out that "most academics and government officials maintain that the level of foreign ownership is not significant in determining the competitiveness" of Canada. Porter disagrees, arguing:

It matters a lot where a multinational calls home, because a company's home base is where the best jobs exist, where core R&D is undertaken, and where strategic control rests.... Home bases are important to an economy because they support high productivity and productivity growth.

Thompson notes that in this difference of opinion, Porter takes a position "closer to economic nationalists" than to the more conventional economic wisdom.

Finally, concludes Professor Thompson, the message is "that we must move quickly or risk a real loss in standard of living."[7]

··· EVIDENCE CONTRADICTING PORTER ··· AND CONVENTIONAL WISDOM[8]

Two reports in *The Globe and Mail* seem to be somewhat at odds with all the bad news about Canada's competitive ability. The first, a Statistics Canada study, shows that exports of Canadian manufacturing products accounted for 47 percent of all our merchandise exports in 1990 (compared to only 32 percent in 1980). These exports began increasing in the latter half of the 1980s, despite the rise of the Canadian dollar against the U.S. dollar making our exports more expensive. Later Statistics Canada figures show that the percentage continued to rise between 1991 and 1993, despite the recession. By 1994 manufactured products constituted 68 percent of all exports.

Even when automotive trade with the United States is excluded, manufacturing exports still increased from 20 percent to 37 percent of overall exports in the 1980s. According to Philip Cross, StatCan's director of current analysis, the big losses in manufacturing appeared to occur in the domestic market. Such industries as textiles, furniture, appliances, food products, printing, and publishing were hit.

Cross's statistics are borne out by the comments of J. Myers, chief economist and senior vice-president of the Canadian Exporters and Manufacturers Association. He says that "the real weakness in manufacturing has not been in exports ... but on the domestic side." Myers notes that Canadian manufacturers' share of the domestic market slipped from 73 percent in 1980 to 55 percent in 1991. By 1994 the figure was down to 45 percent, in large extent due to the FTA and NAFTA. This figure had slipped further by 1998. Perhaps even more impressive, Cross says:

*Manufacturing output has declined at a slower pace than has manufacturing employment during the recession as companies have continued to make productivity gains even as output fell, **which is highly unusual** [authors' emphasis]. Productivity is defined as real output per person-hour worked.*

These statistics are almost startling in view of all the gloomy statements by Porter and so many others about the poor productivity of Canadian manufacturers.

The second report from *The Globe and Mail* covers a study by a University of Toronto political science professor, Joseph Fletcher, about Canadian attitudes to capitalistic and entrepreneurial ideologies. "Canadians, it turns out, are more American than the Americans." On a long list of questions designed to compare Canadian and American attitudes, we seem to be waving ideological business banners "even more zealously" than our cousins to the south.

While it is rather surprising to discover that we are really so different from the image usually projected of Canadians, there is something even more surprising. This study, entitled *Canadian Attitudes Towards Competitiveness and Entrepreneurship*, was commissioned by the federal government. But it was held up by the Department of Industry, Science, and Technology for nearly a year, until well after the delivery of the Porter report in October 1991. The lengthy delay is understandable, since the study conflicts with a basic premise in Porter's report. The article notes that

> *Mr. Porter concluded in his report that the biggest barriers to improving Canada's competitiveness are attitudinal. He said that if his study had only one impact, he hoped it would be the way Canadians think about competitiveness. Although there was not a shred of attitudinal research in the Porter report, big business and government quickly picked up the theme.*

In the meantime, various ratings of Canada's international competitiveness position in the early 1990s by the OECD and the World Economic Forum had us fluctuating annually somewhere at the bottom of the top third or quarter of the 24 or 48 countries evaluated.

Nevertheless, the OECD, consisting of the 29 most advanced industrialized countries and whose current secretary-general is Canadian Donald Johnston, continues to rate Canada's standard of living as being 10 percent above the average of industrial countries. The OECD also said that it had erred in evaluating how productive the Canadian economy had been in the 1980s and 1990s.[9] (See additional discussion of the issue of productivity in the previous chapter and in Chapter 10.) The whole issue of assessing international competitiveness is complex and open to varying opinions. For example, as you can see in Figure 3.7, the prestigious World Economic Forum put Canada fifth in international competitiveness in 1998, only 10 percent behind the U.S. Comparing 1996 with 1998, the U.S. has moved from fourth to third place, while Canada moved from eighth to fifth place.

As we enter the twenty-first century it is clear that more research is required to explain these contradictions. It seems that no one has the answer to the important question: How productive, and therefore how competitive, is Canada?

FIGURE 3.7
· · · ·
WORLD ECONOMIC
FORUM GLOBAL
COMPETITIVENESS
REPORT

This report clearly shows that Canada's competitive position is quite strong. It slipped a little in 1998, but is still much better than it was in 1996. We are only 10 percent behind the U.S.

Country	Competitiveness Index	Rank 1998	Rank 1997	Rank 1996
Singapore	2.16	1	(1)	(1)
Hong Kong	1.91	2	(2)	(2)
United States	1.41	3	(3)	(4)
United Kingdom	1.29	4	(7)	(15)
Canada	**1.27**	**5**	**(4)**	**(8)**

Source: <www.weforum.org>, May 1999.

Progress
Check

- What is the EU? What is it trying to achieve?
- What is the Porter report? What are its main conclusions according to Professor Thompson?
- What is the evidence contradicting some of its conclusions?

···· ━━━ ····

CAREERS AND JOBS IN THE GLOBAL WORLD OF BUSINESS

Business has become global in nature and this fact should be influencing how you prepare yourself for a promising career or job. Your first thoughts might be about what large company could employ you, and there are many such Canadian companies that are deeply involved in international activities. The major Canadian banks —Royal, CIBC, Bank of Montreal, Nova Scotia, and TD—and banks that are subsidiaries of giant international banks like the Hong Kong Bank of Canada are good examples. Some major manufacturing and processing companies are Northern Telecom (Nortel Networks), Magna International, Bombardier, International Nickel, Nova Corp., and the Canadian subsidiaries of the American and Japanese automobile manufacturers. There are also insurance company, forestry and pulp and paper companies, and hundreds of other large companies with major international investments and markets.

Many small software companies are involved in global business. Even small companies can grow quickly by developing an international presence.

Do not overlook the thousands of smaller Canadian companies who are also involved in global business, including software companies. You will see some of the names scattered throughout this book in Profiles or in boxes. Many of them are aided by an extensive federal government program to assist smaller exporters. Or you may even start your own business in Canada or elsewhere as a result of ideas that occur to you while travelling through other countries. A good example is the traveller in Africa who noticed that it was hard to get ice for drinks. He did a little research and found that there was no ice factory in hundreds of kilometres, despite a large market for ice. He found some investors in North America prepared to back him, returned to Africa, and built an ice-making plant. He went on to develop a successful business.

To be better equipped for working in the global business atmosphere, you should be thinking about, and doing, the following:

- learning to speak other languages; French, Spanish, and Chinese would all be very useful
- travelling to other countries to observe first hand how their cultures function
- taking some cross-cultural courses to better understand the attitudes of other peoples
- reading magazines and newspapers that concentrate on business and news from other countries
- forming friendships with students from other countries

REVIEW

Do you recall the ethical problem about nightgowns at the start of the chapter? Here's what our executives think. Bédard says, "I feel the nightgowns are a write-off. The company has already suffered severely because of this fabric. Unless the nightgowns can be treated with fire-retardant material that would be efficient for the life of the garment, I would suggest that they be destroyed and the company must accept the loss."

Reilley believes that "sales of Nightie Nite (NN) products in less restrictive countries may work in the ▲

short term. However, the NN company would become known as being less than ethical and would eventually have to adjust their products to be safe, or lose market share. Emerging-country consumers are becoming more sophisticated all the time and NN's competitors are becoming more ethical on the world market as well." In addition, "world bodies such as the WTO, IME, and UN are demanding more ethical conduct [in] emerging countries."

All of these actions will help to expand your vision and knowledge of how the world functions, helping you to find a useful niche and to function better in whatever job or career you choose.

SUMMARY
• • • • •

1. Discuss the critical importance of the international market and the role of comparative advantage in international trade.

1. The world market for trade is huge. Some 95 percent of the people in the world live outside Canada and the United States.
   - ***Why should nations trade with other nations?***
   (1) No country is self-sufficient, (2) countries need products that other countries produce, and (3) there is a world imbalance of natural resources and technological skills.

   - ***What is the theory of comparative advantage?***
   The theory of comparative advantage contends that a country should produce and sell those products it produces most efficiently and buy those it cannot produce as effectively.

2. Understand the status of Canada in international business.

2. Canada has only 30 million people, yet it ranks seventh in the world in volume of international trade. Canadian companies also invest large sums of money in the United States and in other countries.
   - ***What made Canada's success in international trade possible?***
   Canada is an efficient, modern, industrialized country with a well-trained workforce. It has developed high levels of expertise in agricultural, energy, and other natural resource production. Canada produces huge quantities of these products, as well as automotive vehicles and parts, which are exported to the United States under the special Auto Pact. More recently, electronic and telecommunication products and transportation equipment have become major exports.

3. A company can participate in world trade in a number of ways.
   - ***What are some ways a company can get involved in international business?***
   Ways of entering world trade include exporting and importing, joint venturing, licensing, creating subsidiaries, franchising, and countertrading.

   3. Illustrate the strategies used in reaching global markets.

4. There are many restrictions on foreign trade other than protectionism.
   - ***What are some of the other hurdles that can discourage participation in international business?***
   Potential stumbling blocks to world trade include cultural differences, societal and economic differences, legal and regulatory differences, and fluctuations in values of different currencies.

   4. Discuss the hurdles to trading in world markets.

5. Political pressures are often the most difficult hurdles to international trade.
   - ***How does trade protectionism reduce international trade?***
   Trade protectionism is the use of government regulations to limit the import of goods and services, based on the theory of favouring domestic producers to help them survive and grow and generate more jobs. Some tools of protectionism are tariffs and quotas.

   5. Review what trade protectionism is and how and why it is practised.

   - ***What are tariffs?***
   Tariffs are taxes on imports.

   - ***How does a quota differ from a tariff?***
   A quota limits the quantity of particular imports.

   - ***Is trade protectionism good for domestic producers?***
   That is debatable. Trade protectionism hurt all countries badly during the Great Depression of the 1930s because other countries responded to foreign tariffs with tariffs of their own.

   - ***Why do governments continue such practices?***
   Pressure from industries and their associations, unions, and communities affected by imports nurtures the practice of trade protectionism.

6. One of the most significant developments for the future of world trade is the formation of 15 European countries into one trading bloc, called the European Union (EU).
   - ***What trading partnership is more important to Canada than the EU?***
   The U.S.–Canada–Mexico North American Free Trade Agreement (NAFTA). It is expected to expand ultimately to include all of South and Central America.

   6. Discuss the future of international trade and investment.

   - ***Will future growth in world trade be with large developed nations?***
   Yes, but there will likely be more growth with the rapidly developing Pacific Rim countries such as China and other countries in Southeast Asia. The former communist countries in eastern Europe and what was the Soviet Union also offer great potential for investment and trade.

KEY TERMS
. . . . . .

balance of trade 64
bartering 72
common market 78
comparative
   advantage
   theory 63
consortium 70
countertrading 72
embargo 76
exchange rate 65
foreign subsidiary 69

General Agreement
   on Tariffs and Trade
   (GATT) 77
import quota 74
international joint
   venture (IJV) 70
International
   Monetary Fund
   (IMF) 77
licensing 68
mercantilism 74

producers' cartels
   77
trade deficit 65
trade protectionism
   65
transnational or
   multinational
   corporation (TNC
   or MNC) 61
World Bank 77

DEVELOPING WORKPLACE SKILLS

1. Visit an Oriental rug dealer or some other importer of foreign goods. Talk with the owner or manager about the problems and satisfactions involved in international trade. Visit several such organizations and compile a list of advantages and disadvantages. Compare your list with those of other students in your class.

2. Prepare a short essay describing the benefits and drawbacks of trade protectionism. Have your class divide into two sides and debate this issue: "Resolved—that Canada should increase trade protection to save Canadian jobs and Canadian companies."

3. Many firms have made embarrassing mistakes selling overseas. Sometimes the product is not adapted to the needs of the country, sometimes the advertising makes no sense, sometimes the colour is wrong, and so forth. Discuss the steps Canadian businesses should follow to be more responsive to the needs of foreign markets. Discuss your list with others, and together form a plan for improving trade overseas.

4. What aspect of international business interests you most: importing, exporting, investment, production, finance, marketing, or franchising? Why?

5. How seriously have you explored working in a global economy? What courses might you take to better prepare yourself?

INTERNET CHALLENGES

1. Trade protectionism is a constant issue in the U.S., especially in periods leading up to elections, which take place in November 2000 and 2002. Because the U.S. is by far our largest customer, this issue is of major importance to us. Search the Web sites of your local newspaper, *The Globe and Mail*, and the *National Post* newspapers, and *Canadian Business* or *MacLean's* magazines to see what current news stories there are on this topic, especially reports that affect any Canadian companies or industries.

2. The European Union plan for a single currency—the *euro*—for its 15 members is unfolding with 11 countries now showing prices in the euro as well as in local currency. This new currency will have a major effect on international business. Use the Yahoo search engine <www.yahoo.com> (or any other such search engine) and the keywords *euro currency* to see what information you can gather about the current situation, such as how many countries are using the euro, how the process is unfolding, what problems have arisen, and any special impact on Canada.

Practising Management Decisions

Since the collapse of the Soviet Union in 1989 and the splitting up of the country into a dozen independent states, a whole new world of opportunity has opened up for Canadian, and other, companies. These republics are busily engaged in trying to establish capitalist economies and they need a lot of help: capital, technology, and management skills are desperately needed.

This large potential market has attracted hundreds of thousands of companies and individuals who see a great opportunity to get rich quick. Unfortunately, these opportunities are matched by risks of equal size. Because the collapse was so sudden, the attempt to make a complete change has resulted in a very chaotic situation. Laws are weak, confused, nonexistent, or not enforced. Serious corruption and major crimes such as kidnapping and murder are commonplace. Many business people travel only with bodyguards and in bullet-proof cars. Organized crime represents a strong and growing force in these republics.

One of the ongoing problems of doing business in Moscow is the pressure from gangs to pay them to protect you. The gangs provide a *roof* so no other gangs will threaten you. Usually they start with small demands and then gradually increase their price until they take over the whole business and force you to leave the country. Let us examine how one Canadian company coped with this high-risk situation.

Brad Pielsticker operates an airfreight-forwarding company, AES International Ltd., with offices in the Moscow airport and in downtown Moscow. One day he received a call at the airport

CASE 1
······
INTERNATIONAL EXPANSION: A CAUTIONARY TALE
······

office from his Russian partner, who told him that the mafia had finally caught up with them. Someone had just entered their downtown office and demanded payment for a roof.

Pielsticker remembered what had happened to his brother, who had had his lucrative software-teaching-skills company taken away from him and given 24 hours to flee the country. Pielsticker decided to bluff. He and his partner told the enforcer that they already had a roof and that he should return in three days if he wanted to meet him.

Pielsticker then hired someone he knew, who had underworld connections and a reputation, to pose as their roof. Fortunately the trick worked, because after one meeting the enforcer did not return. Pielsticker feels very lucky—he had a close call and he knows it.

Decision Questions

1. How would you feel about expanding your business into Moscow? Would the temptation of big bucks overcome your worries?
2. How does a company or individual determine what is an acceptable level of risk? Is it better to always stay away from high-risk situations?
3. Suppose your company sent you to Moscow to manage or work in the local office. Would that be different? Why?
4. Is it better to wait a while, hoping the situation will improve? Suppose your competitors are already there?

Source: John Nadler, "Married (Often Happily) to the Mob," *Canadian Business*, April 1996, p. 30ff.

Condor Manufacturing has a joint venture with a local company in an African country we shall call Lorino. Condor sent you out to be the general manager for three years to train a Lorinese to take over from you. You are facing certain problems that you do not know how to resolve.

Bribery and kickbacks are normal methods of getting things done in Lorino. This applies to dealings with other companies and with the government. Salaries are very low and bribes are expected to make up the shortfall so that people can survive.

CASE 2
······
TO BRIBE OR NOT TO BRIBE? THAT IS THE QUESTION
······

The vice-president of international operations for Condor is not very keen about this way of doing business, especially as it violates the company's ethical code. However, he informs you that these are decisions that you will have to make as the general manager. You have tried to pass the buck and it has been passed right back to you.

You have had to bribe people to get certain licences, to get supplies, to have a road repaired, and to get sales contracts signed. You know that other local companies have learned to live with these conditions. Now you are negotiating to buy a piece of land adjacent to the factory because Condor will have to expand in the near future. A substantial bribe is being demanded and you are trying to resist it.

Decision Questions

1. Should you go along with this demand since it is a one-time issue?

2. Should you hold your nose and go along with this "normal" way of doing things?

3. Should you try to get a transfer out of Lorino even if you have to cook up some medical or personal reasons?

4. Do you have any other alternatives? What are the likely results of each of the previous choices?

The Role of Government in Business

Chapter 4

Former Premier of New Brunswick Frank McKenna attracted a lot of attention across Canada, not all of it favourable, for his aggressive campaign to bring new business into his province. McKenna concentrated on making New Brunswick the call-centre capital of Canada.

Most of us are aware that when we call a company today, we never know where the call is being received. Companies used to receive calls at their local offices, but new communication technology has made it more economical to have one centre receive all calls. Modern satellites and fibre optics make it possible for the centre to be anywhere in the world.

Cashing in on this possibility, Frank McKenna was able to attract a wide variety of companies to New Brunswick. The Royal Bank set up its new telebanking centre in Moncton; Hospitality Franchise Systems and ICT Group, a major marketing and information research service, located its centre in Saint John; Sun Life Assurance, IBM Canada, Camco Inc., Pepsi Cola (Atlantic), Xerox, and many others, including important software companies, have also located call centres and related functions in New Brunswick.

 PROFILE

Premier Frank McKenna: New Brunswick's Super Salesman

The result of these and other recruiting activities was a steady increase in jobs and economic activities in New Brunswick. In 1995 alone employment was up by 7000 reaching an all-time high of 314,000 and bringing unemployment in New Brunswick to 11.5 percent, the lowest level since 1980. Added to two consecutive years of increases in employment participation while the national rate dropped for the sixth consecutive year, this was a very impressive performance. The economic results were quite substantial: inflation below the national rate; GDP, manufacturing shipments, and exports above national rates; retail sales and wages at national rates.

Although there were some protests from other provinces that McKenna was stealing companies from them or engaging inn unfair competition, these were not too serious and McKenna continued his campaign of attracting business to New Brunswick.

The efforts of Frank McKenna continued to be felt in New Brunswick at the end of the 1990s, long after his departure from the political scene.

Ethical Dilemma

TACKLING THE DEFICIT

As you saw in Chapter 2, the federal government was under strong pressure from the business community to reduce and wipe out the annual deficit in the federal budget. Business was convinced that these constant deficits and the resulting accumulated debt were dragging the Canadian economy down and making Canada uncompetitive with other major countries. In this chapter you will see that the government has drastically cut its expenditures, resulting in significant reductions in funding to the provinces for health care, higher education, and other important activities. Combined with other budget-cutting measures that have led to lower and

fewer payments to the unemployed, the result has been an increase in poverty levels, especially among children and women. In December 1998 a United Nations committee criticized Canada because of the high percentage of the population in poor circumstances.[1]

These facts lead to some ethical questions: Should such severe budget cuts have been made? Does the business community bear some responsibility for the increase in poverty in Canada? Was there really any other choice given the tough, globally competitive conditions today? We will look for answers at the end of ▲ the chapter.

<www.dbic.com>
<www.cbsc.org>

The Doing Business in Canada and Canada Business Service Centres Web sites are federal government services, but include information on services provided by provincial governments, other institutional and private organizations, and federal government agencies.

GOVERNMENT INVOLVEMENT IN THE ECONOMY

As discussed in Chapter 2, the Canadian economic system is often described as a mixed economy—that is, a capitalist economy in which government plays an important role. If you look at the government of Canada section (and equivalent provincial government sections) in the blue pages of a city telephone directory, you will get some idea of the degree of government involvement in our economy. There are so many services that federal and provincial governments issue publications listing them in detail. For example, the 13th edition of the *Guide to Federal Programs and Services* is a 450-page book. It lists programs and services for 140 government-owned companies, departments, and agencies, with addresses and toll-free phone numbers across the country and other information. Companies owned by the federal or provincial governments are called **crown corporations**.

IMPACT ON CAREERS AND JOBS

crown corporations
Companies owned by the federal or a provincial government.

As you make your way through the chapter and see the complex activities of governments in Canada, you will not be surprised to learn that they are the largest employers in the country. The federal government and the provinces with the largest populations and levels of economic activity—Ontario, Quebec, B.C., Alberta—head the list of employers. In the past it was quite natural for college graduates to find employment with these governments. However, as noted in Chapter 2 and as you will see in the chapter, in the latter half of the 1990s governments cut back many of their activities and reduced their workforces. These measures, combined with continued privatization of government-owned companies, caused a major source of employment to dry up.

HOW GOVERNMENT AFFECTS BUSINESS

<www.cn.ca/cnwebsite/
cnwebsite.nsf/public/
splashC>
<www.aircanada.ca/
about-us>

The CN and Air Canada Web sites provide information about the progress of these two companies since privatization. Visit these sites to learn more.

Government activities can be divided into five categories, as shown in Figure 4.1: laws and regulations, crown corporations, services, financial aid, and purchasing policies. This chapter will look at all of them.

All countries' governments are involved in the economy, but the extent of involvement and the specific ways they participate vary a great deal. In Canada there are particular historical reasons why we developed into a nation in which governments play very important roles. Before looking at this history and the many ways that governments affect business, let us look at the current trends of government involvement.

The federal government has a major disposition campaign underway. It sold the Canadian National Railways (CNR), Air Canada, and the national system of air traffic control. The government also sold the St. Lawrence Seaway, hundreds of ports and ferries, and other maritime installations. This veritable flood of disposals of government assets and companies signals a minor revolution in Canadian history. The whole process of governments selling publicly owned corporations is called **privatization**.[2] In addition, industries that had been regulated, such as airlines and trucking, were partially or completely deregulated—no longer subject to certain regulations. Similar activities were undertaken by provincial governments.

privatization
The process of governments selling crown corporations.

Some people believe this trend should be reversed to get the economy moving again and to deal with the unprecedented structural changes (discussed in Chapter 1) that occurred in the 1990s. They believe that the lack of a comprehensive, coordinated government plan to guide and revitalize the economy, called an **industrial policy**, will undermine our ability to recover from the very severe recession of the early 1990s. Others are strongly opposed in principle to such government action. We will return to this issue at the end of the chapter.

industrial policy
A comprehensive coordinated government plan to guide and revitalize the economy.

••• A HISTORICAL REVIEW •••

When Canada was formed as a country in 1867, the federal government was given the power to "regulate trade and commerce." When the western provinces

---

1. **Laws and regulations.** These cover a wide range, from taxation and consumer protection to environmental controls, working conditions, and labour–management relations.

2. **Crown corporations.** There are hundreds of such companies, and they play an important role in the economy. Crown corporations sometimes compete with regular businesses.

3. **Services.** These include a vast array of direct and indirect activities, among them helping specific industries go international, bringing companies to Canada, training and retraining the workforce, and providing a comprehensive statistics service.

4. **Financial aid.** All levels of government provide a host of direct and indirect aid packages as incentives to achieve certain goals. These packages consist of tax reductions, tariffs and quotas on imports, grants, loans, and loan guarantees.

5. **Purchasing policies.** Governments are very large purchasers of ordinary supplies, services, and materials for military purposes. Because the federal government is the single largest purchaser in Canada, its policies regarding where to purchase have a major effect on particular businesses and the economy of specific provinces and regions.

FIGURE **4.1**
• • • •
**GOVERNMENT
INVOLVEMENT
WITH BUSINESS**

Government activities that affect business can be divided into five categories.

Many previously government-owned corporations, such as the St. Lawrence Seaway, have been privatized in recent years. Privatization and deregulation have been somewhat controversial because these "new" corporations now operate on the profit principle, not necessarily on what is best for consumers.

later joined this confederation, it became clear that it would take special efforts to build a united Canada. The very small population was scattered across a huge country and there was no railway connecting them. Trading patterns were in a north to south configuration because, like today, most people lived near the U.S. border. The cross-border shopping phenomenon is not new.

The United States was developing much faster, with a much larger population and a bigger economy that provided products not available in the provinces, either because they were not made here or there was no transportation to distribute them.

This led Canadian governments, starting with our first prime minister, Sir John A. MacDonald, to develop what was called the **National Policy**. The Policy placed high tariffs on imports from the United States to protect Canadian manufacturing, which had higher costs. In addition, the government began to grapple with the difficult question of building a costly rail line to the west coast.

These two issues set the tone for the continuing and substantial involvement of Canadian governments in developing and maintaining the Canadian economy. The same type of mixed economy can be found in many countries: advanced countries, like Germany and Japan; newly developed countries, like Taiwan and South Korea; and developing ones, like Brazil and Thailand.

National Policy
Federal government policy imposing high tariffs on imports from the United States to protect Canadian manufacturing.

The issue of how much government should be involved in the economy has been the subject of much debate in Canada. In the United States ideology has played a major role in influencing Americans to believe that, in principle, government should "butt out." This thinking ignores the significant role the U.S. government has played and continues to play in its economy. In Canada, we are less negative and perhaps more pragmatic: If it works, let's do it. But where do we go from here? Do we need less or more government involvement? Is it a question of the quality of that involvement? Could it be *smarter* rather than just *less*? What are your thoughts?

<www.aecl.ca>
<www.edc.ca>

Most crown corporations have Web sites on the Internet. Surf the Net to see if you can find them. Visit the Atomic Energy of Canada and Export Development Corporation Web sites to look at a couple of examples. If you are considering getting into a business that exports goods to foreign countries, the EDC can provide help—check it out.

••• CROWN CORPORATIONS •••

In Canada, an important aspect of the role of government is expressed through crown corporations. Some major federal ones are Canada Post Corporation, Atomic Energy of Canada Ltd., Canada Mortgage and Housing Corporation, the Canadian Broadcasting Corporation (CBC), the Canadian Wheat Board, and the Export Development Corporation. There are many more large and small federally owned crown corporations.

Each province also owns such corporations. Typically, a crown corporation owns the province's electric power company. New Brunswick Electric Power, B.C. Hydro, Ontario Hydro, and Hydro-Quebec are some examples. Some of the telephone systems in western Canada are owned by provincial crown corporations. The provinces also own other specialized corporations.

The Export Development Corporation (EDC) is a Crown corporation that operates as a commercial financial institution. EDC has been helping Canadian businesses grow through exports and international investment since 1944. The trade finance solutions offered by EDC can help exporters compete in more than 200 countries, including higher-risk and emerging markets.

Alberta owns a bank called Alberta Treasury Branches (ATB), originally set up to help farmers in bad times.

Governments set up crown corporations either to provide services that were not being provided by businesses (which is how Air Canada came into being in the 1930s), to bail out a major industry in trouble (which is how the Canadian National Railways, now privatized, was put together in 1919), or to provide some special services that could not otherwise be made available, as in the case of Atomic Energy of Canada Ltd. or the Bank of Canada. Two important examples in Alberta and Quebec are discussed below.

SPECIAL FINANCIAL ROLE OF TWO PROVINCIAL CROWN CORPORATIONS The Alberta Heritage Savings Trust Fund was established in the 1970s, when the Alberta economy was prospering as a result of the oil boom and the government set aside part of its oil royalty revenue to start the fund. The Fund's assets total $13 billion. It must operate on a sound financial basis, but as much as possible, it makes investment decisions that will benefit Alberta.

Quebec has the Caisse de dépôt et placement du Québec, a giant fund that was established to handle the funds collected by the Quebec Pension Plan. At $69 billion, it is one of the largest pools of funds in North America. This plan was set up parallel to the Canada Pension Plan in 1966. The fund also handles other Quebec government funds and is a very powerful investment vehicle that is used to guide economic development in Quebec. Although it too must operate on a sound financial basis, it has a lot of scope to make decisions that will benefit the Quebec economy.

A closer look at what Quebec and New Brunswick have been doing reveals some important initiatives of government in close cooperation with business. The last section of the chapter will look at this important issue again, in more detail.

The federal and provincial governments in Canada are continually reducing their involvement in the economic life of the country. For example, the federal government has sold Crown corporations such as Petro-Canada and Air Canada.

··· A SMALLER ROLE FOR GOVERNMENT ···

Elections in Canada in the 1990s saw provincial and federal governments of all parties embark upon a series of measures designed to continue the reduction of governments' role in the economic life of the country. Former large crown corporations like Teleglobe Canada, Air Canada, Alberta Government Telephone, and Petro-Canada have been

Spotlight on Small Business

<www.bdc.ca>

Business Development Bank of Canada

One crown corporation that is particularly helpful to business is the federal Business Development Bank of Canada (BDC). The bank has been in operation since the mid-1940s and has been invaluable for small and medium-sized businesses. The BDC originally functioned only as a lender—the bank of last resort—but over the years it has developed into a multiservice organization. In the late 1990s the BDC embarked on an aggressive marketing campaign explaining its services to small and medium-sized businesses.

The BDC not only lends money to businesses that cannot get loans from commercial banks, but it also invests in enterprises that are just starting up or expanding. The owners have the right to buy out the BDC holdings in their companies any time in the future at the value then prevailing. When the BDC takes an equity position (buys shares in a company), this often encourages other investors or lenders who might otherwise have been reluctant to participate.

In addition, the bank provides management services through its Counseling Assistance to Small Enterprises (CASE). CASE uses the services of retired business people and experts as consultants to smaller companies. This large group of people, with every conceivable

background in business, is made available at reasonable rates. It is a useful service, since many entrepreneurs are weak in some aspect of management, be it marketing, finance, production, or planning. Over the years thousands of CASE consultants have helped tens of thousands of business people to prosper.

Another service provided by the BDC is the Automated Information for Management (AIM). This large database contains useful information for small and medium-sized businesses. It lists all assistance programs available from all levels of government in Canada, sources of information, and various business opportunities all over the country.

Among BDC's publications is a bimonthly publication, *Profits*, with useful articles and information for entrepreneurs and small businesses. The autumn issue highlights Small Business Week. This annual event started in British Columbia in 1979, takes place in a different province each year, and includes "business fairs, exhibits, workshops, conferences, luncheons, award ceremonies, and much more."

▲ Sources: Various publications of BDC: *Profits*, annual reports.

sold off. Saskatchewan reduced its interest in giant uranium producer Cameco Corp., Quebec is selling its stake in Domtar Inc., and Alberta is trying to dispose of the Alberta Petroleum Marketing Commission.

Progress Check

• What are three of the five categories of government intervention in the economy?

• What does privatization refer to? Can you cite any examples?

• What are crown corporations? Why are they set up? Can you name three?

···· ▬▬▬ ····

REGISTRATION, REPORTING, AND INFORMATION

··· REGISTRATION ···

Governments need to know what businesses are in operation to ensure that a wide range of laws and regulations are being followed. Ensuring that names of businesses are not duplicated is important to avoid confusion. Additionally, governments have to be sure that all taxes are being paid. To achieve these and other goals, every company must register at the appropriate provincial authority when it commences business. This is a simple, routine, and inexpensive procedure.

In addition, all corporations must obtain **articles of incorporation**. This is a legal authorization from the federal or a provincial government for a company to use the corporate format. Incorporation is usually done through a legal firm and is discussed in detail in Chapter 6. Governments, and the public at large, thus have a record of the existence of every corporation in Canada.

articles of incorporation
The legal documents, obtained from the federal or provincial governments, authorizing a company to operate as a corporation.

··· REPORTING AND INFORMATION ···

Businesses receive many documents from governments during the course of the year. Some are just information about changes in employment insurance, Canada or Quebec Pension Plan, or tax legislation as it affects them and their employees. Then there are various statistics forms that all companies must complete so that governments can compile reports that businesses, individuals, research organizations, and governments need to operate more effectively.

Statistics Canada (StatCan) maintains vast databases that it creates from these reports and from many other sources, including international databases. StatCan issues many quarterly, semi-annual, or annual reports on a host of topics. It also publishes a variety of special reports at irregular intervals. Some of them are quoted in this text.

All corporations must also file annual reports containing basic data about themselves: for example, how many shares have been issued, who the officers and directors are, and where the head office is located. Of course, every company must also file annual tax returns containing financial statements and pay the necessary income and other taxes during the year.

TAXATION OF COMPANIES

Each level of government collects some kind of taxes from companies to give it the income it needs to discharge its legal obligations. The main source of income for municipalities is taxes on property, but there are a variety of other taxes and fees as well. Federal and provincial governments rely mostly on income taxes on individuals and corporations. Provincial sales taxes are also an important source of revenue for the provinces (only Alberta has no sales tax), while the goods and services tax (GST) brings very substantial moneys to the federal government. In some provinces, health care is financed by a tax on the total wages and salaries paid by companies.

Taxes on businesses are considered part of the cost of doing business and thus are included in the prices they charge. Small corporations get a tax break; they pay about half the normal income tax rates. Manufacturing corporations also get a reduced rate. Various other fiscal (taxation) devices are discussed in the next section.

··· FISCAL MEASURES TO INFLUENCE THE ECONOMY ···

One purpose of taxation, as we have just seen, is to raise funds for government needs. Governments also use taxation to help the economy move in a desired direction. For example, taxes may be lowered to stimulate the economy when it is weak. Similarly, taxes may be raised when the economy is booming to cool it off and slow down inflation.

fiscal policy
The use of taxation to stimulate or restrain various aspects of the economy or the economy as a whole.

Taxation is often used in more subtle ways to stimulate or restrain various aspects of the economy or the whole economy. This is called **fiscal policy**. For example, to stimulate the economy government may ease the taxation load of the construction industry, a basic industry that affects many others. When that industry begins to move, the spinoff effect means more equipment, vehicles, and material supplies purchased. More homes, offices, and factories built and sold lead to more sales of furniture and appliances and new mortgages and insurance, thus stimulating a wide range of industries and services. When government deems the economy to be overheated and inflation is a problem, it implements the opposite policy.

Federal and provincial governments constantly use the lever of fiscal policy to stimulate specific geographic and industrial areas. They offer special tax credits to companies that open plants in areas of chronically high unemployment, such as Cape Breton, the Gaspé, or Newfoundland. All companies that invest in specific activities considered desirable (such activities vary from time to time but usually include manufacturing, processing, or scientific research) receive a tax credit that reduces the income tax they have to pay. Many of these programs have been scaled back or eliminated due to budgetary restraints.

···· ▬▬▬ ····

HOW GOVERNMENTS SPEND TAX DOLLARS TO HELP BUSINESS

Governments in Canada disburse tens of billions of dollars annually in old-age pensions, allowances to low-income families or individuals, employment insurance, welfare, workers' compensation, and various other payments to individuals. These vast sums put a lot of consumer buying power into the hands of Canadians. As they spend these dollars, large numbers of Canadian companies and their employees benefit. Governments, in turn, collect taxes on the profits of these companies and on the salaries and wages of their employees. Increasing or lowering the rates or eligibility for these payments results in further fine-tuning of the economy. Again, lack of money has resulted in the reduction of such payments in recent years.

··· GOVERNMENT PURCHASING POLICIES ···

Most governments are very large purchasers and consumers of goods and services; indeed, in Canada they are the largest buyers. The federal and provincial governments use this enormous purchasing power to favour Canadian companies. The provinces favour those companies in their own territories, and have even set up important trade barriers between provinces (discussed below). When advanced technology items, civilian or military, must be obtained from foreign companies, our governments usually insist that a certain minimum portion must be manufactured in Canada. This enables Canadian companies to acquire advanced technology know-how and to provide employment.

Contracts are awarded most often to help Canadian businesses even if they are sometimes more expensive than bids by non-Canadian companies. This is particularly true in the significant military acquisitions programs. Whatever can be produced or serviced in Canada—ships, electron-

A Canadian CF-18 hornet fighter pilot takes off from Aviano Air Base in Italy. The military acquisitions program in Canada requires that whatever can be produced or serviced in Canada be acquired from Canadian companies.

ics, trucks, artillery, ammunition—is acquired from Canadian companies. These federal and provincial policies are being modified as a result of the NAFTA and the GATT as part of the general movement to freer trade. Oddly enough, in many cases, it is easier to trade with foreign countries than between provinces. We look at this anomaly next.

••• NO FREE TRADE BETWEEN PROVINCES •••

The provincial governments have erected walls between the provinces that practically rule out interprovincial government acquisitions. The municipal governments within a province also follow this procedure. These protectionist policies favour the companies in each province, but almost eliminate normal free trade and competition. They also create other distortions by insisting, for example, that a beer company must have a plant in a province if it wants to sell beer there, preventing the normal cost savings that could be achieved with fewer but larger plants. Larger-scale production would result in lower costs, called **economies of scale**, and therefore lower prices to consumers. Lower costs would make many Canadian companies more competitive on the international scene, especially with American firms.

economies of scale
The cost savings that result from large-scale production.

A case that drew a lot of attention a few years ago was a paving job in the town of Aylmer, Quebec, near the Ontario border. The town bought bricks from an Ontario company, but was forced by the provincial government to pull them up and replace them with Quebec bricks. This is an extreme example of a common problem in Canada. "By one estimate there are more than 500 trade barriers between provinces," according to an article in the *Montreal Gazette*:[3]

> *For a country that was supposed to have eliminated barriers to trade [within the country] 125 years ago, Canada in some ways behaves more like a collection of warring principalities than a single economic unit. Ontario consumers can't buy milk from Quebec or Manitoba. Quebec wouldn't buy busses from an Ontario plant until the plant moved to Quebec. A phone company in one province won't buy telephone wire from another [province]. Nova Scotia's Moosehead beer is readily available in the U.S., but not in other provinces.* [Author's note: American beer is readily available in Canada.]

There is mounting pressure for the provinces to end this uneconomic behaviour, which is estimated to cost the Canadian economy up to $6 billion annually. When we are in a recession and Canada's ability to compete internationally is in doubt, we cannot afford such additional costs.

The question of protectionism comes up regularly at annual meetings of provincial ministers. Everybody agrees that something must be done, but as each year passes no detectable changes take place. The reason is clear: removal of barriers would mean a difficult period of adjustment as each province loses jobs due to the closing of uncompetitive operations. It is strange that provinces that supported the FTA and NAFTA enthusiastically seem to fear provincial competition more than they fear American companies.

Progress Check

- What is Statistics Canada? How is it useful to Canadian businesses?
- What is fiscal policy? What are two purposes of the federal taxation system?
- How do government expenditures affect business? What are three broad categories of such expenditures?
- Are there any barriers to trade between the provinces? What developments are going to have an effect on this situation?

••• OTHER GOVERNMENT EXPENDITURES •••

Governments spend huge sums of money on education, health, roads, ports, waterways, airports, and various other services required by businesses and individuals. They also provide direct aid to business.

There are many direct and indirect government programs designed to help businesses. Governments also intervene on an ad hoc (special, unplanned) basis in important cases. The Chrysler and de Havilland cases, discussed later in the chapter, are examples of this. Aid to Saskatchewan farmers and Newfoundland and B.C. fishermen when their industries faced severe hardships are other examples.

DIRECT INTERVENTION   All levels of government offer a variety of direct assistance programs to businesses, including grants, loans, loan guarantees, consulting advice, information, and other aids that are designed to achieve certain purposes. One of the largest special cases occurred early in the 1980s, when a combined Canadian and U.S. government loan guarantee to banks in excess of $1 billion was required to save Chrysler Corp. from collapsing. Had it gone bankrupt, many companies that were creditors of Chrysler would have

Spotlight on
Big Business

<www.bombardier.com>

A Rescue Package for an Ailing Giant

In January 1992, in a joint scheme, the Ontario and federal governments announced a $490 million aid package to facilitate a deal whereby Bombardier Inc. of Montreal bought 51 percent and the Ontario government 49 percent of the shares of de Havilland Aircraft in Toronto to save the company from closing. There were many reasons why saving this company was considered vital: it is the largest employer in the Toronto area, with some 4500 employees still working there after several reductions in workforce; and it had the potential to compete globally since the previous owner, giant Boeing Aircraft Co. of the United States, had spent hug sums acquiring, modernizing, and updating production facilities (with generous grants from both levels of government in Canada). Unfortunately, the deep recession and other factors led Boeing to throw in the towel after several cuts in the workforce.

Bombardier had earned a solid reputation with its successful acquisition of similar troubled companies in the United States and Northern Ireland. As a result Bombardier had become a world leader in the small-air-

craft field, which many believe is one of the high-tech industries of the future. In addition, the recession and other factors had seen hundreds of plant closings and hundreds of thousands of jobs lost in Ontario. This combination of social, political, and economic factors led the Ontario and federal governments to ask Bombardier to continue its string of successful takeovers. Bombardier, with its record of sound financial analysis and management, insisted on the substantial aid package from the governments to lay a foundation for the future of de Havilland. Subsequent developments indicate that this deal worked well for all parties.

The continued successes and growth of Bombardier shows how a carefully planned government aid package can be a great advantage to all parties: more Canadians got jobs, governments at all levels collected more taxes, Bombardier developed advanced technology and planes and became a leading exporter and transnational corporation, and the company generated more profits for its shareholders. In sum, the Canadian economy received many times over what the government invested.

been dragged down as well and hundreds of thousands of jobs would have been lost in both countries.

Some government aid is designed to help industries or companies that are deemed to be very important—at the cutting-edge of technology, providing highly skilled jobs, and oriented toward exports. Thus Ottawa was considering a $150 million aid package for the aerospace industry "to keep this high-tech industry from moving to other countries which offer such inducements."[4]

Similarly, the federal and Ontario governments and Spar Aerospace Ltd. took a "huge gamble" developing an all-weather radar satellite that has the potential "to start a new multibillion-dollar industry in Canada." Both governments combined bore 51 percent of the cost and have the rights to 51 percent of the data. The U.S. government did likewise for a 15 percent stake. The first results made the space scientists at Spar "whoop for joy" as they saw a clear image of Cape Breton Island produced through the rain and in the dark.[5]

Pratt & Whitney Canada Inc., after getting nearly $12 million from the federal and Quebec governments to develop a new aircraft engine—the PW 150 for the de Havilland Dash 8-400 commuter aircraft—was "threatening to move the project outside Canada unless Ottawa [gave] it more." In 1998 the company again warned that it might have to close down. Since this is a $200 million project, both governments agreed to an $11.7 million interest-free loan as part of a $45.7 million program under the Canada-Subsidiary Agreement for Industrial Development.[6]

Major companies often hint or even announce outright that they are planning to close a large plant that they claim is not efficient enough to be competitive. They often suggest they will consolidate operations with other plants in Canada or the United States. These announcements naturally result in a flurry of efforts by all affected parties to prevent the closure. Unions, municipalities, and provincial and federal governments all work to save the jobs and economies of the area. There are many examples of such cases in the last decade.

Auto plants, pulp and paper mills, food processing plants, oil refineries, shipbuilding yards, meat-packing plants, steel mills, and other industries across the country have faced such closures. In many cases the closures could not have been prevented. But the General Motors plant north of Montreal and the de Havilland plant north of Toronto, among others, were saved by such concerted action. (See Spotlight on Big Business.)

A newspaper report shows how the Ontario and federal governments combined with the steelworkers' union, banks, and shareholders to prevent the Algoma Steel mill in Sault Ste. Marie, Ontario, from closing. This involved government aid and employee purchase of the plant.[7] A similar rescue of the troubled Sydney Steel complex in Sydney, Nova Scotia, in 1981 ended with the Nova Scotia government buying the company. In Alberta, the government intervened to keep some meat-packing plants alive.

Many of these rescue efforts end in costly failures. For example, the Nova Scotia government announced in February 1992 that it would have to sell or close Sydney Steel, after having spent almost a billion dollars over a decade to modernize it and make it competitive. In January 1999 the federal government announced to a shocked community that it was going to end its long-time financial support of the Cape Breton Development

Government and private business sometimes join forces to save a company from closing. This happened in the case of the Algoma Steel Mill in Sault Ste. Marie, Ontario.

<www.acoa.ca>

A visit to the Web site for the Atlantic Canada Opportunities Agency will introduce you to the range of projects it has engaged in as it seeks to facilitate development in its region. Start by selecting the *About ACOA* button, and then explore its range of activities. See if you can find other Web sites for parallel agencies.

Corp. (Devco), a coal mining operation. After pouring more than a billion dollars into covering deficits, the government decided to close or sell off the mines as there was no hope of profitable operations.[8] Was it worth it to spend such sums to provide hundreds of jobs in chronically depressed Cape Breton? Was it the best way to help the unemployed in this area of high unemployment? These types of questions are constantly being asked in Canada.

EQUALIZATION TRANSFER PROGRAMS   Canada is a very large country with uneven resources, climate, and geography, which have led to uneven economic development. Ontario and Quebec, with large populations, proximity to the United States, an abundance of all kinds of natural resources, and excellent rail and water transport, were the earliest to develop industrially.

Nova Scotia and New Brunswick began to suffer when wooden ships gave way to metal ships in the last century and their lumber industries declined. The west was sparsely populated until well into this century. Alberta and British Columbia became strong industrially only in the last 30 years as oil, gas, coal, hydroelectric power, and forestry became significant competitive resources for them. Saskatchewan and Manitoba are essentially tied to the volatile agricultural industry. Newfoundland, which became part of Canada in 1949 and was far behind the average Canadian living standard, has relied mainly on fisheries and pulp and paper. With the collapse of the cod fishery, Newfoundland now looks to the development of the off-shore Hibernia and other oilfields to become major factors in its economic growth in the twenty-first century. The Yukon, the Northwest Territories, and Nunavut are very lightly populated and have difficult climates.

A long-standing system of payments (transfers) to poorer provinces, which was financed by the wealthier ones (Ontario, B.C., Alberta), is being gradually reduced by the federal government.

Critical Thinking

Advances in technology are extremely important to keep a country globally competitive. Since governments do not have unlimited amounts of money to spend, they may have to focus on a few areas. Would it be wise for Canadian governments to concentrate on advanced technology? Should they, in conjunction with business, pick some high-tech industries and give them substantial support? Should this include a major effort to get more students to pursue scientific and engineering careers?

•••• ▬▬▬ ••••

THE EFFECT OF OTHER DEPARTMENTS AND REGULATIONS ON BUSINESS

We have seen how provincial and federal governments carry on a wide variety of government activities that affect business. We will now take a closer look at some of the major departments of the federal government that handle these activities. There are corresponding departments in many of the provinces, especially the four largest, most developed ones: Ontario, Quebec, B.C., and Alberta.

••• DEPARTMENT OF INDUSTRY (INDUSTRY CANADA) •••

For many years the federal government has had a variety of programs to help small businesses get started. In Chapter 7 you will see a detailed account of how this aid works. The programs are part of a larger one that involves setting up Canada Business Service Centers in every province and territory. These centres are operated jointly with provincial governments and certain local organizations. Industry Canada publishes brochures, booklet, and guides informing business people of the help available and how and where to get it.

Other programs are designed to encourage businesses to establish themselves or expand in economically depressed areas of the country. Populated regions that are industrially underdeveloped have high unemployment and lower standards of living. Such regions that were previously mentioned in this book include Cape Breton Island of Nova Scotia, the Gaspé area of Quebec, and Newfoundland. The programs include help for the tourist industry and for aboriginal residents of remote areas who want to establish businesses.

Industry Canada also administers a variety of laws affecting consumers and businesses. A later section in this chapter reviews a number of important laws relating to consumer protection. Companies wanting to incorporate federally must apply to this department for articles of incorporation. Industry Canada maintains a complete registry of all companies incorporated under federal law. Companies may also be incorporated under an equivalent provincial department. Annual reports are required to keep the register up to date; it is open to public inspection.

<www.ic.gc.ca>

Industry Canada's corporate information Web site provides a wealth of information about the department, its mandate, and the corporate outlook in Canada.

The department also administers the Competition Act, which aims to make sure that mergers of large corporations will not restrict competition and that fair competition exists among businesses. The act covers discriminatory pricing, price fixing, misleading advertising, and refusal to deal with certain companies, among other activities.

The federal Bureau of Competition Policy and the Competition Tribunal are busy organizations whose work is constantly in the news. Three recent examples: they challenged the Interac monopoly on electronic payments;[9] they ended a monopoly that A.C. Neilsen had on the "vast data generated by checkout scanners at supermarkets and drugstores across Canada";[10] they investigated a proposed takeover by American food giant Archer-Daniels-Midland of four Maple Leaf flour mills.[11]

In 1998 the Bureau was faced with perhaps one of the most important issues it had ever dealt with. Two proposals involving mergers of the largest banks in Canada, one of the Royal Bank and the Bank of Montreal and the other the CIBC and Toronto Dominion, generated fierce and widespread discussion across the country. The Bureau had the difficult tasks of deciding whether the proposed mergers would reduce competition, and if so, if they would stop them. The issues were complex, with the banks arguing that they had to merge to stay in the race with the global banking giants, many of which arose out of mergers in the U.S. and Switzerland. Once again we see how the globalization of business has a direct impact on Canada. Opponents argued that competition would decline in Canada and service, especially to seniors, would also decline as more branches would close, and many employees would lose their jobs. The Bureau finally recommended against allowing the mergers and the minister of finance, who has the final say on matters relating to banks, accepted that recommendation.

••• DEPARTMENT OF COMMUNICATIONS •••

The Department of Communications is responsible for the Canadian Radio-Television and Telecommunications Commission (CRTC). The CRTC grants licences to radio stations, TV stations, and cable companies for limited periods, usually one to three years. Public hearings are held at licence-granting and renewal times so that anyone can criticize or voice opposition to such renewals. The CRTC also regulates the types of programs and the minimum percentage of Canadian content. It must approve at public hearings all rate and service changes of cable and federally incorporated telephone and telegraph companies.

A typical example of CRTC activities is their ruling ordering Teleglobe Canada Inc., which has a monopoly on all overseas calls, to reduce its rates by 35 percent over a four-year period.[12] The CRTC has also made many difficult decisions regarding control of satellite dishes and disputes between cable and telephone companies as technology opens up new possibilities for formerly very different companies that now seek to exploit the same technology or markets.

··· TRANSPORT CANADA ···

Transport Canada administers a number of acts, including the Motor Vehicle Transportation Act and the National Transportation Act. These Acts cover all modes of interprovincial transportation in Canada. The National Transportation Agency grants licences, hears complaints, makes sure safety regulations are being followed and investigates train and plane accidents. The department has inspectors on the road. You can sometimes see their cars beside trailer trucks stopped for inspection.

··· DEPARTMENT OF FINANCE ···

One of the most influential ministries is the Department of Finance. It has overall responsibility for setting tax (fiscal) and financial policy and thus has a major impact on Canadian business. The annual budget presented to Parliament, usually every spring, by the minister of finance is a major event. The budget is a comprehensive document that reveals government financial policies for the coming year: it shows how much revenue the government expects to collect, any changes in income and other taxes, and whether expenditures will exceed income (resulting in a deficit).

BANK OF CANADA   A major agency of the Department of Finance is the Bank of Canada, an independent body run by a board of governors appointed by the government. The minister of finance (or his or her deputy-minister) attends board meetings but has no vote. The Bank of Canada has two main responsibilities. One is to oversee the operations of all federally chartered banks, which means nearly all the banks in Canada. The banks all report to the Bank of Canada regularly. Some reports are required daily, some weekly, and some monthly.

The second responsibility is to set **monetary policy**, which means to control the supply of money in the country and influence the level of interest rates. Controlling the supply of money in Canada is very complex and involves a variety of methods. You may be most familiar with the determination of the appropriate level of interest rates at any particular time. From time to time the bank announces the rate it will charge commercial banks for borrowings, mostly a symbolic gesture, as these banks do not do much borrowing from the Bank of Canada. The bank rate mainly gives the banks guidelines as to whether they should be raising or lowering their interest rates or leaving them unchanged.

In 1998 the Canadian dollar dropped to historic lows against the U.S. dollar, falling to 63 cents. Many voices were heard demanding that the Bank of Canada, now under a new governor, Gordon Theissen, raise interest rates to help boost the dollar to a higher exchange value. Many other voices said the

<www.bank-banque-canada.ca>

Visit the Bank of Canada Web site for information about the Bank and a wide range of financial information and data about Canada. See, for example, the discussion of monetary policy at <www.bank-banque-canada.ca/english/bg-p-1.htm>.

monetary policy
The Bank of Canada's exercise of control over the supply of money and the level of interest rates in the country.

The Bank of Canada, located in Ottawa, oversees the operations of all federally chartered banks and sets monetary policy for the country.

Bank should do nothing. By mid-1999 the dollar was up to 68 cents. The Bank of Canada keeps a constant eye on the value of the Canadian dollar and other matters to carry out its mandate of setting proper monetary policy.

Progress Check

- What are three forms of direct government aid to business? Two forms of indirect aid?
- Name four large companies that owe their existence to such aid. Why was such aid extended?
- How do governments help poorer regions of Canada?
- Why is the Department of Finance so important? What is the annual budget it prepares and why does it attract so much attention?

PROTECTING CONSUMERS

The Department of Industry administers many laws designed to protect consumers. These laws have a great impact on companies, which must make sure their policies and operations conform with legal requirements. Some of the major consumer protection laws are shown in Figure 4.2.

All of these acts, and others under the jurisdiction of other federal or provincial departments, are designed to protect and inform consumers. Every time you buy an agricultural product, you are assured that someone has inspected it or a sample of the batch it came from. The list of ingredients and expiration date are there because of a regulation. The same applies to the clothes you wear, which have a label showing country of origin, size, type of fabric, and washing instructions.

Similarly, you are assured that all the food, drugs, toys, and other products you buy do not contain anything hazardous. Whether you buy a kilogram of grapes or 25 litres of gasoline, you can feel confident that you have gotten

Agricultural products such as fruit and vegetables are inspected before they ever make their way onto store shelves. Such inspection is required to ensure the public consumes safe and healthy produce.

FIGURE 4.2

....

SOME MAJOR CONSUMER
PROTECTION LAWS

These laws all provide
consumers with informa-
tion and protection, in
various ways.

Canadian Agricultural Products Standards Act covers a wide range of farm products, such as meat, poultry, eggs, maple syrup, honey, and dairy products.

Consumer Packaging and Labelling Act applies to all products not specifically included in other acts.

Food and Drug Act covers a whole range of regulations pertaining to quality, testing, approval, packaging, and labelling.

Hazardous Products Act covers all hazardous products.

National Trademark and True Labelling Act includes not only labelling, but also accurate advertising.

Textile Labelling Act includes apparel sizing and many other special areas.

Weights and Measures Act applies to all equipment that measure quantities (scales, gas pumps, and so forth).

<www.cdic.ca>

Visit the CDIC Web site to find out about its mission statement. The section on *how deposit insurance works* sets out the basic principles of the protection provided.

<www.osc.gov.on.ca>

The Ontario Securities Commission Web site provides a full range of information related to the OSC. Look at the section called *about the OSC* to learn how it operates. Skim its rules and regulations to get the flavour of its mandate.

prospectus
A document, which must be prepared by every public company seeking financing through issue of shares or bonds, that gives the public certain information about the company. A prospectus must be approved by the securities commission of the province where these securities will be offered for sale.

securities commission
The official body set up by a province to regulate its stock exchange and to approve all new issues of securities in that province.

a true measure because there is a sticker on the equipment showing when it was last inspected. The provinces have various laws giving consumers the right to cancel contracts or return goods within a certain time of signing or purchase. It is just about impossible to get through a day without being helped in some way by legislation or regulation. Similarly, a company cannot get through a day without being affected by various laws.

••• CANADA DEPOSIT INSURANCE CORPORATION •••

Another body that plays an important role in protecting the consumer is the Canada Deposit Insurance Corporation (CDIC). The CDIC insures individual deposits in banks and trust companies against these institutions' failure or collapse. The CDIC guarantees deposits up to $60,000 and is funded by annual premium payments from all banks and trust companies that want to have their customers' deposits insured, which in practice means just about all such financial institutions. The CDIC reports to the chair of the Treasury Board, who is a minister of state in the government.

••• PROVINCIAL REGULATION OF BUSINESS •••

The consumer as investor is protected by various laws that lay down the procedures companies must follow to attract investors or lenders through public offerings. Companies seeking public financing must issue a **prospectus**, which provides minimum specified information about the company and its officers and directors to better inform potential investors. This document must be approved by the **securities commission** in the province where public funding is being sought. This is the official body set up by a province to regulate its stock exchange and to approve all new issues of securities in that province.

It is expensive to produce a prospectus because it requires a lot of input from legal and accounting firms before it can be approved. This cost must be borne by the company that is seeking public financing. There are five stock exchanges in Canada—Toronto, Montreal, Calgary, Vancouver, and Winnipeg— and a securities commission in each of the provinces where these cities are located. One of their aims is to ensure that the small investor is not taken advantage of by powerful or unscrupulous companies or individuals. All companies whose shares are listed on the stock exchanges must issue quarterly reports to their shareholders, as well as annual reports. There are many other provisions in these regulations, which vary somewhat from province to province.

One common regulation makes it illegal for *insiders*—those with inside or private information not yet available to the public—to take advantage of the information. Insiders cannot engage in securities transactions (the sale or purchase of stocks and bonds and related instruments) based on inside information for their personal gain.

For example, suppose your sister told you that her company was about to announce that it had had an unusually profitable period, which would likely send the price of the company's share up sharply. You rushed to buy some shares; when they rose quickly after the announcement, you sold them and made a nice profit in a few days. This is insider trading and is illegal.

All businesses must comply with the consumer protection requirements that affect them. Although this may add to the costs of doing business, everybody is in the same boat, so no company has an edge over any competitor. Furthermore, similar conditions exist in most industrialized countries, so the level playing field extends beyond the borders of Canada. The international competitiveness of Canadian companies is not usually weakened by such regulations.

••• THE IMPACT OF MUNICIPALITIES ON BUSINESS •••

Municipalities also play a role in consumer protection. They all have regulations and laws regarding any establishment that serves food. Inspectors regularly examine the premises of all restaurants for cleanliness. If you look carefully in your local newspapers, you will see lists of restaurants fined for not maintaining required standards.

There are similar laws about noise, smells, signs, and other activities that may affect a neighbourhood. These are called zoning laws because certain zones are restricted to residences only and others permit only certain quiet businesses to operate.

Zoning requirements also limit the height of buildings in certain zones and how far back they must be set from the road. Most Canadian cities require that all high-rise buildings have a certain ratio of garage space so that cars have off-street parking places. Parking problems in residential areas due to overflow of vehicles from adjacent businesses have led to parking being limited to residential permit holders on certain streets, so stores and other places of business must offer commercial parking lots for their customers. Of course, we are all familiar with speed limits set by municipal or provincial authorities.

All businesses must usually obtain a municipal licence to operate so the appropriate department may track them to make sure they are following regulations. Many municipalities also have a business tax and charge for water consumption.

LABOUR STANDARDS AND WORKING CONDITIONS

In later chapters you will learn about the many federal and provincial laws and regulations that affect companies' conditions of employment. We tend to take for granted minimum wages, vacation pay, and a host of other working conditions. Figure 4.3 lists some of the major issues that are affected by legislation.

Figure 4.3 is only a partial list of the legal requirements that employers must meet. The many laws across Canada that protect workers have accumulated over more than 100 years. As the standards of civilized or acceptable behaviour evolved in Canada, laws were passed to reflect these rising expectations. It is a continuing process that sees new developments every few years. One of the most recent issues to evolve is pay equity for women (discussed in Part 4).

FIGURE **4.3**

· · · ·

SOME ASPECTS OF EMPLOYMENT AFFECTED BY LEGISLATION

This is only a partial list.

Banning of child labour.

Minimum wages.

Overtime pay after a normal workweek.

Specified number of paid holidays.

Paid vacations of not less than two or three weeks (or equivalent pay if employed less than one year).

No firing without cause after a specified period of employment.

No discrimination by sex, nationality, colour, or religion in hiring, remuneration, promotion, or firing.

Unpaid or paid maternity or paternity leave.

No unhealthy or unsafe working conditions.

No sexual or racial harassment.

Employment insurance contributions.

Canada or Quebec Pension Plan contributions.

Workers' compensation for employees injured at work.

···· ▬▬ ····

ENVIRONMENTAL REGULATIONS

Chapter 5 reviews the importance of concerns with the impact of production activities on our physical environment. These concerns have led to regulatory requirements that are changing how companies operate.

We are all well acquainted with many of the serious consequences to our environment from the uncontrolled operations and growth of industry. We are now faced with the huge problems caused by certain dirty industrial processes and the mountains of waste that are an inevitable result of many business operations.

Some environmental problems are product related. For example, cars are major contributors to pollution, inefficient users of energy, and increasingly less useful for commuting to and from work due to traffic jams. These kinds of problems are what led governments to create ministries of the environment. Now many companies face heavy expenditures of money and management's energy to become *green*, or environmentally responsible. Some farsighted companies are developing technology for waste management and energy-efficient operations that will give them important competitive advantages.

···· ▬▬ ····

EMPLOYMENT AND IMMIGRATION IN CANADA

Two departments of the federal government that have a major impact on business are the Department of Citizenship and Immigration, and the Department of Human Resources Development, which have a direct impact on the nature, size, and skills of the workforce in Canada. A coherent immigration policy helps to ensure a good inflow of required skills for employers. After all, Canada became a modern industrial country with the aid of the skills and financial capital that immigrants brought here.

One of the anomalies of recent times is that despite the very high number of people who are unemployed or working at part-time or temporary jobs, there are still many jobs that cannot be filled because of the lack of applicants with the necessary skills.

Reaching Beyond
Our Borders

<www.dfait-maeci.gc.ca/menu-e.asp>
<www.ic.gc.ca>

Government Aid to High-Technology Companies

The importance of high-technology and global business to a modern economy are repeatedly stressed in this book. Governments in Canada are concerned with the progress of companies in these fields. Two departments play important roles in assisting such companies: Foreign Affairs and International Trade, and Industry Canada. Together with Investment Canada and in cooperation with research and technology associations, they publish many informative brochures and listings of Canadian companies active in specific fields. They distribute these to companies overseas and arrange for their representatives to meet with Canadian company representatives.

High-Technology Opportunity: If Software Is Your Business, Canadian Partners Can Make the Difference is a glossy, full-colour brochure with a multilingual introduction. Included in this attractive package is detailed information on all Canadian software companies with good track records. Some of them are already well known to the international business community. The aim is to promote joint ventures and other tie-ins with these companies. This package is of great benefit to the hundreds of smaller high-tech companies that cannot afford such expenditures themselves.

Sources: Various publications of Investment Canada and Departments of Foreign Affairs and International Trade, and Industry Canada.

Federal and provincial ministries are involved in training and retraining schemes designed to overcome this problem. Such programs encourage unemployed people to enroll in colleges to upgrade their skills and support them financially during their retraining period. Other programs to train or retrain workers are joint efforts of governments, unions, and employers in varying combinations. Some will be discussed in more detail in later chapters.

Education and training are becoming increasingly important as low-skilled jobs disappear due to automation and to companies moving to the United States or Mexico. Rapid changes in technology mean that long-term employment in one job or skill is becoming rare. This issue is forcing increased attention to be paid to the whole question of education and training, and is capturing a lot of headlines.

Controlling the flow of immigrants to Canada is another major responsibility of the Department of Citizenship and Immigration. There is much pressure from people in many parts of the world who would like to live in Canada. The department tries to ensure that immigrants have the proper skills or finances to fit into the needs of the Canadian economy. Immigrants have always been a vital factor in the development of Canada and will continue to play an important role. The department must try to find that delicate balance between admitting too many immigrants faster than the economy can absorb, and not admitting enough.

NATIONAL RESEARCH COUNCIL

One of the best-kept Canadian secrets concerns the National Research Council (NRC), a federal agency that began in 1916. This organization of some 3000 scientists, researchers, and technicians is Canada's principal science and technology agency. The NRC plays a significant role in research that helps Canadian industry to remain competitive and innovative. Its Canadian Institute for Scientific and Technical Information (CISTI) has the largest international collection of information on science, technology, and medicine in Canada. CISTI gets about half a million requests for information annually. Subscribers to its online system can access this vast worldwide database directly from their own computer terminals.

The NRC operates the Industrial Research Assistance Program (IRAP) and 16 specialized institutes in some major industries of tomorrow, including biotechnology, industrial materials, environmental science and technology, information technology, automated manufacturing, and microelectronics. Eleven of the institutes are in Ottawa and the other five are spread out from St. John's, Newfoundland, to Vancouver, B.C. Every year thousands of Canadian firms receive technical and financial help through the NRC's industry development programs. Its specialized equipment allows companies to conduct tests and experiments that would otherwise not be possible. This service is especially useful for many smaller high-tech firms. The NRC also operates a Research Press and the Canadian Technology Network (CTN), which provide important information for thousands of Canadian businesses.[13]

During the last few years, the budget and staff of the NRC have been repeatedly cut. It is unfortunate that funding has been reduced for such an important organization in an era when technological know-how is one of the major competitive tools for business. There are constant complaints that the amount of spending on R&D in Canada is lower than that of any other advanced industrial country. The federal government has repeatedly committed itself to raise the level of R&D spending, which makes it difficult to understand the reduction in NRC funding. In 1998 the government announced some additional funding to partially offset previous reductions.

···· ▬▬▬ ····

GOVERNMENT IMPACT OF FARMING BUSINESS

marketing boards
Organizations that control the supply or pricing of certain agricultural products in Canada.

In Canada we have a special system of **marketing boards**, which control the supply or pricing of certain agricultural products. This supply management is designed to give some stability to an important area of the economy that is normally very volatile. Farmers are subject to conditions that are rather unique and that have a great effect on their business and on our food supply. Weather and disease are major factors in the operation of farms and are beyond the control of the individual farmer. So are unstable prices and changes in supply resulting from uncoordinated decision making by millions of farmers around the world or the exercise of market power by concentrated business organizations.

In the past, farmers have experienced periods of severe drought, flooding, severe cold, and disease that affect crops, livestock, and poultry. The situation regarding international markets and supply has a serious impact on Canada's grain farmers, since we export much more wheat than we consume domestically. This market fluctuates greatly depending on the supply in other major grain-exporting countries like the United States, Argentina, and Australia. The market also depends on demand from major importers like China and Russia, whose abilities to meet their own requirements are subject to wide variation. Often the Canadian government (like other governments) grants substantial loans with favourable conditions to enable these countries to pay for their imports of our wheat.

As we export some $25 billion of agricultural products annually, the ability to hold our own in international markets has a major impact on the state of the Canadian economy. When Prairie farmers are flourishing, they buy new equipment and consumer goods and their communities feel the effects of ample cash flow. So does the transportation industry. Conversely, when farmers are suffering—which unfortunately was the case for most of the 1980s and well into the 1990s—all these sectors hurt as well.

To smooth out the effect of these unusual conditions on this sector of our economy and to ensure a steady supply of food to consumers at reasonable prices, six government agencies have been set up to control poultry, dairy products, and wheat and barley. The Canadian Wheat Board operates in the three Prairie provinces and is the sole legal exporter of wheat and barley produced in those provinces. The Board is also the sole sales agent domestically for industrial use of these products. The Canadian Diary Commission controls the output and pricing of milk for processing into other dairy products. (Both of these boards are crown corporations.)

The Canadian Egg Marketing Agency, Chicken Farmers of Canada, Canadian Turkey Marketing Agency, and Canadian Broiler Hatching Egg Marketing Agency consist of representatives from the provinces that produce these items.

All of these bodies except the Wheat Board control the amount of production for the products under their supervision by allocating quotas to each province that produces them. Provincial agencies administer these quotas and set prices for their province. Each agency controls products that are sold only in its province.

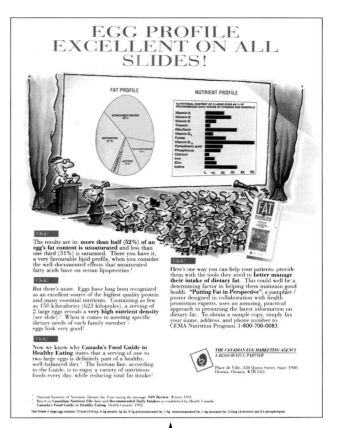

Marketing boards control the supply or pricing of certain agricultural products. They also promote their products by running advertising campaigns such as this one from the Canadian Egg Marketing Agency.

••• SUPPLY MANAGEMENT IN EVOLUTION •••

A system to manage the supply of agricultural products can be found in many countries, although not necessarily in the same format as in Canada. Various subsidy and indirect support methods can be found almost everywhere. Supply management of farm products is an effective barriers to their entry into Canada, because imports are also subject to the quota system.

The Canadian system of marketing boards has been under attack by various organizations because it does not permit normal competitive conditions to operate in this field. This, they argue, distorts the whole industry and raises prices to Canadian consumers. Defenders of the system argue that other countries, including the United States, have different systems that have the same effect as our marketing boards but are just less visible.

In Chapter 3 we referred to the General Agreement on Tariffs and Trade, and to the World Trade Organization that administers it, whose main purpose is to reduce barriers to trade between countries. After lengthy negotiations, Canada agreed in 1994 to a complicated system that replaces the simple restrictive import quota system on these agricultural products. The new system is based on very high tariffs to make it difficult for foreign products to compete with those Canadian agricultural products subject to marketing board control in Canada. Some people are concerned that this is the thin edge of the wedge leading to the end of our long-standing system of marketing boards.

Meanwhile, the United States claimed that these high tariffs are in violation of NAFTA and filed a formal protest to a binational panel with an outside chair, as provided by NAFTA. The panel ruled in Canada's favour.

Periodically, U.S. farmers have protested the growth of Canadian exports of grains, livestock, pork, and red meat to their country, claiming that Canadian farmers are subsidized. The most recent event occurred in 1998 and made a lot of headlines when farmers in North Dakota physically blocked trucks carrying such Canadian products. The farmers were supported by their own governor as well as governors and farmers in adjacent states. These actions are clearly illegal under NAFTA and other U.S.–Canada agreements. Some subsidization still occurs, and this happens on both sides of the border, such as the contribution of the Quebec government to farm income stabilization programs. However, the growth in Canadian export of grain and livestock to the U.S. in the 1990s is more attributable to other factors, including the combination of a very low Canadian dollar and the cancellation of Canadian gain transportation subsidies under the Western Grain Transportation Act, contributing to lower grain prices and increased livestock production in the Prairie provinces. The tendency for U.S. farmers to protest such growth in Canadian exports to the U.S., and the readiness of U.S. politicians to join the debate, increases during an election year, which was the case in 1998, especially when world commodity prices are also low.

The United States, which often complains about other countries' unreasonable trade barriers, as noted above, or about Japanese trade barriers forcing consumers to pay much higher than free market prices for rice, has its own restrictions, such as on peanut and sugar imports. The result is that American consumers pay about 25 percent more than the free market price for sugar.[14]

A spate of articles and reports in Canadian media in 1995 and 1996 indicated that the whole Canadian agricultural marketing system was undergoing a significant change. The same pressures that led to a freer world market for products and services began to have a serious impact on agriculture. In our country some Alberta wheat farmers are battling the Wheat Board for the right to sell wheat and barley directly and not through the board. The co-op Saskatchewan Wheat Pool has become a public corporation, as has the United Grain Growers of Winnipeg.

Agricultural economists foresee a very different picture emerging worldwide over the next decade: limited protection for domestic markets, reduced tariffs and other restrictions, and the market having a much greater impact on prices and production. The effect on Canadian farmers, and on the whole agricultural industry in general, will be enormous. The next decade will see everyone trying to cope with the necessary adjustments to the new conditions.[15]

We end this chapter with a closer look at national industrial policy.

ROLE OF THE CANADIAN GOVERNMENT DOMESTICALLY AND GLOBALLY

In 1996 most of Canada was still suffering from the very severe recession that had begun in 1990. In the 400 days from the end of 1990 to the beginning of 1992, 1000 jobs per day were lost, 400,000 in all. Manufacturing was particularly had hit. And the carnage continued unabated into 1993.

By the mid 1990s the economy was improving, but it was clear that a new phenomenon had appeared in Canada and in other developed countries: the *jobless recovery*. Our unemployment rate seemed stuck in the 9 to 10 percent range and wasn't expected to improve soon; bankruptcies were at record levels, and plant and office closings and layoffs were still occurring despite many companies reporting record profits.

In early 1996 there were mixed signals about the Canadian economic outlook. Inflation low, interest rates staying down, GDP climbing modestly, exports booming—these were all good signs. British Columbia and Alberta were in better shape and wheat prices had climbed to levels not seen in more than 10 years, giving Prairie farmers a long-awaited boost. New Brunswick was still moving in the right direction, as discussed in the Profile at the start of the chapter. But unemployment and increasing welfare rolls remained serious problems.

By mid-1999 the unemployment situation was better, hovering in the 8 to 8.5 percent range, and forecasts for the economy as measured by GDP growth were more optimistic. The main problem was still the economic weakness and instability in Russia, East and Southeast Asia, and South America. The *Asian flu* was showing signs of abating. (See Chapter 2 for details on all of these points.)

Many people believe that the best way to protect the Canadian economy is for the federal government to reverse its current direction. Instead of withdrawing from active direction and participation in the economy, as noted in the previous chapter, it should develop a long-term industrial policy of leadership and an active role in shaping the future of the economy. An industrial policy requires close consultation with business and labour to develop a comprehensive program for long-term sustainable industrial development.

Others are opposed in principle to such government involvement. As mentioned previously in this chapter, the 1980s witnessed a movement toward deregulation, privatization, and less government involvement in Canada and in other countries. But the seriousness of the global and economic situation and its impact on Canada are bringing this issue to the forefront once more.

Those who want government to fashion a strategy to lead us back to prosperity and improve Canada's competitive edge point to other countries where this has worked. The best examples are to be found, they say, in Germany, Japan, and the so-called Four Tigers of East Asia: South Korea, Taiwan, Hong Kong, and Singapore. All of these countries are extremely competitive, have trade surpluses, and have developed rapidly economically in the past two decades. These governments continue to play active roles in helping their economies recover from prolonged recessions. In the latter half of the 1990s, financial pages carried many reports of the German and Japanese governments initiating multi-billion dollar projects to give their economies a kickstart and to create jobs. So did the Taiwanese government.[16]

Starting in 1997 and continuing through to early 1999, the East Asian Tigers, as well as Indonesia and Thailand, were having serious economic problems and currency valuation crashes, leading to the *Asian flu*. Even in Hong Kong, where the government had played a much less interventionist role, it was forced to change tactics. The government intervened strongly when the stock market collapsed and it engaged in substantial buying of shares to shore up the Hong Kong currency and the stock market.

In all of these cases there is no denying that strong government leadership in planning, prioritizing, and direction has contributed to their success. The governments of the European Union (EU) of 15 advanced economies also embarked on an ambitious plan to reduce their serious and pervasive unemployment problems. Faced with some 18 million jobless workers, they decided to consider major expenditures such as transcontinental road and rail links and defence.[17] The question is: Can it work in Canada? We have a different culture; we are a large, dispersed, very diverse, low-density population that rarely unites to pull in the same direction. We have a different history and political structure, with much power dispersed to provincial centres. We are also a democracy, while the Four Tigers have a history of dictatorships (ranging from the brutal to the benign in Singapore).

Germany, however, the country with the greatest exports per capita in the world, is a democracy. Is there anything we can learn from these and other countries about the major role of government in the economy? This question is being increasingly discussed in Canada and even in the United States, where the concept of *laissez-faire* or *leave-it-alone capitalism* is very strong. But even in the U.S. there were important business voices, like the prestigious *Business Weekly* (as noted in Chapter 2), that believed that "free markets need government action to work best."

Critical Thinking

You have seen many examples of government initiatives to aid business in Canada. Do we need an overall strategy to plan where our economy should be going? If so, where is the leadership from our major business organizations? Is this a responsibility of government? How relevant are the successful East Asian countries whose governments pursued such a course?

••• DOMESTIC AND FOREIGN OPINIONS •••

A *Financial Post* (now the *National Post*) article disputes that the free market is the best medium for solving society's economic woes. It says, "the only problem with this laissez-faire notion of the world is that it denies history and reality." The article also notes that the management of technology on an international front is long term, large scale, complex, difficult, and risky—and very costly. That is why governments must be involved.

The article gives examples of different countries to show that governments have historically played essential roles in most major developments. The article stresses the role of the American government, as noted in the previous quote, and elaborates on the major contribution of the Japanese government in helping industrial research and development in certain crucial high-tech areas such as superconductivity. In France the government played a critical role in the development of high-speed trains, the supersonic Concorde, and the commercial jet aircraft company Airbus. This company is a joint venture of the governments of France, England, Germany, and Spain.

The article concludes that it would be difficult to find a major technology company in the world that did not depend on direct or indirect government support and involvement. Whether it's Boeing or Airbus, the market has hardly been operating in a free and unfettered manner.

The article ends by reminding readers that Canadian history is replete with many successful "examples of government stepping in to produce solutions when the market couldn't," such as the Canadian Pacific Railway, the Trans-Canada Pipeline, Ontario Hydro, Polysar, and our wartime industries during World War II.[18]

While many commentators support the continuing shrinkage of governments and their smaller role in the economy, a growing number are taking the opposite tack. Magazines, newspapers, radio, and TV from 1996 to 1999 carried many reports of experts questioning the current trend and worrying about social discontent, as increasing homelessness and poverty, job insecurity, and layoffs took high economic and personal tolls. Many people were also concerned that continuing government cutbacks because of deficit and debt-reduction programs were only aggravating these problems and weakening the education and health-care systems in Canada.[19]

In April 1996 the seven leading industrial countries of the world (Canada is number seven), known as the G7 or Group of Seven, met in France to discuss what could be done about their chronic unemployment problems. Between them the G7 had more than 23 million people unemployed, and that number had been resisting all efforts at reduction. According to *The Economist*, one of the most prestigious magazines in the world, "the Group tried to chart a course between free-marketeers and interventionists."[20]

By the end of 1998 the European unemployment situation was showing no improvement and the Asian flu had heightened fears of the situation worsening. This situation led British Prime Minister Tony Blair to consider calling a meeting of the G7 "to deal with the immediate threat posed by the global financial turmoil."[21]

In June 1999 the Group of Eight (now including Russia) met and decided to aid the recovery of the global economy by reducing the enormous debt to foreign banks and governments of developing poorer countries. These countries would be required to invest the resulting substantial reduction in interest and capital payments, which were a great weight on their economies, into their own infrastructures such as education, health, training, and so on.[22]

We have seen some examples of governments, either directly or through international agencies, intervening in the imperfect functioning of the global free-market system. Other important international voices have been heard questioning whether the time has come for controls of international financial activities by governments through international bodies that represent them. This position reflects the globalized natures of business and economies, which weaken the capacity of national governments to influence events in the direction they deem desirable or necessary.

A good example of two such voices are the Prime Minister of Malaysia, Mahathir Mohamad, and international currency speculator, investor, and philanthropist, George Soros. These men have had a running argument since the 1997 collapse of the Malaysian currency and economy that sparked the Asian flu. Mohamad blamed Soros for playing a major role in the Malaysia debacle. In 1999 Mohamad argued that the big powers were controlling the globalization agenda to the detriment of smaller countries like his, and that smaller countries need the freedom to exert some control of their own economies. Soros argued for a change in the roles of the World Bank and the International Monetary Fund so that they could soften the "booms and busts [that] are endemic in financial markets." In effect, Mohamad supports a greater measure of local government involvement, while Soros sees the necessity of government intervention in the global economy via international organizations.[23]

···· ▬▬ ····

THE INTERTWINING OF ETHICAL AND JOB ISSUES

Government cutbacks in spending not only reduced the number of employees directly working for government in Canada and the number of future job openings, but also had the same effect in the education field. School closings occurred nearly everywhere, with similar reductions in employees and job openings. Reduced funding forced colleges and universities to do the same thing. But these cutbacks also raised serious questions about the weakening of the educational system in our country.

With futurists, economists, human resource experts, and others stressing the importance of education in the new information age and the resulting new

Ethical Dilemma

REVIEW

Here's what our two executives have to say about the ways in which Canada tried to reduce its deficit.

Unfortunately, says Bédard, "as the old song would say, when *you owe your soul to the company store* you don't make the decisions or call the shots. Canada was too dependent on the [foreign] banks and their credit rating system to finance current operations." He adds

that "again, I feel that Canada did not cut expenses in the proper fashion."

Reilley comments that what was really unethical and irresponsible was to allow our national debt to grow so large. It was unethical *not* to take steps to reverse the dangerous trend. If any blame is attributable to business it should be "that it didn't, with a loud voice, challenge government's annual deficits much earlier."

economy, how can governments justify such cutbacks? How can we train people for tomorrow's jobs and how will Canada remain competitive in this era of tough, globalized business with fewer teachers and professors, larger class sizes, and less funding for education? Administrators are forced to concentrate on budgets instead of on how to improve, update, and modernize the educational process and keep them relevant in a fast-moving world.

So we end the chapter where we started it: looking at the extent of the role that government plays in business. But now we are asking whether it is time to deepen or keep reducing that involvement. What do you think?

Progress Check

- Can you name four laws that are important for consumer protection? What does the CDIC do? How do all of these affect businesses?
- What is a prospectus? What purpose does it serve? How does it affect companies?
- What are two important functions of the Department of Citizenship and Immigration? How do they affect businesses in Canada?
- How does the NRC help technology advancement in Canada? Can you give three specific examples?
- What are marketing boards? What area of business is affected by them?

SUMMARY
• • • • •

1. Explain the historical role of government in the Canadian economy.

2. List some of the major crown corporations in Canada and understand their role in the economy.

1. The Canadian government played a key role from the beginning of the country in 1867 in protecting young manufacturing industries and getting the railroad built to the west coast, helping to bind the country together.
   - *Why did the government have to do what it did?*
   It had the legal power and responsibility. The United States threatened to overwhelm our industry, which was not strong enough by itself to resist or to build the railway.

2. Crown corporations are one way government did its job.
   - *Why were crown corporations necessary?*
   Companies were not willing or able to assume certain responsibilities or fill some needs in the marketplace. The CNR, Air Canada, Hydro-Quebec,

and Atomic Energy of Canada Ltd. are some important examples. (The CNR and Air Canada are no longer crown corporations.)

3. Companies must be properly registered to have a public record of all business.
   • **Why is registration necessary?**
   Those who do business with a company may want to know who the owners are, when the business started, and other basic information. Governments need to know who is in business to ensure that taxes are paid, statistical data collected, and information supplied.

3. Understand how the start-up and operations of companies take place within a framework of government laws and regulations.

4. Many laws and regulations affect competition in Canada.
   • **What is the major piece of federal legislation?**
   The Competition Act is probably the most important act governing competition in Canada.

4. Identify major legislation affecting competition in Canada.

5. Governments have various methods for stimulating or restraining the economy as they deem necessary.
   • **What are their principal tools?**
   The two main methods are fiscal policy, which adjusts taxation, and monetary policy, which adjusts interest rates and money supply. Monetary policy is the domain of the Bank of Canada.

5. Discuss the role of government in stimulating or restraining the economy.

6. Canadian society demands a certain level of consumer and investor protection.
   • **How is this achieved?**
   Each level of government has legislation designed to give such protection. There is a wide range of laws and regulations supervised by consumer protection divisions in government. Investors are protected by provincial security commissions and the CDIC.

6. Understand the role of government in consumer and investor protection.

7. Many countries have established industrial policies to guide their development.
   • **Why is there controversy in Canada about the desirability of establishing such a policy?**
   Most large businesses lean toward a laissez-faire ideology. They are supported in this thinking by some segments of the population. Other large segments of the country lean toward greater government participation and direction to resolve Canada's economic woes.

7. Understand the controversy over a government industrial policy.

KEY TERMS

articles of
  incorporation 99
crown corporations
  94
economies of scale
  101

fiscal policy 100
industrial policy 95
marketing boards
  112
monetary policy 106

National Policy 96
privatization 95
prospectus 108
securities commission
  108

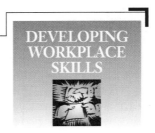

DEVELOPING WORKPLACE SKILLS

1. Scan your local newspapers, *The Globe and Mail,* the *National Post,* or a Canadian magazine like *Canadian Business* for references to government programs of help to Canadian business or a specific company. Bring these articles to class and discuss.

2. Canada is constantly subject to pressure of all kinds from our neighbour to the south. Many American states have strong marketing campaigns to

attract Canadian businesses. They also offer many inducements, financial and others, to lure businesses to move there. Should anything be done about this? Most provincial governments have similar programs to attract foreign companies to their jurisdictions. Check out your provincial government's Web site to see what it is doing in this regard. Bring your information to class to discuss this kind of government expenditure.

3. Cross-border shopping continues to be a popular activity. Many Canadians regularly head south to buy gas, cigarettes, clothing, and other consumer goods. This drains billions of dollars from the Canadian economy, hurting businesses, jobs, and government tax revenues. What, if anything, should be done about this problem? What can governments do?

4. Although unemployment remains very high, especially among young people, business people complain that they cannot find trained employees to fill existing vacancies. Job candidates lack math and science backgrounds and their written English language skills are weak. (In Quebec there are similar complaints, but the language problems are in French.) Further, too many are high-school dropouts. What can be done about this serious problem? Should business or government be working on it? What exactly should they be doing?

5. Do some research to see how many points you can find to support each side of the argument concerning a government industrial policy.

INTERNET CHALLENGES

1. Check out your municipality's Web site to see if you can spot any regulations affecting business that you find surprising. Perhaps the regulation concerns health, parking, necessary permits, or hours of business. Share your findings with your class.

2. Scan the Web site of your local newspaper for any reports of
   a) companies who may have violated any of these municipal regulations
   b) government aid to an existing or new business in your area

   See if you can find some items relating to a) or b) to bring to class for discussion.

Practising Management Decisions

CASE 1

GOVERNMENT-OWNED BANKS IN ALBERTA: AN ANOMALY?

Alberta is the only provincial government that owns and operates a bank. Alberta Treasury Branches (ATB) has become a large banking institution in Alberta. ATB serves 238 communities. In 90 of these communities, it is the sole provider of financial services. ATB has 148 branches, 129 agencies, and $9 billion in deposits. The bank generated a record profit of $110 million in 1999.

How does it happen that conservative Alberta, with a strong antigovernment, free enterprise bent, is the only province that owns a bank? The roots of this situation are to be found in the terrible economic depression of the 1930s. Like the rest of Canada, Alberta was flat on its back, so ATB was set up in 1938 to aid Albertans recovering from the Great Depression.

ATB was designed to be of particular use for rural Albertans, who constituted a much larger percentage of the population at that time. ATB was also intended to help small businesses. Originally it was supposed to have a five-year life, just to get the economy going again. ATB has now become a well-established financial institution in Alberta. According to chief operating officer Elmer Leahy, "ATB has been able to provide a measure of stability" through the ups and downs of economic fluctuations.

The only criticisms have been accusations that ATB has moved away from its mandate of concentrating on helping farmers and small businesses by giving loans to big businesses and speculators. ATB has long-range plans to expand into new services at the beginning of the twenty-first century. There has not been any serious movement to privatize the bank at a time when across Canada, including Alberta, many crown corporations are being sold off.

Decision Questions

1. Should a provincial government be in the banking business? Doesn't this contradict the whole trend toward privatization?
2. Should a crown corporation be privatized on principle? Even if it is well run and profitable?
3. What are the main arguments for "getting the government out of business?"
4. How do you feel about this issue? Can you see any situations that justify government owning or operating businesses?

Source: Brent Jang, "Treasury Branches a Special Case," *Globe and Mail, Report on Business,* February 1, 1996, p. B11; ATB Web site, <www.atb.com>, June 1999.

CASE 2

GAMBLING: A CASH COW FOR PROVINCIAL GOVERNMENTS

Starting slowly in Quebec in the late 1960s, but catching on quickly across the country, lotteries, casinos, video-lottery terminals (VLTs), and other forms of gambling had become, at the end of the century, a major source of revenue for many Canadian provincial governments. Now Quebec is going even further by heading up a $141 million consortium to build a hotel and casino in Pointe-au-Pic. The hotel will be managed by Canadian Pacific Hotels, but the casino will be managed by Loto-Quebec, the government agency that operates all gambling in the province.

You can get some idea of how large the gambling business has become by looking at the revenues and profits for the Ontario and Quebec governments. For the 1997–98 year the Ontario Lottery Corp. took in $1.6 billion from its four casinos, and $2.1 billion from all the other gaming and lottery sources for a grand total of $3.7 billion. For Quebec the 1998–99 figures are $633 million from its three casinos and $1.7 billion from the rest of its activities for a total of $2.33 billion. After all expenses and payouts to loto winners, the Quebec government still netted a handsome $1.2 billion.

Decision Questions

1. Some people and organizations argue that governments should not be in the gambling business, that encouraging gambling is a bad idea. Others argue private enterprise should run that kind of business and argue further that companies would generate more profit for governments. Governments reply that they want to keep organized crime from controlling gambling so they must own and run such operations. What do you think? Is it okay for governments to be in business? Should they be in the gambling?

2. Governments seem to believe that gambling is a great way to raise money because we don't seem to mind creating revenue for them by having some *fun,* and a chance of big winnings, instead of just paying higher taxes. Besides, they argue, nobody is forced to gamble so it's a kind of voluntary tax. How do you feel about that? Do you buy that argument?

3. Some churches and other institutions concerned with personal and family welfare point to the rising number of family and personal breakdowns caused by people becoming gambling addicts. Also easy access to VLTs is very bad for young persons. Do you agree with either of these concerns? Why? What can be done to improve the situation?

4. Suppose you agree with those who are totally opposed to governments encouraging gambling. Wouldn't taxes have to be raised to replace these revenues? Would you mind paying more taxes? Do you think your parents or family members would mind? Or do you have any other suggestions?

Sources: *Montreal Gazette,* June 17, 1999, p. A3, and June 19, 1999, pp. B3, B4.

How Governments
Aid Exporters

Appendix A

Because exports are particularly important to the economic well-being of Canada, we have a very large and elaborate government apparatus to assist companies in their exporting and foreign investment activities. Not only the federal government, but most provincial and all large municipal governments have various ministries, departments, and agencies that provide a variety of services, including information, marketing, financial aid, insurance and guarantees, publications, and contacts. All major trading countries provide similar support to their exporters.

The federal government agency that has the main responsibility for international business is the Department of Foreign Affairs and International Trade (DFAIT). This ministry has trade commissioners in Canadian embassies abroad and in Canada. DFAIT also maintains "one-stop" international trade centres across Canada. This federal organization engages in a variety of activities that are shown in more detail in the next section. A business that is contemplating going international can get almost any information and help it requires from DFAIT. Further information may be obtained from InfoExport's toll-free line: 1-800-267-8376; and its Web site: <www.infoexport.gc.ca/faq-e.asp?>.

ACCESSING THE GLOBAL MARKET:
SERVICES OF THE CANADIAN GOVERNMENT

Because exports have traditionally been such an important issue for Canadians, the federal government has always maintained a high profile in this area. Recently, the government's main efforts have been channelled through DFAIT, which has absorbed previous agencies and developed a comprehensive basket of aid and support for Canadian companies wanting to export, or to engage in investment outside Canada. Advice and aid are administered through some 600 trade commissioners—in a worldwide network of trade commissions in more than 125 cities, in Ottawa, and in more than 13 trade centres across the country. This help is particularly useful for small and medium-sized enterprises who cannot easily get this information. Here is a partial list of some of their important activities.

••• TRADE COUNSELING AND ASSISTANCE •••

- International trade centres in 13 Canadian cities provide one-stop information services. Many of these centres are cooperative efforts of federal, provincial, and local governments, boards of trade, chambers of commerce, and so forth. They are well set up, with extensive facilities for research, and helpful staff.
- Geographic trade divisions dividing the world into five regions.
- Sectoral trade divisions dividing marketing, investment, and financing opportunities into 14 product and service sectors.
- Advice about Canadian regulations restricting exports and imports.

••• PROGRAMS THAT OFFER FINANCIAL ASSISTANCE •••

- Information and aid on providing military services and supplies to U.S. and European governments under various mutual agreements.
- Export orientation programs to help small and medium-sized companies expand into the United States and overseas.
- Investment development programs to help foreign corporations bring new capital and technology into Canada. Also helps to set up joint ventures with Canadian companies.
- Programs for export market development to facilitate a variety of marketing activities such as attending or setting up booths at trade fairs, setting up permanent sales offices abroad, and arranging visits by foreign buyers to Canada.
- Technology Inflow Program (TIPS) to sponsor group missions or individual companies' visits abroad and visits to Canadian companies by foreign technical experts.

••• EXPORT FINANCING AND FOREIGN SALES PROCUREMENT •••

- Industrial Cooperation Program of the Canadian International Development Agency helps Canadian companies seeking investment opportunities and transfer of technology abroad.
- Export Development Corporation provides a full range of financing, insurance, and guarantees to Canadian companies investing or doing business abroad.
- Canadian Commercial Corporation acts as the prime contractor when foreign governments or international agencies want to purchase goods or services from Canada through the government.
- World Information Network for Exports (WINS) lists more than 30,000 Canadian exporters and would-be exporters offering approximately 25,000 products and services. This constantly updated information is used by the trade commissioners mentioned above to find potential buyers for these products. Foreign importers can also access WINS to find products they are seeking.

••• TRADE DATA AND PUBLICATIONS •••

- *CanadExport* is a trade newsletter published twice monthly and sent to more than 60,000 readers. It contains a variety of useful information

Business Agenda

International Trade Practices Course

MONTREAL—September 17–December 4—*The Practice of International Trade* is a certified 63-hour evening course on the terms and techniques used in import and export transactions.

Organized by the Quebec Association of Export Trading Houses, it is one of the most comprehensive and complete international trading courses offered in Canada. For information, contact Lilly Nguyen, Tel.: 1-800-465-9615; Fax: (514) 848-9986; e-mail: amceq@amceq.org.

Cross-Canada Seminars on Taiwan

CANADA—A series of information *seminars on business opportunities, challenges and strategies for succeeding in Taiwan* will be held in four Canadian cities beginning in late September.

Hugh Stephens, director of the Canadian Trade Office in Taipei, will give an update on this dynamic market in a series format that includes breakfast, followed by a question period and one-on-one meetings.

Stephens will address such areas as market trends, joint ventures with Taiwan partners, global investment opportunities, trade, tourism, educational services, and other matters relevant to the Canada–Taiwan bilateral relationship. He will also explain the services available through the

Canadian Trade Office in Taipei to help Canadian businesses capture some of this market.

Individual appointments with Stephens are on a first-come, first-serve basis. Cities and dates for the information seminars are: Calgary (September 26); Winnipeg (September 27); Toronto (September 30); and Montreal (October 2).

For a complete program outline or for more information on the seminars, contact Elsie Lee, Canada-Taiwan Business Association, Ottawa, Tel.: (613) 238-4000 ext. 240; Fax: (613) 238-7643.

Doing Business With the UN

MONTREAL—October 1—Canadian exporters, especially small and medium-sized firms, are invited to attend a one-day seminar, *How To Do Business With the UN*. Representatives from key United Nations procurement agencies will be present.

In addition to briefings—all speakers are bilingual—there will be afternoon workshops to allow for focused discussions between suppliers and buyers.

The $150 (including lunch and a business guide) event is organized by the United Nations Association in Canada (UNAC), in collaboration with the Department of Foreign Affairs and International Trade, the Canadian Commercial Corporation, the Canadian International Development

Agency, and the Quebec Ministry of Industry, Commerce, Science and Technology.

To register, contact Mrs. Sylvie Thibault, World Trade Centre, Montreal, Tel.: (514) 849-1999; Fax: (514) 847-8343.

Cross-Canada Seminars Planned for Canada Expo in Chile

CANADA—A series of seminars across Canada will be held in October 1996 to assist exhibitors prepare for the *Canada Expo* trade fair in Santiago, Chile, December 3–6, 1996.

Following the success of Canada Expo '94 in Mexico City, Expo '96 promises to provide significant potential for new business opportunities, partnerships, and contacts in a variety of sectors. These include industrial, machinery, power and energy, advanced technologies, environmental equipment, health care, construction, infrastructure and building materials, packaging, education, agri-food, consumer products, and professional services.

Canadian companies interested in learning more about Canada Expo '96 and the seminar series should contact the Canada Expo Coordinator, Latin America and Caribbean Trade Division (LGT), Department of Foreign Affairs and International Trade, 125 Sussex Drive, Ottawa K1A 0G2, or facsimile at (613) 944-0479.

Sample pages from *CanadExport* magazine.

for Canadian companies who export or invest outside of Canada. The newsletter also has a business agenda page that lists seminars, meetings, courses, and conferences across Canada, of interest to those engaged in, or planning to engage in, international business. Many are sponsored by DFAIT or other government agencies. Sample pages are shown at the end of this Appendix and above.

- A variety of directories and special studies of use to actual or potential exporters.
- An International Trade Data Bank that stores a wide range of information from the United Nations and various trade blocs about international trade.

Most of this information is available free on the Internet, including the regular issues of *CanadExport*. The main Internet access address is <www.dfait-maeci.gc.ca>.

http://www.dfait-maeci.gc.ca/english/news/newsletr/canex

Vol. 17, No. 20 — December 1, 1999

Pettigrew Announces Canada's Position on WTO Negotiations

On November 15, 1999, International Trade Minister Pierre Pettigrew presented Canada's position for upcoming negotiations at the World Trade Organization (WTO) to Parliament.

The report, *Canada and the Future of the World Trade Organization*, describes in detail the approach Canada will take when the world's trade ministers meet in Seattle this week. It directly answers 45 recommendations made by an all-party Parliamentary committee, the Standing Committee on Foreign Affairs and International Trade (SCFAIT).

"Our position is detailed and balanced – the result of extensive consultations with Canadian business and citizens," said Minister Pettigrew. "Parliamentarians and citizens have told us that they support Canada's role in international trade talks, as long as they benefit

TelPlus Systems makes a successful swipe in Japan
See story on page 2

Canadians as a whole, that they reflect our heritage of democracy and openness and our ongoing quest for a just society."

Earlier this year, the SCFAIT held 30 public sessions and heard from more than 400 Canadians from a variety of business, labour, environmental, academic and human rights groups. The Department of Foreign Affairs and International Trade and other departments also directly consulted industry sectors and citizen groups throughout the spring and summer and will continue to do so during the negotiations.

Continued on page 3 — Canada's Position

REVOLUTIONARY WASTEWATER TREATMENT COMPANY SUCCESSFULLY TESTS EXPORT WATERS

Years of research and hard work have finally paid off for Brampton-based (near Toronto) Dry Biofilter Inc. now that it has broken into the world of exports — first in Poland and almost immediately after in the United States – with its new revolutionary wastewater treatment system, the Dry Biofilter (DBF™).

These successes did not come without much preparation, lengthy investigations and protracted negotiations involving each deal.

"As a matter of fact," says company President and CEO Don Prazmowski, "it took us 10 years to develop our product and

Continued on page 6 — Dry Biofilter Inc.

Chapter 5

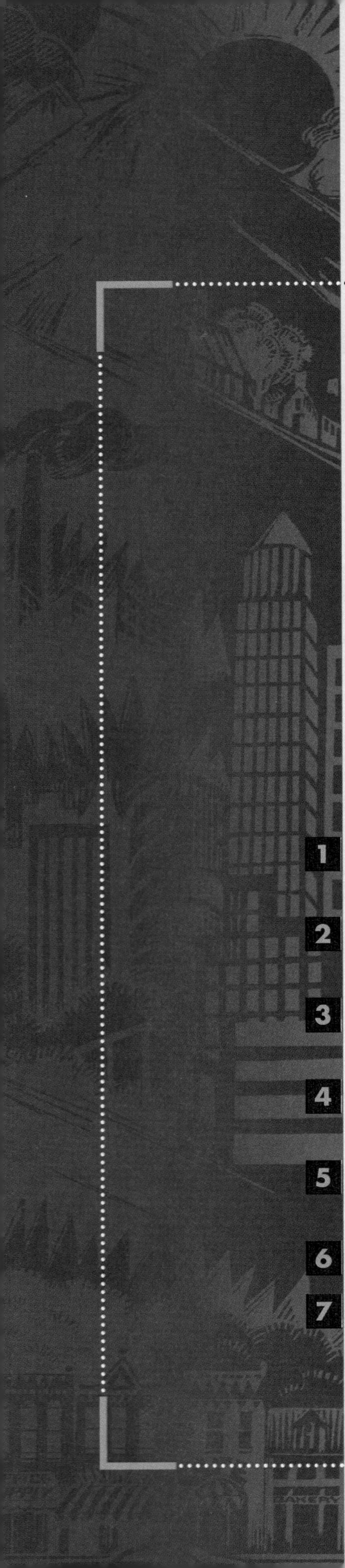

Ethical Behaviour, the Environment, and Social Responsibility

LEARNING GOALS

After you have read and studied this chapter, you should be able to

1 discuss how business in the early capitalist period ignored ethical standards of behaviour.

2 describe the modern beginnings of business ethics, and understand why ethical issues are so important now.

3 define management's role in setting ethical standards, and list the six-step approach to ethical decisions.

4 identify what first led to concern about the environment, and list some of the major environmental problems.

5 understand why business sees a conflict between a clean environment and competitive ability.

6 describe the rule of 72, and explain its relationship to growth.

7 explain how sustainable development has become the major international goal for reconciling growth with environmental constraints.

Each year, International Earth Day is celebrated around the world on April 22. The Canadian branch is called *Earth Day Canada*, and its president is Jed Goldberg. One of Goldberg's main jobs is to elicit corporate financial support for his organization, about which he is very optimistic. Starting in 1994 with 25 Canadian companies whose contributions totalled $200,000, he pushed this amount up to $595,000 in 1995 with 45 companies participating, and support continued to grow steadily.

Earth Day Canada relies mainly on corporate support as governments contribute only 10 percent of the budget. However, this does not mean that Goldberg will accept help from any company. Goldberg chooses sponsors that he feels are really interested in environmental issues and show that concern through specific company policies.

For example, he accepted an offer from MAC Cosmetics to manufacture, sell, and contribute all proceeds of a $24 necklace because the company's products are developed without animal testing. Goldberg happily accepts contributions from Xerox because it recycles its toner cartridges. There is no problem about this criterion because companies whose policies do not support environmental improvement usually do not seek to support Earth Day Canada.

The organization sponsors environmental awareness programs like Canadian Natural Highway Tree-Planting and assists other groups such as Ottawa's Friends of the Earth, Toronto's Evergreen Foundation of Canada, and La Societé de verdissement du Montréal Métropolitain.

For Earth Day April 22, 1996, Jed got support from Radke Films, which produced a 30-second TV commercial, and from HMV Canada, which produced an Earth Day Album featuring 17 Canadian artists with all proceeds going to Earth Day Canada.

We will be looking at environmental issues in more detail in the second half of this chapter, but we turn first to business ethics.

PROFILE

Jed Goldberg Marshals Corporate Support for Earth Day Canada

Sources: James Pollock, "The Earth Day Payback," *Marketing*, April 15, 1996, p. 10; interviews with Jed Goldberg, June 13, 1996, and October 30, 1998.

CORPORATE RESPONSIBILITY: HOW DOES IT MEASURE UP?

In this chapter you will see a review of issues that relate to the principal question of the need and ability of Canadian companies, governments, and all organizations to behave in a responsible way to our society. You will see that some people believe in a limited responsibility for companies, while others believe that corporations, like individuals, cannot duck full responsibility for the level of ethical standards that they have and for the impact of their actions on the environment. Some commentators go so far as to say that business ethics is an oxymoron. That is, it's an absurd contradiction, like saying someone is tall and short or rich and poor. Most people do not take such an extreme position. You can see examples in the Profiles of many things companies do to show their responsibility to society. However, some say this is merely PR—window dressing. What do you think? Is it possible, indeed necessary, that companies adopt, apply, and maintain responsible ethical standards in their policies and practices? As you will see, this is not an easy question in our complex world. We will return to this issue after you have explored the many aspects of the problem in the chapter.

ETHICAL BEHAVIOUR IN BUSINESS AND GOVERNMENT

Throughout this book you will see many comments about the issue of business ethics. Why so much emphasis on ethical behaviour of business people and companies? The reason is that the past decade saw a rising tide of criticism in Canada (and other countries) of various business practices that many Canadians found unacceptable.

Knowing what's right and wrong and behaving accordingly is what ethical behaviour is all about. This goes beyond legal and regulatory requirements or obeying the laws of a country. Social responsibility means that a business shows concern for the welfare of society as a whole. In this chapter we look at ethics from an organizational perspective and how the behaviour of companies and organizations rates on the social responsibility scorecard.

EFFECT ON CAREER CHOICE

How will what you learn in this chapter be likely to affect your choice of career? Most employees are more comfortable working for a company whose policies and practices are solidly based on a responsible approach to their community and country and to the global environment. After all, as an employee you must live by the rules of your company and carry out the orders and wishes of your superiors. Further, some day you will occupy a managerial position and have the responsibility of not only doing what your superior expects from you, but you will also be helping to shape company policy and practices. As you work your way through this chapter, you will have plenty of food for thought about these issues.

.... ▬ ....

A BRIEF HISTORY OF ETHICS IN BUSINESS

The recent criticism of business practices in North America can perhaps be traced back to the 1960s in the United States, when a young lawyer named Ralph Nader almost single-handedly took on mighty General Motors. He started challenging GM because of its defective Corvair, which had been responsible for many fatal accidents because of sudden, erratic, and uncontrollable behaviour.

At first, GM regarded Nader as an elephant might regard a pesky mosquito. Gradually, however, his efforts draw more and more support. Despite GM's strenuous opposition, including hiring private detectives to look for dirt on Ralph Nader's personal life to discredit him, GM was forced, for the first time in the history of automobile manufacturing, to recall cars to correct problems. Now, of course, recalls have become standard procedure for all auto manufacturers. This was perhaps the first important signal of a move toward **corporate social responsibility**, the recognition by corporations that their actions must take into account the needs and ethical standards of society.

corporate social responsibility
The recognition by corporations that their actions must take into account the needs and ethical standards of society.

People have been concerned about business practices for a long time. The advent of the Industrial Revolution at the end of the 1700s led to serious criticism of its drawbacks (see Chapter 2). Critics of the new capitalist-industrial societies that emerged in the 1800s in western Europe, Canada, and the United States were numerous. Many of them condemned greed and the cruel treatment of workers: harsh and dangerous conditions that caused many accidents, low pay, long hours, child labour, and so on.

These inhumane practices were the subject of many novels that achieved wide acclaim. Charles Dickens in England and later Sinclair Lewis in the United States are but two novelists who described and condemned these and other business practices of the day. In Chapter 14 you will see how similar harsh conditions in Canada led to the formation of the union movement and eventually laws banning various unacceptable practices.

••• A MURKY ROAD TO WEALTH •••

The accumulation of large fortunes in the 1800s and 1900s (before the days of income taxes) was usually aided by many shady if not criminal acts, including the alleged killing of competitors and union leaders. In the United States, those early, wealthy capitalists were dubbed **robber barons**, a term that became very popular and is still used today. The classic robber baron was John D. Rockefeller, who established a near monopoly in the oil business using power tactics. His huge Standard Oil Co. (from which we get the name Esso, S.O.) was finally forced by the U.S. courts at the beginning of this century to split up into a number of companies, each still quite large.

robber barons
Capitalists of the nineteenth century whose wealth came, in part, through shady if not criminal acts.

In Canada, one of the most notorious developments occurred during the building of the first railway line to the west coast in the 1870s and 1880s. This vast project, like most railway construction in North America, was accompanied by many scandals and corruption, leading to the resignation in 1873 of the federal government of Canada's first prime minister, John A. MacDonald. The first scandal involved Sir Hugh Allan. His company (which became the CPR) was given contracts, vast sums of money, and huge tracks of land across western Canada, often under questionable circumstances. Many men made fortunes, including Donald A. Smith (later Lord Strathcona) and Sir William Van Horne. Similar scandals in the province of Quebec, on a smaller scale, led to the fall of the government of Honoré Mercier in the 1890s.

••• MODERN CAPITALISM •••

laissez-faire capitalism
The theory that, if left alone and unhindered by government, the free market, in pursuit of economic efficiency, would provide an abundance of goods at the lowest prices, improving everyone's life.

The nineteenth century saw the emergence of the modern industrial-capitalist system. The economic philosophy that underpinned it was first elaborated upon by Adam Smith, whom we met in Chapter 2. Smith's book *The Wealth of Nations*, published in 1776, gave birth to the concept of **laissez-faire capitalism**. This theory emphasized that, if left alone and unhindered by government, the free market, in pursuit of economic efficiency, would provide an abundance of goods at the lowest prices, improving everyone's life. The workings of this "invisible hand" would reward capitalists for their work and financial risks, thus providing jobs for the population and plentiful goods to satisfy human needs and improve living standards.

For some years this seemed to work as Smith predicted. But (as noted in Chapter 2) there were many booms and busts, the economic cycles we now take for granted. There were also the serious problems of poverty, job-related illnesses, the lack of pensions or compensation to workers for the many industrial accidents, and other such problems. Life for the average person was said to be "short, nasty, and brutish."

••• THE END OF LAISSEZ-FAIRE CAPITALISM •••

The twentieth century saw the beginnings of serious attempts to deal with the shortcomings of the capitalist system. In Chapter 4 we saw how Canadian governments were forced to implement a variety of programs to smooth out the rough edges of capitalism and cope with its contradictions of extreme wealth and poverty. Of course, we now take for granted the great productive capacities that capitalism developed, which resulted in greatly improved living standards for the majority of people.

We accept and usually welcome what new technologies make available to us—faster travel, electronic gadgetry and communications, and more—but we also express more concern for human values. Canadian society condemns discrimination in hiring, promotion, or firing; continued high unemployment; poverty; homelessness; and children going to school hungry. We expect solutions. We insist that business managers, company directors, and politicians behave ethically. Activities such as bribery, influence peddling, favouritism, discrimination, and expense padding are denounced. The dumping of wastes and toxic material and many other formerly common practices are now either severely frowned upon or illegal.

These concerns have also found expression on the international scene. For many years, nearly all countries supported the sanctions against South Africa and helped to bring an end to its official racist party of apartheid, which had kept its black majority in a permanent state of oppression. Canada had laws and policies that banned most dealings with South African government and businesses. Banks and companies that had investments there were severely criticized by shareholders, church leaders, and community groups. Eventually many responded by curtailing or ceasing their activities in that country.

A NEW EMPHASIS ON CORPORATE SOCIAL RESPONSIBILITY

Today there seems to be a heightened interest in, and awareness, of the importance of the social responsibility of business, especially for large corporations. An increasing number of comments by Canadian and international business leaders are stressing the obligations that companies have to society. The Spotlight on Big Business gives one important example. A brief review of other comments reported in *The Economist, Time* magazine, *The Globe and Mail*, and the *Montreal Gazette* will give some idea of the extent to which this has become a major concern of many business, government, and academic leaders.

The Globe and Mail report on the opening addresses at the prestigious World Economic Forum meeting in Davos, Switzerland, in February 1996 is headlined, "Capitalism must develop a heart" and "Davos forum kicks off with a warning that greed is ultimately bad for business." The president of Switzerland, a former U.S. Cabinet member and philosopher, and a well-known Harvard professor and business consultant, addressed the gathering of "1,000 [senior] executives and their spouses, 200 government officials and 40 heads of government." All speakers had the same message: unless business demonstrates real commitment to its workforce and to the communities in which it operates, there will be strong, popular reactions, including a resurgent union movement. There is even "a risk globalization [of business] will collapse."[1]

Palliser Furniture is a company that has found success by producing environmentally friendly furniture. The company's A.A. DeFehr Foundation receives 10 percent of the company's income, which is distributed among various charities.

••• ETHICAL BEHAVIOUR IS PROFITABLE •••

At a conference on ethics in business organized by York University and the Canadian Centre for Ethics & Corporate Policy in Toronto in December 1995 Canadian entrepreneur Isadore Sharp, founder of Four Seasons Hotels, pointed out that a Gallup poll showed that the corporation was one of the least trusted institutions in the United States. He also noted the contrast between what corporate leaders and their employees think about their companies. A 1993 poll showed that while 96 percent of the Fortune 500 companies thought their companies behaved ethically, 41 percent of the employees disagreed with their leaders. Another survey, reported Sharp, showed that 70 percent of consumers said they would not buy products from a company they believed to be unethical. A Canadian survey indicated that consumers would overwhelmingly go out of their way, or pay more, to buy ethically produced clothing.[2]

Sharp contrasted the behaviour of two American companies, Johnson & Johnson and Exxon. The former, faced with a major problem when seven people died in Chicago from poisoned Tylenol capsules, made the whole issue public and told retailers to return all their Tylenol stock for full credit. This cost Johnson & Jonson several millions of dollars but restored public confidence in their products quickly. A different story emerged concerning Exxon after the 1989 oil spill catastrophe off Alaska when the giant Exxon *Valdez* tanker went aground. Exxon's delay in assuming responsibility for one of the worst maritime oil disasters ever cost it dearly in public and business ratings and landed it with a $5 billion fine. Sharp concluded by stating that a growing body of evidence indicates that ethical behaviour pays off in higher profits.[3]

Proof that ethical behaviour pays off can be found in the profitable existence of companies like The Body Shop International and Ben & Jerry's. Both companies emphasize responsibility to the community and the environment and have successful operations in Canada. Other examples are ethical mutual funds that have good performance records through investing only in companies deemed to be socially responsible. For example, the Clean Environment

<www.depaul.edu/ethics>

The DePaul University Institute for Business and Professional Ethics Web site indicates that it is "one of the first ethics-related resources to pioneer a hypertext linked ethics network throughout the Internet." Check it out. Find out about the Institute and its activities. Who are its members? What does membership entail?

The pressure has been building for twenty years.

A Little History. Ben & Jerry's, Vermont's Finest Ice Cream and Frozen Yogurt, was founded in 1978 by childhood friends Ben Cohen and Jerry Greenfield. They soon became popular for their innovative flavours, made from fresh Vermont milk and cream. Early in 1998, Ben & Jerry's granted Delicious Alternative Desserts Ltd. the license to manufacture its ice creams. DAD is a publicly traded Canadian company with manufacturing facilities in Stoney Creek, Ontario. The 65 year-old Stoney Creek Dairy plant has been completely rebuilt at a cost of over $10 million to meet Ben & Jerry's exacting quality standards. In the U.S., Ben & Jerry's products are distributed in all 50 states, and you'll find over 160 Ben & Jerry's franchised scoop shops in 20 states. In 1988 Ben & Jerry's Homemade, Inc. created a document called the Statement of Mission.

The company is dedicated to the creation and demonstration of a new corporate concept of linked prosperity. Its mission consists of three interrelated parts: product, economic and social. DAD has embraced Ben & Jerry's social marketing philosophies and is actively engaged in forging partnerships in Canada to continue the founders' mission.

Ben & Jerry's Philanthropy. Ben & Jerry's Homemade, Inc. gives away 7.5 percent of its pre-tax earnings in three ways: the Ben & Jerry's Foundation; employee Community Action Teams at five Vermont sites; and through corporate grants made by the Director of The Social Mission. The company supports projects that are models for social change—projects which exhibit creative problem solving and hopefulness. The Foundation is managed by a nine member employee board and considers proposals relating to children and families, disadvantaged groups, and the environment.

Enjoy the explosion.

BEN & JERRY'S

At your grocer's. At Last.

Ben & Jerry's is a great example of how ethical behaviour pays off in higher profits. This highly successful company stressess responsibility to the community and to the environment.

Equity Fund outperformed the average Canadian mutual fund in 1995 and for the three years ending in 1995.[4] The fund continued its excellent performance for the next three years.

SOME QUESTIONABLE PRACTICES

A growing number of "normal" business activities are coming under increasing scrutiny in Canada (and elsewhere) because of their doubtful ethical practices. As society's values are changing, certain practices are now being deemed controversial or unacceptable. Let us look at some of them.

••• WEAPONS SALES •••

Many people are concerned about the question of selling military equipment, supplies, and sophisticated industrial machinery and products to brutal dictatorships. In 1991 we witnessed a UN-sponsored attack on Iraq, in which Canada participated, because it had invaded its neighbour, Kuwait, in 1990 and refused to withdraw. Saddam Hussein, the dictator who rules Iraq, has an extremely unsavory record and has often been condemned by Amnesty International and other human rights groups.

Despite this fact many countries, including Canada, had sold him billions of dollars worth of military equipment and supplies—including the capability to produce chemical and nuclear weapons and missiles. There are many media reports that much military equipment continues to be sold to Iraq by various countries, including the United States and Canada. Other countries with odious records send representatives to arms shows in Canada and can pretty well buy whatever they wish from Canadian companies. This problem is not only a Canadian one. The UN Office of Disarmament Affairs and other organizations are concerned about the continuing proliferation of arms sold by the major industrial powers.[5]

••• ATOMIC REACTORS SOLD TO ROMANIA •••

Atomic Energy of Canada Ltd. (AECL), a crown corporation, was under heavy fire for having sold our nuclear reactors in the 1980s to the late dictator Nicolae Ceausescu of Romania. These contracts were important to AECL because for years it had been unable to sell any Canadian reactors. It was later learned that the workers who had built the massive reactor housings were practically slave labourers. This was a classic example of the pressures businesses and governments face: a badly needed sales opportunity versus a customer who is ethically very distasteful. The question is made all the more complex when competitors in some countries seem to have no ethical standards at all.

••• LAND MINES •••

A notorious issue relates to land mines, which are cheap to buy and are now strewn over many countries in Africa and Asia. Long after fighting has ceased, these mines continue to maim and kill innocent children, women, and men who are working in fields. In countries like Angola, Vietnam, and Cambodia, thousands of people become amputees annually. At a UN-sponsored conference to ban land mines, in Geneva in January 1996, it was reported that there are 110 types of mines, in uncounted millions, spread throughout 69 countries, killing 10,000 civilians annually and maiming another 20,000. At this conference, Canada announced "a moratorium on the production, export, and use of antipersonnel mines." Unfortunately, only about 20 countries were in favour of such a ban.

Jody Williams, Nobel Prize laureate, is a strong advocate for a global ban on land mines.

A report on *60 Minutes* in July 1996 said that there were some 100 million land mines threatening people globally. The report also noted that in Cambodia, a small country of nine million people, there were 60,000 amputees, not to mention all the small children who had been killed. The worst offending nations, according to *60 Minutes*, are China, Pakistan, Russia, and the United States. These countries harbour the main producers and exporters of land mines, some of which sell for as little as two dollars, and have so far refused to support the movement to ban mines. Canada hosted a UN conference in September 1996 to push them and other countries to stop the production of these deadly instruments of destruction.[6]

Canada finally succeeded when 122 countries signed an agreement in Ottawa in December 1997, banning the production, sale, and use of land mines effective when the governments of 40 countries ratified the treaty. Unfortunately three major powers who are all significant manufacturers and exporters of land mines, the U.S., Russia, and China refused to sign the treaty for various reasons. One year later, there was good news according to the executive director of Mines Action Canada, the coordinating body of 15 Canadian organizations monitoring the implementation of the treaty. He reported that 11 more countries had signed the treaty, bringing the number to 133, and equally if not more important, 55 countries had already ratified the treaty. It came into force March 1, 1999. Furthermore, the U.S. has indicated that it expects to sign on by the year 2000 and has contributed $100 million toward the important mine-clearing program. Russia has banned the export of mines and there are indications they may also become a signatory in the near future.[7]

••• HIV-INFECTED BLOOD SUPPLY •••

One of the big news stories in Canada in 1995 and 1996 concerned the official inquiry by Justice Kever into the serious allegations that the Canadian Red Cross and the federal and seven provincial governments allowed hepatitis-C and HIV-infected blood to be transfused to hemophiliacs. This error resulted in hundreds of hemophiliacs becoming HIV positive and many getting full-blown AIDS and hepatitis-C and subsequently dying. The families and the hemophiliac organizations alleged that unpurified blood stocks were being used at a time when testing procedures were known and available, to avoid financial loss.

The long and complex hearings, costing many millions of dollars, were coming to an end, and Justice Kever announced that the final report would name individuals and organizations responsible for this tragic incident. The Red Cross and all the governments involved immediately took legal action to prevent Justice Kever from doing that. They claimed that they were not given the opportunity to adequately present their side of the case as required by law.

This set off a round of public statements and editorials condemning them for such action. Many felt that it was ridiculous to spend so many months and millions of dollars to uncover what happened, why it happened, and who was responsible, and then to try to prevent a full report from being issued. It is clear that any person, organization, or government found responsible for this tragedy would face substantial legal claims by the families of the sick and deceased. Some thought it particularly ironic that the federal government that set up the inquiry should now be trying to block its results from becoming known.

Eventually Justice Kever was prevented from naming individuals, government ministries, or organizations who were responsible for this disaster. One of the sad effects of this case was that Canadians lost confidence in the Canadian Red Cross. After more than a half-century of yeoman service getting and storing blood donations and providing hospitals with the blood needed for transfusions, the Red Cross gave up this responsibility.

••• THE WESTRAY COAL MINE DISASTER •••

Another problem that received a lot of attention in Canada from 1992 to 1996 concerned the Westray coal mine explosion that occurred May 1992 in Plymouth, Nova Scotia, taking the lives of 26 men. Accusations were made by family and friends of the victims and by members of Parliament and the Nova Scotia legislature that both levels of government, acting for political reasons, financed the opening of the mine despite warnings from their mining departments that it was a dangerous mine with a long record of explosions and deaths. After much delay, an official inquiry was launched in 1995 to examine all matters relevant to the disaster.

Company and government officials as well as mine inspectors have testified, often making contradictory statements. Nearly all deny any responsibility for the explosion. Miners have stated that the coal dust hazard was constantly high and that mine officials and government inspectors brushed aside or ignored complaints made to them. Miners claim they were also told not to make complaints if they wanted to keep their jobs.

The Westray disaster is another example of the complex ethical problems that can arise in seemingly ordinary business decisions. Here was a community of miners desperately in need of jobs. The federal and provincial governments were anxious to help provide the jobs as elections were due to take place shortly and a company was prepared to operate the mine. So all parties, including the union, backed the scheme even though there were known risks. The governments helped finance the reopening of the mine.

After the explosion, former federal cabinet minister Tom Hockins, interviewed on the CBC, said that economic considerations rather than safety factors led to the mine opening. The area has a persistently high unemployment rate so the mine opening was welcome news despite the risks.

Some miners claimed that after operations commenced, they began to worry about the growing risk of an explosion; but it appears that the other parties were too far into the project to want to stop.

According to Nova Scotia reporter Dean Jobb, who wrote a book about the Westray mine disaster, "almost $100 million of public funds" were spent on the mine. He notes that

In December 1997, an inquiry headed by Justice Peter Richard of the Nova Scotia Supreme Court condemned Westray management as "derelict" in its duty to run a safe mine. Singled out were Currah [Inc.;

the Toronto-based mine owner] chairman Clifford Frame; [on-site managers] Gerald Phillips and Roger Parry. The latter two were charged in 1993 with manslaughter and criminal negligence causing death.

But the last straw came at the end of June 1998. After spending $3 million and preparing for five years, the Crown attorneys announced that they no longer believed they had a case against the operators of the Westray coal mine.[8]

··· DISCRIMINATION AGAINST WOMEN ···

In other chapters we discuss how women have been discriminated against in hiring, promotion, and pay and how this situation has improved. Companies have changed their policies as federal and provincial governments pass laws banning discrimination. Nevertheless, women still earn much less than men for work of equal value. To remedy this situation, governments and companies have agreed in principle to pay equity for women.

However, there are difficulties in the actual implementation of pay equity laws. In various ways, the Ontario and Quebec provincial governments and the federal government are delaying or diluting the commencement or application of their own laws. Claiming severe budgetary limitations they either restricted the periods for which they will make up for past injustices or they delayed actual implementation of current pay equity.

Some Quebec business associations expressed strong opposition to instituting pay equity for women. Ghislain Dufour, president of the Conseil du Patronat, Quebec's largest employer group, said his group opposes a pay equity law. Michel Decary, Quebec vice-president of the Canadian Federation of Independent Business, called the proposal a "colossally bad idea."[9]

In 1998 the Canadian Human Rights Council finally ruled on a case going back to 1984. The Council ordered the federal government to obey its own laws by compensating its employees (mostly women) who had suffered pay discrimination for 14 years. A fierce public debate developed in Canada on this issue because very large sums of money were involved. Various estimates placed the amount that the federal government would have to pay out in the range of $4 to $6 billion. Had it been a smaller amount, there likely would have been far less disagreement about the principle involved—pay equity. The federal government launched an appeal of this ruling, claiming that the determination of what constitutes work of equal value was flawed.

Progress Check

- What issue launched concern about unethical business practices in the United States? How was it resolved?
- What was the major business scandal in Canada in the 1800s?
- Can you name some Canadian business practices that were once acceptable but now are perceived as unethical or are even illegal?

··· WHITE-COLLAR CRIME ···

Bob Crampton of the Metro Toronto fraud squad spent many years tracking **white-collar crimes**. These are crimes, usually thefts, committed by executives and other white-collar, or office, workers. Crampton said, "ethics are a rare commodity in the business community." He quoted Mario Puzo, author of *The Godfather*, who maintained that "behind every great fortune is a crime."[10] This is obviously an exaggeration, but it is often true.

Den of Thieves by *Wall Street Journal* editor James Stewart is about greed run amok in some brokerage firms on Wall Street in the 1980s. A number of

white-collar crimes
Crimes, usually theft, committed by executives or other white-collar office workers.

Spotlight on Big Business   <www.weforum.org>

Backlash Against Globalization: Corporate Social Responsibility

The World Economic Forum, based in Geneva, Switzerland, is one of the top global business organizations in the world. Its membership includes many governments and the largest companies in the world, all of which send their leading figures to the annual conference in Davos, Switzerland. Prime ministers and presidents of countries rub shoulders with corporation presidents, chairpeople, and CEOs. The Forum also accumulates economic data and issues reports from time to time that attract a lot of attention. So when the founder and president of the Forum makes a public comment, it is a noteworthy event. This is exactly what happened in 1996. Klaus Schwab wrote a joint article with Forum managing director Claude Smadja in the *International Herald Tribune*, one of the great, long-established, truly global newspapers.

The central point of the article is the serious backlash that has developed against the negative effects of the globalization of business and what should be done about it. Schwab and Smadja stated that this backlash has become so serious that it "is threatening to disrupt economic activity and social stability" in the industrial democracies. They used the example of the month-long national strikes and protests that seriously disrupted the French economy in December 1995 (personally witnessed by the Canadian author of this text). Other events before and after the article was published give further support to this argument.

In Canada, Ontario unionists led many major protests and strikes of tens of thousands of people in Toronto, London, and elsewhere in Ontario in 1995 and 1996. In Germany, millions of unionists staged significant protests in June 1996. In the Untied States, various candidates for the presidential election in 1996 catered to the same widespread sentiments of restrictions against foreign imports. This inward-looking protectionist attitude in the U.S. continues to be a constant problem according to a 1999 report.

All of these protests related to increasing and persistent unemployment, reduced wages and salaries, reduced social benefits, or higher cost of these benefits. Protesters all expressed deep concern, worry, and anger due to an increasing feeling of insecurity, lower incomes, or both.

The article noted that it is not surprising that there is so much concern because rapid globalization of economic activities and technological change have drastically altered life all over the world. Although East Asian countries were benefitting, promised or expected benefits had not been forthcoming in the industrialized democracies. There we have seen downsizing, restructuring, and, despite increased productivity and exports and rapid technological developments, fewer or poorer-quality jobs and lower incomes and benefits. Even in the U.S., where the end of the 1990s saw reduced unemployment, employees' real incomes and benefits were down.

The authors believed that globalization must avoid being seen as a "brakeless rain" caused by an uncontrolled free market. Global corporations have a responsibility to deal with these serious problems by helping governments set national priorities in areas such as training, education, and fiscal policies that provide incentives for entrepreneurs.

This involves going beyond "traditional concept[s] of economic policy." The authors stressed the urgent need for innovative policies to avoid what could become a serious backlash against the effects of the technological revolution and the globalization of business because these trends cannot be reversed.

Source: Klaus Schwab and Claude Smadja, "Globalization Backlash is Serious," *International Herald Tribune*, February 21, 1996, p. 18; Shawn McCarthy and Heather Scoffield, "Inward-looking U.S. Threatens Canada's Interests, Ministers Fold," *Globe and Mail*, June 30, 1999, p. A4.

major court cases sent brokers to prison and led to some record fines ($100 million in one case) and serious damage to the reputations of some U.S. investment and brokerage houses. A Canadian investment dealer bought 300 copies of this book for its staff so they would learn how *not* to give in to ever-present temptations for the "easy and fast buck."[11] However, it is not just this temptation that leads to crime or unethical behaviour.

HOW GLOBALIZATION AND TECHNOLOGY AFFECT WHITE-COLLAR CRIME It is important to realize that international financial transactions now involve the movement of vast sums of money, 24 hours a day. Time zone differences mean that when our business day ends, it is just starting in the Pacific Rim countries of Asia and vice versa. Advances in technology and the growth of international investment and trade have made around-the-clock transfers of huge amounts of funds, in a variety of currencies, possible.

This has brought many advantages, but has also created a dangerous situation for some large banks, financial houses, and the employees who work in their international departments. Employees have occasionally made errors in judgment, which have resulted in substantial losses for their companies. In certain cases, employees have engaged in transactions beyond their authority or scope in attempts to cover up errors.

The repercussions of doing so can be disastrous. One of the most prominent cases in the early 1990s involved a 27-year-old British currency trader, Nick Leeson, who worked in the Singapore branch of Barings Bank. This 200-year-old bank was one of the most respected private banks in the world. It served as banker to the Queen and other members of the royal family in England. Leeson became involved in the kind of situation described above while trading in Japanese yen. He was soon trading hundreds of millions of dollars worth of yen. The end result was that the huge losses he caused the bank forced Barings to go out of business, and it was taken over by a Dutch company. Leeson served a prison sentence in Singapore.

Unfortunately, this story is not unique. The giant Daiwa Bank of Japan and some other Japanese banks have had similar occurrences with individuals in their American branches, but they have survived. Similar, perhaps smaller, incidents are believed to be happening in many parts of the world, including Canada. These are often hushed up by the companies involved, which do not want to publicize a possible lack of control by senior officers.

••• PRICE FIXING AND BID RIGGING •••

The Competition Act was passed to ensure that the Canadian marketplace remains fair and competitive. This assurance is vital for the health of the free enterprise system. Companies that conspire to get around that law should be curbed. An editorial in the *Financial Times* commended Howard Wetson, director of the Bureau of Competition Policy, for finally applying the law as it was meant to be applied. (The implication is that companies previously engaging in such activities got away with them.)

Canadian Liquid Air Ltd., Union Carbide Canada Ltd., and Liquid Carbonic Inc. pleaded guilty to changes of "conspiracy to fix prices for gases such as oxygen used in hospitals" and were each fined $1.7 million, the largest fines ever imposed under the Act. Canadian Oxygen Ltd. was fined $700,000, and a fifth company, Air Products Canada Ltd., will be charged later.

In a previous case, eight companies were charged with **bid rigging**, a secret agreement among competitors to make artificially high bids, for Third

<www.weforum.org>

The World Economic Forum does much more than hold the annual Davos conference to bring world business and political leaders together to exchange views and ideas. Its regular publication, *World Link Magazine*, is circulated to top business leaders around the world. Visit the WEF Web site and find out about *World Link's* editorial policy. What does its content emphasize?

bid rigging
Secret agreement among competitors to make artificially high bids.

World food-aid contracts. After a probe by the competition bureau, four of them were fined a total of $3.25 million. Three of the firms found guilty are among the largest flour-milling farms in Canada: Robin Hood Multifoods Inc., Maple Leaf Mills ltd., and Ogilvie Flour Mills Ltd. Two other firms later pleaded guilty and received fines proportional to their size. The *Financial Times* editorial condemns this anticompetitive behaviour as being "especially offensive in the sale of medical products or famine aid."[12]

Critical Thinking

Consider the case of the Westray mine explosion discussed previously. Think about all the pressures to open the mine in an area of high unemployment with poor prospects for any new jobs. At the same time, think about the high explosion record in the past. As a government official, what would you have done if you had to decide whether to open? As a company officer? A union official?

··· DRUGS AND PHARMACEUTICALS ···

Newspapers, magazines, and TV programs like *Fifth Estate* on the CBC, and *60 Minutes* and *20/20* in the United States have long reported on faulty products made by pharmaceutical companies that then refuse to take the products off the market. These companies spend many years and hundreds of millions of dollars developing and testing new products to make sure they are safe and effective. Every once in a while they slip up, but they are reluctant to withdraw such products because of the heavy investment in R&D, testing, approval, and marketing. The companies also face many lawsuits and costly settlements from injured users of these products if they admit guilt.

One of the most infamous cases occurred in the 1970s and involved an intrauterine contraceptive device called the Dalkon Shield. This IUD caused severe medial problems, including sterility, for many women. For years the manufacturer, A. H. Robins, denied that there were any problems, but ultimately it was forced to withdraw the product and pay substantial court-awarded damages to these women.

Pharmaceutical companies have spent millions of dollars settling lawsuits alleging negligence in informing the medical community of the potential risks of silicone gel. Baxter Healthcare Corporation, a silicone implant manufacturer, negotiated a settlement worth $22 million in damages.

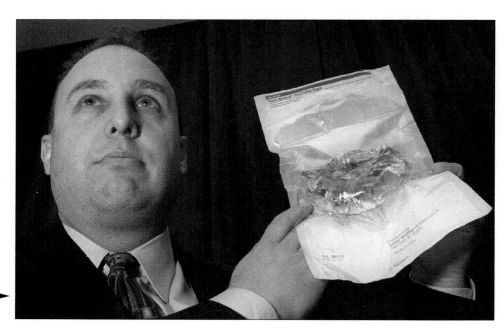

In February 1996 a mini-scandal erupted in the Health Protection Branch (HPB) of Health Canada when a senior federal drug-safety reviewer resigned. Interviewed on the CBC program *Fifth Estate*, February 27, 1996, Dr. Michelle Brill-Edwards claimed that a common drug used to treat high blood pressure, nifedipine, was dangerous. Various studies had found a higher death rate among long-term users of the medication. Two companies were marketing this drug in Canada.

Further, she argued, two Canadian doctors who were part of a committee to review the drug's safety and who supported its usage were not impartial because of certain previous procompany activities. When Brill-Edwards did her own review of HPB files on this matter, she found a 15-year-old memo pointing to potential problems with long-term usage. Brill-Edwards resigned because, despite her efforts to have higher department officials reexamine the safety issue, nothing was done. Two other doctors interviewed on the *Fifth Estate* program also were concerned about the long-term problems.

This long-simmering friction in the HPB broke into public view again in 1998 when various media stories and reports again hit the headlines. Quoting doctor Brill-Edwards and researchers in the Health Protection Branch, the media reported that the whole unit was becoming ineffective and unreliable for a number of reasons. Federal government budget cuts leading to funding by the very companies whose products the HPB has to approve or reject, had destroyed its ability to do this important work impartially. Furthermore, there were reports that senior officials had put pressure on researchers to approve drugs—specifically BGH, bovine growth hormone. This drug, which is given to cattle to stimulate greater milk production, was approved in the U.S. despite much opposition. The HPB has been examining BGH for several years, but has been reluctant to approve it because of many possible negative effects on cattle and on humans.

The issue came to a head with reports that the staff was muzzled—not allowed to speak to anyone about this issue. Because of the intense public interest in possible interference with the normal functioning of the HPB, the Senate set up a special committee to examine both the BGH issue and the situation at HPB. Staff of the branch who were afraid to speak at this parliamentary hearing because of reported threats from their senior officials, demanded and got iron-clad guarantees from the Minister of Health that they would not be penalized for testifying before the committee. The senators on the committee were stunned. They could not believe that this was happening in our democratic country. At the time of this writing, the senate committee had not yet completed its report.

••• ASBESTOS •••

One of the most famous issues in Canada involved asbestos. For many years, Quebec was one of the largest producers of asbestos in the world. Asbestos has the wonderful quality of being completely fireproof, which seemed to make it a perfect product for building materials, firefighters' clothing, and many other uses. Unfortunately, it was learned that the tiny, invisible asbestos fibres adhere to the lungs and cause asbestosis, which is usually fatal. For years the Quebec CSST (workers' compensation board) refused to acknowledge this as a work-related illness despite the very high incidence of asbestosis among workers and their families in the plants and communities in which asbestos was mined and processed. The major companies were American and they fought hard for many years against compensation for workers who died or were laid off due to illness.

Eventually the proof was overwhelming, and by the early 1980s the asbestos industry was almost totally shut down. In the United States, thousands

<www.louisville.edu/ admin/dehs/ hsasbes.htm>

Visit the University of Louisville Web site and look at its article on the health and safety issues surrounding asbestos to learn more.

of lawsuits were launched by workers in various plants in which asbestos was used, including some facilities of the U.S. Navy. There were so many lawsuits that it became an industry in itself. One of the major asbestos companies, Johns-Manville, went into bankruptcy because of all the claims against it. In the meantime, all over Canada, schools and other institutions started tearing out walls, floors, and ceilings that contained asbestos. The total cost in human lives, medical costs, suffering, and building material replacement is incalculable.

CIGARETTES   We finish this section with the story of the cigarette. For many years, doctors and researchers warned about the dangers of cigarette smoking; lung cancer was killing hundreds of thousands of people annually in Canada and the United States. Year in and year out, cigarette manufacturers denied any connection between smoking and cancer. Doctors in white lab coats would appear on TV ads and give their okay for smoking.

It is obvious why the companies refused to yield—cigarettes are the most profitable product made in Canada or the United States. Governments in both countries were also not keen on giving up the revenue from cigarette taxes. In Canada, taxes make up about 80 percent of the price of cigarettes and provide governments with hundreds of millions of dollars annually.

Finally, the accumulating evidence could no longer be ignored. The actual medical and hospital costs of care for those afflicted with lung cancer and related illnesses were contributing to skyrocketing health care costs. Campaigns warned people of the hazards of smoking, advertising was severely restricted in Canada, and taxes were increased to make cigarettes smoking a very expensive habit.

···· ▬▬ ····

PROGRESS IN CORPORATE SOCIAL RESPONSIBILITY

Despite all the ethical problems reviewed so far, the fact is that most large companies are concerned about their public image, and many executives support the notion of companies acting in a socially responsible way. Many companies have established their own department of corporate ethics. This was addressed by a report in *Canadian Business*:

> *David Nitkin, founder of EthicScan Canada Ltd. and publisher of* The Corporate Ethics Monitor *newsletter, keeps tabs on the social and environmental performance of 1500 Canadian companies. He is consultant to many companies and organizations, including such giants as Imperial Oil Co., who want to improve their social performance and image. Until recently he would have been dismissed as a nut.*[13]

··· FORMAL ETHICS CODES ···

These are encouraging signs that Canadian business is making significant changes in its attitudes and practices. Change is always difficult, particularly when it involves additional immediate costs at a time when international competitiveness is forcing Canadian companies to find every possible way to reduce costs. Nevertheless, formal corporate ethics codes are popular these days. Companies without them are scrambling to commit corporate values to paper. Companies that already have codes are rushing to update, distribute, and interpret them.

To be effective, all ethics codes must be enforced and employees must be held responsible for their behaviour. A long-term improvement of business ethics calls for a six-step approach:[14]

1. Top management must adopt and unconditionally support an explicit corporate code of conduct.

2. Employees must understand that expectations for ethical behaviour begin at the top and that senior management expects all employees to act accordingly.

3. Managers and others must be trained to consider the ethical implications of all business decisions.

4. An ethics office must be set up. Phone lines to the office should be established so that employees who don't necessarily want to be seen with an ethics officer can inquire about ethical matters anonymously.

5. Outsiders such as suppliers, subcontractors, distributors, and customers must be told about the ethics program. Often pressure to put aside ethical considerations comes from the outside, and it helps employees resist such pressure when everyone knows what the ethical standards are.

6. The ethics code must be enforced. It's important to back any ethics program with timely action if any rules are broken. That's the best way to communicate to all employees that the code is serious and cannot be broken.

<www.streetweb.nl/csr/>

See the Corporate Social Responsibility Web site. The site acts as an open forum for discussion about relevant issues and has links to other related sites. What is the stated purpose of this Web site? Who established it? When? Do you think Web sites like this perform a useful function? Why?

CORPORATE RESPONSIBILITY IN THE TWENTY-FIRST CENTURY

stakeholders
Those people who can affect or are affected by the achievement of an organization's objectives; they include shareholders, employees, customers, suppliers, distributors, competitors, and the general public.

What should be the guiding philosophy for business in the twenty-first century? For most of the twentieth century, there has been uncertainty regarding the position top managers should take. The question revolves around the treatment of stakeholders. **Stakeholders** are those people who can affect or be affected by the achievement of an organization's objectives; they include shareholders, employees, customers, suppliers, distributors, competitors, and the general public. There are two different views of corporate responsibility to these stakeholders:

1. *The strategic approach.* The strategic approach requires that management's primary orientation be toward the economic interests of shareholders. The rationale is this: as owners, shareholders have the right to expect management to work in their best interests, that is, to optimize profits. Furthermore, Adam Smith's notion of the invisible hand suggests that the maximum social gain is realized when managers attend only to their shareholders' interests.

   For example, IBM's John Akers said that an IBM decision about whether to cease operations in a country would be a business decision: "We are not in business to conduct moral activity; we are not in business to conduct socially responsible action. We are in business to conduct business." The strategic approach encourages managers to consider actions' effects on stakeholders other than owners, but others' interests are secondary. Often those

Children provide cheap labour in some countries. Craig Kielburger has pleaded that Canadian companies comply with moral standards and not let business overshadow concern for human rights. This 10-year-old boy from New Delhi, India, works as a food vendor in a marketplace.

interests are considered only when they would adversely affect profits if ignored.

2. *The pluralist approach.* This approach recognizes the special responsibility of management to optimize profits, but not at the expense of employees, suppliers, and members of the community. This approach recognizes the moral responsibilities of management that apply to all human beings. Managers don't have moral immunity when making managerial decisions. This view says that corporations can maintain their economic viability only when they fulfill their moral responsibilities to society as a whole. When shareholders' interests compete with those of the community, as they often do, managers must decide, using ethical and moral principles.

The guiding philosophy for the twenty-first century will be some version of the pluralist approach. Managerial decision making won't be easy, and new ethical guidelines may have to be drawn. But the process toward such guidelines has been started, and a new era of more responsible and responsive management is beginning. Many corporations are publishing reports that document their net social contribution. To do that, a company must measure its social contributions and subtract its negative social impacts. We'll discuss that process next.

••• SOCIAL AUDITING •••

It's nice to talk about having organizations become more socially responsible. It's also good to see some efforts made toward creating safer products, cleaning up the environment, designing more honest advertising, treating women and minorities fairly, and so forth. But is there any indication that organizations are making social responsiveness an integral part of top management's decision making? The answer is yes, and the term that represents that effort is *social auditing.*

social audit
A systematic evaluation of an organization's progress toward implementing programs that are socially responsible and responsive.

A **social audit** is a systematic evaluation of an organization's progress toward implementing programs that are socially responsible and responsive. One of the more difficult problems with social auditing is how to define *socially responsible* and *responsive.* Is it being socially responsible to delay putting in the latest technology (e.g., robots and computers) to save jobs, even if that makes the firm less competitive? Hundreds of such questions make the design of social audits difficult. Another major problem is establishing procedures for measuring a firm's activities and their effects on society. What should be measured? Figure 5.1 outlines business activities that could be considered socially responsible.

There's some question as to whether positive actions should be added and then negative effects (e.g., pollution or layoffs) subtracted to get a net social contribution. Or should just positive actions be recorded? In general, social auditing has become a concern of business. It's becoming one of the aspects of corporate success that business evaluates, measures, and develops.

•••• ━━━━ ••••

THE IMPACT OF ENVIRONMENTAL ISSUES ON BUSINESS

The modern concern with environmental issues traces its beginnings to a famous book, *Silent Spring,* written by U.S. government biologist Rachel Carson in the early 1960s. She had noticed that for several years she had not

- Community-related activities such as participating in local fundraising campaigns, donating executive time to various nonprofit organizations (including local government), and participating in urban planning and development.
- Employee-related activities such as equal opportunity programs, flextime, improved benefits, job enrichment, job safety, and employee development programs. (You'll learn more about these activities in Chapters 13 and 14.)
- Political activities such as taking a position on issues like nuclear safety, gun control, pollution control, and consumer protection; and working more closely with local, provincial, and federal government officials.
- Support for higher education, the arts, and other nonprofit social agencies.
- Consumer activities such as product safety, honest advertising, prompt complaint handling, honest pricing policies, and extensive consumer education programs.

FIGURE **5.1**

. . . .

SOCIALLY RESPONSIBLE BUSINESS ACTIVITIES

A wide variety of activities fall under this heading.

heard many birds singing in spring. That led to the discovery that DDT, a widely used domestic and commercial pesticide, was a deadly poison that was affecting all wildlife and humans as well. That was the beginning of the serious investigation of how modern technology was affecting our environment.

Nearly everyone is now aware that the physical environment of the Earth has been seriously damaged by various activities of human beings. Scientists over a broad range of studies—ecology, genetics, meteorology, botany, chemistry, zoology—warn us about the serious threats that require prompt action if we are to continue living on this planet. Many international conferences have been held on this topic. Perhaps the most important took place in Brazil in 1992. It was called the United Nations Conference on the Environment and Development (UNCED). See Reaching Beyond Our Borders on page 147 for the story. Its chairman was Canadian Maurice Strong, who has been an important international figure for many years.

In 1972 Strong chaired the Stockholm Conference on the Human Environment, the first international conference to put the *green* agenda on the international stage. "We've all lost our innocence," said Strong. "I don't think we can wait another 20 years. The Earth has cancer. In the early stages, the symptoms are minimal, but by the time they become acute it's too late.[15]

Twenty-five years later, in 1997, an important international environmental conference took place in Kyoto, Japan. This meeting resulted in the Kyoto Protocol whereby many of the nations of the world agreed on a timetable to cut back on the production of greenhouse emissions to the levels of 1990. Unfortunately even that first step is in doubt. Follow-up summits at Buenos Aires and Bonn, aimed at "finding ways to implement the emission-reduction targets" are keeping the treaty signed by 80 nations alive, but no real progress is expected until another meeting in The Hague in 2000 or 2001. There is still strong opposition from American oil companies, some U.S. senators, and OPEC members. It is really up to the United States, Canada, and other leading industrial countries that produce most of the climate-warming emissions to bite the bullet and start reducing them. Our Parliament passed a bill in June 1999 that was supposed to give effect to Canada's commitment at Kyoto, but there were criticisms from many sources that the bill had been so watered-down that it would do little to reduce our greenhouse emissions.[16]

••• TRADE AND ENVIRONMENTAL ISSUES •••

Former U.S. trade representative Carla Hill, who negotiated all trade matters for her country during much of the 1980s, has said, "I do think that [environ-

The Sierra Club of British Columbia (SCBC) began its work in 1969 in support of efforts to protect the famous West Coast Trail. SCBC's campaign tactics include public education and awareness raising with the goal of minimizing the destructive effects that logging, mining, and other developments have on the environment.

<www.sierraclub.ca/bc>

A visit to the B.C. Sierra Club Web site will tell you more about the issues associated with the environmental impact of harvesting practices in the B.C. forestry industry.

mental] issues are going to intersect more and more with trade in this decade, and that we're going to have to analyze them and come up with a multilateral way of dealing with them."[17]

The Sierra Club is a major environmental group in the United States and Canada. Its chairman, J. Michael McCloskey, criticized Arthur Dunkel, then director general of GATT, as a glaring example of narrow economic thinking. Dunkel said nations can no longer play a role as environmental leaders. He also insisted that agreements concerning ozone depletion, international waste, and endangered species are "possible sources of conflict with the GATT rules." We can see that Dunkel has a different point of view from Hill's. McCloskey went on to state that

The Sierra Club is not opposed to expanded trade but it is opposed to policy that suggests that trade is free of costs to society. Trade agreements can and should become important tools for a more comprehensive form of development, not just narrow economic growth.[18]

••• THE FORESTRY INDUSTRY •••

One of the most serious environmental hazards is created by the giant pulp and paper industry, which may be the largest employer in Canada. From British Columbia to Newfoundland, they spew their deadly wastes into our rivers, lakes, and ocean bays, causing incredible problems: drinking water is contaminated; aboriginals die from eating mercury-poisoned fish; the population at large is warned not to eat fish often; the rare white beluga whales in the St. Lawrence are dying off, so contaminated that their bodies are handled as highly toxic waste.

Unfortunately, according to some reports, mercury pollution has worsened. The *Montreal Gazette* carried a report from the *New York Times*:

Two decades after the government thought that the problem had been put to rest, mercury is accumulating in fish in thousands of lakes across the United States and Canada, poisoning wildlife and threatening human health. Twenty U.S. states have warned people to limit or eliminate from their diets fish they catch in certain lakes because of dangerous levels of mercury.

Canadian scientists have found elevated levels of mercury in fish caught in 95 percent of lakes they tested in Ontario. (In Ontario and Quebec, the pulp and paper industry is a major contributor to the problem.) Scientists say the principal source of contamination [in the United States] is rain containing traces of mercury from coal-burning power plants, municipal incinerators, and smelters. Other contamination comes from lake and ocean sediments previously polluted by mercury.[19]

Some steps have been taken to improve the situation. Companies have shortened the bleaching process to avoid the use of chlorine. More paper is recycled—we have become familiar with brown envelopes and other recycled paper products. The companies have begun to clean up their operations and waste problems. There are also hopeful signs in new technology emerging to deal with pulp mill sludge.

GOOD NEWS FROM THE PULP AND PAPER INDUSTRY   In 1992 the Alberta Newsprint Co. reported that a $2 million pilot project on the use of effluent sludge as a soil conditioner was showing very good results. By 1996 the results were even more encouraging. Technical director Gary Smith reported that, working closely with the Alberta Research Council and Olds College, the project was continuing to show excellent promise. A group of farmers and greenhouses found that the conditioned sludge was very good for the soil and the crops being produced. For example, canola yields had improved considerably. There was now a waiting list for the company's processed effluent.

Smith pointed out that the effluent combined well with peat moss to produce an improved product. He was also pleased to note the whole process provided a useful illustration of conservation, efficiency, and profitability. Wood chips are being recycled into the raw material required to produce newsprint. The effluent is then recycled into agricultural nutrients in combination with peat moss, thus reducing the amount of peat moss used, and peat moss is a nonrenewable resource.

Alberta Newsprint is looking at a whole new market for what was formerly a waste product that was costly to dispose of. The company was getting inquiries from potential users who were now importing similar material from Oregon. Furthermore, Alberta Newsprint was even investigating the possibility of a joint venture with a horticultural company to take charge of the entire output.

In Montreal, the chairman of the Canadian Pulp and Paper Association (CPPA) stated that by the end of 1992, 15 mills would be producing recycled newsprint from de-inked paper. In 1998 director of recycling, David Church, reported that 22 such mills were on stream. Church indicated that the industry faced many complex problems in its attempts to recycle and to reduce pollution. The cyclical nature of the industry, with sharp ups and downs, and the wide variety of products, which results in a variety of different effluent wastes, compound the difficulties and make solutions slow and costly. Church indicated that despite these problems and the extreme competitive pressures from international markets, the industry continues to develop new technology leading to new methods of reducing pollution.

More good news concerns the multi-pronged effort by the industry on a number of important environment issues. The CPPA reports that the recovery rate of recyclable paper doubled from 1988 to 1997. In addition there has been a steady reduction in toxic wastes, with projections that by 2000 this will be less than one-third of 1993 output. There are similar reductions in water usage in processing, of suspended solids and organochlorides in effluent, in biochemical oxygen demand of effluent, fossil fuel usage, and perhaps even more important, in use of elemental chlorine in bleaching, and in the almost complete elimination of deadly dioxins and furans (see Figure 5.2). Achieving these and other beneficial results for our water and air quality has required that the industry invest many billions of dollars.[20]

Another piece of good news is that in 1993, "22 organizations representing virtually all aspects of the Canadian forest products industry" from coast to coast formed the Canadian Sustainable Forestry Certification Coalition. The aim is to develop a national sustainable forest management system under standards developed by the Canadian Standards Association (CSA). The CSA is an organization accredited by a government agency, the Standards Council of Canada, which coordinates the national standards system.[21]

There is no doubt that the pressure on the forestry companies to make all of these improvements came from a variety of sources: regulations in U.S. cities and in Canada, environmental groups, competitors' activities, the company's feelings of social responsibility and awareness that some of these changes will ultimately reduce their costs. Regardless of the reasons, the results

<www.
newforestsproject.com>

Closely aligned to the pollution issues associated with the pulp and paper business is the deforestation issue on a global scale. For the past two decades there has been a growing level of alarm and concern regarding the rate of forest clearing being carried out. The New Forests Project, based in Washington, DC, is a demonstration of this concern and an attempt to respond positively through encouraging the development of reforestation projects.

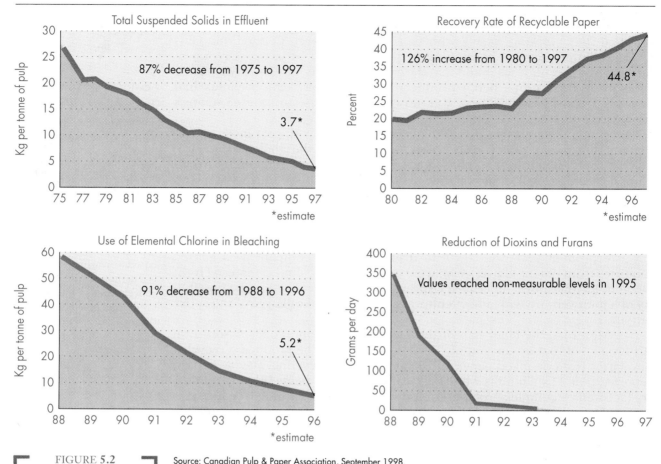

FIGURE **5.2**

· · · ·

**SIGNIFICANT
IMPROVEMENTS IN
PULP AND PAPER
PROCESSING AND WASTE**
Four examples of
where the industry is
reducing its damage to
the environment.

Source: Canadian Pulp & Paper Association, September 1998.

are good news for all Canadians. You should also remember that this industry
is one of the largest in Canada and provides employment for more than one
million people directly and indirectly. Their actions have a lot of impact.

OTHER PROBLEMS   The forestry industry, especially in B.C., has run into
serious criticism for its rapid depletion of Canada's first-growth forests, which
are irreplaceable. A major battle has been fought for some years by aboriginal
peoples and environmentalists to save the huge trees that are hundreds of
years old in the Carmanah Valley and Clayoquot Sound in B.C.

This problem does not lend itself to a quick fix. Many large lumber companies, numerous sawmills, and thousands of employees work in this industry. Stopping logging operations completely means disaster for the sawmill
operators, many of them carrying on family operations that have run for generations. The same scenario looms over the employees engaged in the various
components of this industry. What would they do if logging stopped in various
areas of B.C.? What would it mean for the local economies? These kinds of
problems must be solved soon.

••• WORLDWIDE DEFORESTATION •••

Vast deforestation has been taking place in Brazil, Borneo, Indonesia, and
elsewhere in the world. Deforestation leads to soil erosion, since the treeless

Reaching Beyond
Our Borders

<www.un.org>

UN Conference on the Environment and Development

After three years of painstaking planning, negotiations, and organizing, the most ambitious conference in history on environmental issues took place in June 1992 in Rio de Janeiro, Brazil. The United Nations brought together 160 nations in a massive effort to achieve a breakthrough on proposals to improve the world's environment. The leaders of more than 100 countries attended. The conference was chaired by Maurice Strong of Canada, who said, "Rio will produce more than any other UN conference in history. If Rio does not succeed, it will be the greatest breakdown of all time for the international community and perhaps the beginning of a rich–poor war."

The conference goal was to "find a way to bridge that divide between wealth and nature, growth and conservation, developed and developing. Summit supporters hoped they would steer the world in a new direction, one in which the rich North would consume less while the poor South will produce more."

Strong noted that UN members approved 98 percent of Agenda 21, a comprehensive 800-page document that outlined how in the next century the world could clean and save its environment. Agenda 21 deals with almost every environmental issue from overpopulation to overfishing.

The problems this conference faced were staggering. Huge sums of money are required if the goals are to be achieved. The rich, developed North says to the poor, underdeveloped South: Stop cutting down your tropical forests, stop burning so much coal. You are adding substantially to the greenhouse effect and reducing the Earth's ability to absorb carbon dioxide. Malaysia answers: we need space for agriculture for our growing population and we need the money from the sale of our timber. And China says: we cannot afford to convert our 750,000 coal-burning industrial boilers to cleaner methods. Furthermore, they all say: you rich Northerners consume too much energy, aggravating the greenhouse effect. You will have to finance us if you want us not to do what we are now doing and what you yourself have done previously.

Strong and others called for a starting fund of US$10 billion of new green funds for developing countries. Negotiators for most Northern countries said $3 billion was more likely but even this amount had not been raised by 1999. Subsequent annual conferences in Geneva 1996, Bonn 1997, and Kyoto 1997–98, showed that progress was very slow. Many Canadian press reports and editorials were critical of governments for moving so slowly on this important question.

Sources: UN press releases, 1996, 1998, 1999; John Stackhouse, "Canadian on Mission to Save This Planet," *Globe and Mail*, May 2, 1992, p. A1.

soil cannot retain water; silting up of rivers downstream; fewer trees producing less oxygen for a growing world population and absorbing less carbon dioxide; and logs sinking in rivers and lakes, giving off gases as they decay, which adds to the warming of the atmosphere. The solutions are not easy, since many people are trying to survive by clearing forests to farm, raise cattle, or simply earn a living working for logging companies. Tree-planting programs are a partial solution.

••• PESTICIDES AND AGRICULTURE •••

A major problem in agriculture is the very extensive, and intensive, use of pesticides and fertilizer as a regular process. David Suzuki, the prominent Canadian geneticist, broadcaster, and writer on environmental issues, pointed out that after almost a half-century of spraying, not a single insect species has been killed off. Instead, new spray-resistant varieties appear, requiring new

Every year MacMillan Bloedel plants approximately seven million seedlings on land it harvests. Ninety percent of all its working area of the forest are restocked within three years of harvest, either through replanting or natural regeneration.

and more powerful insecticides, in a never-ending vicious circle. Farmers are locked into ever-rising costs just to stand still in their endless battle against insects.

They also face rising personal health hazards from these chemicals. The CBC reported that farmers in Alberta were warned not to wear baseball caps during spraying operations. When they perspire, the chemicals absorbed by the hats leach into their scalps, causing a variety of side effects, including vomitting, nausea, and other hazards.[22] Further, the run-off into rivers and lakes causes an accumulation of metals and algae. Fed by fertilizer nutrients, the algae bloom so profusely that they consume all the oxygen, causing fish and all other living matter to die. The algae then produce toxins as they die off.

A significant movement toward chemical-free **organic farming** has developed across Canada, as in other parts of the world. The change is slow, complex, and costly. Organic farming is still a small percentage of total agricultural production. Federal and provincial departments of agriculture have been slow to support this movement, and some people suspect pressure from the giant companies that produce fertilizers and insecticides. (See the box entitled "The Pesticide Shuffle" on page 157 for other international ramifications of pesticides.)

organic farming
Farming that is done without chemicals.

<www.laidlawenv.com/ 1-about/txtinfo/ abttxt1.htm>

One of the world's leading waste disposal firms is Hamilton-based Laidlaw. See this Web site to learn about one of its operations, called *Safety-Kleen*.

••• SEWAGE WASTE AND AUTO EXHAUSTS •••

In addition to agricultural run-offs and pulp and paper waste, there is waste from sewage plants. Auto exhausts deposits chemicals on the roads and highways that are washed by rain into the seas. A 1978 documentary produced by the New Jersey Network called "Sea under Siege" shows a miles-long algae bloom. The documentary cites dolphins, full of heavy metals and dioxins, that get cancer and other illnesses as their immune systems weaken, and warns of the deadly effect on humans of eating fish and shellfish.

••• AFFECT OF ACCIDENTS AND BANKRUPTCIES •••

When the huge Lavalin conglomerate went bankrupt in Montreal in 1991, nobody knew who was going to pay for the cost of shutting down and cleaning up the petrochemical plant it owned in Montreal. It is fortunate that the

The *Irving Whale* was raised from the bottom of the Gulf of St. Lawrence near Charlottetown. The oil-laden barge was raised to the surface without incident after spending 26 years on the ocean floor.

stranded engineers and employees stayed on without pay to shut down the operation properly to avoid a catastrophe. The provincial government, meaning the taxpayers, was stuck with the cost of the cleanup job.

A more important case that attracted a lot of attention in Canada in 1996 concerned the raising of an oil barge, the *Irving Whale*, that had gone down during a storm in the Gulf of St. Lawrence in 1970. This barge had been leaking its oil cargo and deadly PCBs from its heating system for many years. Residents from adjacent provinces were constantly worried about damage to the fisheries, sea mammals, and other wildlife. There was endless controversy about how to solve this difficult problem, which was threatening to become even more serious as the leaking continued.

There was also the issue of determining who was responsible for this mess and who should, therefore, pay for the very expensive and complex solution, which involved raising the *Irving Wale*. The Irving Oil Company said its barge had sunk in what were then international waters; besides, the company added, it had paid many millions into an oil industry fund that was supposed to take care of such costs. The barge was now in Canadian waters, which further complicated matters. The oil industry fund said the sinking occurred before the fund was set up, therefore, it could not be responsible for the costs.

Finally, after extensive discussions between environmental experts and federal and provincial governments, it was agreed that despite the dangers of breakup and greater leakage, the *Irving Whale* had to be raised. Under the management of the Canadian Coast Guard, an armada of specialized salvage and environment protection ships, equipment, and personnel were assembled in July 1996. Watched by an army of TV and other media people, the very risky and complex job was successfully accomplished and everybody breathed a collective sigh of relief. Only one question remained to be settled: Is the federal government going to have to pick up the tab for the $30 million salvage job? The courts will be deciding that issue.

Contrast this with a case in Alberta involving a bankrupt oil company. A secured lender, who normally can seize the assets securing a loan, was prevented from doing so in this perhaps historic ruling in Canada. The Alberta Energy Resources Conservation Board ruled that the $200,000 cash that was available to the secured lender must be used to cap the company's oil wells to prevent environmental damage.[23]

••• NOT IN MY BACKYARD •••

NIMBY

Not in my backyard, meaning that people don't want waste disposal facilities in their towns, though they agree that such facilities are needed somewhere.

One of the major problems with waste—nuclear, ordinary, or toxic—is that nobody wants it. We seem to want the products or processes that produce waste, but everybody says "not in my backyard" (**NIMBY**) when it comes to disposing of it. All across Canada, any time any level of government proposes setting up some waste storage or disposal facility and hearings are held, the overwhelming response is nearly always NIMBY, regardless of the potential economic benefits or jobs that might flow from erecting and operating the facility. We don't mind if our waste is dumped in other provinces or countries if they will accept it.

Obviously, this attitude is neither rational nor practical and offers no long-term solution to waste disposal. Better ways are gradually being adopted.

Spotlight on Small Business

Potential Environmental Legal Nightmares for Small Business

The potential losses facing business from the mishandling of waste are tremendous. Businesses may require an emission licence, and a conviction for operating without one can bring heavy fines of up to $100,000 a day. Any company that puffs smoke through a stack on the roof—and that includes restaurants, fastfood or otherwise—may already be breaking regulations without knowing it.

Dry-cleaning firms that flush chemicals directly into the sewer system instead of contracting with bona fide waste removal firms may be exposing themselves to heavy fines. The owners or officers of businesses might even find themselves hauled off to jail.

A small firm's truck can swerve to miss a rabbit, flip onto its side, and empty its cargo of toxic material, chemicals, or gasoline into a roadside creek, with resulting financial disaster for the truck's owners. The price for the smallest spill—for instance, toxic waste seeping into the soil from defective storage tanks—will include the cost of cleanup, expert assessment of the damage, legal fees, and fines, and can run up to $100,000 said environmental lawyer Roger Cotton. And that does not

include the large costs of defending against any legal suits brought by any of the surrounding homeowners.

The pressure is on governments to put teeth into environmental regulations. Unfortunately, insurance is not yet available for this type of problem, which means that all companies, large and small, must consult with waste and storage disposal experts to ensure that they are not breaking any laws.

This issue also affects every purchase of land, buildings, or businesses. Banks will not lend for such purchases unless an environmental audit has been made and a clean bill of health issued by a reputable company with expertise in environmental problems. Public accounting and management consulting firms also urge their clients to have these audits performed before considering such acquisitions.

Occasional reports in the media indicate that this issue continues to be a problem.

Sources: Claire Bernstein, "Problem of Waste Storage and Disposal Has Even Small Companies Worried," *Toronto Star*, April 6, 1992, p. D3; interviews with Ms. Bernstein, February 12, 1999, and chartered accountant L. Wolman, January 10, 1999.

Loblaw's, Ontario's largest food retailer, has been putting money into going green. Vice-president Patrick Carson noted that

> *If you want to be successful ... you have to be realistic, and the reality is that we are living in an environment that is deteriorating. If we make money destroying this planet, we'll have to spend even more money going back to repair [it].*[24]

This lesson is slowly being learned by managers, senior officers, and boards of directors. But all the environmental experts are warning us that we will have to move a lost faster if we are to avoid extremely serious problems in the near future. One solution is to do as Bell Canada did—use conservation to reduce the volume of waste—and save substantial dollars in the process.

Progress Check

- What are ethical issues relating to arms sales, pharmaceuticals, forestry, and cigarettes?
- How do companies organize to ensure that decisions are made on an ethical basis? What is the six-step approach?
- Explain the difference between the strategic and the pluralist approaches to corporate responsibility.
- What is a social audit? How does social audit help companies improve their ethical behaviour?
- What is NIMBY?

••• CONSERVATION •••

One effective way to deal with waste is to *use* less, so less waste is created. The amount of packaging per item in supermarkets and elsewhere is being reduced. Furthermore, containers and other packaging are being made biodegradable. Many fastfood restaurants have followed this trend. These measures do not reduce the volume of waste, but it makes it less threatening to the environment.

Conservation has many more beneficial side effects. More fuel-efficient automotive, marine, and airplane engines reduces demand on the Earth's natural resources, and transportation and distribution of fuel oils and gasoline. Fewer marine and truck tankers and storage tanks reduce the risk of accidents and spills. Less fuel burned results in less exhaust gas, reducing the warming of the Earth by the greenhouse effect.

Electricity consumption is being reduced through energy-efficient kitchen appliances, electric motors, and light bulbs, as well as better-insulated buildings and lower room thermostat and hot-water settings. Hydro and power companies are educating themselves and consumers about conservation methods and offering various incentives. These activities avoid the necessity for costly new hydroelectric projects that would flood vast territories, creating various environmental hazards and encroaching on indigenous peoples' lands and rights.

An example of an efficient and environmentally sound operation is the CBC building in Montreal, headquarters of the French network Radio-Canada. According to the chief heating engineer, this 30-year-old building employs heat from the bodies of its inhabitants and heat generated by the lights in the TV studios to provide almost all the heating required—with very rare supplementation by a conventional heating system.[25]

All new buildings are now better insulated and have special window installations that reduce heat loss, an important factor in energy consumption in our cold northern climate.

Environment Canada's Green Lane <www.ec.gc.ca> Web site proposes a variety of suggestions to help reduce smog in our communities. One idea is sustainable transportation, which covers many issues such as promoting the use of public transit, car-pooling, and alternative forms of transportation including bicycling and walking.

The combined energy-efficient operations of equipment, appliances, buildings, and vehicles have an enormous cumulative effect in reducing the emission of gases that contribute to the warming of the planet by the greenhouse effect. They also reduce other environmental damage.

··· OZONE PROBLEMS ···

For some time, scientists have warned that the ozone layers in the upper atmosphere have developed holes or are thinning, posing greater risks of cancer because increased amounts of ultraviolet radiation are getting through from the sun to us. Yet too much ozone in the lower atmosphere causes deadly smog. An impressive analysis based on 15 years of data compiled by NASA satellites and using "a new, more accurate analytical technique" shows that "the increases [in ultraviolet B radiation] are largest in middle and high latitudes where most people live and where there is the majority of agricultural activity."[26] This region includes Canada.

The Globe and Mail, carrying a news item from the well-respected *Christian Science Monitor* of Boston, noted that California (a forerunner on many environmental issues) has established controls on a wide variety of products that contribute to smog. This includes items like dusting aids, nonstick cooking sprays, charcoal lighter fluid, household adhesives, insecticides, and personal fragrance items. Placing smog controls on these items is expected to cut air pollution in California by the equivalent of one million new cars. Personal fragrance products alone release four tons of volatile organic compounds into the air daily in California.[27]

General Motors Corporation is helping to address the problems of endless growth for the environment through its development of electric cars. An electric motor vehicle doesn't require emission testing because it doesn't have any emissions. Also, the car does not require gasoline or oil changes, which means cleaner air. The aluminum structure of the car is also 100 percent recyclable.

The California and British Columbia governments have both passed regulations requiring less- or nonpolluting vehicles to be on their roads. These restrictions are being phased in over a 5- to 10-year period to give auto manufacturers the opportunity to gradually reduce exhaust pollutants and to introduce electric vehicles.[28]

⋯ TECHNOLOGICAL SOLUTIONS ⋯

Some people count on technology as a solution to pollution and other environmental problems. Periodically there are encouraging reports of ingenious ideas that seem to offer some hope. A story in the *Minneapolis–St. Paul Star Tribune* told how engineer Emil Pfender, in his lab at the University of Minnesota, had converted the toxins benzene and acetone into tiny industrial diamonds. He expects to be able to do the same with deadly PCBs as soon as he can solve the problem of handling them safely.[29]

Although such advances in science are important, we are a very long way from being able to convert the vast output of waste, toxic or otherwise, into useful substances. It is far more logical to follow the conservation route and start reducing the vast daily outpouring of such products. Conservation has the added advantage of maintaining our resources and natural environment.

⋯ THE GLOBAL ENVIRONMENT ⋯

The environmental problems we face in Canada are duplicated all over the world. Typical headlines from Canadian and American newspapers read: "Mexico extends restrictions as capital chokes on smog," "Scientists say people, pollution threaten 'rain forests of the ocean,'" "Alps caught in vise between tourism and trucks," "The Sphinx in danger of collapse," and "Why the environment is the issue of our lives."

This small sample indicates the damage caused to the natural environment by the activities of humans. Most of the problems stem from the explosion of population and industrial activities that we are seeing: the Earth cannot sustain that growth without suffering serious damage.

THE PROBLEM OF ENDLESS GROWTH

All countries, including Canada, believe that growth is a desirable goal. We even worship growth. More plants, more offices, more production, more sales, even more population are all considered positive achievements. In Canada, we worry about our population declining because of our low birthrate. Various countries have programs to encourage larger families to increase population. Only China has undertaken a serious long-term campaign to control population growth.

David Suzuki pointed out that it is only in this century that growth has become a normal part of our lives. He quoted University of Colorado physicist Albert Bartlett: "The greatest shortcoming of the human race is our inability to understand the **exponential function**." It is simply the mathematical description of anything that changes steadily in one direction over a given period of time. Suzuki gave some interesting examples of where that leads.

The **rule of 72** says that if you divide the rate of increase of any activity into 72, you get the number of years it takes for the result of that activity to double. If the inflation rate is 6 percent, in 12 years prices will double. This holds true whether it is pollution, population, or use of energy that is growing.

The point is that even a small, steady increase can over time have startling effects in one lifetime. A 5 percent inflation rate over a 72-year life span would result in gas going from 50¢ to $16 a litre, an $8 movie admission to $256, a $1 soda pop to $32, and a $20,000 car to $640,000! If all of this sounds fantastic, just ask your grandparents if they remember 3¢-per-litre gas, 25¢ movies, 5¢ pop, and $800 new cars.

exponential function
The mathematical description of anything that changes steadily in one direction over a given period.

rule of 72
Divide the rate of increase of any activity into 72 to get the number of years it takes for the result of that activity to double.

Suzuki continued:

It's the same with exponential increase in our use of energy, forests, or ocean resources.... Yet we continue to demand more. But everything in the universe, including the universe itself, is finite. Nothing in it can grow exponentially indefinitely.... Stanford ecologist Paul Ehrlich is more blunt. Steady, endless growth, he says, is the creed of cancer cells and mainstream economists, and the inevitable result is the same for both.

If you look at the history of mankind on this planet, it is only in this century that growth has become such an obvious part of life. On a graph of our numbers—use of food, air, water, soil—the curves are virtually flat for 99 percent of our history. They begin to turn up perceptibly only in the past century; and then in our lifetime, through exponential growth, they leap off the page.[30]

Suzuki's point is clearly demonstrated if we look at population growth. William K. Stevens, writing in the *New York Times*, pointed out that it took all of human history for the world population to reach 2.5 billion in 1950. But it took only 40 more years for that number to double to 5 billion in 1990. If this exponential growth rate of 1.75 percent continues, the population will double again to 10 billion people by the year 2030.

Stevens quoted from *Beyond the Limits* by Meadows, Meadows, and Raders. Their updated computer simulations indicate that

If human activity continues as at present, it will "overshoot" the carrying capacity of the biosphere and precipitate a collapse within the next few decades.... The new analysis puts more emphasis on the deterioration of the biosphere, says Dennis Meadows. He notes that "Twenty years ago it seemed to us that there was a period out to 2030 or 2040 in which to fashion a sustainable society." Now, he says, it looks as though if a new set of attitudes and policies is not in place in the next 20 years [2012], it will be too late to avoid an eventual collapse.

This same article carried a report from an important business consulting group that denied that there is anything to worry about for the next 100 to 150 years because the market system has repeatedly stretched the so-called finite limits of the Earth to become "roughly infinite." But researchers in these fields disagree with this optimistic assessment. They see population and emission increases leading to drastic climate and other changes in the biosphere because of overloading.[31]

In Chapter 9 you will find reference to an important book on this question: *Small Is Beautiful* by E. F. Schumacher. In 1972 Schumacher pointed out the dangers inherent in mindless growth for growth's sake alone. This book is being looked at seriously again because it is so relevant today.

 Critical Thinking

Do you think that environmental concerns are overstated? Even if they are not overstated, technology has always produced ingenious ways of solving many problems. Why not rely on some new process to take care of pollution, the greenhouse effect, the ozone problem, and the rest?

···· ▬ ····

WHAT IS THE ANSWER?

The problem of business and the environment in Canada is quite complicated. An article in the prestigious *Harvard Business Review* by Charles Hampden-

Turner, a senior research fellow at the London Business School and at the Centre for International Business Studies in Amsterdam, addressed the issue globally:

> *Environmental clean-up in the United States has been stalled for a decade by a sterile debate about the "costs" of government regulation to economic competitiveness. In Japan, by contrast, government intervened to encourage the development of antipollution technologies. The result: both cleaner industries and a new generation of companies internationally competitive in the emerging global market for these technologies.* [32]

The difference in attitudes and action between Japanese and American business and governments is clear. Canada has a better track record than the United States, but environmental and community groups generally accuse governments and business of giving mostly lip service to, rather than being genuinely involved in, a serious effort to improve the situation. We also seem to be held back by concerns about the "costs" question and what it will do to our competitiveness.

Here are some interesting examples of what can be done to cut the use of *dirty* fuels. The city of Tokyo has 1.5 million buildings with solar hot-water heating. Germany now produces 3000 megawatts of windpower, while we in Canada produce only 30 megawatts of windpower. In addition Germany created 10,000 new jobs in the windpower industry during the 1990s. Wind is the fastest-growing energy source in the world, with production increasing 25 percent annually during the 1990s, generating some $3 billion in sales in 1998. [33]

The German and Japanese examples are certainly promising ones to follow. In Canada we have also made some technological advances that are helping us export our environmentally friendly expertise.

••• GLOBAL APPLICATION OF CANADIAN TECHNOLOGY •••

Some Canadian companies are already applying their expertise to environmental problems around the world. Some recent examples are:

1. Toronto engineering firm R. V. Anderson Associates Ltd. has an initial $3 million contract to help clean up the sewage system in "one of the world's dirtiest cities," Bombay, India. [34]

2. Spar Aerospace, which built the robotic Canadarm used on American space vehicles, obtained a $22 million contract from the U.S. government to build four robotic backhoes for toxic and other environmental cleanup jobs. [35]

3. Zenon Environmental Inc. of Burlington, Ontario, received a contract from the Egyptian government to provide four membrane-based water purification systems. [36]

4. Scientists at the University of Guelph have developed a genetically engineered pig whose manure contains "very little phosphorus, a water pollutant that promotes the growth of algae" in all waters, thus reducing the amount of oxygen available for fish and other flora. The scientists are also hard at work trying to engineer the reduction of nitrogen, another pollutant in pig waste. Nitrogen is also responsible for the terrible odour in pig manure, which is becoming a serious problem to people living adjacent to pig farms. Going by the trade name *Enviropig*, this is believed to be the first animal engineered to solve an environmental problem. [37]

These are but a few examples of the expertise that can develop when Canadian companies start applying themselves to solving environmental problems.

The mission of the International Institute for Sustainable Development (IISD) is to promote sustainable development in decision making internationally and within Canada. IISD was established in 1990 with continuing financial support from Environment Canada, CIDA, and the Province of Manitoba. IISD also receives revenue from foundations and other private sector sources. The institute is registered as a charitable organization in Canada and a tax-exempt, non-profit corporation in the United States.

<www.iisd1.iisd.ca>

Visit the International Institute for Sustainable Development Web site to learn more about the organization and its work. You might find the Institute's definition of *sustainable development* particularly useful.

··· SUSTAINABLE DEVELOPMENT ···

Another useful input into this difficult area is the concept that emerged from the international conference on the environment in Toronto in 1988. The Brundtland report (named after the Norwegian prime minister who chaired the commission) suggested that sustainable development is the responsible way of the future. Only economic and industrial development that can be sustained over time without damaging the environment should be pursued. Most governments now support this concept in theory, but its implementation is another story. (See Chapter 1 for a more complete discussion of this concept.)

In Canada, we have made a good start by establishing the International Institute for Sustainable Development (IISD), set up jointly by the federal and Manitoba governments and headquartered in Winnipeg. The governments appointed the first three members of the board of directors, who then appointed 12 international members from various countries.

> *IISD is an independent, non-profit corporation, funded by the governments of Manitoba and Canada. Its mission is to promote the concept and practice of development which integrates the needs of the economy and the environment in decision making. The institute undertakes programs and projects internationally and in Canada. IISD is governed by an independent international board of directors.*[38]

Business, governments, and labour, too, are beginning to shift their emphasis from thinking in the short term—profits, jobs, and tax revenues now—to thinking of the long-term effects on the environment. It will take a determined effort from everyone concerned to get decision making moving in the direction of sustainable development, but we have no choice if we want to maintain a habitable world for ourselves and our children.

In past years, steps were taken to improve the environment: catalytic converters on vehicles, reduced gas consumption, banning of spray cans that release ozone-depleting chemicals, elimination of toxins like PCBs, and recycling to reduce waste and tree cutting. However, we have not yet made the really hard decisions that must be made.

Making Ethical Decisions

<www.cropro.org>

The Pesticide Shuffle

An article in the respected weekly, *Science News*, pointed out the complexity, danger, and global ramifications of the global trade in dangerous pesticides. The problems relate to the export of pesticides that are banned in the United States or subject to severe restrictions. Only a small portion of the 250,000 tons of pesticides exported annually from the United States is identifiable. And that portion contains DDT and other dangerous items. It is impossible to get information on the unidentified and much larger portion.

The danger is that users in the countries that receive U.S. products assume that they are safe or the United States would not manufacture or ship them. Labels cannot be read or are ignored, and the results can be disastrous for farmers and other users. Not only that, but after being sprayed, many of these pesticides get into the rivers and lakes or get trapped in trees, soil, and other stable material and then float out into the atmosphere where they may be carried far away, according to chemist Donald Mackay of Trent University in Peterborough, Ontario.

These problems were examined at a Vancouver conference of the Society of Environmental Toxicology and Chemistry in November 1995. It is a complex issue, but according to Mackay, airborne pesticides then find their way into the United States and elsewhere. This may explain pesticides found at nesting sites of albatross in the Midway Islands in the Pacific Ocean and in polar bears and in the breast milk of Arctic Innuit women in northern Canada.

According to Ann McMillan of the Canadian Atmospheric Environment Service in Downsview, Ontario, the data from exporting industrialized countries like the United States are so incomplete that they are like Swiss cheese—full of holes. The data from importing countries, mostly developing nations, are even worse, so it is extremely difficult for the United Nations to come up with a proper control program to curb "the airborne trek of persistent volatile pollutants across national borders."

A UN commission has been working on the problem of persistent organic compounds (POPs) since 1979. POPs include very dangerous toxins such as dioxins, PCBs, DDT, toxaphene, and chlordane. Mackay is very anxious to see a treaty signed, compelling "signatory nations to survey which domestic firms [are] making and using the environmentally damaging compounds." Until this is done it will be impossible to control their release. In the meantime, chemical companies continue to produce and export these products.

How long can we afford to wait for a solution to this serious problem? What should be done now given that U.S. companies are only subject to U.S. laws and treaties?

Source: Janet Raloff, "The Pesticide Shuffle," *Science News*, March 16, 1996, pp. 174–175.

••• SUSTAINABLE CONSUMPTION •••

A concept that complements sustainable development is another UN project called the *United Nations Environment Program (UNEP)*, which works in partnership with the UN Commission on Sustainable development. UNEP "goes beyond 'green' consumption and addresses social and equity issues as well." UNEP urges governments and businesses to use procurement and production to "foster demand for cleaner products and services" with the help of advertising agencies. UNEP has worked closely with government agencies in Germany, Japan, Norway, Holland, Spain, and with the OECD and the European Union in a variety of projects including eco-labelling schemes for developing countries.[39]

••• ISO 14,000 RATINGS •••

In Chapter 10 you will read about how the International Standards Organization (ISO) has developed a widely accepted 9000 series for rating companies all over the world. This rating assures customers of companies with the 9000 rating that quality, delivery, service, and so on will be consistent and reliable. Many companies in Europe and North America will only do business with suppliers who have a 9000 rating. Now the ISO also has a 14,000 designation that it issues to companies that operate in an environmentally friendly fashion. If the 14,000 rating gains as much support as is the case with the 9000 designation, a significant step will have been taken in the direction of a better global physical environment. The Canadian Standards Association (CSA) is the agent in Canada for issuing the 14,000 rating. At the end of the chapter you will see a case of a raspberry-growing operation in Quebec that was the first farm in Canada to receive a 14,000 series approval.[40]

A RADICALLY DIFFERENT ANSWER[41]

Paul Hawken is an American entrepreneur, cofounder of Smith and Hawken, catalogue merchandisers, and author of *The Ecology of Commerce* and *Our Future and the Making of Things*. Both books provide some startling answers for the ethical and environmental issues that we face. Hawken believes that a new approach is required if we are to survive on this planet. He claims that if his suggestions were followed they would

- reduce energy and natural resource use in developed nations by 80 percent within a half-century.
- provider secure, stable, and meaningful employment.
- be a "self-actuating" system rather than one that is regulated or moralistic.
- restore degraded habitats and ecosystems rather than merely sustain them at current levels.
- rely on current levels of solar "income."
- be fun, involving, and aesthetic.

This may give the impression of some utopian dream, but Hawken fleshed out his plan in great detail. He has a 12-point program that proposes a radically different system of government taxation and business operation. Ordinary people will also have to change their way of life.

> *At present, the environmental and social responsibility movements consist of many different initiatives connected primarily by values and beliefs rather than by design. What is needed is a conscious plan to create a sustainable future, including a set of design strategies for people to follow.*

The underlying philosophy of his "design strategies" is that the current systems make destructive commercial and industrial behaviour normal and profitable, and it requires high moral principles to act more responsibly. He would change this around so that irresponsible behaviour would be costly and abnormal, whereas socially responsible activities would be cheaper and yield more profits for companies. Hawken says, "we need a system of commerce and production in which each and every act is inherently sustainable and restorative."

Some major aspects of Hawken's 12-point program include:

1. Adjusting prices to reflect all costs. This includes proper waste disposal, damage to environment and to people's health, and so on.

2. Total revision of taxation philosophy so that instead of taxing jobs, payrolls, creativity, and real income, it is degradation, pollution, and depletion that will be taxed.

3. Transformation of the way we design products so that most things will be recyclable or biodegradable. This will involve drastic reduction or elimination of the hundreds of chemicals, metals, plastics, dyes, and pesticides that are part of so many products. This is already being done to a certain extent in Germany and Japan with autos and other items. These are all part of an elaborate scheme that would totally revolutionize how we now function. Hawken insists that we have no choice because even if "every company on the planet were to adopt the environment and social practices of the best companies ... the world would still be moving towards environmental degradation and collapse." He is not alone in this belief.

As with ethical issues, important changes in thinking and actions by corporate and government management show an acceptance of greater social responsibility. The new generation of managers emerging from business schools has been alerted to these concerns, so the future looks promising. Are we ready for the kind of changes Hawken proposed? Do we have a choice?

···· ▬▬▬ ····

IMPACT ON CAREERS

At the beginning of the chapter you were alerted to the possible impact on your career choices of the information provided here. As you have seen, the issues are complex and not open to simple solutions. However, the scope and depth of environmental and ethical problems have resulted in a whole new field of

Ethical Dilemma

REVIEW

Our executives believe that the growing interdependency of companies and countries through the globalization of business is leading to international standards of behaviour. Bédard believes that "we are in an era of a more level global playing field because of NGOs [nongovernmental organizations] and other such groups. All companies are under the same watchful eyes and in the long run everyone will learn that ethical standards must be maintained no matter where an operation is carried out."

Reilley emphasizes that "company growth and ethical behaviour are not mutually exclusive. A company won't survive in the long run if it's not proactive on these issues. Also more and more world bodies (WTO, NAFTA, OECD, ASEAN, IMF) are demanding ethical behaviour ... in all countries. Things are changing very quickly, which may not be obvious to those not directly involved. Being at the forefront of this activity positions Canadian companies to gain, not the other way around."

studies in an effort to find workable solutions. New career opportunities have opened up devoted to studying the problems, finding answers, and implementing them. Universities and governments have whole departments grappling with environmental issues and thousands of articles and books are constantly being written exploring problems and solutions. Companies and environmental organizations require employees who are knowledgeable about environmental and ethical problems. You might find a career in this area interesting, challenging, and rewarding.

Progress Check

- What is the ozone problem? Why is it so important?
- What is the rule of 72? Why is it useful? Can you give some examples?
- Why is population growth a potential time bomb?

SUMMARY
• • • • •

1. Discuss how business in the early capitalist period ignored ethical standards of behaviour.

1. In the 1800s, laissez-faire capitalism was commonly accepted as good and necessary.
   - ***Why were ethical standards ignored or so low?***
   It was believed that everyone would benefit from unregulated and unrestricted production and wealth accumulation by capitalists. The evils of this new system were tolerated as being unavoidable.

2. Describe the modern beginnings of business ethics, and understand why ethical issues are so important now.

2. Prior to the 1960s, there was little real challenge to the ways companies did business. Then something happened in the United States and a great change occurred in the attitudes of Americans and Canadians.
   - ***What was the role of Ralph Nader in changing company attitudes? What are their expectations now?***
   This young lawyer, working almost alone, took on mighty General Motors because of its defective Corvair model. He finally forced GM to recall cars for the first time in automotive history. Greater social responsibility is now demanded from companies, governments, and their officials.

3. Define management's role in setting ethical standards, and list the six-step approach to ethical decisions.

3. Some managers think ethics are individual issues that have nothing to do with management; others believe ethics have everything to do with management. In practice, it's often difficult to know when a decision is ethical.
   - ***What is management's role in setting ethical standards? How can managers determine if their decisions are ethical?***
   Top managers set formal ethical standards and establish company structures to supervise them, but more important are the messages they send through their actions. Tolerance or intolerance of ethical misconduct influences employees more than any written ethics code. (See the six steps that lead to a practical ethical decision-making system.)

4. Identify what first led to concern about the environment, and list some of the major environmental problems.

4. The change in attitudes regarding the environment started with a book published in the United States in the 1960s.
   - ***What was that book and why did it make such an impact?***
   Silent Spring by Rachel Carson showed how the numbers of birds had declined sharply. The cause was the insecticide DDT, previously used as a cure-all spray. This led to the birth of the modern environmental movement.

   - ***What are the most serious, widespread issues now?***
   Global warming, due to an increase in gases trapped in the atmosphere, is causing the greenhouse effect. Ozone depletion at upper levels and an increase at lower levels are other results of certain gas emissions. Pollution of the air, water, and soil is also causing many serious problems.

5. There are heavy costs attached to cleaning up problems from the past and just as great costs in changing how industries operate in the future.
   * ***How does this affect competitiveness?***
   This concern is that companies that do a good job will incur heavier costs than those that do not clean up their act. These additional costs will result in higher prices than those of "dirty" competitors.

5. Understand why business sees a conflict between a clean environment and competitive ability.

6. The rule of 72 is a mathematical formula.
   * ***What information does it yield and what is the significance of this information?***
   It shows how many years it takes for any steady rate of change to result in a doubling of the results of that change. It is determined by dividing a certain rate of change into 72.

6. Describe the rule of 72, and explain its relationship to growth.

7. Endless uncontrolled growth has led to many of our environmental problems.
   * ***How does sustainable development provide a solution for such problems?***
   Planning only as much growth or expansion as the environment can tolerate without deteriorating is the only way to sustain development over the long term.

7. Explain how sustainable development has become the major international goal for reconciling growth with environmental constraints.

KEY TERMS
• • • • • •

bid rigging 137
corporate social
　responsibility 129
exponential function
　153

laissez-faire
　capitalism 130
NIMBY 150
organic farming 148
robber barons 129

rule of 72 153
social audit 142
stakeholders 141
white-collar crimes
　135

DEVELOPING WORKPLACE SKILLS

1. Do you believe most businesses today are socially responsible? What is your evidence to back up that position?

2. Discuss the merits of increased legislation versus self-regulation by companies to prevent deceptive business practices. Which is better in the long run? Defend your position.

3. How would you describe the ethical environment in Canada today? How important is the role of business in creating that environment? Do you see leadership emerging to improve ethical standards in Canada? What can you do to support such leadership?

4. You are the purchasing manager of a small, wholesale, giftware company. You have been grooming Catherine, a bright employee, for a managerial position in your department, but the owner of the company springs a surprise on you. He informs you that he would like to bring his son, Josh, into the business and his background makes him suitable for the same managerial position. You are afraid if you tell Cathy the truth she will quit because she will not get a promised promotion. What would you do—tell her some story and hope she will stay and some other opening might take place? Would you try to make Josh's life difficult so he will quit or his father will let him go? Is there any other course of action open to you?

1. Check out the Web site of Bombardier <www.bombardier.ca>. Click on *social responsibility* and then on *social commitment* and *environment policy* to see what the company's policy is on these matters. What do you think about these policies? Bring a printout to class for discussion.

2. Examine the Web sites of these two Canadian companies to see what you can learn about the ISO 14,000 rating and approval process in Canada:

   MGMT Alliance Inc: <www.mgmt14k.com>.
   Canadian Environmental Auditing Association: <www.ceaa-acve.ca>.

   Print out anything you find interesting and bring it to class.

Practising Management Decisions

CASE 1
......
THE BATTLE BETWEEN THE CORPORATE GIANT AND THE SASKATCHEWAN FARMER
......

Percy Schmeiser has spent 50 years farming his land near Bruno, Saskatchewan. Now suddenly, Schmeiser is fighting what may be the strangest battle in the history of agriculture. "My grandfather and my father homesteaded here," Schmeiser says. "There were no such things as chemical companies, or even seed companies. They were free and independent." Now Schmeiser has been forced to fight the biggest boy on the block; he's battling the world's largest agrochemical company, Monsanto. Monsanto makes the weedkiller called Roundup. Spray it onto a field and it kills everything growing there. Then Monsanto genetically engineered a canola seed so that Roundup doesn't hurt it. That means a farmer can spray Roundup herbicide over an entire field, kill all the weeds growing there, and not hurt the canola crops, as long as it comes from Monsanto's special seed.

In the brave new world of agriculture, it's Monsanto versus the farmer. Farmers buying Monsanto's seed must sign a contract promising to buy fresh seed every year. Then, they must let Monsanto inspect their fields for cheating. Monsanto's regional director in Western Canada is Randy Christenson. He says the company has to be tough. "We've put years of research into developing this technology so we must recoup our investment," Christenson says.

Percy Schmeiser says he's never used Monsanto's seed. He saves the seeds from his own crops, then replants them in the spring. But Monsanto investigators say they've found Monsanto DNA in Schmeiser's crops. Monsanto says Schmeiser never paid for the rights to use its DNA.

Now they're suing Schmeiser. "I've been farming for 50 years, and all of the sudden I have this," Schmeiser says. "It's very upsetting and nerve wracking to have a multi-giant corporation come after you. I don't have the resources to fight this."

Monsanto doesn't apologize for playing hardball. But the Monsanto representatives insist the whole process is very friendly. Monsanto calls its investigations *audits*. "Yes, we do have a group that does audits, they do make farm visits, but they do it in a way that is extremely respectful to the farmers," Christensen says. He insists that farmers who have been through it are very comfortable with what Monsanto is doing because they never go on their property without farmers' permission.

But court documents show Monsanto ordered its investigators to trespass onto Schmeiser's fields and collect samples. Then Monsanto agents paid a secret visit to the company that processes Schmeiser's seeds for planting and were able to get a sample of the seeds. Monsanto says Schmeiser has stolen its DNA. Monsanto has accused dozens of farmers of growing the special seed without paying for it. The problem is, Mother Nature has been moving DNA around for thousands of years. Monsanto's is just the latest. "It will blow in the wind. You can't control it. You can't just, say, put a fence around it and say that's where it stops. It might end up 10 miles, 20 miles away," Schmeiser says.

Schmeiser is backed by scientists from Agriculture Canada who say wind can blow seeds or pollen between fields, meaning the DNA of crops in one field often mixes with another. Seeds or pollen can also be blown off uncovered trucks and farm equipment. But Monsanto seems to be saying it's up to farmers to dig out any crops from seeds they have not bought from Monsanto. Without a microscope, there's no way to tell regular crops from crops carrying the Monsanto DNA.

This means even the seed that farmers keep from their own crops may contain Monsanto's altered gene. Last year, Edward Zilinski of Micado traded seeds with a farmer from Prince Albert. This is an old farming tradition. But the seeds he got in return had Monsanto's DNA. Now Monsanto says Zilinski and his wife owe them more than $28,000 in penalties. "Farmers should have some rights of their own!" Zilinski says.

Monsanto's heavy hand is sparking the anger of many farmers in Western Canada. The Kram family in Raymore say planes and a helicopter have buzzed their fields. The couple says agents dropped weedkiller on their canola field, to see if the crops had the Monsanto's gene. Monsanto says they had absolutely nothing to do with it. The Krams think otherwise: "We are … disgusted with the way things are going," Elizabeth Kram says "Who put the canola in? It was the farmer. It doesn't belong to Monsanto or anybody else and I don't see anybody else's name on the titles of all the land we own. It's my husband and myself. Nobody else. [We're] thoroughly pissed off."

Percy Schmeiser believes Monsanto hopes to force farmers into accepting genetically engineered products. Schmeiser is standing up to Monsanto in court. "I'm going to fight and fight and fight," he says, "because I believe what is happening to farmers is wrong. And I'm fighting this not just for myself, but for my children and my grandchildren. And for my farmer friends."

"As you move to adopt new technology, whether it was from the horse to the car, there was a great deal of controversy, questions being asked, on how to deal with certain issues,"

Monsanto's Christensen says. But the real question is this, can Monsanto or anybody put a patent on a piece of nature? The answer could determine who controls the future of world farming.

Decision Questions

1. In this case we can see how our technologically driven world creates new ethical dilemmas. Genetic engineering in general has sparked a lot of controversy worldwide because of uncertainty about long-term harmful effects. Here the immediate questions are: should a company have the right to patent new forms of plant or animal life? Can Monsanto carry on its investigations in an acceptable manner? How far should it be allowed to go in enforcing its rights?

2. Assuming that Monsanto discovers its DNA in the fields of a farmer who had not purchased its seeds that year, what should it do? Is it reasonable to expect farmers to dig up crops that may have been affected by wind-blown seeds? Are they supposed to get samples of each stalk and have them examined under a microscope?

3. It is apparent that what we have here is a conflict of rights. Monsanto has been granted certain legal rights by the U.S. Patent Office that are conflicting with the normal rights and freedoms of farmers in Saskatchewan. Whose rights are more important? Can such a distinction really be made?

4. Let's return to the first question about genetic engineering in general. This is a recurring issue in medicine, in biology, and in many other fields. Should we draw a line and not permit technology to go beyond a certain point? How do we determine that point? Who will decide what's ethical?

Source: CBC TV, *The National*, June 8, 1999.

Jocelyne Hamelin and her husband Daniel Couture operate a raspberry farm business, La Framboisère, in the Eastern Townships region of Quebec. For many reasons, it is not your ordinary small farm. First, the farm produces 40 tonnes annually, which is a lot of raspberries. The couple have the largest raspberry farm in Quebec. Second, the couple are em-

┌ **CASE 2** ┐
. . . . . .
TWO CHEERS FOR RASPBERRIES
. . . . . .

barked on a plan to make their operation environmentally friendly. This means reducing pesticide use by 70 percent. The farm also has an underground drip system for irrigation with the result that a pond now irrigates 26 acres instead of 15. This conservation of water is not only good for the environment, but has also increased their production by 50 percent.

Other aspects of an environmentally friendly operation include strict rules on fuel storage, waste management, and recyclable packaging.

As a result of such careful attention to these details of their operations, Hamelin and Couture have achieved an important first—theirs is the first farm in Canada to get the ISO 14,001 designation. ISO stands for *International Standards Organization* and it is a very important body. In Chapter 10 you will see how their 9000 series designation has become the major international seal of approval for the ability of companies to consistently and reliably produce, deliver, and service products of good quality. If you observe company signs in your area you may see displays on buildings of companies proudly showing that they have received an ISO 9001 or 9002 rating.

The ISO 14,000 series rating is for environmentally friendly operations and is a more recent development. Couture says that it is not yet an important marketing tool, but that "American buyers are catching on" and soon consumers will be looking for that approval on labels. As Couture puts it, "so when you eat a raspberry you will know that you are really eating a raspberry and not pesticide."

Other farmers in the area are catching on because "seven other farms producing milk, pork or Christmas trees are working towards [ISO 14,000] certification."

Decision Questions

1. Does the example of La Framboisière mean farmers are not afraid to try something new? Does the fact that other farmers are *catching on* support that belief? Would you be more apt to buy a fruit or vegetable with an ISO 14,000 seal of approval?

2. This case demonstrates that being kind to the environment can result in *decreased* and not *extra* costs of operations. Why then do you think that many companies are reluctant to explore more environmentally friendly alternatives? Do you think that consumer products would enjoy greater popularity if they had an ISO 14,000 rating?

3. How important do you think it is to move more quickly in the direction of reducing damage to the environment? Do we need stricter laws? Or would stricter enforcement of existing regulations do the job?

4. Some people believe that showing by example is more effective than passing stronger laws. How can we encourage more companies to take the lead so that others will follow? Would you be in favour of tax concessions to aid companies *going green*?

Source: CBC News Report, CBM Radio, Montreal, June 13, 1999.

Part 2

Business Ownership and Small Business

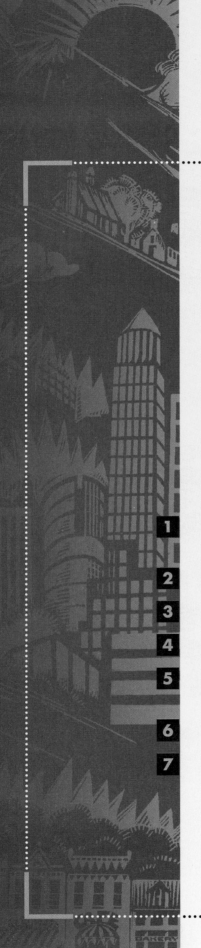

Forms of Business Organization

Chapter 6

LEARNING GOALS

After you have read and studied this chapter, you should be able to

1 list the three basic forms of business ownership and compare the advantages and disadvantages of each.

2 explain the differences between limited and general partners.

3 summarize the important clauses of a partnership agreement.

4 define public and private corporations.

5 compare the advantages and disadvantages of private and public corporations.

6 define franchising and examine its advantages and disadvantages.

7 outline the areas to analyze when evaluating a franchise.

Born in 1907 in Quebec, J. Armand Bombardier was only 15 when he built his first propeller-driven snow vehicles from the wreck of an old Ford. Bombardier's mechanical abilities led him to numerous experiments, resulting in the invention of a revolutionary new sprocket wheel and track system in 1935. In 1937 he started a company to mass produce snowmobiles based on his invention.

Over the next two decades, Bombardier designed numerous all-terrain vehicles. In 1959 he began marketing the first small Ski-Doo snowmobile. Bombardier thus not only solved the problem of individual transportation on snow, but created a new sport. Armand Bombardier died in 1964 without an inkling of the market success his invention was to enjoy.

PROFILE

Armand Bombardier, Founder of Bombardier Inc.

Today Bombardier Inc. is a giant transnational company with production facilities in Canada, the Untied States, Mexico, and eight European countries. It has 42 subsidiaries with activities in all forms of rail transport, aerospace and defence, motorized consumer products, financial services, and real estate development.

Bombardier's company has paid a lot of attention to its social responsibilities by forming the J. Armand Bombardier Foundation. The foundation receives 3 percent of the company's net income before tax and uses these funds to support charitable causes, through student bursaries, donations to educational institutions, and donations to charitable organizations.

Source: *Annual Report*, January 31, 1999, and other documentation from Bombardier Inc.

WHO IS LIABLE?

In this chapter you will read about the different legal structures available to individuals who want to operate a business. For example, two people can set up their business as a partnership or as a corporation in which they are the only shareholders. You will learn that each structure has its advantages and disadvantages and that it is possible to go from one format to another one.

Let's look at the partnership, Travira Wholesalers, Elvira and Trong have been operating for several years, which supplies computer components.

The partners have gotten into a bind and are having difficulty paying their bills. They might have to declare a formal bankruptcy to get out of the mess.

However, as they are not a corporation they will still be personally liable for all the unpaid bills of their company, Travira. Trong suggests that they incorporate Travira, that is, form a corporation that takes over all the assets and liabilities of their partnership and continues to operate the business. Then, he explains to Elvira, if the company goes bankrupt they will not be personally liable for the debts of the company because it is now a corporation.

Do you think it is ethical for Elvira and Trong to try to evade their personal liability in this fashion? We will return to this issue at the end of the chapter after you have had time to absorb the material.

FORMS OF BUSINESS OWNERSHIP

Like Armand Bombardier, tens of thousands of people start new businesses in Canada every year. Chances are you have thought of owning your own business or know someone who has. One key to success in a new business is knowing how to get the resources you need to start. You may need to take on partners or find other ways of obtaining money. To stay in business, you may need help from someone with more expertise than you have in certain areas or you may need to raise more money to expand. How you form your business can make a tremendous difference in your long-run success. The three major forms of business ownership are (1) sole proprietorships, (2) partnerships, and (3) corporations. The advantages and disadvantages of each form are seen in Figure 6.1.

It is easy to start your own business. For example, you can begin a word-processing service out of your home, open a car repair centre, start a new restaurant, or go about meeting other wants and needs of the community on your own. An organization that is owned directly, and usually managed, by one person is called a **sole proprietorship**. That is the most common form of business ownership (more than one million firms).

Many people do not have the money, time, or desire to run a business on their own. They prefer to get together with one or more people to form the business. When two or more people legally agree to become co-owners of a business, the organization is called a **partnership.**

Creating a business that is separate and distinct from its owners has its advantages. A legal entity that has an existence separate from the people who own it is called a **corporation**. Owners hold shares in the corporation. There are about 100,000 corporations in Canada, but they have the largest share of business by far (see Figure 6.2).

As you will learn in this chapter, each form of business ownership has its advantages and disadvantages. It is important to understand these advantages

sole proprietorship
A business that is owned directly, and usually managed, by one person.

partnership
A legal form of business with two or more owners.

corporation
A legal entity with an existence separate from its owners.

Form of Ownership	Advantages	Disadvantages
Sole Proprietorship	Easy to start and end Sole control of company All profits go to owner No restrictions on withdrawal of funds Possible tax advantages	Unlimited (personal) financial liability Ownership not divisible All losses borne by owner No continuity No relief for holidays or sickness Possible tax disadvantages
*Private Corporation	No personal liability Profits are sole property of owner Easy to start and end Owner has sole control Continuity of legal existence Ownership is divisible (up to maximum of 50 shareholders) Possible tax advantages	Funds withdrawal by owner is complex Losses not shared Possible tax disadvantages

Partnership	Not difficult to form but more complex
	    than sole proprietorship
	Responsibilities shared
	Complementary skills
	Partners can help each other
	Greater financial resources than
	    single owner
	Losses shared
	Possible tax advantages
		More difficult to dissolve than sole
		    proprietorship
		Unlimited personal liability of one partner
		    for all partners
		Conflicts between partners
		Lack of continuity
		Profits shared
		Possible tax disadvantages

†Public corporation	Limited liability of shareholders
	Greatest possibility of raising finances
	Unlimited ownership by share issues
	Large size makes possible specialized
	    management skills
		Costly and complex to form
		Many complex regulations
		Conflicts between managers
		Conflicts between managers and
		    shareholders
		High tax rates

* One person or partners can form a private corporation. These are usually smaller companies.

† Any business that contemplates large-scale operations requiring large amounts of capital has no choice but to be set up as a public corporation to raise such financing.

FIGURE **6.1**

• • • •

ADVANTAGES AND
DISADVANTAGES
OF FORMS OF
BUSINESS OWNERSHIP

**WHICH FORM OF
BUSINESS ORGANIZATION
IS MOST COMMON?**

Partnerships (9%) ·············
Corporations (17%) ········

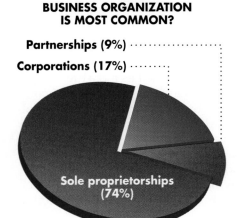

Sole proprietorships
(74%)

**WHICH FORM OF BUSINESS
ORGANIZATION HAS THE
LARGEST SALES VOLUME?**

Partnerships (4%) ······   Proprietorships (9%)

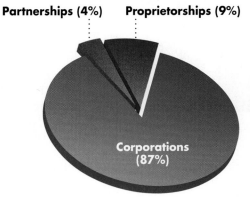

Corporations
(87%)

FIGURE **6.2**

• • • •

FORMS OF BUSINESS
ORGANIZATIONS

Although corporations
make up only 17 percent
of the total *number* of
businesses, they have 87
percent of the sales vol-
ume. Sole proprietor-
ships are the most
common form of owner-
ship (74 percent), but
they have only 9 percent
of sales volume.

Spotlight on Small Business

<strategis.ic.gc.ca/SSG/mi02954e.html>

Selecting an Appropriate Form of Ownership

How does an individual decide on the best form of ownership for a new enterprise? It really depends on several factors. If you are starting a service business, say computer software design, you will not be buying and selling raw material or finished goods, and you will not be incurring major debts. Also, if you are starting small, you do not need much capital. Under these circumstances, the advantage of limited liability the corporate form offers is not very important, because proper insurance can avoid major liabilities that could arise from accidents or from product liability. This means that you can start as a sole proprietorship and avoid the disadvantages of incorporating. The same holds true if two partners start a business. If the business expands and conditions change, you can incorporate later.

If you are starting a manufacturing, wholesale, or retail business, it is a different story. Once you start selling goods, you will be buying on credit and, therefore, accumulating debts. At any one time, the business will normally owe at least one or two months' purchases. There may be a long and expensive lease commitment and perhaps a substantial balance owing for equipment and improvements to the premises. Under these circumstances, it would be prudent to incorporate from the start to avoid the possibility of having to assume personal liability for all these debts.

and disadvantages before starting a business. Keep in mind that just because a business starts in one form of ownership, it doesn't have to stay in that form. Many companies, like Armand Bombardier's, started out as one-person shows, and added a partner or two, and eventually became corporations.

A small business, such as this soda shop, may be set up as a sole proprietorship or a corporation. There are advantages and disadvantages to both forms of ownership.

ADVANTAGES AND DISADVANTAGES OF DIFFERENT FORMS OF OWNERSHIP

Before examining the possible types of ownership of businesses in Canada, it is important to see how the *size* of a business is related to the choice of ownership form and, therefore, to the advantages and disadvantages it will have. This relationship is often not well understood.

··· SMALL BUSINESSES ···

A small business that is owned by one person may be set up as a sole proprietorship or a corporation. Similarly, a small business that is owned by two or more people may be organized as a partnership or a corporation. In each case, the owners have complete freedom to choose the route they wish to follow. Regardless of the choice, a small business has all the advantages and disadvantages of a small-sized operation and also has the advantages and disadvantages of the corporate or noncorporate form selected.

A sole owner has the advantages of having no boss, making all the decisions, not having to share the profits, and having all the pride and satisfaction of ownership and success. But he or she has the disadvantages of not being able to share responsibility or the heavy workload or losses and financing needs. These conditions exist *whether or not the business is incorporated*.

When two or more persons form a small-business partnership or corporation, the workload, decision making, losses, and financial responsibility are shared. But there may be differences of opinion and conflicts, profits must be shared, and it is complicated if one owner dies or wants to leave. Again, this holds true whether or not the business is incorporated.

··· LARGE BUSINESSES ···

When it comes to big businesses, the situation is quite different. As you will later see, all large companies must adopt the corporate form of ownership. These companies regularly require substantial investing or borrowing from the public and this can only be done in the corporate form. In addition, the large number of owners (shareholders) means that the limited liability feature of corporations is also necessary. So, while small-business owners have a choice of form of ownership, large companies really have no such choice. Some of Canada's largest corporations are shown in Figure 6.3.

Various publications regularly compile lists of Canada's largest 50, 500, or 1000 companies; all are corporations. Figure 6.4 is a list of some of the criteria used to measure the largest companies in Canada.

COMPANY	SALES ($ BILLIONS)	ASSETS ($ BILLIONS)	EMPLOYEES (000s)
General Motors of Canada Ltd.	32	n/a	n/a
BCE Inc.	33	33	58
Ford Motor Co. of Canada Ltd.	28	10	n/a
Northern Telecom Ltd.	26	29	75
Seagram Co. Ltd.	11	22	25
Chrysler Canada Ltd.	20	n/a	n/a
TransCanada PipeLines Ltd.	17	26	3
George Weston Ltd.	15	9	118
Thomson Corp.	6	12	39
Onex Corp.	9	7	53
Alcan Aluminium Ltd.	8	10	39
Imperial Oil Ltd.	8	9	7
Loblaw Cos. Ltd.	13	7	113

FIGURE **6.3**

LARGE CANADIAN CORPORATIONS

These are some of Canada's largest non-financial companies.

Sources: Performance 2000, *Canadian Business*, June 25/July 9, 1999; The Top 1000, *Globe and Mail, Report on Business*, July 1999.
n/a: not available.

FIGURE **6.4**

• • • •

CRITERIA USED TO MEASURE LARGE CANADIAN COMPANIES

This figure illustrates different ways of determining which Canadian companies are the largest or most important.

Number of employees: George Weston Ltd.	118,000
Sales: General Motors of Canada Ltd.	$ 34.0 billion
Assets: Nonfinancial: Imasco Ltd	$ 50.0 billion
Financial companies: CIBC	$281.0 billion
Profits: BCE Inc.	$ 4.6 billion

Source: The Top 1000, *Globe and Mail, Report on Business,* July 1999, pp. 129, 140.

SOLE PROPRIETORSHIPS

••• ADVANTAGES OF SOLE PROPRIETORSHIPS •••

There must be some major advantages to being a sole proprietor. After all, hundreds of thousands of people in Canada have formed this kind of business. Sole proprietorships are the easiest kind of businesses to explore in your quest for an interesting career. Every town has some sole proprietorships that you can visit. There's the local produce stand, the beauty shop, the auto repair garage, and the accountant. If you look closely, you'll find sole proprietors who do income taxes, repair appliances and television sets, and provide all kinds of local services. (Ascertain that they are not corporations.) Talk with them about the joys and frustrations of being on their own. Most people will mention the benefits of being their own boss and setting their own hours. They may also mention the following advantages:

1. *Ease of starting and ending the business.* All you have to do to start a sole proprietorship is buy the needed equipment (for example, a saw, a computer, a tractor, a lawnmower) and put up some announcements saying you are in business. It is just as easy to get out of business; you simply stop. There is no one to consult or to disagree with about such decisions. You may have to get a permit or licence from the government to start, but that is usually no problem. Such businesses can start small and grow rapidly.

2. *Being your own boss.* "Working for others simply does not have the same excitement as working for yourself." That's the way sole proprietors feel. You may make mistakes, but they are *your* mistakes—and so are the many small victories each day.

3. *Pride of ownership.* People who own and manage their own businesses are rightfully proud of their work. They deserve all the credit for taking the risks and providing needed goods or services.

4. *Retention of profit.* Other than the joy of being your own boss, there is nothing like the pleasure of knowing that there is no limit to how much money you can make and you do not have to share that money with anyone else (except the government, in taxes). People are often willing to start working early in the day and stay late because the money they earn is theirs to keep.

For these and other reasons, there are more sole proprietorships than any other kind of business in Canada. Tens of thousands of new businesses are formed every year. Most of these are very small companies, so the total amount of business they do is a fraction of the total business done by a much smaller number of very large corporations. And thousands of small businesses fail. Many people dream of owning their own business, but there are also disadvantages to sole proprietorships.

··· DISADVANTAGES OF SOLE PROPRIETORSHIPS ···

Not everyone is cut out to be a sole owner and manager of a business. It is difficult to save enough money to start a business *and* keep it going. Often the cost of inventory, supplies, insurance, advertising, rent, utilities, and other expenses are simply too much to cover alone. There are other disadvantages:

1. *Unlimited liability—the risk of losses.* When you work for others, it is their problem if the business is not profitable. When you have your own sole proprietorship, you and the business are considered one. The businesses is not a legal entity distinct from the owner; therefore, you have **unlimited liability**. Any debts or damages incurred by the business are *your* personal debts and *you* must pay them, even if it means selling your home, your car, and so forth. This is the most serious disadvantage of a sole proprietorship. It requires careful thought and discussion with a lawyer and an accountant.

   unlimited liability
   The responsibility of a business owner for all of the debts of the business, making the personal assets of the owner vulnerable to claims against the business.

2. *Limited financial resources.* Funds available to the business are limited to the funds that the one (sole) owner can gather. Since there are serious limits to how much one person can do, partnerships and corporations have a greater probability of recruiting the needed financial backing to start a business.

3. *Overwhelming time commitment.* It is hard to own a business, manage it, train people, and have time for anything else in life. The owner must spend long hours working. The owner of a store, for example, may put in 12 hours a day, six or seven days a week. That is almost twice the hours worked by an employee, who may make more money.

4. *Few fringe benefits.* If you are your own boss, you lose many of the fringe benefits that come with working for others. For example, you have no disability insurance, no sick leave, no vacation pay, and so on.

5. *Limited growth.* If the owner becomes incapacitated, the business often comes to a standstill. Since a sole proprietorship relies on its owner for most of its funding, expansion is often slow. This is one reason many individuals seek partners to assist in a business.

6. *Limited life span.* If the sole proprietor dies, the business ceases to exist legally. Practically, unless arrangements have been made to pass the ownership and management on to others, the business ends.

Talk with a few small-business owners about the problems they have faced. They know more about the situation in your area than anyone else does. They are likely to have many interesting stories to tell about problems getting loans from the bank, problems with theft, and problems simply keeping up with the business. These problems are the reason that many sole proprietors discourage their children from following in their footsteps, although many would have it no other way. These problems are also the reasons why many sole proprietors choose to find partners to share the load. Remember, though, partnerships have disadvantages, too.

Critical Thinking

Have you ever dreamed of opening your own business? If you did, what would it be? What talent or skills do you have that you could use?

Could you start a business in your home? About how much would it cost to start? Could you begin part-time while you worked elsewhere?

What could you get from owning your own business in the way of satisfaction and profit? What would you lose?

Many of the disadvantages of owning your own business are taken care of when you find a business partner. When one partner is not there, the other can take over.

PARTNERSHIPS

A partnership is a legal form of business with two or more owners. It is not difficult to form a partnership, but it is wise to get the counsel of a lawyer experienced with such agreements. Lawyers' services are expensive, so would-be partners should reach some basic agreements before calling in a lawyer. It is often easier to *form* a partnership than to operate or end one, and many friendships have ended in partnerships.

••• ADVANTAGES OF PARTNERSHIPS •••

There are many advantages of having one or more partners in a business. Often, it is much easier to own and manage a business with one or more partners. Your partner can cover for you when you are sick or go on vacation. Your partner may be skilled at inventory-keeping, accounting, and finance, whereas you do the selling or servicing. A partner can also provide additional money, support, and expertise. Enjoying the advantages of partnerships today, more than ever before, are doctors, lawyers, dentists, and other professionals. They have learned that it is easier to take vacations, stay home when they are sick, or relax a little when there are others available to help take care of clients. With some care, partnerships can have the following advantages:

limited partner
Owner who invests money in the business, but does not have any management responsibility or liability for losses beyond the investment.

limited liability
The responsibility of a business's owners for losses only up to the amount they invest; limited partners have limited liability.

1. *More financial resources.* Naturally, when two or more people pool their money and credit, it is easier to have enough cash to start and to pay the rent, utilities, and other bills incurred by a business. A concept called limited partnership is specially designed to help raise capital (money). A **limited partner** invests money in the business, but cannot legally have any management responsibility and has limited liability. **Limited liability** means that limited partners are not responsible for the debts of the business. Their personal property is *not* at risk. The worst that can happen is that they will lose their investment.

2. *Shared management.* It is simply much easier to manage the day-to-day activities of a business with carefully chosen partners. Partners give each other free time from the business and provide different skills and perspectives. Many people find that the best partner is a spouse. That is why you see so many husband and wife teams managing restaurants, service shops, and other businesses.

••• DISADVANTAGES OF PARTNERSHIPS •••

Any time two people must agree on anything, there is the possibility of conflict and tension. Partnerships have caused splits among families, friends, and marriages. Other disadvantages are:

1. *Unlimited liability.* Each general partner is liable for all the debts of the firm, no matter who was responsible for causing those debts. Like a sole proprietor, partners can lose their homes, cars, and everything else they own if the business cannot pay its debts. Such a risk is very serious and should be discussed with a lawyer and an insurance expert. A **general partner**, then, is an owner (partner) who has unlimited liability and is active in managing the firm. As with sole proprietorships, this is the most serious disadvantage of partnerships. (As mentioned earlier, a limited partner risks an investment in the firm, but is not liable for the business's losses beyond that investment and cannot legally help to manage the company.)

2. *Division of profits.* Sharing the risk means sharing the profit, and that can cause conflicts. For example, two people form a partnership: one puts in more money and the other puts in more hours. Each may later feel justified in asking for a bigger share of the profits. Imagine the resulting conflicts.

3. *Disagreements among partners.* Disagreements over money are just one example of potential conflict in a partnership. Who has final authority over employees? Who hires and fires them? Who works what hours? What if one partner wants to buy expensive equipment for the firm and the other partner disagrees? Potential conflicts are many. Because of such problems, all terms of partnership should be spelled out in writing to protect all parties and to minimize future misunderstandings.

4. *Difficult to terminate.* Once you have committed yourself to a partnership, it is not easy to get out of it. Questions about who gets what and what happens next are often very difficult to solve when the business is closed. Surprisingly, law firms often have faulty partnership agreements and find that breaking up is hard to do. How do you get rid of a partner you don't like? It is best to decide that up front, in the partnership agreement (discussed on the next page).

Again, the best way to learn about the advantages and disadvantages of partnerships is to interview several people who have experience with such agreements. They will give you additional insights and hints on how to avoid problems.

••• CATEGORIES OF PARTNERS •••

Several types of partners can be involved in a partnership. The most common types are the following:

- *Silent partners* take no active role in managing a partnership, but their identities and involvement are known to the public.
- *Secret partners* take an active role in managing a partnership, but their identities as partners are unknown to the public.
- *Nominal partners* are not actually involved in a partnership, but lend their names to it for public relations purposes.
- *Dormant partners* are neither active in managing a partnership nor know to the public.
- *Senior partners* assume major management roles due to their experience, long tenure, or amount of investment in the partnership. They normally receive large shares of the partnership's profits.

general partner
An owner (partner) who has unlimited liability and is active in managing the firm.

- *Junior partners* generally have less tenure, assume a limited role in the partnership's management, and receive a smaller share of the partnership's profit.

••• HOW TO FORM A PARTNERSHIP •••

The first step in forming a partnership is choosing the *right* partner. The importance of this step cannot be overemphasized. Many partnerships dissolve because of disagreements between partners. One should choose a business partner as carefully as a marriage partner. Then, a written **partnership agreement** should be signed. This is a legal document that specifies the rights and responsibilities of each partner. It normally includes the following provisions:

partnership agreement
Legal document that specifies the rights and responsibilities of each partner.

1. The name of the business. All provinces require the firm name to be registered with the province if the firm name is not the name of any partner.
2. The names and addresses of all partners.
3. The purpose and nature of the business and the main location.
4. The date the partnership will start and how long it will last. No mention of termination means that the partnership will continue indefinitely until one of the partners dies or leaves.
5. The amount of cash or other assets each partner will invest.
6. Each partner's management responsibilities and authority.
7. The salaries and drawing accounts of each partner and in what proportion profits and losses will be shared.
8. Provision for the withdrawal of a partner and also for the admission of new partners.
9. Provision for the purchase of a deceased, retiring, or sick partner's share of the business.
10. Provision for how serious disagreements will be resolved.
11. Provision for when and how to dissolve the partnership.

Sole proprietors and partners have to contend with the major disadvantage of unlimited personal liability for company debts. The solution to this problem is to form a corporation. We look at corporations next.

Progress
Check

- Most people who start a business in Canada are sole proprietors, and most of them are no longer in business after 10 years. What are the advantages and disadvantages of this form of business?
- What are some of the advantages of partnerships over sole proprietorships?
- Unlimited liability is one of the biggest drawbacks to sole proprietorships and general partnerships. Can you explain what that means?
- What is the difference between a *limited* partner and a *general* partner?

•••• ▬▬▬ ••••

CORPORATIONS

Although the word *corporation* makes people think of big businesses like Imperial Oil, the Royal Bank, Nova Corp., MacMillan Bloedel, or Irving Oil, it is not necessary to be big to incorporate (start a corporation). Obviously, many

NOVA Chemical's Joffre manufacturing facility lies just east of Red Deer, Alberta, and is one of North America's largest petrochemical complexes.

<www.nova.ca>
<www.irvingoil.com>

Of course, the number of corporations with Web sites describing the corporation and its activities is increasing at a dramatic rate. Soon, virtually all corporations will be on the Net. Check out these two examples of large successful corporations from two different parts of Canada.

public corporation
Corporation that has the right to issue shares to the public, so its shares may be listed on the stock exchanges.

private corporation
Corporation that is not allowed to issue stock to the public, so its shares are not listed on stock exchanges and it is limited to 50 or fewer shareholders.

corporations are big. However, incorporating may be beneficial for small businesses also.

A corporation is a federally or provincially chartered legal entity with authority to act and have liability separate from its owners. The corporation's owners (shareholders) are not liable for the debts or any other problems of the corporation beyond the money they invest. Corporate shareholders do not have to worry about losing their houses, cars, and other personal property if the business cannot pay its bills—a very significant benefit. A corporation not only limits the liability of owners, it enables many people to share in the ownership (and profits) of a business without working there or having other commitments to it.

In Canada commercial corporations are divided into two classes: public and private. A **public corporation** has the right to issue shares to the public, which means its shares may be listed on a stock exchange. This offers the possibility of raising large amounts of capital and is the reason why all large companies are corporations.

A **private corporation** is not allowed to issue stock to the public, so its shares are not listed on a stock exchange, and it is limited to 50 or fewer shareholders. This greatly reduces the costs of incorporating. Most small corporations are in the private category. This is the vehicle employed by individuals or partners who do not anticipate the need for substantial financing, but want to take advantage of limited liability. Some private corporations are very large. For example, the T. Eaton Co. Ltd. was, until recently, owned by the Eaton family.

There is one important advantage Canadian-owned private corporations have over public corporations: the income tax rate on the first $200,000 of annual business profits is half the normal corporate tax rate. It is also about half of what individuals pay when they are not incorporated. This is another feature that leads individuals and partners to incorporate.

Another important advantage for the owner of a private corporation is that he or she can issue shares to a daughter, a son, or to a spouse, making them co-owners of the company. This procedure is not available to a sole proprietor. It is a simple and useful way of recognizing the contribution of these or other family members, or employees, to the company. This procedure may also be a good way for the owner to prepare for retirement by gradually transferring ownership and responsibility to those who will be inheriting the business.

There is a formal procedure for forming a corporation that involves applying to the appropriate federal or provincial agency. For small companies this may be done by the founders themselves, thus avoiding the costs of having a legal firm attend to it. The procedure for large or public corporations is much more complex and expensive and definitely requires hiring a legal firm. These costs can easily run into the hundreds of thousands of dollars.

··· ADVANTAGES OF CORPORATIONS ···

Most people are prepared to risk what they invest in a business, but are not willing to risk everything to go into business. Yet, for businesses to grow and prosper and create abundance, many people would have to be willing to invest their money in business. The way to solve this problem was to create an artificial being, an entity that exists only in the eyes of the law. That artificial being is called a *corporation*. It has a separate legal identity from the owners— the shareholders—of the company. The corporation files its own tax returns. This entity is a technique for involving people in business without risking their other personal assets.

The first three advantages listed here apply only to large public corporations. The last three apply to all corporations.

<www.incoltd.com>

Visit Inco's Web site. What does it produce and sell? How much does it produce? What was its volume of sales last year? How many employees does it have?

1. *More money for investment.* To raise money, a public corporation sells ownership (shares or stock) to anyone who is interested. (We shall discuss shares in Chapter 18.) This means that thousands of people can own part of major companies like INCO, Bombardier, and MacMillan Bloedel. If a company sold one million shares for $50 each, it would have $50 million available to build plants, buy materials, hire people, build products, and so on. Such a large amount of money would be difficult to raise any other way. Laws regulate how corporations can raise this money. The types of shares and the kinds of debt that can be incurred vary from province to province.

2. *Size.* Because they have large amounts of money to work with, corporations can build large, modern factories with the latest equipment. They can also hire experts or specialists in all areas of operation. Furthermore, they can buy other corporations in other fields to *diversify their risk*. (When a corporation is involved in many businesses at once, if one fails, the corporation will survive.) In short, large corporations have the size and resources to take advantage of opportunities anywhere in the world. However, corporations do not have to be large for their shareholders to enjoy the benefits of limited liability and access to more capital.

3. *Separation of ownership from management.* Public corporations are able to raise money from many different investors without getting them involved in management. The corporate hierarchy is shown in Figure 6.5. The pyramid shows that the owners and shareholders are separate from the managers and employees. The owners elect a board of directors. The directors select the officers, who in turn hire managers and employees. The owners thus have some say in who runs the corporation.

4. *Limited liability.* Corporations in Canada have Limited, Incorporated, or Corporation after their names, as in "Shopper's Drug Mart Ltd." The "Ltd." stands for *limited liability* and is probably the most significant advantage of corporations. Remember, limited liability means

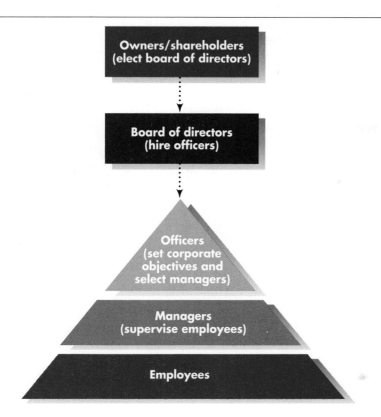

FIGURE **6.5**

• • • •

CORPORATE HIERARCHY

Owners influence how a business is managed by electing a board of directors. The board hires the top managers (or fires them), and sets the pay for top managers. Top managers then select other managers and employees with the help of the human resources department.

that the owners of a business cannot lose more than their investment in that business. The corporation itself is fully liable for all of its debts. Banks and other financial institutions usually require the personal guarantee of the owners of small corporations before making loans to these companies. These owners, therefore, lose the limited liability protection for those debts.

5. *Perpetual life.* Because corporations are separate legal entities from the people who own them, the death or departure of one or more owners does not terminate the corporation. This makes corporations a better risk to bankers and other lenders, so it is easier to get loans.

6. *Ease of ownership change.* Ownership of public corporations is constantly changing as existing shareholders sell all or part of the shareholdings, and other people or companies buy these shares and become shareholders. This happens very infrequently in private companies, but the procedure has its advantages for private companies, as discussed on pages 177 and 178.

••• DISADVANTAGES OF CORPORATIONS •••

There are also disadvantages that come with the corporate form of ownership, including:

1. *More paperwork.* There is more documentation involved in setting up and operating a corporation because of government requirements. This leads to more costly legal and accounting fees, as well as more time-consuming and, therefore, costly operations.

2. *Less flexibility.* In unincorporated companies, proprietors or partners can withdraw funds as they wish with no impact on tax liabilities. In

The National Gallery of Canada is a visual arts museum that holds its collections of art in trust for all Canadians. The mandate of the National Gallery is set out in the 1990 Museums Act. The Gallery is a nonprofit crown corporation of the federal government.

<www.ymca.ca>

You can learn about various YMCAs in different Canadian cities by visiting this Web site. Check out the one nearest you!

corporations, such withdrawals are taxed in one way or another. Certain other transactions also involve formal paperwork.

3. *Starting and winding-up.* The legal procedures involved in starting and ending a corporation are costly and much more complex than for unincorporated companies.

••• OTHER TYPES OF CORPORATIONS •••

When reading about corporations, you may find many confusing terms. A *nonresident corporation* does business in Canada, but has its head office outside Canada. Examples are most foreign airlines. A *personal service corporation* is set up by an athlete, entertainer, or some other high-earning, self-employed person to access some advantages of corporate ownership.

A *nonprofit corporation* is formed for charitable or socially beneficial purposes. It is not run for profit. It has many of the features of business corporations, but it pays no income taxes and does not issue shares. It has no owners or shareholders. The number of nonprofit corporations in Canada runs into the tens of thousands. In some towns, property is tax exempt if it belongs to nonprofit organizations such as churches, hospitals, colleges, museums, YMCAs, athletic, artistic, or charitable organizations.

Figure 6.6 compares different types of ownership.

Progress Check

- What are the major advantages and disadvantages of the corporate form of business?
- What is the role of owners (shareholders) in the corporate hierarchy?
- If you buy shares in a corporation and someone gets injured by one of the corporation's products, can you be sued? Why or why not? Could you be sued if you were a general partner in a partnership?

Critical Thinking

What would Canada be like without major corporations? What products would be hard to get? What would be the benefits?

Now that you've read about the proprietorships, partnerships, and corporations, which sounds like the best place for you to work? Why? Which calls for taking the most risks? Which would be most fun? Most profitable?

What part of your personality most determines where you fit in best?

	Sole Proprietorship	Partnerships		Corporations	
		General Partnership	Limited* Partnership	Public Corporation	Private Corporation
Documents needed to start business	None (may need permit or licence)	Partnership agreement, oral or written	Written agreement; must file certificate of limited partnership	Articles of incorporation, bylaws	Articles of incorporation, bylaws; must meet criteria
Ease of termination	Easy, just pay debts and quit	May be difficult, depending on agreement	Same as general partnership	Difficult and expensive to terminate	Not difficult; pay off debts, sell off assets, withdraw cash, and pay taxes
Life span	Terminates on death, sale, or retirement	Terminates on death or withdrawal of partner[†]	Terminates only on death or withdrawal of general partner[†]	Perpetual life	Perpetual life
Transfer of ownership	Sale terminates sole proprietorship	Requires agreement of partner(s) (per partnership agreement)	Agreement usually allows for such transfers	Easy—just sell shares	Easy—just sell shares[†]
Financial resources	Limited to owner's capital and loans	Limited to partners' capital and loans	Same as general partnership	May issue as many shares and bonds as market will absorb	Owners' capital and loans; no public stock issue allowed
Personal risk of losses	Unlimited liability	Unlimited liability	Limited liability	Limited liability	Limited liability
Income taxes	Taxed as personal income	Taxed as personal income	Taxed as personal income	Corporate income tax plus lower personal tax on dividends	Low corporate rate plus lower personal tax on dividends
Management responsibilities	Owner manages all areas of the business	Partners share management	Cannot participate in management	Management separate from ownership	Owners usually manage all areas

* There must be at least one general partner who manages the partnership and has unlimited liability.
† Unless agreement specifies otherwise.

FIGURE **6.6**

· · · ·

COMPARISON OF TYPES
OF OWNERSHIP

· · · · ▬▬▬ · · · ·

CORPORATE EXPANSION: MERGERS AND ACQUISITIONS

The last decade saw considerable corporate expansion. Nearly every day a new corporate merger or acquisition was announced. A **merger** occurs when two firms unite to form one company. An **acquisition** occurs when one company buys another company. Acquisitions are much more common than mergers.

merger
Two firms unite to form one company.

acquisition
One company buys another company.

FIGURE **6.7**

. . . .

MERGERS AND ACQUISITIONS

Some major acquisitions and mergers in the 1990s involving Canadian companies.

<www.pepsico.com>

Check out this Web site to learn about the company. If you look at *A History of PepsiCo*, you will see that PepsiCo announced in 1997 that it had decided to sell its noncore businesses, including the restaurants. Why do you suppose it has decided to desert its *vertical merger* strategy?

vertical merger
The joining of two firms involved in different stages of related businesses.

horizontal merger
Joins two firms in the same or similar industries to allow them to diversify or expand their products.

franchising
A method of distributing a product or service, or both, to achieve a maximum market impact with a minimum investment.

franchise agreement
An arrangement whereby someone with a good idea for a business sells the rights to use the business name and sell its products or services in a given territory.

franchisor
A company that develops a product concept and sells others the rights to make and sell the products.

franchisee
A person who buys a franchise.

franchise
The right to use a specific business's name and sell its products or services in a given territory.

1. Barrick Gold acquired Lac Minerals, becoming an even larger gold producer.
2. Inco acquired Diamond Resources, whose gigantic mineral discoveries in Labrador made headlines for months.
3. Québecor continued to acquire American and European printing companies to become one of the largest printing companies in the world.
4. Loblaws and Provigo merged to form one of the largest supermarket chains.
5. The giant U.S. chain, Wal-Mart, entered Canada by acquiring Woolco.
6. Microsoft acquired the innovative SoftImage software company of Montreal, whose Hollywood success attracted mongul Bill Gates's eye.
7. Seagram's, the Canadian liquor and beverage giant, acquired control of the huge U.S. entertainment company MCA and the giant Dutch Company Polygram.
8. Two giant American companies each acquired a major Canadian forestry company— MacMillan Bloedel in B.C. and Forex Group in Quebec.

There are two major types of corporate mergers or acquisitions: vertical and horizontal. A **vertical merger** is joining of two firms involved in different stages of related businesses. Pepsi Cola acquired Pizza Hut and KFC to ensure a controlled market for Pepsi beverages. A **horizontal merger** joins two firms in the same or similar industries and allows them to diversify or expand their products. Seagram's acquired the Tropicana fruit juice company when liquor sales were declining. Figure 6.7 lists some important mergers and acquisitions of the 1990s involving Canadian companies. Most were horizontal.

The reason for all of this merger and acquisition mania, as some people have called it, is the continuing pressure that companies feel: to compete in the global marketplace they must be large and powerful. As even old giant American and European companies continue to merge, witness Daimler and Chrysler in 1999, Canadian companies feel they have no choice but to do likewise. The four huge Canadian banks tried in 1998 to merge into two even larger financial entities to better meet the global competition of similar mergers around the world, but were refused permission to do so. (This is discussed in Chapter 4.)

. . . . ▬▬▬ . . . .

FRANCHISING[1]

Not everyone wants to start or operate a business as a sole owner. The personality called for is that of a risk taker and innovator. Some people are more cautious or simply want more assurance of success. For them, a very different strategy is available: the opportunity of franchising. Business students often mistakenly identify franchising as an industry. **Franchising** is a *method* of distributing a product or service, or both, to achieve a maximum market impact with a minimum investment.

Some people develop ideas and build a winning product or service that they attempt to exploit through a franchise agreement. A **franchise agreement** is an arrangement whereby someone with a good idea for a business (the **franchisor**) sells to another (the **franchisee**) the rights to use the business name and sell a product or service in a given territory. As you might suspect, both franchisors and franchisees have a stake in the success of the **franchise**.

The franchise structure of ownership has had an important impact on Canadian business. Franchises employ more than one million people directly, provide many more jobs indirectly, and generate annual sales of $100 billion. While the food services industry alone employs half a million people, there are

38 other categories of franchises that have almost 600,000 employees. The greatest growth is expected in the following sectors:

- business aids and services
- construction
- maintenance and cleaning services
- retailing (nonfood)
- automotive products and services
- home improvement
- home inspection services

Figure 6.8 details more interesting facts about franchise operations in Canada.

The franchise business is even more important in the United States where some 550,000 franchises generate $800 billion in sales annually. The well-known futurist John Naisbitt believes that "franchising is the way of the future" because it "is the most successful marketing concept ever created." In North America alone there are 3000 franchising companies in 60 different industries.

A very large franchisor in the food industry in Canada is Cara Operations Ltd., which controls Harvey's, Swiss Chalet, and Second Cup franchises. Cara provides food services at all major airports in Canada, as well as to Canadian and international airlines. It has eight subsidiaries and two alliances. Cara has 1690 outlets, nearly all in Canada. Second Cup itself is concentrating on its 350 units in Canada after having disposed of its 150 U.S. units.[2] We are all familiar with McDonald's, Pizza Huts, Dairy Queens, and so forth, but there are also Shopper's Drug Marts, Tilden Car Rentals, Uniglobe Travel, Beaver Lumber, Jean Coutu drugstores, and many more large nonfood franchises in Canada.

Number of franchisor companies		1,327
Number of franchised units		73,500
Average number of years the franchisor has been in business		20
Average cash outlay by franchisees to acquire a unit		$155,000

The most common categories of franchise units are:

Products and services	13.2%
Fastfood restaurants	10.2
Automotive products and services	8.3
Miscellaneous retail	7.6
Sub-total	39.0%
All other categories	61.0%
Total	100.0%

On average, a new franchise unit is opened **every two hours every day of the year.**

FIGURE **6.8**
. . . .
FRANCHISING IN CANADA

Here you can see details concerning franchise operations in Canada.

FRANCHISOR HEAD OFFICE LOCATIONS

Ontario	**56%**
B.C.	**13**
Quebec	**12**
Manitoba	**3**
Nova Scotia	**2**
Saskatchewan	**1**
N.B.	**1**
Foreign	**12**
Total	**100%**

This may look like the set of Camelot, but it is actually the Crowne Plaza Hotel in downtown Edinburgh, Scotland. Bass Hotel and Resort franchises try to complement the environment of the areas they serve.

<www.bison1.com/ acad/acad-article.html>

Check out this comprehensive Web site devoted to franchises and franchising issue around the world.

••• ADVANTAGES OF FRANCHISES •••

Franchising has penetrated every aspect of Canadian and global business life by offering products and services that are reliable, convenient, and cost effective. Richard Ashman, chairman of the International Franchise Association (headquartered in Washington, DC), probably put it best when he commented, "you name it and there is a good chance that someone out there is franchising it." Obviously, the growth in franchising throughout the world was not accomplished by accident. Franchising clearly has many advantages.[3]

1. *Training and management assistance.* A franchisee (the person who buys a franchise) has a much greater chance of succeeding in business than an independent because he or she has an established product (for example, McDonald's hamburgers), help with choosing a location, training, promotion, and assistance in all phases of operation. It is like having your own business with full-time consultants available when you need them. Furthermore, you have a whole network of peers facing similar problems who can share their experiences with you.

2. *Personal ownership.* A franchise operation is still *your* business and you enjoy most of the freedom, incentives, and profit of any sole proprietor. However, you must follow rules, regulations, and procedures set by the franchisor.

3. *Nationally recognized name.* It is one thing to open a new hamburger outlet or ice cream store. It is quite another to open another Second Cup coffee shop or a Baskin-Robbins ice cream shop. With an established franchise, you get instant recognition and support from a product group with established customers from around the world.

4. *Financial advice and assistance.* Major problems for small business are arranging financing and learning to keep records. Franchisees get valuable assistance in these areas and periodic advice from experts. Some franchisors will even provide financing to potential franchisees they think will be valuable parts of the franchise system.

The Franchise

Did your lawyer approve the franchise contract you are considering after he or she studied it paragraph by paragraph?

Does the franchise give you an exclusive territory for the length of the franchise?

Under what circumstances can you terminate the franchise contract and at what cost to you?

If you sell your franchise, will you be compensated for your goodwill?

If the franchisor sells the company, will your investment be protected?

The Franchisor

How many years has the firm offering you a franchise been in operation?

Has it a reputation for honesty and fair dealing among the local firms holding its franchise?

Has the franchisor shown you any certified figures indicating exact net profits of one or more franchisees that you have personally checked with the franchisee?

Will the firm assist you with
- – a management training program?
- – an employee training program?
- – a public relations program?
- – capital?
- – credit?
- merchandising ideas?

Will the firm help you find a good location for your new business?

Has the franchisor investigated you carefully enough to assure itself that you can successfully operate one of its franchises at a profit to both the franchisor and you?

You, the Franchisee

How much equity capital will you need to purchase the franchise and operate it until your income equals your expenses?

Does the franchisor offer financing for a portion of the franchising fees? On what terms?

Are you prepared to give up some independence of action to secure the advantages offered by the franchise?

Are you ready to spend much or all of the remainder of your business life with this franchisor, offering its product or service to your public?

Your Market

Have you made any study to determine whether the product or service that you propose to sell under franchise has a market in your territory at the prices you will have to charge?

Will the population in the territory given to you increase, remain static, or decrease over the next five years?

Will the product or service you are considering be in greater demand, about the same, or in less demand five years from now?

What competition already exists in your territory for the product or service you are contemplating selling?

Source: *Small Business*, July–August 1990, p. 51.

FIGURE 6.9

• • • •

CHECKLIST FOR
EVALUATING A
FRANCHISE

··· DISADVANTAGES OF FRANCHISES ···

It may sound as if the potential of franchising is too good to be true. Indeed, there *are* costs associated with joining a franchise. Be sure to check out any such arrangement with present franchisees and discuss the idea with an experienced franchise lawyer. The following are some disadvantages of franchises:

1. *Large start-up costs.* Most franchises demand a fee just to obtain the rights to the franchise. Fees for franchises can vary considerably. The very successful ones demand a fee that will place them out of the reach of a small-business venture. Fees may run well over $250,000 for the well-known franchises, but for newer or unproven ones, it may be anything from zero to $35,000. In addition to this fee are other normal initial cash needs that can easily exceed $100,000. Of course, a home-based franchise will require much less start-up cash.

2. *Shared profit.* The franchisor often demands a large share of the profits, or a percentage commission based on *sales*, not profit. This share is generally referred to as a *royalty*. Often, the share taken by the franchisor is so high that the owner's profit does not match the time and effort involved in owning and managing a business. The royalty demanded by a franchisor is an important factor to consider before going ahead (see Figure 6.9).

3. *Management regulation.* Management assistance has a way of becoming managerial orders, directives, and limitations. Franchisees may feel burdened by the company's rules and regulations and lose the spirit and incentive of being their own boss with their own business.

4. *Coattail effects.* What happens to your franchise if fellow franchisees fail? You might be forced out of business even if your particular franchise was profitable. This is often referred to as a coattail effect. The actions of other franchisees have an impact on your future growth and level of profitability. Remember, franchising is a team effort. If you play with a bad team, chances are you will lose.

··· BUYING A FRANCHISE ···

As we have seen, there are many advantages and disadvantages you need to explore before buying a franchise (see Figure 6.10 for a summary). Buying a franchise is an excellent way to enter business as an owner or a manager and make a nice salary and profit.

A good source of information about franchise possibilities is Franchise Watchdog in Burlington, Vermont. It compares what franchisors have to offer, including fees and support services, and also rates franchisors by sampling franchisees.

Be careful of franchises that are just starting, grow too fast, or change ownership often. For example, Mother's Restaurants changed hands three times between 1986 and 1989, and its debt grew substantially as a result. In 1989, the 15-year-old, 90-unit franchise went bankrupt, dragging many franchisees down with it.[4] Be sure to check out the financial strength of a company before you get involved.

There are many things to do before jumping into a franchise. First, get an accountant. Then, have a lawyer review the contract. Remember, you are making a sizable financial investment. Furthermore, you have to analyze yourself,

---

FIGURE **6.10**

····

BENEFITS AND DRAWBACKS OF FRANCHISING

The start-up fees and monthly fees can be killers. Ask around. Don't be shy. This is the time to learn about opportunities and risks. (This schedule applies to well-established franchises.)

BENEFITS	DRAWBACKS
Nationally recognized name and established reputation.	High initial franchise fee. Monthly fees for advertising.
Help with finding a good location.	A monthly percentage of gross sales to the franchisor.
A proven management system.	Possible competition from other nearby franchisees.
Tested methods for inventory and operations management.	No freedom to select decor or other design features.
Financial advice and assistance.	Little freedom to determine management procedures.
Training in all phases of operation.	Many rules and regulations to follow.
Promotional assistance.	Coattail effect.
Periodic management counseling.	
Proven record of success.	
It's your business!	

Reaching Beyond Our Borders

<www.yogenfruz.com>
<www.mollymaid.com>

Canadian Franchisors Make Their Mark

Two Canadian franchisors that have successfully moved beyond Canada's borders are Molly Maid Inc. and Yogen Fruz Worldwide Inc. Molly Maid got its start in Toronto in 1979 by setting out to provide domestic cleaning services. As more women were moving into the workforce, the company saw an opportunity to cash in by filling a new need in the marketplace. And fill it it did. Soon the company was expanding outside Canada into countries where similar market niches were opening up. By 1996 it was well established in Japan, Australia, and the United States. The company is highly rated in the United States as one of the "top 10 best low-investment franchises" and by various magazines such as *Entrepreneur, Franchise Times,* and *Business Start-Up. Platinum 200* ranked Molly Maid number one among franchisors in 1995 and 1996. The software program the company developed for its franchisees, the Customer Care System, was awarded the Microsoft

Windows World Open prize for 1994. Molly Maid now operates more than 500 franchises in Canada, the United States, England, Japan, and Portugal.

Yogen Fruz, headquartered in Markham, Ontario, has as its mission "to become the world's largest franchisor of frozen yogurt." It is well on the way to achieving that target by acquiring the American franchise I Can't Believe It's Yogurt. Yogen Fruz has acquired about a dozen famous companies in the ice cream and dairy industries and has licensing agreements with many well-known brand names such as Betty Crocker and Yoplait. It now has approximately 4900 outlets in 80 countries. This makes Yogen Fruz the largest franchise outside North America and second largest in the world.

Sources: *Successful Franchising,* April 1996, p. 28; Web sites <www.mollymaid.com>, May 1999, <www.carlsononline.com>, June 1999.

the franchise, and the market. Take some time to go over the checklist in Figure 6.10; it will help you to understand many of the questions franchisees should ask if they want a successful venture.

Critical Thinking

Is it fair to say that franchisees have the true entrepreneurial spirit? What do you think of the franchise opportunities of the future? Could you see yourself as a franchisee or franchisor? Which one?

••• FRANCHISING OPPORTUNITIES OVERSEAS •••

If you are contemplating becoming a franchisor, be aware of the ultimate potential of franchise outlets in other countries. We have all seen the attention paid to two of the largest foreign fastfood franchises, McDonald's (Canada) in Moscow and Kentucky Fried Chicken (now KFC) in Beijing. These successful ventures took many years of patient planning, heavy cost, and much frustration. Smaller franchisors have similar opportunities, but will need to build a solid management team, reputation, and strong financial resources before they can move in that direction.

Progress Check

- What is a franchise? A franchisor? A franchisee?
- What are the advantages of going into business by acquiring a franchise? What are the disadvantages?

Co-operatives are important in agriculture. They enable farmers to purchase seed and equipment at reasonable prices. They also provide an outlet for farm products. One advantage of co-operatives is that they do not pay taxes as corporations do.

CO-OPERATIVES

Some people dislike the notion of having owners, managers, workers, and buyers as separate individuals with separate goals. They envision a world where people cooperate with one another more fully and share the wealth more evenly. These people have formed a different kind of organization that reflects their social orientation: a co-operative, or co-op.

A **co-operative** is an organization that is owned by members and customers, who pay an annual membership fee and share in any profits (if it is a profit-making organization). Often the members work in the organization a certain number of hours a month as part of their duties. In Canada there is a wide range of co-ops. There are *producer co-ops*. Fishermen on both coasts and farmers on the Prairies, in Ontario, and in Quebec each produce their own product, but part or all of their marketing is done through these jointly owned co-ops. Any *profit* is distributed to the co-op members in proportion to the quantity supplied by each. Profit is regarded as additional payment for produce provided.

Producer co-ops on the Prairies and elsewhere use their combined purchasing power to buy equipment, seeds, and other items at reduced prices. This gives them some bargaining power with the large companies they often deal with.

At *consumer co-ops* in cities, consumers get together and establish a food store in the hope of reducing their food costs. The members work in the store, buy their food there, and share any profits as a reduction of their cost of food.

There are also many *financial co-ops*, called credit unions and Caisses Populaires. These serve the purpose of banks, but they have no shareholders. Instead, they distribute their profits annually to their members in various ways. The Caisses Populaires in Quebec have become very large and have a significant share of financial business there.

Because co-ops distribute their profits to members as a reduction in members' costs, these profits are not subject to income tax. From time to time various business organizations assert that many co-ops are now more like large businesses and should be taxed. So far this viewpoint has not been successful and does not appear to have much support. Figure 6.11 lists some of the largest co-operatives in Canada. Some co-ops are also becoming corporations.

WHICH FORM IS FOR YOU?

As you have seen, you can participate in the business world in a variety of ways. You can be involved in a sole proprietorship, a partnership, a corporation, a franchise, or a co-operative. There are advantages and disadvantages to each. However, the risks are high no matter which form you choose. The miracle of free enterprise is that the freedom and incentives of capitalism make such risks acceptable to many people, who go on to create the great Canadian businesses.

One of the best known was the giant department store chain, the T. Eaton Co. Ltd. Eaton's was founded 125 years ago by Timothy Eaton in Toronto as a small store. Canadian Tire is another success story. So is Magna International,

<www.desjardins.com>

This Web site has a wealth of information about the Caisses Populaires and their history in *du Mouvement Desjardins*. Visit it to learn about the development of the Caisses and their current importance in Quebec. How significant are the Caisses Populaires today?

NONFINANCIAL CO-OPERATIVES	FINANCIAL CO-OPERATIVES
Agricore Cooperative Ltd*	Mouvement Caisse Desjardins†
Federated Cooperatives	Caisse centrale Desjardins
Agropur Cooperative Agro-Al	Vancouver City Savings Credit Union
United Farmers of Alta. Co-op	Cooperators Group
Calgary Cooperative Assoc.	FCPD de Montreal
Co-op Atlantic	Credit Union Central (Sask.)
Western Co-op Fertilizers	Richmond Savings
Lilydale Cooperative	Pacific Coast Savings Credit Union
XCAN Grain Pool	Cooperators Life Insurance

FIGURE 6.11

· · · ·

CANADIAN
CO-OPERATIVES

This is a list of some of Canada's largest financial and nonfinancial co-ops, in order of size.

Source: The Top 1000, *Globe and Mail, Report on Business*, July 1999, 186.

* Agricore was created in November 1998 by a merger of the Manitoba and Alberta Wheat Pools.

† The Mouvement Caisse Desjardins operates many bank branches in Manitoba, Ontario, Quebec and New Brunswick. It is a giant co-op with more than 5.5 million members (mostly depositors) and 33,000 employees. Its assets of $70 billion are more than double the *combined* assets of all the other 17 co-ops shown here.

Spotlight on Big Business

<www.bombardier.com>

How Bombardier Took Off

The Profile at the beginning of this chapter highlighted the career of Armand Bombardier. From his tentative beginnings in 1937 with a vehicle to provide mobility on snow, now known as the *Skidoo*, his company, Bombardier, has mushroomed into a giant transnational in the aerospace and rail transportation businesses.

From 1986 to 1992 the company made several major acquisitions in Europe and North America under favourable terms. The best known are Canadair in Montreal, de Havilland in Toronto, Learjet in the U.S., and Short Bros. in Northern Ireland. During this period Bombardier became a technological leader in rail transportation and executive jets. One of the company's major contracts was for 254 train cars and loaders for the English Channel tunnel—the *chunnel*—and *Time* magazine said that the cars would be "among the

world's most technologically advanced rolling stock when they go into service." The company's jets and railcars and rail systems are sold all over the world.

Bombardier's 1999 annual report indicated that the company had 53,000 employees in 42 subsidiaries, operating in 12 countries. It had assets of $11.5 billion, sales of $14.2 billion, and a record backlog of orders of $25.5 billion. In 1999 Bombardier was selected by business leaders as the most respected company in Canada. Armand Bombardier's little company has come a long way.

Sources: *Annual Report*, January 31, 1999; company documents; *Time*, November 12, 1990, p. 27; *Globe and Mail, Report on Business*, April 1999, p. 76.

Ethical Dilemma

REVIEW

Remember our couple, Elvira and Trong, who are planning to incorporate their partnership to avoid personal liability for the debts the business has accumulated? Our executives view this dilemma differently.

Bédard has a simple and clear answer: "No way. It is unethical to carry out such practices." Reilley takes a somewhat different tack. By incorporating, he notes, the company's ultimate bankruptcy will leave the owners personally still solvent so that "these two entrepreneurs could (and very likely would) start again, which would eventually create jobs, tax revenue, and so on."

Note that the manoeuvre contemplated by Elvira and Trong will not help them avoid personal liability. If you are in business as a sole proprietorship or partnership, the debts the business incurs remain personal liabilities even after they are taken over by a corporation. According to the law, it is the status existing at the time the debts were incurred that governs, not what happens subsequently. When a supplier sells to an unincorporated business, it knows and expects that, under the law, the owner remains personally responsible for the debt until it is paid.

the large auto parts manufacturer. Bombardier, Canadian Airlines, CAE, and Steinberg's are only a few of the many companies whose success was due to the confidence, hard work, and abilities of the individuals who founded them. They all started small, accumulated capital from profits, grew, and became leaders in their fields. It is still being done today. Could you do the same? (Eaton's went bankrupt in the late 1990s and Steinberg's was sold off in the late 1970s, but these problems were due to descendants of the founders not being able to carry on as successfully as the founders.)

Many students prefer to take the more cautious route of working for a corporation. The advantages are many: a fixed salary, paid vacations, health coverage, limited risk, promotional possibilities, and more.

The disadvantages of working for others are also significant: limited income potential, fixed hours, repetitive work, job insecurity, close supervision, and limited freedom. Sometimes it is exciting to work for others while starting your own business on the side. Apple Computer was started in a garage. Many firms have started in people's basements and attics. Business offers many different opportunities for tomorrow's graduates.

Of course, the option of becoming a franchisee, as discussed before, is also open to you. The problem here is that getting into a successful franchise requires lots of money. The newer or unproven ones require much less cash, but are a lot riskier. However, you might be one of the fortunate few who has a sound idea for franchising that could lead *you* to become the *franchisor*, and you would be collecting fees and royalties from franchisees.

SUMMARY

1. List the three basic forms of business ownership and compare the advantages and disadvantages of each.

1. A business can be formed in several ways.
   - ***What are the three major forms of business ownerships?***
   The three major forms of business ownership are sole proprietorship, partnerships, and corporations.

   - ***Is there some way to compare the advantages and disadvantages of each form?***
   See Figure 6.6 on page 181.

- *Which form of business is the most common and which does most of the business in Canada?*

Sole proprietorships are most popular, but corporations do most of the business in Canada.

2. Not all partners have the same roles and responsibilities.
   - *What are the differences between limited and general partners?*

General partners are owners (partners) who have unlimited liability and are active in managing the company. Limited partners are owners (partners) who have limited liability and must not be active in the company.

- *What does unlimited liability mean?*

Unlimited liability means that sole proprietors and general partners are personally liable for all debts and damages caused by their business. They may lose their houses, cars, or other personal possessions if the business is unable to pay these.

- *What does limited liability mean?*

Limited liability means that corporate owners (shareholders) and limited partners cannot lose more than the amount they invest. Their other personal property is not at risk for business debts.

3. The first and most important step in forming a partnership is choosing the right partner.
   - *How do you form a partnership?*

The most important step in forming a partnership is choosing a partner wisely. Then, no matter how good of friends you and your partner may be, put your partnership agreement *in writing*. For major points of such an agreement see page 176.

4. There are two major categories of corporation: private and public.
   - *What is the major difference between them?*

Private corporations are limited to a small number of shareholders (usually 50) and cannot sell their shares or bonds (borrowed money) publicly (on the stock exchange). Public corporations have no such limitations and their securities (stocks and bonds) trade on the stock exchange.

5. Private and public corporations each have some advantages and disadvantages.
   - *What are the major ones?*

The principal disadvantages of private corporations are that shares cannot be sold to the public and the number of shareholders is limited. The advantages are the lower tax rate and much smaller costs of incorporating and ongoing legal and accounting costs. The situation is reversed for public corporations.

6. A person can participate in the entrepreneurial age by buying the rights to market a new product innovation in his or her area.
   - *What is this arrangement called?*

A franchise is an arrangement to buy the rights to use the business name and sell its products or services in a given territory.

- *What is a franchisee?*

A franchisee is a person who buys a franchise.

- *What are the benefits and drawbacks of being a franchisee?*

The benefits include a nationally recognized name and reputation (for a well-established franchise), a proven management system, promotional

2. Explain the differences between limited and general partners.

3. Summarize the important clauses of a partnership agreement.

4. Define public and private corporations.

5. Compare the advantages and disadvantages of private and public corporations.

6. Define franchising and examine its advantages and disadvantages.

assistance, and pride of ownership. Drawbacks include high franchise fees, managerial regulation, shared profits, and the coattail transfer of adverse effects if other franchisees fail.

7. Outline the areas to analyze when evaluating a franchise.

7. One should not jump blindly into franchise ownership.
   • ***What areas should you analyze when evaluating a franchise?***
   Before you buy a franchise, analyze yourself, the franchise, the franchisor, and the market.

KEY TERMS
······

acquisition 181	general partner 175	private corporation 177
co-operative 188	horizontal merger 182	public corporation 177
corporation 168	limited liability 174	sole proprietorship 168
franchise 182	limited partner 174	unlimited liability 173
franchise agreement 182	merger 181	vertical merger 182
franchisee 182	partnership 168	
franchising 182	partnership agreement 176	
franchisor 182		

DEVELOPING WORKPLACE SKILLS

1. Find out how much it costs to incorporate a company in your province. Then compare it to the cost of a federal incorporation. Is there a significant difference?

2. Have you ever thought about starting your own business? What kind of business would it be? Think of a friend who you might want for a partner in the business. List the capital and personal skills you need for the business. The make separate lists of the capital and personal skills you might bring and those your friend might bring. What capital and personal skills do you need that neither of you have?

3. Speak to a lawyer, accountant, or stockbroker to find out how popular limited partnerships are. Inquire under what circumstances limited partnerships are used.

4. Look at a listing of all the Toronto Stock Exchange transactions for a week. You can find this in the *National Post, The Globe and Mail*, or perhaps your local newspaper. Look at the column called "Volume" for number of shares of a particular company that were traded that week. Make some reasonable dividing line between very active trading and low-volume trading shares (say, 100,000). Count how many high-volume and low-volume stocks are listed. What does that tell you about large and small Canadian public companies? What useful information does this yield?

5. Get an annual report of a large corporation from the library or on the Internet. What are the firm's annual sales? Net income (profit)? Number of common shares? Dividends paid to shareholders?

INTERNET CHALLENGES

1. Find the Web site of the Canadian Federation of Independent Business and do a search using keywords such as *partnerships, corporations,* and *sole proprietorships.* See if you find some interesting data relevant to this chapter to bring to class.

2. Go to the Web site Be the Boss: The Ultimate Franchising Web site at <www.betheboss.com> and click on Getting Started. Then select Franchising 101, The Basics, and click on Franchising—An Interactive Self-Test. Complete the test, submit it, and see how you rate as a suitable franchise operator. Remember, it's only a guide and not necessarily foolproof.

Also check out the Web site of the Canadian Franchise Association at <www.cfa.ca> to see what type of franchises are available and other useful information you can find about franchising.

Practising Management Decisions

CASE 1
• • • • • •
SHOULD THE PARTNERSHIP INCORPORATE?
• • • • • •

Helen and Dimitri have worked hard at their business for three years. Their wholesale beauty supplies partnership has come a long way from the early days when they were working in the basement of their home. Last year, sales exceeded $1 million, and this year they are running well ahead of last year. They expect their profit this year to be about $100,000 after deducting their own salaries, which amount to $60,000. They expect sales and profits to rise dramatically in the next three years.

Most of their friends who are in businesses are incorporated and Helen and Dimitri have been wondering if they should go that route too. Their accountant has been urging them to take this step because of the many advantages of the corporate form of ownership.

They are somewhat reluctant to do this because they like the simplicity of their partnership format. They are also concerned about the costs of making the switch, the more complex structure, and the ongoing additional legal and accounting costs of operating as a corporation.

Decision Questions

1. What are the major advantages and disadvantages of each type of ownership?
2. Do you think that in this case the advantages of incorporation outweigh the partnership form? Why?
3. Will it be easier for Helen and Dimitri to obtain funding in the future if they make the switch? Explain.
4. If they incorporate, will they run a greater risk of a hostile takeover? Why?

CASE 2
• • • • • •
GOING PUBLIC
• • • • • •

George Zegoyan and Amir Gupta face a difficult decision. Their private auto-parts manufacturing company has been a great success—too quickly. They cannot keep up with the demand for their product. They must expand their facilities, but have not had the time to accumulate sufficient working capital, nor do they want to acquire long-term debt to finance the expansion. Discussions with their accountants, lawyers, and stockbrokers have confronted them with the necessity of going public to raise the required capital.

They are concerned about maintaining control if they become a public company. They are also worried about the loss of privacy because of the required reporting to various regulatory bodies and to their shareholders. Naturally, they are also pleased that the process will enable them to sell some of their shareholdings to the public and realize a fair profit from their past and expected future successes. It will also let them raise substantial new capital to meet the needs of their current expansion program.

The proposed new structure will allow them to retain 60 percent of the outstanding voting shares, so they will keep control of the company. Nevertheless, they are somewhat uneasy about taking this step, because it will change the whole nature of the company and the informal method of operating they are used to. They are concerned about having "partners" in their operations and profits. They are wondering whether they should remain as they are and try to grow more slowly even if it means giving up profitable orders.

Decision Questions

1. Are George and Amir justified in their concerns? Why?

2. Do they have any other options besides going public? Is the franchise route a viable option?

3. Do you think they should try to limit their growth to a manageable size to avoid going public, even if it means forgoing profits now? Why?

4. Would you advise them to sell their business now if they can get a good price and then start a new operation? Explain.

Small Business and Entrepreneurship

Chapter 7

LEARNING GOALS

After you have read and studied this chapter, you should be able to

1 define small business and discuss its importance to the Canadian economy.

2 explain why people are willing to take the risks of entrepreneurship.

3 describe the attributes needed to be a successful entrepreneur, and explain why women have a higher success rate than men.

4 summarize the major causes of small business failures.

5 identify ways you can learn about small businesses.

6 explain what a business plan is, and outline the general areas of information it should include.

7 list the requirements to operate a small business successfully.

Jim Carroll, who runs a small business, believes that "technology levels the playing field." Here's part of a column that he wrote in *The Globe and Mail* on October 1, 1998.

I have been an entrepreneur since 1990. I left a public accounting firm after a round of mergers, having determined not to trust my career and my fate to a group of anonymous executives in a boardroom somewhere. Instead of seeking another job, I decided to establish my own consulting firm, and haven't looked back since. As business activities expanded in the early years, I soon found that I needed some help, so my wife quit her job and joined me in the home office. Today, the business consists of a lot of consulting, speaking, and writing. We work out of perhaps the ultimate wired home—it even has a local area network. I am, I suppose, the only guy in the neighbourhood with a computer-network jack on the patio.

When establishing this small business, one of the first decisions made was that technology would be a key method to ensure its survival. And my experience through the past eight years has left me with a deep appreciation that the effective use of technology by a small business can play an extremely significant role in its success. When it comes right down to it, technology is levelling the playing field for small business in a way that is unprecedented. The combination of laser printers, fax machines, personal computers, the Internet, hand-held organizers, sophisticated telephone technology, cellphones, and countless other innovations have provided small businesses an opportunity to act, think, and look as professional as their larger counterparts.

PROFILE

Technology: A Vital Element of a Small Business

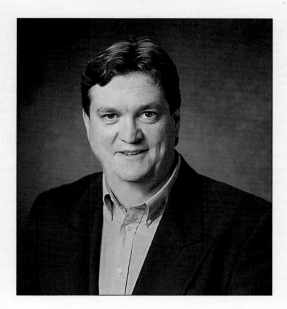

Not only that, small businesses can work with efficiency and low costs on a global basis in a way that has never been seen before. My own experience is bearing this out. I'm winning new clients through the Internet, and I generate my own colour brochures. I produce my own promotional videos and distribute them on CD-ROM and online. I've saved most of the electronic mail messages sent and received since 1984, thus building a powerful personal knowledge resource. I've mastered the skill of "just-in-time knowledge," meaning I can learn about anything at any time. With the Internet, I've become global in such a way that would have been a dream just a few years ago. Just last weekend, a fellow in Japan bought one of my books from my online store.

Technology has not only been powerful, it has been extremely empowering. No longer do I have to waste hours in a traffic jam early in the morning or late in the day; that time is much better spent being productive in the home office. And the lifestyle implications are enormous—I probably get to spend more time with my two young children than most other fathers. My kids are growing up with me as an integral part of their life, a fact for which I credit technology.

I'm a wired entrepreneur and I'm having a ball. When asked to undertake a column about the use of technology within small business, I jumped at the chance. I am convinced that technology will help to make the twenty-first century the era of small business.

Jim Carroll is the co-author of *Small Business Online—A Strategic Guide for Entrepreneurs*. His e-mail address is <jcarroll@jimcarroll.com>.

WHERE TO DRAW THE LINE?

In this chapter you will see that a common route to starting a business is via a job in a company where young potential entrepreneurs can gain valuable experience and connections. When they deem the time is right, these entrepreneurs start their own ventures. Often, ethical dilemmas arise concerning "stealing" customers or clients or using special technology or processes learned from an employer. Some companies protect themselves by having

employment contracts that forbid this happening. However, suppose your venture requires you to compete with your former employer because you are providing similar services and trying to sell them to the same customers? It is, for example, ethical to take knowledge or customers from your previous employer for your own company? What do you think you would do? Think about it and we'll return to this question at the end of the chapter.

SMALL BUSINESS: A DYNAMIC SOURCE OF CAREERS AND JOBS

Jim Carroll is a good example of the 2.6 million self-employed persons in Canada. Almost half of them are operating businesses employing about 50 percent of the workforce and generating 43 percent of the total economic output, or GDP, of our country. Ninety-seven percent of all businesses are small businesses (see Figure 7.1). Of course, these figures also mean that 3 percent of all businesses are large businesses, but they generate 57 percent of Canadian GDP. During the 1990s small business generated most of the jobs while large companies were laying off employees. Another interesting fact is that women constitute 35 percent of all small-business owners and they generate about half of all new business start-ups.[1]

··· AN IMPORTANT PLAYER IN THE CANADIAN ECONOMY ···

Not only do small businesses create many jobs and generate a large segment of the GDP in Canada, but seventy-five thousand small businesses engage in exporting, thus helping to create an international trade surplus for Canada.

FIGURE **7.1**

· · · ·

ANALYSIS OF CANADIAN BUSINESSES BY NUMBER OF EMPLOYEES

Ninety-seven percent of Canadian companies are small businesses with fewer than 50 employees.

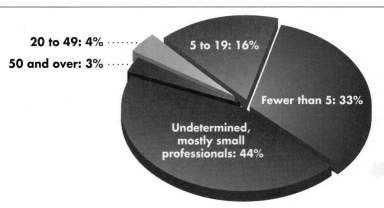

Source: Statistics Canada, CANSIM, Matrix 3451, Series D986059, 986061 May 1999.

Obviously, the small-business sector is a dynamic and vital part of Canadian life. What drives all of these people is often called *entrepreneurship*. **Entrepreneurship** is having the skills and determination to start and operate a business and to accept the calculated risks that are part of such an undertaking. Entrepreneurship helped countries that had little land and few natural resources to prosper. Some excellent examples are Hong Kong, Singapore, Japan, and Taiwan. Canada has both natural resources and entrepreneurs, but its success in the future is more dependent on entrepreneurs than on natural resources. An **entrepreneur** is a person who organizes, manages, and assumes the risks of starting and operating a business to make a profit.

Successful entrepreneurs are usually bold, determined innovators obsessed with an idea that drives them to put up with all sorts of difficulties and discouragement to achieve their goal. Nearly all the modern conveniences and technological advances that we now take for granted were born of the efforts of such entrepreneurs.

The sewing machine, the radio, transistors, TVs, telephones, cars, computers—all were the ideas of various geniuses whose work has been put to practical use by entrepreneurs. Some inventors have also been good entrepreneurs, but that is quite rare. Many entrepreneurs just find better ways to produce or distribute existing products. That's how chain and department stores and supermarkets developed.

Entrepreneurs played a major role in developing the early Canadian economy in fur trading, lumber, shipbuilding, fishing, farming, retail trade, and transportation. Some became giant companies like the Hudson Bay Co., CPR, MacMillan Bloedel, and Irving Oil.

Since entrepreneurship is still the major driving force in the Canadian economy, we are going to examine its implications for you and your future career. We will be looking at entrepreneurship in large corporations and in small businesses.

Intrapreneurs develop new products for corporations that employ them. The Scotch Pop-up Tape Strips are the latest innovation from 3M, a company that welcomes employee ideas.

THE ENTREPRENEURIAL CHALLENGE

There are been many surveys asking people why the opened their own businesses. Thousands of new businesses are started every month, and most of these are small, owner-managed enterprises. Statistics indicate that the number continues to increase, and that women are playing an ever-increasing role. This occurs despite a very high failure rate. Why do so many men and women, young and old, newly arrived immigrants and long-settled residents undertake this difficult, risky task? Here are some of the reasons.

New Idea, Process, or Product. Some entrepreneurs are driven by a firm belief, perhaps even an obsession, that they can produce a better widget, or the old widget at a lower cost, than anybody else. Perhaps they have gotten hold of a new widget or have conceived of an improvement that they are con-

entrepreneurship
Having the skills and determination to start and operate a business and to accept the calculated risks that are part of such an undertaking.

entrepreneur
A person who organizes, manages, and assumes the risks of starting and operating a business to make a profit.

<www.apple.com/pr/
bios/jobs.html>

Check out this Web site
for a detailed biography of
Steve Jobs, one of the most
interesting and successful
entrepreneurs of his generation. Job's achievements
include the introduction
of the personal computer
and the creation of Apple
Computer.

vinced has a large potential market. That's how Apple Computers started. Three young engineers led by Steve Jobs left good positions with Digital Equipment to develop the personal computer. Sometimes you just *know* that you can run that business better than your boss or company.

Independence. Some employees who have imagination and confidence in themselves find their jobs too restrictive. They need breathing space and a lit- tle elbow room! Perhaps their company does not encourage innovation in their operations, so they make the break. Some corporate managers are tired of big-business life and are quitting to start their own small businesses. They bring with them their managerial expertise and their enthusiasm. Many peo- ple cannot conceive of working for someone else. They like doing things their own way without someone standing over them. This type of person gets a great deal of satisfaction out of what he or she achieves. Do you know any- body who feels that way?

Challenge. Closely related to the previous factors are the excitement and the challenge of doing something new or difficult. Many people thrive on over- coming challenges. These people welcome the opportunity to run their own business.

Family Pattern. Some people grow up in an atmosphere in which family members have started their own businesses, perhaps going back several gen- erations. The talk at the dinner table is often about business matters. This background may predispose young men or women to think along the same lines. Sometimes there is a family business, and the next generation grows up expecting to take its place there in due course.

Profit. It's natural for people to benefit monetarily from their ideas and dedication and to be rewarded for the money they risk and their hard work when they run a business. Yet long after a business has produced substantial profits and amassed personal fortunes for its owners, many continue to enjoy the challenge of overcoming the endless problems that every business faces and to enjoy the satisfaction of continued success.

Job Insecurity or Joblessness. A recent phenomenon is the downsizing pol- icy of many large and medium-sized companies since the serious recessions of the 1980s and 1990s. Companies have been on a long campaign of paring staff to the bone to reduce costs. In combination with the significant inroads made by computers in the same period (the technological unemployment referred to in Chapter 2), many employees, including middle-level and even senior-level managers, have been laid off. This has forced many of them to change their orientation from employee to self-employed. The accelerating movement to home-based operations has made this transition easier.

Immigrants. Many immigrants who come to Canada lack educational skills. This, combined with no Canadian job experience and weak language skills in English or French, makes it difficult for them to find employment. However, they often have the drive and desire to succeed, and if they can obtain the capital, they can start their own business. We see this in the many immi- grants who run convenience stores (dépanneurs in Quebec), as well as other types of businesses, such as importing and manufacturing. Other immigrants arrive with capital, skills, and strong entrepreneurial backgrounds. Vancouver and B.C. have been major beneficiaries of such immigrants from Hong Kong.

··· WHAT DOES IT TAKE TO BE A ··· SUCCESSFUL ENTREPRENEUR?[2]

How do you know if you have the qualities necessary to make a successful business person? There is no foolproof formula. Likely winners have proven to be losers and predicted losers have been big winners. External conditions play a major role in determining the success or failure of a business venture. Wars, recessions, inflation, changes in government policies, competitors' actions, technological developments—all can have a significant effect on businesses, especially new companies.

Nevertheless, certain personal qualities are necessary to start and, more important, to operate a small business. Many skills can be learned through work experience and formal education, but the kind of person you are may be the most important factor. Here are some major qualities that will increase your chances of succeeding as an entrepreneur.

1. *Self-direction.* You should be a self-starter, with lots of confidence in yourself. You do not hesitate to step into any situation. Doing your own thing should seem like the *only* way. Furthermore, you are the boss and everything really rests on your shoulders.

2. *Determination.* Closely related to self-direction is the drive you need to see you through all the obstacles and difficulties that you will encounter. You have to keep going when others would give up. This often accompanies the high degree of self-confidence mentioned above.

3. *High energy level.* You must be able to put in long hours every day, six or seven days a week, for the first few years at least. You must be able to take hard work, physically and mentally.

4. *Risk orientation.* Because there is a high risk of failure, you must be able to live with uncertainty. You must accept the fact that all your hard work and money may go down the drain. On a day-to-day basis, you must make decisions that involve varying degrees of risk.

5. *Vision.* Many successful entrepreneurs have some dream or vision they feel impelled to realize. Perhaps it is to make that product better than anyone else can or to provide a new product or service.

6. *Ability to learn quickly.* Making errors is inevitable. Only those who do nothing make no mistakes. What is important is what you learn from them. Good entrepreneurs are quick to learn such lessons. They adapt and shift gears as required instead of letting pride stand in the way of admitting a mistake.

How do you stack up as a potential entrepreneur? You can take the entrepreneurial readiness questionnaire in Appendix B following this chapter to see how you rate. Remember, these are only guidelines. The only rule about starting a business is that there *is* no rule. Some people have had an entrepreneurial bent since they were children. They were always promoting something: delivering papers, organizing other kids to collect bottles or plastic containers, selling, or doing other part-time work at an early age. As adults, they don't ask people if they should go into businesses for themselves—they do it!

A 17-year-old composer once asked Mozart's opinion about the quality of his compositions. After examining the works, Mozart told him they lacked maturity and that he should wait until he was a little older. The visitor, somewhat exasperated, replied that Mozart himself had started composing when he was five! Mozart replied, "That's true, but I didn't ask anybody."

Other entrepreneurs are a little more cautious. They get some education—perhaps a bachelor of commerce (B.Com.) or master of business administration (MBA) degree or a professional designation such as chartered accountant (CA)—as well as some work experience before they decide to venture into

<www/cbsc/org/ ontario/his/houng.html>

See this Web site for more information about the Young Entrepreneurs Association of Ontario. For most other provinces try <www.cbsc.org>, select the province, then click on *programs* and then on *youth services.*

Many young people are finding that creating their own job by starting a business is a good career choice. Although some entrepreneurs do not have formal education or training, these master of business administration (MBA) students believe that a degree will provide them with the skills necessary to operate a small business.

business. Some follow this procedure as part of a deliberate plan; others make the decision to go off on their own later, as a result of business experience they have accumulated.

••• WOMEN ENTREPRENEURS •••

A major phenomenon since the late 1970s is the large number of women who have gone into business for themselves. Throughout this book, you will see many examples of such enterprises. Between 1975 and 1990, the number of male entrepreneurs grew 172.8 percent. In 1998, as noted previously, 35 percent of all self-employed Canadians were women, up from 19 percent in 1975. Women starting their own businesses have tended to concentrate in the service sector. This is not surprising since more than 75 percent of the workforce is in the service area, which contributes between 75 and 80 percent of GDP.[3] Studies and surveys have revealed a variety of reasons for this significant emergence of female entrepreneurs.

Financial Need. The past decade saw the average real incomes of Canadian employees drop and unemployment remain high. This has forced many wives to support the family budget by starting a business, sometimes part-time, sometimes with their husbands.

Lack of Promotion Opportunities. Most positions in higher management are still dominated by men. Although the situation is improving, the rate is extremely slow. Many women who are frustrated by this pace take the entrepreneurial route.

Women Returning to the Workforce. Many women who return to the job market after raising a family find that their skills are outdated. They also encounter subtle age discrimination. These factors encourage many to try self-employment.

Feminism. The feminist movements of the past four decades have given many women the confidence to strike out on their own.

Family and Personal Responsibility. The high divorce rate in recent years has created a situation in which many divorced women find themselves with children and little or no financial support from their ex-husbands. Some even refuse such support to be more independent. The development of affordable personal computers and other modern technology has made it possible for women to start businesses based at home. There are examples in this book of home-based enterprises run by women.

Public Awareness of Women in Business. As more publicity highlights the fact that growing numbers of women have started their own ventures, the idea catches on and gives others the confidence to try. Often two or more women will team up to form a partnership.

Part-Time Occupations. Often, married women with some particular talent—for example, publicity, writing, designing, making clothes, cooking, organizing, or human relations—are encouraged to develop their hobby or skills on a part-time basis to see how far they can go with it. This procedure has resulted in many notable success stories, some of which are reported in this book.

Couples in Partnership. Some ventures are started by couples who cannot find jobs. Or sometimes one member of a couple joins his or her partner, whose business is growing and who needs more help.

Higher Rate of Success for Women. Women entrepreneurs seem to have a better success rate than men. Various factors may account for this. Women feel less pressured than men to achieve quick results. They are a little more cautious, so they make fewer mistakes. They also accept advice more readily than men, who may have a macho image of having to know it all. It will be interesting to follow this process to see if women continue to start ventures at the same rate and maintain their remarkable track record.

Critical Thinking

Do you know anyone who seems to have the entrepreneurial spirit? What about him or her makes you say that?

Are there any similarities between the characteristics demanded of an entrepreneur and those of a professional athlete? Would an athlete be a good prospect for entrepreneurship? Why or why not? Could teamwork be important in an entrepreneurial effort?

If you are a woman, are you motivated by women's success rate?

••• ENTREPRENEURS OF THE FUTURE •••

Many people believe that future entrepreneurs will need better education and preparation than in the past. Business has become much more complex. A complicated mass of governmental laws and regulations, the rapid rate of advances in technology, international competition, and concerns with environmental and ethical issues have all combined to make it far more difficult to start and operate a business now.

International management guru Peter Drucker feels that, in the future, people with college and university training and some corporate experience will do much better as entrepreneurs in the long run. Of course, this will not—and should not—discourage those who are strongly determined to start their own company. Such determination and self-confidence are major requirements for success in business. It is important to remember that there is no formula that guarantees success.

••• ENTREPRENEURIAL TEAMS •••

Large organizations are usually cautious, bureaucratic, and slow to react to changes in the markets they serve. Many companies have set up teams of managers from different areas within the company to overcome such difficulties.

Nancy Mathis invented the TC Probe used to test properties of solid materials such as wood or plastic. She was encouraged to market her device by the National Research Council and with her husband, Chris, formed Mathis Instruments, where they have perfected the TC Probe.

Entrepreneurial teams help the company function efficiently and ensure better cooperation and coordination among different functions of the business.

To encourage the entrepreneurial spirit, employees and managers from different areas of the business who have shown such spirit are organized into special teams. A team can be more effective than an individual because it brings together people with a variety of skills and experience to bounce ideas off each other.

Such teams are said to consist of intrapreneurs. An **intrapreneur** is a person with entrepreneurial skills who is employed in a corporation to launch new products. Such people take hands-on responsibility for innovation in an organization.

Some groups become more daring and enterprising and work on what seem like way-out projects. These are known as *skunkworks* (the name comes from the Li'l Abner comic strip) because no one knows what outlandish ideas they may come up with. **Skunkworks** are highly innovative, fast-moving entrepreneurial units operating at the fringes of a corporation.

Many companies have benefitted enormously from intrapreneurial teams and from skunkworks. An example is the development of the Avro Arrow military plane by de Havilland in the 1960s, the most advanced plane of its kind. Do some research in your library to see what other examples you can find.

One of the most famous examples of intrapreneurial success is the Post-it™ gummed note pad, developed at the 3M Company. Despite its many obvious uses, intrapreneurs had to persist for years before it became a major product.

intrapreneur
A person with entrepreneurial skills who is employed in a corporation to launch new products and who takes hands-on responsibility for innovation in an organization.

skunkworks
Highly innovative, fast-moving entrepreneurial units operating at the fringes of a corporation.

 Progress Check

- What are the advantages of entrepreneurial teams?
- Can you give five reasons why entrepreneurs go into business themselves?
- Why are so many women becoming entrepreneurs? Why do they have such a high success rate?

···· ▬▬ ····

WHAT IS A SMALL BUSINESS?

It would be helpful to define what we mean by the term *small business*. Giant companies like Imperial Oil or General Motors look at nearly all companies as small. Governments have various size guidelines for different aid programs. In the definition we have previously used, a **small business** is independently owned and operated, not dominant in its field, and meets certain standards of size in terms of employees or annual receipts.

By this definition, the vast majority of businesses in Canada are small—fewer than 10 employees and with annual sales under $500,000. This volume of sales, less than $10,000 per week, might be further analyzed as follows (in round numbers):

NUMBER OF DAYS OPEN EACH WEEK	SALES PER DAY LESS THAN
5	$2,000
6	1,700
7	1,500

Of course, many small businesses have sales in the millions and up to 50 employees (see Figure 7.1).

There is constant movement as far as individual businesses are concerned. Many are closing up while larger numbers are starting. Many are steadily growing larger, and some eventually become very large companies. Some merge with others or are sold as owners retire or die.

It is estimated that in the mid-1990s there were about 900,000 businesses in Canada. For this purpose, a business is defined as having at least one paid employee plus the owner. Of all these businesses, only a tiny fraction, about 1 percent, have more than 100 employees. The number of businesses that have no employees may reach into the tens of thousands. Statistics Canada states that more than 2,600,000 person report self-employment income.[4]

··· DYNAMIC SECTOR ···

The small-business sector is a very dynamic part of the Canadian economy. It provided nearly all the new jobs created in the 1980s and repeated this process

small business
Business that is independently owned and operated, not dominant in its field, and meets certain standards of size in terms of employees or annual receipts.

< www.drucker.com/ html/about_peter_f_ drucker.html>

The Web site for The Peter F. Drucker Canadian Foundation for Nonprofit Innovation includes information about the foundation and about Drucker himself and his writings in the field of management. Check it out to learn about this *"guru, legend, and business icon."*

<www.mmm.com>

3M has a reputation for an intrapreneurial culture that goes far beyond the example of Post-It Notes. See this Web site for information on other products and the innovative culture at 3M.

This shop is an example of the many small businesses in Canada. A large number of businesses are started each year by entrepreneurs seeking the challenge of fulfilling a dream.

Spotlight on Big Business

<www.weyerhaeuser.com>

A Small Business Grows to Be a Large Business

In 1961 John Sereny bought a tiny wholesale operation for $1500. In 1994 he sold it for $25 million to forestry giant MacMillan Bloedel. That year Sereny's Green Forest Lumber Ltd., with sawmills and distribution centres in Ontario and the United States, had sales of $377 million and profits of just under $12 million. At 68, with neither of his two musician sons interested in taking over from dad, Sereny felt that the MacMillan Bloedel offer was one he could not refuse.

There was an additional sweetener to the $25 million that Sereny found enticing. He was asked to run the company for three years so that "big Mac" could train his successor. So once a week the 68-year-old entrepreneur took off in his plane at Toronto's airport and flew to inspect the plants in Windsor and Fort Erie, Ontario, and this after a 10- to 12-hour-a-day workweek. Obviously John Sereny loved his work, and the company left him alone so that he could do the job properly.

MacMillan Bloedel had learned its lesson from previous takeovers in which the companies were incorporated into the company's operations rather than ▲ continuing to operate independently, with results that were not entirely satisfactory. Both the company and Sereny had to make adjustments to accommodate to the new situation, but everything worked out well. Is this a story with a happy ending? It certainly is a great success story for John Sereny. The fact that it ceased to be a family-owned business is not unusual. In John Sereny's case, he did what he had to do and his children are doing their thing.

This entire procedure was of an interim or transitional nature. By 1998 Green Forest Lumber had been absorbed directly by its giant parent, MacMillan Bloedel, and ceased to exist as a separate company. John Sereny retired. It's ironic, or perhaps a natural development in the modern world of business, that, in 1999, MacMillan Bloedel itself was acquired by an even larger American forestry firm, Weyerhaeuser.

Source: Patricia Lush, "Green Forest Pilot Still Flies Solo," *Globe and Mail, Report on Business,* February 28, 1996, p. B10; interview with Ruxandra Kovaco, July 2, 1999.

in the 1990s. Small business also is responsible for a big share of innovation and initiative over a wide spectrum of business activities.

Small businesses continue to be feeders for future large businesses. As they prosper and develop new services or products, they are often bought out by large companies, which thus become more competitive. A good example is in the Spotlight on Big Business box. The founders usually profit handsomely from the transaction while retaining managerial positions and acquiring shares in the larger entity. Alternatively, after small businesses establish a good track record, they convert from private to public companies, enabling them to obtain significant financing and become larger companies.

Nearly all small businesses are Canadian-owned and managed, in contrast to large businesses, many of which are foreign-owned and managed. Small business thus plays a big role in helping to maintain the Canadian identity and Canadian economic independence.

••• WIDE DIVERSIFICATION •••

Another significant aspect of small business is the wide diversification of its activities. If you look, you will find small businesses in many sectors:

1. *Service businesses.* You are already familiar with the services provided by dry cleaners, travel agencies, lawncare firms, beauty parlours, and

Spotlight on Small Business

<www.southtower.on/ca>

An Amazing Variety from the Atlantic to the Pacific

In St. John's, Newfoundland, Brian Terry founded Nautical Data International in 1993 by inducing the federal Atlantic Canada Opportunity Agency to grant $400,000 to Cabot College to train fishery workers as prospective geomatics technicians. Now, Bronson Lodge, a 33-year-old former trawlerman, and former fishplant worker Doris King have completed the training program and are working at Nautical Data producing electronic maps and digital nautical products. Some of these products are sold as far away as Japan. The company employs 55 people.

In British Columbia's Fraser Valley, Les Clay and his three employees are experimenting with cloning yellow cedar trees. Clay's Nursery is aiming to be the first commercial-scale tree-cloning operation in Canada. Clay is being helped by Canfor Corp. It is a tricky business, but the business was started by his father and Clay has been at it in one way or another since 1956. He has had big success with his rhododendrons, which he now exports to Japan, New Zealand, the United States, and the United Kingdom.

Between these two coasts we can find Brent Zettl, who grows Saskatoon berries and other plants in a worked-out mine, 1100 feet below the surface, a few

hours drive from Saskatoon. His company, Prairie Plant Systems, has found that underground conditions are ideal for growing. Their 20,000-watt "sun," gentle "rains" controlled by computer, and double the normal amount of carbon dioxide make plants thrive without being subjected to storms, frosts, pests, hail, or other natural disasters. The temperature is ideal, hovering between 18 degrees at night and 25 degrees by day.

Finally, and most exotic of all, in Metcalfe, Ontario, outside Ottawa, Bill and Brenda Brewer-Fedun run the South Tower Armouring Guild, producing medieval armour weapons and clothing. Bill is a retired Canadian Armed Forces aircraft technician and supplies costumes and props for movies and for medieval enthusiasts through a mail-order catalogue. He has even gotten orders for chain-mail miniskirts. In general, Brewer-Fedun has trouble keeping up with the demand. These are but four examples of the hundreds of thousands of small businesses thriving across the country.

Sources: Kevin Cox, "Fish Workers Map Future," *Globe and Mail, Report on Business*, March 1, 1996, p. B7; Edward Kay, "Tree-mendous," *Canadian Business*, October 1995, p. 83; Eric Malling, "Mine Gardening," W5, CTV, February 20, 1996; Edward Kay, "Joust Desserts," *Canadian Business*, November 1995, p. 35.

---

other services that cater to you and your family. In your career search, be sure to explore services such as hotels and motels, health clubs, amusement parks, income tax preparation organizations, employment agencies, accounting firms, rental firms of all kinds, management consulting, repair services (for example, computers, VCRs), insurance agencies, real estate firms, stockbrokers, and so on. A major growth area is in computer consulting and the knowledge-based industries generally.

2. *Retail businesses.* You only have to go to a major shopping mall to see the possibilities in retailing. There are stores selling shoes, clothes, hats, skis, gloves, sporting goods, ice cream, groceries, and more. Much more. Watch the trends, and you will see new ideas like fancy popcorn stores and cafés with Internet access areas.

3. *Construction firms.* Drive through any big city and you will see huge cranes towering over major construction sites. Would you enjoy supervising such work? Visit some areas where construction firms are building bridges, roads, homes, schools, buildings, and dams. There is a feeling of power and creativity in such work that excites many

<www.ndi.nf.ca>

The Nautical Data International Web site invites you to "cruise the digital ocean." Try it to learn more about this producer of electronic maps and digital nautical products.

observers. How about you? Talk to some of the workers and supervisors and learn about the risks and rewards of small construction firms.

4. *Wholesalers.* Have you ever visited a wholesale food warehouse, jewellery centre, or similar wholesale firm? If not, you are missing an important link in the small-business chain, one with much potential. Wholesale representatives often make more money, have more free time, travel more, and enjoy their work more than similar people in retailing.

5. *Manufacturing.* Of course, manufacturing is still an attractive career for tomorrow's graduates. Surveys show that manufacturers make the most money among small-business owners. There are careers for designers, machinists, mechanics, engineers, supervisors, safety inspectors, and a host of other occupations. Visit some small manufacturers in your area and inquire about such jobs to get some experience before starting your own manufacturing business. The high-tech world of today opens up many opportunities, if you are interested.

There are also thousands of small farmers who enjoy the rural life and the pace of farming. Small farms have been in great trouble for the last few years, but some that specialize in exotic crops do quite well. Similarly, many small mining operations attract college and university students who have a sense of adventure. People who are not sure what career they would like to follow have a busy time ahead. They need to visit service firms, construction firms, farms, mines, retailers, wholesalers, and all other kinds of small and large businesses to see the diversity and excitement available in Canadian business.

Critical Thinking

Imagine yourself starting a small business. What kind of business would it be? How much local competition is there? What could you do to make your business more attractive than competitors'? Would you be willing to work 60 to 70 hours per week in such a business?

•••• ▬▬▬ ••••

STARTING A SMALL BUSINESS

There are several ways to get into your first business venture.

1. Start your own company.
2. Buy an existing business.
3. Buy a franchise unit.

Franchising was discussed in the previous chapter. Let us first look at some common procedures you should follow regardless of which path you pursue.

GATHER INFORMATION   The federal Business Development Bank of Canada (BDC) publishes some useful, free material for new entrepreneurs. So do most of the larger banks in Canada and the Canadian Bankers Association. The Canadian Federation of Independent Business (CFIB) is also a useful body for entrepreneurs. It has branches across Canada. Read through some CFIB booklets for important clues as to what you should be doing before starting a business. Other useful federal sources are regional offices of the National Research Council, the Patent Office of the Ministry of Consumer and Corporate Affairs, the Small Business Administration, and the Small Business Data Base of

Statistics Canada. The Statistics Canada database is backed by the federal and provincial governments and provides information on how competitors or potential competitors are performing. Most provincial governments provide a lot of information, assistance, and financing for small business. This is reviewed in some detail in Chapter 4.

OBTAIN PROFESSIONAL ADVICE   Find a good accountant, lawyer, or equivalent professional—they will be your most important advisers for starting and running a business. Ask friends, other entrepreneurs, or family to recommend someone. An experienced accountant will give you invaluable advice and help you through all the procedures of getting your company organized and running (see Figure 7.2).

An account manager at BDC Connex®, BDC's virtual branch, examines an online loan application.

Don't fret about the cost. Remember that you are planning to invest (and borrow) thousands of dollars and invest a long period of hard labour. It is wise to protect that investment by spending a small portion of those dollars at the outset for experienced counsel. Your accountant will also be invaluable on an ongoing basis. He or she will organize your accounting system and your office procedures, produce monthly figures, analyze results, advise on taxation matters, and free you up to concentrate on those functions that only you can and should attend to: buying, selling, servicing customers, collecting payments, and more.

PREPARE A BUSINESS PLAN   It is amazing how many people are eager to start a small business but have only a vague notion of what they want to do. Eventually, they come up with an idea for a business and begin discussing the idea with professors, friends, and other business people. At this stage, the entrepreneur needs a **business plan**, a detailed written statement that describes the nature of the business, the target market, the advantages the business will have over competitors, the resources and qualifications of the owners, and much more.

business plan
A detailed written statement that describes the nature of the business, the target market, the advantages the business will have over competitors, the resources and qualifications of the owners, and much more.

SOURCE	PERCENTAGE USING SOURCE	RANK OF SOURCE
Accountant	78%	1
Other business owners	77	3
Friends/relatives	76	5
Bankers	72	2
Lawyers	63	6
Books/manuals	62	7
Suppliers	59	4
Trade organizations	47	9
Seminars	41	8
Government sources	33	10

FIGURE **7.2**
· · · ·
INFORMATION SOURCES
Small-business managers turn to accountants and bankers for important advice. They also question other business owners and friends for ideas.

A business plan forces potential owners of small businesses to be quite specific about the products or services they intend to offer. They must analyze the competition, the money needed to start, and other details of operation. A business plan forces the entrepreneur to translate hopes and dreams into concrete reality: to see how much cash is required, how much sales and profit must be generated to break even, how much profit will be made if all goes well, whether the target is there, and what the competition is doing. It gives the entrepreneur a good look at what he or she may be walking into.

A business plan also enables investors, bankers, or other lenders to evaluate your proposal properly. You cannot expect to ask for financing without presenting a full picture of what you are all about. A well-prepared business plan provides the vital information these people require to make a decision. It also makes an excellent impression, because it shows that you have gone to a lot of trouble and expense and are very serious about your project.

To prepare a thorough plan, you will most likely need the assistance of a good accountant. In general, a business plan should include the following:

1. A cover letter summarizing the major facets of your proposed business.
2. A brief description of the industry and a detailed explanation of the products or services to be offered.
3. A thorough market analysis that discusses the size and nature of the market, the need for the new product or service, and the nature of the competition.
4. A marketing plan that includes location, signs, advertising, and display.
5. An operating plan that includes a sales forecast, financial projections, accounting procedures, and human resources requirements.
6. A comprehensive capitalization plan describing how much money the owner is committing. Few banks or investors will support a new firm unless the owner has made a substantial financial commitment.
7. A description of the experience and expertise of the owner. This may include résumés, letters of recommendation, and financial statements.

Unless you spend adequate time and effort preparing your business plan, it may end up like thousands of others—in a wastebasket, unread! Of 1200 proposals received in a few months, the Aegis Partners, a Boston venture capital firm, read 600, researched 45, and funded only 14. Why? Because most entrepreneurs don't spend enough time preparing a good business plan but expect potential lenders to spend several hours reading it.[5]

A proper business plan takes months to prepare, as you and your accountant gather information and organize it into the proper format. Unfortunately, you have to convince your busy readers in just a few minutes that it is worth reading. To do that, the plan has to be a real plan, not something cooked up to justify a decision to go into business made on intuition or some other basis.

Many books and articles have been written on how to prepare and write a good business plan. Many include a software disk. Canadian banks have some useful free material, including software. A sample outline of a business plan is provided in Figure 7.3. Your accountant will be well informed on these matters. By working closely with him or her, you will find out what part of the job is yours.

Next, we will discuss some of the many sources of money available to new business ventures. All of them call for a comprehensive business plan. The time and effort invested *before* a business is started pays off many times later. With small business, the big payoff is survival.

Cover Letter

Only one thing is certain when you go hunting for money to start a business: You won't be the only hunter out there. You need to make potential funders want to read your business plan instead of the hundreds of others on their desks. Your cover letter should summarize the most attractive points of your project in as few words as possible. Be sure to address the letter to the potential investor by name. "To whom it may concern" or "Dear Sir" is not the best way to win an investor's support.

Section 1—Introduction

Begin with a two- or three-page management overview of the proposed venture. Include a short description of the business, and discuss major goals and objectives.

Section 2—Company Background

Describe company operations to date (if any), potential legal considerations, and areas of risk and opportunity. Summarize the firm's financial condition. Include past and current balance sheets, income and cash-flow statements, and other relevant financial records. (You will read about these financial statements in Chapter 18.) It is also wise to include a description of insurance coverage. Investors want to be assured that death or mishaps do not pose major threats to the company.

Section 3—Management Team

Include an organization chart, job descriptions of listed positions, and detailed résumés of the current and proposed executives. A mediocre idea with a proven management team is funded more often than a great idea with an inexperienced team. Managers should have expertise in all disciplines necessary to start and run a business. If they do not, mention outside consultants who will serve in these roles and describe their qualifications.

Section 4—Financial Plan

Provide five-year projections for income, expenses, and funding sources. Don't assume the business will grow in a straight line. Adjust your planning to allow for funding at various stages of the company's growth. Explain the rationale and assumptions used to determine the estimates. Assumptions should be reasonable and based on industry and historical trends. Make sure all totals add up and are consistent throughout the plan. (It will be necessary to hire a professional accountant or financial analyst to prepare these statements.)

Stay clear of excessively ambitious sales projections; rather, offer best-case, expected, and worst-case scenarios. These not only reveal how sensitive the bottom line is to sales fluctuations but also serve as good management guides.

Section 5—Capital Required

Indicate the amount of capital needed to commence or continue operations and describe how these funds will be used. Make sure the totals are the same as the ones on the cash-flow statement. This area will receive a great deal of review from potential investors, so it must be clear and concise.

Section 6—Marketing Plan

Don't underestimate the competition. Review industry size, trends, and the target market segment. Discuss strengths and weaknesses of the product or service. The most important things investors want to know are what makes the product more desirable than what's already available and whether it can be patented. Compare pricing to the competition's. Forecast sales in dollars and units. Outline sales, advertising, promotion, and PR programs. Make sure the costs agree with those projected in the financial statements.

Section 7—Location Analysis

In retailing and certain other industries, the location of the business is a crucial factor. Provide a comprehensive demographic analysis of consumers in the area of the proposed store as well as a traffic-pattern analysis and vehicular and pedestrian counts.

Section 8—Manufacturing Plan

Describe minimum plant size, machinery required, production capacity, inventory and inventory-control methods, quality control, plant personnel requirements, and so on. Estimates of product costs should be based on primary research (see Chapter 13).

Section 9—Appendix

Include all marketing research on the product or service (off-the-shelf reports, article reprints, etc.) and other information about the product concept or market size. Provide a bibliography of all the reference materials you consulted. This section should demonstrate that the proposed company won't be entering a declining industry or market segment.

Sources: Eric Adams, "Growing Your Business Plan," *Home-Computing*, May 1991, pp. 44–48; R. Richard Bruno, "How to Write a Business Plan for a New Venture," *Marketing News*, March 15, 1985, p. 10; Ellyn Spragins, "Venture Capital Express," *Inc.*, November 1990, pp. 159–160.

FIGURE 7.3
• • • •
OUTLINE OF A
COMPREHENSIVE
BUSINESS PLAN

Progress Check

- Can you name the five different classes of small businesses?
- What factors are used to classify a firm as a small business?
- What advice would you give a friend who wanted to learn more about starting a small business?
- There are many sections in the business plan. This plan is probably *the* most important document a small-business person will ever create. Can you describe at least four of the sections?

···· ▬▬▬ ····

FUNDING A SMALL BUSINESS

The problem with most new small businesses is that the entrepreneurs have more enthusiasm than managerial skills and capital. Our economic system is called *capitalism* for a reason. It is capital (money) that enables entrepreneurs to get started; buy needed goods, services, labour, and equipment; and keep the business going. Some of the *financial* reasons cited for failure are

- starting with too little capital
- starting with too much capital and being careless in its use
- borrowing money without planning how and when to pay it back
- trying to do too much business with not enough capital
- not allowing for setbacks and unexpected expenses
- extending credit too freely

Entrepreneurs, like most people, are not highly skilled at obtaining, managing, and using money. Inadequate capitalization or poor financial management can destroy a business even when the basic idea behind it is good and the products are accepted in the marketplace. One secret of finding the money to start your business is knowing where to look for it.

One of the major problems for new entrepreneurs is misinformation or lack of information about capitalization and financial management. A new entrepreneur has several sources of capital: personal savings, relatives, former employers, banks, finance companies, venture capital organizations, and government agencies.

Small businesses are key clients of Canada's banks. Approximately 95 percent of all bank business-borrowing customers are small and medium-sized enterprises (SMEs). Banks approve 93 percent of all loans from SMEs, according to the 1998 Thompson-Lightstone national SME survey. Banks compete aggressively in the SME market, tailoring loan packages and services to these customers' special needs, and hosting and participating in seminars and workshops designed to ensure an effective partnership between banks and small business. See Figure 7.4 for further information on the importance of bank and other financing.

In Canada the most common sources of commercial financing are the chartered banks. Since small businesses, especially new ventures, are high-risk undertakings, it is not surprising that banks have been very reluctant to make unsecured loans to small-business people. In response to criticism from many quarters about their lack of support of such an important part of the economy, banks have announced a variety of new programs. For example, the Royal Bank announced a joint operation with the federal Business Development Bank of Canada (BDC) in southern Ontario involving expediting loans of

<strategis.ic.gc.ca>

The marketing research firm mentioned here, Thompson-Lightstone, is listed under the *Business Support and Financing* heading in the Strategis Web site. You can visit this site to learn more about this company. The Strategis Web site itself is a large database provided by Industry Canada as a resource for people who are doing business, or are considering doing business, in Canada. Take some time to explore this site; it has a wealth of very useful information.

$50,000 to $500,000 to export-oriented, high-technology small businesses, the so-called *new economy*.[6] The Royal and the CIBC launched a joint foundation to provide loans of up to $15,000 for unemployed young people who want to start businesses.[7] The Bank of Montreal set up a $200 million financing program for small and medium-sized businesses. It will make traditional loans and also invest in companies.[8]

Entrepreneurs may turn to the federal or provincial governments, which have a variety of agencies and programs to aid new or existing businesses. For example, the Small Business Loans Act authorizes the federal government to guarantee up to 85 percent of loans by authorized lenders, usually banks. The federal BDC is also available for those unable to obtain bank loans. There are also venture capital companies, whose purpose is to seek out worthwhile new ventures and back them. Investors known as **venture capitalists** may finance your project, for a price. Venture capitalists ask for a hefty stake (frequently 60 percent) in your company in exchange for the cash to start your business. Experts recommend that you talk with at least five investment firms and their clients to find the right one for you.

Venture capital companies are interested only in equity positions—buying shares in the company. The BDC may take an equity position or make a loan. Both will insist on seats on the board of directors to keep an eye on the company's operations. In practice, the venture capitalists play a more active role than the BDC. They also will not usually consider a request for less than $500,000. By contrast, the majority of BDC loans are under $100,000. The BDC plays a crucial role because it will invest in businesses with no track record, making it possible for them to obtain additional financing from other sources.

The financing agreement usually provides that, after a certain period, the entrepreneurs may buy back the shares held by these institutions, at their current value.

As Figure 7.4 indicates, 45 percent of SMEs use personal savings for start up and operation. Many entrepreneurs also turn to their families for funds. It is important that, when taking loans from family members or friends, there is a clear understanding of the terms of repayment and if any interest is to be charged. Prepare a brief written document covering these and any other pertinent conditions of the loan that all parties will sign. This will prevent misunderstandings and worse from arising in the future.

You may want to consider borrowing from a potential supplier to your future business. Helping you get started may be in the supplier's interest if there is a chance you will be a big customer later. (See Figure 7.4 for more information).

One of the most common mistakes new small-business owners make is waiting too long to talk to bankers. You would be surprised how long it takes to review and process bank loans. Another common mistake is to ask for too little money.

venture capitalist
Individuals or organizations that invest in new businesses in exchange for partial ownership.

- Half of SMEs report that they currently borrow from a financial institution for business financing (50%).
- Supplier credit is the second most utilized source (48%).
- Credit cards are the third most common source (46%).
- Equipment and vehicle leasing is fourth (28%).

Many companies use multiple sources of financing. In 1998 only 10 percent used a single source. Personal savings were utilized by 45 percent of SMEs.

Source: *Small and Medium-Sized Businesses in Canada*, Thompson, Lightstone & Co. Ltd., 1998, vol. 1, p. 3 (prepared for Canadian Bankers Association).

FIGURE **7.4**
. . . .
SOURCES OF SMALL AND MEDIUM-SIZED ENTERPRISES' (SMES) EXTERNAL FINANCING

As you may have guessed, technology-minded entrepreneurs have the best shot at attracting start-up capital. Such potential businesses are more attractive to venture capitalists and the federal and provincial governments have grant programs that provide funds for such ventures.

PERSONAL CONSIDERATIONS BEFORE GOING INTO BUSINESS

You have been advised several times that the owner and manager must work long hours and perhaps seven-day weeks, especially for the first couple of years. If you are unattached, then you are free to devote all your time to your business. If you want to sleep on a cot in your office there's nothing to stop you.

But what if you are married and have a child or two? Is your spouse ready to back you by undertaking to play daddy and mommy? Will you be torn between your family and business demands? Suppose you have no kids but you have a spouse or companion. How will she or he react to your constant absence? Have you considered what it may do to your relationship? These questions are often overlooked by entrepreneurs until they crop up and create havoc.

Finally, think about what kind of support system you can draw on when required. You may need some no-cost bodies like family members or friends to pitch in sometimes—to answer the phone, do some bookkeeping, help pack or ship. Do you have a shoulder to cry on when things get rough from time to time, as they certainly will?

Once you have passed all these hurdles—business plan, financing, and personal factors—you're ready. So far we have discussed starting a new business. Let us now look at buying a business.

BUYING A BUSINESS

On the one hand, there are many legitimate reasons for owners of a business to want to sell their company. They may want to retire, they may be ill, or they may have other interests that have become more important. Sometimes partners cannot get along or a company wants to divest itself of a subsidiary that does not fit into its core business.

On the other hand, the main reason for selling might be negative business factors. You must be very careful about this. A business whose profits have been declining for a couple of years may be sick. Or perhaps the business seems to be doing all right, but the owners know of some new factor that threatens its viability. This might be a change in a highway route that would result in a loss of vehicle traffic that is the lifeblood of the business. Perhaps a new competing franchising unit is scheduled to be built nearby. Or maybe the area has become run down and regular customers are turning away.

A new technological advance might threaten to make the company's processes, equipment, or product obsolete. (For example, plastic might replace steel and glass.) Imported competing products might be taking away the company's traditional markets (TVs, autos, jeans, and shoes are good examples). The company may be on the verge of losing a major customer. Or perhaps some new environmental regulations are due to kick in shortly that will involve a substantial outlay for new equipment.

To get the real story, do two things. Engage a professional accountant to examine the books and financial statements for the last three to five years. He or she will assess whether the financial statements give you a reliable picture of the company's operations during this period.

While this audit is being conducted, do some intensive investigation of your own. Check out every possible source of information in the municipality or area. Chambers of commerce, business development bodies, local newspapers, adjacent businesses (especially if you are considering a retail business), real estate agents, and local banks are all good sources of information. Drop in on the company unannounced at different hours to see what the operations look like. You might get a chance to speak to employees and customers. Get information from the trade association and trade publications of the particular industry about problems, trends, and developments.

When the audit and your investigation are both done, it is time to sit down with your accountant and review all the facts. (In effect, you have both been assembling some of the data necessary to prepare a business plan.) If you decide to go ahead, the matter of determining a fair price still remains. A business valuation expert can be very useful at this point. Often your accountant can do the job. If you require financing in addition to your own investment, it is time to prepare the formal business plan.

Buying a business requires careful research to determine the owner's reasons for selling and the overall financial stability of the company.

• • • • ▬▬▬ • • • •
CAUSES OF SMALL-BUSINESS FAILURE

Statistics show that most new businesses will fail within five years. There are many reasons for this. Most are avoidable weaknesses, what you might call personal or internal mistakes. They are usually lumped together as signs of *poor management*. (Part 3 of this book contains a thorough discussion of management.)

1. *Lack of finances,* due to any one or a combination of the following:

    Insufficient capital at start.

    Extending too much credit.

    Allowing customers to continually pay late.

    Carrying too much inventory.

    Not making sufficient allowance for slow beginning.

    Inadequate reserve for the unexpected.

    Initial overhead too high.

2. *Lack of experience.*

    Inadequate experience in that line of business.

    No previous work experience at all.

    Poor marketing: pricing, products, or promotion.

3. *Poor allocation of time.*

    Allotting time according to pressure of events.

    Not prioritizing according to importance of activity, such as selling, customer service, and collections.

4. *Weak or no professional guidance.*

Poor planning.

Inadequate accounting system and misleading or outdated information.

Lack of outside objective assessment.

5. *Lack of necessary personal qualities.*

Strong determination and drive needed to overcome setbacks.

Ability to live with uncertainty and risk.

Ability to put in long hours over a long period.

Completely focused on the immediate tasks.

Often external or objective causes that are not subject to the individual's control play an important role in the collapse of a business. For example, if one or two of your major customers go bankrupt while they owe you substantial sums, as often happens in a recession, you may be dragged down with them. If Chrysler had not been saved by U.S. and Canadian government backing, it would have gone bankrupt in 1980 and would have dragged down many small businesses.

Similarly, changes in government policy sometimes have a major impact on business. The Free Trade Agreement has hit many sectors of business in Canada since 1988—wine producers, fruit growers, furniture manufacturers, and more. Some other external factors are the rate of inflation, recession or boom, high or low interest rates, fluctuation in value of the Canadian dollar, and technological advances. The entrepreneur has no control over any of these.

Progress Check

- We gave you six reasons small businesses fail financially. Can you name three?
- Why do so many people continue to start new businesses when the majority of them will be out of business in five years?
- What are three common causes of business failure?

OPERATING A SMALL BUSINESS

In spite of overwhelming odds against them, entrepreneurs set out to conquer the business world confidently and enthusiastically. How hard do they work? Almost half of the owners work 56 hours a week. Nearly 20 percent of new owners keep up full-time or part-time jobs in addition to the long hours working the new business. Clearly, the job as owner of a new small business calls for considerable stamina. Only 11 percent work less than 40 hours; 86 percent put in extra hours on weekends.[9]

Thousands of would-be entrepreneurs of all ages have asked the same question: How do I get started? How can I learn to run my own business? Many of these people had no idea what kind of business they wanted to start; they simply wanted to be in business for themselves. That seems to be a major trend among students today. As you will see shortly, you have to understand business practices or you'll go broke in your own business. Here are some hints for learning about how to run a small business.

••• LEARN FROM OTHERS •••

There are courses available that teach small-business management. You might learn by investigating your local schools and colleges for such classes. A great

Reaching Beyond Our Borders

<www.thinkwaytoys.com>

Toys Are Theirs

In 1995 one of the biggest hit movies was Disney's *Toy Story*. What is perhaps not so well known is that a Canadian company, Thinkway Toys, was the North American licensee for characters based on *Toy Story*. This led to some interesting developments after the movie became a big hit.

Thinkway president Larry Chan got a desperate request from U.S. President Bill Clinton for Buzz Lightyear and Woody. After a frantic effort, the staff came up with 30 playmates ranging form electric toothbrushes to talking money banks, and thus saved the day at the White House Christmas party.

This was just one example of the flood of orders that Larry Chan has had to cope with since October 1995. Eventually he shipped more than $21 million worth of toys around the world. The demand was so heavy that the company could have shipped double that amount, had they been able to produce enough of them.

Larry Chan and his two younger brothers, Michael and Albert, moved to Toronto from Hong Kong in the early 1970s, and they all graduated from the University of Toronto's computer science program. Working with his father-in-law, Larry was importing toys, and eventually Thinkway got its first big break designing and manufacturing the Ninja Turtle Talking Bank.

This success opened the door to a licence from Disney to sell the Little Mermaid Talking Bank in Canada. Chan's proven track record with these products led him to conclude other deals with Disney for characters from the *Lion King* and other Disney features. Subsequently, Chan was able to get other good deals from Lucasfilm and Paramount Pictures. Thinkway Toys is a good example of a small Canadian company that is making it big in the world market.

Source: Gayle MacDonald, "Toy Story's Toy Maker Rides a Hit," *Globe and Mail, Report on Business*, December 21, 1995, p. B11.

---

advantage of these courses is that they bring together entrepreneurs, allowing them to exchange experiences and pass on useful information to new small-business owners. The starting place for budding entrepreneurs is talking with small-business owners and managers. Learn from their experience, especially their mistakes.

They will tell you that location is critical for a retail business. They will caution you not to be undercapitalized. They will warn you about the problems of finding and retaining good workers. And, most of all, they will tell you to keep good records and hire a good accountant and lawyer before you start. Small-business owners can give you hundreds of good ideas, ranging from how to get bank loans, to how to design creative advertising. This free advice is invaluable.

Figure 7.2 shows where entrepreneurs seek advice and how they rank the importance of those sources. As mentioned previously, accountants are the prime, but not the only, source of useful guidance for small business owners.

••• GET SOME EXPERIENCE •••

There is no better way to learn small-business management than by becoming an apprentice or working for a successful entrepreneur. A high percentage of small-business owners got the idea for their businesses from their prior jobs. The prior jobs of almost half of new business owners were in small businesses. The general rule is: get three years' experience in a comparable business.

Advances in technology are allowing more companies, employees, and entrepreneurs to reconsider the traditional workplace environment. Home-based businesses are growing at record levels.

••• THE KEY TO SUCCESSFUL OPERATIONS •••

By following the procedures discussed above, a new entrepreneur should be able to avoid most of the principal causes of failure indicated previously in this chapter: lack of finances and experience; lack of adequate professional guidance; and poor allocation of time. As for having the necessary personal qualities, these were discussed previously. In addition, the entrepreneurial readiness questionnaire that follows this chapter (Appendix B) will help you make a self-assessment.

HOME-BASED BUSINESS

The boom in home-based business operations is one of the major trends in small business. There are estimates that 40 percent of North Americans will be working out of their homes in the year 2000. In the U.S. alone this translates into 55 million people working at home of which some 17.5 million are estimated to be home-based businesses. The U.S. Commerce Department estimates that in 1998 more than half of all small businesses were home-based.[10] Don Dutton, president of the Canadian Home-Based Business Association, noted that the hottest trend is in consulting, with computer management and telecommunications leading the field.[11] It would be a good idea to have another look at Chapter 1, where this important aspect of small business was discussed in detail.

INTERNATIONAL ASPECTS OF ENTREPRENEURSHIP

<www.homebus.com>

You can visit the Business Owners' Network Web site to learn about an organization designed to provide information and contacts for business owners. Can Web sites like this successfully meet the needs of business people who are cut off from the normal means of interaction with other businesses because they operate out of their homes?

Our planet has become a small place. We can no longer do business without considering the international market as both an opportunity and a challenge. Foreign companies come to Canada to compete with domestic companies. We, too, have broadened our horizon to think globally.

If you start your own business, be alert to international investment and export possibilities. As shown in Chapter 4, the Canadian and provincial governments offer extensive financial aid, information, and other support for exports. As you grow, you may consider opening branches, sales offices, or even plants in other countries. You might license a patent to, or enter into a joint venture with, a foreign company. See Chapter 3 for more about doing business internationally.

Small business plays an important role in Canada's export trade. The Canadian government has long recognized this and established the Export Development Corporation (EDC) to assist small and medium-sized businesses in the complex task of exporting to foreign countries. This crown corporation provides a wide variety of excellent services to such companies. It has offices in major cities and puts out many useful brochures and other material. In 1998 EDC reported that 80 percent of the companies they aided, some 3600 firms, were small and medium-sized. It provided $5.8 billion of financing and insurance in more than 150 countries (see Figure 7.5). EDC has a special program to help very small companies, with sales under $1 million, go international.[12]

Number of Companies Served

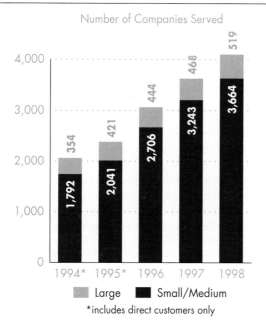

| | Large | Small/Medium |
1994* 1995* 1996 1997 1998
*includes direct customers only

Source: EDC Web site, <www.edc.ca>, June 1999.

┌─ FIGURE 7.5 ─┐
• • • •

**EXPORT DEVELOPMENT
CORPORATION SUPPORT
FOR EXPORTERS**

You can see how **EDC's**
support for Canadian
companies, especially
small and medium-sized
companies that export,
has grown over a five-
year period.

<www.edc.ca>

Visit the Export Develop-
ment Corporation Web site.
What is its function? What
dollar volume of business
does it support?

Ethical Dilemma

REVIEW

Remember the dilemma posed at the beginning of this chapter? Here's what our executives think. Bédard states that "laws and jurisprudence on the ability of people to use formerly gained information or to contact former customers is fairly well established. Regardless of employee contracts that have been signed, if a person does use information previously gained, it is acceptable as long as it has little or no impact on the former employer. If the impact is important, the former employer is in his rights to have the contract enforced. Unfortunately, such things occur and many of these situations will end up in court."

According to Reilley, "proprietary technology and patents are reasonably easy to protect from theft. However, two issues apply here, assuming that theft is not involved. First, the switcher's new company creates competition, which, in turn, applies pressure on the old firm to sharpen its pencil. (This is good.) Second, often the old larger firm is only too happy, in the fullness of time, to seek more efficient suppliers for niche technolo-

gies. The switcher's new firm often fills this need and everyone wins."

Years ago, when the Canadian author of this book decided to leave his last employer to form his own firm of chartered accountants, he was faced with this dilemma. An important client of his employer made him an attractive offer: set up offices on the client's premises with no charge for rent or secretarial services, and take over the auditing and consulting work of his group of companies at a reasonable fee. It was a very tempting offer for a fledgling CA with a young family, who was seeking clients. What would you have done? It was difficult to refuse, but after careful consideration, the author felt it would be unethical to do this, especially since he had had a very good relationship with his employer. He told this client that, after six months, if they still wanted to make the change, it could be done at that time. But the psychological moment had passed and the opportunity was lost.

The Internet computer networks were a mushrooming international phenomenon in the late 1990s. For small business, they offer an unparalleled opportunity for low-cost, fast, international exposure. An increasing number of small companies are taking advantage of this channel to get free information, to advertise their products and services, and to get expert help and advice. There are many reports in various media about the exploding growth of the Internet medium.

SUMMARY
· · · · ·

1. Define small business and discuss its importance to the Canadian economy.

1. Of all the nonfarm business in Canada, more than 95 percent are considered small.
   * *Why are small businesses important to the Canadian economy?*
   Small businesses account for a significant portion of the national economy. Perhaps more important to tomorrow's graduates, 90 percent of the nation's new jobs in the private sector are in small business.

   * *What does the "small" in small business mean?*
   A small business is independently owned and operated, not dominant in its field of operation, and meets certain standards of size in terms of employees (fewer than 100) or sales. (That depends on the size of others in the industry. For example, American Motors was considered small in the auto industry before it merged with Chrysler.)

2. Explain why people are willing to take the risks of entrepreneurship.

2. There are many reasons people are willing to take the risks of entrepreneurship despite the high risks of failure.
   * *What are a few of the reasons why people start their own businesses?*
   Reasons include profit, independence, opportunity, and challenge.

3. Describe the attributes needed to be a successful entrepreneur, and explain why women have a higher success rate than men.

3. Successful entrepreneurship takes a special kind of person.
   * *What does it take to be an entrepreneur?*
   A person must be self-directed, self-nurtured, action-oriented, tolerant of uncertainty, and energetic.

   * *Why are women more successful than men?*
   Generally, women are less pressured to achieve quick success, they are more cautious, and they accept advice more readily.

4. Summarize the major causes of small business failures.

4. More than two-thirds of the small businesses started this year will not survive to celebrate their fifth anniversary.
   * *Why do so many small businesses fail?*
   Many small businesses fail because of managerial incompetence and inadequate financial planning.

5. Identify ways you can learn about small businesses.

5. Most people have no idea how to go about starting a small business. They have some ideas and the motivation; they simply don't have the know-how.
   * *What should you do before starting a small business?*
   First, learn from others. Take courses and talk with some small-business owners. Second, get some experience working for others. Finally, consult with an accountant experienced in small business.

6. Explain what a business plan is, and outline the general areas of information it should include.

6. Begin with a plan. The more effort you put into a business plan, the less grief you'll have later.
   * *What goes into a business plan?*
   See Figure 7.3 on page 211.

• *Should you do it all yourself?*
Most small business owners advise new entrepreneurs to get outside assistance in at least two areas: you need a good lawyer and a good accountant. Also, seek help from government publications and any other sources you can find. The more knowledge you can gain early, the better.

7. The failure rate of new businesses is very high.
    • *What must be done to increase the likelihood of success?*
    You must learn from others, get a few years' experience in the field you are interested in, and get good professional guidance. Make sure you have the necessary personal qualities and conditions for the long haul.

7. List the requirements to operate a small business successfully.

KEY TERMS

business plan 209
entrepreneur 199
entrepreneurship
   199

intrapreneur 204
skunkworks 204
small business 205

venture capitalists
   213

DEVELOPING WORKPLACE SKILLS

1. Select a type of small business that looks attractive as a career possibility for you. Talk to at least three people who manage and own such businesses. Ask them how they started their businesses. Ask about financing, personnel problems (hiring, firing, training, scheduling), accounting problems, and other managerial matters. Pick their brains. Let them be your instructors. Put together a rough business plan of how you would start such a business. Discuss it in class.

2. Go to the library and review some business magazines for the last couple of years. Look for articles about successful entrepreneurs. Write brief profiles of two of them focusing on similarities and differences. Make copies for your career file. Share what you found with the class.

3. Put together a list of factors that might mean the difference between success and failure for a new company in the software industry. Can small start-ups realistically hope to compete with biggies such as Lotus or Microsoft? Discuss the list and your conclusions in class.

4. Visit a franchise other than a fastfood restaurant and see what the owners have to say about the benefits and drawbacks of franchising. Would they buy the franchise again if they could start all over? What mistakes did they make, if any? What advice would they give a student interested in franchising? Share your research with your class.

INTERNET CHALLENGES

1. Using any search engine such as Yahoo, Alta Vista, or Canada.com, see what you can find for *small business*. How many matches did you find under Canada.com? Follow some of the links that interest you. See if you can find anything on home-based businesses. Bring any information to class that you found surprising or that might be useful for students.

2. Check out the Canada Youth Business Foundation Web site at <www.cybf. ca/main.htm> to see what you can find. Is there any help for young persons wanting to start their own business? Is there anything there that stimulates your interest in running your own business?

Practising Management Decisions

It's time to herald a new era of airplane travel. Gone are the days of playing solitaire on food-encrusted tray tops. Airlines are introducing seat backs outfitted with digital screens. Soon you'll be able to order video-on-demand, browse the duty-free catalogue and—thanks to a team of Toronto-based programmers who share a vision for electronic blackjack—zone out playing video games.

The programmers are partners in upstart ISES Corp. The company has finalized a deal with Airtours plc of Manchester, England, and is currently in talks with other major airlines. ISES software will also be used on Air France, which introduced the new seat backs in summer 1999. Steven Johnson, ISES vice-president of marketing, says the company hopes to double its revenue in 1999. But the long-term prospects are the real appeal: as deregulation heightens airline competition, in-flight entertainment (IFE) is expected to explode. ISES hopes to get in on all the action once it has conquered the video game realm.

ISES was founded when five employees of Toronto-based Gametronics Gaming Equipment Ltd. grasped the potential of the nascent IFE industry and left to form their own company. "OK, we thought," says Dean Davis, one of the founders, "we're going to do this ourselves. We're going to be a games supplier." They set up shop in the solarium of fellow-founder Igor Muskatblit's apartment, where they crammed in two picnic tables to serve as computer desks. That was in

CASE 1
······
FIVE ENTREPRENEURS TRY VIDEO GAMES AS A BUSINESS
······

1998. Fuelled by the growth of IFE (ISES also works with Motorola on its version of Web TV), it now has moved into a real office. Most impressively, ISES is beating out major game-makers, largely because its 18-strong roster of games is simple, consisting mainly of mind teasers and familiar board games such as hangman and Chinese checkers. "For a short flight, you're not really going to want to learn a new game," says Davis.

Decision Questions

1. The case illustrates a number of themes from this chapter as well as from other chapters. What issues from the chapter can you find exemplified in this case?
2. What about trends reviewed in the first chapter? Can you see how this case illustrates one or more of the trends? Which ones?
3. Do you think ISES is likely to succeed? What are the factors that might indicate the likelihood of success? Do you see any obstacles?
4. Can you see a future career for yourself starting a software-related business, alone or with some friends? Do you have anything specific in mind? Would you first get a job in that field to get some experience, as the entrepreneurs in this case did, or would you try to launch your business without doing that?

Source: Cynthia Reynolds, "Daddy, Where's the Flight Simulator?" *Canadian Business*, May 28, 1999, p. 74.

You are toying with the idea of starting your own business but are a little nervous about going it on your own. You like the help you would get with a franchise and that you could still run your own show—almost. The problem is that well-known names demand on investment of $150,000 to $1 million, which is much too rich for your blood.

You have heard recently about home-based franchises that require anywhere from $10,000 to $50,000 to start up. Sheldon Adler, who heads a franchising consulting company, says they are pretty easy to get into. He points out that they have been growing steadily in the United States for the last 15 years and are making headway in Canada. He provides you with a sample listing.

CASE 2
······
OPPORTUNITIES IN HOME-BASED FRANCHISING
······

Heels on Wheels, a mobile shoe-repair business operating out of a van. Staff members go directly into offices to fix and polish the shoes of business people. Women often bring three or four pairs to work for repair.

Location Lube, which provides a similar service for automobile lube jobs. Technicians service the cars in office parking lots, saving car owners the trip to a service station.

Colour Your Carpet, a rug-dyeing business that restores your carpet at a fraction the price of buying a new one.

Other home franchises that have appeared recently include cleaning services, computer training, personnel services, and travel and interior design agencies. In most cases, the franchisees start off actually doing the work but soon hire staff and take on a management role.

Nevertheless, Adler warns that home-based franchises demand people who are much more outgoing and marketing oriented than salespeople in retail-shop outlets. "You've got to go out and knock on a lot of doors, because you don't have a storefront for people to walk through," he says. "If you're inhibited, forget it."

Gary Shulz of Victoria is a recent convert to home franchising. Three months ago, he became Canada's master franchiser for Foliage Design Systems, a Florida-based chain that installs and maintains tropical plants in hotels, restaurants, offices, and homes.

"Most businesses have plants," Shulz says. "But they need someone to install and maintain them." A plant lover, he was attracted to the Florida-based franchise chain because the company has 20 years of expertise, enough time to kick the bugs out of the system. Foliage Design Systems gave Shulz horticultural training, marketing assistance, and time-tested business manuals.

The financial returns on home franchises can be lucrative, but Adler cautions would-be owners not to expect overnight success. "It takes a while to build up, because you have to go out and sell," he explained. "It's not like retail."

Vicky Telycenas, coordinator of franchise operations for Trend Tidy's Ltd. of Markham, Ontario, says owners can expect a gross weekly income of up to $4800 after 30 months by managing two or three cleaning teams. She estimates net income at 20 percent, or $960 weekly. Some of the 21 franchisees are ex-housewives who tried returning to the workforce but found their skills were obsolete.

Most are earning more money than they would have in traditional office jobs. They also have more responsibility. Trend Tidy's other franchise operators include former bankers, teachers, and accountants. "In each case, they reached a crisis point in their jobs and decided to leave the rat race," Teleycenas said. "They took control of their lives."

Decision Questions

1. What do you think of the home-based franchise operations discussed above? What questions should you be asking before buying a franchise?

2. Can you find out which franchises seem to be doing well in your area? (Expand your search beyond retail franchises.) Where would you look for such information?

3. Would you be prepared to consider any of the franchises in the case or in the previous question as a possible entry into a small business? What do you find attractive? What is not so attractive?

4. Franchising is increasingly popular, but are the lower risks of franchise organizations worth giving up the freedom of ownership and control? What information do you need to answer this question and how can you get it?

Source: *Globe and Mail, Report on Business,* September 30, 1991, p. B6.

Entrepreneurial Readiness Questionnaire

Appendix B

Not everyone is cut out to be an entrepreneur, but all kinds of people with all kinds of personalities have succeeded in starting small and large businesses. There are certain traits, however, that seem to separate those who will be successful as entrepreneurs from those who may not be. The following questionnaire will help you determine which category you fit into. Take a couple of minutes to answer the questions and then score yourself at the end. **A low score doesn't necessarily mean you won't succeed as an entrepreneur**. It does indicate, however, that you might be happier working for someone else.

Each of the following items describes something you may or may not feel represents your personality or other characteristics. Read each item and then put an X in the column that most nearly reflects the extent to which you agree or disagree that the item seems to fit you best.

Scoring: Give yourself one point for each Column 1 or Column 2 response to these questions: 2, 3, 6, 8, 9, 10, 11, 12, 14, 15, 17, 18, 20, 22, 23, 24. Give yourself one point for each Column 4 or Column 5 response to these questions: 1, 4, 5, 7, 13, 16, 19, 21, 25.

Add your points and see how you rate in the categories below:

21–25 Your entrepreneurial potential looks great if you have a suitable opportunity to use it. What are you waiting for?

16–20 This is close to the high entrepreneurial range. You could be quite successful if your other talents and resources are right.

11–15 Your score is in the transitional range. With some serious work, you can probably develop the outlook you need for running your own business.

 6–10 Things look pretty doubtful for you as an entrepreneur. It would take considerable rearranging of your life philosophy and behaviour to make it.

 0–5 Let's face it. Entrepreneurship is not really for you. Still, learning what it's all about won't hurt anything.

	Agree			Disagree		
	Completely **Column 1**	**Mostly** **Column 2**	**Partially** **Column 3**	**Completely** **Column 4**	**Mostly** **Column 5**	**Partially** **Column 6**
1. I am not generally optimistic.	____	____	____	____	____	____
2. I relish competing intensely regardless of the rewards.	____	____	____	____	____	____
3. I do not hesitate to take a calculated risk.	____	____	____	____	____	____
4. When betting I prefer a high-payoff long shot.	____	____	____	____	____	____
5. I like to follow traditional or conventional thinking.	____	____	____	____	____	____
6. I enjoy games like tennis or hardball with someone who is a little better than I am.	____	____	____	____	____	____
7. Making lots of money is largely a matter of getting the right breaks.	____	____	____	____	____	____
8. I am inclined to forge ahead and discuss later.	____	____	____	____	____	____
9. Reward or praise means less to me than satisfaction of a job well done.	____	____	____	____	____	____
10. I usually go my own way regardless of others' opinions.	____	____	____	____	____	____
11. I am not easily discouraged.	____	____	____	____	____	____
12. I am a self-starter needing little urging from others.	____	____	____	____	____	____
13. I do not take criticism easily.	____	____	____	____	____	____
14. I can criticize others without hurting their feelings.	____	____	____	____	____	____
15. I hate being told what to do.	____	____	____	____	____	____
16. I would rather plan than actually carry out plans.	____	____	____	____	____	____
17. I do not acknowledge errors readily.	____	____	____	____	____	____
18. I communicate well with others.	____	____	____	____	____	____
19. I work best with some guidance.	____	____	____	____	____	____
20. I like to know what's going on and take steps to find out.	____	____	____	____	____	____
21. I am generally casual and easy-going.	____	____	____	____	____	____
22. I like solving my problems myself.	____	____	____	____	____	____
23. I do not give up easily.	____	____	____	____	____	____
24. I enjoy impressing others.	____	____	____	____	____	____
25. I do not accept advice easily.	____	____	____	____	____	____

Part 3

Key Elements in Business Success: Managing, Leadership, Organization, and Production

Leadership and Management

Chapter 8

LEARNING GOALS

*After you have read and studied this chapter,
you should be able to*

1 explain the four functions of management and why the role of managers is changing.

2 distinguish between goals and objectives; distinguish between strategic, tactical, and contingency planning; and explain the relationships of goals and objectives to various types of planning.

3 describe the significance of an organization chart, and explain how organizations are changing to meet the needs of customers.

4 describe the directing function of management, and illustrate how the function differs at various management levels.

5 summarize the five steps of the control function of management.

6 explain the differences between managers and leaders, and compare the characteristics and uses of the various leadership styles.

7 describe the three general categories of skills needed by top, middle, and first-line managers.

8 illustrate the skills you will need to develop your managerial potential, and outline activities you could use to develop these skills.

Mary Parker Follett graduated from Thayer College and Radcliffe. While she was in college, Follett taught political science at a nearby secondary school. She was a part of Boston high society and participated on committees that set minimum wages for women and children. The management theorist of that time (the early 1900s) was Frederick Taylor, the "father of scientific management." His writings favoured command-style, hierarchical organizations. Employees were treated much like robots or computers, things to be manipulated and directed. Taylor did not believe in participative management. Managers acted more like dictators.

Mary Parker Follett, in comparison, believed very strongly that the person doing the job was the person most likely to know how to do the job better. She felt that it was human nature to want to be self-managed. Furthermore, Follett believed in the concept of cross-functional rather than vertical authority. Her idea was for people in various departments to share information with one another to the benefit of all.

Follett believed that managers should be leaders rather than dictators. They were to provide a vision and help focus all the resources of the firm on meeting that vision. Follett also felt that knowledge and experience, not titles and seniority, should decide who should lead.

PROFILE

Mary Parker Follett: Mother of Modern Management

Follett's concepts, written in the 1920s and 1930s, were far ahead of her time. She was relatively ignored while Frederick Taylor grew in importance. But times change and innovative ideas from the past suddenly take on new meaning. That is exactly what has happened to Follett's writings.

A book titled *Mary Parker Follett—Prophet of Management: A Celebration of Writings from the 1920s* was released by the Harvard Business School Press in 1995. In the introduction to the book, guru Peter Drucker stated that it is too bad her works were lost for several decades because she is as pertinent today as she was when she first developed her ideas. In his contribution to this collection of Mary Parker Follett's writings, *Some Fresh Air for Management?* management authority Henry Mintzberg of McGill University wondered what would have happened if "we had spent most of this century heeding Follett instead of Fayol" (see next chapter for a review of Fayol's theories).

London School of Economics chair Sir Peter Parker says that he is not sure who the father of management is, but he is sure who the mother is: Mary Parker Follett. Her ideas about empowerment, self-management, cross-functional cooperation, and conflict resolution are now being implemented in leading firms throughout the world. In this chapter, we shall explore both traditional and new management concepts. Much of it is based on the fundamentals that Mary Parker Follett established 70 years ago.

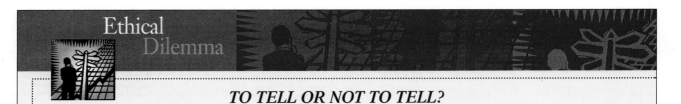

Ethical Dilemma

TO TELL OR NOT TO TELL?

You are an ambitious, hard-working, younger manager. Your department head is an older, experienced manager whose performance has been inconsistent in the past two years. The department has not met its monthly target for the past three months and unless the results improve rapidly, his job may be on the line. By chance, you come across some information that your department head does not have and you know it would help him improve the department's performance significantly. Despite your youth you have excellent evaluations of ▲ your job performance and you think you would have a good chance of succeeding your boss if he was let go. If you are a man, imagine that your wife is about to give birth—you could certainly use a boost in salary. What should you do? If you are a woman, imagine your husband has just lost his job. Would you give the information to your superior to keep quiet? Think about this as you study this chapter and we will try to resolve this dilemma at the end of the chapter.

<www.sunsite.utk.edu/FINS>

This is only one of numerous Web sites presenting quotes from Mary Parker Follett and referring to her work. Surf the Net and see what you can learn about this amazing lady.

<www.ge.com>

You can visit the GE Web site or many other Web sites, to learn more about Jack Welch.

THE MANAGEMENT CHALLENGE OF THE FUTURE

Jack Welch, former CEO of General Electric (GE) is considered by many to be an extremely successful business leader who radically changed the whole approach to corporate management. Changes were necessary because of global competition, technological change, and the growing importance of pleasing customers. Many foreign competitors had the reputation for being more responsive to the market and for bringing out innovations earlier. Canadian firms are changing their management styles to become more responsive and able to produce new products quickly.

To achieve this, managers have delegated more authority and responsibility to lower-level managers and employees who can respond more quickly to consumer requests. Combining this with accelerating technological change increases the need for a new breed of worker, one who is more educated and has higher skill levels. Such workers demand more freedom of operation and a different managerial style.

Closely connected to these changes is a near revolution in the structure and organization of companies. This is discussed in detail in the next chapter. One of the important aspects of restructuring and reengineering companies is a drastic reduction in the number of middle managers and office workers.

••• A DIFFERENT POINT OF VIEW •••

Many notable commentators have expressed doubt that the massive layoffs that have occurred, and continue to take place, will produce the desired results. For example, Thomas Davenport, director of the information management program at the University of Texas, one of the fathers of what some are referring to as *the reengineering craze*, said it has gotten out of hand. The original idea had nothing to do with "mindless corporate bloodshed."[1]

Another world authority and prolific writer on management issues, Henry Mintzberg of McGill University, commented:

While some of the layoffs may be needed, cutbacks have become akin to medieval bloodletting. Whenever there appears to be something wrong with a patient, we cut and bleed him. There may be more creative ways of dealing with the problem, like shorter working hours. A manager must also assess other elements, such as whether the damage to staff morale is worth the savings any layoffs might bring.[2]

Because the jury is still out on this question, we will have to keep an eye on future developments.

In the following sections, we'll describe the foundations of management, but it takes an entire book to learn how to implement the concepts of leadership in today's competitive environment. One book that outlines where organizations are heading in the twenty-first century is Gifford and Elizabeth Pinchot's *The End of Bureaucracy and the Rise of the Intelligent Organization*. The organizations that the book describes are even more flexible and responsive to market changes. To understand where we are going, however, it is important to understand where we have been. Let's begin by exploring some basic managerial principles.

Management is the art of getting things done through people. Today that means working *with* employees rather than simply directing them. Managerial styles are more casual (including casual dress).

··· THE CHANGING ROLE OF MANAGERS ···

Mary Parker Follett defined management as "the art of getting things done through people." At one time, that meant that managers were called *bosses*, and their job was to tell people what to do and watch over them to be sure they did it. Bosses tended to reprimand those who didn't do things correctly and generally acted stern and "bossy." Many managers still behave that way. Perhaps you've witnessed such managers yelling at employees in restaurants, on shop floors, or in offices.

Today, management is moving away from that kind of behaviour. Managers are being educated to guide, train, support, motivate, and coach employees rather than to boss them around. Modern managers in progressive companies emphasize teamwork and cooperation rather than discipline and order giving. Managers in some high-tech and progressive firms dress more casually, are more friendly, and generally treat employees as partners rather than unruly workers.

Management is experiencing a revolution. Managers in the future are much more likely to be working in teams; they'll be appraised by those below them as well as those above, and they'll be assuming completely new roles in the firm. We'll discuss these roles in detail later.

Henry Mintzberg of McGill University is one of the world's authorities on management. He has written extensively on organizational structure and strategy.

The leaders of Labatt Breweries, the Bank of Montreal, and CTV all stress the importance of sharing leadership responsibility. They make a point of regularly spending significant time with their senior executives. In effect this constitutes team leadership.[3]

··· THE MOST EFFECTIVE MANAGERS ···

Effective modern managers have three things in common: they are action oriented, they manage change efficiently, and they are able to build a sense of shared values that will motivate employees and generate loyalty. Executive

<www.management.
mcgill.ca/people/faculty/
profiles/mintzber.htm>

This Web site provides a
brief biography of Henry
Mintzberg and links to an
impressive bibliography of
his writings in the field
of strategic management.

**management by waling
around (MBWA)**
Managers get out of their offices
and personally interact with
employees and customers.

recruiters search for managers with nine attributes that can be divided into two
categories. One is education and experience and the other is personal traits.

The first category includes steady progress through the company ranks,
with an occasional detour to a staff position (see next chapter), and some
background in international business. The personal traits required are excellent communication skills, a vision that can be imparted to others, self-confi-
dency, the ability to take risks without undue worry, and integrity.

Having this kind of background, experience, and personal qualities, makes
top executives attractive to other firms. The favourites typically have a healthy
ego, a fondness for competitive sports, and a lot of experience moving from
city to city or country to country.

Management is experiencing a revolution. Books like *The One Minute
Manager* encourage supervisors to actively praise employees. A concept called
management by walking around (MBWA) encourages managers to get out of
their offices and mingle with workers and customers. This does not mean that
managers are becoming mere cheerleaders; it does mean that they are working
more closely with employees in a joint effort to accomplish common goals.

Henry Mintzberg has written extensively about what managers actually do
and what they should be doing. His speech to the Canadian Club was titled
"Message to Managers: Get Out of Your Offices."

> *Management expert Henry Mintzberg had some pointed advice for an
> audience of blue-chip Montreal business leaders yesterday: don't sit in
> your office and try to manage by remote control. He said Canadians have
> picked up a few bad habits from our American neighbours, and one of
> them is the prevailing management style. Business leaders and decision
> makers can't spend their days sitting in offices poring over numbers and
> flow charts, he said. They have to get out and meet people, be they work-
> ers or customers.*
>
> *Numbers and words are important elements in decision making, but
> they must also be balanced with the insightful elements of images and
> feeling. Those insights can't be obtained by hav-
> ing somebody report to you, Mintzberg said.
> They have to be sensed by the individual. Aloof
> management based only on cold calculations
> of numbers and words is partly responsible for
> the current round of cutbacks and layoffs in
> workplaces.*[4]

Management by walking
around means talking
with employees on the
job. This manager is
going over a report with
an employee so he can
visualize what she wants.

What this means for tomorrow's graduates,
like you, is that managerial careers will demand a
new kind of person. That person is a skilled com-
municator and team player as well as a planner,
coordinator, organizer, and supervisor. These trends
will be addressed in the next few chapters and
should help you decide whether management is
the kind of field you'd like to be in.

•••• ▬▬▬▬ ••••

THE DEFINITION AND
FUNCTIONS OF MANAGEMENT

One reason people go to college is that college prepares them to become managers. Students have told us, "I don't know what I want to do, really. I guess I'd
like to be in management." Management is attractive to students because it

represents authority, money, prestige, and so on. But few students can describe just what managers do. That's what this chapter is for; it describes what managers are, what they do, and how they do it.

Management could be called the art of getting things done through people and other resources. Well-known management consultant Peter Drucker said managers give direction to their organizations, provide leadership, and decide how to use organizational resources to accomplish goals. Both descriptions give you some feel for what managers do. The definition that provides the outline of this chapter is: **management** is the process used to accomplish organizational goals through planning, organizing, directing, and controlling organizational resources. This definition spells out the four key functions of management: (1) planning, (2) organizing, (3) directing (or leading), and (4) controlling (see Figure 8.1).

Planning includes anticipating future trends and determining the best strategies and tactics to achieve organizational goals and objectives. The trend today is to have planning *teams* to help monitor the business environment, to find business opportunities, and to watch for challenges.

Organizing includes designing the organization structure, attracting people to the organization (staffing), and creating conditions and systems that ensure everyone and everything works together to achieve the organization's goals and objectives. Today's organizations are being designed around the customer. The idea is to design the firm so that everyone is working to please the customer while ensuring the continual generation of adequate profits.

Directing is guiding and motivating others to work effectively to achieve the organization's goals and objectives. The trend is to give employees as much freedom as possible to become self-directed and self-motivated. Often that means working in teams. Directing is also referred to as *leading*.

Controlling is checking to determine whether an organization is progressing toward its goals and objectives, and then taking corrective action if it's not. In the past, the greatest attention was given to corporate goals such as profit. The trend today is toward measuring customer satisfaction as well as profit. Continuing customer satisfaction ensures continuing profits.

The four functions just listed are the heart of management, so let's explore them in more detail. The process begins with planning.

---

management
The process used to accomplish organizational goals through planning, organizing, directing, and controlling organizational resources.

planning
Management function that involves anticipating future trends and determining the best strategies and tactics to achieve organizational objectives.

organizing
Management function that involves designing the organizational structure, attracting people to the organization (staffing), and creating conditions and systems that ensure everyone and everything work together to achieve the objectives of the organization.

directing
Management function that involves guiding and motivating others to achieve the goals and objectives of the organization.

controlling
Management function that involves checking to determine whether or not an organization is progressing toward its goals and objectives, and taking corrective action if it is not.

Planning
- Setting organizational goals.
- Developing strategies to reach those goals.
- Determining resources needed.
- Setting standards.

Organizing
- Allocating resources, assigning tasks, and establishing procedures for accomplishing goals.
- Preparing a structure (organization chart) showing lines of authority and responsibility.
- Recruiting, selecting, training, and developing employees.
- Placing employees where they'll be most effective.

Directing (Leading)
- Leading, guiding, and motivating employees to work effectively to accomplish organizational goals and objectives.
- Giving assignments.
- Explaining routines.
- Clarifying policies.
- Providing feedback on performance.

Controlling
- Measuring results against corporate objectives.
- Monitoring performance relative to standards.
- Taking corrective action.

FIGURE **8.1**
• • • •

WHAT MANAGERS DO
Some modern managers perform all of these tasks with the full cooperation and participation of workers. Empowering employees means allowing them to participate more fully in decision making.

Progress Check

- What were some of the factors that have forced executives to change their organizations and managerial styles?
- What's the definition of *management* used in this chapter, and what are the four functions in that definition?

vision
A sense of why the organization exists and where it's heading.

mission statement
An outline of the fundamental purposes of an organization.

goals
Broad, long-term accomplishments an organization wants to attain.

objectives
Specific, short-term statements detailing how to achieve an organization's goals.

operational planning
The process of setting the necessary work standards and schedules to implement the tactical objectives.

The first managerial function is to create a shared vision for the organization. A vision gives a sense of purpose and direction. Goals and objectives are then based on this vision.

PLANNING: CREATING A VISION FOR THE ORGANIZATION

Planning is the first managerial function. Planning involves setting the organizational vision, goals, and objectives. Top managers are expected to create a vision for the firm. A **vision** is more than a goal; it's the larger explanation of why the organization exists and where it's trying to go. A vision gives the organization a sense of purpose and values to unite workers in a common destiny.[5] Managing an organization without a common vision can be counterproductive. It's like motivating everyone in a row boat to get really excited about getting somewhere, but not giving them any direction. As a result, the boat just keeps heading off in different directions rather than speeding toward an agreed-upon goal.

A **mission statement** outlines the fundamental purposes of the organization and becomes the foundation for setting goals and training employees.

Goals are the broad, long-term accomplishments an organization wants to attain. These goals need to be mutually agreed upon by workers and management. Thus, goal setting is often a team process. Nortel's goal was to become the world's leading producer of digital telephone switches by the year 2000.

Objectives are specific, short-term statements detailing how to achieve the goals. One of your goals for reading this chapter, for example, may be to learn basic concepts of management. An objective you could use to achieve this goal is to plan to answer correctly the chapter's Critical Thinking exercises and Progress Checks.

Operational planning is the process of setting the necessary work standards and schedules to implement the tactical objectives. For example, an operational plan would include setting a specific date for a minimum quantity of certain truck parts to be completed and the quality required.

Planning is a continual process. It's unlikely that a plan that worked yesterday would be successful in today's market. Most planning follows a pattern. The procedures you would follow in planning your life and career are basically the same as those used by businesses for their plans. Planning answers three fundamental questions for businesses:

1. What is the situation now? What is the state of the economy? What opportunities exist for meeting people's needs? What products and customers are most profitable? Why do people buy (or not buy) our products? Who are our major competitors?

What threats are there to our business? These questions are part of what is called a **SWOT analysis**. *SWOT* stands for strengths, weaknesses, opportunities, and threats. This type of analysis examines a firm for each of these four characteristics, enabling the company to use its strengths to take advantage of opportunities and meet any threats it faces, while striving to overcome its weaknesses.

2. Where do we want to go? How much growth do we want? What is our profit goal? What are our social objectives? What are our personal development objectives?

3. How can we get there from here? This is the most important part of planning. It takes three forms (Figure 8.2):

    a. **Strategic (long-range) planning** determines the major goals of the organization as well as the policies and strategies for obtaining and using resources to achieve those goals. In this definition, *policies* are broad guides to action, and *strategies* determine the best way to use resources to carry out these policies. At the strategic planning stage, the company decides which customers to serve, what products or services to sell, and the geographic areas in which the firm will compete.

    In today's rapidly changing environment, long-range planning is becoming more difficult and ineffectual. Changes are occurring so fast that plans set for years into the future soon become obsolete. Such plans are often being replaced by ones that allow for quick

SWOT analysis
An analysis of an organization's strengths, weaknesses, opportunities, and threats.

strategic (long-range) planning
Process of determining the major goals of the organization and the policies and strategies for obtaining and using resources to achieve those goals.

FORMS OF PLANNING	EXAMPLES FOR FIBERRIFIC CO.
STRATEGIC PLANNING Broad Long-range Goal-setting By top managers	**STRATEGIC PLAN** Goal set by president: To make Fiberrific the preferred breakfast of health-conscious consumers
TACTICAL PLANNING Specific Short-range Objectives/identification By lower managers	**TACTICAL PLAN** Objective set by director of research and development: To develop a dry cereal that provides 100% of the adult RDA of vitamins, minerals, and fibre by the end of the year
CONTINGENCY PLANNING Backup plans in case primary plans fail	**CONTINGENCY PLAN** Objective set by director of research and development: If dry cereal doesn't meet the market needs, develop a comparable breakfast bar by the end of the year

FIGURE **8.2**
• • • •

PLANNING FUNCTIONS
Very few firms bother to make contingency plans. If something changes the market, such companies are slow to respond. Strategic planning and tactical planning are practised in most firms. This example refers to a company manufacturing a high-fibre breakfast cereal called Fiberrific.

tactical (short-range) planning
Process of developing detailed, short-term strategies about what is to be done, who is to do it, and how it is to be done.

contingency planning
Preparation of alternative courses of action that may be used if the primary plans do not achieve the objectives of the organization.

responses to customer needs and requests. The long-range goal is to be flexible and responsive to the market.

b. **Tactical (short-range) planning** is the process of developing detailed, short-term strategies about what's to be done, who's to do it, and how it's to be done. Tactical planning is normally done by managers or teams of managers at lower levels of the organization, whereas strategic planning is done by the top managers of the firm (for example, the president and vice-presidents of the organization). Tactical planning, for example, involves setting annual budgets and deciding on other details of how to meet the strategic objectives.

c. **Contingency planning** is the preparation of alternative courses of action that may be used if the primary plans don't achieve the organization's objectives. The economic and competitive environments change so rapidly that it's wise to have alternative plans of action ready in anticipation of such changes.

The leaders of market-based companies set direction, not detailed strategy. The idea is to stay flexible, listen for opportunities, and seize opportunities when they come, whether they were planned or not.

 Progress Check

- What's the difference between strategic, tactical, and contingency planning?
- Why would organizations today be less concerned about strategic planning than they once were? What has become of even greater concern? Could strategic planning get in the way of an organization being flexible enough to respond to market changes?

···· ▬▬ ····

ORGANIZING: CREATING A UNIFIED SYSTEM

After managers have planned a course of action, they must organize the firm to accomplish their goals. Basically, organizing means allocating resources, assigning tasks, and establishing procedures for accomplishing the organizational objectives. When organizing, a manager develops a structure or framework that relates all workers, tasks, and resources to each other. That framework is called the *organization structure*. Most organizations draw a chart showing these relationships. This is called an *organization chart*. Figure 8.3 shows a simple one. The organization chart plots who reports to whom and who's responsible for each task. The problem of developing organization structure will be discussed in more detail in the next chapter. For now, it's important to know that the corporate hierarchy illustrated on the organization chart on the next page includes top, middle, and first-line managers.

top management
Highest level of management, consisting of the president and other key company executives who develop strategic plans.

Top management (the highest level of management) consists of the president and other key company executives who develop strategic plans. Three terms you're likely to see often are *chief executive officer (CEO)*, *chief operating officer (COO)*, and *chief financial officer (CFO)*. The CEO is often the president of the firm and is responsible for all top-level decisions and for introducing changes into an organization. The COO is responsible for putting those changes into effect. His or her tasks include structuring, controlling, and rewarding to ensure that people carry out the leader's vision. The CFO is responsible for obtaining funds, budgeting, collecting funds, and other financial matters.

Middle management includes branch and plant managers, deans in colleges and universities, and department heads who are responsible for tactical planning and controlling. **Supervisory (first-line) management** includes people directly responsible for supervising workers and evaluating their daily performance; they're often known as *first-line managers* because they're the first level above workers (see Figure 8.4).

An important part of organizing is staffing, getting the right people on the organizational team. You're probably most familiar with the term *personnel* to describe that function. Today it's called *human resource management* because it's as important to develop employees' potential as it is to recruit good people in the first place. We'll discuss human resource management in Chapter 13.

••• THE CUSTOMER-ORIENTED ORGANIZATION •••

A dominating question of the past 20 years has been how to best organize the firm to respond to the needs of customers and other stakeholders. *Stakeholders* include anyone affected by the organization and its policies and products. That includes employees, customers, suppliers, dealers, environmental groups, and the surrounding communities. The consensus seems to be that smaller organizations are more responsive than large organizations. Therefore, most large firms are being redesigned into smaller, more customer-focused units. For example, Molson Breweries split up into "three regional business units in Canada to improve consumer and market responsiveness."[6]

Small businesses, such as independent tire dealer Direct Tire Sales, realize the importance of pleasing customers, too. The dealership provides services such as loaning customers cars while theirs are in the shop, fixing flats for free on all tires purchased, and guaranteeing linings and brake pads for the

middle management
Level of management that includes plant managers and department heads who are responsible for tactical plans.

supervisory (first-line) management
First level of management above workers; includes people directly responsible for supervising employees and evaluating their daily performance.

FIGURE **8.3**
• • • •
TYPICAL
ORGANIZATION
CHART

This is a rather standard chart with managers for major functions and supervisors reporting to the managers.

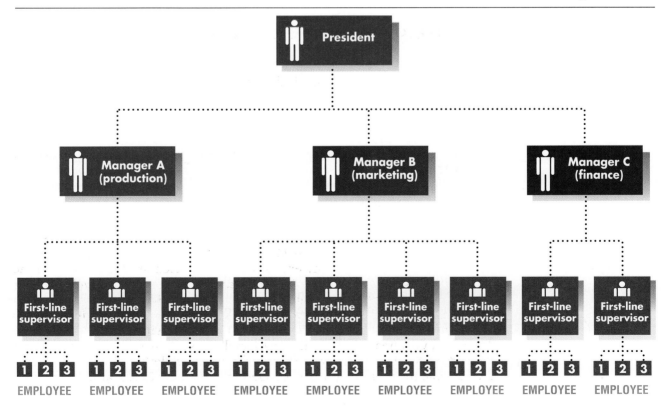

FIGURE **8.4**

· · · ·

**LEVELS OF
MANAGEMENT**

This figure shows the
three levels of manage-
ment. In many firms,
there are several levels
of middle management.
Firms have been elimi-
nating middle-level man-
agers in a cost-cutting
attempt. Computers
have made it possible
to operate with fewer
middle managers.

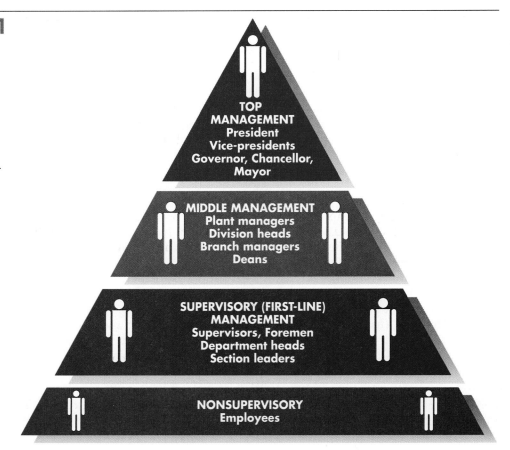

**TOP
MANAGEMENT**
President
Vice-presidents
Governor, Chancellor,
Mayor

MIDDLE MANAGEMENT
Plant managers
Division heads
Branch managers
Deans

**SUPERVISORY (FIRST-LINE)
MANAGEMENT**
Supervisors, Foremen
Department heads
Section leaders

NONSUPERVISORY
Employees

life of the car. They'll even pick up the tab for the cab ride home when you
have your brakes changed. But what really excites customers is the customer
lounge. The spotless, tastefully decorated room sports an aquarium, hot coffee, fresh donuts, and current magazines. Customers ignore the 10 to 15 percent premium for this exceptional service. The dealership was awarded the
Modern Tire Dealer's dealer of the year award.[7]

Other industries, both large and small, are equally customer oriented.
They include investment banking, health care, construction, engineering, and
more. The point is that companies are no longer organizing to make it easy for
managers to have control. Instead, they're organizing so that *customers* have
more influence. The Internet has enabled closer contact with customers and
quicker response time to their requests and needs.

··· ORGANIZATION IS BECOMING INTERFIRM ···

In the past, the goal of organization in the firm was to clearly specify who did
what *within the firm*. Today, the organization task is much more complex
because firms are forming partnerships, joint ventures, and strategic alliances
with other firms that make it necessary to organize the *whole entity*.[8]

There's no way an organization can provide quality goods and services to
customers unless suppliers provide world-class parts and materials with
which to work. Thus, managers have to establish close relationships with suppliers. To make the entire system work, similar relationships have to be established with those organizations that sell directly to consumers—retailers.

Each firm is striving to have every process (e.g., order processing and delivery) as good as the best companies in the world. Often that means finding other firms to perform some of the functions normally carried out internally. This is called *contracting out* or *outsourcing*. Top management must contact those firms and work closely with them to coordinate processes. None of this was possible 20 years ago because the information technology simply wasn't available. Today, however, firms throughout the world are linked by computers and communications technology so that they operate as one.

It makes no sense to introduce the latest management concepts and try to make them work in an organization that's not designed to meet those challenges. And one organization is often not as effective as many organizations working together.[9] Many small businesses are pooling their efforts in such fields as marketing and distribution. Many have formed purchasing co-operatives so they can buy in bulk and get better prices from suppliers.

Creating a unified *system* out of multiple organizations will be one of the greatest management challenges of the twenty-first century. We'll discuss this issue in more depth in Chapter 9.

···· ▬▬▬ ····

DIRECTING AND EMPOWERING EMPLOYEES

After the plans are made and the interfirm connections are made, traditional managers direct the workers in activities to meet the goals and objectives of the organization. In traditional organizations, directing involves giving assignments, explaining routines, clarifying policies, and providing feedback on performance.

In traditional organizations, all managers, from top managers to first-line supervisors, direct employees. The process of directing is quite different, however, at the various levels of the organization. The top managers are concerned with the broad overview of where the company is headed. Their immediate subordinates are middle managers, who are responsible, in turn, for directing employees to meet company objectives. Top managers' directions to subordinates, therefore, are characteristically broad and open-ended. The further down the corporate ladder, the more specific the manager's directions become. First-line managers traditionally allocate much of their time to giving specific, detailed instructions to employees.

··· FROM DIRECTION TO EMPOWERMENT OF TEAMS ···

Progressive managers are less likely to give specific instructions to employees. Rather, they're more likely to empower them to make decisions on their own. Chrysler Canada is a good example (see Chapter 1) of a company where "decision making ... has been moved to the lowest levels." **Empowerment** means giving employees the authority and responsibility to respond quickly to customer requests. In cooperation with employees, managers will set up teams that will work together to accomplish objectives and goals. The manager's role becomes less that of a boss and more that of a coach, assistant, counsellor, and team member. This shift in managerial direction gives employees more participation in decision making and more flexibility in how to get the job done. That usually results in higher employee motivation, more productive workers, and more satisfied customers.

A leading company in the United States, Boeing, tried to upgrade its 747 airplane. Redesigned parts didn't fit together well, and Boeing had to use

empowerment
Giving employees the authority and responsibility to respond quickly to customer requests.

This self-managed team at Boeing is an example of employees who are empowered to make decisions. Management is available for back-up, training, coaching, or other assistance.

thousands of workers to correct the problems. Today, however, Boeing has adopted the team approach, grouping together experts in design, manufacturing, and tooling. The 777 was the first plane designed by a team. Airline customers sat in on the planning sessions. When the plane was finally assembled, the parts fit together within thousandths of an inch. Everything went much smoother than before. Now managers are evaluated by employees as well as the managers above them, and employee morale is up.[10]

Many companies are moving toward self-managed teams. Self-managed, cross-functional teams are groups of employees from various departments such as purchasing, marketing, and engineering. You'll learn more about such teams in Chapter 9. There you will see an excellent example of how Shell Canada has organized its entire workforce in its office at Brockville, Ontario, on the basis of self-managing teams. For now it's important to know that self-managed teams function as independent elements of the firm with an inherent group intelligence of their own. Because they think and act on their own and seek out any information they need, such teams are known as *smart teams*. One purpose of cross-functional teams is to respond quickly to customer needs and market changes. Another purpose is to empower those who know the most about products and what makes them good (the employees themselves) to do what needs to be done to make world-class products. To ensure such responsiveness and responsibility, these teams are self-organizing as well as self-managing.

Training must also be upgraded so that employees become more flexible and ready to take on more responsibility. Customers should be brought into regular contact with the teams, as should suppliers. If they're willing, customers and suppliers can join the teams. Such teams function most effectively when management provides them with all the information the company has (including accounting data) and lets the teams make decisions on their own.

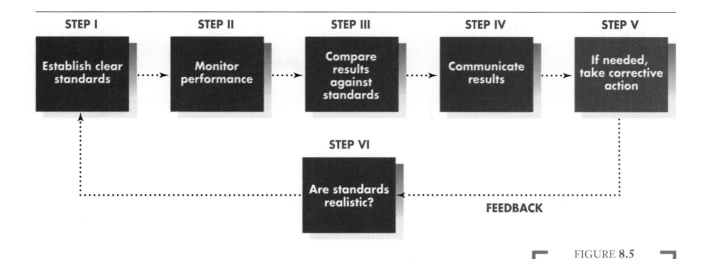

STEP I	STEP II	STEP III	STEP IV	STEP V
Establish clear standards	Monitor performance	Compare results against standards	Communicate results	If needed, take corrective action

STEP VI

Are standards realistic?

FEEDBACK

FIGURE **8.5**

THE CONTROL PROCESS

The whole control process is based on clear standards. Without such standards, the other steps are difficult, if not impossible. With clear standards, performance measurement is relatively easy and the proper action can be taken.

CONTROLLING

Often managers get so involved with the firm's planning process and day-to-day crisis management that they shortchange the control function. The control function involves measuring performance relative to objectives and standards and then taking corrective action when necessary. Thus, the control function (Figure 8.5) is the heart of the management system because it provides the feedback that enables managers and workers to adjust to any deviations from plans and to changes in the environment that have affected performance.

Controlling consists of five steps:

1. Setting clear performance standards.
2. Monitoring and recording actual performance (results).
3. Comparing results against plans and standards.
4. Communicating results and deviations to the employees involved.
5. Taking corrective action when needed.

The control system's weakest link tends to be the setting of standards. To measure results against standards, the standards must be specific, attainable, and measurable.[11] Vague goals and standards such as "better quality," "more efficiency," and "improved performance" aren't sufficient because they don't describe what you're trying to achieve. For example, let's say you're a runner and you say you want to "improve" your distance. When you started your improvement plan last year, you ran two miles a day. Now you run 2.1 miles a day. Did you meet your goal? Well, you did increase your distance, but certainly not by very much. A more appropriate goal statement would be: To increase running distance from two miles a day to four miles a day by January 1. It's important to have a time period established for when specific goals are to be met. Here are examples of goals and standards that meet these criteria:

- Cutting the number of finished product rejects from 10 per 1000 to 5 per 1000 by March 31.
- Increasing the times managers praise employees from 3 times per week to 12 per week.
- Increasing sales of product X from $10,000 per month to $12,000 per month by July 2001.

Spotlight on Small Business

<www.richter.ca>

How Common Is the Practice of Participative Management?

Participative management involves employees in setting objectives and making decisions; democratic and laissez-faire leadership are forms of participative management.

Some firms have had difficulty implementing participative management because some managers hesitate to give up what they feel are their rights. That includes, as they perceive it, the right to be bossy, to tell others what to do, and to punish them if they don't. It certainly does not mean working with people as partners. "Why call me a boss if I am just another worker?" is their attitude. Such people must change if the organization is to develop the teamwork necessary to compete in today's changing environment. Many managers in small firms have always practised participative management.

Stephen Levy, who heads up Richter Management Plus, an arm of chartered accounting firm Richter, Usher & Vineberg, is a consultant in the small-business field in the Montreal area. The 57-year-old Levy has a master's

degree in industrial management from prestigious Massachusetts Institute of Technology and 30 years of tough experience in business. This includes running companies and turning around companies in serious difficulties.

He finds that participative management is the norm rather than the exception in small firms. The atmosphere is generally more informal than at large companies, lending itself to greater employee involvement in decision making. Most small-business owners are overloaded with responsibility so they are happy to have their load lightened by employees assuming more responsibility. This tends to change as the company grows and activities become more formal and structured as more managers are added. That is when the battle to retain the open style that empowers employees usually takes place.

▲ Source: Interview with Stephen Levy, June 13, 1999.

One key to making control systems work is the establishment of clear procedures for monitoring performance. Naturally, management shouldn't be burdened with such control procedures unless the goals are important enough to justify such reporting. Most managers have seen, for example, elaborate accident reports that took hours of management time and that reported, "All is well." To minimize paperwork, such reports could be limited to certain kinds of serious cases.

••• NEW CRITERIA FOR MEASUREMENT: ••• CUSTOMER SATISFACTION

internal customers
Units within the firm that receive services from other units.

external customers
Dealers who buy products to sell to others, and ultimate customers who buy products for their own personal use.

The criteria for measuring success in a customer-oriented firm is customer satisfaction of both internal and external customers. **Internal customers** are units within the firm that receive services from other units. For example, the field salespeople are the internal customers of the marketing research people who prepare research reports for them. **External customers** include dealers who buy products to sell to others, and ultimate customers such as you and I who buy products for their own personal use. One goal today is to go beyond satisfying customers to delighting them with superior products and services.

Other criteria of organizational effectiveness may include the firm's contribution to society or improvements in the quality of air and water surrounding the plant. The traditional measures of success are usually financial, defined in terms of profits or return on investment. Certainly these measures are still important, but they're not the whole purpose of the firm. The purpose of the firm today is to please employees, customers, and other stakeholders. Thus, measurements of success must take all these groups into account. Firms have to ask questions such as:

Do we have good relations with our employees, our suppliers, our dealers, our community leaders, the local media, our stockholders, and our bankers?

What more could we do to please these groups?

Are the corporate needs (such as making a profit) being met as well?

One measure of success used by many firms is whether they delight their customers with their products and services. Relationship building is important for creating a strong bond with customers.

LEADERSHIP: VISION AND VALUES

In the literature of business there's a trend toward separating the notion of manager from that of leader. One person could be a good manager and not a good leader. Another could be a good leader without being a good manager. One difference between managers and leaders is that managers produce order and stability whereas leaders embrace and manage change. **Leadership** is creating a vision for others to follow, establishing corporate values and ethics, and transforming the way the organization does business so that it's more effective and efficient. Management is the carrying out of the vision.

Like managers, leaders plan, organize, direct, and control. But when leaders plan, they plan more globally than managers in setting the agenda for the firm. Leaders organize, but their focus is on structuring or restructuring the organization to be competitive in world markets. Leaders direct and control, but their direction involves creating a vision and their control consists of empowering people and holding them responsible for finding their own means to those ends. Let's look at other ways that leaders differ from managers (see Figure 8.6).

In the future, all organizations will need leaders who can supply the vision as well as the moral and ethical foundation for growth. All organiza-

leadership
Creating a vision for others to follow, establishing corporate values and ethics, and transforming the way the organization does business so it is more effective and efficient.

MANAGERS	LEADERS
Do things right	Do the right thing
Command and control	Inspire and empower
Seek stability and predictability	Seek flexibility and change
Are internally focused	Are externally oriented
Work within the firm	Coordinate the whole system
Are locally oriented	Are globally oriented
Think mostly of workers	Think mostly of customers and other stakeholders

FIGURE **8.6**

MANAGERS AND LEADERS

Generally speaking, leaders are more visionary than managers, who tend to be more rule oriented.

tions will also need managers who share in the vision and know how to get things done with the cooperation of all employees. The workplace is changing from a place where a few dictate what to do to others, to a place where all employees work together to accomplish common goals.

To summarize, leaders are supposed to

autocratic leadership
Leadership style that involves making decisions without consulting others and implies power over others.

democratic (participative leadership)
Leadership style that consists of managers and employees working together to make decisions.

1. *Have a vision and rally others around that vision.* Rather than manage, the leader is supposed to be openly sensitive to the concerns of followers, give them responsibility, and win their trust.
2. *Establish corporate values.* These values include a concern for employees, for customers, and for the quality of the company's products. When companies set their goals today, they're going beyond just narrow business goals and are defining the values of the company as well.
3. *Emphasize corporate ethics.* This means an unfailing demand for honesty and an insistence that everyone in the company gets a fair shake. That's why we've stressed ethical decision making throughout this text.
4. *Not fear change, but embrace it and create it.* The leader's most important job may be to transform the way the company does business so that it's more effective and efficient.

••• LEADERSHIP STYLES •••

Nothing has challenged researchers in the area of management more than the search for the "best" leadership traits, behaviours, or styles. Thousands of studies have been done just to find leadership traits; that is, characteristics that make leaders different from others. Intuitively, you would conclude the same thing that researchers found: the research findings were neither statistically valid nor reliable.[12] We know that some leaders seem to have traits such as good appearance and tact, whereas others appear unkempt and abrasive.

Just as there's no one set of traits that can describe a leader, there's also no one style of leadership that works best in all situations. Let's look briefly at a few of the most commonly recognized leadership styles and see how they may be effective.

Butch Carter, coach of the Toronto Raptors, is a good example of the effectiveness of autocratic leadership in selected situations. This leadership style is not appropriate for all groups. Managers must be able to adapt their leadership style to suit the situation.

1. **Autocratic leadership** involves making managerial decisions without consulting others; it implies power over others. Many business people who were sports leaders seem to use an autocratic style that consists of issuing orders and telling employees what to do. Motivation comes from threats, punishment, and intimidation of all kinds. Such a style is effective in emergencies and when absolute followership is needed (for example, on army manoeuvres). Some football, basketball, hockey, and soccer coaches have successfully used this style.
2. **Democratic** or **participative leadership** consists of managers and employees working together to make decisions. Research has found that employee participation in decisions may not always increase effectiveness, but it usually increases job satisfaction. Many new, progressive organizations are highly successful at using a democratic style of leadership where traits such as flexibility, good listening skills, and empathy are dominant. Chapter 12 gives examples of how this motivates employees.

3. ***Laissez-faire*** or ***free-rein leadership*** involves managers setting objectives and employees being relatively free to do whatever it takes to accomplish those objectives. One example is Nova Scotia Power, as shown in the Spotlight on Big Business. In certain professional organizations, where managers deal with doctors, engineers, and other professionals, the most successful leadership style is often one of laissez-faire leadership. The traits needed by managers in such organizations include warmth, friendliness, and understanding. More firms are adopting this style of leadership.

laissez-faire (free-rein) leadership Leadership style that involves managers setting objectives and employees being relatively free to do whatever it takes to accomplish those objectives.

Individual leaders rarely fit neatly into just one of these categories. Researchers Tannenbaum and Schmidt illustrated leadership as a continuum with varying amounts of employee participation ranging from purely boss-centred leadership to subordinate-centered leadership (see Figure 8.7).

Which leadership style is best? Research tells us that successful leadership depends largely on who's being led and in what situations. It also supports the notion that different leadership styles ranging from autocratic to laissez-faire may be successful depending on the people and the situation.

Any manager may use a variety of leadership styles depending on whom he or she is dealing with and the situation. A manager may be autocratic but friendly with a new trainee; democratic with an experienced employee who has many good ideas that can only be fostered by a manager who's a good listener and flexible; and laissez-faire with a trusted, long-term supervisor who probably knows more about operations than the manager does.

Let's summarize what we've just said.

- There's no such thing as leadership traits that are effective in all situations, nor are there leadership styles that always work best.
- Different styles of leadership can be used effectively. They range from autocratic to laissez-faire. Which style is most effective depends on the people and the situation.
- A truly successful leader has the ability to use the leadership style most appropriate to the situation and the employee involved.
- Leadership depends on followership, and followership depends on the traits and circumstances of the follower. In general, though, good

FIGURE 8.7

· · · ·

VARIOUS LEADERSHIP STYLES

The trend today is toward subordinate-centred leadership.

Boss-centred leadership ◄··· Subordinate-centred leadership

Use of authority by manager						Area of freedom for subordinates
Manager makes decision and announces it	Manager "sells" decision	Manager presents ideas and invites questions	Manager presents tentative decision subject to change	Manager presents problem, gets suggestions, makes decision	Manager defines limits, asks group to make decision	Manager permits subordinates to function within limits defined by superior
Autocratic			**Democratic/participative**			**Laissez-faire/ free rein**

leaders tend to be visionary, value driven, flexible, able to identify with the goals and values of followers, good communicators, sensitive to the needs of others, and decisive when the situation demands it (see Figure 8.8).

••• THE TREND TOWARD SELF-MANAGED TEAMS •••

The trend is toward self-managed teams and away from management, with its emphasis on planning, organizing, directing, and controlling. The trend is toward leadership, with its emphasis on vision and empowerment. What will these trends mean for managers and leaders in the twenty-first century? It means, for one thing, that the trend is away from autocratic leadership toward laissez-faire leadership. This is a real challenge for traditional managers because it means giving up their traditional command-and-control style of management.

Managers in the future will be empowering teams rather than individual employees. This is an entirely different role for managers, one that will take some time to develop. In the end, however, the concept of self-managed teams will enable Canadian companies to compete with anyone in the world.

Spotlight on Big Business

<www.nspower.ca>

New Style Management at Nova Scotia Power

Corporate Canada, struggling with low morale created by the recession, is facing increasing competition, breakneck change, and overwhelming complexity. The result: increased pressure for results and decreased patience when they are not achieved.

It's not enough any more to make the strategic decisions from Olympian heights and then point the way ahead. Executives today must understand and respect their employees, create shared values and goals, and march forward right alongside them, creating better customer value in the process. Nova Scotia Power is a good example of a company moving with the times.

L. R. Comeau, president and CEO of Nova Scotia Power Inc., in his 1995 report, his last as head of the company, commented on the many changes during his 13-year stint. Nova Scotia Power made a successful transition from a crown corporation to a public company. It also transferred much decision-making power down the line.

Our corporate restructuring is itself an exercise in building value into our product. We have

successfully created a more effective organization—one that can do "more with less." Most responsibility for decisions and action now rests with people in the field, rather than in Head Office.

This change encourages closer contact between customers and service employees, resulting in "quicker and more personal response to their needs.... Referral to Head Office is the exception rather than the rule." This helps to increase customer value.

From 1995 to 1999 the company continued to develop these policies and the current director of human resource management feels strongly that the program has achieved company goals. She believes that customers, employees, and managers are all benefitting.

Source: 1995 *Annual Report*, Nova Scotia Power Inc.; documents provided by, and interview with, Elizabeth MacDonald, Nova Scotia Power director, HRM, July 6, 1999.

The 12 Golden Rules of Leadership

1. *Set a good example.* Your subordinates will take their cue from you. If your work habits are good, theirs are likely to be, too.

2. *Give your people a set of objectives and a sense of direction.* Good people seldom like to work aimlessly from day to day. They want to know not only what they're doing but why.

3. *Keep your people informed of new developments at the company and how they'll be affected.* Let people know where they stand with you. Let your close assistants in on your plans at an early stage. Let people know of changes that won't affect them but about which they may be worrying.

4. *Ask your people for advice.* Let them know that they have a say in your decisions whenever possible. Make them feel a problem is their problem too. Encourage individual thinking.

5. *Let your people know that you support them.* There's no greater morale killer than a boss who resents a subordinate's ambition.

6. *Don't give orders.* Suggest, direct, and request.

7. *Emphasize skills, not rules.* Judge results, not methods. Give a person a job to do and let him or her do it. Let an employee improve his or her own job methods.

8. *Give credit where credit is due.* Appreciation for a job well done is the most appreciated of "fringe benefits."

9. *Praise in public.* This is where it will do the most good.

10. *Criticize in private.*

11. *Criticize constructively.* Concentrate on correction, not blame. Allow a person to retain his or her dignity. Suggest specific steps to prevent recurrence of the mistake. Forgive, and encourage desired results.

12. *Make it known that you welcome new ideas.* No idea is too small for a hearing or too wild for consideration. Make it easy for people to communicate their ideas to you. Follow through on their ideas.

The Seven Sins of Leadership

These items can cancel any constructive image you might try to establish.

1. *Trying to be liked rather than respected.* Don't accept favours from your subordinates. Don't do special favours in trying to be liked. Don't try for popular decisions. Don't be soft about discipline. Have a sense of humour. Don't give up.

2. *Failing to ask subordinates for their advice and help.*

3. *Failing to develop a sense of responsibility in subordinates.* Allow freedom of expression. Give each person a chance to learn his or her superior's job. When you give responsibility, give authority too. Hold subordinates accountable for results.

4. *Emphasizing rules rather than skill.* While company rules and procedures are important to maintain an orderly operation, even more important is being alert to customer and employee needs. Let employees find their own ways of achieving this and judge by results.

5. *Failing to keep criticism constructive.* When something goes wrong, do you tend to assume who's at fault? Do you do your best to get all the facts first? Do you control your temper? Do you praise before you criticize? Do you listen to the other side of the story?

6. *Not paying attention to employee gripes and complaints.* Make it easy for them to come to you. Get rid of red tape. Explain the grievance machinery. Help a person voice his or her complaint. Always grant a hearing. Practise patience. Ask a complainant what he or she wants to do. Don't render a hasty or biased judgment. Get all the facts. Let the complainant know what your decision is. Double-check your results. Be concerned.

7. *Failing to keep people informed.* Empowering employees and developing well-functioning teams requires that everyone be kept fully informed of all matters relevant to their responsibilities. This will help to motivate employees. Keeping people in the dark leads to rumours and other negative factors.

Source: "To Become an 'Effective Executive,' Develop Leadership and Other Skills," *Marketing News*, April 1984, p. 1

FIGURE **8.8**
• • • •
RULES AND SINS OF LEADERSHIP

Progress Check

- What are some characteristics of leadership today that make leaders different from traditional managers?

- Explain the differences between autocratic and democratic leadership styles.

- Describe empowerment and explain to which of the four management functions it is related.

Critical Thinking

Do you see any problems with a participative managerial style? Do you think it could be adopted by football teams? It's already practised by some baseball teams. What's the difference between football and baseball players, what they do, and how they're managed? How does that relate to the business world?

Can you see a manager getting frustrated when he or she can't be bossy? Can someone who's trained to give orders (for example, a military sergeant) be retrained to be a participative manager? What problems may emerge? What kind of boss would you be? Do you have evidence to show that?

TASKS AND SKILLS AT DIFFERENT LEVELS OF MANAGEMENT

Anyone who has ever played a sport knows, there's a tremendous difference between being an excellent player and an excellent coach (manager). Often a good player will volunteer to coach the neighbourhood team and be a disaster as a manager. The same thing happens in business. Few people are trained to be managers. Rather, the process of becoming a manager is similar to the sports example. A person learns how to be a skilled accountant or salesperson or production line worker, and then—because of his or her skill—is selected to be a manager. The tendency is for such managers to become deeply involved in showing others how to do things, helping them, supervising them, and generally being very active in the operating task.

The further up the managerial ladder a person moves, the less such skills are required. Instead, the need is for people who are visionaries, good planners, organizers, coordinators, communicators, morale builders, and motivators. Figure 8.9 shows that a manager must have three categories of skills: (1) technical skills, (2) human relations skills, and (3) conceptual skills. Let's pause here to clarify the terms.

technical skills

Ability to perform tasks of a specific department (such as selling or bookkeeping).

human relations skills

Ability to lead, communicate, motivate, coach, build morale, train, support, and delegate.

conceptual skills

Ability to picture the organization as a whole and the relationship between the various parts.

Technical skills involve the ability to perform tasks of a specific department such as selling (marketing) or bookkeeping (accounting).

Human relations skills include leadership, motivation, coaching, communication, morale building, training and development, help and supportiveness, and delegating.

Conceptual skills refer to a manager's ability to picture the organization as a whole and the relationship of various parts, and to perform tasks such as planning, organizing, controlling, systems development, problem analysis, decision making, coordinating, and delegating.

Looking at Figure 8.9, you'll notice that first-line managers need to be skilled in all three areas. Most of their time is spent on technical and human relations tasks (assisting operating personnel, giving direction, and so forth). First-line managers spend little time on conceptual tasks. Top managers, on the other hand, need to use few technical skills. Instead, almost all of their time is devoted to human relations and conceptual tasks. One who's competent at one level of management may not be competent at higher levels and vice versa. The skills needed are different at different levels.

Spend some time reviewing the definitions of conceptual and human relations skills, which are so important to top management. Note that the word *delegate* is in our definition of human relations skills. Another one of the key managerial tasks is decision making. Because of their importance, we'll explore both delegating and decision making in more detail.

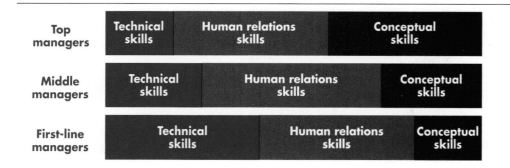

FIGURE 8.9
• • • •
SKILLS NEEDED AT
VARIOUS LEVELS OF
MANAGEMENT

All managers need
human relations skills.
At the top, managers
need strong conceptual
skills. First-line
managers need strong
technical skills. Middle
managers need to have a
balance between techni-
cal and conceptual skills.

··· DELEGATING: BECOMING A TEAM LEADER ···

The most difficult task for most managers to learn is **delegating** (assigning authority and accountability to others while retaining responsibility for results). Remember, managers are usually selected from those who are most skilled at doing what the people they manage are doing. The inclination is for managers to pitch in and help or do it themselves. Of course, this keeps workers from learning and having the satisfaction of doing it themselves. A great leader is one whose workers say, "We did it ourselves."

As we noted earlier, most progressive managers of the twenty-first century will be team leaders. They will set specific goals in cooperation with a team of workers, set up feedback and communication procedures (control procedures), and minimize the tendency to continually look over the team's shoulder to make sure it's doing things the manager's way. Employees will be given the freedom (empowered) to decide the hows and whens of completion of specific tasks as long as the goals are accomplished on time.

delegating
Assigning authority and
accountability to others while
retaining responsibility for results.

··· DECISION MAKING: FINDING THE ··· BEST ETHICAL ALTERNATIVE

Decision making is choosing among two or more alternatives. It sounds easier than it is in practice. Decision making is the heart of all the management functions: planning, organizing, directing, and controlling. As Figure 8.10 shows, the rational decision-making model is a series of steps managers

decision making
Choosing among two or more
alternatives.

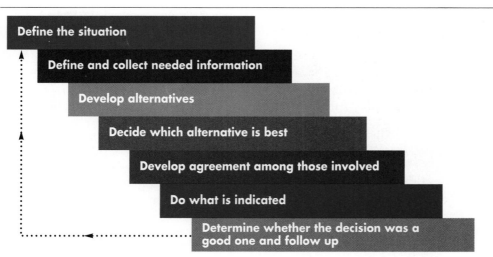

FIGURE 8.10
• • • •
THE DECISION-MAKING
PROCESS

An important step in the
decision-making process
is to choose the best
ethical alternative. Other
alternatives may gener-
ate more money but be
immoral or improper
in some way. After an
evaluation is made of
the decision, the whole
process begins again.

should follow to make logical, intelligent, and well-founded decisions. The six Ds of decision making are:

1. Define the problem.
2. Define and collect needed information.
3. Develop alternatives.
4. Decide which ethical alternative is best.
5. Do what's indicated (implement solution).
6. Determine whether the decision was a good one and follow up.

The best decisions are based on sound information. That's why this is known as the Information Age. Managers have computer terminals at their desks so they can get internal records and external data of all kinds. But all the data in the world can't replace a manager who is creative and makes brilliant decisions. Decision making is more an art than a science. It's the one skill most needed by managers and leaders in that all the other functions depend on it.

···· ▬ ····

LEARNING MANAGERIAL SKILLS

Now that you know some of the broad categories of skills needed by various levels of management, we can look at the more specific skills you'll need to learn to be a good manager. As you build your skills, it helps to think of yourself as a one-person business. Like any business, you must strive for quality and customer satisfaction.[13]

In general, it's a good idea to take as many courses as you can in oral communication, writing, computers, and human relations. In all managerial jobs, these are the skills in greatest demand. Naturally, you'll also have to develop technical skills in your chosen area. Figure 8.11 lists the six skills you'll need to develop your managerial potential: verbal skills, writing skills, computer skills, human relations skills, time management skills, and other technical skills.

FIGURE **8.11**
····

EVALUATING YOUR MANAGEMENT POTENTIAL

If you find yourself needing improvement in any of these areas, it's a good idea to take courses or read books to improve yourself. The best time to do this is *before* you seek work so you're fully prepared when you go job hunting.

Skill needed	Personal evaluation			
	Excellent	Good	Fair	Need work
Verbal skills				
Writing skills				
Computer skills				
Human relations skills				
Time-management skills				
Other technical skills				

··· VERBAL SKILLS ···

The bulk of your duties as a manager will involve communicating with others. You'll have to give talks, conduct meetings, make presentations, and generally communicate your ideas to others. To prepare for such tasks, you should take oral communication courses and become active in various student groups. Become an officer of an organization so that you're responsible for conducting meetings and giving speeches. You may want to join a choir or other group to become comfortable performing in front of others.

At least half of communication is skilled listening. A good manager mixes with other managers, workers, clients, shareholders, and others outside the firm. He or she listens to recommendations and complaints and acts on them. Active listening requires asking questions and feeding back what you've heard to let others know you're truly interested in what they say.

··· WRITING SKILLS ···

Managers must also be able to write clearly and precisely. Much of what you want others to do must be communicated through memos, reports, policies, and letters. Organizations everywhere are complaining about many college graduates' inability to write clearly. If you develop good writing skills, you'll be miles ahead of your competition. That means you should take courses in grammar and composition. To learn to write, you must practise writing! It helps to write anything: a diary, letters, notes, and so on. With practice, you'll develop the ability to write easily—just as you speak. With this skill, you'll be better prepared for a career in management.

··· COMPUTER SKILLS ···

Offices today are full of computers and related technology. Memos, charts, letters, and most of your other communication efforts involve the computer. When you're practising writing, practise on a word processor. The truly efficient manager must be able to effectively use and take advantage of the continuing developments in technology.

··· HUMAN RELATIONS SKILLS ···

A manager works with people; good managers know how to get along with people, motivate them, and inspire them. People skills are learned by working with people. Join student groups, volunteer to help at your church or temple and local charities, and get involved in political organizations. Try to assume leadership positions in which you're responsible for contacting others, assigning them work, and motivating them. Good leaders begin early by assuming leadership positions in sports, community groups, and so on.

Be aware of how others react to you. If you cause negative feelings or reactions, learn why. Don't be afraid to make mistakes and upset others. That's how you learn. But do learn how to work with others. Ask your friends what you could do to be a more effective and attractive leader.

MANAGING DIVERSITY **Managing diversity** means building systems and a culture that unite different people in a common pursuit without undermining their diversity. The problem of diversity is more than dealing with questions about race, gender, ethnicity, sexual orientation, and disabilities. If people are to work on teams, they have to learn to deal with people who have different personalities, different priorities, and different lifestyles. In the past, firms looked

managing diversity
Building systems and a culture that unite different people in a common pursuit without undermining their diversity.

<www.bus.sfu.ca>
<www.mgmt.utoronto.ca>
<business.queensu.ca>

Reaching Beyond Our Borders

Learning About Managing Businesses in Volatile Global Markets

Business schools are seeing a change these days. As students read about countries that make up the former Soviet Union going to a market economy and eastern Europeans opening their doors to western businesses, they're demanding to know more about global business management. Many young people know they'll be involved in international business even if they never leave Canada. They also know that Canadian companies are looking to business schools for managers who know how to work in the new global context.

How are business schools responding to this student demand? Many are revamping their existing curriculums by integrating international examples into basic courses. This reduces the need for specifically international courses. The idea is to bring international dimensions into the mainstream.

Still, some students demand more. They feel that global enterprise is too important to be mixed in with other courses, and they want courses that are entirely international. Many business schools offer semester exchange programs with business schools in other countries. Professors are encouraged to participate in international research to gain teaching experience overseas. Students are encouraged—and in some cases required—to study foreign languages. Students have caught the international fever and have passed the sense of urgency on to colleges.

Businesses, too, are changing the way they educate employees. Rather than send them for a traditional MBA, firms are teaching their managers how to work on teams, how to use the latest technology, and how to operate in a global economy. It's possible, if not likely, that the entire nature of business education will change over the next decade. Much more information will be available and accessible via computers and computer networks. More courses will be customized to fit the needs of individual firms. Many senior managers are expressing dissatisfaction with the MBA program at most Canadian universities and apparently newer dynamic companies are not keen on hiring MBAs. Complaints vary, but it would seem that what companies are seeking are more flexible employees who are tuned in to a fast-moving, fast-changing, volatile global market—employees who can "think on their feet." In any case, the future of management promises to be exciting, and so does the future of management education.

Sources: Brian O'Reilly, "How Execs Learn Now," *Business Week*, April 5, 1993, pp. 52–58; Brian O'Reilly, "Reengineering the MBA," *Fortune*, January 24, 1994, pp. 38–47; Harvey Schacter, "Programmed for Obsolescence?" *Canadian Business*, June 25/ July 9, 1999, pp. 49–51.

for people much like the people already working at the firm. Today such recruiting would probably be illegal, and it certainly would be less than optimal.

Research has shown that heterogeneous (mixed) groups are more productive than homogeneous (similar) groups in the workplace.[14] Men and women, young and old, gay and straight, and all other types of people can learn not only to work together, but to work together with more success. In the future, managers must learn how to deal effectively with people from many different cultures. Managers will also be asked to work in foreign countries. The more skilled you can become now in other languages and in working with diverse cultural groups, the better off you'll be when you become a manager.

••• TIME-MANAGEMENT SKILLS •••

One of the most important skills for new managers to learn is how to budget their time effectively. There are many demands on managers' time that they need to learn to control: telephone interruptions, visits from colleagues, questions from subordinates, meetings scheduled by higher management, and such. See if your school offers courses in time management. Time-management courses or workshops will help you develop such skills as setting priorities, delegating work, choosing activities that produce the most results, doing your work when you're at your best, and dealing with interruptions. Learning these skills now will help you increase your productivity at school and home.

••• TECHNICAL SKILLS •••

To rise through the ranks of accounting, marketing, finance, production, or any other functional area, you'll have to be proficient in that area. Begin now to choose some area of specialization. To rise to top management, you might supplement your undergraduate studies with an **MBA** (master of business administration) or some similar degree in government, economics, or hospital administration. More and more students are going on to take advanced degrees. About 60 percent of top managers have taken courses beyond the bachelor's degree. The most common areas of technical expertise among top managers are accounting and finance together. Marketing came in second. Slightly more than half of the top 1000 chief executive officers in the country have a graduate degree.[15]

Managing diversity means building a culture within an organization that unites people in a common pursuit without ignoring their cultural heritage. An example is Singh Dhillon, a Sikh who became the first graduate of the RCMP training centre to wear a turban and sport a beard.

MANAGERS AND LEADERS ARE NEEDED EVERYWHERE

One exciting thing about studying management and leadership is that it prepares you for a career in any organization. Managers and leaders are needed in schools, churches, charities, government organizations, unions, associations, clubs, and all other organizations. Naturally, an important need for managers and leaders is in business.

When selecting a career in management, a student has several decisions to make.

- What kind of organization is most attractive? That is, would you like to work for government, business, or some nonprofit organization?

- What type of managerial position seems most interesting? A person may become a production manager, a sales manager, a human resource manager, an accounting manager, a traffic (distribution) manager, a credit manager, and so on. There are dozens of managerial positions from which to choose. In the future, you're likely to move among several different functions, so it pays to have a broad education in business.

- What type of industry appeals to you: sporting goods, computers, auto, tourism, aircraft, or something else? Would you prefer to work for a relatively new firm or an established one?

- What courses and training are needed to prepare for various managerial careers? Only careful research will answer this question.

Management will be discussed in more detail in the next few chapters. Let's pause now, review, and do some exercises. Management is doing, not just reading.

Ethical Dilemma

REVIEW

You will recall the beginning-of-the-chapter question. Here's what our executives think. Bédard states that "honesty has always been the best policy. Anyone beginning their career with an approach that would be detrimental to a supervisor or a fellow employee, quickly becomes identified as such and would eventually suffer the consequences."

Reilley believes that "you should always keep your superior informed. Perhaps his performance is spotty only in your opinion and by holding back you are harming both the team and yourself. Also, if you aren't a team player, the word soon gets around and it could work against you. Finally, assuming you get the boss's job by this unscrupulous means, how can you engender loyalty from your new team if you suspect others of

doing what you have done? If the boss is truly inefficient, his day of reckoning will come. Keep the boss informed. Quick gains by underhanded means will eventually work against you."

Suppose your boss has been very good to you, mentoring and supporting you so that you have made rapid progress. Or, perhaps she has been a rotten boss, always giving you heck and never offering a word of praise or recognition. What if she is in her 50s and her chances of getting another job are very slim? This is, obviously, a tough call and no two individuals will make the same decision. It depends on how ambitious you are, the strength of your personal ethical standards, the nature of your relationship with your boss, and how badly strapped you are for funds. What do you think?

Critical Thinking

What kind of management are you best suited for: human resources, marketing, finance, accounting, production, credit? Why do you feel this area is most appropriate?

Would you like to work for a large firm or a small business? Private or government? In an office or out in the field? Would you like being a manager?

Progress Check

- Which managerial skills are used more by supervisors than by top managers and vice versa?
- What are the six **D**s of decision making?
- What are the six skills you should be working on now to become a good manager later?

SUMMARY
......

1. Explain the four functions of management and why the role of managers is changing.

1. Many managers are changing their approach to corporate management.
   - ***What reasons can you give to account for these changes in management?***
   The three major reasons given in this text for management changes are (1) global competition, (2) technological change, and (3) the growing importance of pleasing customers. Managers are now being trained to guide and coach employees rather than boss them. The trend is toward working with employees as a team to meet organizational goals.

   - ***What are the four functions of management?***
   Management is the process used to pursue organizational goals through (1) planning, (2) organizing, (3) directing, and (4) controlling.

2. The planning function involves the process of setting objectives to meet the organizational goals.

- **What's the difference between goals and objectives?**

Goals are broad, long-term achievements that organizations aim to accomplish, whereas objectives are specific, short-term plans made to help reach the goals.

- **What are the three types of planning and how are they related to the organization's goals and objectives?**

Strategic planning is broad, long-range planning that outlines the goals of the organization. Tactical planning, on the other hand, is specific, short-term planning that lists organizational objectives. Contingency planning involves developing an alternative set of plans in case the first set doesn't work out.

3. Managers develop a framework that illustrates the relationship of workers, tasks, and resources.

- **What is this framework or chart called, and what are the three major levels of management illustrated on the chart?**

The organization chart pictures who reports to whom and who is responsible for what task. It illustrates the top, middle, and first-line management levels.

- **How are organizations changing to become more customer oriented?**

Organizations are becoming smaller so that they can respond more quickly to customers. Furthermore, each firm is striving to have every process as good as the best companies in the world. Often that means finding other firms to do various tasks. Top management must make contact with those firms and work very closely with them to coordinate processes so that customers get the highest-quality goods and services possible.

4. The directing function of management involves giving assignments, explaining routines, clarifying policies, and providing feedback on performance.

- **How does the directing function vary at different levels of management?**

The further down the corporate ladder, the more specific the manager's directions become. First-line managers once spent a great deal of their time giving very specific, detailed instructions to their subordinates. Now they're more likely to work with employees to set goals and to allow more freedom for employees to decide how to reach those goals. Top managers direct middle managers, who require only broad, general directions.

5. The control function of management involves measuring employee performance against objectives and standards and taking corrective action if necessary.

- **What are the five steps of the control function?**

Controlling incorporates (1) setting clear standards, (2) monitoring and recording performance, (3) comparing performance with plans and standards, (4) communicating results and deviations to employees, and (5) taking corrective action if necessary.

- **What qualities must standards possess to be used to measure performance results?**

Standards must be specific, attainable, and measurable.

2. Distinguish between goals and objectives; distinguish between strategic, tactical, and contingency planning; and explain the relationships of goals and objectives to the various types of planning.

3. Describe the significance of an organization chart, and explain how organizations are changing to meet the needs of customers.

4. Describe the directing function of management, and illustrate how the function differs at the various management levels.

5. Summarize the five steps of the control function of management.

6. Explain the differences between managers and leaders, and compare the characteristics and uses of the various leadership styles.

6. Executives today must be more than just managers; they must be leaders as well.

- ***What's the difference between a manager and a leader?***
A manager sees that the organization runs smoothly and that order is maintained. A leader does this and more. A leader has vision and inspires others to grasp that vision, establishes corporate values, emphasizes corporate ethics, and doesn't fear change.

- ***Describe the various leadership styles.***
Figure 8.7 shows a continuum of leadership styles ranging from boss-centred to subordinate-centred leadership.

- ***Which leadership style is best?***
The best (most effective) leadership style depends on the people being led and the situation. The challenge of the future will be to empower self-managed teams to manage themselves. This is a move away from command-and-control management.

7. Describe the three general categories of skills needed by top, middle, and first-line managers.

7. Managers must be good planners, organizers, coordinators, communicators, morale builders, and motivators.

- ***What skills must a manager have to be all these things?***
Managers must have three categories of skills (1) technical skills (ability to perform tasks such as bookkeeping or selling), (2) human relations skills (ability to communicate and motivate), and (3) conceptual skills (ability to see organizations as a whole and how all the parts fit together).

- ***Are these skills equally important at all management levels?***
The skills needed are different at different levels. Top managers rely heavily on human relations and conceptual skills and rarely use technical skills, whereas first-line supervisors need strong technical and human relations skills but use conceptual skills less often (see Figure 8.9).

8. Illustrate the skills you will need to develop your managerial potential, and outline activities you could use to develop these skills.

8. Now that you've examined what managers do, you may be considering a career in management.

- ***What skills should you be developing now to help you become a better manager in the future?***
You'll need to develop six skills to sharpen your managerial potential (1) verbal skills, (2) writing skills, (3) computer skills, (4) human relations skills, (5) time-management skills, and (6) technical skills.

KEY TERMS
......

autocratic leadership 244

conceptual skills 248

contingency planning 236

controlling 233

decision making 249

delegating 249

democratic (participative) leadership 244

directing 233

empowerment 239

goals 234

external customers 242

human relations skills 248

internal customers 242

laissez-faire (free-rein) leadership 245

leadership 243

management 233

management by walking around 232

managing diversity 251

middle management 237

mission statement 234

objectives 234

operational planning 234

organizing 233

planning 233

strategic (long-range) planning 235

supervisory (first-line) management 237

SWOT analysis 235

tactical (short-range) planning 236

technical skills 248

top management 236

vision 234

1. Discuss the merits of working as a manager in the following types of organizations: government, business, and nonprofit. To learn the advantages of each, talk to managers from each area and share what you learn with the class.

2. Interview two or more managers of local businesses (preferably of different sizes) and find out what they spend the majority of their time doing. Is it planning, organizing, controlling, or directing? Use a computer graphics program to create a pie chart illustrating the average amount of time spent on each type of activity. If you have a chance to talk with different levels of managers, it would be interesting to create a chart comparing their allocation of time. Discuss the results with the class.

3. Discuss the disadvantages of becoming a manager. Does the size of the business make a difference? Do managers or workers seem to enjoy better lifestyles? Discuss.

4. Review various business journals and read about key executives and managers. How much do they make? How many hours do they work? Do you believe they earn their pay? Discuss.

5. Review Figure 8.7 and discuss managers you have known, worked for, or read about who have practised each style. Which did you like best? Why? Which were most effective? Why?

1. Leadership and management are very hot topics and many articles and discussions about them can be found in nearly all media. Using either or both of these words scan the Web site of your local newspaper to see what recent stories you can find about the topic relating to companies in your area. If you cannot find anything, try the national newspapers or the Web sites of the TV networks like CBC, CTV, Global, CanWest, or your local radio or TV station. If you have no luck, try <www.globeandmail.com/hubs/managing.html> for a recent article on managing. It might be interesting to have some classroom discussion on some of these articles.

2. Use search engines like Yahoo or Alta Vista to extend your search to other countries such as the U.S. and Europe, use the same key words to see if there are any developments there that might be a prelude to what's coming to Canadian companies. Again, this could lead to some useful classroom discussion.

Practising Management Decisions

CASE 1
• • • • • •
CHANGING THE PARADIGM
• • • • • •

Noel Tichy, a business professor at the University of Michigan, advises you not to try this at home. Consider the two ways to boil a live frog. The first way is to drop little Kermit into boiling water. He'll hop right out according to those acquainted with the classic physiological phenomenon. But try placing Kermit in a pot of cold water and gradually raising the temperature. He'll sit there and boil to death. This is meant to be a parable for business leadership in the 1990s, not a lesson in animal torture. Kermit failed to adjust to a shifting paradigm. He ignored a critical, though gradual, change in his environment. Before coming to a full boil, he should have remembered the words of American patriot Thomas Paine, "A long habit of not thinking a thing wrong gives it the superficial appearance of being right."

Used in business, the word *paradigm* (pronounced para-dime) simply refers to the accepted view of how things have always been done and should continue to be done. A paradigm shifter is someone who throws out the rules of the game and starts radical change. Tichy, who worked with General Electric's ultimate paradigm shifter, Jack Welch, adds, "It's not just quantum ideas, but the guts to stick with them. In industry after industry, a lot of frogs are waking up and finding it's too late to jump. Banking is there. Auto has had two chances and may not get a third. And now the computer industry is feeling the heat."

Jack Welch's restructuring of GE meant far fewer middle managers and more power to those who remained. John Trani (the Welch lieutenant who overhauled and ran GE Medical Systems) says, "People come to me and ask, 'Why was I good enough yesterday, but not today?' It's simple. In 1954, Roger Bannister won world acclaim for breaking the four-minute mile. Today many high schoolers can do that. The standard is always changing, but there's always a top 10 and a bottom 10." As a matter of policy, Welch demanded that all GE businesses be number one or number two in their industry.

Decision Questions

1. How is the business environment changing from what it was 10 or 20 years ago? What can managers do to adapt to these changes?
2. Noel Tichy suggests that companies that don't adjust to shifting paradigms face death. As an example, he points to buggy makers who turned up their noses at Henry Ford's smelly exhaust. Can you think of other victims of shifting paradigms?
3. Experts say that for a real paradigm shift to occur within a corporation, top management has to have a strong commitment to change. Says Ram Charan, a consultant to many Fortune 500 companies, "There has to be divine discontent with the status quo at the very top, and courage to do something about it." Explain why top management's commitment to change is crucial to change within a corporation.

CASE 2

THE CHANGING ROLE OF MANAGEMENT

The traditional role of managers has been to plan, organize, direct, and control the work of others to achieve the objectives of the organization. In the past, emphasis was placed on strategic (long-range) planning, on telling employees what to do and how to do it, and on closely supervising employees and discouraging errors and defects. All of that is changing in today's fast-paced industries. One of those rapidly changing industries is telecommunications. The deregulation of phone companies, the introduction of fibre optics, the growth of cellular phone systems, and more are making competition and the need for innovation more important than ever.

Tellabs is one company that has successfully implemented all of the newest management concepts: just-in-time inventory control, total quality management, continuous improvement, and cross-functional teams. The company realizes that customer expectations are what determine quality standards. To get close to customers, the company sends out cross-functional teams to determine customer wants, needs, and expectations. *Planning* takes on a much shorter horizon as the company continually innovates to stay ahead of competition.

An entirely new kind of *organization*, the cross-functional team, is used to facilitate innovation and motivation. The company designed and constructed its plant so that there literally are no walls between functional units.

Directing is minimized at Tellabs. Instead, members of cross-functional teams are encouraged to be self-managed, to make mistakes (if you don't make mistakes, you're being too cautious and not sufficiently innovative), and to respond quickly to customers.

Control is less a matter of looking over the shoulder of workers and more a matter of measuring customer satisfaction and making adjustments when needed. In short, management at Tellabs is largely a matter of leadership. What is the difference? Leadership is more involved with creating a vision. At Tellabs, that vision is one of a global leader. The leadership style is more democratic than most firms; some might say it resembles laissez faire.

A decision by management to give more authority and responsibility to employees doesn't come easily. Managers must give up some of their own authority to become coaches, supporters, and motivators instead. Every employee becomes his or her own manager in that they assume more responsibility. That is what self management is all about. It helps to have people working in teams because shared responsibility and authority also help to optimize the diverse experiences of group members. At Tellabs, that teamwork has led to new innovations and a more motivated workforce.

Decision Questions

1. In the future, more college and university graduates will be working on cross-functional teams. What kind of training in school would help students be more productive on such teams?

2. What kinds of problems might managers experience in the future as a result of the growth of cross-functional teams? Will it be more difficult to evaluate, compensate, and promote people?

3. Is information management more or less important now that the planning horizon for managers is much shorter? Why?

4. Would you rather work at a firm with a traditional organizational structure or one with cross-functional teams? Why?

Organizing a Customer-Driven Business

Chapter

9

LEARNING GOALS

After you have read and studied this chapter, you should be able to

1 describe the traditional hierarchical, bureaucratic, organizational structure, and explain how and why it is being restructured.

2 explain the organizational theories of Fayol and Weber.

3 discuss the various issues connected with organizational design.

4 explain the concepts of span of control and tall or flat structures and their interconnectedness.

5 describe the differences between line, line and staff, matrix, and cross-functional organizations.

6 explain the benefits of turning organizations upside down and inside out.

7 give examples to show how organizational culture and the informal organization can hinder or assist organizational change.

Mei-Lin Cheng and Julie Anderson are both managers at Hewlett-Packard, one of America's most admired companies. They work at HP's North American distribution organization, which manages the flow of billions of dollars' worth of products, from personal computers to toner cartridges, from order to delivery. But Cheng and Anderson had a problem: HP was taking 26 days for products to reach customers, while competitors were shipping out PCs within a couple of days.

Since customer responsiveness is one of the most important competitive advantages today, HP had to do something to improve its response time.

Cheng and Anderson assumed responsibility for reengineering the processing of orders. Once they had permission to make certain necessary changes, the two women assembled a team of 35 people from HP and two other companies and gave them total freedom to do what was needed to improve the process.

A pilot program cut delivery time from 26 to 8 days for one of HP's bigger customers. The customer was then able to cut inventories by 20 percent and increase its service level to its customers.

The two women accomplished this objective by changing all the rules. There was no longer any hierarchy, no titles, no job descriptions, no plans, no step-by-step measures of progress. Instead, team members were encouraged to do whatever it took to make the system work better and faster. Diversity of views and systems thinking were encouraged. The first month was one long meeting, during which employees decided what to do and how to do it. The result, at first, was chaos. Team members included people from Andersen

Mei-Lin Cheng and Julie Anderson of Hewlett-Packard

Consulting and Menlo Logistics. Menlo is the company's transportation and distribution partner. The system they were trying to implement, from SAP (a German company), was designed to create a unified database covering everything from the customer's order through the credit check, manufacturing, shipping, warehousing, and billing. Then orders were traced through the firm to find where the stoppages were. Then each road block was eliminated until the whole process went smoothly and quickly.

As a consequence of this reengineering process, everyone in the organization has learned how to learn. The firm now responds quickly to other challenges. Employees have learned to work and think in teams. In short, HP's distribution organization is now a learning system where everything gets better over time and people are happier and more productive.

The HP experience is just one example of the major changes taking place in organizations today. The old system in which bosses tell others what to do is being replaced by a system in which everyone participates, and specialization by function (e.g., production, marketing, finance) is being replaced by cross-functional teams (people from various departments working together). The implications are tremendous for today's business students. They must be prepared to work in teams and to be self-motivated and self-directed. This chapter will look at past systems and how and why they are changing so that you will get some feel for what the future will bring.

Sources: Stratford Sherman, "Secrets of HP's 'Muddled' Team," *Fortune*, March 18, 1996, pp. 116–120; Debra Phillips, "Rush Hour," *Entrepreneur*, February 1998, pp. 114–118.

Ethical Dilemma

WHEN IS LEARNING UNETHICAL?

In this chapter you will see the term *benchmarking*. This refers to trying to discover what the best practices of your competitors are so that you can adopt them and even improve on them. Benchmarking is one of the key strategies for staying competitive in today's rapidly changing marketplace. The ethical questions that arise relate to how far you can go in this research before it becomes unethical. Should you entice some of your competitors' best researchers to work for you? How far can you go in spying on other companies and learning what they are doing? Suppose your boss wants to give you a leave of absence so you can get a job at a competitor to learn their secrets? We will look at these questions again after you have read the chapter.

<www.hp.com>

The Web site for Cheng and Anderson's company, Hewlett-Packard, will give you a full picture of the company.

<www.ac.com>

Andersen Consulting, referred to in the Profile of Mei-Lin Cheng and Julie Anderson, is one of the largest management consulting firms in the world. Visit its colourful Web site to learn more about this well-known and highly regarded firm.

organizational design
The structuring of workers so that they can best accomplish the firm's goals.

hierarchy
A system in which one person is at the top of the organization and many levels of managers are responsible to that person.

JOBS AND CAREERS IN THE CUSTOMER-DRIVEN COMPANY

As the Profile indicates, working for large companies is taking on a new character. As you work your way through this chapter, you will see that work in the future will not be the same as it was in the past. Employees and managers are now expected to function as independent persons playing a self-motivated role in teams. Narrow job descriptions and waiting for your boss to tell you what to do are part of the past, offering today's students a wonderful challenge and opportunity. The job you are likely to get should be interesting because it will give you a chance to use your initiative, take part in teamwork, and get to know many aspects of your company. It is unlikely that you will find yourself doing the same boring thing day after day. In today's fiercely competitive global climate, companies need bold, dynamic employees who can use the freedom they are given to show what they can do.

THE CHANGING ORGANIZATIONAL HIERARCHY

Moving from a boss-driven to an employee-driven or team-driven company isn't easy. Managers may resist giving up their authority over workers, while workers often resist the responsibility that comes with self-management. Nonetheless, many of the world's leading organizations are moving in that direction.[1] They're trying to develop an organizational design that best serves the needs of customers, stockholders, employees, and the community.

Organizational design is the structuring of workers so that they can best accomplish the firm's goals. In the past many organizations were designed so that managers could control workers, and most organizations are still organized that way, with everything set up in a hierarchy. A **hierarchy** is a system in which one person is at the top of the organization and many levels of managers are responsible to that person. Since one person can't keep track of thousands of workers, the top manager needs many lower-level managers to help. Figure 9.1 shows a typical hierarchical organization structure.

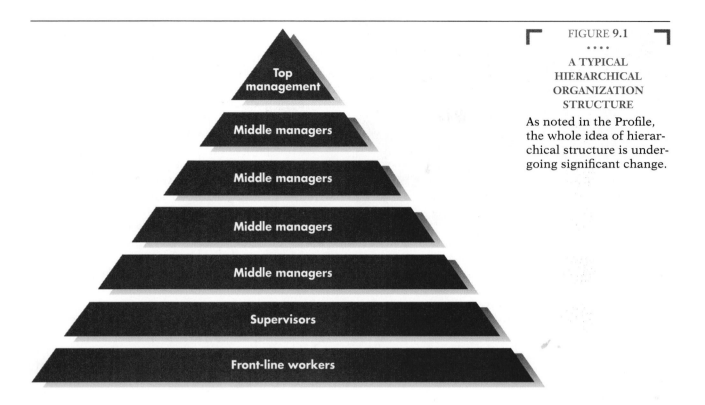

Some organizations have had as many as 10 to 14 layers of management between the chief executive officer (CEO) and the lowest-level employees. If employees wanted to introduce work changes, they would ask their supervisors, who would ask their managers, who would ask the manager above them and so on. Eventually a decision would be made and passed down from manager to manager until it reached the employee. Such decisions could take days, weeks, or months. **Bureaucracy** is the term used for an organization with many layers of managers who set rules and regulations and oversee all decisions. But bureaucracy is on its way out.

Recently, a survey found that 28 percent of companies have no more than four layers of management. Five years ago, only 8 percent had so few layers. It should be noted, however, that 8 percent of the companies still had more than eight layers of management.[2] As you can see, organizations are eliminating managers and giving more power to lower-level employees. This process is called *downsizing* because it allows the organization to operate with fewer workers. According to a recent study, many companies that have downsized have not experienced the full impact they anticipated on earnings or a long-run rise in the price of their stock.[3]

bureaucracy
An organization with many layers of managers who set rules and regulations and oversee all decisions.

. . . . ▬▬▬ . . . .

THE FUNDAMENTALS OF BUREAUCRACY

In a bureaucratic organization, a chain of command goes from the top down. There are many rules and regulations that everyone is expected to follow. To make the process easier, organizations are set up by function. That is, there are separate departments for design, engineering, purchasing, production, marketing, finance, human resource management, accounting, legal, and so on. People tend to specialize in one function on the job. Communication among depart-

Bureaucracy frequently means delays in meeting the needs of customers. Instead of being empowered, employees follow rules and procedures that are slow and inefficient.

restructuring
The process of reorganizing the structure of companies to make them more efficient.

ments is minimal. The typical career is to move up within a functional area. For example, one might move up from salesperson to sales trainer, to sales manager, to regional manager, to marketing manager, to marketing vice president. Such a career progression doesn't regularly expose people to other functions in the firm and, therefore, doesn't create much interdepartmental cooperation.

In the past such an organizational structure worked well because employees could specialize in one area and learn to do it well. The problem today is that such organizations are not responsive to customers. Employees tend to follow the rules and aren't very flexible in responding to changing customer wants and needs. One major characteristic of all countries, developed or developing, is the rapid rate of social, technological, and economic changes. Companies that want to be successful have to be able to respond quickly to the constantly changing marketplace. Slow response cuts dramatically into sales and can be very costly.

Giant firms like General Motors and IBM found that out when they were slow to react: GM to Japanese cars and IBM to personal computer developments. They eventually responded by restructuring their firms. **Restructuring** means redesigning an organization so that it can more effectively and efficiently service customers. Often that means breaking down barriers between functions. It also means giving more authority to lower-level managers and to all employees, thus moving from a top-down to a participatory style of management. Organizations that have made such changes—like Nova Scotia Power (profiled in the previous chapter) or Hewlett-Packard (profiled in this chapter)—have regained market leadership. Many others are quickly following their lead.

There are still many remnants of stifling bureaucracy among today's organizations. Most universities are still slow to adapt to customers' (students') wants and needs. So are most government agencies. Often you can see the consequences of bureaucracy in agencies such as a department of motor vehicles or Canada Post. However, even agencies such as these are now starting to explore new ways of organizing. Otherwise, they may lose their function to more efficient organizations. For example, the postal service in England has been taken over by private firms. There are occasional rumours that the same will happen with Canada Post.

Start noticing how many clerks and other customer-contact people say things like, "that's not our policy," or "we don't do things that way," when you request some unusual service. Such answers are the result of bureaucratic rules and regulations that employees are forced to follow. Can you imagine a day when employees are empowered to adjust to the wants and needs of customers? What organizational changes would have to be made? Would the results be worth the effort?

For an answer to these questions look at what happened at a Hampton Inn hotel when a customer service representative overheard a customer complaining that the complementary breakfast he had just eaten did not offer his favourite breakfast cereal. This employee felt that this was not just another "disgruntled guest" so he decided that this was an opportunity to make a guest happy. He gave him a cash refund for one night's stay at the hotel. Furthermore, he did it on the spot, without having to check with his supervisor or the general manager and without having the guest fill out a long complaint form. This is an excellent example of what is meant when companies talk about reorganizing to better provide customer satisfaction. You can imagine what this gesture is worth to Hampton Inn in terms of word-of-mouth publicity.[4]

HOW ORGANIZATIONAL STRUCTURE HAS EVOLVED

To understand traditional managers and their approach to business, you have to understand traditional organizational theory. In the next few sections, we will review these theories. Then we'll outline the new approaches that will guide organizations in the twenty-first century.

··· HISTORY OF ORGANIZATIONAL THEORY ···

Until the 1900s most organizations were rather small, the processes for producing goods were rather simple, and organization of workers was fairly easy to do. Not until the twentieth century and the introduction of mass production did business organizations grow complex and difficult to manage. The bigger the plants, the more efficient production became, or so it seemed. The concept was called *economies of scale*. This means that the larger the plant, the more efficient it could be because all the employees could specialize in particular aspects of production, marketing, or finance, which would result in more productivity per employee and, therefore, lower costs. The problem was that managers began to think that bigger was better without limit and in all cases. That's how some companies became too large to be efficient.

It was in this period that organizational theorists emerged. In France, Henri Fayol published his book *Administration Industrielle et Générale* in 1919. It was popularized on this side of the Atlantic in the late 1940s under the title *General and Industrial Management*. Max Weber (pronounced *Vayber*) was writing organizational theories in Germany a little before Fayol. It was only about a half a century ago that organizational theory became popular this side of the Atlantic Ocean.

Bombardier is one company that demonstrates the need for good organization. In this airplane hangar, many projects are being worked on at once and management needs to create the right organizational design to get the projects completed on time.

⋯ FAYOL'S PRINCIPLES OF ORGANIZATION ⋯

Fayol introduced principles such as:

- *Unity of command.* Each worker was to report to one, and only one, boss. The benefits of this principle are obvious. What happens if two different bosses give you two different assignments? Which one should you follow? To prevent such confusion, each person reports to only one manager.
- *Hierarchy of authority.* Fayol suggested that each person should know to whom they should report and managers should have the right to give orders and expect others to follow.
- *Authority.* Managers have the right to give orders and the power to exact obedience. Authority and responsibility are related: whenever authority is exercised, responsibility arises (see Figure 9.2).
- *Degree of centralization.* The amount of decision-making power vested in top management should vary by circumstances. In a small organization, it's possible to centralize all decision-making power in the top manager. In a larger organization, however, some decision-making power should be delegated to lower-level managers and employees on both major and minor issues (see the discussion of participative management in Chapter 8).
- *Equity.* A manager should treat employees and peers with respect and justice.
- *Clear communication channels.* Everyone should understand how to obtain and send information throughout the organization.
- *Division of labour.* Functions are to be divided into areas of specialization such as production, marketing, and finance.
- *Subordination of individual interests to the general interest.* Workers are to think of themselves as a coordinated team. Goals of the team are more important than the goals of individual workers.
- *Esprit de corps.* A spirit of pride and loyalty should be created among people in the firm.
- *Order.* Materials and people should be placed and maintained in the proper locations.

Management courses in colleges and universities throughout the world taught these principles, and they became synonymous with the concept of management. Organizations were designed so that no person had more than one boss, lines of authority were clear, and everyone knew to whom they were to report. Naturally, these principles tended to become rules and policies as organizations got larger. That led to more rigid organization and a feeling among workers that they belonged to an inflexible system rather than to a group of friendly, cooperative workers joined together in a common effort. It is unfortunate that the ideas of Mary Parker Follett—who was profiled in the previous chapter—were not well known. They would have offset this rigid approach.

⋯ MAX WEBER AND ORGANIZATIONAL THEORY ⋯

Weber used the term *bureaucrats* to describe middle managers whose function was to implement top management's orders. His book *The Theory of Social and Economic Organizations* was introduced here in the late 1940s. Weber's concept of a bureaucratic organization basically consisted of three layers of authority: (1) top managers who were the decision makers, (2) middle managers (the bureaucracy) who developed rules and procedures for implementing the decisions, and (3) workers and supervisors who did the work.

It was Weber, then, who promoted the pyramid-shaped organizational structure that became so popular in large firms (see Figures 9.1 and 9.2). Weber put great trust in managers and felt that a firm would do well if employees simply did what they were told. The less decision making employees had to do, the better. Clearly, this is a reasonable way to operate if you are dealing with uneducated, untrained workers—often the only workers available around 1900. Today, however, most firms feel that workers are the *best* source of ideas and that managers are there to support workers rather than boss them around.

Today's more educated workforce has made much of what Weber and Fayol said obsolete. Let's see whether these concepts of Weber's still apply:

- job descriptions—every job was to be outlined in detail in writing

- written rules, decision guidelines, and detailed records

- consistent procedures, regulations, and policies

- staffing and promotions based on qualifications

You can thank Weber when you go to a store or government agency and have trouble getting things done because the clerk says, "that's not company policy," or "I can't do that; it's against the rules." Weber felt large organizations demanded clearly established rules and guidelines that had to be followed precisely. This would ensure the consistent application of policies, regulations, and rules, as well as the equal treatment of all people affected by the organization.

The benefits of such concepts and practices are obvious, but zealous enforcement led to inflexibility and insensitivity to customers' needs. Although the word *bureaucrat* did not have negative connotations when used by Weber,

Max Weber was the first to use the word *bureaucrats* to describe managers.

FIGURE **9.2**

• • • •

BUREAUCRATIC ORGANIZATIONAL STRUCTURE

This chart shows Weber's concept of a bureaucratic organization, one with clear lines of authority and several layers of management.

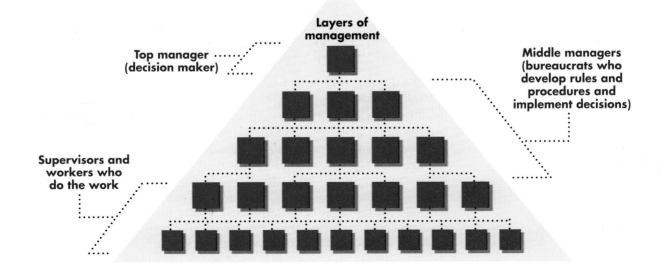

Layers of management

Top manager (decision maker)

Middle managers (bureaucrats who develop rules and procedures and implement decisions)

Supervisors and workers who do the work

the practice of establishing and enforcing rules and procedures became so rigid that *bureaucracy* has become a nasty word for organizations with too many managers who seem to do nothing but make and enforce rules. What is needed today is a way to implement these concepts creatively and flexibly to establish an atmosphere of freedom and incentive, enabling employees to work more productively alone and in teams.

••• BUREAUCRACY: YESTERDAY, TODAY, AND TOMORROW •••

Joan Woodward and her associates studied 100 industrial firms in England between 1953 and 1971 to see if there was a relationship among how an organization was structured, the technologies it used, and its success. Success was measured by the net income of the corporation (profit) and by increases in market domination. What Woodward found was that there was no one best way to organize a corporation. Rather, the structure depended on the technical complexity of the company's production process. However, today even the most technically complex companies find that reducing bureaucracy results in better performance.

The trend today is for companies to shed layers of management (bureaucracy) to speed up their response to customer needs and demands and to cut costs. Technological developments such as automation and computers have hastened the reduction of the workforce and, therefore, the numbers and levels of management. The advent of computers has reduced the layers of middle management, as senior managers can now access information and exercise control directly from their own terminals.

As can been seen in the Profile, Hewlett-Packard and many other businesses are adopting other radical ideas, such as doing away with job descriptions and masses of rules to permit more flexible deployment of the workforce. In other words, they are seeking ways to become more efficient and more competitive. All of these innovations have become possible because the educated workforce can, and wants to, take on more responsibility and decision making. Flexibility and adaptability are features of many successful companies that are managing in this new mode.

That is not to say that there is no room at all for the classic method of bureaucratic operation that Fayol and Weber advocated. (McDonald's functions well under their strict procedures.) What must be understood is that the trend today is away from such structures and management styles. International competitive pressures are forcing all companies to react and adapt much more quickly than they used to and to use all their human resources more effectively. Both of these goals are best achieved by opening up company structures and procedures and breaking down rigid bureaucracies. Here are some Canadian examples of this trend:

- David Killins, president of Legacy Storage Systems says that "the giant, centrally managed monolith is basically obsolete as a corporate model."[5]
- Shell Canada opened a lubricants plant in Brockville, Ontario, where "hierarchical structures and the control-and-command mentality have been swept aside by a dynamic organization driven by commitments rather than reward and punishment. 'I feel more independent. I'm given more responsibility,' says Theresa Hetherington."[6]
- The Department of National Defence started a project in its support services whose "aim is to demonstrate that local-level managers can maintain current levels of service more efficiently and economically if given greater authority over assigned resources.[7]

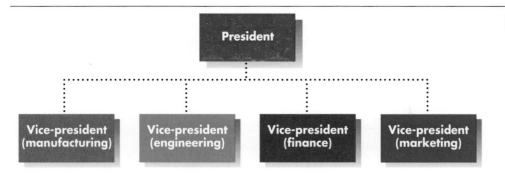

• PanCanadian Petroleum decided to "push decision making down the ranks. It means, for example, giving field operators signing authority for up to $1000 of purchases; previously, they needed a foreman's approval to buy a broom."[8]

FIGURE **9.3**
• • • •
FUNCTIONAL ORGANIZATION
The top management of a functionally oriented organization. Large organizations prospered in the past because of a division of labour. That division is reflected in departmentalization—the assigning of different functions to different departments. This chart shows a typical breakdown of functions.

Progress Check

• What were some of the reasons why organizations became large? What are some of the drawbacks of large firms?

• Can you name four of Fayol's principles and show how they link with Weber's principles?

• Why are many large organizations moving away from these principles? Are any still valid?

• • • •   ▬▬▬▬   • • • •

DESIGNING MORE RESPONSIVE ORGANIZATIONS

One of the most common ways to organize a company is by the different functions or departments, such as marketing, finance, production, and so on. The relationship between the different departments and their personnel is traditionally shown in an organization chart, a visual diagram of an organization that shows who reports to whom. The top segment of such a chart is shown in Figure 9.3. The entire organization chart tended to look like a pyramid (as shown in Figures 9.1 and 9.2).

In large companies, workers, clerks, or salespeople reported to supervisors, who reported to plant, office, or sales managers, who reported to regional managers, who reported to national managers, who reported to vice-presidents, who reported to the president, who reported to the chair of the board of directors. Such complex organizations required many rules, guidelines, and procedures. (They were bureaucracies.)

By their nature, such organizational structures are slow and unwieldy. One Canadian management consultant reported that

Research shows that 85 to 95 percent of service, quality, or productivity problems stem from the organization's structure and processes.... Ask the question: "For whose convenience are systems designed?" Too often they serve accountants, technocrats, or management. Get the cart behind the horse. Your systems should serve your customers or those producing, delivering, or supporting your products or services.[9]

That is why current trends are toward smaller, more flexible structures that let companies react more quickly to today's fast-changing, technologically competitive business climate. They also unleash employees' initiative and enable them to participate in decision making. We next examine some of the issues that arise from these changing organizational structures. These issues (some of which are not new) include

1. tall versus flat structures
2. span of control
3. departmentalization
4. centralization versus decentralization

••• TALL VERSUS FLAT ORGANIZATIONAL STRUCTURES •••

As organizations got bigger, some began adding layer after layer of management, sometimes resulting in a dozen or more managerial steps in firms such as Bell Canada. Such organizations have what are called *tall organizational structures*—the organization chart is quite tall because of the various levels of management. The army is an example of how tall an organization can get. There are many layers of management between a private and a general (e.g., sergeant, lieutenant, captain, major, colonel). You can imagine how a message may be distorted as it moves up through so many layers of management or officers.

Many business organizations took on the same style of organization as the military. The organizations were divided into regions, divisions, centres, and plants. Each plant might have had several layers of management. The net effect was a huge complex of managers, management assistants, secretaries, assistant secretaries, supervisors, trainers, and so on. Office workers were known as *white-collar workers*, as opposed to the *blue-collar workers* who worked on the assembly line. As you can imagine, the cost of keeping all these managers and support people was quite high. The paperwork they generated was unbelievable, and the inefficiencies in communication and decision making became intolerable.

Teamwork, whether in the field or in the office, builds trust, cooperation, and joint commitments to achieve common objectives. This concept was a key part of Fayol's principles.

The trend now is toward *flat organizational structures*. That is, organizations are continuing to cut layers of management so that lower-level managers do not have to pass through many levels to reach higher managers; they simply report directly to these higher-level managers. This process has been greatly facilitated by the advent of desktop computers, which are now the common method of communication between these levels of managers who were formerly quite removed from each other.

One benefit of having these managers reporting to a higher-level manager is that the higher-level manager simply does not have time to get involved in the day-to-day work of the managers below. This gives lower-level managers more freedom to make changes as they see fit, makes organizations more responsive, and raises the morale of lower-level managers.

Those organizations that do cut management are often creating teams. Business majors, therefore, need to practise working and thinking in teams. You may get a job because of functional expertise (e.g., as a finance major), but your career is likely to take you into many different areas of the firm and demand more general skills. You may have to be a jack-of-all trades and a master of at least one.

An important question is: how many managers (or employees) should report to one manager? This matter requires some explanation and we look at that issue next.

··· SPAN OF CONTROL ···

Span of control refers to the number of subordinates a manager supervises. Many factors must be considered when determining span of control. At the lower levels, where the work is standardized, it is possible to implement a wide span of control (15 to 40 workers). However, the number should gradually narrow at higher levels of the organization because work is less standardized and there is more need for face-to-face communication. Variables in span of control include

span of control
The number of subordinates a manager supervises.

1. *The complexity of the job*, broken down into five areas:
   a. Functional complexity. The more complex the functions are, the narrower the span of control (fewer workers report to one supervisor).
   b. Functional similarity. The more similar the function, the broader the span of control.
   c. Need for coordination. The greater the need for coordination, the narrower the span of control.
   d. Planning demands. The more involved the plan, the narrower the span of control.
   e. Geographic closeness. The more concentrated the work area, the broader the span of control. (This has become somewhat redundant because of the excellent information linkages that exist now.)

2. *The capabilities of the manager*. The more experienced and capable the manager, the broader the span of control.

3. *The capabilities of the subordinates*. The more subordinates and supervisors need supervision, the narrower the span of control.

Other factors to consider include the professionalism of superiors and subordinates and the number of new problems that occur in a day. In business the span of control varies widely. The number of people reporting to the president may differ widely.

Figure 9.4 ties together span of control and tall and flat organizational structures. The tall organization with a narrow span of control might describe

NARROW VERSUS WIDE SPAN OF CONTROL

This figure describes two ways to structure an organization with the same number of employees. The tall structure with a narrow span of control has two managers who supervise four employees each. Changing to a flat surface with a wide span of control, the company could eliminate two managers and perhaps replace them with one or two employees, but the top manager would have to supervise 10 people instead of two.

departmentalization
Dividing an organization's structure into separate homogeneous units.

functional structure
Grouping of workers into departments based on similar skills, expertise, or resource use.

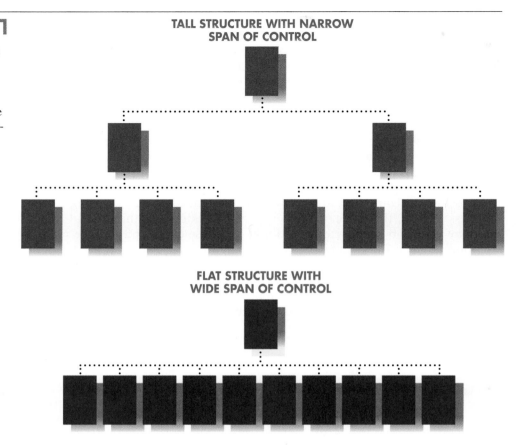

TALL STRUCTURE WITH NARROW SPAN OF CONTROL

FLAT STRUCTURE WITH WIDE SPAN OF CONTROL

Most larger companies in the past were divided into separate departments. Many departments have now merged, but some, such as the service department, often remain separate.

a lawncare service with two supervisors who manage four employees each (two of whom are more experienced). The flat structure with a wide span of control may work in a plant where all 10 workers are picking crabmeat. The wider the span of control, the greater the decision-making power of each employee. The trend now is to expand the span of control as organizations reduce the number of middle managers. Two factors that are helping this process are the constant improvements in information technology and the increasing professionalization of employees. These developments allow managers to handle more information and employees to take more responsibility for self-management.

••• DEPARTMENTALIZATION •••

The dividing of an organization's structure into separate homogeneous units is called **departmentalization**. The traditional technique for departmentalizing an organization is by function. **Functional structure** is the grouping of workers into departments based on similar skills, expertise, or resource use. There might be, for example, a production department, a transportation department, a finance department, an accounting department, a marketing department, a data-processing department, and so on. Such units enable employees to specialize and work together more efficiently. The advantages of such a structure include the following:

1. Skills can be developed in depth, and employees can progress within a department as their skills develop.
2. It allows for economies of scale in that all the resources needed can be centralized and various experts can be located in that area.
3. There is good coordination within the function, and top management can easily direct and control the activities of the various departments.

The disadvantages include the following:

1. There is a lack of communication among the different departments. For example, production may be isolated from marketing so that the people making the product do not get the proper feedback from customers.
2. Individual employees begin to identify with their department and its goals rather than the goals of the organization as a whole.
3. Response to external changes is slow.
4. People are not trained to take different managerial responsibilities; rather, they tend to become narrow specialists.

Given the limitations of departmentalization, businesses are now trying to redesign their structures to optimize skill development while increasing communication among employees in different departments. The goal, remember, is to better serve customers and to win their loyalty.

DIFFERENT WAYS TO DEPARTMENTALIZE   Figure 9.5 shows five ways a firm can departmentalize. One is by *product*. A book publisher might have a trade book department, a textbook department, and a technical book department. The development and marketing processes vary greatly among such books because customers for each type of book are very different, so each department specializes in those functions.

The most common way to departmentalize, as discussed above, is by *function*. This text is divided by business function because such groupings are common. Production, marketing, finance, human resources, and accounting are all distinct functions calling for separate skills.

It makes more sense in some organizations to departmentalize by *customer group*. A pharmaceutical company, for example, might have one department that focuses on the consumer market, another on hospitals (institutional market), and another that targets doctors.

Some firms group their units by *geographic locations*. Canada is usually considered one market area. Japan, Europe, and Korea may involve separate departments. The decision about which way to departmentalize depends greatly on the nature of the product and the customers served. A few firms departmentalize by *process* because it is more efficient to separate the activities that way. For example, a firm that makes leather coats may have one department cut the leather, another dye it, and a third sew the coat together.

Often firms use combinations of these methods.

··· CENTRALIZATION VERSUS ···
DECENTRALIZATION OF AUTHORITY

Imagine for a minute that you are a top manager for a large retail chain such as Reitman's. Your temptation may be to maintain control over all your stores to maintain a uniformity of image and merchandise. You have noticed such control works well for McDonald's, why not Reitman's? The degree to which an organization allows managers at the lower levels of the managerial

FIGURE **9.5**

. . . .

**VARIOUS WAYS TO
DEPARTMENTALIZE**

A publisher may want
to departmentalize by
product, a leather manu-
facturer by process, a
pharmaceutical company
by customer group, a
manufacturer by func-
tion, and a computer
company by geography
(countries). In each case,
the structure must fit the
goals of the firm. Often
a company will depart-
mentalize by function,
process, and product at
different levels. While B
is by function, E may be
the same company one
level lower, departmen-
talized by product.

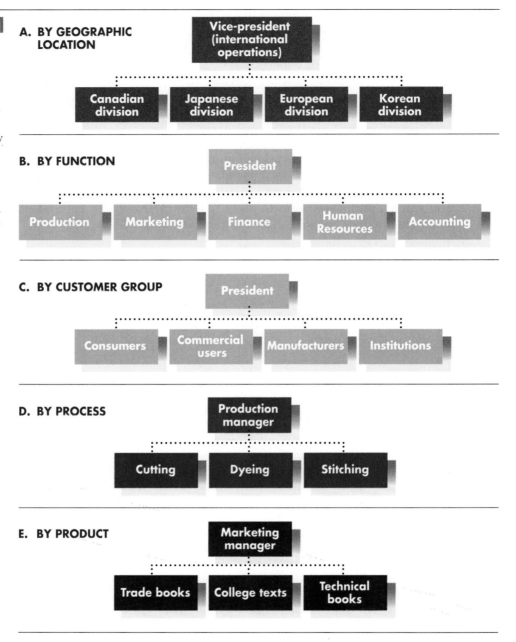

hierarchy to make decisions determines the degree of decentralization that an
organization practises.

centralized authority
Maintaining decision-making
authority at the top level of
management.

decentralized authority
Delegating decision-making
authority to lower-level managers
who are more familiar with local
conditions.

- **Centralized authority** means that decision-making authority is maintained at the top level of management at headquarters, or central
  management.
- **Decentralized authority** means that decision-making authority is
  delegated to lower-level managers who are more familiar with local
  conditions.

At Reitman's, for example, the customers in Vancouver are likely to demand
clothing styles different from those in Montreal or Toronto. It makes sense, therefore, to give regional managers in various areas the authority to buy, price, and

Campbell makes a variety of products, as this picture shows. Since the firm restructured, it has narrowed its product lines and revitalized its management and workforce. As a result, costs are down, and profits are up.

promote merchandise appropriate for each area. Such an assignment of part of a manager's duties to subordinates is called a *delegation of authority* and is an example of decentralized management.

On the other hand, McDonald's feels that purchasing, promotion, and other such decisions are best handled centrally. There is little need for each McDonald's store to carry different food products. McDonald's, therefore, leans toward centralized authority.

Today's rapidly changing markets, added to the global differences in consumer tastes and specific local problems, favour more decentralization and thus more delegation of authority. McDonald's in England, for example, has learned that its restaurants have to provide tea, management in Germany knows it must serve beer, in Japan they have rice, and management in France provide wine in their restaurants.

Most organizations have some degree of centralized authority and some decentralized authority. The Spotlight on Big Business on page 281 concerning the Campbell Soup Co. illustrates this point.

Critical Thinking

Can you see the connections between flat and tall structures, span of control, and centralization and decentralization? Does a flatter structure mean a wider span of control and thus more decentralization? Does a taller structure mean a narrower span of control and thus more centralized decision making?

Progress Check

- What is bureaucracy, and why has it led to the need for restructuring organizations?

- Are businesses moving toward taller or flatter organizational structures? Centralized or decentralized decision making? Why?

- What are some reasons for having a narrow span of control? Is there any advantage to a wide span of control?

- What are the five ways to departmentalize a company?

ORGANIZATION MODELS

Now that we have explored the basic principles of organizational design and learned the benefits of flat versus tall organizations, we can explore in more depth the various ways to structure an organization to accomplish its goals. We will look at (1) line organizations, (2) line and staff organizations, (3) matrix organizations, and (4) cross-functional, self-managed teams. Figure 9.6 compares their advantages and disadvantages.

··· LINE ORGANIZATIONS ···

A line organization is one in which there are direct two-way lines of responsibility, authority, and communication running from the top to the bottom and

FIGURE **9.6**
• • • •
**TYPES OF
ORGANIZATIONS**
Each form of organiza-
tion has its advantages
and disadvantages.

	Advantages	Disadvantages
Line	• Clearly defined responsibility and authority • Easy to understand • One supervisor for each person	• Too inflexible • Few specialists to advise • Long lines of communication • Unable to handle complex questions quickly
Line and staff	• Expert advice from staff to line personnel • Establishes lines of authority • Encourages cooperation and better communication at all levels	• Potential overstaffing • Potential overanalyzing • Lines of communication can get blurred • Staff frustrations because of lack of authority
Matrix	• Flexible • Encourages cooperation among departments • Can produce creative solutions to problems • Allows organization to take on new projects without adding to the organizational structure • Provides for more efficient use of organizational resources	• Costly and complex • Can confuse employees • Requires good interpersonal skills and cooperative managers and employees • Difficult to evaluate employees and to set up reward systems
Cross-functional, self-managed teams	• Greatly increases interdepartmental coordination and cooperation • Quicker response to customers and market conditions • Increased employee motivation and morale	• Some confusion over responsibility and authority • Perceived loss of control by management • Difficult to evaluate employees and to set up reward systems • Requires self-motivated and highly trained workers

back to the top of the organization, with every employee reporting to only one specific supervisor. A line organization has the advantages of having clearly defined responsibility and authority, being easy to understand, and providing one supervisor for each person. It meets the principles of good organization design (see Figure 9.7). Most small companies are organized this way.

However, a line organization has the disadvantages of being too inflexible, having few specialists or experts to advise people along the line, having lines of communication that are too long, and being unable to handle the complex decisions involved in an organization with thousands of sometimes unrelated products and tonnes of paperwork.

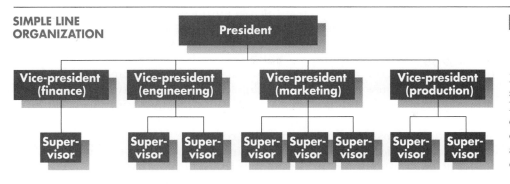

SIMPLE LINE ORGANIZATION

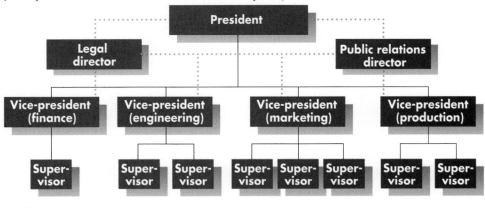

SIMPLE LINE AND STAFF ORGANIZATION
(staff personnel act as advisors, in-house experts)

Staff relationships ·············
Line relationships ——————

FIGURE **9.7**
· · · ·

LINE VERSUS LINE AND STAFF ORGANIZATIONS
Note that in the line and staff organization, the legal and public relations directors are not in the chain of command. They are advisors to the president and vice-presidents.

··· LINE AND STAFF ORGANIZATIONS ···

To minimize the disadvantages of simple line organizations, most organizations today have both line and staff personnel.

- **Line personnel** perform functions that contribute directly to the primary goals of the organization (e.g., making the product, distributing it, and selling it).
- **Staff personnel** perform functions that *advise* and *assist* line personnel in achieving their goals (e.g., marketing research, legal advising, and human resources.

Most organizations have benefitted from the expert advice of staff assistants in areas such as safety, quality control, computer technology, human resources, and investing. Staff positions strengthen the line positions and are by no means inferior or lower paid. It is like having well-paid consultants on the organization's payroll.

line personnel
Employees who perform functions that contribute directly to the primary goals of the organization.

staff personnel
Employees who perform functions that advise and assist line personnel in achieving their goals.

··· MATRIX ORGANIZATIONS ···

Both line and line and staff structures suffer from a certain inflexibility. Both have established lines of authority and communication and both work well in organizations with a relatively stable environment and slow product development (such as firms manufacturing consumer products like toasters and

matrix organization
Organization in which specialists from different parts of the organization are brought together to work on specific projects but still remain part of a line and staff structure.

refrigerators). In such firms, clear lines of authority and relatively fixed organizational structures are assets that assure efficient operations.

Today's economic scene is dominated by new kinds of organizations in high-growth industries unlike anything seen in the past. These include industries such as telecommunications, robotics, biotechnology, and aerospace. In these industries, new projects are developed quickly, competition with similar projects elsewhere is stiff, and the life cycle of new ideas is very short. The economic, technological, and competitive environments are changing rapidly. In such organizations, emphasis is on new-product development, creativity, special projects, rapid communication, and interdepartmental teamwork.

That environment led to the popularity of the **matrix organization** in which specialists from different parts of the organization are brought together to work on specific projects, but still remain part of a line and staff structure (see Figure 9.8). In other words, a project manager can borrow from different departments to help design and market new-product ideas or complete complex projects.

Matrix structures were developed in the aerospace industry at firms such as Boeing, Lockheed, and McDonnell Douglas and also at the United States National Aeronautics and Space Administration (NASA). The structure is now used in banking, management consulting firms, accounting firms, agencies, and school systems.

Although it works well in some organizations, it does not work in others. A matrix structure has some advantages:

- It gives flexibility to managers when assigning people to projects.
- It encourages intraorganizational cooperation and teamwork.

FIGURE 9.8

· · · ·

A MATRIX ORGANIZATION

In a matrix organization, project managers are in charge of teams made up of members of several departments. In this case, project manager 2 supervises 11 employees. These employees are accountable not only to project manager 2, but also to the heads of their individual departments, in manufacturing, marketing, finances, and engineering.

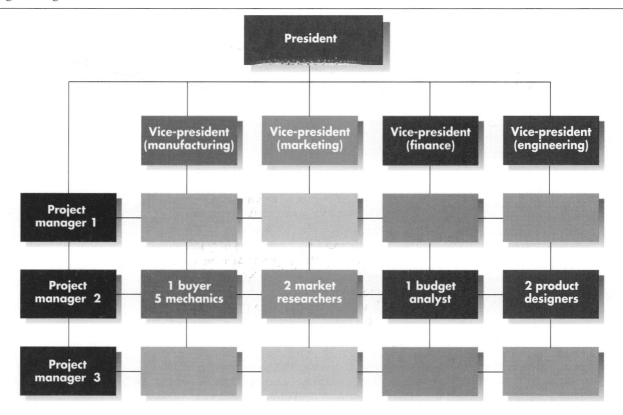

- It is flexible and can result in creative solutions to problems such as new product development.
- It provides for more efficient use of organizational resources.

The disadvantages are:

- It is complex and costly.
- It can cause confusion among employees as to where their loyalty belongs—to the project manager or their functional unit. (There is a potential conflict between two bosses.)
- It requires good interpersonal skills and cooperative employees and managers.

If it seems to you that matrix organizations violate some traditional managerial principles, you are right. Normally a person cannot work effectively for two bosses. (Who has the *real* authority? Which directive has the first priority—the one from the project manager or from one's immediate supervisor?) Figure 9.9 shows how decisions regarding a matrix organization fit in with other organizational decisions. In reality, the system functions more effectively than you may imagine.

To develop a new product idea, a project manager may be given temporary authority to "borrow" line personnel from engineering, production, marketing, and other line functions. Together, they work to complete the project and then return to their regular positions. Thus, no one really reports to more than one manager at a time.

The effectiveness of matrix-style organizations in high-tech firms eventually led to the adoption of similar concepts in many firms, including such low-tech firms as Rubbermaid. Rubbermaid now turns out an average of one new product every day using the team concept from matrix management.

••• CROSS-FUNCTIONAL, SELF-MANAGED TEAMS •••

The matrix style of organization eventually led to cross-functional teams. **Cross-functional teams** are groups of employees from different departments

<www.boeing.com>

A visit to Boeing's Web site will show why it needs an innovative organization structure! Boeing's products and their underlying technology and production are extremely complex.

cross-functional teams
Groups of employees from different departments who work together on a semipermanent basis (as opposed to the temporary teams established in matrix-style organizations).

Departmentalization	How should departments be established—by product, function, customer, geographic location, process, or some combination of these?
Span of control	How many employees should report to each manager? (A narrow span means few people reporting to one manager; a wide span means many people reporting to one manager.)
Lines of authority	What will be the lines of authority and responsibility in the firm? Which positions will be staff (support positions) and which will be line (directly in the chain of command)?
Delegation of authority	Should all key decisions be made by top management? What decisions should be delegated to managers and supervisors, if any?
Matrix formation	Who should be assigned to various committees? What authority should be given line managers to borrow employees from other areas for special committee assignments (see matrix organization discussion)?

FIGURE **9.9**

••••

QUESTIONS FOR VARIOUS ORGANIZATIONAL DESIGN ASPECTS

<www.oticonus.com>

Reaching Beyond Our Borders

Self-Managed Teams Overseas

Oticon A/S is the oldest and one of the largest manufacturers of hearing aid instruments. Founded in 1904 Oticon continues to be one of the most important in the industry, with advanced technology, and operations and sales all over the world. Few companies in the world were more conservative and bureaucratic than Oticon. The organizational structure wasn't working well, however, and in 1987 the company lost half of its equity. Something had to be done. The company decided to completely overhaul its organizational structure. As a consequence, profits rose sixfold and are still growing. Employee satisfaction is at an all-time high even though 15 percent of the staff had to be let go. Oticon's reorganization will give you some feel for the radical changes now occurring in organizations.

Workers at Oticon no longer have a job; instead they have a portfolio of jobs that they choose for themselves. For example, a woman in accounting serves as the company's contact for all Spanish-language calls. Between calls, she does her accounting work. An engineer may sign up to write the company's newsletter or help with the marketing plan. The idea is to fit the work to the people rather than fit the people to the work. ▲

Employees set their own hours and vacations. Everyone knows how the company's projects are doing and what the financial results are. If something needs to be done, anyone can volunteer to do it. There's no hierarchy.

All titles have been eliminated so there are no bosses or managers, but there are leaders. Employees are organized into highly flexible project teams. Chaos is prevented by a high level of communication. Everyone knows the strategies and policies of the firm. Project leaders keep the self-managed teams coordinated and a leadership group decides which projects to follow. Project leaders also set salaries.

As a result of cross-functional, self-managed work teams and open communication, time to market for new products has been cut in half. Oticon, in other words, has taken a lead in designing a nonbureaucratic office.

The results of these policies are shown in the continuing expansion and profitability of the company, seen in the 1998 annual report.

Source: Gifford Pinchot and Elizabeth Pinchot, *The End of Bureaucracy and the Rise of the Intelligent Organization* (San Francisco: Berrett-Koelher, 1993); <www.oticonus.com>, July 1999.

who work together on a semipermanent basis (as opposed to the temporary teams established in matrix-style organizations). Often the teams are empowered to make decisions on their own without seeking the approval of management. That's why the teams are called *self-managed*. The barriers between design, engineering, marketing, distribution, and other functions fall as members of each department work on teams.

Campbell Soup Canada (see Spotlight on Big Business) was very successful in converting to self-managed teams. These cross-functional teams of 10 to 30 people were also able to effectively carry out continual improvement.

Working together in teams is much different from working on your own. You must become multi-skilled, performing your own function, but also be able to understand and relate to people in other activities.

Spotlight on
Big Business

<www.campbellsoup.com>

Campbell Soup in Canada:
A Succes Story of Self-Managed Teams

Campbell Canada is a subsidiary of the Campbell Soup Co. in the United States. In the late 1980s and early 1990s, the parent company undertook a drastic restructuring of the entire organization. It merged Canada and the United States into one division under the FTA to improve its profitability, which had slipped badly. As part of that process, nine Canadian plants were sold or closed, leaving only two plants here, one at Listowel and the other in Toronto.

David Clark, former president of Campbell Canada, knew its future was at stake. As part of Campbell's restructuring, Clark told the head office he would produce fewer, more specialized products, do it cost effectively, and export at least half the volume to the United States.

To attain these difficult targets, Clark undertook a radically different tack from the traditional strategies. He set out to restructure employees' minds—to transform the way workers related to their jobs and their company. He hired Toronto-based motivational guru Bix Bickson.

The results were very impressive. A variety of "unreasonable, irrational, and impossible" targets were set by teams. When Clark saw some of the plans, he thought the teams were out of their minds. In the end, most surpassed these incredible objectives. The Toronto team had started on a breakthrough regime a year ear-

lier, when it cost $3.87 more to produce one case of soup in Toronto than at Campbell's best plant in Maxton, North Carolina. They narrowed the gap to 32 cents.

By 1995 the entire operation at Toronto had converted to self-managed teams, and by 1996 the Toronto plant was racking up some high value results. Production of soup went from 11.8 cases per labour hour in 1991 to 16.2 cases. Costs of producing a case dropped from U.S. $3.22 to $2.22. Total output rose from 6.4 million cases annually to 15.2 million cases. In 20 out of 22 calendar months ending March 1996, the Toronto plant led all Campbell plants in North America. One of the results was that Toronto was getting an ever larger share of U.S. business.

The role of self-managed teams was crucial according to director of operation for Canada, Ned Hennighausen. The early impressive results led the company to invest $45 million in the last four years to modernize production. It also increased its workforce to cope with the rising demand from the United States.

All of these efforts continue to show up in the company's financial results. In 1998 sales reached their highest level ever at $6.69 billion dollars.

Sources: Interview with Ned Hennighausen, May 10, 1996; Wendy Trueman, "Alternate Visions," *Canadian Business* 64, no. 3 (March 1991); <www.campbellsoup.com>, July 1999.

Shell Canada has organized its entire workforce in its plant at Brockville, Ontario, into self-managing teams. This $75 million lubricants factory employs only 75 people, of whom 15 are senior managers (called coordinators) or purely administrative staff. There are 60 team operators (of whom one-third are women). All of these employees are expected to manage everything themselves as individuals or team members. "The teams are responsible for discipline, cost control (including absenteeism), and arranging their own vacation and training schedules."[10]

There are many examples of Canadian companies that have embraced the new management and organization styles to become more efficient and thus more competitive. Many corporations are experimenting with self-managed, cross-functional teams, which are expected to lead to important productivity breakthroughs. The Reaching Beyond Our Borders box illustrates how one such firm in Denmark has applied the concepts.

<www.oticonus.com>

Visit Oticon's Web site to see how its new approach to management and organizational structure has contributed to renewed success.

Networking to Win

Networking helps large and small organizations to compete in global markets. Beginning in 1989, for example, 3500 small Danish firms organized into networks, small groups of businesses that work together. In less than two years, they had made a substantial contribution to completely reversing a three-decade-long deficit in the country's trade exports. Networking thus creates jobs. CD (Corporate Design) Line is one of the Danish success stories. A network of 14 textile firms produces part of a complete collection: shirts, suits, skirts, women's knitwear, ties, scarves, and more. Marketing the entire collection together benefits all the firms. Together they hired a quality manager and set up salespeople in their best foreign markets: Sweden and Germany. They jointly contract with famous designers. They even share an electronic data interchange network on a cost-sharing basis.

Together, this network can now compete with large companies. Smaller organizations use networking to purchase cooperatively, to market jointly, to combine research and development, to establish quality programs, to share in distribution research and costs, and more.

This kind of network is now called an *extranet* and is discussed below. Some people believe extranets have become essential for small business to compete.

Source: Jessica Lipnack and Jeffrey Stamps, *The TeamNet Factor* (Essex Junction, VT: Oliver Wight Publications, 1993); Jason Myers, "Rewire Your Business Plan," *Canadian Business*, June 25/July 9, 1999, p. 198.

<www.campbellsoup.com>

To learn more about Campbell's, visit its Web site and read *The Story of Campbell Soup Company*.

networking
Using communications technology and other means to link organizations and allow them to work together on common objectives.

extranet
An extension of the Internet that connects suppliers, customers, and other organizations via secure Web sites.

CROSS-FUNCTIONAL TEAMS LEAD TO NETWORKING Cross-functional teams work best when the "voice of the customer" is brought into organizations. That's why it's a good idea to include customers on cross-functional product development teams. To ensure that suppliers and distributors are part of the process, they should be included on the team as well. Now you have cross-functional teams that cross organizational boundaries.

The net result of cross-functional teams, therefore, is that organizational design has now expanded way beyond the design of a single firm. It has become the design of an integrated system of firms that all work together to satisfy the wants and needs of customers and other stakeholders of the *system*.[11] Imagine, for example, a piece of hockey equipment designed in Scandinavia, engineered in the United States to meet the needs of the Canadian market, manufactured in Korea, and distributed in a global market with initial distribution from Japan. Such linked organizations reflect what's happening today. As such systems become global, the orientation of managers becomes global as well, and barriers between cooperating countries are reduced.

Some of these suppliers and distributors may be in other countries. Thus, such teams may share market information with teams across national boundaries. The government may encourage this networking of teams and government coordinators may assist such projects. In that case, cross-functional teams also break the barriers between government and business cooperation. Whether it involves customers, suppliers, distributors, or government, **networking** in this context means using communications technology and other means to link organizations and allow them to work together on common objectives.[12]

••• EXTRANETS LINK COMPANY INTRANETS •••

The latest trend is to link firms on an extranet. an **extranet** is an extension of the Internet and connects suppliers, customers, and other organizations via secure Web sites. It is made up of linked intranets. The Spotlight on Small Business on

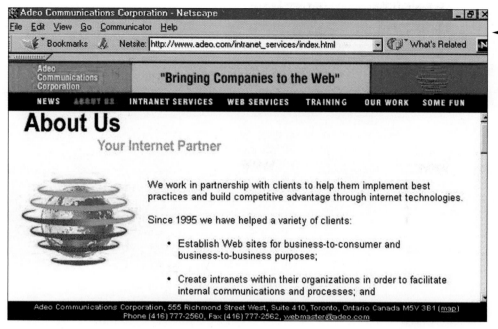

Adeo Communications Corporation is an example of a successful company that creates intranets within business organizations to facilitate internal communications. In addition, the company also establishes secure extranets to support specific business-to-business communications. Adeo's client list includes well-known companies such as Ford of Canada, M&M Meat Shops, Noranda, and Ontario Power Generation.

the previous page gives an example of how small companies combine to form an extranet. An **intranet** is a set of communication links within a company that travels over the Internet.[13] Service organizations like Wells Fargo Bank and manufacturing firms like Silicon Graphics both use intranets. Although intranets are used mostly at larger firms, smaller firms are using them as well.[14] The ideas is to link everyone in the firm electronically so they can communicate freely and work together on projects. For example, workers at Hallmark Cards once pasted creative ideas on a bulletin board for others to comment on. Because of limited space on the board, old cards were simply not available for easy comparison. Today, old and new cards are available on the intranet, where comments can be made and cards can be adapted by anyone. Any information a Hallmark employee wants others in the firm to see can be placed on the intranet.[15] Such information can also be made available to employees at suppliers and dealers if they are part of a linked intranet system (an extranet).

intranet
A set of communication links within a company that travels over the Internet.

LIMITATIONS OF CROSS-FUNCTIONAL TEAMS   Setting up cross-functional teams isn't easy. Often managers of functional areas will resist the move toward teams. Furthermore, team members are often unsure of what their duties are, how they'll be compensated, and who's responsible if mistakes are made. Working on a team takes different skills from working alone. Additional training is needed to prepare workers for teamwork. The change to such teams is often so disruptive that a company may falter for years while the changes are being made. That has been the case at IBM, for example.[16]

The most common problem with teams is that companies rush out and form the wrong kind of team for the wrong kind of job. Figure 9.10 illustrates five different types of teams. Sometimes teams can be overused. Cross-functional teams aren't the answer to every management problem. Some problems can be solved faster by a single person. For example, making creative types sit in a team meeting waiting to reach a consensus can stifle creativity.

Progress Check

- Can you cite the advantages and disadvantages of line, line and staff, matrix, and cross-functional organizational forms?
- Why do cross-functional teams often lead to networking?

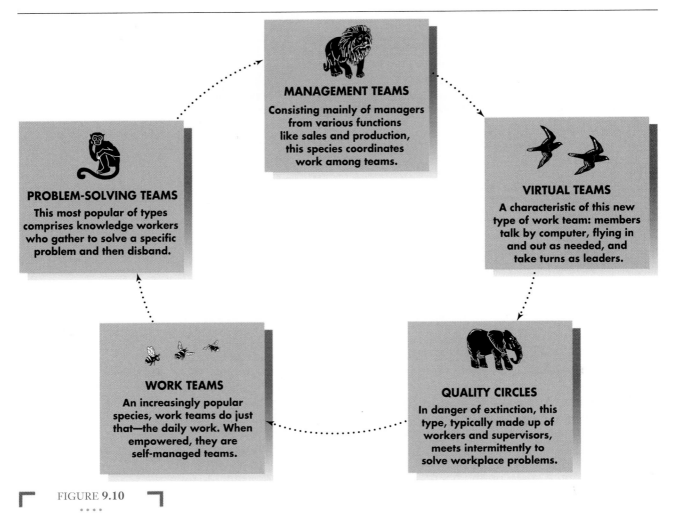

MANAGEMENT TEAMS
Consisting mainly of managers
from various functions
like sales and production,
this species coordinates
work among teams.

PROBLEM-SOLVING TEAMS
This most popular of types
comprises knowledge workers
who gather to solve a specific
problem and then disband.

VIRTUAL TEAMS
A characteristic of this new
type of work team: members
talk by computer, flying in
and out as needed, and
take turns as leaders.

WORK TEAMS
An increasingly popular
species, work teams do just
that—the daily work. When
empowered, they are
self-managed teams.

QUALITY CIRCLES
In danger of extinction, this
type, typically made up of
workers and supervisors,
meets intermittently to
solve workplace problems.

FIGURE **9.10**

FIVE TYPES OF TEAMS

Note the differences
between each type of
team. Together they are
able to fill all the needs
of a modern company.

**total quality
management (TQM)**
Striving for maximum customer
satisfaction by ensuring quality
from all departments.

**continuous
improvement (CI)**
Constantly improving the way the
organization does things so that
customer needs can be better
satisfied.

THE RESTRUCTURING PROCESS
AND TOTAL QUALITY

It's not easy to move from an organization dominated by managers to one that
relies heavily on self-managed teams. How you restructure an organization
depends on the status of the present system. If the system already has a customer
focus, but isn't working well, a total quality management approach may work.

Total quality management (TQM) is the practice of striving for maximum customer satisfaction by ensuring quality from all departments. Total
quality management calls for *continual improvement of present processes.*
Processes are sets of activities strung together for a reason, such as the process
for handling a customer's order. **Continuous improvement (CI)** means constantly improving the way the organization does things so that customer
needs can be better satisfied.

The movement is catching on in Canada. Many of the companies spot-
lighted in this book practise it. Meat-packer Schneider Corp. of Kitchener,
Ontario, attributes its success in overcoming difficult adjustments to market changes to CI.[17] Another Canadian enthusiast for CI is PanCanadian
Petroleum Ltd., which has been applying it in engineering and production.

Two years into CI, PanCanadian smells a winner. The program has moved in-house, with a squad of company coaches taking over from the TeamPro consultants. Plans are afoot to introduce it into the finance department and to create work teams from different departments.

The early experiments uncapped a vast reserve of creativity. The next step is to give this force some direction without slipping back into the old autocratic style.[18]

It's possible, in an organization with few layers of management and a customer focus, that new computer software and employee training could lead to a team-oriented approach with few problems. In bureaucratic organizations with many layers of management, however, TQM is not useful. Continual improvement doesn't work when the whole process is being done incorrectly. When an organization needs dramatic changes, only reengineering will do. **Reengineering** is the fundamental rethinking and radical redesign of organizational processes to achieve dramatic improvements in critical measures of performance. Note the words *radical redesign* and *dramatic improvements*.[19]

A word of caution may be in order about these theories. In management, as in other fields, new fads are always cropping up. Some are old ideas recycled in new clothes. Others represent some new thinking and require attention. The essence of the current trends of restructuring, reengineering, downsizing, and such are an attempt to become more competitive by (1) reducing costs, (2) doing away with bureaucratic thinking and organization, and (3) providing excellent customer service as a normal way of operating.

A useful book on this topic concentrates on "what customers value most." Based on a survey of 1800 North American companies by management consultants Coopers & Lybrand, the book concludes that the "slash and burn" that accompanies the process of restructuring is useless unless the customers really get better value where they can see it. Unless order-taking, billing, complaints, sales force—everything that touches the customer—improves sharply, the whole wrenching procedure will only produce short-term advantages.[20]

At IBM Credit Corporation, for example, the process for handling a customer's request for credit once went through a five-step process that took an average of six days. By completely reengineering the customer-request process, IBM Credit cut its processing time from six days to four hours! In reengineering, narrow, task-oriented jobs become multidimensional. Employees who once did as they were told now make decisions on their own. Functional departments lose their reason for being. Managers stop acting like supervisors and instead behave like coaches. Workers focus more on the customers' needs and less on their bosses' needs. Attitudes and values change in response to new incentives. Practically every aspect of the organization is transformed, often beyond recognition. Because of the complexity of the process, many reengineering efforts fail.

<deming.org>

One of the founding fathers of the movement toward total quality as a focus of management attention was Edwards Deming. Visit this Web site and follow some of its links to learn more about this intriguing man. You might want to try your hand at the *Deming Puzzle*, on the Internet at <deming.edu/DP/Puzzle11Print.htm>.

reengineering
The rethinking and radical redesign of organizational processes to achieve dramatic improvements in critical measures of performance.

Critical Thinking

Why do some reengineering efforts fail? Given the dramatic changes that occur when companies adopt cross-functional, self-managed teams, what prevents the majority of companies from adopting such an organizational structure?

Given the flexibility and education requirements of empowered employees, what changes must occur in Canadian schools to prepare students for such jobs?

inverted organization
Organization method that has contact people at the top and chief executive at the bottom.

Working in an inverted organization is much different from working in a firm with a more traditional structure. Frontline employees are given more training and responsibility, and are expected to do more. These factors make the job more exciting and motivating.

⋯ TURNING THE ORGANIZATION UPSIDE ⋯ DOWN TO EMPOWER EMPLOYEES

Many firms are discovering that the key to long-term success in a competitive market is to empower front-line people (often in teams) to respond quickly to customer wants and needs. That means major restructuring of the firm to make front-line workers the most important people in the firm. For example, doctors have long been treated as the most important people in hospitals, pilots are the focus of airlines, and professors are the central focus of universities, while front-desk people in hotels, clerks in department stores, and tellers in banks haven't been considered key personnel in the past. Instead, managers were considered the key people, and they were responsible for managing the front-line people. The organization chart in a typical firm, therefore, looked something like the pyramid in Figure 9.11.

The most advanced service organizations have turned the traditional organizational structure upside down. These **inverted organizations** have contact people at the top and the chief executive officer at the bottom. There are few layers of management, and their job is to assist and support front-line people, not boss them around. Figure 9.12 shows the new inverted organizational structure.

A good example of an inverted organization is NovaCare, a provider of rehabilitation care in the United States. At its top are some 5000 physical, occupational, and speech therapists. The rest of the organization is structured to serve those therapists. Managers consider the therapists as their bosses, and the manager's job is to support them by arranging contacts with nursing homes, handling accounting and credit activities, and providing training for the therapists.

Companies based on this organizational structure support front-line personnel with internal and external databanks, advanced communication systems, and professional assistance. Naturally, this means that front-line people have to be better educated, better trained, and better paid than in the past. It takes a lot of trust for top managers to implement such a system—but when they do, the payoff for

FIGURE 9.11
• • • •
TRADITIONAL ORGANIZATION CHART

This is the traditional, bureaucratic, organizational structure.

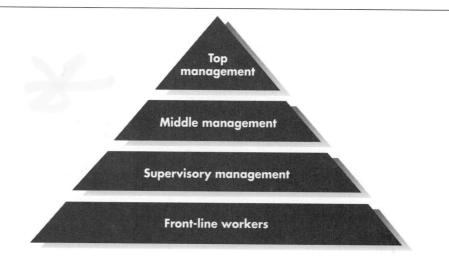

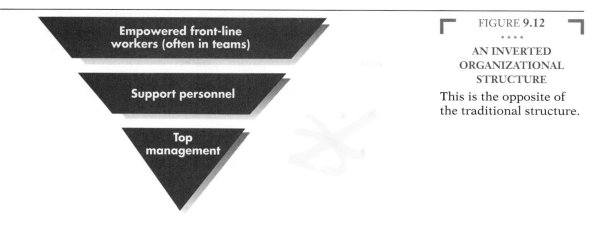

FIGURE **9.12**
· · · ·
AN INVERTED ORGANIZATIONAL STRUCTURE
This is the opposite of the traditional structure.

customers and profits is often well worth the effort.[21] In the past, managers controlled information, and that gave them power. In more progressive organizations, everyone shares information and that gives everyone power.

··· TURNING THE ORGANIZATION ··· INSIDE OUT—OUTSOURCING

In the past, organizations tried to do everything themselves. That is, each organization had a separate department for accounting, finance, marketing, production, and so on. Today's organizations are turning inside out. TQM demands that organizations benchmark each function against the best in the world. **Competitive benchmarking** is rating an organization's practices, processes, and products against the world's best. Benchmarking has become a significant activity in Canada. Governments and large and small companies are all involved in procedures to discover and apply the best practices available. Industry Canada and Statistics Canada have accumulated extensive statistics of the use of benchmarking in a variety of industries. Some examples are breweries, flour mixing and cereal production, electronic computing, paperboard manufacturing, musical instruments and the recording industry. The Alliance of Manufacturers and Exporters has established an extensive Promoting Business Excellence (PROBE) program relying largely on the IBM Consulting Group in Canada.[22]

As global competition continues to heat up, the idea of benchmarking is attracting increasing attention. Sometimes managers can become overzealous in their attempts to find out what their strongest competitors are doing, whether in marketing, production or research. It is important that companies monitor these activities to ensure that managers do not overreach the boundaries of ethical behaviour. (See the Ethical Dilemma box at the start of the chapter.)

If the organization can't do as well as the best, the idea is to outsource the function to an organization that *is* the best. **Outsourcing** is assigning various functions, such as accounting and legal work, to outside organizations. Some functions, such as information management, may be too important to assign to outside firms. In that case, the organization should benchmark on the best firms and reengineer their departments to be equally good. The next chapter continues the discussion of outsourcing.

When a firm has completed its outsourcing process, the remaining functions are the firm's core competencies. **Core competencies** are those func-

competitive benchmarking
Rating an organization's practices, processes, and products against the world's best.

outsourcing
Assigning various functions, such as accounting and legal work, to outside organizations.

core competencies
Functions that the organization can do as well as or better than any other company in the world.

tions that the organization can do as well as or better than any other company in the world. Gallo Winery, for example, doesn't grow most of its own grapes. Instead, it sticks to what it does best: producing and marketing (including distributing) wine products. Gallo spends more money on market research than its primary competitors and thus knows more about the market for wines. It also has the most up-to-date information and distribution system. Gallo isn't as skilled in retailing and promotion, so it outsources those functions.

CREATING INTERNAL CUSTOMERS   Some departments in organizations are reluctant to join the total quality revolution. They would rather function the old way, when each department had its own agenda and method of operating. Executives who believe in TQM have a way of transforming such departments. They create internal customers within the firm. To improve such internal services, management sets up buy–sell relationships among teams and business units in the organization. If the team isn't happy with the products and services provided by an *internal* unit, the team can purchase them from *outside vendors*. This creates a competitive situation, forcing internal units to become more internally customer oriented or lose their business to outsiders.

Large, transnational companies are continuing the process of transferring authority and decision making to lower levels of management and also dividing themselves into smaller, more independent, more efficient business units. This development naturally leads to more intensive efforts to please internal customers if the units want to avoid losing business to outside competitors.[23]

···· ▬▬ ····

ESTABLISHING A SERVICE-ORIENTED CULTURE

Figure 9.13 summarizes the charges that occur as an organization moves from being bureaucratic to being customer oriented.

FIGURE **9.13**

····

BUREAUCRATIC VERSUS CUSTOMER-FOCUSED ORGANIZATIONAL STRUCTURES

This shows the great contrast between the old and the new structures.

BUREAUCRATIC	CUSTOMER-FOCUSED
Coordination from the top	Self-management
Top-down chain of command	Bottom-up power relationships
Many rules and regulations	Employees free to make decisions
Departmentalization by function	Cross-functional teams
Specialization	Integration and cooperation
One firm does it all	Outsourcing
Management controls information	Information goes to all
Largely domestic orientation	Global orientation
Focus on external customers	Focus on both internal and external customers

Any organizational change is bound to cause some stress and resistance among members of the firm. Therefore, any change should be accompanied by the establishment of an organizational culture that facilitates such change.[24] **Organizational culture** may be defined as widely shared values within a organization that provide coherence and cooperation to achieve common goals. Usually the culture of an organization is reflected in stories, traditions, and myths.

Anyone who has been to Disneyland or Disney World can't fail to be impressed by the obvious values instilled by Walt Disney that permeate the organization. You may have heard about or read about the focus on cleanliness, helpfulness, and friendliness, but such stories can't prepare you for the near-perfect implementation of those values at the parks.

It's also obvious from visiting any McDonald's restaurant that every effort has been made to maintain a culture that emphasizes "quality, service, cleanliness, and value." Each restaurant has the same "feel," the same "look," and the same "atmosphere." In short, each reflects the organizational culture.

Disney and McDonald's are two examples of favourable organizational cultures that led to successful operations. But an organizational culture can also be negative. Have you ever been in an organization in which you feel that no one cares about service or quality? The clerks may seem uniformly glum, indifferent, and testy. The mood often seems to pervade the atmosphere so that patrons become moody and upset. You know the feeling. Are there examples in your area?

The very best organizations have cultures that emphasize service to others, especially customers. The atmosphere is one of friendly, concerned, caring people who enjoy working together to provide a good product at a reasonable price. Those companies that have such cultures have less need for close supervision of employees, not to mention policy manuals, organization charts, and formal rules, procedures, and controls (see Figure 9.13).

Good organizational leaders create a culture that emphasizes cooperation and satisfaction in serving customers and that culture results in self-motivated employees who need minimal supervision. Within that atmosphere, self-managed teams can develop and flourish. The key to productive culture is mutual trust. You get it by giving it. The very best companies stress high moral and ethical values such as honesty, reliability, fairness, environmental protection, and social involvement.

Thus far, we have been talking as if organizational matters were mostly controllable by management. The fact is that the formal organizational structure is just one element of the total organizational system. In the creation of organizational culture, the *informal organization* is of equal or greater importance. Let's explore this notion next.

organizational culture
Widely shared values within an organization that provide coherence and cooperation to achieve common goals.

<www.tompetersgroup.
com>

One of the strongest advocates of the role of organizational culture and the importance of leadership's role in shaping it is Tom Peters. The culture of several of the most successful companies in the world is described in the best-selling book *In Search of Excellence*, written by Peters and Robert Waterman. Two of the companies included are Disney and McDonalds. Visit Peters' Web site and learn about his work.

Critical
Thinking

What is the organizational culture at your university or college? Is it known for its excellence, quality, and student orientation? If not, what is it known for? How is that reflected in student attitudes, community support, and faculty attitudes? How could the culture be improved?

···· ▬▬▬▬ ····

THE INFORMAL ORGANIZATION
HELPS CREATE TEAMWORK

All organizations have two organizational systems. One is the **formal organization**. This is the official system that details each person's responsibility,

formal organization
The official system that details responsibility, authority, and position; it is the structure shown on the organization chart.

informal organization
The system of relationships and lines of authority that develop spontaneously outside the formal organization; it is the human side of the organization and does not show up on any organization chart.

authority, and position. It is the structure shown on organization charts. But there is also an **informal organization**. It consists of the various cliques, relationships, and lines of authority that develop spontaneously outside the formal organization. This system is the human side of organization and does not show up on any organization chart.

Only very small companies can operate effectively without both types of organization. The formal system is often too slow and bureaucratic to enable the organization to adapt quickly. However, the formal organization does provide helpful guidelines and lines of authority to follow in routine situations.

The informal organization is often too unstructured and emotional to allow careful, reasoned decision making on critical matters. It is extremely effective, however, in generating creative solutions to short-term problems, providing a feeling of camaraderie and teamwork among employees, and overcoming bottlenecks created by the formal system.

In any organization, it is wise to learn quickly whom the important people are in the *informal* organization. There are rules and procedures to follow for using certain equipment, but those procedures often take days. Who in the organization knows how to get you the equipment immediately, without following the normal procedures? Which assistants should you see if you want your work given first priority?

Key figures are usually older, respected employees who have earned that position of influence. It is interesting to speculate on whether the importance of the informal organization will be diminished in the future because of the radical reorganizations we have discussed. This change often involves drastic reductions in staff, including the early retirement of employees with many years' seniority—precisely those people who are likely to be key in the informal organization. This might be an interesting topic for a research paper.

The informal organization's nerve centre is the *grapevine*, the system through which unofficial information flows between and among managers and employees. It consists of rumours, facts, suspicions, accusations, and all kinds of accurate and inaccurate information. The key people in the information system usually have the most influence in the organization.

In the old "we versus they" system of organizations in which managers and employees were often at odds, the informal system often hindered effective management. In the new, more open organizations in which managers and employees work together to set objectives and design procedures, the informal organization can be an invaluable managerial asset that promotes harmony among workers and establishes the corporate culture. That is a major advantage, for example, of self-managed teams. Two of the more important aspects of the informal organization are the following:

1. *Group norms.* Group norms are the informal rules and procedures that guide the behaviour of group members. They include often unspoken but very clear guidelines regarding things like proper dress, language, work habits (e.g., how fast one works, how many breaks one takes, where one turns for assistance, and so on), and social behaviour (where one goes for recreation, with whom, how often). Deviants from the norm are often verbally abused, isolated, or harassed.

2. *Group cohesiveness.* Often a work group will develop alliances and commitments over time that tie them together strongly. The term used to describe such feelings of group loyalty is *cohesiveness*. Historically, unions have been a strong cohesive force as workers united to fight management. The goal today is to generate such cohesiveness among all corporate employees to create excellence in all phases of operation.

Ethical Dilemma

REVIEW

You can see that working for a large modern company can be interesting and challenging but it can also be difficult. As the Ethical Dilemma box at the beginning of the chapter shows, sometimes you may be called upon to do things that you consider questionable. Let's see what our executives think.

Bédard feels that "there are limits to what the law will allow in the gathering of information on other companies. Some information is available through various technical sources and some companies will willingly share information. If the information requested is confidential, there are reasons [for this]. Honest competition is the only viable option."

Reilley states that information in the public domain will provide a company with what it needs to know about its competitors. He adds, "however, an integrated intelligence approach is necessary to gain this public domain information. I've never heard of seeding an employee via a leave of absence into another firm to

gain information. Not only is it entirely unethical, but how can one be certain about the information being provided? Once embarked upon an unethical endeavour, a firm engenders a culture of dishonesty that will manifest itself at all levels [and] in turn, will result in major inefficiencies. Ethical companies always win in the long run. Good guys don't finish last!"

Most companies today operate under ethical guidelines, but you may disagree about whether something your company wants you to do falls within its ethical guidelines. As you saw in Chapter 3, competition is intense and global, and managers and employees are sometimes faced with difficult decisions that lie at the boundaries of ethical behaviour. They might, perhaps, be tempted to steal a senior employee from a top competitor. In a major European case General Motors successfully sued Volkswagen for just such a reason and got a multimillion dollar award for damages. How do you feel about this issue?

For such cohesiveness to develop, employees must feel that they are part of a total corporate team. Often, the informal network created by corporate athletic teams, unions and other such affiliations can assist in the creation of teamwork and cooperation.

In summary, the informal organization of a firm can strongly reinforce a feeling of teamwork and cooperation or can effectively prevent any such unity. Managers who maintain open, honest communication with employees can create an informal atmosphere that promotes willing commitment and group cohesiveness. As effective as the informal organization may be in creating group cooperation, it can be equally powerful in resisting management directives. Learning to create the right corporate culture and to work with the informal organization is a key to managerial success.

Progress Check

- What's the difference between continuous improvement and reengineering?
- What does it mean to turn an organization chart upside down?
- What's an internal customer?
- How important is the informal organization to the success of organizational change?

SUMMARY
· · · · · ·

1. Describe the traditional hierarchical, bureaucratic organizational structure, and explain how and why it is being restructured.

1. Organizational design is the coordinating of workers so that they can best accomplish all the firm's goals.
   - ***What's the traditional organizational structure and how is it being restructured?***
   The typical organization is hierarchical and bureaucratic. Restructuring means redesigning an organization so that it can more effectively and efficiently service customers. Often that means breaking down the barriers between functions. It may also mean giving more authority to lower-level employees and ending top-down management.

2. Explain the organizational theories of Fayol and Weber.

2. Economy of scale means that the larger the plant, the more efficient it can be because all the employees can specialize in a function that they can do efficiently.
   - ***What concepts did Fayol and Weber contribute?***
   Fayol introduced principles such as unity of command, hierarchy of authority, division of labour, subordination of individual interests to the general interest, authority, clear communication channels, order, and equity. Weber added principles of bureaucracy such as job descriptions, written rules and decision guidelines, consistent procedures, and staffing and promotions based on qualifications.

3. Discuss the various issues connected with organizational design.

3. Organizational issues that have led to design changes include (1) tall versus flat organizational structures, (2) span of control, (3) departmentalization, and (4) centralization versus decentralization.
   - ***What are the major issues of each?***
   The issue of tall organizations is that they slow communication. The trend is to eliminate managers and flatten organizations. The span of control is getting larger as employees are becoming self-directed. Departments are often being replaced or supplemented by matrix organizations and cross-functional teams. In matrix organizations, people can be borrowed from departments to be put on project teams. Cross-functional teams have been very effective in making organizations faster and more responsive to the market. They've also led to decentralization of authority.

4. Explain the concepts of span of control and tall or flat structures and their interconnectedness.

4. The current trend is for organizations to move from a tall to a flat structure and from a narrow to a wide span of control for managers.
   - ***What do flat and tall structures and span of control mean?***
   Span of control refers to the number of subordinates who report to a manager. The span may be narrow (i.e., a small number of subordinates report to each manager) or wide (i.e., a larger number of subordinates report to each manager). Tall and flat refer to the shape of the organization chart. As organizations are eliminating levels of management, these shapes are becoming flatter. Another effect is that remaining managers must supervise greater numbers of subordinates, resulting in a movement to wider span of control.

5. Describe the differences between line, line and staff, matrix, and cross-functional organizations.

5. The four forms of organization explored in the text are (1) line organizations, (2) line and staff organizations, (3) matrix-style organizations, and (4) cross-functional, self-managed teams.
   - ***What are the advantages of each?***
   A line organization has the advantages of having clearly defined responsibility and authority, of being easy to understand, and of providing one supervisor for each person. Most organizations have benefited from the line and staff organization because it provides expert advice of staff assis-

tants in areas such as safety, quality control, computer technology, human resource management, and investing. Matrix organizations give flexibility to managers in assigning people to projects and encourage intraorganizational cooperation and teamwork. Cross-functional, self-managed teams are more permanent and have all the benefits of the matrix style.

6. Reengineering is the fundamental rethinking and radical redesign of organizational processes to improve critical measures of performance.
   * ***What are the benefits of turning organizations upside down and inside out?***
   By turning organizations upside down, more authority and responsibility are given to front-line workers so they can better serve customers. Managers serve workers instead of the other way around. Outsourcing is assigning various functions, such as accounting and legal work, to outside organizations. By setting up competition between internal and external functions, a corporation can become world class.

6. Explain the benefits of turning organizations upside down and inside out.

7. Organizational culture may be defined as widely shared values within an organization that provide coherence and cooperation to achieve common goals.
   * ***How can organizational culture and the informal organization hinder or assist organizational change?***
   The informal organization can strongly reinforce a feeling of teamwork and cooperation or can effectively prevent such unity. Managers who maintain open, honest communication with employees can create an informal atmosphere that promotes willing commitment and group cohesiveness. The informal organizaton can be equally powerful in resisting management directives. Learning to create the right corporate culture and to work with the informal organization is a key to managerial success.

7. Give examples to show how organizational culture and the informal organization can hinder or assist organizational change.

KEY TERMS

bureaucracy 263	**departmentalization** 273	**matrix organization** 278
centralized authority 274	**extranet** 282	**networking** 282
competitive benchmarking 287	**formal organization** 289	**organizational culture** 289
continuous improvement (CI) 284	**functional structure** 273	**organizational design** 262
core competencies 287	**hierarchy** 262	**outsourcing** 287
cross-functional teams 279	**informal organization** 290	**reengineering** 285
decentralized authority 274	**intranet** 283	**restructuring** 264
	inverted organization 286	**span of control** 271
	line personnel 277	**staff personnel** 277
		total quality management (TQM) 284

DEVELOPING WORKPLACE SKILLS

1. Form groups in class and discuss jobs you have had from the point of view of what organizational structure was in place. Do you know what span of control your boss had? Discuss whether it seemed to be the right span of control. What is your evidence?

2. Go to a local financial institution and find out from the manager how many levels of management there are between him or her and the president.

Ask if there have been any recent changes in the number of levels. Inquire if the current structure seems to work well. If the answer is no, find out what the problems are.

3. The lean-and-mean approach has been criticized by some business commentators as very shortsighted. They argue that when a recession ends and business picks up, those companies who have let go many experienced managers are going to be at a great competitive disadvantage. How should a company balance the need to hold onto its valuable managers with financial pressures to cut costs?

4. Ten years from today, you are operating a successful small business with 35 employees. What kind of organizational structure will you favour, centralized or decentralized? What factors will help you decide? Explain.

5. Write a short description of a situation in which you were frustrated because a clerk in a bank, or some other business, government agency, school, or hospital followed the rules or policy to the letter and caused you much grief and lost time. Share your story with others in the class. Compare stories and then discuss strategies for minimizing such bureaucratic hassles in organizations.

INTERNET CHALLENGES

1. Using a search vehicle like Canada.com, Yahoo, or Alta Vista, click on a business, finance, or economics choice and scan some recent business headlines for names of well-known large Canadian companies. Try to contact a company by e-mail and ask human resource management for an *organization chart* or an *organogram*. If you have no success try a major bank, Nortel Networks <www.nortelnetworks.com>, or Bombardier <www.bombardier.com>. When you get a couple of charts, study them and record how many levels of management you can find. Bring the charts to class for discussion about how they meet the modern challenge of less bureaucracy.

2. Using the same search vehicles, try to establish contact with other colleges or universities to see if you can network with other students taking business courses. Perhaps you can discuss common problems or difficulties relating to courses you are taking. Report to the class whether you have found this networking helpful. Can you see how small companies can use networking for information or contacts to help overcome difficulties?

Practising Management Decisions

Every company follows its own path to restructuring. Some close regional offices and plants; others sell off previously acquired companies to concentrate on their core businesses. Still others downsize drastically or adopt massive training and development programs for their managers and employees. But Bill Duncan did something quite different at Mohawk Oil Canada Ltd. of Burnaby, B.C.

When he became CEO in January 1991, the company was in very serious trouble. He had been with Mohawk since 1976 when, at age 24, he was

CASE 1
• • • • • •
A DRASTIC RESTRUCTURING AT MOHAWK OIL
• • • • • •

hired as controller. Now he was in charge of a company that had not reacted to changing conditions in its market. From a tiny start in 1961, Mohawk had grown to a major independent oil distributor in western Canada with 1260 employees and 250 retail outlets. Price wars and meeting new environmental regulations had hit Mohawk hard, and it was practically bankrupt.

Despite the urgency of the situation, Bill Duncan did not rush into action. After lengthy, careful meetings with outside consultants and a team of Mohawk employees, he led the company through a revolutionary change. The company-owned stations would become franchise dealers and outlets. Many Mohawk employees became franchisees. The plan would see the number of employees drop to 200, and revenue would not include franchise fees and royalties.

Because the employees were involved in the whole process and in the decisions, the suggestions were well received and the transformation was successful. Mohawk emerged from a string of losses to show a profit of $4 million in 1992, and by 1994 it was in good enough shape to go public.

Decision Questions

1. Why do you think Duncan took such a radical step rather than the more common one of cutting staff to reduce costs?
2. The results were good, but does that mean that an alternative course could not have been successful?
3. Do you agree with Duncan's decision? Why?
4. As a general rule, do you think drastic surgery in a serious situation is better than small doses of medicine?

Source: Liz Davis, "Back From the Brink," *Profit*, December–January 1996, p. 28.

CASE 2
• • • • • •
RESTRUCTURING HITS MANAGEMENT POSITIONS
• • • • • •

Tom Peters, co-author of *In Search of Excellence*, believes the staffs of the Fortune 500 companies are still hopelessly bloated. Peters feels that many of those managers with MBA degrees got to top positions without ever getting real-world experience in designing, making, selling, and servicing products. They tend to rely on technology rather than people for their answers—and ignore the retraining and redeployment of the workforce.

Peters recommends that managers get out of their offices and ask their workers how to make the firm more productive. Then they should visit customers and ask what they would like to see changed. Management is no longer viewed as simply an intellectual position involving planning, organizing, leading, and controlling. It is now a hands-on job, with managers and employees working as a team to make the firm more productive. Those who used to sit and ponder are gone and more cuts will be coming.

Since Peters's comments about U.S. businesses in 1991, Canadian businesses have made drastic reductions in managerial staff. Many smaller companies have let people go. Even top-flight managers with good work records are not immune to the budget axe. Various studies have indicated that typical 40-year-old white-collar workers will change jobs two or three times during the rest of their careers, at lease once voluntarily. This includes a vast group of real estate managers, central purchasing agents, human resource specialists, futurologists, economists, planners, and analysts of all kinds.

Decision Questions

1. What does the reduction in middle-management jobs mean for tomorrow's undergraduate and graduate business students?
2. How would you, as the president of a firm, decide which managers to let go?
3. What are the advantages and disadvantages of cutting staff in areas like human resources, quality control, planning, and auditing? Could there be serious consequences from rapid cutbacks in management?
4. What alternative does a company have when it seems top-heavy with staff other than firing them all and becoming leaner and meaner in one swift action?

Providing World-Class Products and Services

Chapter

10

LEARNING GOALS

After you have read and studied this chapter, you should be able to

1 describe the production process, and explain the importance of productivity.

2 explain the importance of site selection in keeping down costs, and identify the criteria used to evaluate different sites.

3 classify the various production processes and how materials requirement planning links organizations in performing those processes.

4 describe manufacturing techniques such as just-in-time inventory control, flexible manufacturing, lean manufacturing, and competing in time.

5 show how CAD/CAM improves the production process.

6 illustrate the use of Gantt and PERT charts in production planning.

7 explain the importance of productivity in the service sector.

Erik Brinkman's design team at Interactive Design Studios, based in Victoria, B.C., came up with a simple, revolutionary invention that eliminates friction wherever things turn, such as with wheels, shafts, and so forth. Scroller rotary motion allows rotation around a shaft, motors, or bicycle wheels by using a continuous band between the shaft and four rollers.

The whole process is now well advanced and the company is discussing financial and organizational progress with investment advisers. Three major American TV programs, *Good Morning America, Nightline*, and *20/20*, aired segments in September 1999 on Erik Brinkman and his company, Interactive Design Studios.

Since Brinkman's patenting of the invention, "corporations have beaten a path to the design group's door," reports Brinkman. So have reporters from around the world. He says there are endless applications for this invention. He encourages inquiring companies to play around with the idea a little before coming up with a specific request for a licence to use the patent.

Brinkman and his wife made a crude working model by cutting a broom handle into five pieces, with one serving as a shaft and four as rollers around it. The whole contraption was held together by a strip of paper wound partially around the shaft and then around the four rollers. The strip of paper was made into a continuous piece with scotch tape.

Modern communication technology made it possible for members of Interactive's design team to be located on three continents—North America, Europe, and Asia (Japan). Six of them worked on the scroller technology. Actually, the original problem facing the team was how to produce a greaseless bicycle for Third World countries where grease is not readily available.

Development has now reached the stage where the bike has actually been designed. Imagine a bicycle without spokes, cables or brakes, requiring no grease, that is foldable, and completely recyclable. furthermore it "takes a lot of the load off the rider's knees and makes it look like it wants to jump." Brinkman "designed it to look like an animal on the run." Canada is indeed fortunate to have a man of Erik Brinkman's calibre as one of the great inventors of our era.

This story reflects how great ideas do not have to be complex. It also shows how important innovation is and that it does not necessarily have to be an expensive process. It further demonstrates how trying to solve a problem often leads to unexpected and important results. Innovation has emerged as an essential component for companies, large and small, that want to remain competitive.

One final note: Erik Brinkman is almost totally blind.

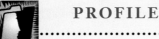

PROFILE

Erik Brinkman
Reinvents the Wheel

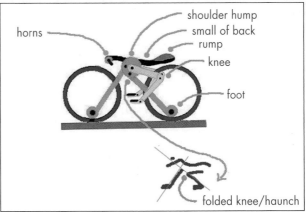

- 100% recyclable
- wheel bearing in the rim
- anti-lock brakes
- belt driven
- suspension rebound moves bike forward
- foldable design

Sources: Communications from Erik Brinkman, September 1999; interview with Erik Brinkman, July 11, 1996; "Canadian Reinvents the Wheel," *Globe and Mail, Report on Business*, December 27, 1995, p. B7.

Ethical Dilemma

EFFECT OF RELOCATION ON SMALL TOWNS

In this chapter you will see that companies engage in a never-ending battle to improve productivity to be more competitive. They automate, integrate newer technologies, use less or better material, modernize, and downsize their workforces, but they also relocate factories and offices and contract out a lot of their work to other companies.

The last two activities often mean that ethical issues are raised. When a company closes down a facility in a small town where it may be the main, or the only, source of jobs, it obviously has a serious impact on the lives of the inhabitants in that town. The same problem, perhaps to a lesser extent, arises when the company outsources work previously done in its town location. This has happened in several Canadian (and American) small towns and is still occurring today. Does the company have an obligation to consider the serious impact of such actions on its employees, their families, and the small retailers who depend on them as customers? Should a company, can it, do anything? Think about these questions as you review the chapter. At the end we will attempt to answer them.

<www.ids.bc.ca>

This is the Web site of Interactive Design Studios, Erik Brinkman's company. You will see a lot of imaginative designs here, mostly of a revolutionary nature.

CAREERS IN MANUFACTURING IN CANADA

Erik Brinkman's story illustrates what is happening in Canadian industry. The changes are coming fast and furious. Worldwide competition and advances in technology have made these changes necessary. Competition in the workplace means you have to keep up. Some of the ideas are new and complex. Even the terminology is confusing at first. Nonetheless, this chapter is one of the more important ones in the text, because it represents the future of Canada and, therefore, your future as well.

THE BASICS OF PRODUCTION MANAGEMENT

production and operations management
All the activities of managers to create goods and services.

One purpose of this chapter is to introduce the basic concepts and issues in production management. **Production and operations management** includes all the activities of managers to create goods and services. Today, most of what gets done actually falls into the service category. There are two aspects to the service category. As noted in the first chapter, service companies such as financial institutions, computer consultants, software designers, Internet service providers, communication companies, and host of other companies employ a large percentage of working Canadians. These *new economy* industries are the result of the transformation of the so-called *rust belt* industries into the new information technology firms in which brains rather than brawn are important. You will see examples such as Chrysler and IPSCO later in the chapter.

Furthermore, only a very small percentage of employees in manufacturing companies are actually working on the production line. Most are engaged in other important functions of a service nature, such as research and development (R&D), human resource management (HRM), accounting, marketing, finance, law, and so on. Concepts that apply to service organizations, such as consumer orientation, apply generally to manufacturing companies as well.

In Chapter 1, we saw why manufacturing is so important for a modern economy. All the countries that have a high standard of living—Japan, Sweden, Germany, Switzerland, the United States, Canada—rest on a strong industrial base. We also saw how the emergence of a strong service sector complements the manufacturing base. Managing the production of goods and services in today's high-technology world, in which competition has become global and fierce, is the major challenge facing Canadian companies.

New production techniques make it possible to virtually custom-build products for individual industrial buyers. The job then becomes one of getting closer to customers to find out what their product needs are. This requires effective marketing combined with effective production and management to make Canadian producers globally effective competitors. At the same time companies must be alert to new technologies that are constantly emerging. For example, in the next chapter you will see that Wal-Mart was the first retailer to adopt the barcode scanner system, which gave them an important edge over their competitors.

Today there are relatively few college students majoring in production and operations management, inventory management, and other careers involving manufacturing. That means more opportunities for those student entrepreneurs who can see the future trends and have mathematical and analytical skills to own, or work in, tomorrow's highly automated, efficient factories. For example, when IPSCO Inc. of Regina built a steel mill in Iowa, the first employees hired were 27 college graduates.[1]

In addition, to prepare for a career in production and operations management, you must learn the basics of production. That is the subject of an entire course or courses, but in this chapter we'll simply review some of the fundamentals you should know.

<www.ipsco.com>

IPSCO started out as a pipe manufacturer and has grown into a very large steelmaker. Visit its Web site to learn more about the company, its history, and its long-term goals.

PRODUCTION AND PRODUCTIVITY

Common sense and your experience have already taught you some of the basic inputs you need to produce anything and to manage those operations. You know what it takes to produce a term paper or prepare a dinner. You need a plan, a place to work, you need people with the necessary skills, you need money to acquire materials and equipment, you need information, and you need to be organized to get the task done. Production needs all of the above and it needs managers to oversee the whole operation. All these requirements are called *inputs* and what are produced are called *outputs*. The formal definition states that **production** is the creation of goods and services using the factors of production: land, labour, capital, entrepreneurship, and information. Production creates what is known as *form utility*. **Form utility** is the value added to inputs by the creation of outputs. A finished product is worth more than the sum of the individual inputs.

Production is a broad term that describes the creative process in all industries that produce goods and services. This includes manufacturing, lumber and forestry, mining, banking, transportation, distribution, and processing. **Manufacturing**, an important part of production, means people producing goods using materials, machinery, robots, and computers. This is different from extracting things from the ground or water—mining, oil and gas, farming, fishing—or providing services such as insurance or banking.

To be competitive, manufacturers must keep the costs of inputs down, but also give good service, have reliable and dependable products, and be responsive to changing customer needs. The marketing chapters deal with these

production
The creation of goods and services using the factors of production: land, labour, capital, entrepreneurship, and information.

form utility
The value added to inputs by the creation of outputs.

manufacturing
An important part of production, it means people producing goods using materials, machinery, robots, and computers.

FIGURE **10.1**

• • • •

THE PRODUCTION PROCESS

The production process consists of taking the factors of production (land, labour, and so forth) and using those inputs to produce goods, services, and ideas. Planning, routing, scheduling, producing, and so on are the means to accomplish the objective—output.

INPUTS	PRODUCTION CONTROL	OUTPUTS
• Land • Labour • Capital • Entrepreneurship • Information	• Planning • Routing • Scheduling • Producing • Dispatching • Following up	• Goods • Services • Ideas

topics. In this chapter we concentrate on cost, quality, and productivity. A simple equation is used to measure productivity:

$$\text{productivity} = \frac{\text{outputs}}{\text{inputs}}$$

The higher the output or the lower the input, the higher the productivity and, therefore, the lower the cost of production. Ideally a company would try to do both. Inputs and outputs are discussed in more detail in the next section.

The costs of workers, machinery, and so on must be kept as low as possible. Similarly, the amount of output must be relatively high. The term for output per worker is *productivity*. How does a producer keep costs low and still produce more—that is, increase productivity? This issue is dealt with in the following pages.

Nortel is an example of a Canadian company that is successfully responding to increasing global competition. One of Nortel's key competitivie advantages in designing acoustic devices is its use of sophisticated computer modelling and prediction techniques. Preparing to evaluate the acoustic performance of a Nortel wireless handset, design engineer Larry Hawkins positions a microphone on the head and torso simulator in Nortel's anechoic chamber.

• • • • ▬▬▬ • • • •

CHALLENGES TO CANADA

Canada is a large industrial country with many major industries. We are one of the largest producers in the world of forest products, with plants in nearly all provinces turning out a vast array of wood, furniture, and paper products. Giant aluminum mills in Quebec and B.C.; auto and automotive plants in Ontario and Quebec; aircraft in Ontario, Quebec, and Manitoba; oil, natural gas, and coal produced in Alberta, Saskatchewan, Newfoundland, Nova Scotia, and B.C. and processed there or in other provinces; a vast array of metals and minerals from all parts of Canada—these are only some of the thousands of components, products, and natural resources produced or processed in Canada.

Canada is now facing some serious challenges to its ability to remain a modern, competitive, industrial country. As mentioned in the first chapter, today's business climate is characterized by constant and restless change and dislocation, as ever newer technologies and increasing global competition force companies to respond quickly to these challenges. Many factors account for our difficulties in the world's competitive race. Among them are inadequate improvement in productivity and unrelenting competition from Japan, Germany, and more recently from China and other Southeast Asian countries; inadequate education and retraining programs for our workforce; our "branch plant economy," subservient to U.S. parent companies; our constant brain drain to the United States; too little money for research and development; and problems created by the free trade agreement with the United States and Mexico (as discussed in Part 1).

Despite these challenges, or perhaps because of them, Canada continues to rank high in competitiveness with other nations. Our exact ranking is difficult to determine (see Chapter 3) as there is some dispute among the different bodies that conduct the evaluations. Statistics Canada, the Alliance of Exporters and Manufacturers Canada, the Organization for Economic Cooperation and Development (OECD), the World Economic Forum (WEF), and other bodies are trying to come to some agreement. In its rankings the prestigious WEF has rated Canada eighth in 1996, fourth in 1997, and fifth in 1998 and 1999.[2] One of the factors that gives Canadian manufacturers an edge over their competitors is lower prices. If you can keep your costs down, you can afford to sell at lower prices. There are three ways to do this (see Figure 10.1):

1. Reduce the cost of inputs (for a given amount of output or production).
2. Increase the volume or value of outputs (for a given cost of inputs).
3. Decrease inputs *and* increase outputs.

Any of these achievements results in greater productivity, which reduces cost per unit. Output refers to the number of units produced and the value of those units. Let's look at inputs first to see how they can be kept down. Throughout this chapter, you will see many examples of Canadian companies that have been successful in reducing costs.

REDUCING INPUT COSTS

Input costs include such items as wages and salaries, raw materials and parts, energy, interest, and costs of operating the factory (overhead) like rent, taxes, insurance, maintenance, and depreciation of equipment. The question of labour costs generally gets a lot of publicity.

••• KEEPING COSTS LOW: THE •••
IMPORTANCE OF SITE SELECTION

It is a common misconception that, to reduce costs, companies should look at wages first. Labour costs as a percentage of total manufacturing costs have been dropping steadily for a long time. StatCan figures show that in the 38 years from 1960 to 1998, the number of people employed in the Canadian manufacturing industry remained constant at about 2 million, rising to 2.2 million in 1999.[3] Due to automation and other efficiencies, manufacturing output rose enormously, so labour as a percentage of manufacturing cost dropped dramatically (see Chapter 1).

It makes sense to select a site, domestic or foreign, for your operations that will give you the most advantages. Factors to consider include wages, markets, raw materials, access to energy, government inducements, workforce, local taxes, and quality of life, and other factors.

Lower Wages. Despite the decreasing importance of labour as a component of production costs, the fact remains that where operations are labour intensive or assembly work is relatively unskilled, many Canadian companies have moved these operations to the southern United States or Mexico. Wages there are considerably lower (as was discussed in Part 1). Northern Telecom set up factories in China for the same reason.

Markets. If a particular plant will serve a certain geographic segment of the market, it is a competitive advantage to be close to that market. It speeds up delivery and reduces transportation costs for your customers. In general, it enables a company to improve its service to customers.

Raw Materials and Parts. Locating near your principal suppliers eases supply problems and reduces transportation costs.

Access to Energy. Some industries consume vast amounts of energy. Quebec, Ontario, Alberta, and B.C. have been successful in attracting such major industries because of their plentiful, low-cost hydroelectric power or oil and gas.

Government Inducements. Most provinces and cities try to tempt businesses to locate in their area by offering such benefits as cash grants, lower taxes, interest-free loans, and free land. Some cities attract business by designing industrial parks. An **industrial park** is a planned area where land, shipping facilities, and waste disposal outlets are readily available so businesses are attracted to the area to build a manufacturing plant or storage facility.

Availability of Workforce. A good source of well-educated, skilled, and semiskilled workers has become a major consideration for companies, given the increasing importance of technology and information in production and operations.

Taxes. Provinces have different tax rates. Those with lower taxes like Alberta are more attractive to companies.

Quality of Life. It is becoming increasingly important to meet the requirements of all employees for a decent quality of life as they define it. Executives, managers, and the workforce in general want access to good schools and child-care facilities and want to avoid noisy, dirty, polluted, or unsafe neighbourhoods. They also want good public transportation and fairly short commuting distances.

industrial park
A planned area where land, shipping facilties, and waste disposal outlets are readily available so businesses are attracted to the area to build a manufacturing plant or storage facility.

••• OTHER ASPECTS OF REDUCING INPUT COSTS •••

The following are discussed at some length in the next section of this chapter, so they are mentioned only briefly here.

- *Materials Handling.* This is a major area of cost for business; inefficiencies here can add substantially to input costs.

- *Inventory.* Most companies producing or selling goods invest large amounts of money in inventory. Reducing the amount you have on hand at any one time results in lower input costs. Just-in-time inventory procedures will be discussed shortly.

- *Equipment.* This may be the most important aspect of cost management in manufacturing. An efficient, motivated worker using outdated machinery at company A will obviously produce less than an equivalent worker with the latest equipment at company B. Lower productivity results in higher labour costs per unit even if wage rates are equal. That may be true even if the worker in company B has a higher wage rate than the worker in company A. This leads us directly into the second theme, increasing outputs.

SITE SELECTION IN THE FUTURE Constantly improving information technology (computers, modems, e-mail, voice mail, teleconferencing, and so on) is giving firms and employees more flexibility in choosing locations while staying in the competitive mainstream. **Telecommuting**, working from home via computer and modem, is a major trend in business. More and more employees are now telecommuting. Companies that no longer need to locate near sources of labour will be able to move to areas where land is less expensive and the quality of life may be preferred by in-house employees.

Telecommuting
Working from home via computer and modem.

.... ▬▬ ....

INCREASING THE VOLUME OR VALUE OF OUTPUTS

The factors discussed below are dealt with in detail in the next sections on production.

Engineering and Design. Just as proper equipment is important for increasing output, so is engineering and design input. The goal is to speed up production by improving the product's design and reducing its number of parts, ensuring the best layout of plant and equipment, and using the most efficient production processes.

Marketing. One responsibility of the marketing department is to find products in demand that are well suited to the company's manufacturing capabilities. This simplifies production and employee training, leading to greater output. Marketing is reviewed in some detail in Chapters 15 and 16.

Employee Motivation. A motivated workforce produces more than an unmotivated one. Management must find ways to motivate employees. This important issue is discussed in great detail in Chapter 12.

.... ▬▬ ....

DECREASING INPUTS AND INCREASING OUTPUTS

Research and development (R&D) can reduce inputs by developing, adapting, or improving technology to reduce the cost of manufacturing. In conjunction with marketing, R&D improves existing products or develops new ones, leading to greater sales and thus to economies of scale—greater output for the same cost of input.

.... ▬▬ ....

RESTRUCTURING FOR GREATER PRODUCTIVITY

In earlier chapters, we referred to the unusual restructuring process that has dominated the Canadian business scene since the beginning of the 1990s. Most large service and manufacturing companies have dismissed thousands of employees. Air Canada, CNR, IBM, GM, and many other large and smaller companies, badly squeezed by the recession and by globally competing products and services, have drastically reduced their workforces. The computer, telecommunication, and automation revolutions have also displaced many employees and managers.

The ultimate goal of these developments is an increase in productivity per employee so that costs per unit come down, making companies more competitive. If all goes as expected, the Canadian workforce will be more skilled and better paid. But the adjustment period is likely to be long and painful.

An article in the *Montreal Gazette* is typical. The writer was commenting on an announcement from Chrysler that it was making its largest investment in Canada—a $600 million expansion of an Ontario plant—but it would not create a single new job.

The article quoted labour analyst Cecile Dumas of StatCan as saying that Canadian manufacturers have "permanently changed their habits." Dumas cited evidence of greatly improved exports as a sign of greater competitiveness. She noted that, during a recession, productivity usually slumps, but in 1990–91 "the productivity of Canadian manufacturers actually rose." Subsequent data indicate continuing improvement.[4] However, as noted earlier, the question of how well we are doing in improving our productivity remains a disputed issue in Canada. If our main competitors, primarily American companies, are able to improve their productivity faster than we are, then Canadian companies will slip behind their competitors.

The road to better jobs and higher wages is through higher productivity and Canada is well launched in that direction, but it is a never-ending process. Unfortunately, as part of this process we will also have to cope with high unemployment during the next few years as we go through the period of adjustment.

···· ▬ ····

PRODUCTION PROCESSES

After a site is selected and a factory has been built, manufacturers begin making products. There are several different processes manufacturers use. Andrew S. Grove, chief executive officer of Intel, used a great analogy to explain the production process.[5]

> *To understand the principles of production, imagine that you're a waiter ... and that your task is to serve a breakfast consisting of a three-minute soft-boiled egg, buttered toast, and coffee. Your job is to prepare and deliver the three items simultaneously, each of them fresh and hot.*
>
> *The task here encompasses the three basic requirements of production. They are to build and deliver products in response to the demands of the customer at a scheduled delivery time, at an acceptable quality level, and at the lowest possible cost....*

process manufacturing
Production process that physically or chemically changes materials.

assembly process
Production process that puts together components.

synthetic system
Production process that either changes raw materials into other products or combines raw materials or parts into finished products.

analytic system
Manuafcturing system that breaks down raw materials into components to extract other products.

From the breakfast example, it is easy to understand two manufacturing processes: process and assembly. In **process manufacturing**, you physically or chemically change materials. For example, boiling physically changes the egg. In **assembly process**, you put together components, such as the egg, the toast, and the coffee to make a breakfast. These two processes are called synthetic systems. A **synthetic system** either changes raw materials into other products (process manufacturing) or combines raw materials or parts into a finished product (assembly process).

The reverse of a synthetic system is called an analytic system. In an **analytic system**, a raw material is broken down into components to extract other products. For example, crude oil can be reduced to gasoline, wax, and jet fuel. So the production process will be either synthetic or analytic. In addition, production processes are either continual or intermittent.

Oil refineries use analytic systems to create gasoline and other products from crude oil. Analytic systems break raw materials down into component parts.

A *continual process* (also referred to as *make-to-stock*) is one in which long production runs turn out finished goods over time. In our breakfast example, you could have eggs on a conveyor belt that lowered them into boiling water for three minutes and then lifted them out on a continual basis. A three-minute egg would be available whenever you wanted one. An chemical plant is run on a continual process.

It usually makes more sense when responding to specific customer orders (job-order production) to use an *intermittent process* (also referred to as *make-to-order*). This is an operation in which the production run is short (one or two eggs) and the machines are shut down frequently or changed to produce different products (like the oven in a bakery or the toaster in the breakfast shop). Manufacturers of custom-designed furniture or metal railings use an intermittent process.

Today, most new manufacturers use intermittent processes. Their computers, automation, and flexible manufacturing processes allow manufacturers to turn out custom-made goods almost as fast as mass-produced goods. We shall discuss how they do that in more detail later.

••• MATERIALS REQUIREMENT PLANNING: THE RIGHT ••• AMOUNT IN THE RIGHT PLACE AT THE RIGHT TIME

The technological changes now taking place in manufacturing have resulted in a whole new terminology for production and operations management. Today's students need to be familiar with this terminology before they can discuss such advances in any depth.

One of the more important terms is **materials requirement planning (MRP)**. Materials requirement planning is a computer-based production and operations management system that uses sales forecasts to make sure needed parts and materials are available at the right place and the right time. In our breakfast example, we could feed the sales forecast into a computer, which

materials requirement planning (MRP)
A computer-based production and operations management system that uses sales forecasts to make sure needed parts and materials are available at the right place and time.

would specify how much of each ingredient to order and print out the proper schedulling and routing sequence.

MRP is most popular with companies that make products with a lot of different parts. IBM Canada is such a company. "I couldn't deal with the 30,000 to 40,000 parts we have here without an MRP system," said Eugene Polistuk, manager of the IBM plant in Toronto. As better MRP systems developed over the past three decades, efficiency increased. "We had 30 to 40 people in process control," Polistuk said. "There are six today."[6]

A more advanced but much more difficult system is MRP II, *manufacturing resource planning.* This encompasses more than materials requirements and still has many difficulties to overcome.

Despite their drawbacks, both systems are being used in modern factories with some success. IBM's computer integration systems have dramatically improved the company's quality and productivity, helping it achieve large sales increases.

"Those companies that struggle with MRPs struggle because they really haven't got their arms around the information processing part," said Keith Powell, director of manufacturing at the Northern Telecom plant in Bramalea, Ontario.[7]

The newest version of such systems is called *enterprise resource planning.* **Enterprise resource planning (ERP)** is a computer-based production and operations system that links multiple firms into one integrated production unit. The software enables the monitoring of quality and customer satisfaction as it's happening. ERP is much more sophisticated than MRP II because it monitors processes in multiple firms at the same time. For example, it monitors inventory at the supplier as well as at the manufacturing plant.

Eventually, such programs will link suppliers, manufacturers, and retailers in a completely integrated manufacturing and distribution system that will be constantly monitored for the smooth flow of goods from the time they're ordered to the time they reach the ultimate consumer.[8]

enterprise resource planning (ERP)
Computer-based production and operations system that links multiple firms into one integrated production unit.

Progress Check

- What is production?
- What are the major factors that determine where a plant locates?
- Can you explain the differences among the following production processes: process, assembly, analytic, continual, and intermittent?
- What is enterprise resource planning?

MODERN PRODUCTION TECHNIQUES

The ultimate goal of manufacturing and process management is to provide high-quality goods and services instantaneously in response to customer demand. Traditional organizations were simply not designed to be so responsive to the customer. Rather, they were designed to make goods efficiently. The whole idea of mass production was to make large quantities of a limited variety of products at very low cost. A pioneer of such techniques was the Ford Motor Co., which increased its output in 1909 from 17,771 cars to 202,667. By continuing these efforts Ford produced 1.8 million vehicles in 1924. This also resulted in lower costs and, therefore, lower prices, which dropped from $950 in 1909 to $550 in 1913 and to $355 in 1923. This price even included automatic starters![9]

Over the years low cost often came at the expense of quality and flexibility. Furthermore, suppliers didn't always deliver when they promised so manufacturers had to carry large inventories of raw materials and components. Such inefficiencies made companies subject to foreign competitors who were using more advanced production techniques. The Spotlight on Big Business box discusses *benchmarking*, or how companies compare themselves with the world's leading companies to find the best practices possible. (See also the previous chapter.)

Organizations that encourage and measure the efficiency of companies are the International Quality & Productivity Centre <www.ipqc.co.uk>, the National Quality Institute in Canada <www.nqi.ca>, and the American Productivity & Quality Center <www.apqc.org>. All these organizations have Web sites where companies can go to find other companies to benchmark and other useful information that will help them find the best practices and procedures.

As a result of global competition, companies today must make a wide variety of high-quality custom-designed products at very low cost. Clearly, something had to change on the production floor to make that possible. Also, something had to change in supplier-producer relationships. Seven major developments have radically changed the production process: (1) just-in-time inventory control, (2) revised purchasing arrangements, (3) flexible manufacturing, (4) lean manufacturing, (5) mass customization, (6) competing on the basis of time, and (7) computer-aided design and manufacturing.

··· JUST-IN-TIME INVENTORY CONTROL ···

One major cost of production is holding parts, motors, and other items in warehouses. To cut such costs, the Japanese perfected an idea called **just-in-time (JIT) inventory control**. This means the delivery of the smallest possible quantities at the latest possible time to keep inventory as low as possible. Some Canadian manufacturers have adopted the practice and are quite happy with the results, although it is much more difficult to implement because of the greater distances involved in Canada.

Here is how it works: A manufacturer sets a production schedule using ERP, as described previously, and determines what parts and supplies will be needed. It then tells its suppliers what will be needed and when. Each supplier must deliver the goods just in time to go on the assembly line. Naturally, this calls for more effort by the suppliers, who resist what seems at first like a major change of operations. They soon learn, however, that they, too, can end up with greater savings. Efficiency is maintained by linking the supplier by computer to the producer (as explained in ERP) so the supplier becomes more like another department in the firm than a separate business. The supplier delivers the materials just in time to be used in the production process, so a bare minimum must be kept in storage just in case the delivery is held up for some reason.

At an auto parts factory, a truck pulls up to the shipping dock and loads wheels right off the production line. Later, the wheels arrive at the auto plant,

The National Quality Institute offers awards to public or private companies as part of the Canada Awards for Excellence program. Organizations considered for an award must show outstanding continual achievement in seven key areas: leadership, planning for improvement, customer focus, people focus, process optimization, supplier focus, and organizational performance. Previous award recipients include TELUS Mobility Inc., John Deere Limited, and Amex Canada Inc.

just-in-time (JIT) inventory control
The delivery of the smallest possible quantities at the latest possible time, to keep inventory as low as possible.

Spotlight on Big Business

<www.nqi.com>

Benchmarking the Best

Today's trend toward globalization means that the world's best manufacturers can enter almost any market at almost any time. In other words, if you aren't one of the world's best manufacturers, you're likely to go out of business. You can be one of the world's best producers and still lose the bulk of your business if you aren't also one of the most innovative and cost-efficient producers. Mercedes and BMW, for example, had long been known as two of the best car manufacturers in the world. Along came Lexus and Infiniti not only to challenge their technological lead but to offer similar quality at a much lower price. Consequently, Mercedes was forced to produce less expensive car models. If Mercedes hadn't responded, it would have continued to lose its market share.

Even being an industry leader doesn't ensure world dominance for long. Japan, for example, introduced high-definition television (HDTV) in 1988 at the Olympics in Seoul, Korea. U.S. manufacturers considered this a challenge much like the old challenge to get to the moon. Working together, U.S. manufacturers developed a better technology that leapfrogged Japanese products. European companies are doing the same. Similarly, IBM once led the world in computer technology, but it's now just one of many competitors, no longer the dominant industry leader.

Staying on top means meeting the world's standard (that is, benchmarking on the best companies in the world). A company must compare each one of its processes to that same process as practised by the best. It must then bring its processes up to world-class standard or outsource the process to someone who can. But it can't rest there; it must empower its workers to become the best in the world and to continually improve processes and products to maintain a leadership position. Often that means the company must develop products that will make its own products obsolete. So be it. If it doesn't do so, someone else will. The American Productivity & Quality Center has an International Benchmarking Clearinghouse where companies can learn the best practices of companies throughout the world.

The National Quality Institute in Canada gives annual Awards for Excellence to Canadian companies who provide products or services of outstanding quality. Among the 1998 award recipients was John Deere Ltd. for top quality agricultural equipment and service from its branches in Grimsby, Ontario, and Regina, Saskatchewan. A winner in the small company division was the Trade Electric Co. in Concord, Ontario, a provider of electric and electronic products. It was "awarded a Certificate of Merit recognizing its dynamic environment that weaves quality into every aspect of their business with outstanding results."

Sources: National Quality Institute, <www.nqi.ca>, July 31, 1999; "Two New Benchmarking Studies Released," *Quality Digest*, January 1997, p. 10; Vicki J. Powers, "Selecting a Benchmarking Partner: Five Tips for Success," *Quality Digest*, October 1997, pp. 37–41.

where they are unloaded and moved a few metres. They reach the assembly line just in time to be bolted on to the next batch of cars coming down the line.

JIT eliminates the need for warehousing and saves hours of materials handling time. Quality improves dramatically; less handling means less damage. The total cost savings can be enormous.

You can imagine how the system would work for Andrew Grove's breakfast example. Rather than ordering enough eggs, butter, bread, and coffee for the week and storing it, he would have his suppliers deliver every morning.

But implementation is far from simple: it requires spending months—or years—preparing and reorganizing your production. Your suppliers also have to be geared into it. Suppliers and customers must be in constant communication. After two years, Ford's Oakville, Ontario, assembly line had only 130 of 1456 parts on the just-in-time system. At General Motors' massive Oshawa,

Ontario, complex, almost all parts are on the system. That means that about 1200 trucks unload each day.[10]

The latest version of JIT is called *JIT II*. This system is designed to create more harmony and trust than JIT did. In JIT II there is much more sharing of information: an employee from the supplier may work full-time at the buyer's plant or store, facilitating the smooth flow of material or goods. To have such close working relationships, a whole new approach to suppliers was required. We look at this shortly.

OTHER MATERIAL AND INVENTORY CONTROL SYSTEMS   Several large organizations have adopted systems all aimed at reducing the cost of handling inventory. The Halifax plant of Pratt & Whitney, which manufactures gear casings for its line of aircraft engines, has been hailed as a showcase of modern technology in this regard. It uses an integrated materials handling (IMH) system in conjunction with a flexible manufacturing system (described in next section) to produce a state-of-the-art facility.[11]

In British Columbia, the B.C. Purchasing Commission had a tough problem. The public sector spends in excess of $5 billion annually. Controlling such vast expenditures was a mammoth task. After scouring North America and finding nothing suitable, the commission developed its own system. Working with two Canadian companies, Cognos Inc. of Ottawa and OGMA Consulting Ltd. of Victoria, it integrated an HP 3000 minicomputer into a very sophisticated system.

After two years, the system was expanded to include complete tracking of all materials and equipment. This computer-assisted materials management system (CAMMS) identifies all materials in stock and their purchase costs. The CAMMS program tracks the total lifetime of all consequential goods, from the time they are first ordered to the time the commission disposes of them.[12]

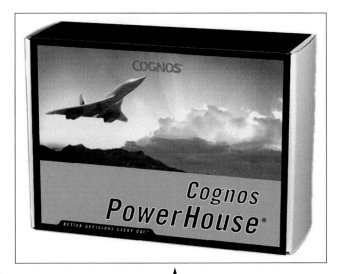

The Cognos® PowerHouse product is the inventory control system developed by the B.C. Purchasing Commission.

••• FLEXIBLE MANUFACTURING •••

When researchers from America visited the Toyota-Takaoka auto plant in Japan, they were stunned by the contrast they saw with the GM plant in Framingham, Massachusetts. The GM plant had wide aisles full of indirect workers; that is, workers on their way to relieve a fellow employee, workers en route to troubleshoot a problem, and so forth. These workers were adding no immediate value to the product, whereas in Japan almost all workers were engaged in adding value to the auto. Furthermore, the Framingham plant had several weeks' worth of inventory piled around the plant. The Toyota plant had no more than an hour's worth of materials near the workstation and there was no warehouse to store surplus inventory.

In addition to just-in-time inventory control, the Toyota plant practises **flexible manufacturing**. This involves designing and using individual machines that can do multiple tasks so that each can produce a variety of products. That allows Toyota, using a few machines, to produce a wide variety of cars.[13]

Today, U.S. car manufacturers have also adopted flexible manufacturing at their plants in the United States and in Canada. Ford Motor Company, for

flexible manufacturing
Designing and using individual machines that can do multiple tasks so that each can produce a variety of products.

example, has designed V-8 and V-6 engines around a basic building block (a combustion chamber designed for maximum fuel economy). As many as six new V-8s and V-6s can be built from the same machinery.[14]

Many Canadian companies, large and small, are successfully using flexible manufacturing. Some Ontario examples are Celestica Manufacturing Co., which does contract manufacturing for IBM and other computer companies; Eaton Yale Co. of St. Thomas, maker of automobile air conditioners, which won the prestigious University of Utah Shingo Award for excellence; Johnson Controls of Orangeville, which produces industrial and automobile controls; and a smaller Toronto company, Canadian Ice Manufacturing Co. (CIMCO).[15]

Critical Thinking

Earlier we talked about continual processes versus intermittent processes. Can you see how flexible manufacturing makes it possible for intermittent processes to become as fast as continual processes? What are the implications for saving time on the assembly line, saving money, and cutting back on labour?

••• LEAN MANUFACTURING •••

lean manufacturing
The production of goods using less of everything compared to mass production.

Lean manufacturing is the production of goods using less of everything compared to mass production: less human effort, less manufacturing space, less investment in tools, less engineering time to develop a new product in less time.[16] A company becomes lean by continually increasing the capacity to produce more higher-quality results with fewer resources.[17]

Investing eight years and $3.5 billion, GM redesigned its production process, abandoning the assembly line. The name given the changeover was Project Saturn. The fundamental purpose of the restructuring was to cut dramatically the number of worker-hours needed to build a car.

In addition to these changes, GM designed a casting process for building the engine block that uses 40 percent less machinery. This, too, saves time and money. And finally, GM greatly expanded its use of robots in the manufacturing process. A **robot** is a computer-controlled machine capable of performing many tasks requiring the use of materials and tools. For example, robots spray paint cars and do welding. They are usually fast, efficient, and accurate. GM did have trouble implementing the whole process. Other companies have also had trouble implementing new technologies. That doesn't mean the idea isn't good—the problem is in learning how to manage change.

robot
A computer-controlled machine capable of performing many tasks.

Arnold Norris, a vice-president of Honda Canada, said the fear that robots would replace workers has proven to be unfounded. Workers end up being more highly trained to operate the robots. David Robertson of the Canadian Auto Workers (CAW) union agreed that the new jobs created are more highly skilled and better paying and the jobs that disappear are the ones no one wants to do. However, he said, wherever robotics have been introduced, there are fewer people working than before.

••• MASS CUSTOMIZATION •••

mass customization
Tailoring products to meet the needs of individual customers.

Mass customization means tailoring products to meet the needs of individual customers. The National Bicycle Industrial Company in Japan, for example, makes 18 bicycle models in more than two million combinations, with each combination designed to fit the needs of a specific customer. The customer chooses the model size, colour, and design. The retailer measures the buyer and faxes the data to the factory, where robots handle the bulk of the assembly.[18]

GiftMaker is a software program that lets you sit at your computer and custom-design T-shirts, baseball caps, and other gift items for your friends.

My Design allows you to choose a special friend of Barbie's hair, eyes, fashion, and more—you can even give her a name and personality! Mattel, Inc. will custom-make your doll and send her directly to your door.

Once you're finished with the design, you enter the addresses where you want the items sent, enter a credit card number, and send it by modem to the manufacturer. The manufacturer will then custom-make your products and send them to your friends.[19]

More and more manufacturers are learning to customize their products. For example, General Nutrition Centers (GNC) has put machines in some of its stores that enable customers to custom-design their own vitamins, shampoos, and lotions. Porsche 911 sports cars are offered with custom colours, custom leathers (including leather from a customer's own herd), custom wood inlays, and custom accessories like refrigerators and compartments for revolvers. You can buy custom-made books with your children's names inserted in key places or create custom-made greeting cards. The Custom Foot stores use infrared scanners to precisely measure each foot so shoes can be crafted to fit perfectly. InterActive Custom Clothes offers a wide variety of options in custom-made jeans, including four different colours of rivets.[20]

<www.gnc.com>
<www.ic3d.com>

Visit GNC's and InterActive Custom Clothes Company's Web sites. Each provide descriptions of the company's history and current position, as well as its future direction. See how they operate!

··· COMPETING IN TIME ···

Competing in time is essential to competing at all in a global marketplace. McKinsey & Co., a major consulting firm, estimated that going over budget by 50 percent to get a new product out on time reduces profit 4 percent. However, staying on budget and getting the product out six months late reduces profit 33 percent. Speed is of the essence. Ford estimated that it must be 25 percent faster than it is now in creating new products to match the best.

In their book *Competing Against Time*, Tom Hout and George Stalk, Jr., described *the 0.05 to 5 rule:* "Most products and many services are actually receiving value [something is actually happening to them] for only 0.05 to 5 percent of the time they are in the systems of their companies."[21] For example, a manufacturer may take 45 days to get a special-order car to a buyer, but it only takes 16 hours to assemble the car. Hout and Stalk said we routinely waste 95 percent of our time. That gives us lots of opportunity for improvement!

Next we'll explore dramatic changes that are crucial to Canadian competitive strength in manufacturing: computer-aided design and computer-aided manufacturing. They enable firms to compete in time and efficiency.

••• COMPUTER-AIDED DESIGN AND ••• MANUFACTURING (CAD/CAM)

computer-aided design (CAD)
The use of computers in the design of products.

computer-aided manufacturing (CAM)
The use of computers in the production process.

If one development in the 1980s changed production techniques and strategies more than any other, it was the integration of computers into the design and manufacturing of products. The first thing computers did was help in the design of products. The idea is called **computer-aided design (CAD)**. The next step was to involve computers directly in the production process. That was called **computer-aided manufacturing (CAM)**.

The use of both CAD and CAM has made it possible to custom-design products to meet the needs of small markets, with very little increase in costs. A producer programs the computer to make a simple design change, and that change can be incorporated right into the production line.

An example reveals how helpful the computer can be. A Viennese architect named Josef Hoffman designed a beautiful silver-plated bowl as a gift for Albert Einstein. The original bowl has disappeared; only a photograph remains. To duplicate the bowl by hand through trial and error would have been costly and difficult. Instead, two men used the CAD process to program the dimensions of the bowl. They made 100,000 copies and sold them for $120 each. They could now make a slight change in the design on the computer and produce a new, unique design of their own.

Computer-aided design and manufacturing are also invading the clothing industry. A computer program establishes a pattern and cuts the cloth auto-

Computer-aided design (CAD) has greatly enhanced manufacturing productivity, and has changed the nature of many jobs. This picture shows a car being designed on a CAD system.

matically. Soon, a person's dimensions will be programmed into the machines to create custom-cut clothing at little additional cost. Computer-aided manufacturing is used to make cookies in those fresh-baked cookie shops. On-site, small-scale, semiautomated, sensor-controlled baking makes consistent quality easy.

CAD has doubled productivity in many firms, but the problem in the past was that computer-aided design machines couldn't talk to computer-aided manufacturing machines. It's one thing to design a product; it's quite another to set the specifications to make a machine do the work. Recently, however, new software programs have been designed to unite CAD with CAM: *computer-integrated manufacturing* (CIM). The new software is expensive, but it cuts 80 percent of the time needed to program machines to eliminate parts and many errors.[22]

••• COMPUTER-INTEGRATED MANUFACTURING ••• FOR SMALL BUSINESSES

The bulk of manufacturing automation is in large companies. For instance, 80 percent of the robots used in the United States are in companies like Ford and IBM. Although experts have been saying for more than a decade that factory automation will soon be common in small companies, it just hasn't happened yet.

As the gap widens between the skills workers need and the skills they have, small companies' need for sophisticated equipment increases. To attract quality workers, small companies must have the right equipment.

Why are small companies slower to automate? There are lots of reasons. At the top of the list are the high initial equipment costs and the high cost of training. Many small firms simply don't have the money to do it. Large companies have greater resources and can spread the cost of technology over several products; small-business owners spend their own money and can lose the business if the technology doesn't pay for itself. One way to overcome these disadvantages is for several smaller manufacturers to pool their resources and buy or lease equipment.

The software for implementing CAD/CAM often costs $30,000 or more. Small businesses must think of creative ways to finance such an expense or to share the expense with others. Often larger firms will help finance such a purchase for their suppliers. They do this because they want their suppliers to have the most modern equipment so they can supply them with the best parts and materials. They also want their suppliers to become compatible with their automated systems. Vendors of automated equipment now recognize the problems caused by their customers' skill deficiencies. Their sales pitches now emphasize training and technical support. Small businesses can also work closely with local educational institutions for employee training. Community colleges across the country have increased their attention to "manufacturing education." Their aim is to teach current workers basic literacy, critical thinking, and technical skills.

As computer integration becomes more popular, the price of CAD/CAM systems should go down. Then even the smallest firms should be able to take advantage of the technology.

Progress Check

- What is just-in-time inventory control?
- How does flexible manufacturing differ from lean manufacturing?
- What is meant by competing in time?

OUTSOURCING

The previous chapter noted that many companies now try to divide their production between *core competencies*, work *they* do best in-house, and *outsourcing*, letting outside companies service them by doing what *they* are experts at. The result sought is the best-quality products at the lowest possible costs. This process of contract manufacturing has become a hot practice in North America. One example of this common trend was Nortel Networks' decision to outsource certain products that it would no longer produce in-house. This decision would affect about 3000 employees, who would be leaving to become employees of the contractors.[23] Some studies indicate that there are some 500 large contract manufacturers in the electronics, computer, and telecommunications industries in Canada and the United States.

Two large Canadian companies providing manufacturing services for these industries are Celestica Inc. and Span Manufacturing Ltd., both in the Toronto area. Celestica, a world leader in electronics manufacturing services (EMS), provides design and manufacturing services to its customers, which include industry leading original equipment manufacturers (OEMs), primarily in the computer and communications sectors. In 1998 Celestica

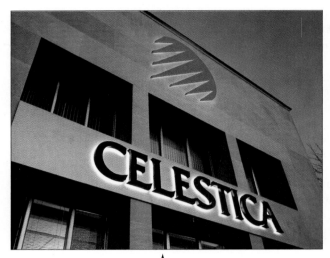

Celestica, a world leader in electronics manufacturing services (EMS), provides design and manufacturing services to its customers, which include industry leading original equipment manufacturers (OEMs), primarily in the computer and communications sectors.

had revenues of $3.2 billion (U.S.). Mark Chipman, vice-president of Span Manufacturing, said the business is "growing too fast to track." He can't even count the number of competitors that have sprung up in Ontario alone, including ex-employees of Span.

Technology Forecasters of California believes that contract manufacturing now accounts for 15 percent of the electronics industries. They expect total business in this area to top U.S. $50 billion shortly. Because these products are very complex, manufacturers have found it best to outsource them to highly specialized contract firms that can deliver on time and with the high quality required. These factors have become more important than looking for the very lowest labour cost.[24]

THE COMPUTERIZED FACTORY

Because of new ideas such as CAD/CAM, we are now on the brink of a new era in production and operations management. The force behind the change is new technology, especially computers and robots. Terms you'll be seeing over the next decade include the following:

1. *Computer-aided engineering (CAE)*. CAE includes the designing and analysis of products, the programming of robots and machine tools, the designing of molds and tools, and the planning of the production process and quality control. In the past engineering involved a lot of paperwork—blueprints, drawings, and so forth. Many inefficiencies resulted from the shuffling of such papers from desk to desk to shop floor and so on. Today, the whole engineering process from conception to production can be and is being done by computer in some firms.

2. *Flexible manufacturing systems (FMS)*. These are totally automated production centres that include robots, automatic materials handling equipment, and computer-controlled machine tools that can perform a variety of functions to produce different products. GM's new plants use flexible manufacturing systems.

3. *Design for manufacturability and assembly (DFMA)*. This innovation is based on the premise that the best-engineered part may be no part at all. Reducing the number of parts needed to build a product reduces the product's cost. Savings come from less time to assemble, ease in installation and maintenance, and less field service. NCR's newest electronic cash register has only 15 parts (85 percent fewer parts from 65 percent fewer vendors than its previous model). The terminal takes only one-fourth of the time previously required to assemble.

4. *Computer-aided acquisition and logistics support (CALS)*. This communications system allows manufacturers to send design specifications to suppliers over a phone line directly to the machine that will do the work. This system makes it possible to reduce inventories even further because new parts can be ordered and processed at once, and sent almost immediately.

What you should learn from all this is that factories are being fully automated. That is, most of the jobs that traditionally have been involved in the manufacturing process are being eliminated. Everything from customer order processing, to inventory control planning, to forecasting through production, quality control, and shipping is being made more productive through the use of computers and robots. The remaining workers are and will be highly skilled technical workers who have the training needed to use, maintain, and develop such equipment.

···· ▬▬ ····

CONTROL PROCEDURES: PERT AND GANTT CHARTS

An important function of a production manager is to be sure that products are manufactured and delivered on time. The question is, how can one be sure that all of the assembly processes will go smoothly and end up completed by the required time? A popular technique for maintaining some feel for the progress of the production process is called the *program evaluation and review technique*, a process developed in the 1950s for constructing nuclear submarines. The **program evaluation and review technique (PERT)** is a method for analyzing the tasks involved in completing a given project, estimating the time needed to complete each task, and identifying the minimum time needed to complete the total project.

The steps involved in using PERT are (1) analyzing and sequencing tasks that need to be done, (2) estimating the time needed to complete each task, (3) drawing a PERT network illustrating the information from steps 1 and 2, and (4) identifying the critical path. The **critical path** is the sequence of tasks that takes the longest time to complete. The term *critical path* is used because any delay in the time needed to complete this path would cause the project or production run to be late.

Figure 10.2 illustrates a PERT chart for producing a music video. Note that the squares on the chart indicate completed tasks and the arrows leading to the squares indicate the time needed to complete each task. The path from one completed task to the other illustrates the relationships among tasks. For example, the arrow from "set designed" to "set materials purchased" shows

program evaluation and review technique (PERT)
A method for analyzing the tasks involved in completing a given project, estimating the time needed to complete each task, and identifying the minimum time needed to complete the total project.

critical path
The sequence of tasks that takes the longest time to complete.

┌   FIGURE **10.2**   ┐
····

PERT CHART FOR PRODUCING A VIDEO

The minimum amount of time it will take to produce this video is 15 weeks. To get that number, you add the week it takes to pick a star and a song to the four weeks to design a set, the two weeks to purchase set materials, the six weeks to construct the set, the week of rehearsals, and the final week when the video is made. That's the critical path. Only delays in that process will delay the final video. See text for more details.

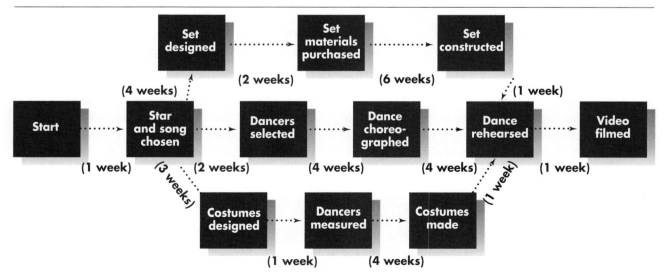

The Rolls-Royce of Auto Parts Scrapyards

The customer is in a rush. Potholes have claimed a wheel on his 1989 Honda Civic, and he is desperate for a replacement. The request is no big deal for the uniformed saleswoman, one of 78 sales consultants of Pintendre Autos Inc. She calmly punches the make, model year, and coded part number into a computer.

Within seconds she confirms that, yes, Pintendre has a dozen such wheels in its vast stock of used parts. The screen flashes the range of prices and conditions—as well as the location of each wheel on Pintendre's rambling premises. It's another small coup for Quebec's largest used auto parts dealer.

In layperson's language Pintendre Autos is a scrapyard. But Francis Carrier, founder and president, bristles at any suggestion that he is a mere scrap dealer. For the past 30 years, this distributor of used auto, truck, and motorcycle components has pioneered notions of service, technology, and strategic alliance in an industry with a seedy, backward image.

"Our aim from the start was to change the image of recycling," said Carrier, 58, a former insurance adjuster who founded Pintendre with his brother Bruno and friend Emilie Couture.

Established in 1972 Pintendre Autos did not re-invent the wheel, but it set out to re-define the industry by coming up with a dismantling and classification system that stressed efficiency both internally and from the customer's point of view. Pintendre also vowed to become the industry leader by the turn of the century. This goal was accomplished a few years ago and annual sales surpassed 28 million dollars in 1997. (As a private corporation the company does not reveal current financial data.)

Back then, scrap dealers knew what they had in stock only by scouring unsightly fields full of rusted cars behind their shops. Today, Pintendre's has a flexible information system that tracks and manages an inventory of more than 200,000 parts.

Employees—225 in all—handle up to 2500 telephone requests a day. They know at the touch of a button what's in stock, what they can sell and for how much, and what they need to stock up on. Carrier figures he has spent more than $1 million on computer hardware

and software since 1978. "Without the computers, it would be hell," he confessed during a tour of his 51-hectare "recycling centre." He added that "people often ask what I would buy first if I were just starting out. It would be a computer—not a building, not a tow truck."

Bolstered by such technology, Pintendre can offer fast and reliable service: 24-hour delivery anywhere in the province. And it guarantees everything it sells.

Some customers may be drawn by the business's outlandish appearance. To drive home his service image, Carrier has styled the front facade of his two-story warehouse and showroom in the shape of a Rolls-Royce car, complete with headlights, silver grille, and hood ornament. Kitschy perhaps, but it leaves visitors with the clear—and entirely accurate—impression that this is no ordinary scrapyard.

Pintendre has also imposed on itself strict environmental guidelines to prevent any future crisis and promotes reuse and recycling of waste materials.

The company buys in excess of 7000 cars, in addition to big rigs and recreational vehicles, a year. Those that can be repaired are sold at the company's used-car lot down the street.

Every morning an inspector drives a pickup truck through the huge lot to inspect the previous day's arrivals. He gives the cars a cursory inspection, checks the condition of major parts, and applies a separate eight-digit code to as many as 16 large parts on each car. He punches the information into a laptop computer so the sales staff has a quick snapshot of what's in the lot.

On a weekly basis, the eight-employee computer department sets the work schedule for the body shop. Based on recent sales and a review of its inventory, it will designate 75 to 100 cars for dismantling. At this point, the company's mechanics do a more thorough inspection to identify salvageable parts, estimate the work required to refurbish them, and grade them for quality. That information is immediately logged in one of the company's 70 computer terminals to let salespeople know what's in stock.

An auto contains as many as 450 identifiable parts—everything from complete front ends to ashtrays. Those that Pintendre feels it can use are cleaned, repaired (when necessary), catalogued, and carefully stored in one of its several buildings. The inventory does not hold parts from cars more than 10 years old. Those are immediately resold as scrap metal or sometimes sent as far away as Mexico and the Netherlands, where older cars are still on the road.

Carrier won't divulge the company's profits, but he said its margins are well above the industry average.

Over the years, Pintendre Autos has received local and international recognition and awards. In 1990 the ▲

Automotive Recyclers Association (ARA) honoured the company for overall development of the firm. In 1992 they received a Canada award in the entrepreneurship category. In 1996 competing with 1600 recyclers in 18 different countries, Pintendre was selected as the "best structured automotive recycling facility."

Source: <www.pintendre.com>, August 2, 1999; Barrie McKenna, "More than the Sum of Its Parts," *Globe and Mail, Report on Business,* February 23, 1993, p. B24.

---

that designing the set must be completed before the materials can be purchased. The critical path (indicated by the bold black arrows) reflects that producing the set takes more time than auditioning dancers and choreographing dances as well as designing and making costumes. The project manager now knows that it's critical that set construction remain on schedule if the project is to be completed on time, but short delays in the dance and costume preparation shouldn't affect the total project.

A PERT network can be made up of thousands of events over many months. Today, this complex procedure is done by computer. Another, more basic, strategy used by manufacturers for measuring production progress is a Gantt chart. The **Gantt chart** (named after its developer, Henry L. Gantt) preceded the development of the PERT method, and is a bar graph that clearly shows what projects are being worked on and what stage they are at on a daily basis. Figure 10.3 shows a Gantt chart for a doll manufacturer. The chart shows that the dolls heads and bodies should be completed before the clothing is sewn. It also shows that at the end of week 3, the dolls' bodies are ready,

<westrek.hypermarket. net/scientific>

Visit this Web site to find brief biographies of Henry Gantt and several other key contributors to the field of *scientific management.* We'll be looking at this topic next.

Gantt chart
Bar graph that show managers what projects are being worked on and what stage they are at on a daily basis.

On an annual basis, Pintendre Autos buys in excess of 7000 automobiles, 250 big rigs, and 350 recreational vehicles such as motorcycles, snowmobiles, and personal water crafts. Approximately 95 percent of these vehicles are acquired through agreements with responsible insurance companies.

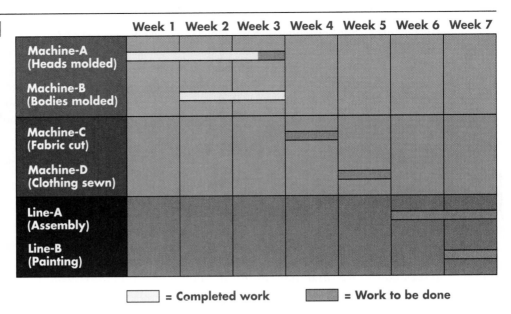

FIGURE 10.3
. . . .
A GANTT CHART FOR A
DOLL MANUFACTURER

A Gantt chart enables a production manager to see at a glance when projects are scheduled to be completed and what the status now is. For example, the dolls' heads and bodies should be completed before the clothing is sewn, but could be a little late, as long as everything is ready for assembly in week 6. This chart shows that at the end of week 3, the dolls' bodies are ready, but the heads are about half a week behind.

but the heads are about half a week behind. All of this calculation was once done by hand. Now the computer has taken over. Using a Gantt-like computer program, a manager can trace the production process minute by minute to determine which tasks are on time and which are behind. Adjustments can be made to allow the company to stay on schedule.

. . . . ▬▬▬▬ . . . .
TOTAL QUALITY IN PRODUCTION MANAGEMENT

quality control
The measurement of products and services against set standards.

Quality control is the measurement of products and services against set standards. Previously, quality control was often done at the end of the production line by a quality control department. Today, things have changed.

As mentioned in the previous chapter, *total quality management (TQM)* means satisfying customers by building in and ensuring quality from product planning to production, purchasing, sales, and service. Emphasis is placed on customer satisfaction and the fact that quality is the concern of everyone, not just the quality control people at the end of the assembly line. In TQM, the structure is so organized that everybody contributes to quality improvement as part of their job. This includes ongoing monitoring and evaluating of performance.

Remember that the purpose of quality goods and services is to make the consumer happy. So a TQM program begins by analyzing the market to see what quality standards need to be established. Quality is then designed into products, and every product must meet those standards every step of the production process.

Total quality management in an organization means[25]

1. Quality is a companywide process involving everyone from the president to the lowest-level employees.

2. Quality does not mean higher cost; doing things right the first time results in *less* cost.

3. Quality involves both individual workers and teams of workers; it has to be part of the corporate culture.

4. Quality improvement is continuous improvement (CI), and that means empowering employees to implement quality changes on a constant or regular basis. Quality and innovation are mutually dependent. The best-quality obsolete product will not sell (see the discussion of CI in the previous chapter).

5. Quality must be a part of the total system, involving suppliers, distributors, repair facilities, and all other organizations that affect consumer satisfaction.

Quality and quality control have been hot topics in Canadian manufacturing management since the mid-1980s. The pressure on Canadian and American companies to pay more attention to quality arose primarily from the superiority of Japanese automobiles, electronics, and other products. What happens if we accept 99.9 percent quality instead of 100 percent quality is illustrated in Figure 10.4.

As more consumers turned away from the Big Three automakers and started buying Toyotas, Hondas, Nissans, and other Japanese products they found to be more reliable and less costly, North American producers were forced to sit up and take notice. It is ironic that it was Edwards Deming, an American ignored by U.S. companies, who went to Japan in 1950 to sell his ideas there. The Japanese became very enthusiastic about his emphasis on the importance of quality and how to achieve quality control. Today, the most prestigious prize in Japan, awarded annually to the company judged to have produced the highest-quality products, is called the *Deming Award*. This elder statesman of production, born in 1900, lectured tirelessly in North America until his death in 1993, stressing that our quality is just not good enough.

Traditionally, our manufacturing system had a quality inspector at the end of the production process who was supposed to reject all the units that did not meet quality standards. Deming taught that quality had to be built right into the production process so that there would be no rejects at the end. We have finally begun to listen to him, but the transition to this new philosophy is difficult. Let's have a look at what Deming's system consists of.

Deming [aimed] his sharpest barbs at top management for not paying attention to quality, especially statistical methods for quality assurance. His recipe for quality control is deceptively simple: tally defects, examine them to find their source, correct the cause, and then keep a record of what happens afterward. He [preached] that statistical analysis, not investments in equipment and automation, is the way for America to garner the gains the Japanese have enjoyed, offering the following advice to do so:

99.9 percent quality would yield:

In Medicine

- 50 newborn babies would die daily
- 500 faulty surgical procedures would be performed weekly
- 20,000 drug prescriptions would be improperly filled annually

In the Postal Service

- 16,000 pieces of mail would be lost hourly

Source: M. E. Mengelsdorf, "Why 99.9 Percent Won't Do," *Inc.*, April 1989, p. 26.

FIGURE **10.4**

····

WHY ZERO DEFECTS?

One aspect of TQM is making the product or service with zero defects. What happens when you have only 99.9 percent quality rather than 100 percent? Here is a U.S. example.

- *Rely on statistical evidence of quality during the process, not at the end of the process. The earlier an error is caught, the less it costs to correct it.*
- *Rely on suppliers that have historically provided quality, not on sampling inspections to determine the quality of each delivery. Instead of a number of vendors, select and stick with a few sources that furnish consistently satisfactory quality.*
- *Rely on training and retraining to give employees the skills to use statistical methods in their jobs, not slogans to improve quality. Employees should feel free to report any conditions that detract from quality.*
- *Rely on supervision guided by statistical methods to help people do their work better, not on production work standards. Statistical techniques detect the sources of waste and teams of designers, supervisors, and workers eliminate the sources.*
- *Rely on the doctrine that poor quality is unacceptable. Defective materials, workmanship, products, and service will not be tolerated.*

\<deming.org\>

You will recall that we met W. Edwards Deming earlier. Do a bit of Net surfing, to see what else you can learn about this man and his contribution to the modern view of management.

According to the Deming philosophy, there is little use in exhorting hourly workers to improve quality, because they do not control the resources needed to do it, such as tools, materials, scheduling, and facilities. Management controls the resources, and 85 percent of all quality problems originate in the system itself, not from the workers. The other 15 percent result from special causes, such as defective tools and negligent acts. Deming placed the responsibility for improvement squarely on management, believing that when managers remove the barriers that stand between hourly workers and their right to pride of workmanship, quality soon surfaces.[26]

Today, TQM has become a major concentration in service and manufacturing companies. Case 2 at the end of this chapter presents some examples of Canadian companies that are not enthused about TQM or see it as just a new name for existing practices. Like every new idea, TQM must be carefully studied and applied if it is to have a chance of succeeding. As you can see from Deming's list, it is not easy to institute his system without total, long-term commitment by the entire management team from the president down. TQM will not work if a company is looking for a quick fix with some new fad.

The following are examples of how quality is being introduced into the production process:

- Motorola set a goal of attaining "six sigma" quality—just 3.4 defects per million products.
- In the past, Xerox found 97 defects for every 100 copiers coming off the assembly line. Now it finds only 12. As a consequence, it raised its market share for small-business copiers from 1 percent to 20 percent.
- Holiday Inn authorized its hotel staff to do almost anything to satisfy an unhappy customer, from handing out gift certificates to eliminating the charge for a service. Managers were given the authority (empowered) to waive charges for the night's stay if the customer was still unhappy.

ISO 9000
Quality management and assurance standards published by the International Organization for Standardization (ISO).

··· ISO 9000 AND GLOBAL STANDARDS OF QUALITY ···

The new global measures for quality are called ISO 9000 standards. **ISO 9000** is the common name given to quality management and assurance standards

How a Quebec Bathtub Company Competes in the United States

Dagmar Egerer has marketed condos in Spain, peddled Maple Leaf gold coins in Belgium, and worked for a hotel chain in Lebanon and Iran. But Egerer, U.S. sales manager for Maax Inc., a Quebec bathtub and shower manufacturer, had rarely faced as persnickety a customer as Home Depot Inc.

One of her jobs is to make sure Maax's bathtubs and showers show up on time at Home Depot's New England outlets. When the giant chain says the period from order to delivery is 18 days, it means 18, not 17 or 19.

The bathtubs weren't shipped to some convenient central warehouse, but to widely scattered stores up to 900 kilometres from Maax's factory. Egerer and her colleagues performed somersaults to arrange trucking schedules. What's more, Home Depot's obsession with defect-free products meant Maax had to package each fibreglass shower in a box to avoid mishaps in transit.

The wooing, winning, and servicing of Home Depot was a big coup for little Maax, located 30 minutes south of Quebec City, with sales of $21 million in 1992. It had secured a toehold with the largest U.S. warehouse retailer of building materials, whose 194 monster outlets did 1992 sales of US$5.4 billion.

After filling in as an emergency supplier of fibreglass showers for two stores, Maax began shipping to 34 Home Depot outlets in the U.S. northeast, as far away as Maryland. Home Depot became its third largest customer, accounting for 15 percent of sales. Maax's U.S. sales grew 58 percent in the six months to August 31, 1992, compared with the previous year.

By plugging into Home Depot, Maax joins the ranks of masochistic suppliers who thrive on being abused by tough customers. In the United States, companies that sell to Wal-Mart stores have to be bent on self-improvement. Softhearted clients are no good for succeeding in the global competitive game, argued Michael Porter, a Harvard University professor and authority on competitive advantage. "A demanding market, rather than a welcoming or easy-to-serve one, is what underpins success," he wrote in a 1991 report for the federal government (see Chapter 3).

To complicate matters, Maax fills every truck before it's sent out to minimize transport costs. A typical order might include shipments to two Long Island, New York, outlets and to one in Connecticut. One Long Island store may set a delivery time for midnight, whereas the other, only 20 kilometres away, may insist on 10 hours later. The traffic manager has to juggle to minimize truckers' downtime.

Adaptability was also the rule on the factory floor. Frequent changes in models had so far discouraged much automation (Maax had only one robot). But Placide Poulin, president and major shareholder, says the just-in-time demands of customers led to flexible manufacturing.

Take thermoforming, the process whereby a sheet of acrylic is heated and then drawn by a vacuum to form the shape of the tub or shower. The existing thermoformers required two to seven hours for a mold change. With 18 models of tubs and showers available, the loss of precious time was immense. So employees ordered a new thermoformer of their own design that could handle two different models at the same time and continue operating while the molds were being changed.

This eagerness to please paid off. Home Depot agreed to stock Maax's higher-end acrylic tubs and showers, as well as its lower-end fibreglass lines. It wasn't an easy sell, because acrylic is a luxury for practical do-it-yourselfers. But when a Home Depot buyer requested a "real good price" on a five-foot acrylic whirlpool tub, Egerer came up with a number and the chain ordered a thousand. With this big order, Maax could bargain harder with its own suppliers. The first tubs carried a retail price of $391, a few hundred dollars cheaper than the competition. Subsequently, Home Depot repeatedly reordered.

By 1996 the picture had changed enormously. Maax was the largest producer of bathtub fixtures in Canada, with 25 percent of the market. It produced 365 different fixtures, had more than 700 employees, nine manufacturing plants, and three distribution centres in North America. Maax had acquired two companies and sales had quadrupled, with the U.S. market providing almost 65 percent.

In 1999 the company was showing record sales and profits, with its sales figure likely to surpass $400 million, well ahead of its 1996 goal of $225 million by the year 2000. Maax continues to do intensive R&D, leading to a steady stream of new products, productivity, and manufacturing improvements, and is continually ▲

automating. These activities, combined with the ongoing acquisition of Canadian and U.S. companies, augur well for the company's future.

Sources: RBC Dominion Securities report, June 30, 1999; Paul Delean, "Maax Reports Bright First Quarter," *Montreal Gazette,* June 27, 1996, p. E7; interview with Dagmar Egerer, July 17, 1996; Alan Freeman, "Company Enjoys a 'Shower' of Business," *Globe and Mail,* classroom edition, January 1993, p. 16.

<www.iso.ch>

You can find out a lot more about ISO and its standards by visiting its Web site. Learn about its history, and the ISO 9001 standards that apply to industries in all aspects of producing and providing goods and services.

published by the International Organization for Standardization (ISO). Prior to the establishment of such standards in 1987, there were no international standards of quality against which to measure companies. Now ISO standards, established in Europe, provide a "common denominator" of business quality accepted around the world.

To be ISO certified a company must show that all procedures are documented and that employees consistently follow those procedures. This assures customers of consistent quality. The process of getting certified usually improves company quality performance.

What makes ISO 9000 so important is that the European Union (EU) of 15 leading European countries requires that any company that wants to do business with EU countries must be certified by ISO standards. Several accreditation agencies in Europe, the U.S., and Canada can provide this certification. In Canada the Canadian Standards Association (CSA) is the organization that does this certification. (You may have noticed the CSA approval on various appliances.) This ensures that the company meets the necessary standards for all phases of its operations, from product development through production and testing to installation. If you look carefully in your area, you may notice various companies have erected signs showing that they are ISO 9000 (or 9001, 9002) approved.

MEASURING PRODUCTIVITY IN THE SERVICE SECTOR

The greatest productivity problem in Canada is reported to be in the service economy. Although productivity growth was relatively good for manufacturers during the 1980s, it was reported to be next to nothing (0.2 percent) for service organizations. We've already learned that 7 of 10 jobs are now in the service sector, with more to come. A truly strong economy, therefore, has to be progressive in introducing the latest technology to services as well as to manufacturing.

There's strong evidence that productivity in the service sector *is* rising, but the government simply doesn't have the means to measure it.[27] The quality of service is greatly improving, but quality is difficult to measure. The traditional way to measure productivity involves tracking inputs (worker hours) compared to outputs (dollars). New information systems must be developed to measure the *speed* of delivery of services, the quality, and customer satisfaction.

Using computers is only the beginning of improving service sector productivity. Think about labour-intensive businesses like McDonald's and Burger King where automation plays a big role in controlling costs and improving service. Today, at Burger King, you fill your own drink cup, which gives servers more time to fill orders. Because the people working at the drive-up window now wear headsets instead of using stationary mikes, they aren't glued to one spot anymore and can do four or five tasks while taking an order.

Most of us have been exposed to similar productivity gains in banking. For example, people no longer have to wait in long lines for harassed tellers to help them deposit and withdraw money. Instead, they use automatic machines, the Internet, or telephones, that take a few seconds and are available 24 hours a day.

Another service that was once annoyingly slow was the checkout counter at the grocery store. The system of marking goods with universal product codes enables computerized checkout and allows cashiers to be much more productive when providing this service.

Airlines are another service industry experiencing tremendous productivity increases through the use of computers for everything from processing reservations, to the heavy use of prepackaged meals on board, to more standardization of all movements of luggage, passengers, and freight. There are also automated ticketing machines, ticketing via Internet, and even ticketless boarding to speed up the process.

In short, operations management has led to tremendous productivity increases in the service sector. Those gains haven't been reflected in national productivity figures because the government doesn't yet know how to accurately measure them. Nonetheless, service workers are losing jobs to machines just as manufacturing workers are. Again, the secret to obtaining and holding a good job is to acquire appropriate education and training. That message can't be repeated too frequently.

Operations management has added greatly to the productivity of the service sector. This machine dispenses movie tickets to customers using bank or credit cards.

LESS RIGID JOB DESCRIPTIONS AID PRODUCTIVITY

Some companies have been moving away from the traditional, rigid job description as a basis for organizing their operations management. Tom Peters pointed out that companies that want to be most productive and react quickly to competitive demands have moved toward flexibility; managers and employees do whatever is required and are not bound by job descriptions. This allows for greater employee initiative and participation, leading to more motivated employees. In today's fast-moving world, reacting quickly gives businesses a competitive edge. In small companies, employees have long functioned as generalists, not limited by strict job descriptions. For bigger businesses, this represents a new trend.

The very large companies have been pushing their unions for some time to allow for greater flexibility in moving employees to do what is required. Unions have usually been suspicious of this demand because they worry that it will be used to reduce pay rates. The Big Three auto companies have begun to get important concessions in this regard from the autoworkers' unions in Canada and the United States. They have drastically reduced the number of job descriptions, allowing for more efficient deployment of their workforces. These companies are waging a tough fight to be more competitive with Japanese automakers, and this is one way to improve their productivity.

W. Edwards Deming went much further than that. He stressed the importance of cooperation among workers, saying that "workers in Japan learned how to cooperate because it was the only chance for the country's survival, given its limited resources and land.... People must learn to work together, but it will take time. North American industry must change its philosophy of every man for himself."[28]

SERVICES GO INTERACTIVE

The service industry has always taken advantage of new technology to increase customer satisfaction. Jet travel enabled Federal Express to deliver goods overnight. Computer databases enabled AT&T to have individualized customer service. Cable TV led to pay-per-view services. And now interactive computer networks, such as the Internet and the World Wide Web, are revolutionizing services. Interactive services are already available from banks, stock brokers, travel agents, and information providers of all kinds. Consumers may soon be involved in all kinds of interactive systems, including participating in community and national decision making.[29]

You can now buy a greater variety of books and CDs on the Internet than you can in retail stores. You can also search for and buy new and used automobiles and new and used computers. As computers and modems get faster, the Internet may take over much of traditional retailing. In short, the service sector is experiencing the same kind of revolution as the manufacturing sector. The success of service organizations in the future will depend greatly on establishing a dialogue with consumers so that service organizations can adapt to consumer demands faster and more efficiently. Such information systems (to make a dialogue easier) have been developed and should prove highly useful.

PREPARING FOR THE FUTURE

What does all this mean to you? It means that university and college graduates of the future will have marvelous new technological advances available to them. It means new opportunities and a higher standard of living and quality of life. But it also means preparing for these opportunities.

Clearly, the workplace is already dominated by an impressive array of computer hardware that is getting progressively smaller, cheaper, and more powerful. A bewildering array of software to make use of this growing capability is opening up an incredible world of high technology. Cellular phones, faxes, and modems are advancing in similar fashion.

If all of this sounds terribly cold and impersonal, you recognize one of the needs of the future. People will need much more human contact outside the work environment. There will be new demands for recreation, social clubs, travel, and other diversions. The Canada of the twenty-first century will be radically different from the Canada of today. It will take both technically trained people and people skilled in human relationships to guide us through the transition.

Many universities offer courses in manufacturing management and robotics. Some require such courses for an MBA degree. Many have research programs in robotics and intelligent machines. McGill University and the University of Toronto, for example, have substantial research centres. These centres often maintain close relations with industry and do contract work for companies. McGill's clients include such major companies as CAE, Hydro-Quebec, and SPAR Aerospace. SPAR developed the robotic arm for U.S. space vehicles, the Canadarm.

REVIEW

Now let's take another look at the ethical dilemma raised at the beginning of this chapter. Companies in Canada are required by law to give employees sufficient notice of such plant closings, sometimes of up to six months. But do companies have obligations beyond those set out in law? Here's what our executives think.

Bédard believes that companies do have responsibilities to their employees and must meet those responsibilities by informing employees of the situation, getting their cooperation, and trying to avoid a closure. If the company opens its books to its employees, they may be able to propose improvements and avoid a plant closure. Further, "companies that think too much in the short term and focus only on the short term will one day pay a price."

Reilley says that companies owe their loyal employees a measure of support when plant closures occur. This support can include relocation to another site,

retraining, or termination packages. The company should also try to attract other firms to the town. Remember, too, outsourcing is not all bad. Redundant employees often form their own enterprises and compete for outsourcing contracts. The company should also try to protect employees through reassignment and early retirement incentives. Reilley notes that "increasing productivity doesn't necessarily mean layoffs and plant closings. Productivity enhancement, if done right, leads to greater market share and thus tends to protect jobs (and even creates new jobs)."

Many companies in Canada and around the world have leap-frogged from country to country chasing lower wages. Some Canadian companies have moved factories first to the northern U.S., then to the southern U.S., and finally to Mexico. Nike and Reebok have followed the same trail from the U.S., outsourcing work to contractors in South Korea and then in Indonesia.

The trend is toward making production and operations management courses a requisite for graduate degrees in management. Such courses, in combination with those on organizational behaviour, train students to manage the high-tech workers and managers of the new era. Emphasis is on participative management and the design of a work environment suitable to the twenty-first century. A new era is opening up for both manufacturing and the service sector. There will be many exciting, challenging careers in this field.

Progress Check

- Could you draw a **PERT** chart for making a breakfast of three-minute eggs, buttered toast, and coffee? Which process would be the critical path, the longest process? How could you use a Gantt chart to keep track of production?
- Why does service productivity seem to lag behind industrial productivity, and what can be done about it?

SUMMARY

• • • • • •

1. Production and operations management consists of those activities managers do to create goods and services.
    - ***What is the production process, and how does productivity relate to it?***
    Production is the creation of finished goods and services using inputs—land, labour, capital, entrepreneurship, and information. *Productivity* is the term used to describe output per worker. Output could mean goods like cars and furniture, or services such as education and health care.

1. Describe the production process, and explain the importance of productivity.

2. Explain the importance of site selection in keeping down costs, and identify the criteria used to evaluate different sites.

2. A major issue of the 1990s was the shift of manufacturing and service organizations from one city or province to another in Canada or to foreign countries.

• *Why is site selection so important, and what criteria is used to evaluate different sites?*

The very survival of the manufacturing industry depends on its ability to remain competitive, and that means either cheaper inputs, such as cheaper costs of labour and land, or increased outputs from present inputs (increased productivity). Cheaper labour and land are two major criteria for selecting the right sites. Other criteria include whether (1) resources are plentiful and inexpensive, (2) skilled workers are available or are trainable, (3) taxes are low and the local government offers support, (4) energy and water are available, (5) transportation costs are low, and (6) the quality of life and the quality of education are high.

3. Classify the various production processes and how materials requirement planning links organizations in performing those processes.

3. Process manufacturing physically or chemically changes materials. Assembly processes put together components. These two processes are called *synthetic systems*.

• *Are there other production processes?*

Yes, the reverse of a synthetic system is called an *analytic system*. Analytic systems break down raw materials into components to extract other products. In addition, production processes are either continual or intermittent. A continual process is one in which long production runs turn out finished goods over time. An intermittent process is an operation in which the production run is short (e.g., one or two eggs) and the machines are changed frequently to produce different products.

• *What relationship does MRP have with the production process?*

A manufacturer sets a production schedule. It then informs its suppliers of what will be needed. The supplier must deliver the goods just in time to go on the assembly line, making the supplier part of the process.

4. Describe manufacturing techniques such as just-in-time inventory control, flexible manufacturing, lean manufacturing, and competing in time.

4. Flexible manufacturing is the design of machines to do multiple tasks so that they can produce a variety of products.

• *What's the relationship between flexible manufacturing and lean manufacturing?*

Lean manufacturing is the production of goods using less of everything compared to mass production: half the human effort, half the manufacturing space, half the investment in tools, half the engineering time to develop a new product in half the time. Flexible manufacturing enables the firm to use less equipment to make more goods; thus, it could be considered part of lean manufacturing.

• *What is mass customization?*

Mass customization means making custom-designed goods for all customers. Flexible manufacturing makes mass customization possible. Given the exact needs of a customer, flexible manufacturing machines can produce a customized good as fast as mass-produced goods.

• *How do competing in time and JIT fit into the process?*

Getting your product to market before your competitors is essential today, particularly in the electronic sector. Thus competing in time is critical. JIT inventory control allows for less inventory and fewer machines to move goods. This allows for more flexibility and faster response times.

5. Show how CAD/CAM improves the production process.

5. CAD/CAM has made it possible to custom-design products to meet the tastes of small markets, with very little increase in cost.

- *How might CAD/CAM lead to people problems?*
Workers must be trained to deal with the new technology. Better relationships must be established between the firm and suppliers, customers, and other stakeholders.

6. The program evaluation and review technique (PERT) is a method for analyzing the tasks involved in completing a given project, estimating the time needed to complete each task, and identifying the minimum time needed to complete the total project.

    6. Illustrate the use of Gantt and PERT charts in production planning.

   - *How can one learn to draw such a chart? Is there any relationship between it and a Gantt chart?*
Figure 10.2 shows a PERT chart. A Gantt chart (Figure 10.3) is a bar graph that clearly shows what projects are being worked on and how much has been completed on a daily basis. Whereas PERT is a planning tool, Gantt is a tool used to measure progress.

7. Because Canada is a service society now, automation of the service sector is extremely important.

    7. Explain the importance of productivity in the service sector.

   - *Why is service productivity not increasing as rapidly as manufacturing productivity?*
One important reason is that the service sector is labour-intensive. Keep in mind, however, that productivity and quality are rising in the service sector, but they're harder to measure than outputs of the industrial sector.

KEY TERMS
· · · · · ·

analytic system 304
assembly process 304
computer-aided design (CAD) 312
computer-aided manufacturing (CAM) 312
critical path 315
enterprise resource planning (ERP) 306
flexible manufacturing 309
form utility 299
Gantt chart 317

industrial park 302
ISO 9000 320
just-in-time (JIT) inventory control 307
lean manufacturing 310
manufacturing 299
mass customization 310
materials requirement planning (MRP) 305

process manufacturing 304
production 299
production and operations management 298
program evaluation and review technique (PERT) 315
quality control 318
robot 310
synthetic system 304
telecommuting 303

DEVELOPING WORKPLACE SKILLS

1. Mass customization means that you will be able to purchase custom-designed goods and services for about the same price as mass-produced items. Discuss how these changes will affect your own purchases of goods and services such as shoes, vacations, and video games.

2. Review all the terms in this chapter: CAD, CAM, CIM, MRP, JIT, and so on. These are the business terms of the twenty-first century. Try to use them in class so that they become familiar in different settings. Soon you will be thinking of new ways to advance business yourself, based on your understanding of these terms.

3. Compose a list of the applications of advanced technology in the service sector that have already occurred; include as many as you can. Using this information, brainstorm further uses of technology in areas such as recre-

ation, travel, retailing, wholesaling, insurance, banking, finance, and government. Prepare a two-minute summary report to give to your class.

4. Scan recent issues of your local newspaper, *The Globe and Mail*, the *National Post*, and *Canadian Business* magazine for reports on companies in your area that are shifting more of their production to outsourcing. Bring these reports to class and discuss the possible impact of these developments on your community in terms of unemployment, retail sales, housing prices, and so on.

5. Debate the following proposition: "Canadian manufacturers should halt the spread of computers and robots used in manufacturing to save jobs for Canadian workers." Again, take the other side of this issue from your normal position.

INTERNET CHALLENGES

1. Using Yahoo, key in the words *flexible manufacturing* and see how many references you can find over the last 12 months. Click on *Alliance Automated Systems* and follow some of links on flexible manufacturing. What impact do you think these developments may have on you and other consumers? Bring these reports to class for discussion.

2. Using the same search engines, key in *telecommuting* and see what results you get. In August 1999 there were 73 site matches on Yahoo. Has there been more written about telecommuting since then? Read some of these articles and think about your work future. Can you see yourself working at home as an employee? As a self-employed person?

Practising Management Decisions

Matthew Kiernan, based in Unionville, Ontario, is a management consultant whose views command attention. He has a Ph.D. degree in strategic management from the University of London and was a senior partner with an international consulting firm, KPMG Peat Marwick. Subsequently he founded his own firm, Innovest Group International, with a staff operating out of Geneva, London, and Toronto. He was also a director of the Business Council for Sustainable Development based in Geneva.

His book *Get Innovative or Get Dead* took aim at big corporations for their poor record on innovation. Any five-year-old could tell you that companies must innovate to survive, he said, so what's the problem? According to Kiernan, it's one thing to understand something in your head but quite another thing to really feel it in your gut. This is further complicated by the difficulty of getting a big company to shift gears, to turn its culture around so that innovation becomes the norm rather than the special effort.

CASE 1

• • • • • •

WHY BIG COMPANIES FAIL TO INNOVATE

• • • • • •

Kiernan called for a company to develop a style and atmosphere that favours individual risk taking, the intrapreneurial approach discussed in Chapter 7. That means that if a team tries something that doesn't work, you don't shoot them down. Encouraging innovation, which inevitably involves taking risks with the unknown, means accepting the fact that it may take two or three attempts before something useful is developed. Further, it requires "creative thinking to see the potential" in something new or untested.

The 3M company is often used as a great example of a company that encourages creativity. Its policy dictates that 30 percent of annual sales come from products less than four years old. But 3M wasn't always that progressive. When the now legendary Post-it Notes were first developed by an employee, he had a hard time getting the company to see the potential in his idea. This ultimately triggered a major change in the company's policy.

Kiernan pointed out that most companies give lip service to the necessity of innovation but do not act in a credible way as far as their employees are concerned. If you mean business you must take that "bright guy out of the basement, [the one] everybody knows is a genius, but whose last two enterprise efforts came to grief, and visibly promote him."

Decision Questions

1. Do large companies find it difficult to innovate because they resist change? Is it because they are big or because they are afraid of the unknown? Why is that?
2. Do smaller companies do better at innovation because they are not so risk-averse? Is that because most of them are private companies and not accountable to outside shareholders?
3. Can you see any connection between innovation and continuous improvement? Does CI require innovation?
4. If you were vice president in charge of production at a big corporation, how would you encourage innovation?

CASE 2
......
TOTAL QUALITY MANAGEMENT: IS IT A CURE-ALL?
......

"The current rage for total quality management as a miracle cure-all has a lot of executives tearing their hair in exasperation." So said *The Globe and Mail* in a summary of its article on TQM. It then attempted to sort "through the facts and fiction of business's favourite fad." What is the problem?

In 1984, long before most Canadian companies had even heard of TQM, Culinar Inc. became the Canadian pioneer of TQM. Then CEO Roger Neron hired consultants and sent a key executive to "see what foreign companies were doing." They were hoping to "grab a larger piece of the North American snack food industry."

By 1992 the $587-million-a-year junk food giant had no formal TQM program at all. Jean-Rene Halde, appointed CEO in 1987, scratched it because it was "billed as the solution to all our problems but it was only one solution to *some* of them." Nobody would talk about it at Culinar and "TQM has become a dirty acronym." They still use some TQM tools, such as statistical process control and business process redesign, but the "politically correct term for these activities is 'continuous improvement.'"

Apparently Culinar's story is not unusual. Florida Power & Light Co., winner of Japan's coveted Deming prize, cut back on its quality program. After a scrutiny of companies in North America and Europe, McKinsey & Co. Inc., the giant international consulting firm, said "lack of results kills as many as two-thirds of TQM programs that are more than two years old." Similar results are reported from other large surveys in England and the United States, which show that only one-third to one-fifth of companies report

"tangible benefits" or "significant impact on their competitive positions" as a result of their TQM programs. Nevertheless, most claimed that they reaped some benefits.

Henry Mintzberg of McGill University's management faculty has done considerable research and writes often on management theory and practices. He said that any company that goes through the TQM exercise asking itself "Who are we? What is there in here for us? How can we adapt this to our needs?" will probably get some useful results. But any company that thinks that "all we've got to do is to plug this in" will "do worse than fail—it will make everyone cynical."

These sentiments were echoed by Yvan Allaire, a professor at the Universite du Quebec's school of management and chairman of strategy consultants Secor Groupe Inc. of Montreal. He said, "I'm critical of the sloganeering, the faddishness, the overblown expectations and the inevitable disappointments." He warned that TQM should not be seen as a cure-all that solves everything while producing better financial results.

That is the bad news; but what have the proponents of TQM said? Plenty.

Problems arise "from a lack of commitment, understanding, and patience on the part of CEOs." The 1992 *Globe and Mail* article looked at three Canadian companies that have benefitted from TQM. Toronto-based Cadet Uniform Services Ltd. uses a modest-sized organization with few management layers and sales of $30 million. Winnipeg's Reimer Express Lines Ltd. had sales of more than $250 million, 1400 vehicles, and 1000 employees. It has a complex operation with facilities across the country. General Electric Canada

Inc. has an aircraft-engine component plant in Bromont, Quebec, with 600 employees. Like Cadet, it has few layers of management.

Did these companies have anything in common that enabled them to adopt TQM successfully? All three had

- top executives who were highly committed to the program.
- cultures that were inherently TQM-friendly. They possessed many TQM values and some of its practices.

Cadet and GE also had few layers of management and were of modest size. Reimer reorganized itself to act as if it were a group of smaller companies.

It seems all of these characteristics are necessary for a TQM program to succeed. President of Cadet Quentin Wahl, whose management style is democratic, encountered difficulties until he realized that TQM is not a management program but a "people" program that must involve all employees. TQM manager Andrew McNab reported that by 1996 the program was proceeding smoothly and continued to show good results.

At GE, Diane Buck, engineer in charge of quality, said that TQM was a useful reminder to employees when they started to forget they were part of a larger entity whose interests superseded their own." At GE quality and teamwork have always been stressed. This made adoption of TQM much easier. In 1996 Buck reported that TQM helped GE to improve and increase production despite a reduction in the workforce to 500 employees.

Decision Questions

1. The surveys of companies showed a low rate of success with TQM. Do you think that may be due to executives looking for results that will show up in their bottom line quickly? Is this part of a general problem of North American management's orientation toward too short a time frame? If so, what could be done about that?

2. Should TQM be applied very selectively? Should only companies with the "right" climate, as noted in the case, attempt to obtain its benefits?

3. Some managers claim that TQM is just a fancy name for practices they have always employed—concern with quality, participative style, teamwork, and so on. Does TQM heighten everyone's consciousness about these issues? Does it bring together under one umbrella various practices and thus help an organization to function better?

4. In the high-tech world of production and operations that now prevails, is there less need for TQM because fewer people are employed? Or is TQM even more important precisely because of this?

Sources: Sandy Fife, "The Total Quality Muddle," *Globe and Mail, Report on Business*, November 1992, p. B64ff; interviews with Andrew McNab and Diane Buck, July 17, 1996.

Information Technology:
A Vital Component
of Management

Chapter

11

LEARNING GOALS

*After you have read and studied this chapter,
you should be able to*

1 outline the changing role of business technology.

2 compare the scope of the Internet, intranets, and extranets as tools for managing information.

3 list the steps in managing information, and identify the characteristics of useful information.

4 review the hardware most frequently used in business, and outline the benefits of the move toward computer networks.

5 classify the computer software most frequently used in business.

6 evaluate the human resource, security, and privacy issues in management that are affected by information technology.

7 identify the careers that are gaining or losing workers because of the growth of information technology.

One of the disadvantages of being self-employed is that it is difficult to take time off. With today's technology, however, many entrepreneurs are finding that they don't need to be chained to their desks to keep their businesses running smoothly.

Vance Webster, an insurance services entrepreneur, traded his office for a 44-foot yacht and sailed to the San Juan Islands, taking his business with him. Armed with a cell phone, notebook computer, and pager, Webster kept his business afloat while he enjoyed the sights. He updated his voice mail each morning by referring to the day's date and telling callers that he'd check back for messages later in the day. He sent routine replies (such as those to customers who needed to register cars for insurance) to the database on his notebook computer. He was able to handle long-distance emergencies as well. For example, one client phoned in that his wife had hit a post supporting his carport, which had caused the roof to collapse on top of his car. Webster checked the client's policy on his notebook, called him back right away to say everything was covered, and gave him the claims-office phone number.

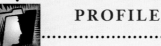

PROFILE

Vance Webster, Insurance Services Entrepreneur

Technology is changing the way we do business. Technological improvements have made the Internet friendlier and less expensive than it was in the beginning. This technology includes powerful microprocessors and network computers, inexpensive digital storage, improved software development tools, simplified user interfaces, and a low-cost communications bandwidth (the "pipeline" data flows through). For millions of business people, using a computer is now as commonplace as using a telephone.

Businesses small and large will succeed or fail based on their ability to manage information. New technology will enable managers to make informed decisions and to communicate with each other, with customers, and with other companies, including suppliers. The rapid technological developments along the information superhighway make this one of the most exciting times in history. The question is, will you be able to keep up?

Sources: Dale D. Buss, "Take a Break," *Home Office Computing*, May 1997, pp. 60–64; Joia Shillingford, "Teleworking," *Financial Times*, September 10, 1997, p. 13.

SOFTWARE: TO COPY OR NOT TO COPY?

A common practice today is copying software from a friend or company onto disks and then loading it into your computer. Of course, you are then not a registered owner with the all the advantages of upgrading and such. When you do this you have stolen a company's product. Is this more acceptable than shoplifting, which is also stealing something without paying for it? We seem to treat software copying like rolling through a stop sign on a deserted street at 2:00 a.m. or exceeding the speed limit by 10 kilometres per hour. The difference is that these driving actions are illegal and may be dangerous but property is not being stolen. It is obviously almost impossible to stop such thefts given the ease and privacy with which it can be done. What would you do if you were operating a small business? Would you encourage your employees to do it or would you do it yourself?

THE ROLE OF INFORMATION TECHNOLOGY

Throughout this text, we have emphasized the need to manage information flows among businesses and their employees, businesses and their customers, and so on. Those managers who rely on the old ways of doing things will simply not be able to compete with those who have the latest technology and know how to use it.

Business technology has often changed names and changed roles. In the 1970s business technology was known as **data processing (DP)**. Although many people use the words data and information interchangeably, they are different. Data are raw, unanalyzed, and unsummarized facts and figures. Information is the processed and summarized data that can be used for managerial decision making. DP was used to support an existing business; its primary purpose was to improve the flow of financial information. DP employees tended to be hidden in a back room and rarely came in contact with customers.

In the 1980s business technology became known as **information systems (IS)**. IS moved out of the back room and into the centre of the business. Its role changed from supporting the business to *doing* business. Customers began to interact with a wide array of technological tools, from automated bank machines (ABMs) to voice mail. As business increased its use of information systems, it became more dependent on them.

Until the late 1980s business technology was just an addition to the existing way of doing business. Keeping up to date was a matter of using new technology on *old* methods. But things started to change as the 1990s approached. Businesses shifted to using *new* technology on new methods. Business technology then became known as **information technology (IT)**, and its role became to change business.

••• HOW INFORMATION TECHNOLOGY CHANGES BUSINESS •••

Time and place have always been at the centre of business. Customers had to go to the business during business hours to satisfy their needs. We went to the

data processing (DP)
Technology that supported an existing business; primarily used to improve the flow of financial information.

information systems (IS)
Technology that helps companies do business; includes such tools as automated bank machines (ABMs) and voice mail.

information technology (IT)
Technology that helps companies change business by using new technology on new methods.

store to buy clothes. We went to the bank to arrange for a loan. Businesses decided when and where we did business with them. Today IT allows businesses to deliver products and services whenever and wherever it is convenient for the *customer*. Thus, you can order clothes and do banking or send flowers via the Internet, at a time you choose.

Consider how IT has changed the entertainment industry. If you wanted to see a movie 30 years ago, you had to go to a movie theater. Twenty-five years ago you could wait for it to be on television. Fifteen years ago you could wait for it to be on cable television. Ten years ago you could go to a video store and rent it. Now you can order video on demand by satellite or cable.

As IT breaks down time and location barriers, it creates organizations and services that are independent of location. For example, NASDAQ and **SOFFEX** are electronic stock exchanges without trading floors. Buyers and sellers make trades by computer.

Being independent of location brings work to people instead of people to work. With IT, data and information can flow more than 12,800 kilometres a second, allowing businesses to conduct work around the globe continually. We are moving toward what we call **virtualization**; that is, accessibility through technology that allows business to be conducted independent of location. For example, you can carry a virtual office in your pocket or purse. Such tools as cellular phones, pagers, laptop computers, and personal digital assistants allow you to access people and information as if you were in an actual office. Likewise, virtual communities are forming as people who would otherwise not have met communicate with each other through the virtual post office created by computer networks.

Satellites have transformed the entertainment industry. Consumers no longer have to leave their homes to view the latest movies.

virtualization
Accessibility through technology that allows business to be conducted independent of location.

Organization	Technology is breaking down corporate barriers, allowing functional departments or product groups (and factory workers) to share critical information instantly.
Operations	Technology shrinks cycle times, reduces defects, and cuts waste. Companies use electronic data interchange to streamline ordering and communication with suppliers and customers.
Staffing	Technology eliminates layers of management and cuts the number of employees. Companies use computers and telecommunication equipment to create virtual offices with employees in various locations or at home.
New products	Information technology cuts development cycles by feeding customer and marketing comments to product development teams quickly so that they can more readily revive old products or develop new products and target specific customers.
Customer relations	Customer service representatives can solve customers' problems instantly by using companywide databases to complete tasks from changing addresses to adjusting bills. Information gathered from customer service interactions can further strengthen customer relationships.

FIGURE **11.1**
. . . .
HOW INFORMATION TECHNOLOGY IS CHANGING BUSINESS

Here are a few ways that information technology is changing businesses, their employees, suppliers, and customers.

knowledge technology (KT)
Technology that adds a layer of intelligence to filter appropriate information and deliver it when it is needed.

Lucent Technologies provides businesses with tools to increase their technological capabilities. Accessibility through technology, or virtualization, allows business to be conducted independent of location.

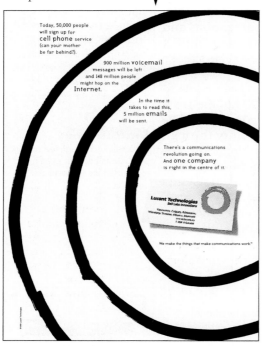

Doing business drastically changes when companies increase their technological capabilities. See Figure 11.1 for other examples of how information technology changes business.

··· MOVING FROM INFORMATION TECHNOLOGY ··· TOWARD KNOWLEDGE TECHNOLOGY

In the mid-1990s, yet another change occurred in the terminology of business technology as we started moving away from information technology and toward **knowledge technology (KT)**. Knowledge is information charged with enough intelligence to make it relevant and useful. KT adds a layer of intelligence to filter appropriate information and deliver it when it is needed. For example, consider the number 70. Alone, it doesn't mean much. Change it to 70 percent and it means a little more but still doesn't tell us a lot. Make it a 70 percent chance of rain and we have more meaning.

Now let's imagine you are the first one on your block with a wristwatch featuring KT. As you walk out the door, the watch signals you that it has a message: "70 percent chance of rain in your city today." KT just gave you relevant and useful information at the moment you needed it. Now you can head for class with an umbrella under your arm, knowing that you made an informed decision.

KT changes the traditional flow of information; instead of an individual going to the database, the data come to the individual. For example, using KT business training software, Bell Canada can put a new employee at a workstation and then let the system take over to do everything from laying out a checklist of the tasks required on a shift to answering questions and offering insights that once would have taken up a supervisor's time. Knowledge databases may one day replace the traditional mentors who helped workers up the corporate ladder.[1]

KT "thinks" about the facts based on an individual's needs, reducing the time that person must spend finding and getting information. Business people who use KT can focus on what's important: deciding how to react to problems and opportunities. According to some market analysts, by 2005 more money will be spent on knowledge-based IT than on traditional systems.[2]

Critical Thinking

Knowledge technology allows the database to go to the individual; the individual will no longer need to search through a database. Can you imagine how you could use such a system? If you could design it yourself, what would it look like and what would it do?

Progress Check

- How has the role of information technology changed since the days when it was known as data processing?
- In what way is knowledge technology different from information technology?

···· ▬▬▬ ····

THE ROAD TO KNOWLEDGE: THE INTERNET, INTRANETS, AND EXTRANETS

A key issue for business today is how to get the right information to the right people at the right time. Knowledge, more than physical assets, is now the key to successful competition. That is why knowledge has become one of the more important factors of production.[3] The importance of business knowledge is nothing new—what is new is the recognition of the need to manage it like any other asset. To manage knowledge, a company needs to learn how to share information throughout the organization and to implement systems for creating new knowledge. This need is leading to new technologies that support the exchange of information among staff, suppliers, and customers. At the heart of this technology are the Internet, intranets, and extranets.[4]

You already know that the Internet is a network of computer networks. An **intranet** is a companywide network, closed to public access, that uses Internet technology. Some companies use intranets only to publish information for employees, such as phone lists and employee policy manuals. These companies do not enjoy as high a return on their investment as other companies that create interactive intranet applications. Such applications include allowing employees to update their addresses or submit company forms such as supply requisitions, timesheets, or payroll forms online. These applications save money and generate greater revenue because they eliminate paper handling and enable faster decision making.[5]

By 2002 between one-half and two-thirds of all businesses will be running intranets.[6] One problem with an intranet occurs when companies don't want others, particularly the competition, to see their site. To solve that problem, companies can construct a *firewall* between themselves and the outside world to protect corporate information from unauthorized users. A firewall can be hardware, software, or both.[7]

Many businesses choose to open their intranets to other selected companies through the use of extranets.[8] An **extranet** is a semiprivate network that uses Internet technology and allows more than one company to access the same information or allows people on different servers to collaborate. One of the most common uses of extranets is to extend an intranet to outside customers.[9]

The Internet is changing the way we do business. No longer are the advantages of electronic data interchange (EDI) available only to the large companies that can afford such a system. Now almost all companies can use the Internet to share data and process orders, specifications, invoices, and payments.[10] "Only about 2 percent of organizations have EDI—but 99 percent have a PC and a telephone. The Internet creates a critical mass of people who can exchange data over the network," explains Matthew Wall, the business unit director at software company EDS.[11]

Another way that the Internet is changing how we do business is by making it easier for small businesses to sell their goods and services globally. Read the Reaching Beyond Our Borders box on page 349 to learn more about how technology can facilitate global business.

If there are no changes in network capacity, the more people who use Internet technology, the slower it will become. But Internet computing isn't the only reason for traffic jams on the information superhighway. Remote and mobile workers trying to connect to the corporate networks also add to the

As more and more people go online, the Internet will continue its informational influence on many facets of our lives. In business, intranets have that same effect on the job. Intranets are companywide networks that use Internet technologies, but are closed to public access.

intranet
A companywide network, closed to public access, that uses Internet technology.

extranet
A semiprivate network that uses Internet technology and allows more than one company to access the same information or allows people on different servers to collaborate.

Delta Vancouver Suites has become one of the first hotels in the country to offer high-speed Internet access to its guests. RoomLinx Inc. has made available to both guest and meeting rooms the high-speed service, which not only provides users with an accelerated connection to the Internet, but also allows them to access and download text, audio, and video files up to 300 times faster than through the use of a standard modem.

Internet 2
The new Internet system that will link government supercomputer centres and a select group of universities; it will run 100 to 1000 times faster than today's public infrastructure and will support heavy-duty applications.

<www.ecommercetimes. com/news/viewpoint/ view-990505.shtml>

The *E-Commerce Times* is a newspaper on the Internet focusing on electronic commerce. Search for items on Internet 2 to learn about new developments.

congestion.[12] The traffic on the information superhighway has become so intense that early Net settlers—scientists and other scholars—have found that they have been squeezed off the crowded Internet and are unable to access, transmit, and manipulate complex mathematical models, data sets, and other digital elements of their craft. Their answer? Create another Internet, reserved for research purposes only.

The new system, **Internet 2**, will run 100 to 1000 times faster than today's infrastructure and will support heavy-duty applications, such as videoconferencing, collaborative research, distance education, digital libraries, and full-body simulation environments known as teleimmersion. A key element of Internet 2 is a network called vBNS, or very high-speed Backbone Network Service, which was set up in 1995 as a way to link government supercomputer centres and a select group of universities.[13] Although Internet 2 became available to a few select organizations in the U.S. in late 1997, it is expected to be available to the private sector by 2000. Cynics say that by then Internet 2 itself will be overrun by networked undergrads involved in role-playing games and other resource-hogging pursuits. But the designers of Internet 2 are thinking ahead. Not only do they expect Internet history to repeat itself, they are counting on it. They are planning to filter the Internet 2 technology out to the wider Internet community in such a way that there is plenty of room on the road for all of us—at a price, of course.[14]

MANAGING INFORMATION

Even before the use of computers, managers had to sift through mountains of information to find what they needed to help them make decisions. Today business people are deluged with information from voice mail, the Internet, fax machines, and e-mail. More than 2.7 *trillion* e-mail messages alone were sent in 1997. One study revealed that the average office worker sends 57

Spotlight on Small Business

Time is Money

One of the most common sights at airports, on planes, and in hotels is the busy business traveller either carrying a laptop computer or sitting with the laptop perched on his or her knees, hard at work. Today there is no rest for managers, executives, and other employees on the move. There is constant pressure to communicate with colleagues, supervisors, customers, or your office as timely information is a vital business asset. To meet this need, airlines and hotels have been adding facilities that allow travellers to plug in their units and send or receive e-mail, faxes, and other information. However, there have been many complaints about inadequate or slow connections, especially when downloading big files.

Along comes a Vancouver company, RoomLinx Inc., that offers a high-speed downloading facility in hotel ▲ rooms. By establishing a network installed in the hotel, president Jason Arnold notes that his Internet feed operates at 10,000 KB per second, which is almost 200 times faster than the *fast* dial-up modem available via the phone lines. He claims that his RoomLinx system can download a huge 18-megabyte file—that would fill 12 floppy disks—in only 15 seconds!

RoomLinx also offers 24-hour technical help and the total cost to the user is $9.95 for a 24-hour, noon-to-noon usage. Arnold says that his system is also capable of constant upgrading. Two Vancouver hotels, a Delta and a Sheraton unit, were the first to sign up.

Source: Nora Underwood, "Traveller's Check—Cussing and Swearing Be Damned," *Globe and Mail, Report on Business*, August 1999, p. 59.

---

e-mail messages a day.[15] Business people refer to this information overload as "infoglut."[16] Too much information can confuse issues rather than clarify them. How can managers keep from getting buried in the infoglut? Stepping back to gain perspective is the key to managing the sea of information.

The first step toward gaining perspective is to identify the four or five key goals you want to reach. Eliminating the information that is not related to those top priorities can reduce the amount of information flowing into your office by half. For example, when we were gathering information to include in this chapter, we collected more than 400 journal articles. Feeling the pressure of information overload, we identified the goals we wanted the chapter to accomplish and eliminated all the articles that didn't address those goals. As we further refined our goals, the huge stack of paper gradually dropped to a manageable size.

Obviously, not all of the information that ends up on your desk will be useful. The usefulness of management information depends on four characteristics:

1. *Quality.* Quality means that the information is accurate and reliable. When the clerk at a fastfood restaurant enters your order into the cash register, it may be automatically fed to a computer, and the day's sales and profits can be calculated as soon as the store closes. The sales and expense data must be accurate, or the rest of the calculations will be wrong.

2. *Completeness.* There must be enough information to allow you to make a decision but not so much as to confuse the issue. Today, as we have noted, the problem is often too much information rather than too little.

3. *Timeliness.* Information must reach managers quickly. If a customer has a complaint, that complaint should be handled within a day. In the

past a salesperson would make a report to his or her manager; that report would go to a higher-level manager, and the problem would not be resolved for days, weeks, or months. E-mail and other developments make it possible for marketing, engineering, and production to hear about a problem with a product the same day the salesperson hears about it. Product changes can be made instantly using computer-integrated manufacturing, as discussed in Chapter 10.

4. *Relevance.* Different managers have different information needs. Again, the problem today is that information systems often make too much data available. Managers must learn which questions to ask to get the relevant answers they need.

push technology
Software that delivers information tailored to a previously defined user profile; it pushes the information to users so that they don't have to pull it out.

Sorting out the useful information and getting it to the right people are the goals to solve information overload. There are software programs and services available that do just that by filtering information so that users can get the customized information they need. Known as **push technology** because they push the information to users so they don't have to pull it out, these services deliver customized news to individual computers after sorting through thousands of news sources to find information that suits the user's identified needs. The major Web browsers, Netscape Navigator and Microsoft Internet Explorer, include push technology features.[17]

You may be concerned that only getting the information the computer thinks you need will eliminate a lot of other useful information you may find by luck. Software developers envision a program with a dial that will allow you to regulate the amount of random information you receive with your customized news.

People can connect their analog cell phones to their computers and access e-mail and the Web from remote locations, but connections are slow and expensive. The Teledesic satellite network is projected to be up and running by 2003. This "Internet in the sky" will use 288 low-Earth-orbit satellites to create a global, high-speed data network, providing Internet access at cable modem speeds from almost anywhere in the world.

The important thing to remember when facing information overload is to relax. You can never read everything that is available. Set goals for yourself and do the best you can. Remember, just because there is a public library doesn't mean you should feel guilty about not reading every book in it. And so it is with the information superhighway: you can't make every stop along the route, so plan your trip wisely and bon voyage!

THE ENABLING TECHNOLOGY: HARDWARE

We hesitate to discuss the advances that have been made in computer hardware because what is powerful as we write this may be obsolete by the time you read it. In the mid-1970s the chairman of Intel Corporation, Gordon E. Moore, predicted that the capacity of computer chips would double every year or so. This has since been called Moore's Law. The million-dollar vacuum-tube computers that awed people in the 1950s couldn't now keep up with a pocket calculator. A greeting card that plays "Happy Birthday" contains more computing power than existed before 1950.

The speed of evolution in the computer industry has slowed little since Moore's remark, although in 1997 Moore did say that his prediction cannot hold good for much longer because chipmakers will sooner or later run into a fundamental law of nature; that is, the finite size of atomic particles will prevent infinite miniaturization.[18] That won't stop chipmakers from improving chips in ways other than miniaturization. Rapid advances make one product after another obsolete, helping create demand for newer chips. For example, a three-year-old personal computer is considered out of date. So rather than overload you with potentially outdated facts, we offer you a simple overview of the kind of computer technology available now, at the start of the new millennium.

Hardware includes computers, pagers, cellular phones, printers, scanners, fax machines, personal digital assistants (PDAs), and so on. The mobile worker can find travel-size versions of computers, printers, and fax machines that are almost as powerful and feature-laden as their big brothers. All-in-one devices that address the entire range of your communications needs are now available. For example, there are handheld units that include a wireless portable phone, fax, e-mail, Web browser, and personal information manager (PIM).

Researchers are working on a human–computer interface that combines a videocamera and computer. When you approach the PC, it recognizes you, asks you how you feel, and determines what tasks you want to complete that day.[19] Instead of hearing a mechanical beep to remind you of your next class, you'll hear a soothing voice say, "Jamie, your Introduction to Business final will begin in 30 minutes." Sorry, it won't take the test for you—some things you still have to do for yourself.

The desk of today's office worker would not be complete without a computer, modem, and access to a printer.

<www.intel.com/ pressroom/kits/bios/ moore.htm>

Visit this Web site to learn more about Intel and Gordon Moore. What does the revised version of *Moore's Law* now say?

··· COMPUTER NETWORKS ···

Perhaps the most dynamic change in business technology in recent years is the move away from mainframe computers that serve as the centre of information processing and toward network systems that allow many users to access information at the same time. In an older system, a central computer (mainframe) performed all the tasks and sent the results to a terminal that could not perform those tasks itself. In the new **network computing system** (also called **client/server computing**), the tasks, such as searching sales records, are handled by personal computers ("clients"). The information needed to complete the tasks is stored in huge databases controlled by the "server." Networks connect people to people and people to data.[20]

The major benefits of networks are the following:

network computing system (client/server computing)
Computer systems that allow personal computers (clients) to obtain needed information from huge databases controlled by a network server.

- *Saving time and money.* SynOptics Communications found that electronic delivery of mail and files increased the speed of project development by 25 percent.

- *Providing easy links across functional boundaries.* With networks, it's easy to find someone who can offer insightful solutions to a problem. The most common questions on computer bulletin boards begin, "Does anyone know …?" Usually someone does.

- *Allowing employees to see complete information.* In traditional organizations, information is summarized so many times that it often loses its meaning. For example, a sales representative's two-page summary may be cut to a paragraph in the district manager's report and then to a few numbers on a chart in the regional manager's report. Networks, on the other hand, catch raw information.

<www.lotus.com>

Learn more about Lotus by visiting its Web site. What is *Lotusphere*?

Here's how networks helped Lotus Development. Instead of waiting for the information gained from four million annual phone calls to be summarized by technical support people, Lotus Development now sends information straight into a database, where it's available on demand. Rather than accept someone else's idea of what information is needed, any Lotus Development employee can access the data and search according to his or her needs. The result is that many more employees have direct access to market information and can act accordingly.

The move toward networks does not mean that mainframes are dead. Far from it. Using networks requires so many organizational changes that some companies (as many as a third) that try networking go back to mainframes. For the next decade or so, while organizations learn to let go of hierarchical management styles (discussed in Chapters 8, 9, and 10) and feel more comfortable entrusting employees with the power of information, the computing world will be a hybrid. PCs will take on more jobs with their speed, flexibility, and utility, while mainframes will handle the larger corporations' big jobs of storing, transferring, and processing large amounts of data.

One problem with computer networks is that technical glitches can interrupt the lines of communication. See the Spotlight on Big Business box for a remarkable story about how scientists have been able to use what they have learned about ants to improve computer network systems.

 Critical Thinking

What are the implications for world peace and world trade given the increased ability firms and government organizations now have to communicate with one another throughout the world? Could the cooperation needed among telecommunications firms worldwide lead to increased cooperation among other organizations on other issues such as world health care and worldwide exchanges of technical information?

shareware
Software that is copyrighted but distributed to potential customers free of charge.

•••• ▬▬▬ ••••

SOFTWARE

Computer software programs provide the instructions that enable you to tell the computer what to do. Although many people looking to buy a computer think first of the equipment, it is important to find the right software before finding the right hardware. Software is like a sound recording. If you want to hear a certain singer or orchestra, you buy that particular recording. The recording may be an old 78 or a new CD. The type of recording you want dictates the kind of equipment you need.

Some software programs are easier to use than others. Some are more sophisticated and can perform more functions than others. A business person must decide what functions he or she wants the computer to perform and then choose the appropriate software. That choice will help determine what brand of computer to buy and how much power it should have.

Cisco has played a leadership role in the development of many new world networks. Companies and individuals are migrating to Internet-based applications at unprecedented rates and Cisco is helping Canadians stay ahead of this change.

While most software is distributed commercially through suppliers like retail stores or mail-order houses or directly via the Internet, there is some software, called **shareware**, that is copyrighted but distributed to potential customers free of charge. The users are asked to send a specified fee to the developer if the program meets their needs and they decide to use it. The shareware concept has become very popular and has dramat-

Spotlight on Big Business

<www.bt.com>

It's Only Natural

Researchers at British Telecommunications (BT), one of the world's leading telecommunications companies, studied ant colonies, jellyfish, and slime molds. Why? They hoped that nature could help them solve one of their most critical business problems—overloaded or damaged network lines. It could take BT a decade and more than $46 billion to overhaul its phone network the traditional way. So BT asked biologists and entomologists to search the natural world for alternative solutions. "Biological organisms do complex things with very simple software, while man's unbelievably complex systems can only do very simple things," says Peter Cochrane, BT's research director. One of Cochrane's teams modelled a software program on ant colonies. The program sends out "ants," or intelligent agents, to explore alternate routes through overloaded or damaged networks. As each ant returns almost instantaneously with information on how long it takes to travel to different parts of the network, the network can reconfig-

ure itself to bypass the problem in less than a second— much faster than the several minutes it now takes to do the same task.

Where is technology headed? Cochrane envisions people and technology converging to create what he calls "homo cyberneticus." For example, we will dress in vests that will use heat from our bodies to power all the technology we will wear. Picture a visor that can project TV-like images or data directly onto the retina, allowing you to read e-mail or study a map while walking down the street. "People will be walking around online in the early twenty-first century," predicts Cochrane. He also believes that desktop boxes will disappear, replaced by more cuddly interfaces. His favourite example is a computerized robot that "looks like a kitten but doesn't bring in dead mice."

Source: Julia Flynn, "British Telecom: Notes from the Ant Colony," *Business Week*, June 23, 1997, p. 108.

---

ically reduced the price of software.[21] **Public domain software** is software that is free for the taking.

    Business people most frequently use software for six major purposes: (1) writing (word processors), (2) manipulating numbers (spreadsheets), (3) filing and retrieving data (databases), (4) presenting information visually (graphics), (5) communicating (e-mail), and (6) accounting. Today's software can perform many functions in one kind of program known as *integrated software* or *suites*. A new class of software program, called *groupware*, has emerged for use on networks. We'll explore all of these software applications next.

> **public domain software**
> Software that is free for the taking.

••• WORD-PROCESSING PROGRAMS •••

Many computer users spend most of their time using word-processing programs. The most popular of these programs can handle everything from a quick memo to a multichapter book. They can also produce designs that once could be done only by powerful page-layout design programs.

    Businesses use word processors to increase office productivity. Standardized letters can be personalized quickly, documents can be updated by changing only the outdated text and leaving the rest intact, and contract forms can be revised to meet the stipulations of specific customers.

    Desktop publishing software combines word processing with graphics capabilities. A keystroke or a click of a mouse can change the style of type, the placement of a chart, or the width of the text columns. Businesses can now publish their own professional-looking newsletters and presentations.

Of the many word-processing software packages on the market, three of the most popular are Corel WordPerfect, Microsoft Word, and WordPro.

••• SPREADSHEET PROGRAMS •••

spreadsheet program
The electronic equivalent of an accountant's worksheet, plus such features as mathematical function libraries, statistical data analysis, and charts.

A **spreadsheet program** is simply the electronic equivalent of an accountant's worksheet with such features as mathematical function libraries, statistical data analysis, and charts. A spreadsheet is a table made up of rows and columns that enables a manager to organize information. Using the computer's speedy calculations, managers have their questions answered almost as fast as they can ask them. For example, suppose we use a spreadsheet to figure the break-even point for Fiberrific cereal. The spreadsheet contains the appropriate formula for calculating the break-even point. Our calculations show that at a price of $2 a box, we must sell 2000 boxes weekly to break even. We now think we can raise our price, however, since a government study linking eating oat bran with lowering cholesterol levels has caused an increase in demand. We can ask, "What if we raise the price of Fiberiffic to $2.50?" Once we simply insert $2.50 in the price cell (a specific line or row in a specific column) the computer will tell us instantly that we must sell only 1333 boxes to break even (see Figure 11.2). Of course, this is a simple example. Businesses often develop highly complex spreadsheets, sometimes using hundreds of columns and rows. Some of the most popular spreadsheet programs are Lotus 1-2-3, Quattro Pro, and Excel.

••• DATABASE PROGRAMS •••

database program
Computer program that allows users to work with information that is normally kept in lists: names, addresses, schedules, inventories, and so forth.

A **database program** allows users to work with information that is normally kept in lists: names, addresses, schedules, inventories, and so forth. Simple commands allow you to add new information, change incorrect information, and delete out-of-date or unnecessary information. Most programs have features that let you print only certain information, arrange records in the order you want them, and change the way information is displayed. Using database programs, you can create reports that contain exactly the information you

---

FIGURE 11.2
· · · ·

HOW A SPREADSHEET PROGRAM WORKS

In this case, the question is, what would happen to the break-even point if the price of the product was raised to $2.50? You simply type $2.50 in column B row 5 and the program does the calculations. The answer is 1333 boxes weekly.

	A Weekly Fixed cost	B Price	C Unit variable cost	D Weekly Break-even point
1				
2				
3				
4	2000	2.00	1	2000
5	2000	2.50	1	1333

want in the form you want it to appear in. Leading database programs include Q&A, Access, Approach, Paradox, PFS: Professional File, PC-File, R base, and FileMaker Pro for Apple computers.

Personal information managers (PIMs), or contact managers, are specialized database programs that allow users to track communication with their business contacts. Such programs keep track of everything—every person, every phone call, every e-mail message, every appointment.[22] Some programs have planners that help you identify free blocks of time for yourself and others in your workgroup. The program Goldmine even has a feature that lets you see who's in, who's out, and how long a person has been away from his or her keyboard. Popular PIMs include Goldmine, Lotus Organizer, ACT, and ECCO Pro.

••• GRAPHICS AND PRESENTATION PROGRAMS •••

A picture is worth a thousand words. Why should we study a thousand-word report to identify the leading Fiberrific salesperson when a glance at a computer-generated bar graph can show us in an instant? Computer graphics programs can use data from spreadsheets to visually summarize information by drawing bar graphs, pie charts, line charts, and more. Do you need to change a figure or label? No need to search for the eraser, ruler, and compass. Simply insert the new data and, presto, the computer makes the changes and your new chart is ready for presentation. Would you rather have a pie chart than a bar graph? No problem—for a computer with a good graphics program.

Your software can make your presentation more appealing to the audience's senses. Inserting sound clips, video clips, clip art, and animation could turn a dull presentation into an enlightening presentation. Some popular graphics programs are Illustrator and Freehand for Macintosh computers, PowerPoint, Harvard Graphics, Lotus Freelance Graphics, Active Presenter, and Corel Draw.

••• COMMUNICATIONS PROGRAMS •••

Communications software makes it possible for different brands of computers to transfer data to each other. The software translates the data into a code known as the American Standard Code for Information Interchange (ASCII—pronounced *ask-ee*), which is the common standard all computer manufacturers have agreed to adopt. Communications programs enable a computer to exchange files with other computers, retrieve information from databases, and send and receive electronic mail. Such programs include Microsoft Outlook, ProComm Plus, Eudora, and Telik.

Message centre software is more powerful than traditional communications packages. This new generation of programs has teamed up with fax or voice modems to provide an efficient way of making certain that phone calls, e-mail, and faxes are received, sorted, and delivered on time, no matter where you are.[23] Such programs include Communicate, Message Center, and WinFax Pro.

••• ACCOUNTING AND FINANCE PROGRAMS •••

Accounting software helps users record financial transactions and generate financial reports. Some programs include online banking features that allow users to pay bills through the computer. Others include "financial advisers" that offer users advice on a variety of financial issues. Popular accounting and finance programs include Peachtree Complete Accounting, Simply Accounting, and QuickBooks Pro.

communications software
Computer programs that make it possible for different brands of computers to transfer data to each other.

message centre software
A new generation of computer programs that uses fax or voice modems to receive, sort, and deliver phone calls, e-mail, and faxes.

··· INTEGRATED PROGRAMS ···

integrated software package (suite)
A computer program that offers two or more applications in one package.

It may occur to you that loading your computer with many different software packages might become cumbersome. It may be difficult to cut or copy information generated in one program (such as a spreadsheet) and paste it into, say, a word-processing document. One solution is an **integrated software package** (also called a **suite**), which offers two or more applications in one package. With these programs, you can share information across applications easily. Most such packages include word processing, database management, spreadsheet, graphics, and communications. Suites include Microsoft Office, Lotus SmartSuite, and Corel WordPefect Suite.

··· GROUPWARE ···

groupware
Software that allows people to work collaboratively and share ideas.

As businesses moved toward networking, a new class of software called groupware has emerged. **Groupware** is software that allows people to work collaboratively and share ideas. The programs we discussed above (word processing, databases, and so on) were designed for people working alone at individual computers. Groupware runs on a network and allows people to work on the same project at the same time. Groupware also makes it possible for work teams to communicate together over time. Team members can swap leads, share client information, keep tabs on news events, and make suggestions to one another. The computer becomes a kind of team memory where every memo and idea is stored for quick retrieval at any time. Groupware programs include Lotus Notes, Frontier's Intranet Genie, Metainfo Sendmail, and Radnet Web Share.

 Progress Check

- What are the four characteristics of information that make it useful?
- How do computer networks change the way employees gather information?
- Can you list and describe the major types of computer software used in business?

EFFECTS OF INFORMATION TECHNOLOGY ON MANAGEMENT

The increase of information technology has already begun to affect management and will continue to do so. Three major issues arising out of the growing reliance on information technology are human resource changes, security threats, and privacy concerns.

··· HUMAN RESOURCE ISSUES ···

Many bureaucratic functions can be replaced by technology. We talked in Chapter 9 about tall versus flat organization structures. Computers often eliminate middle-management functions and thus flatten organization structures.

Perhaps the most revolutionary effect of computers and the increased use of the Internet and intranets is that of telecommuting. In 1997, 11.1 million U.S. employees were classified as telecommuters; by 2000 their ranks are expected to exceed 23 million.[24] The trend toward telecommuting is very pronounced in Canada, as discussed in Chapters 1 and 10. As noted, some futurists believe that in the early years of the twenty-first century, as much as 40 percent of the Canadian workforce, including employees and self-employed persons, will be working mainly at home. Using computers linked to the company's network, employees working at home can transmit their work to the office and back as easily as (and sometimes more easily than) they can walk into the boss's office.

Naturally, such work involves less travel time and fewer costs, and often increases productivity.[25] Telecommuting helps companies save money by allowing them to retain valuable employees during long pregnancy leaves or to tempt experienced employees out of retirement. Companies can also enjoy savings in commercial property costs, since having fewer employees in the office means a company can get by with smaller, and therefore less expensive, offices than before.[26] Telecommuting enables men and women to stay home with small children and is a tremendous boon for workers with disabilities.[27] Employees who can work after hours on their home computers rather than at the office report less stress and improved morale. For these and other reasons, as seen in Chapter 7, many self-employed people work at home or start their small business there. Studies show that telecommuting is most successful among people who are self-starters, who don't have home distractions, and whose work doesn't require face-to-face interaction with co-workers.

Even as telecommuting has grown in popularity, however, some telecommuters report that a consistent diet of long-distance work gives them a dislocated feeling of being left out of the office loop. Some feel a loss of the increased energy some people get through social interaction. In addition to the isolation issue is the intrusion that work brings into what is normally a personal setting. Often people working from home don't know when to turn the work off.[28] Some companies are pulling away from viewing telecommuting as an either–or proposition: either at home or at the office. Such companies are using telecommuting as a part-time alternative. Industry now defines telecommuting as working at home a minimum of two days a week.

Electronic communication can never replace human communication for creating enthusiasm and esprit de corps. Efficiency and productivity can become so important to a firm that people are treated like robots. In the long run, such treatment results in less efficiency and productivity. Computers are a tool, not a total replacement for managers or workers, and creativity is still a human trait. Computers should aid creativity by giving people more freedom and more time. Figure 11.3 illustrates how information technology changes the way managers and workers interact.

MANAGERS MUST	EMPLOYEES MUST
• Instill commitment in subordinates rather than rule by command and control.	• Become initiators, able to act without management direction.
• Become coaches, training workers in necessary job skills, making sure they have resources to accomplish goals, and explaining links between a job and what happens elsewhere in the company.	• Become financially literate so they can understand the business implications of what they do and changes they suggest.
• Give greater authority to workers over scheduling, priority setting, and even compensation.	• Learn group interaction skills, including how to resolve disputes within their work group and how to work with other functions across the company.
• Use new information technologies to measure workers' performance, possibly based on customer satisfaction or the accomplishment of specific goals.	• Develop new math, technical, and analytical skills to use newly available information on their jobs.

FIGURE **11.3**

· · · ·

WHEN INFORMATION TECHNOLOGY ALTERS THE WORKPLACE

Spotlight on Small Business

<www.ernie.ey.com>
<www.retailadvz.com>

Dear Ernie: Online Advice for Small Businesses

Many entrepreneurs can't afford to hire consultants to help them set up their new businesses and they don't have time to search for answers to all their questions. Some of them turn to virtual consultants such as David Wing at the Retail Business Resource Center, an online consulting service specializing in small retail and service companies.

Susie Sherman turned to Wing when she decided to start her own office-design business. For $75 a month she communicates with him via e-mail, getting answers within 72 hours—usually sooner. She can either chat with him online in real time or attend a group chat for clients. Wing helped Sherman focus her business plan and taught her how to market her service. He also provided moral support during her business's fragile infancy.

Lee Penn, vice-president of finance at the SLAM Collaborative, an architectural engineering and design firm, turns to another virtual answer man—Ernie, the folksy name for Ernst & Young's online consulting service. Penn finds that Ernie answers his questions more easily and quickly than the legions of people he once had to search out when he worked at Xerox. Ernie charges a flat $6000 annual fee for providing a worldwide network of experts to answer business questions related to human resources, real estate, taxes, and infor-

mation technology. Clients e-mail their questions to Ernie and they are filtered down and passed along through the company's intranet to the appropriate Ernst & Young expert. Answers arrive within 48 hours. When SLAM needed to hire information technicians, Penn needed to know an appropriate pay scale to offer. Instead of buying a salary book for another industry for hundreds of dollars, Penn asked Ernie and quickly received the compensation ranges in his region for that job category.

In addition to providing clients affordable consulting, Ernie also benefits the Ernst & Young experts by keeping them in tune with what their market segment is thinking about. Over time, they will be able to identify trends by industry segment and job function more clearly. Brian Baum, director of Internet service delivery at Ernst & Young, considers Ernie the natural extension of a worldwide business. He says, "it's really using the platform, the medium, in the most efficient manner. It's applicable to many industries in terms of creating a connected environment."

Source: Robin D. Schatz, "Smaller Businesses Can Turn to Virtual Advisors for Help," *The Wall Street Journal Interactive Edition*, February 20, 1997; "Small Business Web Sites: Getting Down to Business," *PC Magazine*, January 6, 1998, p. 40.

Information technology also changes the way that small-business owners can access management advice. Read the Spotlight on Small Business box to learn more about how business people who are on the move can benefit from some new information technology.

<fullcoverage.
yahoo.com>

This Yahoo Web site provides access to many current newspaper articles on the issue of hackers and crackers. Try clicking on *Tech* and then on *Hackers*.

••• SECURITY ISSUES •••

One current problem with computers that is likely to persist in the future is that they are susceptible to *hackers*, or people who break into computer systems for illegal purposes such as transferring funds from someone's bank account to their own without authorization. In 1994 officials were unable to find the hackers who broke into Pentagon computers through the Internet and stole, altered, and erased numerous records. Ironically, one of the Pentagon systems the hackers gained access to was that of computer security research.

Computer security is more complicated today than ever before. When information was processed in a mainframe environment, the single data centre was easier to control since there was limited access to it. Today, however,

Reaching Beyond Our Borders

<insight.cas.mcmaster.ca/org/efc>

Does the Internet Need Taming?

During the 1990s, a decade that saw an explosion in the practical use of significant technological wonders from powerful computers and cell phones to fibre optics and fast modems, there was no disputing the rise of the Internet as perhaps the major revolutionary tool for communication and business transactions. All forecasts point to exponential growth of e-commerce, e-stock and bond trading, and e-mail. Forecasts mention more than a trillion dollars of business and half a billion people on the Internet by 2000. Obviously, the Internet is having an enormous impact on the way business is done. Unfortunately, all of this activity also includes a number of undesirable and problematic transactions and communications.

At least five types of problems have been identified: viruses, invasion of privacy, theft of information, profusion of child and other pornography, and many scams to defraud innocent people. All of these come in a variety of forms and have received a lot of publicity. You

may have experienced some of these problems or you may know someone or some business that was the object of these activities. Many voices have been raised urging governments to do something to regulate the Internet and restrict or eliminate such activities, just as many voices are opposed to government regulation of this totally free and unrestricted international medium of communication. Not that government regulation of this global monster is that easy, technically. It is obviously undesirable to have international regulatory systems that restrict the important benefits that the Internet yields to individuals and companies.

These are problems that will not go away unless something is done about them. The international aspect of the Internet makes solutions much more complicated. In the meantime we struggle to live with them. Every technological advance whether telephone, automobile, or airplane has brought benefits and problems. The Internet is certainly no exception.

---

computers are accessible not only in all areas within the company but also in all areas of other companies with which the firm does business.

Another security issue involves the spread of computer viruses over the Internet. A **virus** is a piece of programming code inserted into other programming to cause some unexpected and, for the victim, usually undesirable event. Viruses are spread by downloading infected programming or e-mail over the Internet or by sharing an infected diskette. Often the source of the file you downloaded is unaware of the virus. The virus lies dormant until circumstances cause its code to be executed by the computer. Some viruses are playful ("Kilroy was here!"), but some can be quite harmful, erasing data or causing your hard drive to crash. There are software programs, such as McAfee Antivirus Scan or Norton's AntiVirus, that inoculate your computer so that it doesn't catch a known virus. However, new viruses are being developed constantly so that antivirus programs may have only limited success. Therefore, you should keep your antivirus protection program up to date and, more important, practise safe computing by not downloading files from unknown sources and by using your antivirus program to scan diskettes before transferring files from them.

Existing laws do not address the problems of today's direct, real-time communication. As more and more people merge onto the information superhighway, the number of legal issues will likely increase. Already copyright and pornography laws are crashing into the virtual world. Other legal questions—such as those involving intellectual property and contract disputes, online

virus
A piece of programming code inserted into other programming to cause some unexpected and, for the victim, usually undesirable event.

<www.mcafee.com>

Cyberspace is as loaded with antivirus companies, as it is with viruses! Check out the McAfee Web site and click on *Antivirus Centre* to see some examples.

sexual and racial harassment, and the use of electronic communication to promote crooked sales schemes—are being raised as millions of people log on to the Internet.[29]

••• PRIVACY ISSUES •••

<fullcoverage.
yahoo.com>

Revisit the Yahoo Web site, click on *Tech* and then click on *Internet Privacy* to access current articles on this topic.

Major concerns about privacy are created by the increase of technology, particularly the Internet, as more and more personal information is stored in computers and people are able to access that data, legally or illegally. The Internet allows Web surfers to access all sorts of information about you. For example, some Web sites allow people to search for vehicle ownership from a licence number or to find individuals' real estate property records. One key question in the debate over protecting our privacy is, "Isn't this personal information already public anyway?" Civil libertarians have long fought to keep certain kinds of information available to the public. If access to such data is restricted on the Internet, wouldn't we have to reevaluate our policies on public records entirely? The privacy advocates don't think so. After all, the difference is that the Net makes obtaining personal information just too easy.[30] Would your neighbours or friends even consider going to the appropriate local agency and sorting through public records for hours to find out whether you've ever been arrested for drunk driving or to see your divorce settlement? Probably not. But they might if it is as simple as a few clicks of a button.

cookies
Pieces of information, such as registration data or user preferences, sent by a Web site over the Internet to a Web browser that the browser software is expected to save and send back to the server whenever the user returns to that Web site.

Average PC users are concerned that Web sites have gotten downright nosy. Some Web servers do secretly track users' movements online. Web surfers seem willing to swap personal details for free access to online information. This personal information is shared with others without your permission. Web sites often send **cookies** to your computer that stay on your hard drive. These little tidbits often simply contain your name and a password that the Web site recognizes the next time you visit the site so that you don't have to reenter the same information every time you visit. Other cookies track your movements around the Web and then blend that information with a database so that a company can tailor the ads you receive accordingly.[31] Do you mind someone watching over your shoulder while you're on the Web? Tim Berners-Lee, the researcher who invented the World Wide Web, is working on a way to prevent you from receiving cookies without your permission. His Platform for Privacy Preferences, or P3, would allow a Web site to automatically send information on its privacy policies. You would be able to set up your Web browser to communicate only with those Web sites that meet certain criteria.[32] You need to decide how much information about yourself you are willing to give away. Remember, we are living in an information economy, and information is a commodity. The Reaching Beyond Our Borders box on the previous page takes a closer look at the potential of government regulation to protect online privacy and to take care of other problems.

•••• ▬▬▬ ••••

TECHNOLOGY AND YOUR CAREER

If you are beginning to think that being computer illiterate may be occupational suicide, you are getting the point. Workers in every industry come in contact with computers to some degree. Even burger flippers in fastfood chains read orders on computer screens. Nearly 80 percent of the respondents to a 1997 survey said that they believe it is impossible to succeed in the job market without a working knowledge of technology. Respondents who earned $45,000 a year or more were three times more likely to use a computer than those who earned less. More than 80 percent of the women surveyed said that computer proficiency was a key to their entry into traditionally male-dominated fields.[33]

In Canada there is a continuing and severe shortage of skilled software developers and technicians. At the end of Chapter 1 you saw that the Software Human Resources Council in Ottawa states that 20,000 jobs cannot be filled for lack of computer-skilled applicants. Further, with Canada's large and reputable software industry growing by 25 to 30 percent annually, the need for these skills is ever more urgent. Well-paying, challenging, and stimulating jobs are going unfilled, forcing companies to scour the world looking for suitable employees. Figure 11.4 illustrates the effects of information technology on careers in the U.S.

If you are still among those considered computer illiterate, you are not alone. Researchers who have studied computerphobia (fear of computers), find that 55 percent of Americans have the disorder.[34] Amazingly, half of all white-collar workers say they are afraid of trying new technologies. Gender, age, and income level don't appear to lead to computerphobia. The key variable is exposure. That's why Nintendo era kids take to computers so easily.[35] Computerphobes do not do as well in school as their mouse-clicking classmates. They may get passed up for promotions or lose their jobs. On a psychological level, they often feel inadequate and outdated—sort of like technological outcasts in a digitized world. Here's the good news: computerphobia is curable, and computer training, the best medicine, is readily available. You may want to start out with low-tech learning aids such as videos and computer books and then gradually move up to training classes or CD-ROMs.

As information technology eliminates old jobs while creating new ones, it is up to you to learn the skills you need to be certain you aren't left behind.

A bachelor's degree may not be enough to guarantee anyone meaningful employment unless it's accompanied by high-tech skills. Universities, colleges, and private institutions are providing certificate programs designed to fill the high demand for technology skills.

FIGURE 11.4

. . . .

WINNERS AND LOSERS IN THE U.S. RACE DOWN THE INFORMATION HIGHWAY

As the information highway accelerates its evolution, many workers are forced from their obsolete jobs while others find higher-paying jobs.

Technological change and office automation will shrink these jobs . . .

PERCENT EMPLOYMENT CHANGE, 1992–2005	
Computer operators	–39%
Billing, posting, and calculating machine operators	–29%
Telephone operators	–28%
Typists and word processors	–16%
Bank tellers	–4%

Data: Bureau of Labor Statistics.

. . . but technology also generates new openings in the info-tech world.

FIVE FASTEST-GROWING OCCUPATIONS REQUIRING A COLLEGE DEGREE, 1992–2005	
Computer engineers and scientists	112%
Systems analysts	110%
Physical therapists	88%
Special education teachers	74%
Operations research analysts	61%

Data: Bureau of Labor Statistics.

Ethical Dilemma

REVIEW

Recall the question about illegal software copying from the beginning of the chapter. Here's what our executives have to say. Bédard has this comment: "Unfortunately, small businesses rarely have established policies that employees can refer to. Certain practices are tolerated in smaller business that would not be tolerated in more established companies. It is, of course, very difficult to control what employees do when a supervisor or owner is not present. Since it is illegal to copy software, I would recommend having a consistent approach toward honesty. Employees should be informed that this practice is not tolerated by the company. This would send a message that the owner expects his employees to act in a proper fashion in all their dealings."

Reilley has a similar opinion: "No, I would neither do it myself nor encourage my employees to do so. The obvious advantages of not copying software are virus-free and upgradeable software. Copying software is not only an illegal activity, but will contribute to a culture of corporate dishonesty, which can affect a business in many ways.

"For example, an employee might use the same justification ('it's of no consequence') to pilfer company assets, which, of course, would cut into profits. A dishonest mindset could very easily lead to all manner of customer and legal abuses. Dishonest practices will spread across a business and, no matter how seemingly trivial, cannot be tolerated in a serious business venture. Once started they are very, very difficult to stop."

Progress Check

- How has information technology changed the way people work?
- What management issues have been affected by the growth of information technology?
- What careers are losing jobs as information technology expands? What careers are gaining jobs?

SUMMARY

1. Outline the changing role of business technology.

1. Business technology is continually changing names and changing roles.

   • ***What are the various names and roles of business technology since 1970?***
   In the 1970s business technology was called *data processing (DP)* and its role was to support existing business. In the 1980s its name became *information systems (IS)* and its role changed to doing business. By the 1990s business technology became *information technology (IT)* and its role is now to change business.

   • ***How does information technology change business?***
   Information technology has minimized the importance of time and place to business. Business that is independent of time and location can deliver products and services whenever and wherever it is convenient for the customer. See Figure 11.1 for examples of how information technology changes business.

   • ***What is knowledge technology?***
   Knowledge technology adds a layer of intelligence to filter appropriate information and deliver it when it is needed.

2. To become knowledge-based, businesses must know how to share information and design systems for creating new knowledge.
   - *What information technology is available to help businesses manage information?*

   The heart of information technology involves the Internet, intranets, and extranets. The Internet is a massive network of thousands of smaller networks open to everyone with a computer and a modem. An intranet is a companywide network protected from unauthorized entry by outsiders. An extranet is a semiprivate network that allows more than one company to access the same information.

   2. Compare the scope of the Internet, intranets, and extranets as tools for managing information.

3. Information technology multiplies the mountains of information available to business people.
   - *How can you deal with information overload?*

   The most important step in dealing with information overload is to identify your four or five key goals. Eliminate information that will not help you meet your key goals.

   - *What makes information useful?*

   The usefulness of management information depends on four characteristics: quality, completeness, timeliness, and relevance.

   3. List the steps in managing information, and identify the characteristics of useful information.

4. Computer hardware changes rapidly.
   - *What was the most dynamic change in computer hardware in the 1990s?*

   Perhaps the most dynamic change was the move away from mainframe computers that serve as the centre of information processing toward network systems that allow many users to access information at the same time.

   - *What are the major benefits of networks?*

   Networks' major benefits are: (1) saving time and money, (2) providing easy links across functional boundaries, and (3) allowing employees to see complete information.

   4. Review the hardware most frequently used in business, and outline the benefits of the move toward computer networks.

5. Computer software provides the instructions that enable you to tell the computer what to do.
   - *What types of software programs are used by managers most frequently?*

   Managers most often use word-processing, electronic spreadsheet, database, communication, and accounting programs. A new class of software program, called groupware, allows people to work collaboratively and share ideas.

   5. Classify the computer software most frequently used in business.

6. Information technology has a tremendous effect on the way we do business.
   - *What effect has information technology had on business management?*

   Computers eliminate some middle management functions and thus flatten organization structures. Computers also allow workers to work from their own homes. On the negative side, computers sometimes allow information to fall into the wrong hands. Managers must find ways to prevent stealing by hackers. Concern for privacy is another issue affected by the vast store of information available on the Internet. Finding the balance between freedom to access private information and individuals' right to privacy will require continued debate.

   6. Evaluate the human resource, security, and privacy issues in management that are affected by information technology.

7. Identify the careers that are gaining or losing workers because of the growth of information technology.

7. Information technology eliminates old jobs while creating new ones.
   • ***Which careers are gaining and losing workers because of the growth of information technology?***
   Computer operators and word processors are among the shrinking jobs. As more employees can and do access information themselves, they no longer need others to do it for them. Computer engineers and systems analysts are in demand. See Figure 11.4 for other employment changes caused by the growth of information technology.

KEY TERMS
· · · · ·

communications software 345
cookies 350
data processing (DP) 334
database program 344
extranet 337
groupware 346
information systems (IS) 334

information technology (IT) 334
integrated software package (suite) 346
Internet 2 338
intranet 337
knowledge technology (KT) 336
message centre software 345

network computing system (client/server computing) 341
public domain software 343
push technology 340
shareware 342
spreadsheet program 344
virtualization 335
virus 349

DEVELOPING WORKPLACE SKILLS

1. Imagine that a rich relative has given you $3000 to buy a computer system to use for school. Research the latest in hardware and software in computer magazines and then go to a computer store to try out alternatives. Make a list of what you intend to buy and then write a summary explaining the reasons for your choices.

2. Interview someone who bought a computer system to use in his or her business. Ask that person about any problems that occurred in deciding what to buy or in installing and using the system. What would he or she do differently next time? What software does he or she find especially useful?

3. Imagine that you are a purchasing manager for a large computer store near your campus. Design a two-page research survey to determine what software and hardware features students at the school need. (See Chapter 15 for some tips on research.) Discuss your research questions and survey implementation strategy with the class.

4. Choose a topic that interests you and then, on the Internet, use two search engines to find information about the topic. If the initial result of your search is a list of thousands of sites, narrow your search using the tips offered by the search engine. Did both search engines find the same Web sites? If not, how were the sites different? Which engine found the most appropriate information?

5. Computers abound on most college campuses. Where are they and what are they used for on your campus? Use a computer graphics program to create a chart that illustrates the types of software used for various activities. For example, the library may record book checkouts and circulation using a database program. In addition to the library, consider computer use in the student records office, food services, athletic department, business school, alumni office, and business office.

1. One of the big problems with information on the Internet is that anyone can put out anything they want. Without some careful verification, there is no way of knowing how accurate or reliable that information is. To test the value of some Internet information, using a search engine, pick a topic you are interested in, and try to find out how reliable the information you gather from various Web sites is. When picking a topic, make it as specific as possible. For example, do not select *sports* as a topic—it is too general. Better to say *professional hockey* or some other sport you are interested in. Use the following criteria for your evaluation:

   A. *Accuracy.* Is there any information that you personally know is incorrect? Check with people in your college to see if they can spot inaccuracies or errors.
   B. *Authority.* Who are the individuals or groups who created this site? What is their expertise of authority in this field? Have they created any other sites and what reputation do they have?
   C. *Objectivity.* Does the information seem to be intended to sway readers or does it seem to be purely factual? Is there any apparent bias?
   D. *Currency.* How recent is the data? When was the site last updated?
   E. *Coverage.* Does the topic seem to be explored in depth? Does the coverage include reference to various sources? Does it show that there are opposing points of view? Does it have links to other sites that add to the information?
   F. *Technical.* Try any links to see if they are accessible. Is the information they yield current and relevant?

2. Check out the Web site of the Information Technology Association of Canada <www.itac.ca> and follow some of the links to see some current concerns of the association. Is there any progress on some of the problems discussed in the chapter? Are there any new issues being raised? Make a print-out and bring it to class for discussion.

Practising Management Decisions

CASE 1

THE SUPER BOWL OF NETWORKS

Couch potatoes may think of the kick-off of the football season as the time to relax and settle in until Super Bowl Sunday, but for the NFL's information technology's networking groups it's the start of a frantic work marathon that won't stop until the championship rings are engraved. Imagine keeping 30 teams connected to the NFL's New York headquarters not only during game time but also at off-site summer training camps, at the annual owners' meeting, and during draft announcements. And, of course, during the event of the year, on Super Bowl Sunday, last-minute venue changes and different networking configurations present ample opportunities to fumble.

The networking team must create quick-turn networks that are used for a limited amount of time and then quickly dismantled. In just one month in 1996, the NFL wired more than 3000 national and international media people, installed 20 miles of telephone cable, set up 800 phone lines and 600 cell phone lines, and created a 140-node network in New Orleans. To make sure that no one drops the ball, the NFL has teamed up with Sprint to create a best-practices playbook for creating quick-turn networks. Having a game plan is definitely worth the effort since the NFL has to do this on a regular basis, according to Craig Johnson, a research analyst at CurrentAnaylsis Inc.

Every year since its creation in 1993, the Carolina Panthers team has built a network at the team's training camp at Wofford College in Spartanburg, South Carolina, connecting it to the team's headquarters in Charlotte. The network designers use encryption to ensure security. Coaches and team managers in the field can use the network to reach key databases at headquarters to access information such as player statistics or salary figures. Even though the networking team has a system for the physical setup and breakdown of the network, it must still go through planning exercises each year because of constant changes in software and networking hardware. That means the network's performance must be reevaluated every year.

The most important lesson the NFL/Sprint team has learned is to be prepared. Even the best plans can change unexpectedly. For example, just five days before the NFL's highly publicized annual draft announcements, the location was moved from Detroit to Philadelphia. The networking team put a local telecommunications provider in the new locale on alert for establishing a connection in time for the broadcast. You can't plan for everything, so you have to be prepared to move quickly. It's probably safe to say that the venue for the next Super Bowl won't change. But even if it did, the NFL/Sprint networking team will make certain that couch potatoes all over the world aren't denied.

Decision Questions

1. Most businesses don't normally need to create networks quickly, but occasionally it is necessary. Give some examples of situations in which such quick-turn networks might be used.

2. Of course, the NFL doesn't allow general Internet access to its complete network, but you can check out the NFL's Web site <www.nfl.com> to get an idea of the kinds of statistics available. What additional kinds of information do you think the NFL manages? As the general manager of an NFL team, how could you use the NFL network in negotiating your players' contracts for the coming year?

3. As the NFL expands its coverage globally, will its quick-turn networks be of value in locations such as London, Tokyo, and Moscow?

Sources: Aileen Crowley, "Playbook Calls for On-the-Fly Networks," *PC Week*, September 15, 1997, p. 99; Bob Wallace, "LAN Blitz Sharpens Panthers' Claws," *Computer World*, September 29, 1997, p. 53.

CASE 2
• • • • •
TAKING IN THE SITES
• • • • •

The World Wide Web is a fast-flowing river of information. Internet surfers have found that navigating the Web takes them to a wide range of sites, from homemade personal sites to multimedia corporate sites. Why are businesses willing to invest $200,000 to $1 million to create an impressive Web site? Some want to bolster their corporate image; others want to sell their products online.

How companies choose to reach out and hold their audiences' attention depends on what they intend their sites to accomplish. Some Web sites function as general promotion and brand identity tools. For example, General Mills doesn't use its Web site to sell Betty Crocker cake mix, rather it uses the site to present menu plans and household tips. The goal is to link the brand's image with the information the Web site provides.

Another function of some business Web sites is to conduct online business (sometimes called online commerce, e-commerce, or transactional sites). For example, you can book airline tickets, buy a computer on the Gateway 2000, Dell, and Micron sites, or buy stock from many stockbrokers.

Unlike e-commerce sites, some broad-based corporate sites don't sell —they give things away. The aim of these sites is to give surfers easy access to huge banks of free information—particularly information about the companies' products. Microsoft is most likely the largest broad-based corporate site on the Web. The information about Microsoft products is so vast that the site changes about eight times a day as new information is added. Web designers have found that the better the Web site's organization, the more faith visitors have in the site's information and in the company. Corporate Web sites might contain information found in a brochure: description of products, phone numbers, addresses, e-mail address, and so forth. They can also contain information that might be found in an annual report: shareholder information, corporate mission statements, company history, and press releases.

How companies use the Web, then, depends on the type of company and on what the company wants their Web site to accomplish. One thing is certain, though: communication remains the main function of this new medium. People want answers to their questions and the Web can be the most efficient way to get them.

Discussion Questions

1. How could your college or university use a Web site to improve its services to students and the community?

2. The purpose of online commerce Web sites is to sell the company's products online. Do you feel comfortable buying online? What are the advantages and disadvantages of online commerce?

3. Suppose you were to design a Web site for our hypothetical product, Fiberiffic. Which of the Web site functions described in this case would you choose (general promotion/brand identity, online business, or broad-based corporate site)? Describe your proposed Web site. What content would you include? Justify using funds to develop this Web site rather than on more traditional promotional and sales tools.

Part 4

Management of Human Resources

Motivating Employees and Building Self-Managed Teams

Chapter

12

LEARNING GOALS

After you have read and studied this chapter, you should be able to

1 explain Taylor's scientific management.

2 describe the Hawthorne studies, and relate their significance to human-based management.

3 identify the levels of Maslow's hierarchy of needs, and relate their importance to employee motivation.

4 differentiate among Theory X, Theory Y, and Theory Z.

5 distinguish between motivators and hygiene factors identified by Herzberg.

6 explain how job enrichment affects employee motivation and performance.

7 identify the steps involved in implementing a management by objectives (MBO) program.

8 explain the key factors involved in expectancy theory.

9 examine the key principles of equity theory.

Thousands of books and articles have been written about how to motivate a workforce. Not surprisingly, there are many conflicting points of view. In the old days, when you wanted to *encourage* your donkey to move, you could either whack its rear with a stick or dangle a carrot in front of its nose. This was called the *carrot or stick* approach. Something similar holds in the field of motivation theory.

According to Tanja Parsley, vice-president of the consulting firm Outcomes, you cannot use the carrot method (reward system) if your employees work in an atmosphere in which the stick has created fear and victimization attitudes. Change the attitudes, realign the company, and then the carrot will work. Rewards will then lead to attitudinal shifts that will lead to changes in behaviour. That results in a better-motivated workforce.

The precise opposite is argued by Stephen Frey of the United States: If you change the behaviour, you will get a change in attitudes. He is the joint owner of Cin-Made Corporation, a small Cincinnati manufacturer of mailing tubes. After a couple of years of hard struggle with his employees and their union, he finally won them over to a full participatory-style management and a generous profit-sharing scheme. Now they are highly motivated and play a very active role in running the company. Frey said that the employees' attitudes did not change until they tried the new system. That is why he maintains that changed behaviour leads to changes in attitudes and not the other way around.

PROFILE

Choice of Motivational Tools: The Carrot or the Stick

Dr. David Weiss

Author Dr. David Weiss, a partner in the Toronto-based consulting firm Geller, Shedletsky & Weiss, in his book *High-Impact HR* believes that managers must take a flexible approach to motivating their employees and teams. For Weiss, flexibility has two important aspects. First, select the positive motivators that fit the needs of the particular employee. Second, if your positive motivators do not seem to be working, do not simply do more of the same. Think rather of targeting and removing the negative motivators (or *noise* as Weiss calls it) in the work environment that are holding back your employees. As you will see in this chapter, people are not all cut from the same cloth and their needs change over time.

Peter Drucker, probably the most respected management theorist in the world, who has been writing books on the subject for 60 years, presents a different twist on the topic of motivation. In his latest book, *Management Challenges for the Twenty-First Century*, he stresses that the majority of workers are now knowledge workers not manual workers and, therefore, a new approach to motivating them is required. In the new economy employees need autonomy and continual innovation and learning, which should be built into the job.

Sources: Harvey Schachter, "Drucker's Take on Management This Century," *Globe and Mail*, May 26, 1999, p. MI; "A Vision of HR as a Business Within a Business," *Globe and Mail*, May 31, 1999, p. C4; interview with David Weiss, August 26, 1999; Dr. David S. Weiss, *High Impact HR: Transforming Human Resources for Competitive Advantages* (New York: John Wiley & Sons, 1999). Laura Ramsay, "Why Carrot Beats Stick as a Motivational Tool," *Financial Post*, September 18, 1993, p. S30; Robert Frey, "Empowerment or Else," *Harvard Business Review*, September–October 1993, pp. 80–94.

Ethical Dilemma

TEMPTING—BUT IS IT ETHICAL?

As you go through the chapter you will learn how important it is to have a well-motivated workforce. One of the questions that arises is, how far should you go as a manager when attempting to improve employees' motivation? Suppose you are a manager of a department in a large retail store and during the Christmas busy season you always hire temporary help. This year you are having difficulty getting good temp help. Somebody suggests that you should tell the better prospects that the jobs will be permanent, which may entice them to come on board. How ethical is this? Give this some thought as you study motivation in the chapter. We will try to come to grips with this issue at the end of the chapter.

<www.druckerarchives. org>

Peter Drucker is one of the most prolific and most prestigious contemporary writers on business management. Visit this Web site to see his biography and a list of his publications.

intrinsic reward
The good feeling you have when you have done a job well.

extrinsic reward
Something given to you by someone else as recognition for good work; extrinsic rewards include pay increases, praise, and promotions.

THE IMPORTANCE OF MOTIVATION

No matter where you end up being a leader—in school, business, sports, the military—the key to your success will be whether you can motivate others to improve their performance. That is no easy job today when so many people feel bored and uninterested in their work. Yet people are willing to work hard *if* they feel that their work is appreciated and makes a difference. People are motivated by a variety of things, such as recognition, accomplishment, and status. **Intrinsic reward** is the good feeling you have when you have done a job well. An **extrinsic reward** is something given to you by someone else as recognition for good work. Such things as pay increases, praise, and promotions are examples of extrinsic rewards. Although ultimately motivation—the drive to satisfy a need—comes from within an individual, there are ways to stimulate people that bring out the natural drive to do a good job.

One purpose of this chapter is to acquaint you with the concepts, theories, and practice of motivation. The most important person to motivate, of course, is yourself. One way to do that is to find the right job in the right organization, one that enables you to reach your goals in life. Another purpose of this book is to help you in that search and to teach you how to succeed once you get there. One secret of success is to recognize that everyone else is on a similar search. Naturally, some are more committed than others. The job of a manager is to find that commitment, encourage it, and focus it on some common goal.

Why is motivation so important that we devote a whole chapter to this topic? All organizations know that a motivated workforce is much more productive than an unmotivated one. You can easily see this when a baseball, hockey, or football team loses its will to win. The coach will give the players a pep talk to motivate them to win, and the manager will try various other strategies to remotivate them. Same team, same salaries: motivated, they produce; unmotivated, their performance slides. Of course, as the Profile shows, there is some disagreement as to the best way to motivate employees.

Earlier we saw how all companies are striving to increase productivity to be competitive in the tough global environment. Motivation is the key to releasing employee power. You have already seen such key words as *employee empowerment, teamwork, participative management, wide span of control,* and *decentralized decision making.* All these aim to motivate employees to do much more than they have ever done before.

This style of management and leadership is growing rapidly. It is illustrated in this book in many of the profiles, spotlight boxes, and cases about successful companies. You will see such companies in this chapter as well.

Motivation has become even more important as companies have reduced the size of their workforces during the massive restructuring process of the past few years. Fewer employees means more responsibility for each. Every one of them must become a self-starter and use lots of initiative.

This chapter will begin with a look at some of the traditional theories of motivation. You will learn about the Hawthorne studies because they created a whole new interest in worker satisfaction and motivation. Then you will look at some assumptions about employees: Are they basically lazy, or willing to work if given the proper incentives? You will read about the traditional theorists. You will see their names repeatedly in business literature: Mayo, Herzberg, Taylor, Maslow, and McGregor. Finally, we will look at the modern applications of these theories and the managerial procedures for implementing them.

Even the best athletes sometimes need help getting and staying motivated. Coaches use a variety of techniques to keep athletes in top form. Here, champion figure skater Elvis Stojko is shown receiving the Canadian male athlete of the year award.

•••• ▬▬▬ ••••

EARLY MANAGEMENT STUDIES—TAYLOR

Several books on management in the nineteenth century presented management principles. For example, Charles Babbage (1792–1871) designed a mechanical computer and wrote a book on how to manage a manufacturing firm.[1] However, Frederick Taylor earned the title "father of scientific management" because of his book *Principles of Scientific Management*, which was published in 1911. Taylor's goal was to increase worker productivity so that both the firm and the worker could benefit from higher earnings. The way to improve productivity, Taylor thought, was to study it scientifically. **Scientific management** thus became the study of workers to find the most efficient ways of doing things and then teaching people those techniques. Three elements were basic to Taylor's approach: time, methods, and rules of work. His most important tools were observation and the stopwatch. It's Taylor's ideas that today determine how many burgers McDonald's expects its flippers to flip and how many callers the phone companies expect operators to assist.[2]

A classic Taylor story involves his study of men shovelling rice, coal, and iron ore with the same shovel. Taylor felt that different materials called for different shovels. He proceeded to invent a wide variety of sizes and shapes of shovels and with stopwatch in hand, measured output over time in what were called **time–motion studies**: studies of the tasks performed to complete a job and the time needed to do each task. Sure enough, an average person could shovel more (an increase from 25 tonnes to 35 tonnes per day) with the proper shovel using the most efficient motions. This finding led to time–motion studies of virtually every factory job. The most efficient ways of doing things were determined and these became the standards for measuring efficiency of performance.

Taylor's scientific management became the dominant strategy for improving productivity in the early 1900s. There were hundreds of time–motion

scientific management
The study of workers to find the most efficient way of doing things and then teaching people those techniques.

time–motion studies
Studies of the tasks performed to complete a job and the time needed to do each task.

This Web site provides
information about the
Gilbreths and their work. It
focuses primary attention
on Lillian Gilbreth, calling
her *The Mother of Modern
Management.* An amazing
achievement; she was also
the mother of 12 children!

**principle of
motion economy**

Theory that every job can be
broken down into a series of
elementary motions.

specialists in plants everywhere. One follower of Taylor was H. L. Gantt. He
developed charts on which managers plotted the work of employees down to
the smallest detail a day in advance (see previous chapter). Frank and Lillian
Gilbreth used Taylor's ideas in a three-year study of bricklaying. They developed the **principle of motion economy**, which showed that every job could
be broken down into a series of elementary motions called *therbligs*—a slight
variation of Gilbreth spelled backward. They then analyzed each motion to
make it more efficient.

Scientific management viewed people largely as machines that needed to be
properly programmed. There was little concern for the psychological or human
aspects of work. Taylor felt simply that workers would perform at a high level
of effectiveness (that is, be motivated) if they received high enough pay.

As mentioned earlier, some of Taylor's ideas are still being implemented.
Management guru Peter Drucker even calls Taylor's ideas "the most lasting
contribution America has made to Western thought since *The Federalist
Papers*.[3] Some companies still place more emphasis on conformity to work
rules than on creativity, flexibility, and responsiveness. For example, United
Parcel Service (UPS) tells drivers how fast to walk (three feet per second), how
many packages to pick up and deliver a day (average of 400), and how to hold
their keys (teeth up, third finger). Drivers even wear ring scanners, electronic
devices on their index fingers wired to a small computer on their wrists that
shoot a pattern of photons at a barcode on a package to let a customer know
exactly where his or her package is at any given moment.[4] Nonetheless, the
benefits of relying on workers to come up with creative solutions to productivity problems have long been recognized.

Critical Thinking

We live in a time when human rights are an important part of our legal system
and our cultural and social standards. This awareness has had a significant
impact on the workplace because employers must pay attention to regulations
and attitudes concerning employees' working conditions. In this regard, can
you see any ethical question arising out of the rigid application of *Taylorism* as
exemplified in the cases of UPS and the fastfood chain mentioned previously?

<westrek.hypermart.net>

This site has descriptions
of the work of Mayo,
Herzberg, McGregor,
Taylor, and the other
key contributors to the
understanding of human
motivation in a manage-
ment context.

•••• ▬▬ ••••

THE HAWTHORNE STUDIES—MAYO

One of the studies that grew out of Taylor's research was conducted at the
Western Electric Co.'s Hawthorne plant in Cicero, Illinois. The study began in
1927 and ended six years later. The study became famous in management literature as one of the early major studies in productivity.

Elton Mayo and colleagues from Harvard University set out to test the
degree of lighting associated with optimum productivity. In this respect, the
study was a forerunner of the traditional scientific management study: keep
records of productivity performance, varying one factor affecting employees'
working conditions.

The idea was to keep records of the workers' productivity under different
levels of illumination. But the initial experiments revealed a problem: The productivity of the experimental group compared to that of other workers doing
the same job went up regardless of whether the lighting was bright or dim.
This was true even when the lighting was reduced to about the level of moon-
light. These results confused and frustrated the researchers, who had expected
productivity to fall as the lighting was dimmed.

The Hawthorne plant is a classic in the study of motivation. It was at the Hawthorne plant that Elton Mayo and his research team from Harvard University developed human-based motivational theory. Before the studies at Hawthorne, workers were often programmed to behave like human robots.

A second series of experiments was conducted with similar results. The experiments were considered a total failure at this point. No matter what the experimenters did, productivity went up. What was causing the increase?

In the end, Mayo assumed that some human or psychological factor was involved. He and his colleagues then interviewed the workers, asking them about their feelings and attitudes toward the experiment. The researchers' findings began a profound change in management thinking that continues today. Here is what they concluded:

- The workers in the test room thought of themselves as a social group. The atmosphere was informal, they could talk freely, and they interacted regularly with their supervisors and the experimenters. They felt special and worked hard to stay in the group. This motivated them.

- The workers were involved in the planning of the experiments. For example, they rejected one kind of pay schedule and recommended another, which was used. The workers felt that their ideas were respected and that they were involved in managerial decision making. This, too, motivated them.

- The workers enjoyed the atmosphere of their special room and the additional pay they got for more productivity. Job satisfaction increased dramatically.

Now we understand that these employees were motivated because they were being empowered and their social and esteem needs (see Maslow's hierarchy on the next page) were being met.

Researchers now use the term **Hawthorne effect** to refer to the tendency for people to behave differently when they know they're being studied. The Hawthorne study's results encouraged researchers to begin to study human motivation and the managerial styles that lead to more productivity. The

Hawthorne effect
The tendency for people to behave differently when they know they are being studied.

emphasis of research shifted away from Taylor's scientific management to Mayo's new human-based management.

Mayo's findings led to completely new assumptions about employees. One of those assumptions, of course, was that pay was not the only motivator. In fact, money was found to be a relatively low motivator. That change in assumptions led to many theories about the human side of motivation. One of the best-known motivation theorists was Abraham Maslow, whose work we discuss next.

···· ▬▬▬ ····

MOTIVATION AND MASLOW'S HIERARCHY OF NEEDS

Abraham Maslow believed that to understand motivation at work, one must understand human motivation in general. He also believed that motivation arises from need. That is, people are motivated to satisfy *unmet* needs; needs that have been satisfied no longer provide motivation. He thought that needs could be placed on a hierarchy of importance.

Maslow's hierarchy of needs
Theory of motivation that places different types of human needs in order of importance, from basic physiological needs to safety, social, and esteem needs, to self-actualization needs.

Figure 12.1 shows **Maslow's hierarchy of needs**, whose levels are as follows:

- *Physiological needs:* basic survival needs, such as the need for food, water, and shelter.
- *Safety needs:* the need to feel secure at work and at home.
- *Social needs:* the need to feel loved, accepted, and part of the group.
- *Esteem needs:* the need for recognition and acknowledgement from others, as well as self-respect and a sense of status or importance.
- *Self-actualization needs:* the need to develop to your fullest potential.

FIGURE 12.1
····
MASLOW'S HIERARCHY OF NEEDS

Maslow's hierarchy of needs is based on the idea that motivation comes from need. If a need is met, it's no longer a motivator so a higher-level need becomes the motivator. This chart shows the various levels of need.

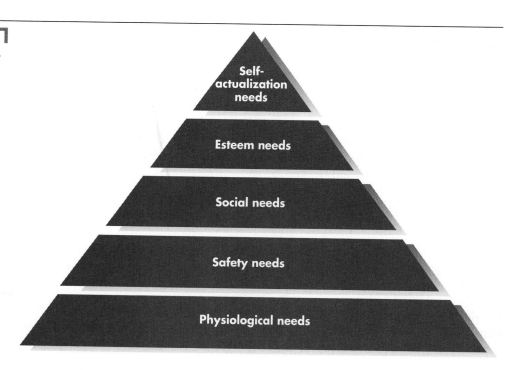

When one need is satisfied, another, higher-level need emerges and motivates the person to do something to satisfy it. The satisfied need is no longer a motivator.[5] For example, if you just ate a full-course dinner, hunger would no longer be a motivator. Also, lower-level needs (e.g., thirst) may emerge at any time they are not met, and take our attention away from higher-level needs such as the need for recognition or status.

Most of the world's workers struggle all day simply to meet the basic physiological and safety needs. In developed countries, such needs no longer dominate, and workers seek to satisfy growth needs (social, esteem, and self-actualization needs).

To compete successfully, firms must create a work environment that motivates the best and the brightest workers. That means establishing a work environment that includes goals such as social contribution, honesty, reliability, service, quality, dependability, unity, and participation in decision making.

Your job right now is to finish reading this chapter. How strongly would you be motivated to do that if you were sweating in a 40°C room? Imagine now that your roommate turns on the air-conditioning. Now that you are more comfortable, are you more likely to read? Look at Maslow's hierarchy of needs to see what need would be motivating you each time. Can you see how helpful Maslow's theory is in understanding motivation by applying it to your own life?

••• APPLYING MASLOW'S THEORY •••

Andrew Grove, CEO and chairman of Intel, has observed Maslow's concepts in action in his firm. One woman, for example, took a low-paying job that did little for her family's standard of living. Why? Because she needed the companionship her work offered (social/affiliation need). One of Grove's friends had a midlife crisis when he was made a vice-president. This position had been a lifelong goal, and when the man reached it he had to find another way to motivate himself (self-actualization need). People at a research and development lab were motivated by the desire to know more about their field of interest, but they had little desire to produce results, and thus little was achieved. Grove had to find new people who wanted to learn to achieve results.

Once you understand the need level of employees, it is easier to design programs that will trigger self-motivation. Grove believes that all motivation comes from within. He believes that self-actualized persons are achievers. Personally, Grove was motivated to earn a doctorate from the University of California at Berkely and to write a best-selling book, *Only the Paranoid Survive*.[6] He also proceeded at Intel to design a managerial program that emphasized achievement. Now Intel's managers are highly motivated to achieve their objectives because they feel rewarded for doing so.[7]

The contemporary approach to Maslow is to use his model as a framework for needs assessment, recognizing that it provides a relative ranking technique of employee needs. Note that individual need categories can and do shift in either direction when circumstances change.

<207.15.178.1:80/ gelman/maslow>

Be sure to visit this Web site to see an interesting summary of the highlights of Maslow's theory regarding human needs and an example of how it can be applied in the context of motivating employees.

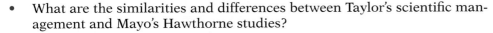

Progress Check

- What are the similarities and differences between Taylor's scientific management and Mayo's Hawthorne studies?
- How did Mayo's findings influence scientific management?
- Can you draw Maslow's hierarchy of needs? Label and describe the parts.
- According to Andrew Grove, what is the ultimate source of all motivation?

···· ■ ····

McGREGOR'S THEORY X AND THEORY Y

The way managers go about motivating people at work depends greatly on their attitudes toward workers. Douglas McGregor observed that managers' attitudes generally fall into one of two entirely different managerial styles, which he called *Theory X* and *Theory Y*.

··· THEORY X ···

The assumptions of Theory X management are as follows:

- The average person dislikes work and will avoid it if possible.
- Because of this dislike, workers must be forced, controlled, directed, or threatened with punishment to make them put forth the effort to achieve the organization's goals.
- The average worker prefers to be directed, wants to avoid responsibility, has relatively little ambition, and wants security.
- Primary motivators are fear and money.

The natural consequence of such attitudes, beliefs, and assumptions is a manager who is very busy and who hangs over people telling them what to do and how to do it. Motivation is more likely to take the form of punishment for bad work rather than rewards for good work. Workers are given little responsibility, authority, or flexibility. Those were the assumptions behind Taylor's scientific management and other theorists who preceded Taylor. That is why management literature focused on time–motion studies that calculated the one best way to perform a task and the optimum time to be devoted to a task. It was assumed that workers needed to be trained and carefully watched to see that they conformed to the standards.

Theory X management still dominates some organizations. Many managers and entrepreneurs still suspect that employees cannot be fully trusted and need to be closely supervised.[8] No doubt you have seen such managers in action. How did this make you feel? Were these managers' assumptions accurate regarding your attitudes?

··· THEORY Y ···

Theory Y makes entirely different assumptions about people:

- Most people like work; it is as natural as play or rest.
- Most people naturally work toward goals to which they are committed.
- The depth of a person's commitment to goals depends on the perceived rewards for achieving them.
- Under certain conditions, most people not only accept but also seek responsibility.
- People are capable of using a relatively high degree of imagination, creativity, and cleverness to solve problems.
- In industry, the average person's intellectual potential is only partially realized.
- People are motivated by a variety of rewards. Each employee is stimulated by a reward unique to that person (time off, money, recognition, and so on).

Rather than emphasize authority, direction, and close supervision, Theory Y emphasizes a relaxed managerial atmosphere in which workers are free to set objectives, be creative, be flexible, and go beyond the goals set by management.[9] A key technique in meeting these objectives is *empowerment*. Empowerment gives employees the ability to make decisions and the tools to implement the decisions they make. For empowerment to be a real motivator, management should follow these three steps: (1) find out what people think the problems in the organization are, (2) let them design the solutions, and (3) get out of the way and let them put those solutions into action.

Delta Hotels is known to its employees as a company where they can contribute and grow and also as a great place to work.

Often employees complain that they're asked to become involved in company decision making, but their managers fail to actually empower them to make decisions. Have you ever worked in such an atmosphere? How did that make you feel?

The trend in many businesses is toward Theory Y management. One reason for this trend is that many service industries are finding Theory Y helpful in dealing with on-the-spot problems. Leona Ackerly of Mini Maid Inc. says, "if our employees look at our managers as partners, a real team effort is built."[10]

Delta Hotels offers an excellent example of how effective employee empowerment is in increasing morale and motivation. Senior vice-president

Spotlight on Small Business

<www.richter.ca>

Motivating Employees in Small Businesses

Small businesses run into specific problems when it comes to motivating their employees. This is particularly true with companies that have grown from a very small beginning to a point where the owner or founder is having difficulty delegating authority. The owner, feeling that he or she must make every decision, as was done from the start, finds it difficult to let go, and this causes dissatisfaction among the workforce.

Picture a workforce of 35 or 40 people with several managers who feel frustrated because of the limited authority given to them by an anxious employer. Management consultant Stephen Levy commented that this is one of the most common problems he has found in successful small businesses; that is, the founders are actually holding back further progress without being aware that they are the source of the problem.

The notion of teams given authority and responsibility for decision making and results is still foreign to many small-business owners. And Levy finds it difficult to

convince them that they could solve many of their problems by empowering employees to play a much greater role in the daily operations of the company.

As the many examples in this and the preceding chapters make clear, the combined energy and resources of a team-based operation yield far superior results to those possible in a boss-centred organization. As a small firm grows it is impossible for one person to continue to be totally aware of every detail of the operations. Teams of employees who are intimately aware of the causes of problems with suppliers, customers, or production are in a much better position to provide solutions or to prevent problems from occurring in the first place. Empowerment of employees and recognition of their achievements lead to a highly motivated staff, as indicated by the theories of Herzberg and Maslow.

Source: Interview with Stephen Levy of Richter Management Plus, June 8, 1999.

Activities such as picnics and sports events like this parking lot hockey game create an atmosphere in which employees can feel like part of the group. This meets their social needs and they can move on to accomplish things at work to satisfy their self-esteem and self-actualization needs.

of people and quality, Bill Pallett, seeks to empower "more than 9000 employees across North America to make daily business decisions without having to turn to their managers for approval." This enables front-line employees to offer better service to customers by making on-the-spot decisions such as cancelling a disputed minibar charge or offering a complimentary room when a guest makes a reasonable complaint.[11]

··· APPLYING THEORY X AND THEORY Y ···

The trouble with these neat theories is that no company is run in strict accordance with either Theory Y or Theory X, not even the army. There are employees who prefer to be told what to do, who do not want responsibility for making crucial decisions, but who, when given precise instructions, perform their assigned tasks with care and diligence. There are also employees who are self-starters and perform best only when they share in the decision-making process; they resent being given orders. Both types can be found in the same company. If you were the chief executive, how would you run that company, by Theory X or Theory Y? Or would you use your common sense and act according to the circumstances at hand? You cannot run a business, or anything else, by blindly following one theory.

Managers must be flexible in applying Theory X or Y to those they supervise. Some people do better with direction; others do better with more freedom. Your natural inclination may be to prefer a Theory Y-type manager as your supervisor, whereas your friend may prefer a Theory X-type supervisor.

The trend in most businesses is toward Theory Y management. As repeatedly noted, participative management, employee empowerment, and team effort all require a democratic style of management. This enables firms to be flexible and to react quickly, putting them in a good position to meet competition from domestic or foreign firms.

This is a good time to have another look at the Profile at the beginning of the chapter. Remember David Weiss's view that flexibility is a key to motivation? Just as important is Peter Drucker's comment about the new information worker being motivated by more autonomy. It is interesting that in the same book review, Schachter notes how Drucker's opinion has changed as the nature of the workforce has changed. Half-a-century ago, in *The Practice of Management*, he advocated Theory X as the best way to motivate employees.

··· OUCHI'S THEORY Z ···

In addition to the stated reasons for the trend toward Theory Y management, another reason for a more flexible managerial style was to meet competition from foreign firms such as those in Japan, China, and the European Union. In the 1980s William Ouchi, a professor of business at UCLA, wrote a best-selling book on management called *Theory Z: How American Business Can Meet the Japanese Challenge*. The book highlighted how organizations in Japan are run quite differently from those in the United States. Out of the Japanese system evolved a concept called Theory Z.[12] Major elements of Theory Z include virtually lifelong employment, collective decision making, slow evaluation and promotion, and few levels of management.

Several U.S. firms attempted to adopt elements of this managerial style. Ouchi cited Hewlett-Packard as one such American firm. The corporate philosophy at Hewlett-Packard is to have overall objectives that are clearly stated and agreed to and to give people the freedom to work toward those goals in ways they determine best for their own areas of responsibility. Many large Canadian companies—the large banks, Bell Canada, and others—used to offer many of the features of the Japanese system of employment noted above.

When Harold Geneen was chief executive officer of ITT, he reviewed Theory Z. He noted that U.S. corporate life is just the opposite from the basics of Theory Z: relatively short-term employment, rapid promotions and dismissals, individual decision making and responsibilities, and a sense of personal rather than corporate loyalty.

Geneen questioned whether Americans would want to trade their heritage of personal freedoms and individual opportunity for the ingrown paternalism, humility, and selflessness of the Japanese system. He doubted whether Americans could instill such feelings, even if they wanted to.[13] Geneen concluded that Theory Z would not work as well in the United States as in Japan because of cultural differences. Ouchi recognized that fact in his book and did not expect Theory Z to catch on in many U.S. firms, nor do it seem applicable to Canadian companies. (See Figure 12.2 for a summary of Theories X, Y, and Z.)

FIGURE **12.2**

A COMPARISON OF THEORIES X, Y, AND Z

Note how Theory X differs from Theories Y and Z, which have some similarities.

THEORY X	THEORY Y	THEORY Z
1. Employees dislike work and will try to avoid it.	1. Employees view work as a natural part of life.	1. Employee involvement is the key to increased productivity.
2. Employees prefer to be controlled and directed.	2. Employees prefer limited control and direction.	2. Employee control is implied and informal.
3. Employees seek security, not responsibility.	3. Employees will seek responsibility under proper work conditions.	3. Employees prefer to share responsibility and decision making.
4. Employees must be intimidated by managers to perform.	4. Employees perform better in work environments that are not intimidating.	4. Employees perform better in environments that foster trust and cooperation.
5. Employees are motivated by financial rewards.	5. Employees are motivated by many different needs.	5. Employees need guaranteed employment and will accept slow evaluations and promotions.

Despite these significant cultural differences, Canadian and American companies have adopted some of the features of the Japanese system (Theory Z) listed above. As noted in previous chapters, these include

- collective decision making (teams)
- expectation of individual responsibility
- few levels of management

The combined effect of such changes is the creation of a sense of involvement, closeness, and cooperation in the organization, which is another of the Theory Z features. At the same time, the protracted and serious recession in Japan has begun to seriously erode the remaining Theory Z features of the system listed earlier. In Canada we have also witnessed extensive layoffs as large companies downsize and restructure. This has also eroded the motivation provided by security of employment and promotion.

As these trends evolve, it will be interesting to see how closely the two systems of motivation will resemble each other in the future.

···· ▬▬▬▬ ····

HERZBERG'S MOTIVATING FACTORS

Theories X, Y, and Z are concerned with styles of management. Another direction in managerial theory is to explore what managers can do with the job itself to motivate employees (a modern-day look at Taylor's research). In other words, some theorists are more concerned with the content of work than with style of management. They ask: Of all the factors controllable by managers, which are most effective in generating an enthusiastic work effort?

The most discussed study in this area was conducted by Frederick Herzberg.[14] He asked workers to rank the following job-related factors in order of importance as motivators. That is, what creates enthusiasm for them and makes them work to full potential? The results were

1. sense of achievement	8. pay
2. earned recognition	9. supervisor's fairness
3. interest in the work itself	10. company policies and rules
4. opportunity for growth	11. status
5. opportunity for advancement	12. job security
6. importance of responsibility	13. supervisor's friendliness
7. peer and group relationships	14. working conditions

Herzberg noted that the factors receiving the most votes were all clustered around job content. Workers like to feel that they contribute (sense of achievement was number one). They want to earn recognition (number two) and feel their jobs are important (number six). They want responsibility (which is why learning is so important), but they want that responsibility to be recognized with a chance for growth and advancement. Of course, workers also want the job to be interesting.

Herzberg noted further that factors having to do with the job environment were not considered motivators by workers. It was interesting to find that one of those factors was pay. Workers felt that the absence of good pay, job security, friendly supervisors, and the like could cause dissatisfaction, but the presence of those factors did not motivate them; they just removed the dissatisfaction.

Herzberg concluded that certain factors, called **motivators**, gave employees a great deal of satisfaction and made them more productive (see Figure 12.3). These factors mostly had to do with job content and were grouped as follows:

motivators
Factors that provide satisfaction and motivate people to work.

- work itself
- achievement
- recognition
- responsibility
- growth and advancement

Other elements of the job were merely what Herzberg called **hygiene factors**. These had to do mostly with job environment and could cause dissatisfaction but would not necessarily motivate if the source of dissatisfaction were removed. They were:

hygiene factors
Factors that cause dissatisfaction but do not motivate if they are removed.

- company policy and administration
- supervision
- working conditions
- interpersonal relations
- salary, status, job security

Combining McGregor's Theory Y with Herzberg's motivating factors, we can conclude:

- Employees work best when management assumes that they are competent and self-motivated. Theory Y calls for a participative style of management.
- The best way to motivate employees is to make the job interesting, help them to achieve their objectives, and recognize that achievement through advancement and added responsibility.

··· APPLYING HERZBERG'S THEORIES ···

Pat Blake, a Sunnen Products Co. employee, says that what motivates her to work extra hours or to learn new skills is less tangible than money or

MOTIVATORS	HYGIENE FACTORS
(These factors can be used to motivate workers.)	(These factors can cause dissatisfaction, but changing them will have little motivational effect.)
Work itself	Company policy and administration
Achievement	Supervision
Recognition	Working conditions
Responsibility	Interpersonal relations (co-workers)
Growth and advancement	Salary, status, job security

FIGURE 12.3
····
HERZBERG'S MOTIVATORS AND HYGIENE FACTORS
There's some controversy over Herzberg's theory. For example, sales managers often use money as a motivator. Recent studies have shown that money can be a motivator if used as a part of a recognition program.

The best motivators in business are achievement, recognition, and a chance for advancement. Westshore Terminals achieved the 400 million tonnes of coal shipped milestone in 1999. The 400 millionth tonne was loaded on board the Greek dry bulk carrier *Aquagrace*. Here Westshore transportaion manager Ron Dion awards a plaque to the ship's master, Captain Dimosthenis Kapetanios.

bonuses—it's a kind word from her boss. "When something good happens, like we have a shipping day with so many thousands of dollars going out the door, they let us know about that." Blake said. "It kind of makes you want to go for the gold."[15] Improved working conditions or better wages are taken for granted after workers get used to them. This is what Herzberg meant by *hygiene factors*: their absence causes dissatisfaction, but their presence doesn't motivate. The best motivator may be a simple and sincere "I really appreciate what you're doing."

Many surveys have been conducted to test Herzberg's theories. They support Herzberg's finding that the number one motivator isn't money, but a sense of achievement and recognition for a job well done. A 1994 survey by *Industry Week* showed that 80 percent of the employees asked to pick the most important factor in fostering company loyalty chose recognition of good work.[16]

When asked what makes them content with their current jobs, more than half of those surveyed listed open communication with higher-ups, the nature of the work, the quality of management, control over work content, the opportunity to gain new skills, the quality of co-workers, and the opportunity for intellectually stimulating work. Only a third mentioned salary as important.[17]

Similar answers were obtained in more recent surveys.[18] Figure 12.4 shows that there is a strong resemblance between Maslow's and Herzberg's theories.

JOB ENRICHMENT

job enrichment
A motivational strategy that emphasizes motivating the worker through the job itself.

Both Maslow's and Herzberg's theories were extended by job enrichment theory. **Job enrichment** is a motivational strategy that emphasizes motivating the worker through the job itself. Work is assigned to individuals so that they

Job enrichment motivates workers by appealing to personal values such as achievement, challenge, and recognition. Harley-Davidson is a company committed to the principles of job enrichment. At Harley-Davidson, self-managed teams of workers are trained to perform different tasks and have clear autonomy over how their job is organized.

Spotlight on Big Business

<www.mckinsey.com>

Designing a Motivating Workplace

One of the largest and most prestigious management consulting firms in the world is McKinsey & Co. For more than four years the Toronto office planned the design of their new premises, which they finally occupied at the end of June 1999. The overriding principle governing the design was to have a structure that would take care of all the major needs of their highly skilled, well-paid, and hard-working professional staff of 150. If they succeeded, then they would have a well-motivated workforce that would be very productive. That is why partner Mehrdad Baghai started planning four years before their lease expired. He engaged architect Siamak Hariri, a long-time friend, to draw up plans for the project. Other architects were hired to plan the actual building.

After many meetings and discussions, the decision was reached that three main criteria had to be met: a midtown location, lots of natural light, and fresh air. These criteria were not too difficult to meet. They found a good location, an atrium and open-style work spaces gave lots of light, and windows that opened provided fresh air. Much planning, many meetings, and lots of discussion went into decisions about hundreds of other details.

The open style means that employees can walk down a hall to the central atrium where they can meet other people or have a meal. The work they do requires consulting with each other often. This is made easy by a series of informal meeting rooms off the atrium where staff can brainstorm with each other or with clients. The whole idea is to have an atmosphere that will stimulate employees' creativity in a profession where creativity is

a vital component. Workstations, which are located in two long arms that branch off the central atrium or *hive*, are near large windows that provide lots of light.

One of problems was the fact that employees spend most of their time away from the office at clients' premises, generally returning on Friday. Some companies might take advantage of this to cut office space requirements by having common desk space that anyone could use. McKinsey did not like this solution; they felt that to feel like part of a community, you need to have your own work area where you can place personal objects like pictures of your family.

Another interesting feature is that space is organized so that entry-level employees can easily be mentored by experienced staff. These employees each have a work area, with their own shelves and drawers. On the other side of this area are senior employees whom the juniors can watch at work and from whom they can absorb important lessons like how to talk to clients on the phone. Also unusual is having smaller rooms for senior partners, who normally get large, bright, corner rooms. These prime quarters are now assigned to senior employees who work with the entry-level staff.

Such an approach to workplace design, while still experimental, shows staff that the company is going to great pains to provide the best possible solutions for their employees' physical and perhaps psychological needs as they relate to their job. This effort is bound to be a significant motivator.

Source: Elizabeth Church, "McKinsey Experiments with its Workspace," *Globe and Mail*, June 21, 1999, p. M1.

have the opportunity to complete an identifiable task from beginning to end. They are held responsible for successful completion of the task. The motivational effect of job enrichment can come from the opportunity for personal achievement, challenge, and recognition. Go back and review Maslow's and Herzberg's work to see how job enrichment grew out of those theories (see Figure 12.4). Five characteristics of work are believed to be important in affecting individual motivation and performance.

1. *Skill variety*. The extent to which a job demands different skills of the person.

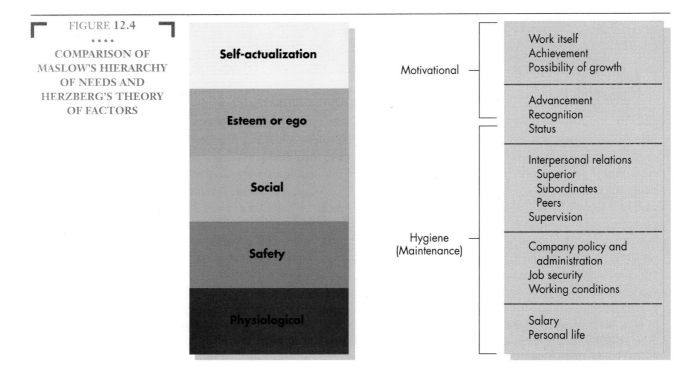

FIGURE **12.4**
• • • •
COMPARISON OF
MASLOW'S HIERARCHY
OF NEEDS AND
HERZBERG'S THEORY
OF FACTORS

2. *Task identity.* The degree to which the job requires working with a visible outcome from beginning to end.

3. *Task significance.* The degree to which the job has a substantial impact on the lives or work of others in the company.

4. *Autonomy.* The degree of freedom, independence, and discretion in scheduling work and determining procedures.

5. *Feedback.* The amount of direct and clear information that is received about job performance.

The same procedure was employed by many Canadian companies with similar satisfactory results. In the previous two chapters we saw how Campbell Soup Canada and Shell Oil successfully applied the team method to obtain a highly motivated workforce. In this chapter, in Reaching Beyond Our Borders on page 383, you'll see how the same is true for GSW Water Heating Co. In the following pages, the example of Motorola Canada Ltd. also shows successful use of teamwork to motivate employees.

As mentioned previously, job enrichment is based on Herzberg's higher motivators such as responsibility, achievement, and recognition. It stands in contrast to **job simplification**, which produces task efficiency by breaking down the job into simple steps and assigning people to each of those steps. There isn't much motivation in doing boring, repetitive work, but some managers who still operate on the Taylor level of motivation use job simplification. Job simplification is sometimes necessary, particularly when people are learning new skills.

Another type of job design used for motivation is **job enlargement**, which combines a series of tasks into one assignment that is more challenging and interesting. For example, Maytag, the home appliance manufacturer, redesigned its work so that employees could assemble an entire water pump

job simplification
Process of producing task efficiency by breaking down the job into simple steps and assigning people to each of those steps.

job enlargement
Job enrichment strategy involving combining a series of tasks into one assignment that is more challenging and interesting.

instead of just one part. **Job rotation** also makes work more interesting and motivating by moving employees from one job to another. One problem with job rotation, of course, is having to train employees to do several different operations. However, the resulting increase in employee morale and motivation leads to greater productivity; thus, it usually offsets the additional costs.

Job enrichment is one way to ensure that workers enjoy responsibility and a sense of accomplishment. Another way is to get everyone to agree on specific company objectives.

GOAL-SETTING THEORY AND MANAGEMENT BY OBJECTIVES

Goal-setting theory is based on the notion that the setting of specific ambitious but attainable goals is related to high levels of motivation and performance if the goals are accepted, accompanied by feedback, and facilitated by organizational conditions.[18] Nothing makes more sense intuitively than the idea that all members of an organization should have some basic agreement about the overall goals of the organization and the specific objectives to be met by each department and individual. It follows, then, that there should be a system to involve everyone in the organization in goal setting and implementation. Such a system is called *management by objectives (MBO)*.

Peter Drucker developed this system in the 1960s. Drucker asserted that "managers cannot motivate people; they can only thwart people's motivation because people motivate themselves."[19] Thus, he designed his system to help employees motivate themselves. **Management by objectives (MBO)** is a system of goal setting and implementation that involves a cycle of discussion, review, and evaluation of objectives among top and middle-level managers, supervisors, and employees. Large corporations such as the Ford Motor Company used MBO and taught the method to the U.S. Defense Department. MBO then spread to other companies and government agencies. When implemented properly, MBO meets the criteria of goal-setting theory and can be quite effective. MBO calls on managers to formulate goals in cooperation with everyone in the organization, to commit employees to those goals, and then to monitor results and reward accomplishment. There are six steps in the MBO process (see Figure 12.5). Can you tell how the model is intended to help workers motivate themselves?

MBO was widely used in the 1960s, and the management literature of the 1970s was packed with articles about MBO, but very little was written about it in the 1980s and 1990s. Some critics of MBO now see it as being out of date and inconsistent with contemporary management thought and practice. Does that mean that MBO isn't used any longer? Not according to one 1995 study, which found that 47 percent of the organizations surveyed used some form of MBO.[20]

MBO is most effective in relatively stable situations where long-range plans can be made and implemented with little need for major changes. It is also important to MBO that managers understand the difference between helping and coaching subordinates. *Helping* means working with the subordinate and doing part of the work if necessary. *Coaching* means acting as a resource—teaching, guiding, and recommending—but not

job rotation
Job enrichment strategy involving moving employees from one job to another.

goal-setting theory
Theory that setting specific ambitious but attainable goals can motivate workers and improve performance if the goals are accepted, accompanied by feedback, and facilitated by organizational conditions.

management by objectives (MBO)
A system of goal setting and implementation that involves a cycle of discussion, review, and evaluation of objectives among top and middle-level managers, supervisors, and employees.

Sometimes it's hard to believe that money doesn't motivate. NBA players like Shareef Abdur-Rahim of the Vancouver Grizzlies make lots of money, but when he's on the court, is it the money or the challenge of competition that makes Shareef play harder? What else do you think drives him to the net?

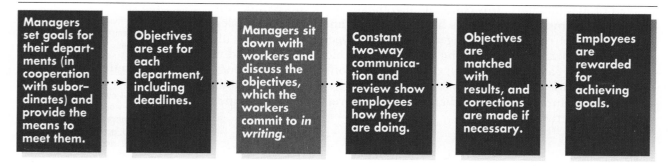

| Managers set goals for their departments (in cooperation with subordinates) and provide the means to meet them. | Objectives are set for each department, including deadlines. | Managers sit down with workers and discuss the objectives, which the workers commit to *in writing*. | Constant two-way communication and review show employees how they are doing. | Objectives are matched with results, and corrections are made if necessary. | Employees are rewarded for achieving goals. |

FIGURE 12.5
• • • •
MANAGEMENT BY OBJECTIVES

The critical step in the MBO process is the one when managers sit down with workers, discuss the objectives, and get the workers to commit to those objectives in writing. Commitment is the key!

helping (that is, not participating actively or doing the task). The central idea of MBO is that employees need to motivate themselves.

Problems can arise when management uses MBO as a strategy for *forcing* managers and workers to commit to goals that are not really mutually agreed on but are set by top management. Employee involvement and expectations are important.

Victor Vroom identified the importance of employee expectations and developed a process called *expectancy theory*. Let's examine this concept next.

• • • • ━━━━━ • • • •

MEETING EMPLOYEE EXPECTATIONS: EXPECTANCY THEORY

expectancy theory
Victor Vroom's theory that the effort employees exert on specific tasks depends on their expectations of the outcomes.

According to Victor Vroom's **expectancy theory**, employee expectations can affect an individual's motivation.[21] Therefore, the effort employees exert on specific tasks depends on their expectations of the outcomes. Vroom contends that employees ask three questions before committing maximum effort to a task: (1) Can I accomplish the task? (2) If I do accomplish it, what's my reward? (3) Is the reward worth the effort?

Think of the effort you might exert in your class under the following conditions: Your instructor says that to earn an A in the course you must achieve an average of 90 percent on coursework plus jump three metres high. Would you exert maximum effort toward earning an A if you knew you could not possibly jump three metres high? Or what if your instructor said students could earn an A in the course but you know that this instructor has not awarded an A in 25 years of teaching? If the reward of an A seems unattainable, would you exert significant effort to try to attain one? Better yet, let's say that you read in the newspaper that businesses actually prefer C-minus students to A-minus students. Does the reward of an A seem worth it? Now think of the same type of situations that may occur on the job.

Expectancy theory does note that expectation varies from individual to individual. Employees establish their own view of task difficulty and the value of the reward. Researchers David Nadler and Edward Lawler modified Vroom's theory and suggested that managers follow five steps to improve employee performance:

1. Determine what rewards are valued by employees.
2. Determine each employee's desired performance standard.
3. Ensure that performance standards are attainable.

4. Guarantee rewards tied to performance.

5. Be certain that rewards are considered adequate.[22]

•••• ━━━━ ••••

TREATING EMPLOYEES FAIRLY: EQUITY THEORY

Equity theory deals with the question "If I do a good job, will it be worth it?" It has to do with perceptions of fairness and how those perceptions affect employees' willingness to perform. The basic principle is that employees try to maintain equity between inputs and outputs compared to others in similar positions. Equity comparisons are made from the information available through personal relationships, professional organizations, and so on.

When workers do perceive inequity, they will try to reestablish equitable exchanges in a number of ways. For example, suppose you compare the grade you earned on a term paper with your classmates' grades. If you think you received a lower grade compared to the students who put out the same effort as you, you will probably react in one of two ways: (1) by reducing your effort on future class projects or (2) by rationalizing (e.g., by saying "Grades are not that important!"). If you think your paper received a higher grade than comparable papers, you will probably (1) increase your effort to justify the higher reward in the future or (2) rationalize by saying "I'm worth it!" In the workplace, perceived inequity leads to lower productivity, reduced quality, increased absenteeism, and voluntary resignation.

Remember that equity judgments are based on perceptions and are subject to errors in perception. When workers overestimate their own contributions—as happens often—they are going to feel that any rewards given out for performance are inequitable. Sometimes organizations try to deal with this by keeping salaries secret, but secrecy may make things worse; employees are likely to overestimate the salaries of others in addition to overestimating their own contribution. In general the best remedy is clear and frequent communication. Managers must communicate as clearly as possible the results that are expected and what will follow when those results are achieved or not.

•••• ━━━━ ••••

REINFORCEMENT THEORY

Another theory of motivation is based on the work of the famous but controversial psychologist B.F. Skinner, who is considered the father of behaviourism—the notion that people will behave according to their awareness of the consequences of their actions. That means that the carrot-and-stick approach, reward and punishment, would be an effective method of motivating people. Although Skinner's influence has been declining recently, his theories gave rise to the reinforcement theory of motivation.

Reinforcement theory states that positive and negative reinforcers will motivate a desired behaviour. Individuals act to receive rewards and avoid punishment. Positive reinforcements are rewards such as praise, recognition, or a pay raise. Negative reinforcement occurs when a person acts to avoid negative consequences such as reprimands. A manager might also withhold praise (positive reinforcement) and this is called *extinction*. Another way of reducing undesirable behaviour is punishment such as a public reprimand. A detailed example of how reinforcement theory applies to motivating appropriate employee behaviour is shown in Figure 12.6.

equity theory
Theory that employees try to maintain equity between inputs and outputs compared to others in similar positions.

<home.mira.net/
~gaffcam/phil/
skinner.htm>

Visit this site to read an article by B.F. Skinner titled *The Origins of Cognitive Thought*. See what the *"father of behaviourism"* has to say!

reinforcement theory
States that positive and negative reinforcers will motivate a desired behaviour.

FIGURE **12.6**

• • • •

REINFORCEMENT
THEORY

How a manager can use positive and negative reinforcement to motivate employee behaviour.

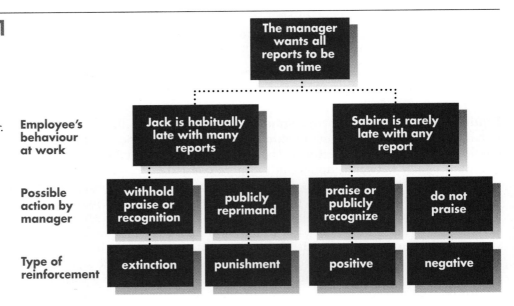

Progress Check

- Briefly describe the managerial attitudes behind Theories X, Y, and Z.
- Relate job enrichment to Herzberg's motivating factors.
- What are the six steps in management by objectives?
- What is the difference between helping and coaching? Which motivates workers more?

• • • • ▬▬▬ • • • •

IMPLEMENTING THE NEW CONCEPTS: MOTIVATION THROUGH COMMUNICATION

Management by objectives teaches us that, in any organization, one key to successful management and motivation is the establishment and maintenance of open communication so that both managers and workers understand the objectives and work together to achieve them. Communication in the organization must flow two ways. The problem is that communication often flows only one way: from top management down. One-way communication takes the form of directives, policies, announcements, memos, rules, procedures, and the like.

The flow upward, from workers to managers, is usually severely restricted. Rarely do organizations have any formal means of upward communication equivalent to directives and announcements. Instead, the burden falls on workers to initiate contact with supervisors and present their ideas and suggestions. As you might imagine, few people in any organization are willing to tell the boss when things are not going well. Children don't tell parents when they've broken something, students don't tell teachers when someone has goofed, and employees don't tell bosses. Such a system creates an atmosphere of "us against them," in which workers feel united in their distrust and avoidance of managers. To create an atmosphere of "us working together," managers have to become active listeners and valued assistants to workers. Such a change often demands radical retraining of managers and careful creation of new attitudes and beliefs among workers.

Teamwork does not happen by itself. The whole organization must be structured to make it easy for managers and employees to talk to one another. Procedures for encouraging open communication include the following:

- Top managers must first create an organizational culture that rewards listening. They must create places to talk (e.g., conference rooms), and they must show employees that talking with superiors counts—by providing feedback, adopting employee suggestions, and rewarding upward communication—even if the discussion is negative. Employees must feel free to say anything they deem appropriate.

- Supervisors and managers must be trained to listen actively. Most people receive no such training in school or anywhere else, so organizations must do the training themselves or hire someone to do it.

- Barriers to open communication must be removed. Having separate offices, parking spaces, bathrooms, dining rooms, and so on only places barriers between managers and workers. Other barriers are different dress codes and different ways of addressing one another (e.g., calling workers by their first names and managers by their last). Removing such barriers may require imagination and a willingness on the part of managers to give up their special privileges.

- Efforts to facilitate communication must be actively undertaken. Large lunch tables where all organization members eat, conference rooms, organizational picnics, organizational athletic teams, and other such outings all allow managers to mix with each other and with workers.

Leaders who don't commit themselves to fostering openness and who continue to create barriers to communicate often pay a heavy price, William Agee, CEO of Morrison Knudson, moved his headquarters to Pebble Beach, California, and left his managers and employees in distant Idaho. This created a spirit of distrust and open resentment that eventually cost Agee his position.[23]

Larger firms are taking the hint, as discussed in the next section. Much of the success of Japanese companies is attributed to their adoption of unifying techniques as a regular practice.

••• OPEN COMMUNICATION AND SELF-MANAGED TEAMS •••

Companies that have developed highly motivated workforces usually have several things in common. Among the most important are open communication systems and self-managed teams. These are both features at the Ford Motor Company. Kenneth Kohrs, vice-president of car product development at Ford, says that an inside group known as "Team Mustang" sets the guidelines for how production teams should be formed. Given the challenge to create a car that would make people dust off their old "Mustang Sally" records and dance into the showrooms, the 400-member team was also given the freedom to make decisions without waiting for approval from headquarters or other departments. The team moved everyone from various departments into cramped offices under one roof of an old warehouse. Draftsmen sat next to accountants, engineers next to stylists. Budgetary walls that divided departments were knocked down as department managers were persuaded to surrender some control over their subordinates.

When the resulting Mustang convertible displayed shaking problems, suppliers were called in, and the team worked around the clock to solve the problem. The engineers were so motivated to complete the program on schedule and under budget that they slept on the floors of the warehouse. The senior Ford

215-HP 4.6L OHC V-8, 4-WHEEL POWER DISC BRAKES, PASSIVE ANTI-THEFT SYSTEM, AND SPORT-TUNED SUSPENSION ARE ALL STANDARD.   www.ford.com

THIS HORSE IS ROCKING.

MUSTANG GT   HAVE YOU DRIVEN A FORD LATELY?   Ford

Highly motivated work teams depend on open communications and self-management. Ford Motor Company provided such an atmosphere for its 400-member "Team Mustang" workgroup.

executives were tempted to overrule the program, but they stuck with their promise not to meddle. The team solved the shaking problem and still came in under budget and a couple of months early.[24]

A 1995 survey of U.S. companies showed that two-thirds were using formal teams. For the giant Winnipeg-based Great-West Life, discussed in Chapter 13, open communication is key to motivating employees. This is also a feature at the Rimouski, Quebec, plant of Toronto-based Phillips Cables Ltd., which produces hair-thin fibre-optic cable in a state-of-the-art factory. This is part of a joint venture with Furukawa Electric of Japan called Phillips-Fitel.

Despite the fact that the Furukawa managers speak no French and the plant employees speak almost no English, there is an open communication system that has helped to create a strongly motivated workforce. According to union president Marcel Rouleau, "the only boss we have is the plant manager. We don't have incompetents telling us what to do when we know better. Now they consult us.... We feel a lot more creative and it's rewarding."

CEO Malcolm Stagg noted that there has been a remarkable change in the attitude of the workforce. The whole experiment is being carefully observed to see if it can be duplicated at other Canadian plants.[25]

Open communication and teamwork have helped make Motorola Canada Ltd. very competitive. Teams compete fiercely in devising ways to reduce costs and increase efficiency. There is a formal competition among all 3700 teams of Motorola's 107,000 employees worldwide.

> *Nine months of intense preparation have come down to a 12-minute performance to a jury of Motorola Canada Ltd. executives on a Saturday morning in a Toronto hotel. "At 4 o'clock in the morning we were still fine-tuning the presentation," says a nervous Jim Kiriacou, one of the nine men and women in Motorola's Toronto paging operations who make up the team.*
>
> *Despite the stress, the UltraEagles team performed flawlessly. Garbed in hockey jerseys with [their] team logo, they used charts and statistics to explain how they saved close to $50,000 a year by improving the accuracy of customer accounts.... They managed to narrowly defeat the Montreal Express, becoming Canadian paging champions for the third year in a row.[26]*

A poll of 1000 large companies in the United States showed that "almost 60 percent of workers and 77 percent of managers ... would work harder if they knew how their jobs keep the company making money."[27]

To implement such groups or teams, managers at most companies must reinvent work. This means respecting workers, providing interesting work, rewarding good work, developing workers' skills, allowing autonomy, and decentralizing authority. Such principles are particularly important to the many workers who are members of what has been called Generation X.[28]

<www.gsw-wh.com>

You can visit GSW's Web site to learn more about the company, its products, its history, and its approach to doing business.

Reaching Beyond Our Borders

<www.gsw-wh.com>

Tapping the Power of Workers' Minds

By any measure, GSW Water Heating Co. should be struggling just to survive. The hourly labour costs of its unionized workforce are the highest of any water-heater manufacturer in North America and as much as double those of U.S. rivals. The company claims no competitive advantage from unique technology or a state-of-the-art plant. Its factory is a concrete dinosaur, having been on its present site since 1911 with only modest updating. The predecessors built the factory in 1874.

Yet at a time of continuing layoffs, GSW Water Heating is expanding its workforce, doubling the capacity of its assembly lines, and competing aggressively and successfully in the United States. All this springs from a collaboration of management, employees, and the union aimed at improving the plant's products and processes and cutting waste and costs. By passing on cost savings to customers, this unit of Toronto-based GSW Inc. has been able to strengthen its competitive position.

"The company said we had to become a world-class manufacturer to survive, and I want to survive," said Robb Rosso, a three-year assembly-line worker who embodies the spirit in the 296-worker plant. Rosso was part of an employee team sifting through worker suggestions to design a bigger production line. The new line doubled the plant's annual capacity to 700,000 heaters, adding another 20 jobs to the workforce.

GSW's survival strategy is one response to the often-heard argument that high labour costs prevent Canadian manufacturers from competing. Rather than dwell on the wage gap, management has worked to reduce other costs and increase productivity by tapping the brainpower of plant workers, whose wage and benefit packages exceed, on average, $24 an hour.

In 1990 GSW Water Heating seemed an unlikely candidate for change. It did not have a rich history of employee involvement. "Our attitude used to be that employees parked their brains at the door when they reported for work and picked them up when they left," said Roger Lippert, director of human resources and a key player in the new approach.

But with the arrival of Canada–U.S. free trade, management, led by president Terry Parsons, was determined to cut costs. It seized on the idea of world-class manufacturing, a generic term for teamwork, training, and continual improvement. The inspiration came from the ideas of W. Edwards Deming, the American consultant who taught total quality management to the Japanese.

In launching the program in 1991, Parsons assured workers this was not a recipe for downsizing. Specific jobs would be lost, he told them, but employment would not be reduced. Sensitive to competitive pressure, the workers accepted the need for change, volunteering in large numbers for training sessions. "Our biggest problem was explaining to employees why they couldn't all participate at the same time," Lippert said. Teams are continually being formed to tackle assignments; there are now more than 14 in the plant, and the number continues to rise.

One team wondered why water heaters had as many as 14 labels dealing with everything from safety to general instructions. By reducing the number of unnecessary labels, the company saved $1 for each heater, or about $350,000 a year. The apparatus for spraying porcelain enamel on the liners of heater tanks was not leaving a uniform deposit. So the problem was handed to a team, whose proposals saved $250,000 a year.

As costs fell, the company embarked on a sales thrust in the United States, where it soon held 2 percent of the water heater market (compared with a 52 percent share in Canada). The target was the U.S. Northeast, within 1000 kilometres of Fergus, Ontario, where GSW has a freight-cost advantage over major competitors in the U.S. Southeast and Southwest. By 1996 the company had doubled its U.S. sales.

Sources: Interview with Roger Lippert, July 15, 1996; Wilfred List, "Tapping the Power of Workers' Minds," *Globe and Mail, Report on Business.* November 10, 1992, p. B26.

In the process of reinventing work, it is essential that managers behave ethically toward all employees. The Ethical Dilemma box illustrates the problem managers may face when filling temporary positions.

···· ▬▬▬ ····

REINVENTING WORK

In 1985 John Naisbitt and Patricia Aburdene co-authored a book called *Re-Inventing the Corporation* (Warner Books, 1985). The goal of management, according to Naisbitt and Aburdene, is to adopt "new humanistic values." Such new values enable employees to motivate themselves because they feel more a part of a unified corporate team.

Naisbitt and Aburdene suggested certain steps for creating a better corporate atmosphere. These included calling everyone by his or her first name, eliminating executive parking spots and bathrooms, having everyone answer his or her own phone, eliminating files, doing business only with pleasant people, and throwing out the organization chart.

The authors also suggested that managers reinvent work. This means respecting workers, providing interesting work, rewarding good work, developing workers' skills, allowing some autonomy, and decentralizing authority.

Other points: (1) The manager's role is that of teacher, mentor, and coach; (2) the best people want ownership in the firm; (3) the best managerial style is not top-down, but a networking, people style of management; (4) quality is the key to success; (5) successful large corporations copy the entrepreneurial flavour of small businesses; and (6) the information age enables firms to locate where there is a high quality of life, since they don't have to be concerned exclusively with such industrial considerations as raw materials.

All of these ideas are consistent with what management was thinking in the 1990s and are discussed throughout this book. Clearly, there *is* a trend toward different management styles. The point of this chapter is that the new management styles are largely motivational tools to bring out the best in more educated, better-trained workers. Those are the workers of the future, and they include you. Look through the points outlined above and see if you don't agree that you would enjoy and be more productive working in such an organization. You would be a more motivated worker and thus do a better job.

••• CHANGING ORGANIZATIONS IS NOT EASY •••

We have come a long way from the time–motion studies of Frederick Taylor. Maslow, Mayo, Herzberg, and others have taught us to treat employees as associates and to get them more involved in decision making. This increases motivation and leads to greater productivity.

The problem is that many managers were brought up under a different system. Some were in the military and are used to telling people what to do rather than consulting with them. Others come from the football-coach school of management. They, too, tend to yell and direct rather than consult and discuss.

Furthermore, employees are often not used to participative management. The transition from Theory X to Theory Y management, from Taylor to Herzberg, is still going on. It is important, then, to have examples to follow when trying to implement the new approaches.

••• WAL-MART: A MODEL FOR THE FUTURE •••

Perhaps the best example of a new company that achieved enormous success in the last 35 years and became the largest retailer in the world is Wal-Mart.

Many of this company's management practices were well ahead of its competitors and of most companies in Canada and the United States. Wal-Mart attributes a good deal of its success to its employee motivation strategies. Because it is such an outstanding example of successful employee motivation and because it is now a major retailer in Canada, Canadians should pay close attention to the Wal-Mart story.

There is much controversy about Wal-Mart in Canada and the United States because it has crushed many small businesses and weakened small U.S. towns. When Wal-Mart entered Canada in 1994 there were dire predictions about the impact on large Canadian retailers. The concern was that they would not be able to compete against this aggressively successful company. However, Canadian Tire and Zellers have successfully countered the Wal-Mart threat, although Eatons may have been a direct casualty. It remains to be seen how they, and other large retailers, will continue to compete successfully against this American behemoth. In any case, it is incumbent upon Canadian companies to learn from successful companies wherever they may be located and regardless of what business they are in. There are such lessons in motivation to be learned from the Wal-Mart experience.

Wal-Mart was founded in 1962 by Sam Walton. Walton, who preferred to be called *Sam*, saw the great potential for discount retailing in the United States. However, Wal-Mart sold the same merchandise as its competitors, so how could the company be different and take advantage of this potential boom? Walton felt the key to success in the industry was in the development of a family-type relationship with the firm's employees, whom he preferred to call *associates*. He believed that if you did not involve employees in the organization, you were making a serious mistake, for employees are the only ones who can make an organization work.

In the 1990s Wal-Mart became the world's largest retailer. The firm operates more than 6000 stores, full-line discount stores, wholesale clubs, Super Centres, and hypermarkets. The company was awarded the Retailer of the Decade award by *Discount Stores News*, and Mr. Sam, who died in 1992, became one of the richest men in the world.

How did all of this happen? Wal-Mart's success can be attributed to many factors. For example, the company was on the cutting edge of technology. It was one of the first firms to implement barcode scanners in all of its stores. It also developed satellite-based transmissions that moved information rapidly from store to store, store to headquarters, and store to suppliers. Wal-Mart demanded a good deal of effort from suppliers but managed to develop positive and long-lasting relationships with them. This efficiency in distribution helped Wal-Mart fulfill its promise of everyday low prices. Many firms, including Sears, have tried to emulate this successful strategy. However, what Wal-Mart did best overall was develop a successful partnership with its associates. Sam Walton firmly believed that only people can make a business grow. He staked his future and that of the company of this basic principle.

Walton laid the foundation of his partnership with employees on three basic principles:

1. *Treat employees as partners.* Share with them both good news and bad so they will strive to excel. Also, let employees share in the rewards they help achieve.

2. *Encourage employees to question and challenge the obvious.* Walton believed the path to success included some failures. It was important to use those failures to advantage by learning from them.

3. *Involve associates at all levels in the decision-making process.* Managers should be facilitators, sharing ideas with employees and soliciting

<wal-mart.com>
<www.canadiantire.ca>
<www.hbc.com/zellers>

You can visit their Web sites to learn more about the three companies discussed here.

ideas from them. Employees should not *ask* to be involved; they should be *required* to be involved.

Although many companies proclaimed such ambitious partnerships, Wal-Mart actually created one. The company regularly provided the good news and bad news just as it promised. Associates were kept informed about costs, freight charges, profit margins, and any other issues considered critical to the firm. Wal-Mart backed up its promise of sharing the wealth by providing a generous bonus plan to deserving employees. Company executives, including Sam Walton, practised participative decision making by visiting Wal-Mart stores throughout the country seeking ideas, advice, and opinions from associates. The company even delegated authority to sales clerks, checkers, and stockpeople to order merchandise they thought they could sell. All employees were encouraged to get involved in operations and make the company better.[29] In Chapter 14 you will see how Wal-Mart handled the issue of unionization attempts at some of its stores.

Critical Thinking

How does Sam Walton's approach to motivation relate to Maslow's theory? Did he try to motivate employees by satisfying their unmet needs? Or do Herzberg's ideas fit better with what Walton did? Is it possible that both Herzberg's and Maslow's theories apply in this case?

···· ▬▬▬ ····

MOTIVATION IN THE FUTURE

What can you learn from all the theories and companies discussed in this chapter? You should have learned that people can be motivated to improve productivity and quality of work if managers know which technique to use and when. You should now be aware that

- The growth and competitiveness of industry and business in general depend on a motivated, productive workforce. As mentioned in previous chapters, to sustain competitive advantage in the global marketplace, a company's workforce must be engaged in continual improvement and innovation. Only motivated employees can achieve improvement and innovation as normal methods of operations.

- Motivation is largely internal, generated by workers themselves; giving employees the freedom to be creative and rewarding achievement when it occurs will release their energy.

- The first step in any motivational program is to establish open communication among workers and managers so that the feeling generated is one of cooperation and teamwork. A family-type atmosphere should prevail.

Today's customers expect high-quality, customized goods and services. That means employees must provide extensive personal service and pay close attention to details. Employees will have to work smart as well as hard. No amount of supervision can force an employee to smile or to go the extra mile to help a customer. Managers need to know how to motivate their employees to meet customer needs.

Tomorrow's managers will not be able to use any one formula for all employees. Rather, they will have to get to know each worker personally and tailor the motivational effort to the individual. As you learned in this chapter, different employees respond to different manager-ial and motivational styles. This is further compli-cated by the increase in global business and the fact that managers now work with employees from a variety of cultural backgrounds. Different cul-tures experience motivational approaches differ-ently; the manager of the future will have to study and understand these cultural factors when designing a reward system. Here's how Digital Equipment dealt with these cultural issues within global teams.

Even though the concept of teamwork is nothing new, building a harmonious global work team is new and can be complicated. Global companies must rec-ognize differing attitudes and competencies in the team's cultural mix and the technological capabilities among team members. For example, a global work team needs to determine whether the culture of its members is high-context or low-context. In a high-context team culture, members build personal relationships and develop group trust before focusing on tasks. In the low-context culture, members often view relationship build-ing as a waste of time that diverts attention from the task. Koreans, Thais, and Saudis (high-context cultures), for example, often view American team members as insincere due to their need for data and quick decision making.

When Digital Equipment Corporation decided to consolidate its operations at six manufacturing sites, the company recognized the need to form multicultural work teams. Realizing the challenge it faced, Digital hired an internal organization-development specialist to train the team in relationship building, foreign languages, and valuing differ-ences. All team members from outside the United States were assigned American partners and invited to spend time with their families. Digital also flew the flags of each employee's native country at all its manufac-turing sites. As communication within the teams increased, the com-pany reduced the time of new-product handoffs from up to three years to just six months.[30]

Radisson Hotels Worldwide recently announced its Employees of the Year at its annual business conference. Three employees from Radisson's 240 North American hotels were chosen from among thousands of employees for the honour. The employees were hon-oured for their talents, skills, outstanding guest service, and "Yes I can!" attitude.

In general, motivation will come from the job itself rather than from exter-nal punishments or rewards. Motivation is certainly difficult if employees do not value their jobs.[31] Managers need to give workers what they need to do a good job: the right tools, the right information, and the right amount of cooperation.

Will happy workers improve corporate performance? The Gallup Organi-zation recently surveyed 55,000 workers to match employee attitudes with company results. The survey found four attitudes that, taken together, corre-late strongly with higher profits. Specifically, the most successful companies are those in which workers feel that (1) they are given the opportunity to do what they do best every day, (2) their opinions count, (3) their fellow workers are committed to quality, and (4) there is a direct connection between their work and the company's mission.[32]

Motivation doesn't have to be difficult. It begins with acknowledging a job well done. You can simply tell those who do such a job that you appreciate them, especially in front of others. It's unfortunate that there are too few "high fives" in business.[33] After all, the best motivator is frequently a sincere "Thanks, I appreciate what you have done."

Ethical Dilemma

REVIEW

Now that you are better acquainted with the importance and significance of motivation, let us have a look at what our executives have to say about the ethical dilemma described at the beginning of the chapter.

Bédard comments that "such a practice would be dishonest and probably illegal. There are other ways to attract temporary help, such as asking for employee referrals and offering a termination bonus if sales attain certain levels."

Reilley believes that "not only is this entirely dishonest, but it can be damaging to the store's reputa-

tion." For him, "the best approach would be to entice the better prospects with the promise that they will be given first consideration for new job openings, if and when they become available."

If you were the manager, would you do what our executives suggest, or do you believe it's just a little white lie? Can you justify such action by thinking that the employee can always look for a permanent job in January without any real harm to their prospects and in the meantime they earn some money? How would you feel if *you* were the employee?

Progress Check

- What are several steps firms can use to increase internal communications and, thus, motivation?
- What are the six steps in reinventing work, and how are they related to motivation?
- What problems may emerge when trying to implement participative management?
- Why is it important today to adjust motivational styles to individual employees? Are there any general principles of motivation that today's managers should follow?

SUMMARY
· · · · ·

1. Explain Taylor's scientific management.

1. Frederick Taylor was one of the first people to study management.
   - ***Who is Frederick Taylor?***
   Frederick Taylor is the father of scientific management. He did time–motion studies to learn the most efficient way of doing a job and then trained workers in those procedures. He published his book on scientific management in 1911. The Gilbreths and H. L. Gantt were followers of Taylor.

2. Describe the Hawthorne studies, and relate their significance to human-based management.

2. Management theory moved away from Taylor's scientific management and toward theories that emphasize human factors of motivation.
   - ***What led to the more humane managerial styles to increase motivation?***
   The greatest impact on motivation theory was generated by the Hawthorne studies in the late 1920s and early 1930s. Elton Mayo found that human factors such as feelings of involvement and participation led to greater productivity gains than did physical changes in the workplace.

3. Identify the levels of Maslow's hierarchy of needs, and relate their importance to employee motivation.

3. Maslow studied basic human motivation and found that motivation was based on need: an unfilled need motivated people to satisfy it; a satisfied need no longer motivated.

- ***What are the various levels of need identified by Maslow?***

Moving up from the bottom of Maslow's hierarchy of needs, the needs are physiological, safety, social, esteem, and self-actualization.

- ***Can managers use this theory?***

Yes, they can recognize a person's unmet needs and design work that satisfies those needs.

4. McGregor held that managers can have two opposing attitudes toward employees. They are called Theory X and Theory Y. Ouchi introduced Theory Z in response to McGregor.
   - ***What are Theory X and Theory Y, and when were they developed?***

   Theory X assumes that the average person dislikes work and will avoid it if possible. Therefore, people must be forced, controlled, and threatened with punishment to accomplish organizational goals. Theory Y assumes that people like working and will accept responsibility for achieving goals if rewarded for doing so. Douglas McGregor published these theories in 1970.

   - ***What is Theory Z?***

   Theory Z comes out of Japanese management. Among other factors, it emphasizes long-term employment.

4. Differentiate among Theory X, Theory Y, and Theory Z.

5. Herzberg found that some things are motivators and others are hygiene factors; the latter cause job dissatisfaction if they're missing, but they aren't motivators if they're present.
   - ***What are the factors called* motivators?**

   The work itself, achievement, recognition, responsibility, growth, and advancement.

   - ***What are hygiene factors?***

   Factors that don't motivate but must be present for employee satisfaction: company policies, supervision, working conditions, interpersonal relations, and salary.

5. Distinguish between motivators and hygiene factors identified by Herzberg.

6. Job enrichment describes efforts to make jobs more interesting.
   - ***What characteristics of work affect motivation and performance?***

   The job characteristics that influence motivation are (1) skill variety, (2) task identify, (3) task significance, (4) autonomy, and (5) feedback.

   - ***Name two forms of job enrichment that increase motivation.***

   Job enrichment strategies include job enlargement and job rotation.

6. Explain how job enrichment affects employee motivation and performance.

7. One procedure for establishing objectives and gaining employee commitment to those objectives is management by objectives.
   - ***What are the steps in an MBO program?***

   (1) Managers set goals. (2) Objectives are established for each department. (3) Workers discuss the objectives and commit themselves in writing to meeting them. (4) Progress is reviewed. (5) Feedback is provided and adjustments are made. (6) Employees are rewarded for achieving goals.

7. Identify the steps involved in implementing a management by objectives (MBO) program.

8. According to Victor Vroom, employee expectations can affect an individual's motivation.
   - ***What are the key elements involved in expectancy theory?***

   Expectancy theory centres on three questions employees often ask about performance on the job: (1) Can I accomplish the task? (2) If I do accomplish it, what's my reward? (3) Is the reward worth the effort?

8. Explain the key factors involved in expectancy theory.

9. Examine the key principles of equity theory.

9. According to equity theory, employees try to maintain equity between inputs and outputs compared to other employees in similar positions.
   • ***What happens when employees perceive that their rewards are not equitable?***
   If employees perceive that they are underrewarded, they will either (1) reduce their effort or (2) rationalize that it isn't important. Inequity leads to lower productivity, reduced quality, increased absenteeism, and voluntary resignation.

KEY TERMS
......

equity theory 379
extrinsic reward 362
expectancy theory 378
goal-setting theory 377
Hawthorne effect 365
hygiene factors 373
intrinsic reward 362

job enlargement 376
job enrichment 374
job rotation 376
job simplification 376
management by objectives (MBO) 377
Maslow's hierarchy of needs 366

motivators 373
principle of motion economy 364
reinforcement theory 379
scientific management 363
time–motion studies 363

DEVELOPING WORKPLACE SKILLS

1. Talk with several of your friends about the subject of motivation. What motivates them to work hard or not work hard in school and on the job? How important is self-motivation to them?

2. Assume you are a branch manager for a large car rental company that continues to lose market share to smaller companies offering superior customer service. Draft a memo to your company's training director describing the steps and policies you recommend the company adopt and implement to motivate your front-line employees to become customer oriented.

3. Examine Maslow's hierarchy of needs and try to determine where you fit into the needs structure. Which category of your needs do you feel is not being met now? Can you see how, if those needs were satisfied, you would be better motivated at school or elsewhere, until the next category of needs was unmet?

4. Herzberg found that pay was not a motivator. If you were paid to get better grades, would you be able to get them? Have you worked harder as a result of a large raise? Discuss money as a motivator with your friends and class. Do you agree 100 percent with Herzberg?

5. Think of all of the groups with whom you have been associated over the years—sports groups, friends, and so on—and try to recall how the leaders of those groups motivated the group to action. Did the leaders assume a Theory X or Theory Y attitude? How often was money used as a motivator? What other motivational tools were used and to what effect?

INTERNET CHALLENGES

1. Scan the Search engine Canada.com using the keywords *employee motivation*. Confine your search to Canada over the past year. You will find many matches. On October 4, 1999, there were 120 matches. Click on an

article that looks interesting to you and see how the report relates to the chapter. Is a company or a manager doing something to improve motivation following any of the theories discussed in the chapter? You might want to bring the article to class for discussion about how this event fits with chapter material.

2. Fastfood chains like McDonald's <www.mcdonalds.com>, Harvey's <www.harveysonline.com>, and Subway <www.subway.com>, generally pay their employees, mostly young students, minimum wages or slightly more and they have a high rate of employee turnover. As you saw in the chapter, Frederick Hertzberg has shown that money is not generally a good long-term motivator of employees. Do you think this is true for fastfood employees? Would an increase in salary motivate them and perhaps reduce the turnover rate? Check out the Web sites of these companies and see if there is any information relating to this topic. Perhaps you can search for stories relating to attempts by fastfood chains to motivate employees. (See also Developing Workplace Skills #1 on the previous page.)

Practising Management Decisions

CASE 1
• • • • • •
THE WORKPLACE: DOES IT HELP OR HINDER MOTIVATION?
• • • • • •

A recent article in the *Report on Business* section of *The Globe and Mail* started with the provocative question: "Does the atmosphere inside your company resemble Calcutta in the summer or France's Fontainbleau forest in the spring?" This question was put to prestigious international business executives in luxurious Davos, Switzerland.

The speaker was Sumantra Ghoshal, an internationally recognized author, professor, and authority on management issues. His weighty audience was attending the annual World Economic Forum, which is probably the most important annual meeting of senior government and business leaders in the world. He was obviously trying to alert them to what he feels is a major problem confronting companies in today's highly competitive global economy.

Ghoshal noted that if you want high performance from your employees, look first at the atmosphere in your company before you start thinking about "changing each individual employee." Before you set out to teach old dogs new tricks, you better change the "smell of the place." It is his belief that most firms create a "stifling atmosphere in which employees feel constrained, controlled, and forced to comply with a rigid contract that governs their behaviour."

Ghoshal's equally famous colleague and co-author, Christopher Bartlett of Harvard University, noted that now that "information, knowledge, and expertise" have become just as important as capital was in the past, emphasis has shifted from the corporation to the individual. This means that whereas earlier managers had to fit into the corporation and become organization people, now the corporation must become flexible and find ways to fit the individual manager.

Decision Questions

1. Do you find it surprising that senior executives have to be reminded of these things? How come they are not already aware of this issue since it has been actively discussed in business schools and business periodicals for some years?
2. Why are companies so slow to adapt to new conditions? Don't they want a better-motivated workforce?
3. Is it possible that corporations' concentration on downsizing in recent years has blinded them to the changed needs of their remaining employees and managers?
4. What is your own experience in jobs you have had? Did you find the atmosphere conducive to employee motivation?

Source: Madeleine Drohan, "Your Workplace: Hole or Haven?" *Globe and Mail, Report on Business*, February 7, 1996, p. B9.

News reports from Canada and the United States indicate a new trend in the job market. A decreasing number of people are being given permanent jobs of the kind we used to expect as normal employment. Security of employment with all the usual fringe benefits is being reserved for a privileged few. U.S. data indicate that up to half of all new jobs are temporary, part-time, or some other unconventional type of employment, and this number is expected to grow. What is behind this trend?

Many Canadian companies have adopted a form of workforce management that they believe will enable them to compete better in the world market. They keep a "core of managers and valued workers whom they favour with good benefits and permanent jobs. They take on and shed other workers as business spurts and slumps." These jobs pay less and have few if any benefits. Many Canadians have lost good jobs and are finding only these unsatisfactory new jobs. Many Canadian students are finding only these poor-quality jobs available upon graduation.

According to Robert Reich, U.S. secretary of labour in the Clinton adminstration, "the entire system has fragmented." He estimates that about 30 percent of the American workforce is composed of contingent workers, but current statistics suggest this estimate is low.

Current Canadian data are not yet available, but various Statistics Canada reports indicate that many new jobs are of a similarly insecure nature.

CASE 2

······

MOTIVATION IN AN ERA OF "DISPOSABLE WORKERS"

······

Apparently Canadian companies that let go hundreds of thousands of employees in the deep recession and restructuring of the 1990s are not rushing to rehire permanent employees if they can avoid it.

Decision Questions

1. What is likely to be the impact of this trend on employee motivation? Will temporary workers be as motivated as permanent employees, especially if they continue to look for a "decent" job?

2. How will this, in turn, affect production and service to customers? Given the growing importance of teamwork and cooperation, is quality production likely to suffer?

3. What are the long-term impacts on the competitiveness of companies? Are companies being too shortsighted in thinking only of current bottom lines?

4. How can companies develop employees' long-term loyalty in such circumstances? Is this still important? Why?

Sources: Peter T. Kilborn, "New Jobs Lack the Old Security in a Time of 'Disposable Workers,'" *New York Times*, March 15, 1993, p. A1; *Globe and Mail, Financial Post*, various issues in February and March 1993; Peter Hadekel, "Very Soon the Working World Will Be Divided into Two Types of People," *Montreal Gazette*, March 10, 1993, p. B14; "What's the Big Deal?" *Globe and Mail, Report on Business*, December 12, 1995, p. B9; Bruce Little, "Canada Pumps out New Jobs in July," *Globe and Mail*, August 7, 1999, p. B3.

Human Resource Management: Managing the Most Important Asset—People

Chapter 13

LEARNING GOALS

After you have read and studied this chapter, you should be able to

1 explain the importance of human resource management, and describe current issues in managing human resources.

2 describe methods companies use to recruit new employees, and explain some of the problems that make recruitment challenging.

3 illustrate the various types of employee training and development methods.

4 summarize the objectives of employee compensation programs, and describe various pay systems and benefits.

5 explain scheduling plans managers use to adjust to workers' needs.

6 describe training methods used in management development programs.

7 illustrate the effects of legislation on human resource management.

Dwayne Leskewich, employee benefits administrator at B.C. forestry giant MacMillan Bloedel, has redesigned and modernized the whole program that he administers. For many years the underlying philosophy found in large companies was the basis of the approach at Mac Blo. Mother MacMillan tended her flock—she made all the decisions. Since January 1995 the employee benefits program has had a totally new look. Choice has been placed in the hands of the employees. The program is called *Partnerships For Success*.

Leskewich points out that the average age of his workforce had edged over 40 and many were asking for the right to choose specific types of benefits rather than having to buy into a fixed package. He knew this was a growing trend in North America and had been thinking about revamping the program to fit modern needs. So Leskewich redesigned it, offering a wide variety of benefits from which employees could select any combination up to a certain maximum dollar amount. Those who opted for a program whose total cost was less than this figure would have the difference added to their pay.

Prior to decision time, employees were given a wide-ranging introduction to the new program and the choices they would have to make. Brochures, lectures, question periods, videos, and one-on-one sessions prepared the way for the changeover. Some employees cautiously opted for a combination that approximated their existing package. Most adopted variations more suited to their particular needs. By May 1996, some 75 percent of the workforce had switched over to the *cafeteria-style* benefits program and were very satisfied with the change.

In addition to the new benefits program, job sharing and flexible working hours have been available for some time and fit the bill for certain employees. People with young children or elders to care for like such options because they reduce stress and absenteeism. Obviously, this works well for the company, too. It is not easy, or always possible, to institute either of these two arrangements, but for those who really want them, the company tries to find ways to accommodate them.

In August 1999 Leskewich reported that the flexible benefits program was well established and strongly favoured by the workforce—75 percent continue to opt for the choices it gives them. A cafeteria-style program not only gives choices, but employees can also make changes annually. The company also offers flexibility in pension planning. Leskewich notes that he is looking at expanding the benefits package to include flexibility in medical coverage for employees after retirement.

Dwayne Leskewich has joined a growing number of benefits managers who have moved away from rigid programs toward employee participation and empowerment, and less rigidity in the workplace overall.

PROFILE

Employee Benefits Get a New Look at MacMillan Bloedel

Sources: Interview with Dwayne Leskewich, May 22, 1996, and August 23, 1999; Deborah Wilson, "Employees Design Benefits Packages," *Globe and Mail*, Report on Business, December 19, 1995, p. B26.

THE TEMPTATION TO GET AROUND THE LAW

You are a manager in the human resource department and one of your jobs is to do the initial interview with job applicants. As you will see in this chapter it is illegal in Canada for a job application form to ask certain questions, such as age, nationality, or religion. Similarly, as an interviewer, you cannot ask a female applicant if she is planning to have children in the near future as it is illegal not to hire a woman who may become pregnant. You are a bit bothered by these restrictions because of problems with some recent hirees. An older man was often absent because his eyes couldn't stand up to the strain of the job, a very orthodox Muslim required much time off for prayer and other religious duties, and a young women proved to have actually been pregnant when hired. Your superior has hinted that you should find some subtle way to get around the legal restrictions when interviewing applicants. He also has hinted that if your track record improves you might get a nice bonus at year-end. Furthermore, if you do not *cooperate*, he has hinted you may find it difficult to get a promotion. What would you do? Let's look at this question at the end of the chapter, after you have had a chance to digest its contents.

THE HUMAN RESOURCE FUNCTION

human resource management (HRM)
The process of evaluating human resource needs, finding people to fill those needs, and motivating employees to get the best work from each one by providing the right incentives and job environment, all with the goal of meeting the organization's objectives.

This chapter will discuss the human resource function, which involves recruiting, hiring, training, evaluating, compensating, and laying off people. **Human resource management (HRM)** is the process of evaluating human resource needs, finding people to fill those needs, and motivating employees to get the best work from each one by providing the right incentives and job environment, all with the goal of meeting the organization's objectives (see Figure 13.1). Let's explore some of the trends in the area of HRM.

••• TRENDS AND ISSUES IN HRM •••

Like many other aspects of Canadian business mentioned in other chapters, HRM has been greatly affected by technology and global competition. Both of these factors have led Canadian companies to downsize workforces for both management and employees. Other employees work at home and only come to company premises occasionally. The nature of work and management has changed enormously. Employees participate more in decision making through teamwork and a greater emphasis on quality and customer satisfaction. Better-trained and better-educated employees are now required to work in a more high-tech global business climate. This is only a short list of some of the major issues that are increasing the importance of, and causing a revolution in, HRM operations.

••• IMPORTANCE OF HRM •••

One reason human resource management is receiving increased attention now is the major shift from traditional manufacturing industries to service industries and high-tech manufacturing organizations that require more technical job skills. Companies now have fewer employees, but the ones who

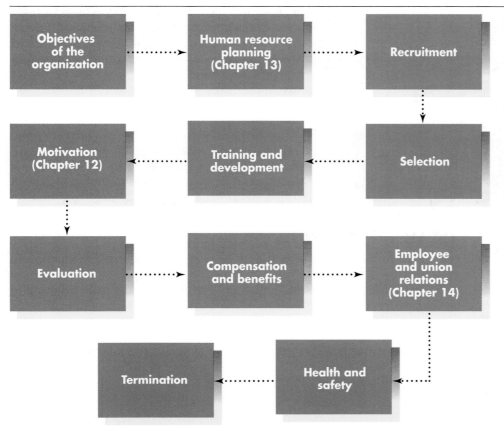

FIGURE **13.1**

• • • •

HUMAN RESOURCE MANAGEMENT

Note that human resource management includes motivation (discussed in Chapter 12) and union relations (discussed in Chapter 14). As you can see from the chart, human resource management involves more than hiring and firing personnel.

remain require more education and skills. A major problem today is retraining workers for new, more challenging jobs.

BC Telephone has set up an education centre in Burnaby, B.C., to provide proper training for its employees. The National Bank of Canada has set up a banking school by teaming up with the Institute of Canadian Bankers and Université de Québec.[1] These are but two examples of how companies are moving to ensure a properly trained workforce. Here are some other examples:

- Canada Mortgage and Housing Corp., a crown corporation, has numerous training programs and job exchanges. Temporary vacancies are often filled by people from other departments wanting to enrich their own experience. Each year, CMHC hires 10 university graduates under a two-year training program that exposes them to 10 or 12 departments.

- Allen-Bradley Canada Ltd. manufactures industrial automation equipment. It has more than a thousand employees in three plants in Ontario and emphasizes training. At its Cambridge plant it employs seven full-time and three part-time instructors. The other locations have four full-time instructors. New marketing employees go through a three-month training and orientation program. All new employees attend a two-week business course.[2]

- The Bank of Montreal spent $40 million setting up an Institute for Learning for its employees. The aim of the director of the complex, Dr. James Rush, is to ensure continuing opportunities for the bank's employees to learn and to be creative.[3]

<www.icb.org/ programs>

Visit the ICB's Web site to see the broad selection of programs and courses it offers to the financial services industry. It even offers an MBA program in collaboration with UQAM (in French) and Dalhousie University (in English).

BC.TELUS Communications Inc. is the second-largest communications company in Canada, delivering unsurpassed service and value to millions of people and thousands of businesses. It employs 25,000 highly skilled Canadians, many of whom receive training at BC Tel's own education centre.

Employees have been called a company's most important resource, and when you think about it, nothing could be truer. People develop the ideas that eventually become the products that satisfy our wants and needs. Take away the creative minds, and organizations such as Bombardier, Du Pont, Nortel, and Magna International cease to be leading firms.

Most firms used to assign the job of recruiting, selecting, training, evaluating, compensating, motivating, and firing people to the various functional departments. For years, the personnel department was viewed more or less as a clerical function responsible for screening applications, keeping records, processing payroll, and finding people when necessary.

Today the job of human resource management has taken on an entirely new role in the firm. In the future, it may become *the* most critical function in that it is responsible for the most critical resource—people. The human resource function has become so important that it is no longer the function of just one department; it is a function of all managers. Most human resource functions are shared between the professional human resource manager and the other managers. In smaller companies with no HRM department, one manager or the owner has this responsibility. Because the job has become so complex (see next section), smaller companies are beginning to turn to outside specialists in HRM.[4]

THE HUMAN RESOURCE CHALLENGE

No changes in the Canadian business system have been more dramatic and had more impact on the future success of the economy than changes in the labour force. Canada's ability to compete in international markets depends on an increase in new ideas, new products, and as we saw in Chapter 10, increased productivity. All of these factors critically depend on the ultimate resource—people. Problems being encountered in the human resource area include the following:

- Shortages in people trained to work in the growth areas of the future such as telecommunications, computers, biotechnology, robotics, and the sciences.

- A huge population of skilled and unskilled workers (from declining industries such as textiles, apparel manufacturing, and steel and modernizing industries such as automobiles) who are unemployed or underemployed and who need retraining.

- A shift in the age composition in the workforce, including many older workers. (See Chapter 1 for a discussion of demographic trends.)

- A complex set of laws and regulations governing hiring, firing, safety, health, unionization, and equal pay that require organizations to go beyond only profit orientation and become more socially responsible.

- An increasing number of single-parent and two-income families resulting in a demand for day care, job sharing, maternity and paternity leave, flexible schedules, and special career advancement programs for women.

- Relentless downsizing, which is taking its toll on employee morale as well as increasing the demand for temporary workers.
- A challenge from foreign labour pools available for lower wages and subject to fewer laws and regulations. This results in many jobs being shifted to other countries.
- An increased demand for benefits tailored to the individual.

Given all these issues, and others that are sure to develop, you can see why human resource management has taken a more central position in management thinking. We will start with a look at planning.

Critical Thinking

Does human resource management seem like a challenging career to you? Do you see any other issues likely to affect this function? What have your experiences been in dealing with people who work in HRM? Would you enjoy working in such an environment?

···· ▬▬▬ ····

DETERMINING HUMAN RESOURCE NEEDS

All management, including HRM, begins with planning. Six steps are involved in the human resource planning process (see Figure 13.2 for a summary).

1. *Preparing forecasts of future human resource needs.*
2. *Preparing a human resource inventory of the organizations' employees.* This inventory should include names, education, capabilities, training, specialized skills, and other information pertinent to the specific organization (for example, languages spoken). Such information reveals the status of the labour force.
3. *Preparing a job analysis.* A **job analysis** is a study of what is done by the employees who hold various job titles. Such analyses are necessary to recruit and train employees with the right skills to do the job. The results of a job analysis are two written statements: job descriptions and job specifications. A **job description** specifies the objectives of the

job analysis
A study of what is done by the employees who hold various job titles.

job description
A summary of the objectives of a job, the type of work to be done, the responsibilities and duties, the working conditions, and the relationship of the job to other functions.

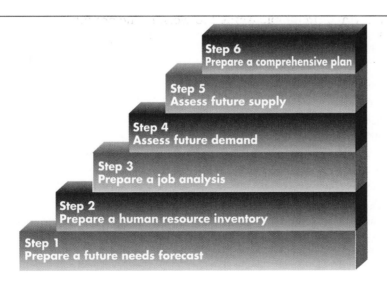

Step 6
Prepare a comprehensive plan

Step 5
Assess future supply

Step 4
Assess future demand

Step 3
Prepare a job analysis

Step 2
Prepare a human resource inventory

Step 1
Prepare a future needs forecast

FIGURE **13.2**
····
STEPS IN HUMAN RESOURCE PLANNING

Human resource planning is a complex process involving several crucial steps.

job specifications
A written summary of the minimum qualifications required of a worker to do a particular job.

<english.monster.ca>
<www.careermosaic.com>
<www.jobtrak.com>
<www.jobmatch.com>

Visit the Web sites of these services to get more information about the services and jobs they offer. See if you can find something that interests you.

job, the type of work to be done, the responsibilities and duties, the working conditions, and the relationship of the job to other functions. **Job specifications** are a written summary of the *minimum* qualifications (education, skills, and so on) required of a worker to fill a specific job. In short, job descriptions are statements about the job, whereas job specifications are statements about the person who does the job. See Figure 13.3 for hypothetical examples of a job description and job specifications.

4. *Assessing future demand.* Constantly changing technology means that training programs must be started long before the need is apparent. Human resource managers who are proactive (in this case that means those who anticipate the future HR needs of their organization) have the trained human resources available when needed.

5. *Assessing future supply.* The labour force is constantly shifting: getting older, becoming more technically oriented, attracting more women, and so forth. There are likely to be increased shortages of some skills in the future (e.g., computer and robotic repair workers) and oversupply of others (e.g., assembly line workers).

6. *Preparing a comprehensive plan.* The plan must address recruiting, selecting, training and developing, appraising, compensating, and scheduling the labour force. Because the previous five steps lead up to this one, this chapter will focus on these elements of the strategic human resource plan.

Useful tools for external recruiting of employees are Internet services such as CareerMosaic, JobTrak, JobMatch, and The Monster Board (which is a Canadian one). The Spotlight on Small Business outlines some of the affordable ways businesses can address their recruiting needs. Although recruiting

---

FIGURE 13.3
• • • •

EXAMPLE OF A JOB ANALYSIS

A job analysis yields two important statements: a job description and job specifications. Here you have a job description and job specifications for a cereal sales representative.

Job Analysis

Observe current sales representatives doing the job.

Discuss job with sales managers.

Have current sales reps keep a diary of their daily activities.

Job Description	**Job Specifications**
Primary responsibility is to sell cereal to food stores in Territory Z. Other duties include servicing accounts and maintaining positive relationships with clients. Examples of duties required: • Introducing the new cereal to store managers in the area. • Helping the store managers estimate the volume to order. • Negotiating prime shelf space. • Explaining sales promotion activities to store managers. • Stocking and maintaining shelves in stores that want such service.	Characteristics of the person qualifying for this job include the following: • Two years' sales experience. • Positive attitude. • Well-groomed appearance. • Good communication skills. • High-school diploma and two years of college credit.

Spotlight on Small Business

<www.careermosaic.com>

Small Businesses Must Compete to Attract Qualified Workers

It's harder now than ever before for businesses to find qualified employees, and it is becoming more expensive. Small-business owners across the country agree that competition for qualified employees is intensifying. Small businesses want top talent but often can't afford corporate-level benefits or expensive recruiters to hunt them down. Despite the hurdles, small-business management consultants say there are many ways to lure desirable workers:

- *Transform ads into promotional tools.* For example, Ecoprint, a small print shop in Maryland, brags about the benefits of working for this collegial company in its advertisements.

- *Post job openings on the Internet.* Running a 20-line ad on an online service like CareerMosaic or The Monster Board costs $100 to $150 for 30 days. A comparable ad in a major newspaper can cost 20 times that amount.

- *Let your staff help select hires.* The more people involved in the interview process, the better chance you have to find out if the person has the personality and skills to fit in.

- *Create a dynamic workplace to attract local, energetic applicants.* Sometimes word of mouth is the most effective recruiting tool.

- *Test-drive an employee.* Hiring temporary workers can allow you to test candidates for a few months before deciding whether to make an offer or not.

- *Hire your customer.* Loyal customers sometimes make the smartest employees.

- *Check community groups and local government agencies.* Don't forget to check out province-run employment agencies. The new welfare-to-work programs may turn up excellent candidates you can train.

- *Lure candidates with a policy of promotions and raises.* Most employees want to know that they can move up in the company. Give employees an incentive for learning the business.

Sources: "Break the Rules to Hire Smart," *Your Company*, February 3–17, 1997; "Netting a Job," *PC Magazine*, February 4, 1997, p. 10.

from most external sources seems straightforward, sometimes this may involve difficult ethical decisions. At the beginning and end of Chapter 9 the question of enticing desirable employees from other companies was reviewed. It might be a good idea to take another look at those pages now.

RECRUITING EMPLOYEES

Recruitment is the set of activities used to obtain a sufficient number of the right people at the right time and to select those who best meet the needs of the organization. One would think that, with a continual flow of new people into the workforce, recruiting would be easy. But the truth is that recruiting has become very difficult for several reasons.

- Legal restrictions, such as the Charter of Rights and Freedoms, make it necessary to consider the proper mix of women, minorities, people with disabilities, and other qualified individuals.

recruitment
The set of activities used to obtain a sufficient number of the right people at the right time and to select those who best meet the needs of the organization.

JCI Technologies presents JobsCanada, the most advanced employment Web site on the Internet today. JCI has spent the last four years and millions of dollars to develop this advanced employment service.

- The emphasis on corporate cultures, teamwork, and participative management makes it important to hire skilled people who also fit in with the culture and leadership style of the organization.

- Firing unsatisfactory employees is getting harder to justify legally. This is especially true of discharges involving possible discrimination by factors such as age, sex, or ethnicity. Therefore, it's necessary to screen and evaluate applicants carefully to be sure they'll be effective long-term members of the organization.

- Some organizations have unattractive workplaces or offer low wages, which makes recruiting and keeping employees difficult.

Because recruiting is a difficult chore that involves finding, hiring, and training people who are an appropriate technical and social fit, human resource managers turn to many sources for assistance (see Figure 13.4). These sources are classified as either internal or external. *Internal sources* include hiring from within the firm (transfers, promotions, and so forth) and employee recommendations. Internal sources are less expensive than recruiting outside the company. The greatest advantage of hiring from within is that it helps maintain employee morale. However, it isn't always possible to find qualified workers within the company, so human resource managers must use *external recruitment sources* such as ads, public and private employment agencies, college placement bureaus, management consultants, professional organizations, referrals, and applicants who simply show up at the office (walk-ins).

···· ▬ ····

SELECTING EMPLOYEES

selection
The process of gathering information to decide who should be hired, under legal guidelines, for the best interests of the organization and the individual.

Selection is the process of gathering information to decide who should be hired, under legal guidelines, for the best interests of the organization and the individual. The cost of selecting and training employees is prohibitively high in large firms. Think of the costs involved: interview time, medical exams, training costs, unproductive time spent learning the job, moving expenses, and so on. It's easy to see how such expenses can run more than $50,000 for a

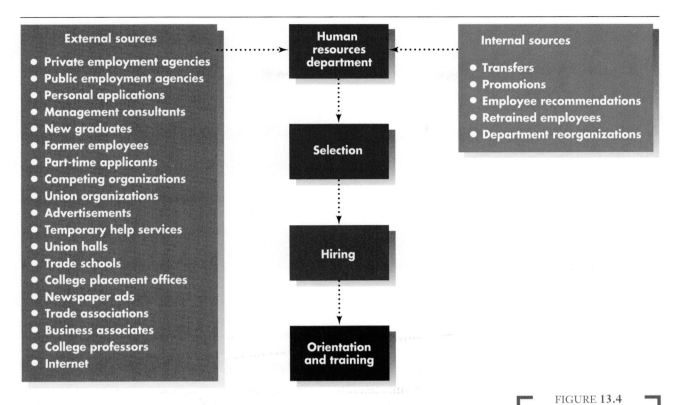

External sources

- Private employment agencies
- Public employment agencies
- Personal applications
- Management consultants
- New graduates
- Former employees
- Part-time applicants
- Competing organizations
- Union organizations
- Advertisements
- Temporary help services
- Union halls
- Trade schools
- College placement offices
- Newspaper ads
- Trade associations
- Business associates
- College professors
- Internet

Human resources department

Selection

Hiring

Orientation and training

Internal sources

- Transfers
- Promotions
- Employee recommendations
- Retrained employees
- Department reorganizations

FIGURE 13.4
• • • •
EMPLOYEE SOURCES

Internal sources are often given first consideration. Therefore, it's useful for you to get a recommendation from a current employee of the firm you want to work for. College placement offices are also an important source. Be sure to learn about such facilities early so you can plan a strategy throughout your college career.

manager. Even entry level workers can cost thousands of dollars to recruit, process, and train. Companies try to avoid the substantial costs of a high turnover rate. Thus, the selection process becomes an important element in any human resource program. A typical selection process involves six steps (see Figure 13.5).

1. *Completion of an application form.* Once this was a simple procedure. Today, legal guidelines limit the kinds of questions you can ask. (Sex, ethnicity, religion, age, or nationality are taboo). Nonetheless, such forms help managers discover educational background, past work experience, career objectives, and other information directly related to the requirements of the job.

2. *Initial and follow-up interviews.* Applicants are often screened in a first interview by a member of the HRM staff. If the interviewer considers the applicant a potential employee, the manager who will supervise the new employee interviews the applicant as well. It's important that managers prepare adequately for the interview process to avoid selection errors they may regret. They must avoid asking the wrong question such as asking a female about her family plans. No matter how innocent the intention, that could be used as evidence if the applicant files discrimination charges.

3. *Employment tests.* Employment tests have been severely criticized on charges of discrimination. Nonetheless, organizations continue to use them to measure basic competencies, test specific job skills (for example, welding or word processing), and help evaluate applicants' personalities and interests. It's important that the employment test be directly job related. This will make the selection process more efficient and often satisfy legal requirements.

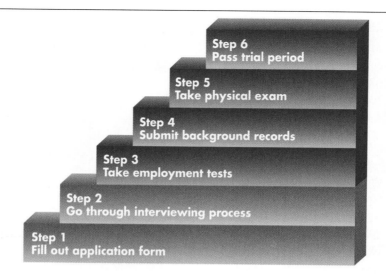

Step 6
Pass trial period

Step 5
Take physical exam

Step 4
Submit background records

Step 3
Take employment tests

Step 2
Go through interviewing process

Step 1
Fill out application form

4. *Background investigations.* Most organizations are more careful than they have been in the past about investigating a candidate's work record, school record, and recommendations. It is simply too costly to hire, train, and motivate people only to lose them, and then have to start the process over. Background checks help weed out candidates least likely to succeed and identify those most likely to succeed in a specific position. It is not always easy to obtain this information, however. Many companies no longer provide references for fear of liability suits if they give negative reports.

5. *Physical exams.* A complete medical background and checkup help screen candidates. There are obvious benefits in hiring physically and mentally healthy people. However, medical tests cannot be given just to screen out specific applicants—that could lead to a charge of discrimination. If such tests are given, they must be given to everyone at the same point in the selection process. A major controversy erupted in the late 1980s related to pre-employment testing to detect drug or alcohol abuse or AIDS.

More than 70 percent of CEOs endorse drug testing in some instances. The Toronto Dominion Bank asked 250 top executives to undergo drug tests and made testing mandatory for all new employees. The Canadian Civil Liberties Association asked the Canadian Human Rights Commission to quash this program as discriminating on the basis of disability but lost the case. However, in 1998 the Federal Court of Appeal ruled that the bank's "mandatory random and universal pre-employment urinary drug-testing policy is discriminatory." In a similar case in Ontario involving the Imperial Oil Co.'s drug-testing policy, both the Human Rights Tribunal and a lower court ruled that the policy was discriminatory and the case has now gone to the Ontario Appeal Court. David Korn, president of The Donwood Institute, a public hospital in Toronto, said company funds should not be used in the search for a quick technological fix to a very complex issue. Levi Strauss & Co. (Canada) Inc. does not test prospective employees for AIDS but has a thorough educational program for them. By contrast, the Canadian AIDS Society, in a survey of 500 businesses, discovered that only 4 percent are developing policies and programs to deal with AIDS; 22 percent said it was not their job to inform employees about AIDS.[5] Some of these issues are still unresolved as cases work their way slowly through the courts.

6. *Probationary periods.* Often an organization will hire an employee conditionally. This enables the person to prove his or her worth on the job. After a period of perhaps six months or a year, the firm has the right to discharge that employee based on evaluations from supervisors. Such systems make it easier to fire inefficient or problem employees but do not eliminate the high cost of turnover.

The selection process is often long and difficult, but it's worth the effort because of the high costs of replacing workers. The high costs consist of all that's involved in recruiting, selecting, hiring, orienting, and training new employees, as discussed in the preceding and following pages. The process helps assure that the people an organization hires are competent in all relevant areas, including communications skills, education, technical skills, experience, social fit, and health.

··· HIRING CONTINGENT WORKERS ···

When more workers are needed in a company, human resource managers may want to consider creative staffing alternatives rather than simply hiring new permanent employees. A company with a varying need for employees, from hour to hour, day to day, week to week, and season to season may find it cost-effective to hire contingent workers. **Contingent workers** are defined as workers who do not have the expectation of regular, full-time employment. Such workers include part-time workers, seasonal workers, temporary workers, independent contractors, interns, and co-op students.

contingent workers
Workers who do not have the expectation of regular, full-time employment.

A varying need for employees is the most common reason for hiring contingent workers. Companies may also look to hire contingent workers when full-time employees experience downtimes, there is a peak demand for labour, and quick service to customers is a priority. Companies in which the jobs require minimum training or that are located in areas where qualified contingent workers are available are most likely to consider alternative staffing options.

Temporary staffing has evolved into a major industry. Contingent workers receive few benefits; they are rarely offered insurance or private pensions. They may also earn less than permanent workers. On the positive side, many of those on temporary assignments are eventually offered full-time positions. Managers see using temporary workers as a way of weeding out poor workers and finding good hires. Furthermore, in an era of downsizing and rapid change, some contingent workers have even found that temping can be more secure than full-time employment.

Progress
Check

- What is human resource management?
- What are the six steps in human resource planning?
- What factors make it difficult to recruit qualified employees?
- What are the six steps in the selection process?

···· ▬▬ ····

TRAINING AND DEVELOPING EMPLOYEES FOR OPTIMUM PERFORMANCE

Because employees need to learn how to work with new equipment such as word processors, computers, and robots, companies are finding that they

This UBC finance student is able to gain valuable hands-on work experience through her internship at CIBC Wood Gundy headquarters in Toronto.

training and development
All attempts to improve productivity by increasing an employee's ability to perform.

employee orientation
The activity that introduces new employees to the organization; to fellow employees; to their immediate supervisors; and to the policies, practices, and objectives of the firm.

on-the-job training
Training program in which the employee immediately begins his or her tasks and learns by doing, or watches others for a while and then imitates them, right at the workplace.

apprentice programs
Training programs involving a period during which a learner works alongside an experienced employee to master the skills and procedures of a craft.

off-the-job training
Training that occurs away from the workplace and consists of internal or external programs to develop any of a variety skills or to foster personal development.

must offer training programs that often are quite sophisticated. **Training and development** include all attempts to improve productivity by increasing an employee's ability to perform. Training is short-term skills oriented, whereas development is long-term career oriented. But both training and development programs include three steps: (1) assessing the needs of the organization and the skills of the employees to determine training needs, (2) designing training activities to meet the identified needs, and (3) evaluating the effectiveness of the training. Some common training and development activities are employee orientation, on-the-job training, apprentice programs, off-the-job training, vestibule training, job simulation, and management training.

- **Employee orientation** is the activity that introduces new employees to the organization; to fellow employees; to their immediate supervisors; and to the policies, practices, and objectives of the firm. Orientation programs include everything from informal talks to formal activities that last a day or more and include scheduled visits to various departments and required reading of lengthy handouts. All firms try to recruit people who have the potential to be productive employees. They realize that potential involves effective training programs and proper managerial incentives. Carefully orienting individuals to their new environment can be an important step for the human resource manager.

- **On-the-job training** is the most fundamental type of training. The employee being trained on the job immediately begins his or her tasks and learns by doing, or watches others for a while and then imitates them, right at the workplace. Salespeople, for example, are often trained by watching experienced salespeople perform. Naturally, this can be either quite effective or disastrous, depending on the skills and habits of the person being watched. On-the-job training is obviously the easiest kind of training to implement and can be effective when the job is relatively simple, such as clerking in a store, or repetitive, such as collecting refuse, cleaning carpets, or mowing lawns. More demanding or intricate jobs require a more intense training effort.

- **Apprentice programs** involve a period during which a learner works alongside an experienced employee to master the skills and procedures of a craft. Some apprentice programs also involve classroom training. Many skilled crafts, such as bricklaying and plumbing, require a new worker to serve as an apprentice for several years. Trade unions often require new workers to serve apprenticeships to ensure excellence among their members as well as to limit entry to the union. Workers who successfully complete an apprentice program earn the classification of *journeyman*. In the future, there are likely to be more but shorter apprentice programs to prepare people for skilled jobs in changing industries. For example, auto repair will require more intense training as new automobile models include more advanced computers and other electronic devices.

- **Off-the-job training** occurs away from the workplace and consists of internal or external programs to develop any of a variety of skills or to foster personal development. Training is becoming more sophisticated as jobs become more sophisticated. Furthermore, training is expanding

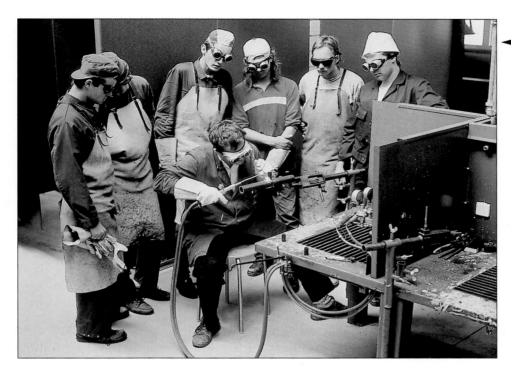

These apprentice welders learn their craft from a skilled professional. Practical hands-on experience is usually combined with class-room training.

to include education (through the Ph.D.) and personal development—subjects may include time management, stress management, health and wellness, physical education, nutrition, and even art and languages.

- **Vestibule training** is done in schools where employees are taught on equipment similar to that used on the job. Such schools enable employees to learn proper methods and safety procedures before assuming a specific job assignment in an organization. Computer and robotics training is often completed in a vestibule school.

- **Job simulation** is the use of equipment that duplicates job conditions and tasks so that trainees can learn skills before attempting them on

vestibule training
Training done in schools where employees are taught on equipment similar to that used on the job.

job simulation
The use of equipment that duplicates job conditions and tasks so that trainees can learn skills before attempting them on the job.

John Cleese, the Monty Python comic, co-founded Video Arts, a company that develops multimedia business training programs. The innovative CD-ROMs provide witty and highly effective training. The program also monitors what workers input and is ready to give them instructions if they become confused about what to do next.

the job. Job simulation differs from vestibule training in that the simulation attempts to duplicate the *exact* combination of conditions that occur on the job. This is the kind of training given to astronauts, airline pilots, army tank operators, ship captains, and others who must learn highly skilled jobs off the job.

<www.oilspill.state.ak.us>

You might find it interesting to learn just how pervasive the consequences of the *Valdez* oil spill have been. Visit this site to see how much is still going on more than 10 years after it happened.

The damage caused by the Exxon *Valdez* oil tanker off Alaska shows how important such training is. A very large crude carrier (VLCC) like the *Valdez* takes six miles to stop when running at 15 knots. By reversing the engines, you can cut the stopping distance to two miles. At any of the half-dozen training institutions in Canada, trainees learn how to pilot such ships on a simulator that resembles a giant video game. You can imagine piloting a ship that is as long as the C.N. Tower is high through a narrow passage with boats all around you. Any accident can cause serious environmental damage. You don't want to learn such skills on the job in a trial-and-error fashion!

••• MANAGEMENT DEVELOPMENT •••

Managers need special training. They need to be good communicators and especially need to learn listening skills and empathy. They also need time-management, planning, and human relations skills.

management development
The process of training and educating employees to become good managers and then developing managerial skills over time.

Management development is the process of training and educating employees to become good managers and then developing managerial skills over time. Management development programs have sprung up everywhere, especially at colleges, universities, and private management development firms. Managers participate in role-playing exercises, solve various management cases, and are exposed to films, lectures, and all kinds of management development processes.

In some organizations, managers are paid to take university courses through the doctoral level. Most management training programs also include several of the following features. (See Bank of Montreal Institute for Learning, discussed earlier in the chapter.)

- *On-the-job-coaching.* A senior manager assists a lower-level manager by teaching him or her needed skills and generally providing direction, advice, and helpful criticism. On-the-job coaching is effective only when the senior managers are skilled themselves and have the ability to educate others. This is not always the case.

- *Understudy positions.* Job titles such as "undersecretary of" and "assistant to" reveal a relatively successful way of developing managers. They work as assistants to higher-level managers and participate in planning and other managerial functions until they are ready to assume such positions themselves. Such assistants may take over when higher-level managers are on vacation or on business trips.

- *Job rotation.* To expose managers to different functions of the organization, they are often given assignments in a variety of departments. Top managers, and potential top managers, must have a broad picture of the organization; such rotation gives them that exposure.

- *Off-the-job courses and training.* Managers periodically go to schools or seminars for a week or more to hone their technical and human relations skills. Such courses expose them to the latest concepts and create a sense of camaraderie as the managers live, eat, and work together in a college-type atmosphere. This is often where case studies and simulation exercises of all kinds are employed.

<www.ml.com>

You may be considering a career in the financial services sector. If so, be sure to visit the Merrill Lynch Web site. Of particular interest are its comments regarding careers offered and its corporate culture.

NETWORKING **Networking** is the process of establishing and maintaining contacts with key managers in your own organization and in other organizations and using those contacts to weave strong relationships that serve as an informal development system. Of equal or greater importance to potential managers are **mentors**, corporate managers who supervise, coach, and guide selected lower-level employees by introducing them to the right people and generally being their organizational sponsors. In reality, an informal type of mentoring goes on in most organizations on a regular basis as older employees assist younger workers. However, many organizations, such as Merrill Lynch and Federal Express, use a formal system of assigning mentors to employees considered to have strong potential.[6]

It's also important to remember that networking and mentoring can go beyond the business environment. For example, college is a perfect place to begin networking. Associations you nurture with professors, with local business people, and especially with your classmates might provide you with a valuable network you can turn to for the rest of your career.

networking
The process of establishing and maintaining contacts with key managers in your own organization and other organizations and using those contacts to weave strong relationships that serve as an informal development system.

mentor
An experienced employee who supervises, coaches, and guides lower-level employees by introducing them to the right people and generally being their organizational sponsor.

DIVERSITY IN MANAGEMENT DEVELOPMENT When women moved into management, they also learned the importance and value of networking and having mentors. But since most older managers are male, women often have more difficulty attracting mentors and entering the network. A series of court rulings has made men-only clubs illegal in Canada, so women are now entering these formerly male preserves and making all the usual business contacts. More and more, women are entering the system or, in some instances, creating their own networking systems. According to Dr. Nina Colwill, consultant on HRM in Brandon, Manitoba, "men, seeing networks as utilitarian, are more likely to receive utilitarian benefits. Women, seeing them as social, may reap mainly social rewards." She believes that it is easy for each side to feel that their approach is superior, whereas it would be much better if each were to learn from the other.[7]

Companies that take the initiative to develop female and minority managers understand three crucial principles: (1) grooming women and minorities for management positions isn't about legality, morality, or even morale; it is about bringing more talent in the door—the key to long-term profitability; (2) the best women and minorities will become harder to attract and retain; and (3) having more women and minorities at all levels means that businesses may be able to serve their increasingly female and minority customers better. If you don't have a diversity of people working in the back room, how are you going to satisfy the diversity of people coming in the front door?

Networking and mentoring are particularly important for women and minorities. Although it has traditionally been difficult for women and minorities to attract mentors, progressive companies now actively take the initiative to develop these employees.

APPRAISING EMPLOYEE PERFORMANCE TO GET OPTIMUM RESULTS

Managers must be able to determine whether or not their workers are doing an effective and efficient job, with a minimum of errors and disruptions. They

performance appraisal
An evaluation in which the performance level of employees is measured against established standards to make decisions about promotions, compensation, additional training, or firing.

do so by using performance appraisals. A **performance appraisal** is an evaluation in which the performance level of employees is measured against established standards to make decisions about promotions, compensation, additional training, or firing. Performance appraisals consist of six steps.

1. *Establishing performance standards.* This is a crucial step. Standards must be understandable, subject to measurement, and reasonable.

2. *Communicating those standards.* Often managers assume that employees know what is expected of them, but such assumptions are dangerous at best. Employees must be told clearly and precisely what the standards and expectations are and how they are to be met.

3. *Evaluating performance.* If the first two steps are done correctly, performance evaluation is relatively easy. It is a matter of evaluating the employee's behaviour to see if it matches standards.

4. *Discussing results with employees.* Most people will make mistakes and fail to meet expectations at first. It takes time to learn a new job and do it well. Discussing an employee's successes and areas that need improvement can provide managers with an opportunity to be understanding and helpful and to guide the employee to better performance. Additionally, the performance appraisal can be a good source of employee suggestions on how a particular task could be better performed.

5. *Taking corrective action.* As an appropriate part of the performance appraisal, a manager can take corrective action or provide corrective feedback to help the employee perform his or her job better. Remember, the key word is *performance*. The primary purpose of conducting this type of appraisal is to improve employee performance, if possible.

6. *Using the results to make decisions.* Decisions about promotions, compensation, additional training, or firing are all based on performance evaluations. An effective performance appraisal system is also a way of satisfying certain legal conditions concerning such decisions.

Effective management means getting results through top performance by employees. That is what performance appraisals are for—at all levels of the organization. Even top-level managers benefit from performance reviews made by their subordinates. The latest form of performance appraisal is called the 360-degree review because it calls for feedback from all directions in the organization: up, down, and all around. Figure 13.6 illustrates how managers can make performance appraisals more meaningful.

FIGURE 13.6
· · · ·
MAKING APPRAISALS AND REVIEWS MORE EFFECTIVE

1. **DON'T** attack the employee personally. Critically evaluate his or her work.

2. **DO** allow sufficient time, without distractions, for appraisal. (Take the phone off the hook or close the office door.)

3. **DON'T** make the employee feel uncomfortable or uneasy. *Never* conduct an appraisal when other employees are present (such as on the shop floor).

4. **DO** include the employee in the process as much as possible. (Let the employee prepare a self-improvement program.)

5. **DON'T** wait until the appraisal to address problems with the employee's work that have been developing for some time.

6. **DO** end the appraisal with positive suggestions for employee improvement.

This requires a Theory Y management style, not Theory X (see Chapter 12). Technology is introducing a whole new approach to performance appraisal, according to one well-known Harvard authority. Rosabeth Moss Kanter has stated that, "in the wired workplace of the future, people will be able to keep track of their own performance on their computers." She believes that they will even be able to calculate their own rewards in the same fashion.[8]

Progress Check

- Can you name and describe four training techniques?
- What is the primary purpose of a performance appraisal?
- What are the six steps in a performance appraisal?

COMPENSATING EMPLOYEES TO ATTRACT AND KEEP THE BEST

<www.onepine.demon. co.uk/pkant.htm>

Rosabeth Moss Kanter identified the key skills for managers who see the need to bring about change within their organizations. She has identified a list of things to be avoided, what she calls *"Ten rules for stifling change."* Visit this Web site to learn these rules and the skills required to bring about successful change.

Employee compensation is one of the largest operating costs for many organizations. The long-term success of a firm—perhaps even its survival—may depend on how well it can control employee costs and optimize employee efficiency. For example, service organizations such as hospitals, airlines, railways, and banks have recently struggled with managing high employee costs. This is not unusual since these operations are considered *labour intensive;* that is, their primary cost of operations is the cost of labour. In the 1990s firms in the airline, auto, and steel industry asked employees to take reductions in wages to make the organizations more competitive. The alternative was to risk going out of business and losing jobs forever. In other words, the competitive environment is such that compensation and benefit packages are being given special attention and are likely to remain of major concern in the near future. (See Figure 13.7 for some common compensation methods.)

A carefully managed compensation and benefit program can accomplish several objectives. They include the following:

- Attracting the kind of people needed by the organization and in sufficient numbers.
- Providing employees with the incentive to work efficiently and productively.
- Keeping valued employees from leaving and going to competitors or starting competing firms.
- Maintaining a competitive position in the marketplace by keeping costs low through high productivity by a motivated workforce.
- Protecting employees from unexpected problems such as layoffs, sickness, and disability.

Service industries, such as the airline industry, are heavily labour intensive. It is imperative in such industries to control employee costs.

••• COMPENSATION FOR WOMEN •••

For many years statistics have shown that Canadian women earn less than men do. As more women obtain university degrees, the salary differential in professional and executive categories is decreasing. However, for the past decade there has been little progress in the huge gap between the earnings of the average woman and the average man. Women have remained stuck at about 65 percent of men's earnings.

In July 1993 the *Toronto Star* carried a report from an annual United Nations study that showed that "Canadian women make 63 percent of the wages of Canadian men." Later statistics show little change. Reporter Debra Black quoted Ms. Menon, the policy analyst in the human development report office of the UN: "In Japan it's 51 percent. In no industrial country is it 90 percent or above. Sweden has the best record with 89 percent." The reports conclusion was that "Canadian women are still getting short shrift when it comes to politics and wages. Women in Canada just aren't treated the same as men." Menon noted, "Canada has done a lot in terms of literacy and education, but not enough has been done in terms of employment wages."[9] There are many historical reasons for this large wage gap. The traditional *women's* jobs—teacher, nurse, secretary—have always paid poorly. But there is much evidence of outright salary discrimination in other types of jobs. By 1998 women's earnings had made some progress but were still way behind men's. Statistics Canada figures[10] showed that the average weekly salary for women in all occupations and industries was $473.00 compared to $683.00 for men. That means that the average woman earned 69 percent of what the average man earned. The highest and lowest percentage of men's earnings that women achieved in 1998 were as follows:

	BEST %	WORST %
By industry categories		
Management and administration	83	
Health care and social assistance	81	
Construction		61
Trade and other services		61
By occupations		
Natural and applied sciences and related occupations	84	
Recreation, sports, travel, and accommodation	82	
Teachers and professors	81	
Retail clerks, cashiers, and supervisors		57
Occupations unique to primary industries		53

As noted in Chapter 1, there are now laws banning such discrimination. Pay equity legislation is beginning to make its way through the provinces and has passed federal hurdles. Unfortunately the governments of Canada, Ontario, and Quebec are setting bad examples by delaying or whittling down the implementation of their laws as they affect their own employees. Officials cite budget cutbacks and the huge costs of making up for past inequitable compensation to female employees as the reasons. Pay equity requires equal pay for work of comparable value, which requires defining *comparable*. For example, which job has more value, nurse or trash collector? This is a difficult and controversial issue because it involves a complex system of job evaluation. HRM departments are alert to this problem and for new job hires most firms are practising equality of pay for women and men.

··· PAY SYSTEMS ···

Like other aspects of HRM, pay systems have undergone an evolutionary development. When work was done at home or in small factories, individuals were paid by piecework—so much for each unit produced. When production became more complex and large numbers of employees worked in big factories where the processes involved joint efforts, piecework was replaced by hourly or daily wages.

Today piecework is prevalent only in low-wage countries or industries. In Canada and all modern industrial countries, this method of compensation has been replaced by a whole range of methods in conformity with a better understanding of employee motivation (as discussed in Chapter 12), the realities of modern production, union contracts, competitive standards, and modern social attitudes. With the overwhelming number of Canadians employed in the service sector, hourly and salary remuneration has become the norm. Commissions are the only payment method that are in effect piecework (see Figure 13.7.)

··· EMPLOYEE BENEFITS ···

Employee benefits include sick leave pay, vacation pay, pension plans, health plans, and other benefits that provide additional compensation to employees. They may be divided into three categories. One group derives from federal or provincial legislation (which varies somewhat from province to province) and requires compulsory deductions from employees' paycheques, employer contributions, or both. These include the Canada/Quebec pension plan, employment insurance, health care, and workers' compensation. You have probably seen some of these deductions from your pay. The second group consists of legally required benefits, including vacation pay, holiday pay, time and a half or double time for overtime, and unpaid maternity leave with job protection.

The third category includes all other benefits and stems from voluntary employer programs or from employer–union contracts. Some are paid by the

Payment Method	Description
Straight salary	Weekly, monthly, or annual amount
Hourly wages	Number of hours worked times agreed-on hourly wage
Commission system	Sales times some fixed percentage
Salary plus commission	Base salary (weekly, monthly, or annual) plus sales times some fixed percentage
Piecework	Number of items produced times some agreed-on rate per unit
Added Compensation	
Overtime	Number of hours worked beyond standard (for example, 40 hours a week) times hourly wages at time and a half or at double time for weekends, after hours, and holidays
Bonuses	Extra pay for meeting or exceeding objectives
Profit sharing	Additional compensation based on company profits
Cost-of-living allowances (COLAs)	Annual increases in wages based on increases in consumer price index

FIGURE **13.7**

COMMON COMPENSATION METHODS

Talk to someone who gets paid in each of the ways described. You will learn how quickly the money can accumulate when you receive overtime. Ask about the pressure of piecework versus the added potential for earnings. Each compensation plan has its benefits and drawbacks. See if you can learn what they are.

Spotlight on Big Business

<www.gwl.ca>

Why Are These Employees So Pleased?

The employees of Great-West Life Assurance Co. work for a major player in the insurance and mutual fund business in North America. The head office is in Winnipeg, and there are offices in all Canadian provinces and American states. They're pleased because the company has an unusual array of employee benefits. The Canadian Mental Health Association honoured the company with a Work and Well-Being Award for its impressive integrated programs, services, and policies designed to look after employees' health and other needs as well as for providing satisfying work and workplaces. A poll conducted by outside consultants found that the employees gave Great-West a higher than 90 percent approval rating.

That is no surprise considering the extensive array of benefits. Besides the typical ones, the company offers such things as insulin supply coverage for diabetics up to $700 annually and a onetime $350 allowance for equipment. It offers mortgages at 80 percent of current rates and contributes $1 for each $3 a worker saves in an employee savings plan. Workers can also buy life insurance free of commission charges.

Employees can take time for work-related courses, and the company pays the cost of tuition and up to $500 for successful graduates. There is a 20,000-volume library and a beautiful art collection, as well as large comfortable lounges, a fitness club, a 240-seat theatre, and a bank on the premises. Postage stamps and bus passes are also available. If an employee is concerned about his or her health, a staff nurse will check his or her blood pressure or give an eye examination. Employees can also get free financial and personal counselling.

Great-West also has a job-sharing program and other flexible work arrangements that are proving attractive to some employees with young children. In addition to all of this, the company has good pay levels, promotion opportunities, and job security. Wouldn't you smile if you worked for such a company? Of course the company is also smiling because it believes it is benefitting from a satisfied workforce.

Sources: Interview with J. Domenico, manager of employee benefits at Great-West, May 22, 1996; E. Innes, J. Lyons, and J. Harris, *The Financial Post 100 Best Companies to Work for in Canada* (Toronto: HarperCollins, 1996), pp. 57–60.

---

employer alone and others are jointly paid by employer and employee. Among the most common are bonuses, company pension plans, group insurance, sick leave, termination pay, and paid rest periods.

The list of benefits is long and has become quite significant—around 35 percent of regular pay. Often, labour negotiations are more likely to concern employee benefits than wage rates. They are no longer at the fringe of negotiations.

For executives and more highly paid managers, the benefits package is more important than additional remuneration. They are already in a high tax bracket and any additional direct income would be taxed at 50 percent or higher, so increases in such nontaxable benefits as dental and health insurance, company contributions to pension plans, and stock options are very attractive.

Employee benefits can also include everything from paid vacations to group insurance plans, recreation facilities, company cars, country club memberships, day-care services, and executive dining rooms. Managing the benefits package is a major HRM issue. Employees want packages to include dental care, legal counselling, maternity leave, and more. (Some types of benefits are recognized as taxable by Revenue Canada.)

cafeteria-style benefits
Benefit plans that allow employees to choose which benefits they want up to a certain dollar amount.

To counter these growing demands, many firms are offering **cafeteria-style benefits** from which employees can choose the type of benefits they want up to a certain dollar amount, such as the example in the chapter-opening Profile. *Choice* is the key to flexible cafeteria-style benefit plans. Employees' needs are more and more varied. Managers can equitably and cost-effectively meet these individual needs by providing benefit choices. For example, older employees might be more interested in good pension plans and holidays, whereas younger employees might concentrate on child care, maternity or paternity leave, or an education package.

••• COMPENSATING TEAMS •••

Thus far we've talked about compensating individuals. What about teams? Since you want your teams to be more than simply a group of individuals, would you compensate them as you would individuals? If you can't answer that question immediately, you are not alone. A 1996 team-based pay survey found that managers continue to be more positive about the use of teams (87 percent) than about how to pay them (41 percent). This suggests that team-based pay programs are not as effective or as fully developed as managers would like. Measuring and rewarding individual performance on teams while at the same time rewarding team performance can be tricky. Nonetheless, it can be done. Football players are rewarded as a team when they go to the play-offs and to the Super Bowl, but they are paid individually as well. Companies are now experimenting with and developing similar incentive systems.

Jay Schuster, co-author of an ongoing study of team pay, found that when pay is based strictly on individual performance, it erodes team cohesiveness and makes it less likely that the team will meet its goals as a collaborative effort. Schuster recommends basing pay on team performance.[11] Skill-based pay and profit-sharing are the two most common compensation methods for teams.

Skill-based pay is related to the growth of both the individual and the team. Base pay is raised when team members learn and apply new skills. The drawbacks of the skill-based pay system are twofold: the system is complex, and it is difficult to correlate skill acquisition and bottom-line gains.

It is important to reward individual team players also. Outstanding team players—those who go beyond what is required and make an outstanding individual contribution to the firm—should be separately recognized for their additional contribution. Recognition can include cashless as well as cash rewards.

A good way to avoid alienating recipients who feel team participation was uneven is to let the team decide which members get what type of individual award. After all, if you really support the team process, you need to give teams freedom to make these decisions.

•••• ▬▬▬ ••••

ADOPTING FLEXIBLE WORK SCHEDULES

By now, you are quite familiar with some of the trends occurring in the workforce. You also know that managers and workers are demanding more from jobs in the way of flexibility and responsiveness. From these trends have emerged several new or renewed ideas such as job sharing, flextime, compressed workweeks, and in-home employment. Let's see how these innovations affect human resources management.

••• JOB SHARING •••

Job sharing is an arrangement whereby two part-time employees share one full-time job. The concept has received great attention in the past 10 years as

job sharing
An arrangement whereby two part-time employees share one full-time job.

more and more women with small children enter the labour force. Job sharing enables mothers or fathers to work part-time while the children are in school and to be home when the children come home. Job sharing has also proved beneficial to students, older people who want to work part-time before fully retiring, and others who prefer to work only part-time. The advantages are:

- Employment opportunities for people who cannot or prefer not to work full-time.
- An employee is more likely to maintain a high level of enthusiasm and productivity for four hours than for eight hours.
- Problems such as absenteeism and tardiness are greatly reduced as part-timers have the free time to attend to personal matters.
- Employers are better able to schedule people into peak demand periods when part-time people are available.

However, as you might suspect, disadvantages include having to hire, train, motivate, and supervise twice as many people and to prorate some employee benefits. Nonetheless, most firms that were at first reluctant to try job sharing are finding the benefits outweigh the disadvantages.

⋯ FLEXTIME PLANS ⋯

flextime plans
Work schedule that gives emloyees some freedom to adjust when they work, within limits, as long as they work the required number of hours.

core time
The period when all employees must be present in a flextime system.

Flextime plans give employees some freedom to adjust when they work, as long as they work the required number of hours. The most popular plans allow employees to come to work at 7, 8, or 9 a.m. and leave between 3:30 and 6:30 p.m. (see Figure 13.8). Usually flextime plans incorporate **core time**, particular hours of the day when all employees are expected to be at their job stations. For example, an organization may designate core time hours between 9:30 and 11:00 a.m., and 2:00 and 3:30 p.m. During these hours, *all* employees are required to be there. Flextime plans, like job-sharing plans, are designed to allow employees to adjust to the new demands of the times, especially the trend toward two-income families. Flextime has been found to boost employee productivity and morale. Specific advantages of flextime include

- Working parents can schedule their days so that one partner can be home to see the children off to school and the other partner can be home soon after school.
- Employees can schedule doctor's appointments and other personal tasks during working hours by coming in early and leaving early or by coming in late and leaving late.

┌   **FIGURE 13.8**   ┐
• • • •
A FLEXTIME CHART

Employees can start any time between 6:30 and 9:30 a.m. They then take half an hour for lunch and can quit from 3:30 to 6:30 p.m. Everyone works an eight-hour day. The blue arrows show a typical flextime day.

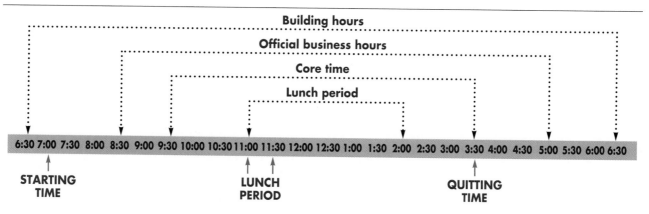

Building hours

Official business hours

Core time

Lunch period

6:30 7:00 7:30 8:00 8:30 9:00 9:30 10:00 10:30 11:00 11:30 12:00 12:30 1:00 1:30 2:00 2:30 3:00 3:30 4:00 4:30 5:00 5:30 6:00 6:30

STARTING TIME   LUNCH PERIOD   QUITTING TIME

- Traffic congestion is greatly reduced as employees arrive and leave over several hours instead of all at once.

- Employees can work when they are most productive; some people are most alert in the morning, whereas others can't get going until 10 a.m.

- Having some choice about sleeping late once in a while or taking off early on Friday afternoon in the spring gives a person a big psychological boost.

- It has obvious advantages for creative people who are most productive at certain times of the day. But it's also helpful for anyone who must work long hours when a proposal is due.

- It helps companies keep employees who might leave otherwise.

There are some real disadvantages to flextime as well. It does not work in assembly line processes where everyone must be at work at the same time. Nor is it effective for shift work.

Another disadvantage to flextime is that managers often have to work longer days to be there to assist and supervise employees. Some organizations operate from 6 a.m. to 6 p.m. under flextime, a potentially long day for supervisors. Flextime also makes communication more difficult; certain employees may not be there when others need to talk to them. Furthermore, some employees could abuse the system if not carefully supervised, causing resentment among others.

Phoebe Wright, a CIBC vice-president, has found that part-time work hasn't hurt her career. Her part-time job also allows her to spend more time with her children.

··· COMPRESSED WORKWEEKS ···

Another option in some organizations is a **compressed workweek.** That means that an employee works four 10-hour days and then enjoys a three-day weekend, instead of working five eight-hour days with a traditional weekend. There are obvious advantages of working only four days and having three days off, but some employees get tired working such long hours, and productivity could decline. Some employees find such a system of great benefit, however, and are quite enthusiastic about it.

compressed workweek
Work schedule made up of four 10-hour days.

··· AN EXAMPLE OF A MODERN HRM DEPARTMENT ···

The Royal Bank is a good example of a large organization whose HRM department has adopted a very progressive and modern approach. For some years the bank has been experimenting with a wide array of options to make the workplace as flexible as possible to meet the changing needs of its workforce. Manager Norma Tombari says that paying careful attention to employees needs is the only way to go. The work and family program consists of an elaborate series of services covering a wide range of issues.

Each service is explained in an attractive brochure and includes information on elder care and child care and how to access the employee and family assistance program. Employees can access magazines, articles, books, and videotapes. There are also three detailed brochures concerning flexible work arrangements: part-time/job sharing, flextime and compressed workweek, and flexiplace.

Tombari says flexible working arrangements are becoming increasingly popular. She notes however, that compressed workweeks do not lend themselves to branches that are open evenings and weekends. As of 1999, some

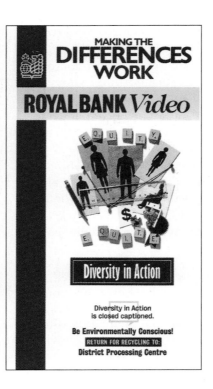

The Royal Bank provides an abundance of information to its employees outlining such services as child care, elder care, and the employee and family assistance program. Royal Bank is a good example of a large organization whose HRM department has adopted a very progressive and modern approach.

<www.royalbank.com/hr/world/workplace.html>

Check out this Web site for current data on the Royal Bank's comprehensive flexible work arrangements plan.

30 percent of Royal Bank employees (about 14,000) were on some form of nontraditional workweek arrangement, and the number was growing steadily. The most popular are job sharing and flexible hours. Tombari reported that a survey by independent consultants showed a 30 percent productivity improvement among employees opting for flexible arrangements.

A 1998 report by the same consultants, Canadian Work/Family Directions, Co., showed that the flexible work arrangements (FWA) program was yielding important positive results for the Royal Bank. Employees and managers agreed, even nonusers of FWA, that it reduced stress and absenteeism, gave greater employee satisfaction and motivation, and enhanced customer services and workforce development while reducing expenses. The report noted that such a program will not work unless managers give it strong support. A notable effect was that employees interpreted the bank's introduction and support of FWA as a sign of a "desirable employer." Finally, the study found no evidence to support concerns that activities like job sharing or flexible hours resulted in less efficiency, disruptions of customer service, or higher costs. As noted above the results were all positive.[12]

••• WORKING AT HOME •••

Until the late eighteenth century, there were no factories or plants as we know them today. People who sewed, knitted, wove, or did a variety of other jobs did them at home. This still survives in many countries, including Canada. Go into any large city and you will find contractors or subcontractors who farm out work. Usually the workers are women, recent immigrants who have no other skills, who do not speak English or French, or who have small children. They are paid by piecework.

Reaching Beyond
Our Borders

<www.bcni.com>
<www.cfib.ca>

Social Benefits, Motivation, and the Free Trade Agreements

Ever since the Free Trade Agreement between Canada and the United States was signed in 1988, various business leaders have suggested that the costs of Canada's social benefits are hindering the ability of our companies to compete with American companies. The Business Council on National Issues (BCNI), which represents the very largest companies in Canada, the Canadian Manufacturers Association (CMA), the Canadian Federation of Independent Businesses (CFIB), and individual business people have made such comments. They have pointed out that such costs are lower in the United States, which weakens the competitiveness of Canadian companies.

When the FTA was being fiercely debated before the 1988 election, these same organizations and other groups who supported the FTA (including former Prime Minister Brian Mulroney) repeatedly assured Canadians that the agreement would pose no threat to our social safety net and our social programs. Now we see them claiming that Canada cannot afford such programs and still remain competitive.

In early 1992 the federal government announced that it was not going ahead with its oft-promised national child-care scheme. The program has been a major demand of a large number of working parents who cannot afford the high cost of private arrangements. Ottawa also abolished family allowances in 1993 and employment insurance benefits were reduced. Our heath-care system is also under considerable attack as being too expensive. So once again the question of social benefits is on the agenda, especially as Mexico was brought into the North American Free Trade Agreement.

We have seen how important a highly motivated workforce is in boosting productivity, thus reducing costs and making businesses more competitive. Successful companies consider expenditures on employee benefits a very good investment. Far-seeing, progressive companies realize that well-motivated employees more than pay for the costs of keeping them motivated. The evidence is very clear on this point. (See Profile and Spotlight on Big Business).

A working parent who has no anxiety about whether his or her children are being well looked after in affordable child-care facilities is a better-functioning employee. Similarly, knowing that the health of your family is looked after by our national health-care system boosts morale and therefore productivity. It seems very short-sighted to think only about immediate dollar outlay rather than about the long-term benefits to companies of having a less worried workforce.

North American executives are often faulted for having a short-term outlook. This is in contrast to companies and governments from the Pacific Rim and Europe who are top international competitors because they have a long-term focus.

We have quoted various commentators who say we have to learn to work smart, not cheap, and point out that Germany, one of the most competitive countries in the world, has better social benefits than we have. That also applies to Scandinavian countries. In Japan, large companies provide a very extensive network of benefits to their employees. All of these countries are now cutting back on these programs, but still remain well above Canadian standards. Which path will we follow?

In the last decade a new phenomenon has arisen—a modern homeworker of a totally different type. Typically he or she has a computer and other electronic communication equipment and may be self-employed or employed by a large company. When these workers are employees, they are paid like other employees, but they can perform their duties at home, thus reducing costs as well as travelling time. They save on eating out, extra clothing, commuting costs, and so on. Employers also cut costs by needing less office space and furniture and having more motivated employees. Working at home is especially attractive for single parents and dual-career families.

Mobile workers create virtual offices that allow them to work from places other than the traditional office. They can use portable computers, cell phones, pagers, fax machines, and network services to conduct business wherever it is convenient.

The old term for working at home is *telecommuting*.[13] The new term is *virtual office* to reflect the practice of carrying office technology in your briefcase or car so you're ready to work anywhere.[14] Peter Firestone, a senior manager in Ernst & Young's information technology consulting division, has no permanent office. His clients provide him with a desk for the duration of each project and he stays linked to his employers by computer and voice mail. The flexibility is a plus, but the downside is not having the camaraderie of fellow workers.[15]

Telecommuting can be a cost saver for employers. For example, IBM used to have a surplus of office space, maintaining more offices than there were employees. Now the company has more mobile workers, with employees telecommuting, "hotelling" (being assigned to a desk through a reservations system), and "hot-desking" (sharing a desk with other employees at different times). About 10,000 IBM employees now share offices, typically with four people to an office.

As mentioned in the first chapter, working at home is expected to become a major aspect of life by the year 2000. How does this affect the responsibility of HRM? The solutions are now being discussed as HRM strives to cope with this new factor.

Critical Thinking

What effect have dual-career families had on the human resource function? Have you noticed any changes in nepotism rules with so many marriages involving two professionals? (*Nepotism* means favouring relatives when hiring.)

What problems can arise when family members work together in the same firm? What is your reaction to employees who date one another?

Progress Check

- Can you name and describe five alternative compensation techniques?
- Can you list five important employee benefits?
- Why is flextime useful?

.... ▬ ....

MOVING EMPLOYEES UP, OVER, AND OUT

Employees don't always stay in the position they were initially hired to fill. They may excel and move up the corporate ladder or fail and move out the front door. In addition to promotion and termination, employees can be moved by reassignment and retirement.

Employment is normally terminated in one of three ways: retirement, voluntary departure, and layoff or dismissal. In all cases HRM is involved as it is responsible for employees during their entire period of employment. Each of these issues is discussed below.

··· PROMOTING AND REASSIGNING EMPLOYEES ···

Many companies find that promotion from within the company improves employee morale. Promotions are also cost-effective in that the promoted employees are already familiar with the corporate culture and procedures and managers do not need to spend valuable time on basic orientation.

Because of the prevalence of flatter corporate structures, there are fewer levels for employees to reach now as compared to the past. Therefore, it is more common today for workers to move *over* to a new position than to move *up* to one. Such transfers allow employees to develop and display new skills and to learn more about the company overall. This is one way of motivating experienced employees to remain in a company with few advancement opportunities.

··· TERMINATING EMPLOYEES ···

As we discussed in previous chapters, downsizing and restructuring, increasing customer demands for greater value, the relentless pressure of global competition, and shifts in technology have human resource managers struggling to manage layoffs and firings.

The issue of layoffs has become very important because of the large number of people let go in the early 1990s. Often, older employees are offered early retirement packages. Many companies counsel these employees to enable them to better cope with their loss of job and to help them find new jobs. Some set up in-house outplacement facilities so that employees can get counselling on obtaining a new job. For senior managers, the company usually pays for private agency career counselling.

The threat of job loss has introduced a strong feeling of insecurity into the Canadian workforce. Insecurity undermines motivation, so HRM must deal with this new issue. Keeping employees fully informed and having a clear policy on termination pay helps to remove some uncertainty. It is important to note that most Canadian jurisdictions require that larger companies give three to six months notice before large layoffs.

Termination usually involves special costs such as terminal pay or penalties, which may be determined by contract for executives, or by union contracts or government regulations. When large companies announce a substantial downsizing you will usually see reference to a special cost charge for the current year that can easily run into many tens of millions of dollars. This is another attraction for companies to employ temporary help, which avoids such costs. Outsourcing is another way around this problem.

··· VOLUNTARY DEPARTURE ···

When an employee leaves as a normal departure, there is no problem. However, if someone leaves because of perceived discrimination—whether because of age, nationality, sex, religion, or ethnicity—then it is a different story. Similarly, if a woman leaves because she feels sexually harassed, the situation is quite different from a person quitting to get a better job or to go back to school. HRM must be alert to any signs or complaints of discrimination or sexual harassment. Not only are these undesirable practices, indicating some potentially serious problems, they are also illegal.

Unfortunately, sexual harassment and discrimination cases continue to crop up regularly across the country. A female engineer working for a subcontractor on the refurbishing of the Peace Tower in Ottawa charged that the main contractor's project manager constantly abused her because she was a woman.[16] The female coordinator of a company in Strathroy, Ontario, filed a complaint with the Ontario Labour Relations Board because she had to go on "stress-induced medical leave." She claimed that she was exposed to "nude calendars, pornographic pictures, and lewd comments." Furthermore, she was told she was "overly sensitive" for complaining.[17]

••• RETIRING EMPLOYEES •••

In addition to laying off employees, another tool used to downsize companies is to offer early retirement benefits to entice older (and more expensive) workers to resign. Such benefits usually involve such financial incentives as one-time cash payments (golden handshakes). The advantage of offering early retirement benefits over laying off employees is that early retirement offers increase the morale of the remaining employees. Retiring senior workers also increases promotion opportunities for younger employees. The better companies help employees prepare for retirement in various ways. They range from seminars on how to plan your financial affairs as income drops to how to develop activities to keep you busy.

•••• ▬▬ ••••
LAWS AFFECTING HUMAN RESOURCE MANAGEMENT

Canada has many laws affecting nearly all aspects of human resource management. We have referred to these laws earlier in this chapter, but now we'll take a closer look.

Because Canada is a confederation of provinces, jurisdiction over many aspects of our lives is divided between the federal and provincial governments. The federal government legislates on national issues, such as employment insurance and pensions; however, the provinces have jurisdiction over most matters, including minimum wages, hours of work, workers' compensation, and discrimination in the workplace.

But it's a little more complicated than that. The federal government also has jurisdiction over certain types of businesses that are deemed to be of a national nature. Banks, insurance companies, airlines, railways, shipping companies, telephone, radio, TV, cable companies, and others are subject to federal law, as are all federal employees. Fewer than 10 percent of all Canadian employees are subject to federal legislation. However, the national Charter of Rights and Freedoms, which is part of the Canadian constitution, overrides all other laws. The federal government had to amend the Unemployment Insurance Act because the Supreme Court had ruled that the act went against the charter in denying coverage to employees over age 64.

What all this means is that there are literally hundreds of laws and regulations, federal and provincial, that apply to all aspects of human resource management. Furthermore, they are constantly being revised because of social pressure or rulings by human rights commissions or courts. One of the most regulated areas involves discrimination.

Laws in all jurisdictions in Canada make it illegal to discriminate against employees because of age, sex, nationality, ethnicity, religion, or marital status. Only Yukon fails to ban discrimination due to physical disability; Saskatchewan, Alberta, and Yukon do not ban discrimination in the case of mental disability. Only Quebec, Ontario, and federal law forbid discrimination based on sexual orientation. Some other forms of discrimination are banned in some provinces or under federal law.

When an employer selects, hires, trains, pays, promotes, transfers, retires, lay off, or fires an employee, HRM must ensure that what is being done and how it is being done do not break any laws. HRM must also make sure health and safety laws are obeyed. So you can see how important the job of HRM is. Managers working in this area must be very sensitive not only to legal requirements but also to union contracts and social standards and expectations, which may be even more demanding.

Ethical Dilemma

REVIEW

Remember the dilemma introduced at the beginning of the chapter? Your boss wants you to find a way, that is not too obvious, of bypassing legal restrictions when interviewing job applicants. He is dangling some monetary bait to tempt you to go along with his plan and threatening not to promote you if you don't. Let's take a look at the opinion of our executives.

Bédard believes that "there are, of course, many subtle questions that are legal and tend to be used to obtain certain information. I have found that when being very honest with candidates, they will often advance information on their own. Employees are usually looking for long-term relationships with an employer and will not want to start off on the wrong foot. Many times accommodations can be made with little disruption."

Reilley has a somewhat different approach. He says that "the law is clear: discrimination of any sort is illegal and unethical. I would communicate my misgivings in writing to my superior. If our working relationship deteriorated, I would seek an interview with my boss's boss and probably start seeking another job if matters didn't improve."

This is what happened in one case, as reported to the Canadian author. At first the employee started thinking up ways to achieve what his boss wanted, perhaps by developing a little secret code for comments about likely age, nationality, and so on, which he would determine by indirect questioning and by making notes on an official-looking sheet. After the interview he would copy the codes to a sticky-note memo, stick it on the application, and then shred the original sheet. The boss could destroy the memo after he had read it. For a while he felt quite satisfied with himself because he thought he had devised a neat system that would satisfy his boss and for which there would be no evidence of anything illegal.

A few days later the employee began to have second thoughts about the scheme. His mother had told him how she was discriminated against when she was first in the job market, and how his Sikh uncle suspects that he had suffered similar discrimination. By the time he reached his apartment he was troubled about his plan. He was in a tough spot because he liked his job and the company he worked for, and believed that he had a good shot at early promotion.

He decided to try what Bédard suggests instead.

••• EMPLOYMENT EQUITY (AFFIRMATIVE ACTION) •••

A well-known 1980s case of discrimination highlights a major problem and how it was solved. A group of women accused the CNR of not hiring them because they were women. The CNR, like many other companies, did not hire women for jobs that were thought to be traditional men's jobs, those for which heavy physical labour was required. In this case the jobs involved maintenance and repairs of the tracks. The Canadian Human Rights Commission ruled in favour of the women. The CNR appealed and the courts ruled against it all the way to the Supreme Court of Canada. There the CNR was told that it had to adopt an affirmative action plan to ensure that women would gradually form a significant part of the maintenance crews.

employment equity (affirmative action) Employment activities designed to right past wrongs endured by females and minorities by giving them preference in employment.

Affirmative action or **employment equity** refers to employment activities designed to right past wrongs endured by females and minorities by giving them preference in employment. This means that CNR had to develop a plan that would result in more women than men being hired for such jobs until the balance was more even. The result is that when a man and a woman are equally qualified the woman must be given preference for a number of years to allow the balance to be adjusted.

reverse discrimination The unfairness unprotected groups may perceive when protected groups receive preference in hiring and promoting.

Some people argue that affirmative action is really a form of reverse discrimination. **Reverse discrimination** refers to the unfairness unprotected groups (say, white men) may perceive when protected groups receive preference in hiring and promoting. The Canadian Charter of Rights specifically allows for affirmative action as a method to overcome long-standing discrimination against groups. Therefore, the courts accept it as being nondiscriminatory in the legal sense. In the United States, and to a lesser extent in Canada, there has been a growing movement against affirmative action because of the reverse discrimination aspect. This has now become a controversial issue.

Progress Check

- Can you name five areas of HRM responsibility affected by government legislation?
- Explain what affirmative action is and give one example.
- Why should HRM be concerned about legislation or court rulings when terminating employment?

SUMMARY
• • • • •

1. Explain the importance of human resource management, and describe current issues in managing human resources.

1. Human resource management is the process of evaluating human resource needs, finding people to fill those needs, and optimizing this important resource by providing the right incentives and job environment, all with the goal of meeting organizational objectives.

   • ***What are some of the current problems in the human resource area?***
   Many current problems revolve around the changing demographics of workers: more women, minorities, immigrants, and older workers. Other problems concern a shortage of trained workers and an abundance of unskilled ones; skilled workers in declining industries requiring retraining; changing employee work attitudes; and complex laws and regulations.

2. Describe methods companies use to recruit new employees, and explain some of the problems that make recruitment challenging.

2. Recruitment is the set of activities used to legally obtain enough of the right people at the right time and to select those that best meet the needs of the organization.

   • ***Why has recruitment become more difficult?***
   Legal restrictions complicate hiring and firing practices. Finding suitable employees can also be difficult if companies are considered unattractive workplaces. Also, it is increasingly difficult to find candidates with the higher educational levels and technical skills needed now.

3. Employee training and development includes all attempts to increase an employee's ability to perform through learning.
   - **What are some of the procedures used for training?**
   They include employee orientation, on- and off-the-job training, apprentice programs, vestibule training, and job simulation.

3. Illustrate the various types of employee training and development methods.

4. Employee compensation is one of the largest operating costs for many organizations.
   - **What compensation systems are used?**
   They include salary systems, hourly wages, piecework, commission plans, bonus plans, and profit-sharing plans.

   - **What are employee benefits?**
   Benefits include sick leave, vacation pay, pension plans, health plans, and other services that provide additional compensation to employees.

4. Summarize the objectives of employee compensation programs, and describe various pay systems and benefits.

5. Workers' increasing need for flexibility has generated innovations in scheduling workers.
   - **What scheduling plans can be used to adjust to employees' needs for flexibility?**
   Such plans include job sharing, flextime, compressed workweeks, and working at home.

5. Explain scheduling plans managers use to adjust to workers' needs.

6. Management development is the process of developing managerial skills over time.
   - **What methods are used to develop managerial skills?**
   Management development methods include on-the-job coaching, understudy positions, job rotation, and off-the-job courses and training.

   - **How does networking fit into this process?**
   Networking is establishing contacts with key managers within and outside the organization to get additional development assistance.

   - **What are mentors?**
   Mentors are experienced staff members who coach and guide selected lower-level people and act as their organizational sponsors.

6. Describe training methods used in management development programs.

7. There are many laws that affect human resource planning.
   - **What areas do these laws cover?**
   All areas are affected because of laws prohibiting discriminatory practices, setting standards such as minimum wages, and regulating health and safety conditions, hours of work, holiday and vacation pay, retirement and firing, pensions, and employment insurance.

7. Illustrate the effects of legislation on human resource management.

KEY TERMS
· · · · · ·

affirmative action or employment equity 424
apprentice programs 406
cafeteria-style benefits 414
compressed workweek 417
contingent workers 405
core time 416
employee orientation 406

flextime plans 416
human resource management (HRM) 396
job analysis 399
job description 399
job sharing 415
job simulation 407
job specifications 400
management development 408
mentor 409
networking 409

off-the-job training 406
on-the-job training 406
performance appraisal 410
recruitment 401
reverse discrimination 424
selection 402
training and development 406
vestibule training 407

DEVELOPING WORKPLACE SKILLS

1. If you experience a typical career you are likely to have about eight different jobs in your lifetime. Therefore, you will have to prepare several résumés and cover letters. Write a cover letter and résumé seeking employment for an entry level position in your local area using the formats suggested in Appendix C following this chapter. Keep it in your file for use when you are job hunting. Don't forget to update it.

2. Read the current business periodicals to find the latest court rulings on issues such as pay equity, affirmative action, unjustified firing, discrimination, and other HRM issues. What seems to be the trend? What will this mean for tomorrow's graduates?

3. Recall the various training programs you have experienced including both on-the-job and off-the-job training. What is your evaluation of such programs? How would you improve them? Share your ideas with the class.

4. Look up the unemployment figures for individual provinces. Notice there are pockets of very high unemployment. What causes such uneven employment? What can be done to retrain workers who are obsolete because of a restructured economy? Is that the role of government or of business? Discuss. Could government and business cooperate in this function?

5. Find several people who work under flextime or part-time systems and interview them regarding their experiences and preferences. Using this information, draft a proposal to your company's management advocating an option for a four-day workweek. Debate this proposal with your class.

INTERNET CHALLENGES

1. Access these job info sites: <english.monster.ca>
   <www.careermosaic.com>
   <www.jobtrak.com>
   <www.jobmatch.com>

   and examine what they contain. Do you find any important differences? List their strengths and weaknesses, from your point of view. Which do you think would be most useful to you if you were job-hunting now? Why?

2. Can you see yourself searching those sites when you graduate? Do you see any positions now available that interest you? Do you see any category that lists many job openings? Are you tempted to plan the rest of your courses so that, on graduation, you would qualify for that type of job?

Practising Management Decisions

CASE 1

· · · · · ·

THE DANGERS OF FIRING AN EMPLOYEE

· · · · · ·

If someone is fired, HRM must be certain the employee's legal and union (if there is one) rights are not abrogated and relevant federal and provincial laws are followed. The history of employer–employee relations has been one of movement from the absolute right of the employer to do as it wishes to important protections for employee rights. One area of protection relates to termination of employment.

Claire Bernstein, a Montreal lawyer and syndicated columnist, has written many columns about this issue. She cited a case of an Alberta employer who fired an employee for refusing to work on Easter Monday. Mondays were the busiest day in his company and all employees knew they had to work that day. The employee took the owner to court and the case went all the way to the Supreme Court, which ruled in the employee's favour. The court agreed with his contention that his religious rights had been violated since his religion forbade him from working on Easter Monday.

Other cases concern workers fired without notice and without cause. For a long-time employee, even a year's pay has been held insufficient. Courts have awarded increased amounts as well as punitive damages for "brutal and callous firing," meaning without notice or cause.

Decision Questions

1. What are the implications for the HRM department of legal rulings against firing for unjust cause?

2. If you were an employer, would you put more effort into screening and training employees, given these rulings? How would this help? Who might benefit or be hurt by such changes?

3. In some cases, an arbitrator has been brought in to settle wrongful discharge cases. What are the benefits of arbitration rather than legal action? Who benefits?

Source: Claire D. Bernstein, *That's Business, but Is It Legal?* (Toronto: Methuen, 1995).

┌ **CASE 2** ┐

• • • • • •

**EMPLOYERS'
LIABILITY
TAKES SOME
SURPRISING TWISTS**

• • • • • •

The potential liability that an employer may have concerning the actions of employees has recently been extended by a decision of the Supreme Court of Canada. The case concerned an employee, Donald Curry, of The Children's Foundation of Vancouver, who was found guilty of 19 pedophilic attacks on children in the Foundation's care. The Foundation is a nonprofit institution that cares for emotionally disturbed children aged 6 to 12. It fired Mr. Curry when it became aware that he had abused another child.

One of the victims, Patrick Bazley, now a 41-year-old resident of Alberta, sued the Foundation claiming that it was responsible for its employees' criminal actions and should be held legally liable for damages. In a unanimous decision, 7 to 0, the Court ruled that The Children's Foundation was liable despite the fact that it was not negligent and had honourable motives. It was supposed to care for "innocent, helpless, and vulnerable" children so it had a legal responsibility to see that they came to no harm.

In a different event, a university department, trying to address the problem of a persistently low percentage of female faculty ran into a possible legal challenge when it tried to correct this imbalance. When professor Angelo Santi became chairperson of the psychology department July 1, 1999, he found that only 3 of 21, or 14 percent, of full-time department faculty were females. The department had been having difficulty attracting women, and three who had been offered positions had accepted offers at other universities. The vice-president, academic, and the university's lawyer were concerned that the university could be found in violation of federal and Ontario employment-equity legislation. So Santi took a bold and unusual step: he placed an ad for a psychology professor specifying that only women should apply. The ad noted that this was an attempt to correct a gender imbalance and that such a procedure was allowed by the Ontario Human Rights Commission.

This ad caused an explosion of opposition in the academic community led by the Society for Academic Freedom and Scholarship (SAFS). Its president, Dr. Doreen Kimura, "internationally acclaimed [retired] scientist ... at Simon Fraser University was 'appalled.'" A fierce dialogue broke out between various camps across Canada. Dr. Kimura pointed to statistics that only 20.5 percent of applicants across all disciplines at universities in Canada were women, but that 34 percent of all hirees were women. This showed that women were twice as likely as men to be hired and that the problem was that not enough females applied for positions. Female Ph.D. and graduate students interviewed thought the ad was a great idea. The SAFS is planning a legal challenge.

Decision Questions

1. If you were a senior manager at The Children's Foundation what would you suggest as a procedure that would ensure that employees are not harming children? Do you see any way that companies can make sure that

employees are not being sexually harassed? What can be done other than issuing clear policy statements that such behaviour is illegal and will not be tolerated?

2. Have you personally witnessed any such behaviour at any job you had? Was anything done about it? Do you feel the situation was properly handled by your employer? If you were in charge what would you have done?

3. What do you think of this attempt by the psychology department of the university to remedy its problem? Do you think it was too extreme or was it necessary under the circumstances? Can you think of any other way that the department could correct the gender imbalance?

4. The United States has long had many affirmative action laws and regulations to help correct the lack of minority, primarily African-American, representation in many aspects of U.S. life. The opponents of affirmative action have long argued that such laws are unfair and undemocratic. In various states affirmative action has been declared a violation of the U.S. constitution. Are you familiar with the specific arguments opponents used? Would any of them apply in the university case?

Sources: "Employer Found Liable for Sexual Abuse," *Globe and Mail*, June 16, 1999, p. A9; Jenefer Curtis, "All's Fair for the Fair Sex," *Globe and Mail*, August 14, 1999, p. D6.

Getting the Job You Want

Appendix C

Now that we have explored human resource management from the business side, let's look at the process from your perspective. You now know that businesses are actively searching for good employees who can produce. Similarly, you are looking for an organization where your talents will be used to the fullest and where you will enjoy working. How can you find a job that will provide the optimal satisfaction for both you and the organization? That is the goal of this Appendix.

If you are older and looking for a new career, your self-assessment has probably revealed that you have impediments and blessings that younger students do not have. First of all, you may already have a full-time job. Working while going to school is exhausting. Many older students must juggle family responsibilities in addition to the responsibilities of school and work. But take heart; you have also acquired many skills from these experiences. Even if they were acquired in unrelated fields, these skills will be invaluable as you enter your new career.

Whether you are beginning your first career or your latest career, it's time to develop a strategy for finding and obtaining a personally satisfying job.

A FIVE-STEP JOB SEARCH STRATEGY

There are many good books available that provide guidance for finding the right job. This Appendix will summarize the important steps.

1. *Complete a self-analysis inventory.* A couple of such programs were discussed earlier. If you want to do an assessment on your own, see Richard Nelson Bolles's *What Color Is Your Parachute?* (Berkely: Ten Speed Press, latest edition). See Figure C.1 for a sample assessment. Career Navigator is a software program that will walk you through five modules of job-seeking strategies from "Know Yourself" to "Land That Job." This program will also help you establish an interviewing strategy.

FIGURE **C.1**
• • • •
**A PERSONAL
ASSESSMENT SCALE**

This assessment will help you in the process of looking for jobs that fit with your personal profile.

Interests

1. How do I like to spend my time?
2. Do I enjoy being with people?
3. Do I like working with mechanical things?
4. Do I enjoy working with numbers?
5. Am I a member of many organizations?
6. Do I enjoy physical activities?
7. Do I like to read?

Abilities

1. Am I adept at working with numbers?
2. Am I adept at working with mechanical things?
3. Do I have good oral and written communications skills?
4. What special talents do I have?
5. In which abilities do I wish I were more adept?

Education

1. Have I taken certain courses that have prepared me for a particular job?
2. In which subjects did I perform best? Worst?
3. Which subjects did I enjoy the most? The least?
4. How have my extracurricular activities prepared me for a particular job?
5. Is my GPA an accurate picture of my academic ability? Why or why not?
6. Do I aspire to a graduate degree? Do I want to earn it before beginning my job?
7. Why did I choose my major?

Experience

1. What previous jobs have I held? What were my responsibilities in each?
2. Were any of my jobs relevant to positions I may be seeking? How?
3. What did I like most about my previous jobs? Least?
4. Why did I take these jobs?
5. If I had it to do over again, would I work in these jobs? Why?

Personality

1. What are my good and bad traits?
2. Am I competitive?
3. Do I work well with others?
4. Am I outspoken?
5. Am I a leader or a follower?
6. Do I work well under pressure?
7. Do I work quickly? Am I methodical?
8. Do I get along well with others?
9. Am I ambitious?
10. Do I work well independently of others?

Desired Job Environment

1. Am I willing to relocate? Why or why not?
2. Do I have a geographic preference? Why or why not?
3. Would I mind travelling in my job?
4. Do I have to work for a large, nationally known firm to be satisfied?
5. Must I have a job that initially offers a high salary?
6. Must the job offer rapid promotion opportunities?
7. In what kind of job environment would I feel most comfortable: a centralized or decentralized structure?
8. If I could design my own job, what characteristics would it have?

Personal Goals

1. What are my short- and long-term goals?
2. Am I career oriented, or do I have broader interests?
3. What are my career goals?
4. What jobs are likely to help me achieve my goals?
5. What do I hope to be doing in five years? In 10 years?
6. What do I want out of life?

Source: Eric N. Berkowitz, Roger A. Kerin, and William Rudelius, *Marketing* (Homewood, IL: Richard D. Irwin, 1989), p. 630.

2. *Search for jobs you would enjoy.* Begin at your university or college placement office, if it has one. Search the Internet at sites indicated in this Appendix and by your placement office. Keep interviewing people in various careers, even after you have found a job. Career progress demands continual research.

3. *Begin the networking process.* Start with your family, relatives, neighbours, friends, professors, and local business people. Be sure to keep a file with the names, addresses, and phone numbers of contacts, where they work, the person who recommended them to you, and the relationship between the source person and the contact.

4. *Prepare a good résumé and cover letter.* Samples are provided in this Appendix.

5. *Develop interviewing skills.* We'll give you some clues about how to do this.

••• THE JOB SEARCH •••

The placement or career service at your school is a good place to begin reading about potential employers (see Figure C.2). On-campus interviewing is an important source of jobs. Another important source of jobs involves sending companies a good résumé and cover letter (see Figures C.4, C.5, and C.7). You can find help identifying companies to contact in your university or college library. Your library may also have annual reports that will give you even more information about your selected companies.

An excellent source of jobs is networking: contacting the people listed in item 3 of the job search strategy at the beginning of this Appendix. Ask them if they know of any job openings, and if they do, whether they know someone who could recommend you. Track those people down and try to arrange a meeting to seek their recommendation.

SOURCES OF JOBS

Personal networking

Internet job sites

On-campus interviewing

Write-ins

Current employee referrals

Job listings with placement office

Want ads

Walk-ins

Cooperative education programs

Summer employment

University/college faculty/staff referrals

Internship programs

High-demand major programs

Minority career programs

Part-time employment

Unsolicited referrals

Women's career programs

Job listings with employment agencies

Referrals from campus organizations

FIGURE **C.2**

• • • •

JOB SOURCES

When looking for a job, be sure to check these sources.

A popular networking tool and source of jobs is the Internet. Web sites are constantly changing, but there are at least two useful sites for job seekers, according to Gregg Blachford of the McGill University Placement Service. The Monster Board can be reached at <monster.ca> and the Riley Guide at <www.dbm.com/jobguide>. Both list Canadian and American job openings. Blachford believes that the Internet is particularly useful for graduate students.

Other good sources of jobs include want ads, summer and internship programs, and walking into firms that appeal to you and asking for an interview. (See Figure C.2 for a detailed list). The *Occupational Outlook Quarterly,* produced by the U.S. Department of Labor, says that "the skills that make a person employable are not so much the ones needed **on the job** as the ones needed to **get the job**, skills like the ability to find a job opening, complete an application, prepare the résumé, and survive an interview."

Read the interview rating sheet in Figure C.3. Note what the recruiters want. Interviewers will be checking your appearance (clothes, haircut, fingernails, shoes), your attitude (friendliness is desired), your verbal ability, and your motivation (be enthusiastic). Speak loud enough to be heard clearly. Note also that interviewers want you to have been active in clubs and activities and to have set goals. Have someone evaluate you on these scales now to see if you have any weak points. You can then work on those areas before you have any actual job interviews.

It is never too early in your career to begin designing a résumé and thinking of cover letters. Preparing such documents reveals your strengths and weaknesses more clearly than most other techniques. Your résumé lists your education, work experience, and activities. By preparing it now, you may discover that you have not been active enough in outside activities to impress an employer. That information may prompt you to join some student groups, become a volunteer, or otherwise enhance your social skills. You may also discover that you are weak on experience, and seek an internship or part-time job to fill in that gap. In any event, it is not too soon to prepare a résumé. It will certainly be helpful in deciding what you would like to see in the area marked "education" and help you to choose a major and other coursework. Let's discuss how to prepare these materials.

••• WRITING A RÉSUMÉ •••

A *résumé* is a document that lists all the information a potential employer needs to evaluate you and your background. It describes your immediate goals and career objectives. This information is followed by an explanation of your educational background, experience, interests, and other relevant data.

If you have exceptional abilities but you do not communicate them to the employer on the résumé, those abilities are not part of the person he or she will evaluate. You must be comprehensive and clear in your résumé to communicate *all* your attributes. Your résumé is an advertisement for yourself. If your ad is better than the other person's ad, you are more likely to get the interview. In this case, *better* means that your ad highlights your attributes in an attractive way.

In discussing your education, for example, be sure to highlight your extracurricular activities such as part-time jobs, sports, and clubs. If you did well in school, put down your grades. The idea is to make yourself look as good on paper as you are in reality. The same is true for your job experience. Be sure to describe what you did, any special projects in which you participated, and any responsibilities you had.

If you include a section on "other interests," do not just list your interests, but describe how deeply you are involved. If you organized the club, volun-

For each characteristic listed below there is a rating scale of 1 through 7; 1 is generally the most unfavourable rating of the characteristic and 7 the most favourable. Rate each characteristic by circling just one number to represent the impression you got in the interview you just completed.

Name of Candidate _____

1. Appearance

Sloppy   1   2   3   4   5   6   7   Neat

2. Attitude

Unfriendly   1   2   3   4   5   6   7   Friendly

3. Assertivness/Verbal Ability

     a. Responded completely to questions asked

        Poor   1   2   3   4   5   6   7   Excellent

     b. Clarified personal background and related to job opening and description

        Poor   1   2   3   4   5   6   7   Excellent

     c. Able to explain and sell job abilities

        Poor   1   2   3   4   5   6   7   Excellent

     d. Initiated questions regarding position and firm

        Poor   1   2   3   4   5   6   7   Excellent

     e. Expressed thorough knowldege of personal goals and abilities

        Poor   1   2   3   4   5   6   7   Excellent

4. Motivation

Poor   1   2   3   4   5   6   7   High

5. Subject/Academic Knowledge

Poor   1   2   3   4   5   6   7   Good

6. Stability

Poor   1   2   3   4   5   6   7   Good

7. Composure

Ill at ease   1   2   3   4   5   6   7   Relaxed

8. Personal Involvement/Activities, Clubs, Etc.

Low   1   2   3   4   5   6   7   Very high

9. Mental Impression

Dull   1   2   3   4   5   6   7   Alert

10. Adaptability

Poor   1   2   3   4   5   6   7   Good

11. Speech Pronunciation

Poor   1   2   3   4   5   6   7   Good

12. Overall Impression

Unsatisfactory   1   2   3   4   5   6   7   Highly satisfactory

13. Would you hire this individual if you were permitted to make that decision right now?

     Yes   No

FIGURE **C.3**

· · · ·

INTERVIEW RATING SHEET

Some employers use an interview rating sheet like this. When you go for a job interview, put your best foot forward.

---

teered your time, or participated more often than usual in an organization, say so in the résumé. Figure C.4 shows a poorly organized version of a résumé. Look it over and see what you think. Then turn to Figure C.5 for an improved version. Can you see how important planning and writing a résumé can be? See Figure C.6 for the type of words you should use in your résumé.

FIGURE **C.4**

· · · ·

INADEQUATE, POORLY ORGANIZED RÉSUMÉ

Stamp out bad résumés. A good résumé should:

1. Invite you to read it; have a clear layout, top-quality printing; eliminate extraneous information.

2. Start sentences with action verbs such as organized, managed, and designed, rather than with lead-ins ("I was responsible for . . .").

3. Highlight those accomplishments related to future work.

4. Be free of spelling, punctuation, and grammatical errors.

5. Speak the reader's language by using the vocabulary of the industry you are targeting.

6. Make a strong statement. This means using only the most relevant information —nothing less, nothing more.

Maria Adzony **18 Nautical Lane** **Windsor, Ont.**	**Age 21** **Height: 1.68 m** **Weight: 55.8 kg** **Hair: Red** **Eyes: Hazel** **Marital Status: Single** **Health: Good**
OBJECTIVE	**To apply management experience and French language skills in a corporation overseas**
EDUCATION	**B.Com., McGill University, Montreal** **Also completed a semester of study abroad in London, England (McGill University)** **Additional Areas of Academic Competence:** **8 Credit Hours in computers using Lotus 1-2-3, Small Business Counseling.** **University Courses included Marketing, French, English Literature, Computer Programming, Data Processing, Statistics, Sociology, Economics** **High School Diploma: St. Agatha's High School, Windsor, Ont.: College Preparatory, National Honour Society, Graduated in top 25% of class.**
WORK EXPERIENCE	
6/92–Present	**Les fleurs Johanne, Montreal, Que. Responsibilities included: bookkeeping, inventory, floral design, selling merchandise, both person to person and by use of computer.**
5/96–8/96	**Waitress, Citronella's Taverna, London, England. Learned to work effectively with an international clientele.**
5/95–9/95	**Hostess, The Clam Shell, Windsor, Ont.**
Activities	**Canadian Marketing Association, Student Marketing Association, Fencing Club**

··· WRITING A COVER LETTER ···

A cover letter is used to announce your availability and to introduce the résumé. The cover letter is probably one of your most important ads when job hunting so it must be done carefully.

1. The cover letter should show that you have researched the organization in question and are interested in a job there. Mention what sources you used and what you know about the organization in the first paragraph to get the reader's attention and show your interest.

2. You may have heard that it is not what you know but whom you know that counts. This is only partly true, but it is important nonetheless. If you do not know anyone, you can get to know someone. Do this by using your network to see if somebody can steer you to a person who either works at the company or can introduce you to someone who is an employee. Ask about training, salary, and other relevant issues. Then, in your cover letter, mention that you have talked with some of

Maria Adzony, B.Com.
18 Nautical Lane
Windsor, Ontario H5J 2K3
(519) 555-1212
fax: (519) 555-1111
e-mail: madzony@isp.ca

EDUCATION

1997	Bachelor of Commerce (Marketing), McGill University
	Among courses taken: marketing research, sales, management, consumer behaviour
1996	Semester abroad, McGill/London, England
1995	39 credit hours, Lotus 1-2-3, small business training—computer science

CAPABILITIES/SKILLS

- Perceive motivations in others, allowing them to produce results based on their goals and commitments.
- Listen to subtle communications and convert them into active resolutions.
- Provide spirit of trust and enthusiasm so that business transactions can occur harmoniously.
- Handle administrative details under pressure to allow boss to pursue higher levels of thinking and decision making.
- Speak and write French fluently.

EXPERIENCE

- Sold floral arrangements at $800 to $1200/month, in person and by telephone and computer.
- Managed all administrative details of medium-size floral shop for five seasons.
- Recognized by British restaurant manager for outstanding courtesy and efficiency.
- Served as restaurant hostess/junior manager when patronage increased more than 33 percent in a three-month period.

| 1992–present | Les Fleurs Johanne, Montreal, Quebec
Sales Assistant |
| 1996 (summer) | Citronella's Taverna, London, England
Waitress |
| 1995 (summer) | The Clam Shell, Windsor, Ontario
Hostess/Junior Manager |

PROFESSIONAL ASSOCIATIONS

Member: Canadian Marketing Association; Student Marketing Association

the firm's employees and that this discussion increased your interest. You thereby show the letter reader that you "know someone," if only casually, and that you are interested enough to actively pursue the organization. This is all part of networking.

3. When describing yourself, be sure to say how your attributes will benefit the organization. For example, do not just say, "I will be graduating with a degree in marketing." Instead say, "You will find that my university/college training in marketing and marketing research has prepared me to learn your marketing system quickly and begin making a contribution right away."

FIGURE **C.5**
. . . .
WELL-ORGANIZED COMPLETE RÉSUMÉ

Check out the new, upgraded version of Maria's résumé, and compare it's impact with the former version.

Things to notice:

1. You would be surprised how many people forget to include their home (permanent) phone number. You can use a second—school—number as well.

2. Eliminate high-school data if they don't add to the total picture. Employers will get this information on the application form anyway.

3. Use action words (see Figure C.6) at the beginning of sentences and paragraphs where you can.

4. Use numbers and quantities where possible.

5. It simplifies matters to eliminate month designations.

6. Rewards and citations help.

7. Note more detail on real results, and the communication of value stressed over simple "duties."

8. It is permissible to claim a piece of the overall successes.

9. If you have any awards or distinctions, they should be listed as a separate category. (Distinction can include being captain of a team.)

Managed	Wrote	Budgeted	Improved
Planned	Produced	Designed	Increased
Organized	Scheduled	Directed	Investigated
Coordinated	Operated	Developed	Sold
Supervised	Conducted	Established	Served
Trained	Administered	Implemented	Handled

4. Be sure to "ask for the order." That is, in your final paragraph state that you are available for an interview at a time and place convenient for the interviewer.

Look at the sample cover lettre in Figure C.7 for guidance. Notice how Maria subtly showed that she read business publications and drew attention to her résumé. Some principles to follow in writing a cover letter and preparing your résumé are:

- Be self-confident. List all your good qualities and attributes.
- Do not be apologetic or negative. Write as one professional to another, not as a humble student begging for a job.
- Research every prospective employer thoroughly before writing anything. Use a rifle approach rather than a shotgun approach. That is, write effective rifle marketing-oriented letters to a few select companies rather than to a general list.
- Prepare your cover letter and résumé using a word processor that has the capability of turning out multiple individualized letters and use letter quality paper and a laser printer. Make sure you spellcheck your documents.
- Have someone edit your materials for spelling, grammar, and style. Don't be like the student who sent out a *second* résumé to correct "sum mistakes." Or another who said "I am acurate wit numbers."

Dear Mr. Franklin,

A recent article in the *National Post* mentioned that your company is expanding its operations into the east. I have always had an interest in your firm, so I read more about you in *The Globe and Mail* Business Report. It seems as though you will be needing good salespeople to handle your expanding business. Mr. Lee Yo, your Toronto sales representative, is a neighbour of mine. He confirmed the newspaper report about your expansion.

I will be graduating from McGill University in June with a Bachelor of Commerce degree, having majored in marketing. My employers have commended me for having very good communication skills, for being resourceful, and for learning quickly in new situations. I believe that these would be useful qualities if I were selling for your company.

I would be pleased to provide additional information at a personal interview to be arranged at your convenience.

Respectfully yours,

[signed] Maria Adzony

- How would you describe yourself?
- What are your greatest strengths and weaknesses?
- How did you choose this company?
- What do you know about the company?
- What are your long-range career goals?
- What courses did you like best? Least?
- What are your hobbies?
- Do you prefer a specific geographic location?

- Are you willing to travel (or move)?
- Which accomplishments have given you the most satisfaction?
- What things are most important to you in a job?
- Why should I hire you?
- What experience have you had in this type of work?
- How much do you expect to earn?

FIGURE **C.8**

. . . .

FREQUENTLY ASKED INTERVIEW QUESTIONS

Be prepared for these frequently asked questions.

- Do not send the names of references until asked.
- Keep both the résumé and the cover letter short to increase their chances of being read. As Figures C.5 and C.7 show, one page for each is best.

••• PREPARING FOR JOB INTERVIEWS •••

Companies usually do not conduct job interviews unless they think the candidate meets the requirements for the job. The interview, therefore, is pretty much a make-or-break situation. If it goes well, you have a very good chance of being hired. So it is critical that you be prepared for your interviews. Following are five stages of interview preparation.

1. *Research prospective employers.* Learn what industry the firm is in, who its competitors are, the products or services it produces and their acceptance in the market, and the title of your desired entry-level position. You can find such information in the firm's annual reports, in Standard & Poor's, and Moody's reports. Dominion Bond Rating Service or the Canada Bond Rating Service reports can also be helpful. In addition, various national newspapers such as the *National Post* and *The Globe and Mail*, and your local papers have useful business sections. There are also business magazines such as *Canadian Business*, *Profit*, and *Les Affaires*. Ask your librarian for help. Together, you can look on the Internet or in the Canadian Business Index and find the company name to look for articles on it. This is a very important first step. It shows your initiative and interest in the firm.

2. *Practise the interview.* Figure C.8 lists some of the more frequently asked questions in an interview. Practise answering these questions and more at a placement office and with your roommate, parents, or friends. Do not memorize your answers, but be prepared—know what you are going to say. Figure C.9 shows some sample questions you might ask the interviewer. Review the action words in Figure C.6 and try to fit them into your answers.

3. *Be professional during the interview.* "You don't have a second chance to make a good first impression," the saying goes. That means that you should look and sound professional throughout the interview. Do your homework and find out how the managers dress at the firm. Then dress appropriately.

FIGURE **C.9**

· · · ·

**SAMPLE QUESTIONS TO
ASK THE INTERVIEWER**

These questions will give
you more information
about the job and will
also show the inter-
viewer that you are
asking intelligent and
relevant questions.

- Who are your major competitors and how would you rate their products and marketing relative to yours?
- How long does the training program last and what is included?
- How soon after school would I be expected to start?
- What are the advantages of working for this firm?
- How much travel is normally expected?
- What managerial style should I expect in my area?
- How would you describe the working environment in my area?
- How would I be evaluated?
- What is the company's promotion policy?
- What is the corporate culture?
- What is the next step in the selection procedures?
- How soon should I expect to hear from you?
- What other information would you like about my background, experience, or education?
- What is your highest priority in the next six months and how could someone like me help?

When you meet the interviewers, greet them by name, smile, and maintain good eye contact. Sit up straight in your chair and be alert and enthusiastic. If you have practised, you should be able to relax and be confident. Other than that, be yourself, answer questions, and be friendly and responsive.

When you leave, thank the interviewers. If you are still interested in the job, tell them so. If they don't tell you, ask them what the next step is. Maintain a positive attitude. Figure C.10 outlines what the interviewers will be evaluating. A few important things *not* to do at an interview to maintain a professional image:

- Do not use vulgar or colloquial language.
- Do not knock previous employers or reveal information about their operations, even if pressed to do so.
- Do not go on at length when answering questions. Keep your replies concise and to the point.
- Do not volunteer negative information about yourself. But, if asked directly, reply honestly.
- Do not rush to ask about salary. Wait for an indication that you are being seriously considered for the job.

4. *Follow up on the interview.* First, write down what you can remember from the interview: names of the interviewers and their titles, any salary figures mentioned, dates for training, and so on. Put the information in your career file. Send a follow-up letter thanking each interviewer for his or her time. You can also send a letter of recommendation or some other piece of added information to keep their interest. "The squeaky wheel gets the grease" is the operative slogan. Your enthusiasm for the company could be a major factor in hiring you.

5. *Be prepared to act.* Know what you want to say if you do get a job offer. You may not want the job after hearing all the information. Do not expect to receive a job offer from everyone you meet, but do expect to

FIGURE **C.10**

· · · ·

TRAITS RECRUITERS
SEEK IN JOB PROSPECTS

1. **Ability to communicate.** Do you have the ability to organize your thoughts and ideas effectively? Can you express them clearly when speaking or writing? Can you present your ideas to others in a persuasive way?

2. **Intelligence.** Do you have the ability to understand the job assignment? Learn the details of the operation? Contribute original ideas to your work?

3. **Self-confidence.** Do you demonstrate a sense of maturity that enables you to deal positively and effectively with situations and people?

4. **Willingness to accept responsibility.** Are you someone who recognizes what needs to be done and is willing to do it?

5. **Initiative.** Do you have the ability to identify the purpose of the work and to take action?

6. **Leadership.** Can you guide and direct others to achieve the recognized objectives?

7. **Energy level.** Do you demonstrate a forcefulness and capacity to make things move ahead? Can you maintain your work effort at an above-average rate?

8. **Imagination.** Can you confront and deal with problems that may not have standard solutions?

9. **Flexibility.** Are you capable of changing and being receptive to new situations and ideas?

10. **Interpersonal skills.** Can you bring out the best efforts of individuals so they become effective, enthusiastic members of a team?

11. **Self-knowledge.** Can you realistically assess your own capabilities? See yourself as others see you? Clearly recognize your strengths and weaknesses?

12. **Ability to handle conflict.** Can you successfully contend with stressful situations and antagonism?

13. **Competitiveness.** Do you have the capacity to compete with others and the willingness to be measured by your performance in relation to that of others?

14. **Goal achievement.** Can you identify and work toward specific goals? Do such goals challenge your abilities?

15. **Vocational skills.** Do you possess the positive combination of education and skills required for the position you are seeking?

16. **Direction.** Have you defined your basic personal needs? Have you determined what type of position will satisfy your knowledge, skills, and goals?

Source: *So You're Looking for a Job?* The College Placement Council.

The more of these qualities you possess the better are your chances of getting and keeping a job.

learn something from every interview. With some practice and persistence, you should find a rewarding and challenging job.

· · · · ▬▬▬ · · · ·

HOW TO MAKE THE BEST USE OF REFERENCES

There is a right time and a wrong time to give interviewers your references or letters of recommendation. It is generally not a good idea to hand over your list of references at a first interview. According to experienced career counsellors, if you wait until after the interview you should have a better idea of what the interviewer is looking for. You can then decide which of your references would be most appropriate for this particular situation. This has two advantages. First, you can call that person and ask for a letter that covers your experience in those relevant areas. For example, if the interviewer tells you that the job entails a lot of travelling and you have done this before, you can tell your reference person to make sure to mention that you travelled regularly for that job. Secondly, you should at the same time tell that person that he or she may be receiving a call from the interviewer. Imagine how embarrassing it would be to have an interviewer call a reference and that person doesn't remember you because you may have worked there a couple of years ago.

···· ▬▬▬ ····

BE PREPARED TO CHANGE JOBS

In the volatile world of business you should expect that you will be following several different career paths over your lifetime. This enables you to try different jobs and stay fresh and enthusiastic. The key to moving forward in your career is a willingness to change jobs, always searching for the career that will bring the most personal satisfaction and growth. Of course, sometimes you will find yourself out of a job, which may require that you look at new career paths as well. This means that you will have to write many cover letters and résumés and go through many interviews during your career. Each time you change jobs, go through the steps in this Appendix to be sure you are fully prepared. Good luck.

Dealing with Employee–Management Issues and Relations

Chapter

14

LEARNING GOALS

After you have read and studied this chapter, you should be able to

1 understand that the most difficult issues facing labour and management today are retraining, job security, and job flexibility.

2 trace the history and role of labour unions in Canada.

3 discuss the major legislation affecting labour and management.

4 outline the collective bargaining process.

5 describe union and management pressure tactics during negotiations.

6 explain a strike and a lockout and who uses these procedures.

7 explain the difference between mediation and arbitration.

For almost a quarter of a century, some of the toughest and most stubborn characters in Canada have succumbed to the charms of Alan Gold. From grizzled longshoremen to armed Mohawk warriors, he has succeeded in winning their trust and reaching agreements where few people expected any progress.

Gold, former chief justice of Quebec Superior Court, gained fame in 1968 when he headed off a strike by longshoremen at the port of Montreal. He mediated a strike by 56,000 rail workers in 1973, ended a bitter postal strike in 1981, and has played a key role in resolving many other labour disputes in construction and airlines as well as at the Royal Mint and the Department of External Affairs.

He was chief arbitrator under the collective agreements between the Quebec government and its employees from 1966 to 1983, when he was appointed chief justice of the Superior Court. He is an honorary life member of the National Academy of Arbitrators (USA), a founding member of the Society of Professionals in Dispute Resolution (USA) and an honorary member of the Corporation professionelle des conseilliers en relations industrielles du Québec.

In the summer of 1990, Gold astonished many observers by negotiating an agreement on human-rights issues in the Oka crisis in Quebec. It was a complex three-way negotiation among the federal government, the Quebec government, and Mohawk warriors at Oka. Before his arrival on the scene, the Oka standoff had seemed virtually impossible to resolve. But his mediation led to the only significant breakthrough in the entire 78-day crisis.

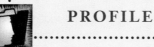

PROFILE

Chief Justice Alan Gold, A Star Labour Mediator

"Whether people are carrying guns or they have economic guns to your head, there are all kinds of pressures ... in these situations," said Gold's son, Marc Gold, who is a law professor at Osgoode Hall Law School (Toronto). He said his father always enjoys a tough job, even if it is regarded as hopeless. He likes to be challenged.

Stewart Sax, a labour lawyer who has worked with former chief justice Gold in labour negotiations, noted that Gold has a history of handling the most intractable disputes "where nobody has the slightest idea of how anyone is ever going to solve the mess."

The key to his father's success, said Marc, is that "he's known to be fair and people trust him to do the fair thing. He's also a very good listener. Most important, he understands that all these issues are human issues. He deals with them on a very human level. He's wonderfully good with people—he likes people." At crucial moments in negotiations, former chief justice Gold is not afraid to use humour to defuse a tense situation.

The long and distinguished career of former chief justice Gold as a jurist, conciliator, arbitrator, and mediator has led to many honours and degrees being showered on him. He has sat on or chaired the boards of many major educational and cultural institutions in Quebec. In retirement he is still active in his specialized field of mediation and arbitration.

Sources: Geoffrey York, "Peacemaker Has Fine Record," *Globe and Mail*, September 7, 1991, p. A8; *Thursday Report*, Concordia University, September 12, 1991; interviews with Alan Gold, May 14, 1996, and December 28, 1998.

A CONFLICT OF VALUES

The main thrust of this chapter concerns labour–management or company–union relations. Sometimes ethical issues arise in these often difficult relations. Suppose you are a chemist working for a small paint company and you are aspiring to a management position. You are a member of the union in your plant, but you are not very pleased with Mike, who is president of your union local. You find him a bit too argumentative and aggressive for your taste, but the majority of employees keep electing him because they are pleased with the contracts he has been able to work out with the owners of the company.

Negotiations have commenced for renewal of the union agreement, which expires shortly. You are on the negotiating team. Both sides are expecting the negotiations to be tough and drawn out. You are friendly with your supervisor, Norman, and he knows you are not enamoured of your union local president. Norman also

knows that you would like to be promoted to a junior management position. One evening, when you are having a beer with him after work, he asks you how you would feel about keeping him posted about what is discussed at the negotiating team meetings. You are a little taken aback by this request. Norman explains that the company is in a weak financial position and Mike seems to have convinced the team to take a firm stand on their demands, which will raise labour costs considerably. All Norman really wants to know is if the union is bluffing so that the company will know how to play its negotiating hand. Norman hints that if you do him this favour he will recommend your promotion to a managerial job. You tell him that you want to think about his request and you will let him know in a couple of days. What would you do? Think about this as you peruse the chapter and we'll come back to the question at the end of the chapter.

THE MAJOR ISSUES FACING LABOUR–MANAGEMENT RELATIONS

Throughout this book we have highlighted the importance of technological change and its impact on the economies of modern industrial societies. You have also seen how maintaining the ability to compete in a globalized trading system is essential if companies want to survive. The North American Free Trade Agreement has added competitive pressures as well as opportunities.

The relationship between management, representing owners or shareholders, and unions, representing employees, has a built-in adversarial basis. Management has the responsibility of operating as profitably as possible and generating growth, with maximum productivity (see Chapter 10) being one of the important tools in achieving those goals. Unions' primary responsibility is the welfare of their members. This includes such factors as decent working conditions, respect and dignity for workers, a reasonable share of the wealth their labour produces for the employer, and assurance the conditions of the contract and government labour laws will not be abrogated. As you will see shortly, with so many employees having lost their jobs in the 1990s, the issues of job security and retraining for the new information-age jobs have become key concerns for unions and the people they represent.

As Canadian companies try to compete more effectively under the demands of technology and world competitiveness, management has been laying off employees, automating operations, and demanding more flexibility in how it uses its remaining workforce. Management must do what its strongest competitors everywhere are doing: adopt the most advanced technological methods, simplify and thin out the organizational structure, and increase productivity.

··· PLANT CLOSINGS AND LAYOFFS ···

These pressures on companies led to numerous layoffs of employees, plant closings, and the loss of more than 300,000 manufacturing jobs in Canada in the early 1990s. Skilled employees with 15, 20, or 25 years experience at their companies found themselves without jobs and wondering what had hit them.

Hardly a week went by without announcements of companies closing, laying off people, or moving all or part of their operations to the southern United States, to Mexico, or even to Asia. These changes were the reason unions in Canada (and in the U.S.) were so opposed to the North American Free Trade Agreement (NAFTA) as discussed in Chapter 2. In both countries there was concern about a wholesale movement of companies' operations to low-wage Mexico. This trend had abated somewhat by the late 1990s, but most Canadian employees had begun to worry about the security of their jobs. Everybody knew somebody, even long-term employees, who had lost their jobs. Thus, job security, as well as job retraining, became major demands of unions in contract negotiations with companies.

The stage was set for sharp conflicts between unions and management. Unions try desperately to hold onto jobs for their members while management fights determinedly to stay alive in the fiercely competitive world in which they find themselves. Unions say: our members need job security, training, and retraining to qualify for the new jobs that require more education and different skills. Management says: we need more flexibility in how we deploy our

The Canadian Auto Workers (CAW) has negotiated with companies such as General Motors to ensure that clauses related to job security and job retraining are included in their contract.

workforce. We must be free to have employees perform multiple tasks and not be bound by rigid job descriptions spelled out in union contracts.

As more traditional labour-intensive jobs are lost due to technology and competition from lower-wage countries, training and retraining become high priorities to prepare the Canadian labour force for the jobs of today and tomorrow. Demands for job security must be tied to job flexibility. To secure a job today, an employee must be able to do a variety of tasks and work well in teams.

How management and labour adapt to these issues will determine our economic and political well-being in the years ahead, and will require substantial cooperation and new attitudes on both sides. In addition, significant funding and close cooperation among government, management, and unions will be necessary to launch and maintain useful training and retraining programs. There are some promising signs of labour–management cooperation that augur well for the future (see Spotlight on Big Business), but the process is proving difficult; it will take years to become a significant factor in Canada.

··· THE IMPACT OF OLD ATTITUDES ···

The problems are greatly complicated by old attitudes that each side brings to the bargaining table. You will recall from Chapter 12 that some managers believe in Theory X for managing people: Work is unpleasant and workers have to be treated by the carrot-and-stick method. Most managers follow the Herzberg/Maslow/Theory Y approach: Workers must be treated as humans. They have different needs and like to participate in decision making.

Similarly, many union representatives are suspicious of management's intentions. They believe that management's goals are to cut wages, reduce the number of jobs, and weaken the union. More far-seeing union leaders realize that there are major, long-term problems that require cooperative efforts to solve.

The result is that specific negotiations succeed or fail depending to a large extent on which of these attitudes the negotiators bring to the table. These issues are not going to disappear. So you can see why there is a continuing need for skilled conciliators like Alan Gold.

··· TRANSFORMATION OF THE CANADIAN ECONOMY: ··· PART OF A UNIVERSAL PROCESS

We are in the midst of a historic transformation of modern industrial society from labour-intensive manufacturing to an automated manufacturing and service economy in which machinery does most of the hard, dirty, dangerous, boring, repetitive jobs, and human beings use their brains rather than their muscles on the job. This process has been developing slowly over the past 200 years, but it picked up speed in the early 1950s and is now rolling along in high gear. Its impact on jobs and relations between management and labour were, and continue to be, significant and considerable, requiring endless adjustments. Let's start by looking at the role played by trade unions in attempting to cope with these critical developments.

···· ▬▬▬ ····

HISTORY AND ROLE OF TRADE UNIONS IN CANADA

A long, rocky road has been travelled in Canada to arrive at the current stage of relatively civilized relationships between owners and managers of businesses and their employees. A complex and often bitter series of events over the last century and a half has involved workers, owners and managers, and government in a long process of evolution that has transformed the rights and obligations of all the parties. This evolution was occurring not only in Canada but in England, the United States, and other countries experiencing the Industrial Revolution.

<www.caw.ca/policy/index.html>

··· THE RISE OF INDUSTRIAL CAPITALISM ···

The nineteenth century witnessed the emergence of modern industrial capitalism. The system of producing the necessities of society in small, home-based workplaces gave way to production in large factories driven by steam and later electricity, both new inventions. Large numbers of people left their homes (or homelike workplaces) to work in large, noisy, dark, dangerous, cold or hot, impersonal places. Accidents were frequent and injured workers were just thrown out and replaced by others. Many writers described these depressing conditions in dramatic terms; the phrase "dark, satanic mills" (coined 200 years ago by famous British artist and poet William Blake) became well known.

This period of almost total disregard of the human needs of workers—especially marked by a dawn-to-dusk work day for miserable wages—was infamous for the brutal exploitation of very young children. Charles Dickens became world-famous in the mid-1800s because of his novels about the maltreatment of children in England. It was not very different in Canada.

A century ago, eight-year-old Canadian children still worked in textile mills on a 12-hour shift for less than $100 a year. Small boys worked long hours in mines, in areas that were inaccessible to adults, for a few cents an hour. A workweek of 80 hours was not uncommon.

The Canadian Auto Workers union has a section on its Web site in which it formally states its policy on significant current workplace issues. One of these, titled "Work Reorganization: Responding to Lean Production," details the Union's position regarding the impact of work reorganization and downsizing. The CAW points out that their goal is to develop "an effective working relationship with management based not on any superficial partnership, but on a negotiated compromise that addresses both worker and corporate concerns."

Be sure to visit this site to learn how the CAW views these issues.

··· BEGINNINGS OF TRADE UNIONISM ···

These conditions gave impetus to the fledgling union movement, started earlier in the new railway and printing industries. Unions set out to establish more humane working conditions and provide workers with a living wage. The struggle was not an easy one because, before 1872, it was illegal to attempt to form unions in Canada. The pioneers in the early struggles were treated as common criminals—arrested, beaten, and often shot.

Long after it was no longer illegal, the idea of workers forming unions to protect their interests was still regarded with suspicion by employers and governments in Canada. Democratic rights for all was still a weak concept and the idea of people getting together to fight for their rights was not accepted as it is today. The union movement was greatly influenced by immigrants from Britain and Europe, who brought with them the ideas and experiences of a more advanced and often more radical background. The growing union movement in the United States also influenced Canada. Many Canadian unions started as locals of American unions and this relationship persists today, as shown later in Figures 14.5 and 14.6. As democracy gradually gained strength, the union movement grew with it. Its participation, in turn, helped democracy sink deeper, wider roots in Canada.

Retraining is a critical issue facing labour–management relations today. This photo shows a Rockwell training instructor explaining a new linking system.

Spotlight on Big Business

<www.cstec.ca>
<www.algoma.com>

Labour, Management, and Government Cooperate in Retraining

When put to the test, labour and management *can* work together. It happened at Algoma Steel Corporation Ltd., where former NDP premier Bob Rae of Ontario appointed some union heads to a special task force. The steel industry's cooperation with labour at Algoma and other sites, well before the special Ontario committee was formed, is seen as one of the few bright lights of labour relations. The Canadian Steel Trade and Employment Congress, a union–management initiative with federal funding, arranged for retraining for 5000 steelworkers over a three-year period. In some cases, that has meant entirely new careers, such as teaching and nursing. In 1993 the Congress was working with 1300 labourers at Algoma and with 6000 workers by 1996.

The forest sector is organizing similar retraining initiatives, while high-tech electronics manufacturing and ▲ communications companies have even more innovative programs. The powerful Canadian Auto Workers (CAW) (formerly led by Bob White, probably the most important union leader in Canada and former leader of the Canadian Congress of Labour) is moving along the same lines. In the 1990 contract with the Big Three auto companies, the union negotiated an income-security clause to assist workers laid off due to technological changes. The CAW also insisted on a three-year program to certify 10,000 workers as having trained on specific types of technical equipment. This retraining program will increase their job mobility.

The recession of the 1990s saw hundreds of thousands of workers lose their jobs without finding new ones, making the question of retraining a pressing economic, social, and political issue.

<www.cpp-rpc.gc.ca>

The Canada Pension Plan has come under considerable attack in recent years. CPP was introduced in the late 1960s to ensure that all working Canadians and their dependants would have a pension income after retirement. Rapid changes in the demographic landscape and cost structures have resulted in a rise in required contribution from employees and employers.

The CPP Web site features "An Information Paper for Consultations on the Canada Pension Plan." Visit the site to learn more about the history and future of the Canada Pension Plan.

••• WORKERS' RIGHTS ENTRENCHED IN LAW •••

As with other movements for greater fairness and equality in our society—women's right to vote, equal rights for minorities and women, protection of children, and so on—when support for employees' rights became widespread in Canada, laws were passed to enforce them. Today we have laws establishing minimum wages, paid minimum holidays and vacation, maximum hours, overtime pay, health and safety conditions, workers' compensation for accidents, employment insurance, the Canada/Quebec Pension Plan, and a host of other rights. It is strange to realize that at one time or another these were all on the agenda of unions and were opposed by employers and governments for many years. They often denounced these demands as radical notions.

The effect of unions goes far beyond their numbers. Companies that want to keep unions out often provide compensation, benefits, and working conditions that match or exceed those found in union plants or offices. Thus, the levels established by unions spill over to nonunion companies. Michelin Tire plants in Nova Scotia are good examples.

•••• ━━━ ••••

LEGISLATION AFFECTING LABOUR–MANAGEMENT RELATIONS

Due to the nature of confederation in Canada, under the Constitution Act of 1867, power and authority are divided between the provinces and the federal government. The federal government has control over specified fields of activity that are national in nature, that is, they operate in more than one province—for example, banks, railways, airlines, telephone companies, broadcasting, and pipelines. So federal legislation applies to unions and labour–management relations in these businesses, as well as to all federal crown corporations and federal civil servants. All other companies are subject to provincial laws, covering perhaps 90 percent of all employees.

Over the years the federal government has passed various laws affecting labour–management relations for those areas under its jurisdiction. These were all consolidated in 1971 into the Canada Labour Code, which is administered by the Department of Labour of the federal government through the Canada Labour Relations Board. The **Labour Relations Board (LRB)** is a quasi-judicial body consisting of representatives of government, labour, and business. It functions more informally than a court but has the full force of law. Similar provincial codes and labour relations boards operate in each province for those areas under their jurisdiction. The laws, regulations, and procedures vary from province to province.

- What are the major issues facing labour–management relations?
- What is being done to solve these problems?
- Can you name the legal body that regulates these relations?

•••• ▬▬▬ ••••

THE COLLECTIVE BARGAINING PROCESS

The Labour Relations Boards (LRBs) oversee **collective bargaining**, the process by which a union represents employees in relations with their employer. Collective bargaining includes how unions are selected, the period prior to a vote, ongoing contract negotiations, and behaviour while a contract is in force and during a breakdown in negotiations for a renewal of a contract. The whole bargaining process is shown in detail in Figure 14.1. It is now illegal for employers to fire employees for union activities.

As you can see, the process is quite regulated and controlled, so that employer and employees, as well as unions, have to follow a strict procedure to ensure that everybody is playing by the rules. The procedure is democratic, and as in any election, the minority has to accept the majority's decisions. The actual contract is quite complex, covering a wide range of topics, as shown in Figure 14.2. We look at some of the major ones next.

••• HIRING CONDITIONS •••

One of the important clauses in a union contract concerns the conditions attached to hiring employees. There are basically four types of conditions.

1. The one favoured by unions is called a **closed shop**, which means that all new hires must be union members. In effect, hiring is done through the union. Unemployed members of the union register for employment or show up daily at a union hiring hall.

2. One step down is a union shop. In a **union shop**, the employer is free to hire anybody but the recruit must then join the union within a short period, perhaps a month.

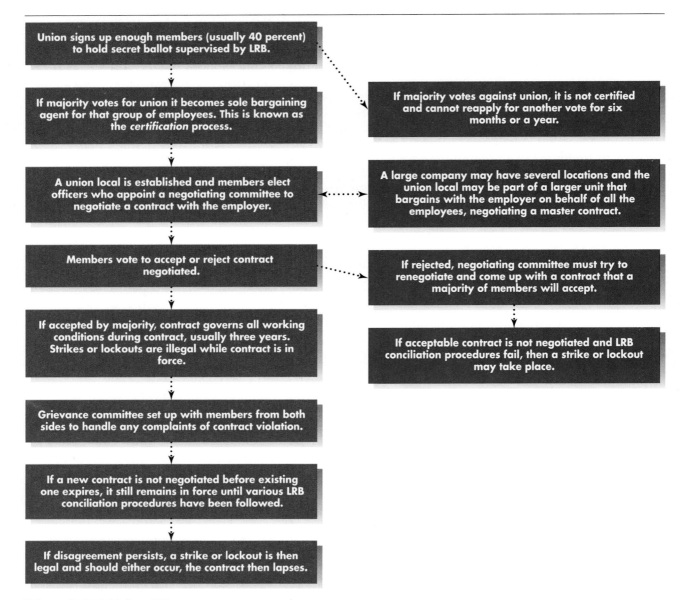

FIGURE **14.1**
• • • •

STEPS IN COLLECTIVE
BARGAINING

**agency shop
(Rand formula)**
Workplace in which a new
employee is not required to join
the union but must pay union
dues. This historic formula was
devised by Justice Rand.

open shop
Workplace in which employees
are free to join or not join the
union and to pay or not pay
union dues.

3. One of the most common conditions is an **agency shop**, which is based on the **Rand formula**. The new employee is not required to join the union but must pay union dues. This historic formula was devised by Supreme Court Justice Rand in 1946 when he arbitrated a major case involving Ford of Canada Ltd. The argument for this requirement is that all employees who benefit from a contract signed by the union should help to pay for the costs of maintaining that union—its officers, union expenses, negotiating committee, shop stewards, and so forth.

4. The hiring condition least popular with unions and one favoured by employers is the **open shop**, where employees are free to join or not join the union and to pay or not pay union dues.

Regardless of which hiring condition prevails, the contract usually contains a **check-off** clause requiring the employer to deduct union dues from employees' pay and remit them to the union (except for nonmembers in case 4). It would obviously be a lot harder to collect union dues individually.

1. Wages, salaries, and other forms of compensation, including the important cost-of-living adjustment clause (COLA).

2. Working hours and time off—regular; overtime; mealtimes; paid holidays, vacations, rest periods, and sick leave; leaves of absence; flextime.

3. Seniority rights—promotions; transfers; layoffs and recalls.

4. Benefit programs—group insurance: medical, dental, and life insurance; pensions; child and elder care; supplementary employment insurance; termination pay; maternity and paternity leave.

5. Grievances—composition of committee; processing of grievances.

6. Health and safety—provision of special clothes or equipment and safe working conditions.

7. Union activities—collection of union dues by the employer (check-off); shop stewards on the floor; union notices.

8. Hiring conditions—closed shop, union shop, agency shop, or open shop.

9. Discipline—rights of management regarding suspension, fines, and termination; hearing process.

FIGURE 14.2

· · · ·

WHAT IS IN A UNION CONTRACT

In general, the contract defines the rights of each party, union and management. There is a long list of topics included in such contracts. The major points are listed here.

Critical Thinking

You have seen how the nature of work is changing. Companies are downsizing and modernizing, so few workers are to be found in large workplaces. More and more people are working out of their homes. What adjustments do you think unions will have to make to accommodate these developments? What signs are there that they are making such changes? Will the nature of unions change?

··· GRIEVANCE PROCEDURE ···

No matter how carefully union contracts are drafted, it is impossible to avoid disagreements. There are always differences of opinion on the exact meaning or interpretation of certain words or clauses. Every day management takes action on transfers, promotions, layoffs, discipline, change in work procedures, and more. Sometimes these actions cause individual workers or the union local to perceive that the contract has been violated. So they file a **grievance**, a formal protest by an individual employee or a union when they believe a particular management decision breaches the contract.

Companies in which relations between management and union are poor or deteriorating usually have a big backlog of unresolved grievances. Where relations are good, there are few grievances and those that arise are quickly settled.

Figure 14.3 indicates all the steps, specified by the contract, in the processing of a grievance. Typically there are five or six levels in this procedure. If the grievance cannot be settled at one level, it moves up to the next level. The final step is an outside arbitrator or arbitration board, but in practice this is quite rare. Many complaints are settled informally and never put in writing.

··· ARBITRATION ···

Arbitration is the process of resolving all disputes, not only grievances, through an outside, impartial third party. The arbitrator renders a decision that is binding on both disputing parties. The arbitrator may be a single person

check-off
Contract clause requiring the employer to deduct union dues from employees' pay and remit them to the union.

grievance
A formal protest by an individual employee or a union when they believe a particular management decision breaches the union contract.

arbitration
The process of resolving all disputes, not only grievances, through an outside, impartial third party.

FIGURE **14.3**
. . . .
STAGES IN PROCESSING GRIEVANCES

The representatives from each side are listed with the stages.

MANAGEMENT		UNION
Stage 1	First-level supervisor	Shop steward
Stage 2	Second-level supervisor	Chief steward
Stage 3	Plant manager	Chief grievance officer
Stage 4	Director of industrial relations	National or international union official
Stage 5	CEO or president	President of union or central labour body
Stage 6	Dispute goes to arbitration (quite rare)	

or a three-person board that is acceptable to both sides. The arbitrator decides in favour of one of the parties.

Arbitration may be *voluntary*: both sides decide to submit their case to an arbitrator. Or it may be *compulsory*: imposed by the government or by Parliament or a provincial legislature. Compulsory arbitration usually occurs in a major or prolonged strike with serious consequences for the public. Usually, nongrievance arbitration (say, for contract disputes) is voluntary and grievance arbitration is compulsory.

••• MEDIATION •••

Sometimes, in bitter disputes between management and labour, arbitration may not be acceptable to both sides. When the differences between the two are extreme or there is much distrust or neither side wants to risk an all-or-nothing decision by an arbitrator, they may opt for mediation. **Mediation** is the use of a third party to attempt to bring the parties to a resolution of their dispute. The mediator tries to get both parties to modify their positions.

mediation
The use of a third party to attempt to bring disputing parties to a resolution by modifying their positions.

Mediators must possess certain important qualities to undertake such a difficult task. After all, they are attempting to bring together parties that are far apart or may hardly be talking to each other. They obviously must be well respected, have excellent negotiating skills, and be patient and determined. It is a high-pressure job involving long sessions and sometimes around-the-clock meetings.

We are fortunate in Canada to have a number of excellent people who possess such qualities and who have resolved some very bitter disputes. One of them is William Kelly, who is now retired after many years of outstanding service. Kelly was a railway man, an officer in one of the rail unions, who was appointed to head up the conciliation branch of the Federal Department of Labour. He settled many notable disputes, thus avoiding strikes in the rail and telephone industries, the postal service, and grain shipping. He was awarded the Order of Canada for his successful mediation efforts.

Former chief justice Alan Gold, of Quebec Superior Court, is another outstanding individual with a notable record of achievement in mediation. Gold has also settled many bitter labour–management conflicts involving longshoremen in Quebec, the postal service, and others. He is profiled at the beginning of this chapter.

WHEN UNIONS AND MANAGEMENT DISAGREE

Because the media give a lot of attention to strikes, you might get the impression that this is the usual pattern of negotiations. But in reality, only a small fraction of contract negotiations between unions and management end in such bitter altercations. Let us examine what happens when an agreement is not reached. What tactics and strategies are available to each side?

Usually, the union is demanding some improvement in benefits, working conditions, job security, or pay increases. The employer usually offers less or very little or sometimes nothing. The union must take actions to try to force the employer to meet its demands. These actions may include such tactics as work-to-rule (working to the exact letter of the agreement), slowdowns, refusal to work overtime, and booking off sick. A favourite negotiating tactic of the police is to refuse to hand out tickets, thus reducing the flow of income to provincial or municipal governments that are unwilling to budge from their bargaining position.

••• STRIKES AND LOCKOUTS •••

If union leaders feel there is strong support among the members, they will call for a strike vote, which is a secret ballot authorizing the union leadership to call a strike when they see fit. If they get a strong mandate, say more than 80 percent in favour, they use this as a lever to convince management to accept their demands without actually going on strike. If management does not give in, the union will have to strike. Of course, if there is a slim majority, say 55 percent, for a strike, union leaders will be very hesitant to call a strike.

Before a strike can be called, all legal requirements must be met. In most jurisdictions in Canada the union must first ask the government to appoint a conciliator, who has a certain time limit to try to bring the parties together. If he or she fails, the union is then legally able to go on strike. The employer is then also free to declare a lockout.

In a **lockout** the *employer* locks the premises against the employees. In either a strike or a lockout, employees are no longer paid their wages or salaries. Clearly, a strike is a weapon of last resort, used only when all else fails. Similarly, management is reluctant to lock out its employees and call a halt to operations. No product, no profits.

Some disputes that received a lot of publicity in 1994 were the acrimonious strike of the major league baseball players, the lockout by baseball owners of the umpires, and the lockout by the NHL owners of the hockey players. Two 1996 disagreements that drew much attention in British Columbia were the lockouts by Safeway and Overwaitea Foods. Both companies were adamant that they would not negotiate with their employees until the unions lowered their demands.

A lockout that was a major news item in the latter half of 1998 concerned another sport, basketball. The main issues were a salary cap on the multimillion-dollar salaries of many veterans, minimum wages levels, and the percentage of total team revenue that would go to the players. The team owners of the NBA locked out the players by refusing to start the 1998–99 season in June 1998. After six months of on-and-off negotiations, there was still no settlement of this bitter dispute. In December the board of

lockout
A drastic negotiating strategy in which the employer locks the premises against the employees.

Bell Canada employees demonstrate in front of the Yellow Pages offices to further their contract demands. During a strike action, employees do not receive wages or a salary.

governors and the commissioner of basketball threatened to cancel the remaining season if no settlement was in place by the seventh of January 1999.[1]

The dispute was finally resolved in February 1999 with everybody agreeing to a shortened season so that the playoffs could commence on time. We can see how important the public's attitude is in such conflicts by looking at the slogans the league used. Prior to the lockout the well-known NBA slogan was "I love the game." To win back public support after the lockout the slogan became "I STILL love this game."

••• BATTLES FOR PUBLIC SUPPORT •••

In major cases where the public is affected—the postal service, nurses, doctors, teachers, transportation, telecommunication, civil servants at all levels—each side plays a propaganda game to win the public to its side. It can be difficult for those not directly involved to really sort out the issues. Sometimes management, if it thinks the public is on its side and the union is perhaps not well organized or lacks strong support, will provoke the union into an unsuccessful strike, weakening the union's bargaining position.

boycott
Urging union members and the public at large not to buy a particular company's products or services.

Unions sometimes ask the public and other union members to **boycott**, or not buy the employer's products or services. One of the most famous and lengthy boycotts in recent history was led by Cesar Chavez of the United Farm Workers, centred in California. The workers were low-paid Mexican immigrants who waged a multiyear battle to improve miserable conditions. In the 1970s they asked people to boycott California grapes to force the growers to negotiate with them.

Their cause was taken up by many organizations in Canada and the United States. At supermarkets in both countries, people picketed and paraded with signs asking shoppers not to buy California grapes. After several years, the growers finally relented and negotiated more reasonable conditions. Most boycotts, in contrast, tend to fizzle out without achieving their goal.

••• OTHER TACTICS •••

Union tactics include rotating strikes—on and off or alternating among different plants or cities—rather than a full-fledged strike in which all employees are off the job for the duration. With rotating strikes, employees still get some pay, which would not be the case in an all-out strike. Many unions build up a strike fund from union dues and use it to give their members strike pay, but that's usually a fraction of their normal wages. Sometimes, in important or long-lasting strikes, other unions will give moral or financial aid.

Management may announce layoffs or a shortened workweek and blame it on declining business. It may say the company is having trouble competing due to high labour costs. It may even adopt the lockout tactic when it seems less costly to close down and cease paying wages than to put up with slowdowns, rotating strikes, or work-to-rule union tactics, all of which can be very disruptive. This tactic may force the union to reduce its demands if individual members cannot do without an income for very long or if there is a weak strike-vote majority.

Remember that arbitration and mediation are always available to the parties in dispute. They may take advantage of these procedures before, during, or after a strike or lockout.

Progress Check

- Can you list the eight steps in the collective bargaining process?
- What are the major areas included in a union contract?
- What is the difference between arbitration and mediation?

STRIKES, LOCKOUTS, AND THE LAW

When a strike is in progress, striking workers usually picket the place (or places) of employment. **Picketing** is the process whereby strikers carrying picket signs walk back and forth across entrances to their places of employment. The aim of these picketers is to publicize the strike and to discourage or prevent people, vehicles, materials, and products from going in or out. They usually allow management personnel through, since they are not union members.

Sometimes, when a company tries to bring in strikebreakers (called **replacement workers** by management and **scabs** by the union) to carry on normal activities, bitter feelings are engendered. This often leads to violence. Picketers mass in large numbers to block buses carrying these strikebreakers. Shouts are uttered, articles are thrown, vehicles are attacked, and so on.

If management's tactics are not successful, it may ask for police protection for the vehicles or ask the courts for an injunction to limit the number of picketers. An **injunction** is an order from a judge requiring strikers to limit or cease picketing or to stop some threatening activity. Injunctions are not as commonly granted now as they used to be.

In Quebec and British Columbia it is illegal for companies to hire replacement workers when a legal strike is in progress. Quite often management employees may continue to work and try to do some of the tasks formerly done by the striking workforce.

picketing
The process whereby strikers carrying picket signs walk back and forth across entrances to their places of employment to publicize the strike and discourage or prevent people, vehicles, materials, and products from going in or out.

replacement workers
Management's name for strikebreakers.

scabs
Unions' name for strikebreakers.

injunction
An order from a judge requiring strikers to limit or cease picketing or stop some threatening activity.

··· RESTRICTIONS ON RIGHT TO STRIKE ···

There are restrictions on the right to strike of various levels of civil servants and quasi-government employees such as hospital workers and electric and telephone utility workers. The provinces and the federal government forbid some employees under their jurisdiction from striking. In other cases, certain minimum levels of service must be provided. For example, when the federal civil service went out on strike in the fall of 1991, employees of the customs service, prison guards, meat inspectors, airport firefighters, and certain other employee were not allowed to strike. When employees of the public bus system in Montreal went on strike in 1990, the provincial Essential Services Council decided what minimum level of services had to be provided during the strike. The same thing happened when Quebec nurses went on strike in 1999. In nearly all provinces, firefighters and police officers are not allowed to strike.

Government sometimes implement back-to-work legislation that forces striking workers back to their jobs. This 15-year-veteran postal worker went back to his route after back-to-work legislation ended a two-week postal strike.

··· LEGISLATING STRIKERS BACK TO WORK ···

Governments have the power to end a particular strike by passing specific legislation to that effect. Provincial and federal governments have done this from time to time to end strikes by teachers, nurses, postal workers, bus drivers, and others. Governments pass back-to-work legislation when they believe they have enough support among the population for such action because of serious hardship to businesses or individuals. For example, the government in British Columbia ordered teachers back to work during the spring of 1993, and so did the Quebec and Saskatchewan government when the nurses went on strike in 1999.

Back-to-work legislation is a denial of the legal right to strike, so it is to a certain extent a restriction of the democratic rights of individuals. Consequently, there is often much contro-

versy about such legislation. It is rarely used to deal with strikes against private businesses.

Striking union locals often turn to affiliated unions for help. Let us now look at the structure of unions in Canada so we can better understand these relationships.

···· ■ ····

STRUCTURE AND SIZE OF TRADE UNIONS IN CANADA[2]

The organization structure of unions in Canada is quite complex. The most basic unit is the union local. One local usually represents one school, government office, or a specific factory or office of a company. However, that local can also cover several small companies or other work units. A local is part of a larger structure that may be a national or an international body. For example, a local of the Ford plant in Windsor is part of the Canadian Auto Workers (CAW) union, which is a national body. A local of the Stelco plant in Hamilton is part of the United Steel Workers (USW) union, which is an international (Canadian and American) body based in the United States.

In turn, both the CAW and USW are part of a central labour organization called the *Canadian Labour Congress (CLC)*. But the USW is also affiliated with another central body, the *AFL-CIO*, based in the United States. Other union locals are part of a union that is affiliated with a different central body called the Canadian Federation of Labour (CFL). Some of these are also affiliated with the AFL-CIO and some are not. In addition, some Canadian locals are part of international unions that are only affiliated with the AFL-CIO central body. There are also provincial and some regional bodies to which various unions belong. These are usually unions that are part of the CLC, the AFL-CIO, or both.

The Canadian Union of Public Employees (CUPE) and the Public Service Alliance of Canada (PSAC) are two of the largest unions in Canada. Together, they represent about 435,000 government employees and are affiliated with the CLC.

To make matters even more complex, while all of the unions referred to above exist in Quebec, there are additional unions in that province that are not connected to any of the central bodies previously mentioned. The Confederation of National Trade Unions (CNTU or CSN in French) is a federation of mostly Quebec-based unions, as is the Centrale des Enseignants de Québec (CEQ), which is a federation of some Quebec teachers' unions. There are also some smaller organizations.

As indicated by Figure 14.4, the total number of union members was under four million in 1998. There has been a small gradual decline in union membership since 1989. About 59 percent of union members are male and 41 percent female. Fifty-six percent are in national unions, 30 percent in international, and 14 percent are government employees. About 35 percent of all Canadian employees are union members.

Figure 14.5 shows the breakdown by different central organizations. The CLC is by far the largest group with some 67 percent of all union membership, including those who are also affiliated with the AFL-CIO. The next largest group at 16 percent are unaffiliated national unions. The general trend over the last few decades has been to more independent Canadian unions. Figure 14.5 shows that just under 28 percent have any affiliation with American-based AFL-CIO.

Unionization rates are highest in the public service and the educational sector. On a provincial basis, Newfoundland has the highest rate of

<www.clc-ctc.ca/policy>

The Canadian Labour Congress plays the role of being the political voice of its member unions. For example, 1998 saw a major controversy regarding the attempt by large Canadian banks to merge. The CLC made a submission to the House of Commons Standing Committee on Finance. In it, the CLC argued very strongly against permitting these bank mergers, taking the position that the public interest requires that they be carefully regulated by government. Visit this Web site to see the CLC submission.

<www.psac.com>

Most unions act as advocates for the political interests of their members, or workers in general. PSAC, for example, has taken a very strong position in favour of pay equity for women. When the Federal Court of Appeal rendered its decision in the *Muldoon case*, PSAC immediately circulated bulletins, press releases, and letters to government officials urging the immediate implementation of pay equity. Visit this Web site to see PSAC's summary of the government's actions and its responses.

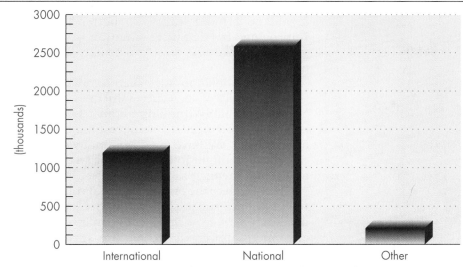

Source: *Directory of Labour Organizations in Canada*, Human Resource and Development Canada, 1998.

FIGURE **14.4**

• • • •

TOTAL NUMBER OF UNION MEMBERS IN CANADA, 1998

The chart shows the breakdown by affiliation as follows:

National	2,556,000
International	1,177,000
Other	204,000
Total	3,937,000

unionization. Although it is difficult to pin down these figures precisely, it has been estimated that if the agricultural sector were omitted and nonunion members in shops with union contracts were included, nearly half the workforce would be covered by union contracts.

• • • • ▬▬▬▬ • • • •

FUTURE OF LABOUR–MANAGEMENT RELATIONS

What about the future of labour–management relations? Obviously we have come a long way in working conditions, hours of work, and wage levels. Many of these gains are now protected by law. Are unions still necessary? We are fortunate to be living in a democratic country where free and private enterprise is the vital feature of our capitalist economic system. We believe that all

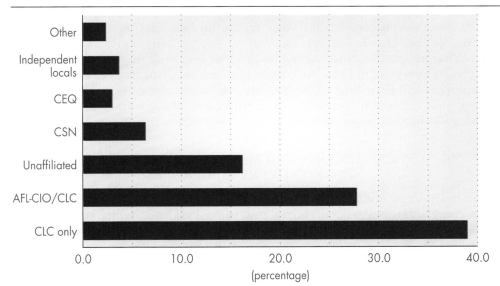

Source: *Directory of Labour Organizations in Canada*, Human Resource and Development, 1998.

FIGURE **14.5**

• • • •

UNION MEMBERSHIP BY CONGRESS AFFILIATION

This figure shows how union membership is distributed by type of affiliation to central labour federations. The chart indicates that about 72 percent of Canadian unionists have no affiliation with American federations. (See text for explanations of the different organization symbols.)

The Canadian Labour Congress (CLC) is the largest and most important labor organization in Canada. Here, outgoing CLC president Bob White celebrates with president-elect Ken Georgetti.

citizens have the right to do what they can, within legal and ethical limits, to better themselves. Improving your financial situation is an admired goal, and those who do so are usually seen as good examples.

In this book you have seen many profiles and other examples of such successful men and women. You are probably thinking about what skills and education you need to achieve financial success and security. We have given you many suggestions of paths you might follow as either an employee or an entrepreneur.

If you select the entrepreneurial route, you will try to build a successful company by providing a necessary service or product in a manner that your customers appreciate. If you are successful, you will ultimately accumulate profits and personal wealth. Perhaps you will be very successful and accumulate great wealth and financial security for yourself and your family. One of the costs of doing business that you will be keeping an eye on is wages, salaries, and benefits paid to employees. Will you want a well-trained, smart workforce capable of keeping up with the rapid pace of technological advances, or will you want your employees to work "cheap"? Will you consider unions nothing but a hindrance?

Suppose you do not see yourself as an entrepreneur and instead go the employee route. Imagine yourself 10 years down the road: You are married with two children and are now a computer software specialist working for a large company in a nonmanagerial role. Will you seek the best salary you can possibly get? Will you want to be part of a group insurance plan to protect your family? How about working hours? Your spouse also works and you need flexible arrangements to be able to spend time with your children and deliver them to school and various other activities. How about overtime demands on the job that cut into time with your children? Will you have adequate, affordable child care?

Can you and your co-workers arrange these and a host of other issues—bonuses, sick leave, termination pay, pensions, retraining, holidays, and more—on a personal basis? Or are you better off with an organization—a union—to represent all of you in making proper contractual arrangements with your employer so that your rights and obligations as well as the employer's are clearly spelled out?

What about all the workers who are less skilled than you are? Some are illiterate; many did not graduate from high school. Hundreds of thousands of employees lost their jobs in the 1990s through no fault of their own. Do they need a strong union to protect their interests? These questions have to be addressed by the people affected.

⋯ CAN UNIONS AND MANAGEMENT STILL ⋯ AFFORD ADVERSARIAL ROLES?

Obviously there are conflicting interests between employers and employees. But every firm seeks to have a highly motivated workforce, which requires good labour–management relations. That means that each side has to appreciate the needs of the other. A progressive union with modern attitudes can cooperate with a progressive, modern management to arrive at workable compromises. Unfortunately, there are as yet very few examples of such cooperation. One good illustration is the Spotlight on Big Business in this chapter, which shows

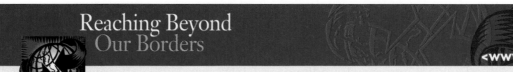

Reaching Beyond Our Borders

<www.gsw-wh.com>

The Future of Labour–Management Relations

Canada faces a choice of the road that labour–management relations will travel. We can either stay on the embattled road we have travelled so far or look to other countries like Germany, the Scandinavian countries, Austria, and Japan, where a different ideology is at work. All of these countries are making or have made the transition to modern high-tech competitive economies where workers are well educated and trained for the new skilled jobs so they can enjoy high incomes and social benefits. There they are learning to work smart, not cheap.

A good Canadian example is the GSW Water Heating Co. of Fergus, Ontario. As shown in Chapter 12, in the box Reaching Beyond Our Borders, GSW is successfully expanding its sales in the U.S. market despite the high wages of its workforce. The secret is a close and trusting relationship with its union, the United Steel Workers. This unusually, for Canada, close rela-

tionship has led to increasing productivity based on excellent and flexible teamwork. The high degree of active employee participation has also led to many cost-saving suggestions. The result has been a Canadian company able to successfully compete with U.S. firms that pay lower wages. Instead of downsizing, GSW continues to hire more employees.

This path requires significant changes in the attitude of workers, unions, managements, and governments. All of us have to change our ways. What is required is a massive, long-term cooperative program involving better education, on-the-job training and retraining programs, substantial investments in new equipment, and government-led incentives to help make it all happen. Nothing less than such an all-out effort will make us more competitive, develop new job opportunities, and keep those opportunities expanding. Are we prepared for such a great challenge? Do we have a choice?

how steel giant Algoma Steel, the Ontario and federal governments, and the United Steel Workers Union worked out a retraining program for redundant Algoma employees. Another good example is the GSW Water Heating Co. discussed in the box Reaching Beyond Our Borders, also in this chapter.

In recent years these relations have been greatly strained because of the massive layoffs and plant closings that have dominated the industrial and commercial landscape of Canada. The most important concern of the average workers has become job security. How can any worker be sure that a job will continue to exist next week, next month, or six months from now? This is a period of great stress in the lives of tens of thousands of Canadian families.

At the same time, businesses are desperately trying to hang on in the face of the many problems that are hurting their ability to compete in the marketplace. These issues have been discussed in various chapters of the book. Bankruptcies have been occurring at record levels, so business owners and managers also wonder if they will still be around next year, or even next month.

These serious economic problems have made labour–management relations very difficult as each side struggles for existence in the highly competitive, technological, globalized business world that now exists. The 1990s saw many tough battles

This nurse is taking a break as her colleagues walk the picket line during an illegal strike staged in 1999 by Quebec nurses.

such as those at Air Canada and Canadian Airlines, and those at the Big Three auto companies and many other companies where unions and management went through long and bitter negotiations that often ended in strikes or just narrowly adverted them. In 1999 nurses went on strike in Saskatchewan, Quebec, and Newfoundland and were very unhappy all across Canada. In Quebec by August, 1999 looked as if it would hit record levels of lost work-days due to strikes and lockouts.[3] These issues are made more complicated by the lingering suspicions that each party is trying to take advantage of the other. Until these barriers are replaced by cooperation, it will be impossible to move into the new era demanded by the competitive conditions of today and tomorrow. Both sides will have to take a good hard look at themselves if progress is to be made.

··· SOME IMPORTANT ISSUES UNIONS ··· ARE CURRENTLY CHAMPIONING

Recent newspaper reports indicate some of the interesting things that unions are doing. For example, the Public Service Alliance of Canada (PSAC) has been fighting a long battle for settlement of wage discrimination by the federal government in female-dominated jobs. The union figures that as much as $1.5 billion is involved in retroactive pay due to female employees going back to 1984. The employees involved were clerks, secretaries, typists, data processors, librarians, hospital service staff, and educational support staff. There are tens of thousands of people involved, and the union argues that the federal government's pay equity legislation has not been adhered to.[4]

As mentioned in Chapter 4, in 1999 the Canadian Human Rights Council finally ruled on the case going back to 1984. It ordered the federal government to obey its own laws by compensating employees (mostly women) who had suffered pay discrimination for 14 years. A fierce public debate developed in Canada on this issue because very large sums of money were involved. Various estimates placed the amount that the federal government would have to pay out in the range of $4 to $6 billion. If it had been a smaller amount, there likely would have been far less disagreement about the principle involved—pay equity. The federal government has launched an appeal of this ruling.

It is somewhat ironic that *The Globe and Mail* of March 9, 1999, carries a reprint of its front page of March 9, 1951, 48 years earlier, with these headlines:

Sex Discrimination Barred
Equal Pay for Men, Women on Same Job, New Bill Rules

The report goes on to note that the then Premier Frost said that the bill was prepared after careful study of similar laws in U.S. states and after a study by a British Royal Commission of the "equal pay problem" in England. Frost further stated that the law was in conformity with the United Nations Universal Declaration of Women's Rights (of which Canada is a signatory). A half-century later we are still struggling with pay equity.

In another case, the Canadian Union of Public Employees (CUPE) has been attempting to provide pensions for same-sex spouses of two of its staff. It is prevented from doing so by certain regulations in the federal Income Tax Act, and so far it has not been successful. It is fighting this case, not only for its own staff, but to set a precedent that governments and companies would have to follow.[5]

In a third cases, Air Canada Pilots' Union and CUPE complained that Air Canada was overworking its staff because of workforce reductions. This caused some dangerous situations, and the company was pressured to increase its staff. Air Canada finally agreed to do so.[6]

<www.eax.se/iwh.htm>

As was noted in this and preceding chapters, the role of unions and the nature of labour–management relations differ in different countries. Visit this Web site to see an example from Sweden. It deals with the issue of working hours and flextime. Notice the underlying view that workers and management are *social partners*, and the Swedish assumption that the best solution to these issues lies in direct discussion and agreement between the parties, rather than in precise government regulations.

Many other issues involve labour–management relations, some of which have been discussed in the previous chapter: testing for drugs and AIDS, working with employees who have AIDS, pay equity for women, affirmative action, and so on. These issues are often difficult to address because of differences of opinion among union members and among managers.

.... ▬▬ ....

HOW ETHICAL ARE UNIONS?

An oft-heard opinion is that unions are too powerful in Canada. This opinion is demonstrated by the inconvenience caused by strikes that disrupt public services from time to time. We also hear charges that some union leaders are more interested in building and protecting their little empires than in protecting their members' interests. Added to this list of criticisms is the charge of a lack of democracy in union operations and even some cases of corruption. It is important to maintain a proper perspective when considering these and other charges against unions. An overall assessment is difficult in this complex situation.

We should remember that occasionally businesses are accused of illegally trying to fix prices. They are also charged with polluting the environment or breaking environmental laws. Companies that provide food or pharmaceutical products are sometimes accused of playing with people's health. Some of these companies are found guilty of the charges. Obviously this does not mean that all managements should be condemned. Similarly, we should exercise caution when evaluating the charges of corruption or careerism in unions. We should not forget unions' significant achievements of improving the living standards and working conditions of millions of Canadians.

.... ▬▬ ....

EXECUTIVES AS EMPLOYEES OF COMPANIES

We normally think of senior and middle managers as people who run companies. While they are not labour and are not eligible to join unions, they are also employees and are subject to company policies. Some important issues concerning executives are discussed below.

••• EXECUTIVE COMPENSATION •••

Most senior executives are well paid and have generous benefits such as stock options, pensions, and bonuses. They carry heavy responsibility, and their compensation should be proportional to that responsibility. In the United States compensation information relating to public companies must be published, but it is not required under Canadian law, except in Ontario. The Ontario Securities Commission requires most publicly listed companies to divulge the compensation of their top executives.

Ironically, we also get a peek into compensation for some Canadian executives if their companies operate in the United States because they are subject to American disclosure regulations. As a result, there has been much criticism in Canada about the high levels of such compensation and some generous settlements when CEOs are terminated. These are called *golden parachutes* because they provide a gentle landing.

Critics have directed their fire at companies that were being particularly generous with their top people despite doing poorly or incurring substantial losses as a corporation. An article in *Canadian Business* showed that many Canadian CEOs were getting multimillion-dollar annual salaries and bonuses;

but the author called the whole system a "crapshoot" because often compensation bears no relationship to performance.[7] The whole issue of rising executive compensation is becoming more contentious in Canada. As the gap between executive and employee compensation continues to widen, union leaders and other Canadians are concerned that this issue is symptomatic of the general divergence in income between the upper 20 percent of the population and everyone else. The gulf is not yet as wide as in the U.S., where this issue is also attracting a lot of attention.

One of the most prestigious management consultants in the world, Peter Drucker, has been critical of executive pay levels since the mid-1980s, when he suggested that CEOs should not earn much more than 20 times the salary of the lowest-paid employee. Some companies have followed Drucker's advice. For example, at Herman Miller Inc., a Michigan producer of office furniture, the chief executive is limited to 20 times the average worker's pay. The company has a long record of being at the forefront of the movement to make employees feel that they are an integral part of the company, resulting in excellent labour–management relations. Unfortunately, many companies have ignored Drucker's suggestion. If you were a hot-dog vendor making minimum wage at any of the Walt Disney theme parks, it would take you 17,852 years to make as much as CEO Michael Eisner earned in 1996. Today the average chief executive of a major corporation makes 209 times the pay of a typical factory worker.

An editorial in *The Globe and Mail (G&M)* on June 6, 1999, strongly supports a chorus of shareholder complaints criticizing the incredible remuneration of the chairman of Repap Enterprises Inc., which *The G&M* calculates at $38 million for a company that has posted losses for three years. The editorial notes a string of well-known Canadian companies—and it cites examples such MacMillan Bloedel, the Loewen Group, and Spar Aerospace—where shareholders have been expressing disapproval of high compensation for company chiefs. These are signs, says *The G&M*, that the days of the "old boys' network" that never embarrassed members of the club openly, are over.

••• EXECUTIVE RESPONSIBILITY AND RISK •••

In many companies, senior executives are also on the board of directors that has the final legal and managerial responsibility for the company on behalf of the shareholders. Some people argue that given this heavy burden, executives are entitled to adequate compensation. Several recent cases highlight this issue.

The Ontario Court of Appeal ordered three directors, two of whom were executives, to personally pay almost half a million dollars to 100 former employees for wages and termination pay because they were laid off when the plant was closed. In another case, the Canada Labour Relations Board ordered four directors who were executives of STN Inc. to pay $567,000 in vacation, severance, and termination pay to 316 former employees of bankrupt STN.[8]

In a different case, General Motors filed a suit against a former top executive and VW in Europe accusing him of stealing thousands of company documents and turning them over to Volkswagen when he left GM to become a senior executive at VW. He denied the charges and says he merely took his expertise to his new job.[9] Eventually VW agreed to pay a multimillion-dollar settlement.

••• PROBLEMS OF MIDDLE MANAGERS •••

The main problem facing middle managers today is the decimation in their ranks. Computers, the recession, employee empowerment, and fiercer global competition have all combined to play havoc with the role of these managers. Entire levels of management have been removed, and bureaucracies have become flatter as companies become decentralized. This reduces costs while enabling greater participation in decision making by all employees and faster responses to market conditions. Thus a major problem of this group of managers is insecurity of employment.

···· ▬ ····

CARING FOR CHILDREN AND ELDERS

One of the growing problems in employee–manager issues arises as a result of the entry of large numbers of women into the workforce. One of the issues has to do with caring for children and the elderly. Although men are increasingly shouldering responsibility in these areas, most of the responsibility still falls on women, which has resulted in very heavy burdens being placed on them. These burdens lead to greater stress and absenteeism.

In general, employers have been slow to respond to this situation. "What often puts elder care on the agenda," according to Anne Martin-Matthews, a professor of family studies at the University of Guelph, who did a survey on this issue, "is when a (senior) executive ... has a mother who breaks her hip." That's when the company's traditional evaluation of what a good employee is begins to be questioned.[10]

Whereas managers might have said the first in and the last to leave is the best employee, they are now being encouraged to focus on output rather than time spent in the office. So a women who works fewer hours because of elder-care or child-care responsibilities is not automatically rated below best. What is accomplished rather than when it is done becomes more important in progressive companies. As noted in previous chapters, companies like the Royal Bank, Bank of Montreal, MacMillan Bloedel, Great-West Life, and others have become sensitive to these needs of their employees. Flexible hours and job sharing go a long way to reducing employee stress and absenteeism.

Many companies recognize the need to adjust to the changing demands of the workforce by offering employees day-care centres such as this one. Child care and elder care are two issues gaining the attention of employers.

REVIEW

Remember the dilemma about a supervisor's request that you keep him posted about discussions at the union negotiating committee's meetings? Our executives have similar outlooks on this one. Bédard believes that "the situation is delicate because of the relationship with Mike, the union's president. A person in a position of trust must not betray that trust. Information tends to eventually leak out and once credibility is lost, it is lost forever. Whether within the union or in a management position, honesty is the best policy."

Reilley believes employees must respect social norms and suggests some specific behaviour. "I would not provide Norman [with] any inside union information. Nor would I inform the union president of Norman's

intervention as this could be very damaging to the negotiations and labour–management relations. I would at least remain entirely neutral. I would also consider resigning from the contract negotiating team."

It is definitely unethical to reveal information concerning confidential negotiating team meetings. The proof is in how you would feel if what you had done leaked to your co-workers. You should also be aware that Norman's request is probably an infringement of the particular labour code governing these negotiations. Furthermore, the bait Norman is dangling might even be interpreted as a bribe, which could be a criminal offence. This situation is more than one of ethics.

Critical Thinking

Top executives' high pay creates tremendous incentives for lower-level executives to work hard to get those jobs. Their high pay also creates resentment among workers, some shareholders, and some members of the general public. What's your position on the proper level of top-executive compensation? Is there a way to make the pay more equitable?

How do you justify the fact that many sports and entertainment stars make millions of dollars? Should top executives take a cut in pay when these people don't? What's the difference between the two groups?

Progress Check

• What is the relationship between injunctions and picketing?
• When is back-to-work legislation used?
• How do labour and management have to cooperate to solve current problems?

SUMMARY
• • • • •

1. Understand that the most difficult issues facing labour and management today are retraining, job security, and job flexibility.

1. There are many difficult issues facing labour and management.
   • ***What are the most difficult?***
   The tough recession, and competitive and technological pressures, force management to push for job flexibility and to pare labour costs to the bone. This results in large job losses at a time when new jobs are hardest to find, so systematic retraining on a large scale has emerged as a key issue. Retraining requires substantial funding and close cooperation among government, management, and unions.

2. Trace the history and role of labour unions in Canada.

2. Unions have a long history in Canada.
   • ***What was their main objective and was it achieved?***

Their main purpose was to improve workers' poor conditions and wages by forming unions that would fight for workers' rights. All this has been largely achieved and many early demands are now entrenched in law.

3. Much labour legislation has been passed by federal and provincial governments.
   • **What is the major piece of legislation?**
   The Canada Labour Code of 1971 consolidated all the federal laws into one. It set up the Canada Labour Relations Board to administer the code. There are equivalent provincial laws and boards.

3. Discuss the major legislation affecting labour and management.

4. The whole process of employees bargaining with their employers through a union is called collective bargaining.
   • **What are the steps in this process?**
   See Figure 14.1 for the steps in collective bargaining.

4. Outline the collective bargaining process.

5. During negotiations, each side employs various tactics to further its strategy.
   • **What tactics are commonly used?**
   Labour may engage in slowdowns, booking off sick, refusing to work overtime, work-to-rule, or it may take a strike vote. Management may announce layoffs or shorter work weeks, claiming lack of orders due to uncompetitiveness because of high labour costs.

5. Describe union and management pressure tactics during negotiations.

6. When negotiations break down, management and labour can employ their ultimate weapons.
   • **What are these?**
   Employees can go on strike, withdrawing their services. Management can lock out its employees—literally shut the doors and prevent them from coming to work.

6. Explain a strike and a lockout and who uses these procedures.

7. There are methods of settling differences when the parties are at a stalemate.
   • **What are these methods?**
   Arbitration is one option. This means a third party is asked to settle the points of disagreement by ruling in favour of one side or the other. Mediation is another option. This involves asking a third party to try to reconcile the parties. This means asking both to modify their demands.

7. Explain the difference between mediation and arbitration.

KEY TERMS
• • • • • •

agency shop (Rand formula) 450	collective bargaining 449	mediation 452
arbitration 451	grievance 451	open shop 450
boycott 454	injunction 455	picketing 455
check-off 451	**Labour Relations Board (LRB)** 449	replacement workers 455
closed shop 449	lockout 453	scabs 455
		union shop 449

DEVELOPING WORKPLACE SKILLS

1. Debate the following in class: Unions are necessary because the only way employees can protect their interests is by having their own organization to represent them and fight for their rights.

2. Develop a list of three issues of importance to employees that are not mentioned in this chapter. Talk to a union official or a human resource manager of a large company about these issues.

3. Your union is divided on the question of employment equity to correct the inferior position of women in your industry. Some men say that it is unfair

to them to allow preferential hiring for women. What do you think? Is this reverse discrimination? Is it justifiable?

4. Debate the following in class: Business executives receive a total compensation package that is far beyond their value. Take the opposite side of the issue from your normal stance to get a better feel for the other point of view.

5. Child care, parental leave, and flexible working hours are important issues for many fathers and mothers. Should businesses and government agencies be required to provide these? Do you think that legislation is necessary to meet these requirements? Is there any other way to achieve these?

INTERNET CHALLENGES

1. Search through the Web sites of your local newspapers for reports on union–management controversies or agreements in your area. If you cannot find anything search <www.newswire.ca> for news about Ford and the CAW (Canadian Auto Workers), who were involved in important negotiations in September 1999. Search under CAW and Ford. Do these reports indicate any interesting new developments in the relations between these two parties? Do you see any signs of conciliation or compromise so that together they can face the difficult adjustments of competing globally in the new millennium, as discussed in this chapter?

2. Do some surfing through the major search engines by inputting the keywords *labour* (*or labor*) *unions*. Try also *union-management*. Confine your search to the last two years. Can you find any references to speeches by union or management leaders about the need to be less adversarial? If you can't find much, try *Canadian Labour Congress* as the keywords.

Practising Management Decisions

The 1990s were disastrous for hundreds of thousands of Canadian employees, especially in the manufacturing area. Hundreds of plants and offices closed because of bankruptcy, consolidation, or transfer of operations to the United States or Mexico. In some cases, management advised unions that the only way they could avoid closing would be substantial concessions in wages and other changes in existing contracts.

Union leaders and their members are in a quandary when faced with such decisions. Sometimes they think management is bluffing. Sometimes they are reluctant to give up contract conditions they fought long and hard for. Accepting wage cuts or benefit reductions when the cost of living continues to rise is not easy. Agreeing to staff reductions to save other jobs is also a tough decision. Unions worry about where these concessions will end. Will there be another round of layoffs or even worse in a few months?

A good example is Phillips Cable Ltd., in Brockville, Ontario, where 350 workers lost their

CASE 1

· · · · · ·

PLANT CLOSINGS, UNIONS, AND CONCESSIONS

· · · · · ·

jobs when the plant was closed. This occurred despite drastic worker concessions in 1991 that were supposed to be "the miracle cure to keep the operations afloat." Brian McDougall, president of Local 510 of the Communications, Energy, and Paperworks Union, Canada, said that everyone was devastated and in shock and disbelief.

This example highlights the dilemma facing unions. Many reports indicate that the new millennium will see tough bargaining, with labour–management peace imperilled.

Decision Questions

1. What would you recommend to union workers whose employer is threatening to close down unless they agree to wage or other concessions?

2. Is there some alternative to cutting wages or closing down? What is it?

3. Union workers often feel that the company is bluffing when it threatens to close. How can such doubts be settled so that more open negotiations can take place?

4. Laws have been passed that require plants with more than a certain number of employees to give up to six months' notice of intention to close. Do you think that such legislation helps businesses to show employees that they are serious about closing a plant and thus get concessions from labour? Are such tactics ethical? Do these laws have any effect on investment decisions?

Sources: Susan Bourette, "Labour Peace May Be in Peril," *Globe and Mail, Report on Business*, February 5, 1996, p. B1; Margot Gibb-Clark, "Unions Predict Bargaining 'Tension' in 1996," *Globe and Mail, ROB*, January 3, 1996, p. B15; Gayle MacDonald, "Workplace Experiment Fails to Save Plant," *Globe and Mail, ROB*, February 21, 1996, p. B6.

CASE 2

MOMMY AND DADDY TRACKS

In 1989, an article by Felice N. Schwartz called "Management Women and the New Facts of Life" appeared in the *Harvard Business Review*. The article dealt with the increase of women in the workplace and the career challenges they would face in the highly competitive work environment of the 1990s. Schwartz said that the problem in the past has been that women had to choose between the fast track at work or staying home to care for their children. What she proposed was called a "mommy track" in business.

Fundamentally, a woman could opt for one of two choices in her work career. She could choose not to have children and to get on the fast track, thus competing equally with men. Then she would have a shot at making partner in the law firm or chief executive officer in her business career. Or she could choose the mommy track, where options for taking extended leave or working part-time would allow for balancing work and family. The second choice would pretty much preclude a woman from making partner or becoming the top executive. Many women cheered the article because they felt it brought attention to a major issue in employee relations. The National Association of Female Executives membership endorsed the idea with more than a 60 percent majority.

The mommy-track controversy was not overlooked by business. Extended parental leaves, flexible work schedules, and job sharing were just a few of the creative ways business sought to deal with the problem of balancing work and home. Today the controversy has taken a new turn. Daddy tracking is a key employee issue that emerged in the 1990s. The daddy track appears to be reserved mostly for professionals, such as Mark Janosky of Eastman Kodak, who took off four months from the company (with benefits but no pay) to be a full-time father. Janosky is typical of many men trying to balance the questions of career and family. James A. Levine, director of the New York-based Fatherhood Project, suggested that if legal trends continue, firms that offer maternity leaves for women may have to provide paternity leaves for men.

How far will men go toward pursuing the daddy track? It's hard to tell. Men do earn on the average almost 40 percent more than women, so the family budget could suffer a big setback. Also, many men feel the hint of a daddy track could be detrimental to their career and provoke negative reactions from family and work peers.

Even the thought of such a tracking system causes much controversy. The debate is healthy and productive because it is an important question. Canada can only benefit from getting this issue out into the open and trying to develop practical, ethical solutions.

Decision Questions

1. Divide the class into two groups: those who like the idea of mommy and daddy tracks and those who do not. Each group should defend the position it is normally against so you have a chance to view the controversy from the other side. Debate the issue and see if you can come to some consensus.

2. In some European countries companies pay full salaries for up to 15 months to men and women who take family leave. Is such a benefit possible or acceptable in the Canadian system?

3. Is the issue of family responsibility the same for men and women or do you see some real differences? What specific differences, if any, do you note? Should companies put equal emphasis on both mommy tracks and daddy tracks?

4. Do you think it's possible for a man or woman to be on the mommy or daddy track at one stage in life and then move to the career fast track when the children get older?

Sources: "The Mommy Track Debate," *The Wall Street Journal*, May 23, 1989, p. A1; Keith H. Hammonds, "Taking Baby Steps Toward a Daddy Track," *Business Week*, April 15, 1991, pp. 90–92; interviews with LC Consultants, Montreal, June 1996; a variety of newspaper, magazine, and TV news reports, 1999.

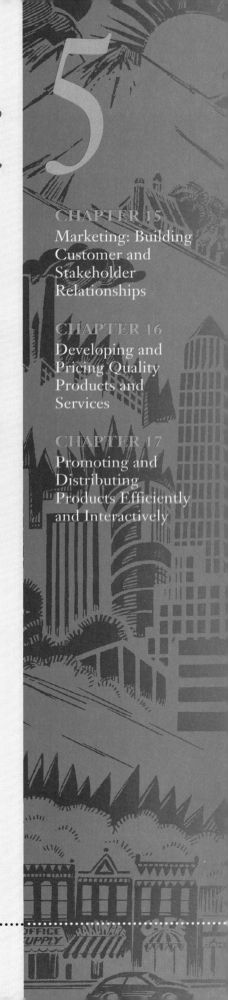

Part 5

Marketing: Developing and Implementing Customer-Oriented Marketing

Marketing: Building Customer and Stakeholder Relationships

Chapter

15

LEARNING GOALS

After you have read and studied this chapter, you should be able to

1 define marketing and summarize the steps involved in the marketing process.

2 describe marketing's changing role in society and the merging of the marketing concept with total quality management.

3 describe how relationship marketing differs from traditional marketing.

4 list the four Ps of marketing.

5 apply the four parts of the marketing research process to a business problem.

6 differentiate between consumer and industrial markets.

Akran Networks Ltd. in Ottawa made such rapid progress in a few years that it made the top 100 list of *Profit* magazine. Its rapid progress from $2 million sales in 1990 to $29.5 million in 1995 was due to the drive and marketing know-how of its president, Raman Agarwal. At first, he was making and selling computers, but when the big retailers began to dominate the consumer market in 1991, he gave that up and concentrated exclusively on corporate and government business. This is an important lesson for all business people: you must know your market well so that you will know where to focus your efforts.

Once Agarwal had determined his target market, he decided that superior service was an essential ingredient for establishing a first-class reputation. Agarwal states that customer service and competitive pricing are his main tools for competing with bigger rivals. Akran's smaller size means low overhead, which enables it to underprice the competition.

As far as service is concerned, the company guarantees that it can respond to problems in half an hour. The result is that it retains 98 percent of its customers, which is an extremely high rate of retention. Akran has built partnerships with companies across Canada and around the world so that it can extend its service to customers' needs anywhere.

A case in point: When the Department of National Defence in Halifax ran into a problem, it called Akran's toll-free number at 9 p.m. Akran was able to send one of his partners to replace a hard drive that same night. Another case: When the Governor General's office ran into a printer problem that no firm could solve, Akran was able to get a part shipped from the United States within 24 hours. This

kind of service led the comany to get a half-million dollar contract to supply a computer network for the Governor General's office. Such service leads to very effective word-of-mouth publicity.

To be able to deliver this kind of service, Akran has developed a highly motivated workforce of 35 people. They all have their own business card and are called *associates*. They get cash bonuses ranging from $25 to $100 for things like letters from satisfied customers, implementing ideas from the firm's suggestion box, and identifying promising new products.

By 1999 Raman had again shifted the focus of his company and was concentrating on "complete systems solutions to small and medium-sized public and private sector companies with full product procurement, implementation, support, and training." Akran continues to win awards and Agarwal is often interviewed on national and local TV and radio. In 1995 and 1996 he was nominated for the Entrepreneur of the Year award by international management consultants Ernst & Young. Agarwal has also been invited to participate in the Team Canada trade missions to various countries.

Raman Agarwal is an excellent example of an entrepreneur in a cutting-edge industry who knows his market and is quick to anticipate and adapt to rapid changes in that market, so that he can meet the needs of his business customers. Now Akran is concentrating on research and development of new technologies including Distant Interactive Satellite Learning and Direct PC Satellite Internet Solutions.

Sources: Interviews with Raman Agarwal, June 6, 1996, and August 23, 1999; "Growing Your Business in Four Easy Lessons," *Profit*, June 1996, pp. 44–45; Akran Web site <www.akran.ca>.

PROFILE

Raman Agarwal Knows his Market

Ethical Dilemma

WIRED FOR ACTION

Roy, Maria, and Hector are three aging baby boomers, all having crossed the 50-year line this year. They've known each other for several years, through work and recreational contact. At different times each has expressed a desire to start their own business. After lengthy discussions they decide to set up shop together providing recreational products to their contemporaries. Since demographic data point to a surge in the baby boomer population bubble, they feel they can develop a profitable business utilizing their considerable work experience in this area.

Their first hurdle is doing some market research to get specific reliable information about what unfulfilled niches there are in the market. Since all three friends mix extensively with their contemporaries at work, at play, and when socializing, they came up with the idea of wearing concealed tape recorders that will pick up what

the people around them are saying. They can throw innocent questions at friends, associates, and so on about products or services they would like to have but cannot seem to get. They expect everyone to speak freely, without concerns about being recorded. Their plan is to tape conversations for month, then sit down and screen the tapes carefully to see what useful ideas emerge. They could then compare these ideas with information from business magazines, newspapers, the Internet, and TV programs to see how they compare.

What do you think about the idea of secretly taping people's conversations and comments? Is there anything unethical about this procedure? Would you undertake such a procedure for market research? Would you feel upset about someone taping you secretly? Think about these questions as you go through the chapter and we'll ▲ have a look at possible answers at the end.

<www.the-cma.org>

The Canadian Marketing Association is a professional association for people in the marketing area. It has established a code of ethics and standards of practice. If you are thinking about a career in marketing, be sure to check out this Web site!

marketing
The process of determining customer wants and needs and then profitably providing customers with goods and services that meet or exceed their expectations.

CAREER PROSPECTS IN MARKETING

If you were to major in marketing, a wide variety of careers would be available to you. You could work in a retail store or for a wholesaler. You could do marketing research or get involved in product management. You could go into selling, advertising, sales promotion, or public relations. You could get involved in transportation, storage, or international distribution. As you read through this marketing chapter, consider whether a marketing career would interest you.

WHAT IS MARKETING?

From an organizational perspective, such as that of Akran Systems Ltd., **marketing** is the process of determining customer wants and needs and then profitably providing customers with goods and services that meet or exceed their expectations. More simply, the marketing process used to be described as:

FIND A NEED AND FILL IT

In the past businesses made products first and marketing was then responsible for selling and distributing those products. For a number of reasons that approach, as you will see in this chapter, is obsolete. Today productive

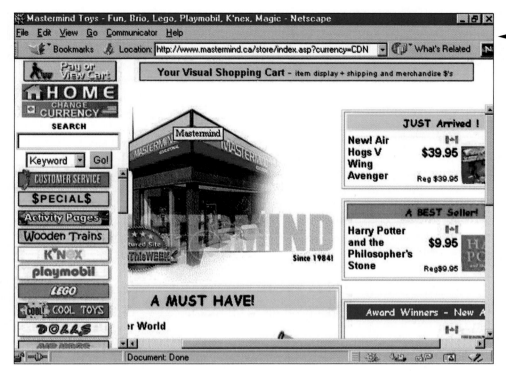

Mastermind Toys has made its products widely accessible throughout Canada and the United States by offering their products for sale through the Internet.

capacity is enormous and the customer is king, so competition is fierce. Businesses must determine exactly what customers (and potential customers) need and want, and then deliver those goods and services in a way that gives customers so much satisfaction that they will want to remain customers and not look elsewhere. The Profile of Raman Agarwal's Akran is a good example of such a company. However, today's conditions also demand that companies continually try to improve their products and how they make them accessible to customers. Offering your products and services for sale through the Internet is a good example of making purchase easier for your customers. In addition businesses must also create new products that they believe will lead to new consumer needs. Nobody was asking for television broadcasting, computers, VCRs, CDs, or cell phones, but these products all quickly became major items demanded by consumers and companies. Thus, creating and filling new needs is also a major marketing activity.

This chapter and the following two will explore all of these aspects of marketing. You will see why marketing has become one of the crucial activities of businesses, employing a substantial segment of the workforce. Many job opportunities exist in this field. Think about that as you study these three chapters. Try to visualize what aspect of marketing intrigues you as a starting career or as a possible long-term job.

···· ▬▬ ····

UNDERSTANDING THE MARKETING PROCESS

The best way for you to understand marketing is to take one product and follow the marketing process that led to the development and sale of that product (see Figure 15.1). You may start the process by remembering that the basis

FIGURE **15.1**
- - - -

THE MARKETING PROCESS

Note the logical progression from the first to the last step.

> **Find a need**
>
> **Conduct research**
>
> **Design a product to meet the need based on research**
>
> **Set a price and do product testing**
>
> **Determine a brand name, design a package and logo**
>
> **Select a distribution system**
>
> **Design a promotional program**
>
> **Build a relationship with customers**

product
Any physical good, service, or idea that satisfies a want or need.

brand name
A word, letter, or group of words or letters that differentiates your product from those of competitors.

of marketing is finding a need and filling it. Your first step is to find a need. Imagine that you and your friends want something for breakfast that's fast, nutritious, and good tasting. Some of your friends eat Quaker's 100% Natural cereal but are not happy with its sugar content.

You ask around among your acquaintances and find a demand for a good-tasting breakfast cereal that's nutritious, high in fibre, and low in sugar. That leads you to conduct a more extensive marketing research study to determine whether there's a large market for such a cereal. Your research supports your hypothesis: there's a large market for such a cereal. "Aha," you say to yourself. "I've found a need." As part of your research you will have also learned what price range will be acceptable to your market. A lot of people may like the idea of your proposed cereal but they will not buy it if the price is too high. That's why *pricing information* must be part of your research.

You've now completed one of the first steps in marketing. You've researched consumer wants and needs and found a need for a product that's not yet available.

••• DESIGNING A PRODUCT TO MEET NEEDS •••

The next step is to develop a product to fill that need. A **product** is any physical good, service, or idea that satisfies a want or need. In this case, your proposed product is a multigrain cereal made with an artificial sweetener. Note that this broad definition of product includes services. Banks, insurance and brokerage firms, and other providers of services regularly refer to the services they offer as *products*. Because services constitute such a large part of the economy, more than half of all marketing efforts are devoted to services.

It's a good idea at this point to do *concept testing*. That is, you develop an accurate description of your product and ask people whether the concept (the idea of the cereal) appeals to them. If it does, you might go to a manufacturer that has the equipment and skills to design such a cereal and begin making prototypes. *Prototypes* are samples of the product that you take to consumers to test their reactions. The process of testing products among potential users is called *test marketing*.

The purpose is to test whether there are enough potential consumers prepared to buy your product at a certain price. This is necessary to determine whether it would be profitable to start manufacturing your product. You can either produce it yourself or have another company produce it for you. (Remember *outsourcing* discussed in previous chapters?) At the same time you have to design an appropriate package, a brand name, and a logo. A **brand name** is a word or group of words or letters that differentiates your product from those of competitors.

Cereal brand names, for example, include Cheerios, Special K, and Raisin Bran. You name your cereal *Fiberrific* to emphasize the high fibre content and terrific taste. We'll discuss the product development process, including packaging, branding, and pricing, in the next chapter. Now, we're simply picturing the whole process (see Figure 15.1) to get an idea of what marketing is all about.

••• GETTING THE PRODUCT TO CONSUMERS •••

Once the product is manufactured, you have to choose how to get it to the consumer. You may want to sell it directly to supermarkets or health food stores, or you may want to sell it through organizations that specialize in distributing food products. Such organizations are called *marketing intermediaries* because they're in the middle of a series of organizations that distribute goods from producers to consumers. We'll discuss intermediaries and distribution in detail in Chapter 17. We'll also look at the Internet as a growing medium of direct distribution to consumers.

··· ESTABLISHING A RELATIONSHIP ···
WITH CUSTOMERS

One of the last steps in the marketing process is to promote the product to consumers. Promotion consists of all the techniques sellers use to capture markets. They include advertising, personal selling, publicity, word of mouth, and various sales promotion efforts such as coupons, rebates, samples, and cents-off deals. Promotion is discussed in Chapter 17.

The last step in the marketing process consists of relationship building with customers. That includes responding to any suggestions they may make to improve the product or its marketing. Postpurchase service may include exchanging goods that weren't satisfactory and making other adjustments to ensure consumer satisfaction, including recycling. Marketing is an ongoing process. A company must continually adapt to changes in the market and to changes in consumer wants and needs.

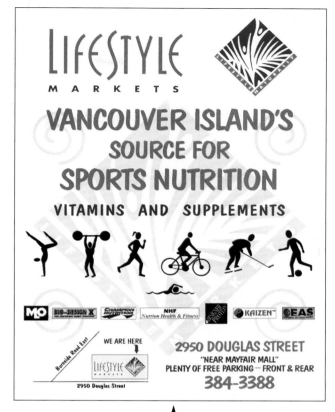

TOTAL QUALITY AND THE MARKETING CONCEPT

Marketing has changed over time as the wants and needs of consumers have changed. A brief review of marketing's history will show its adaptability and give you a glimpse of what's likely to come next.

··· THE MARKETING CONCEPT ···

From the time the first European settlers began their struggle to survive in Canada, until the start of this century, the general philosophy of business was: produce as much as you can because there is a limitless market. Given the limited production capabilities and the vast demand for products in those days, such a philosophy was both logical and profitable. Business owners were mostly farmers, carpenters, and trade workers who were catering to the public's basic needs for housing, food, and clothing. There was a need for greater and greater productive capacity, and businesses naturally had a *production orientation*. That is, the goals of business centred on production rather than marketing. This was satisfactory at that time, because most goods were bought as soon as they became available. The important marketing needs were for distribution and storage.

In the early twentieth century, businesses developed mass-production techniques. Automobile assembly lines are a prime example of this development. Production capacity often exceeded the immediate market demand. The business philosophy turned in the 1920s from a production orientation to a *sales orientation*. Businesses turned their attention to promoting their products and mobilized their resources toward selling, advertising, publicity, and other promotional efforts.

<www.nobella.com>
<www.successlink.net>

Many businesses are now providing services to companies considering online marketing. These are just two examples of such a service.

marketing concept
A three-part business philosophy:
(1) a customer orientation,
(2) training of all employees in
customer service, and (3) a profit
orientation.

After World War II (1945), there was tremendous demand for goods and services among the returning servicemen and women who were starting new lives with new families. These postwar years launched the baby boom (the large increase in the birth rate after the war), which continued for two decades, and the resulting boom in consumer spending. Competition for the consumer's dollar grew. Business owners recognized the need to be more responsive to consumers, and a new orientation emerged called the *marketing concept*. The **marketing concept** had three parts:

1. *A customer orientation*. Find out what customers want and provide it to them.
2. *Training in customer services*. Employees from all departments should be trained in customer service so that everyone in the organization has the same objective: consumer satisfaction. This is a total and integrated organizational effort discussed in some detail in previous chapters.
3. *A profit orientation*. Market goods and services that will earn the firm a profit and enable it to survive and expand to serve more customer wants and needs.

In the late 1980s, the marketing concept was extended by the addition of two important elements to customer orientation:

The marketing concept calls for a customer orientation. Companies often use surveys to determine how satisfied customers were with their experience. This kiosk, developed by In-Touch Survey Systems of Ottawa, records and analyzes customer feedback electronically.

4. *Total quality managment*. The concept of customer orientation was greatly expanded to include total quality management, or TQM. (Also discussed in detail in Chapters 9 and 10 and elsewhere in this book.) In the following section you will see how TQM and the marketing concept have merged.
5. *A societal orientation*. Marketers now recognize that customers' (and all stakeholders') concern for ethically responsible behaviour, including sound environmental practices, has become an important issue. (Chapter 5, devoted to this topic, recognizes how important it has become. In addition, the Ethical Dilemmas discussed in each chapter highlight this issue.)

••• FROM A CUSTOMER ORIENTATION TO DELIGHTING ••• CUSTOMERS AND OTHER STAKEHOLDERS

The phrase "delighting the customer" comes out of the literature of TQM. Marketing's goal in the past was merely to provide customer satisfaction. Today the goal of total quality firms is to please, dazzle, or delight customers by providing goods and services that meet or surpass their requirements. One objective of the marketing effort, therefore, is to make sure that the response to customer wants and needs is so fast and courteous that customers are truly surprised and pleased by the experience. You can see how TQM is just an extension of the marketing concept.

You don't have to look far to see that most organizations haven't yet reached the goal of dazzling customers. Many companies irritate customers as often as they please them. Nonetheless, global competition is relentlessly forcing organizations to adopt total quality concepts, which means, above all, adapting organizations to customers.

Businesses have learned that employees can't provide first-class goods and services to customers unless they receive first-class treatment themselves.

Marketers, therefore, must work with others in the firm, such as human resource personnel, to help make sure that employees are satisfied. In a growing number of firms, employees are now called *internal customers.*

••• FROM TRAINING ALL EMPLOYEES ••• TO UNITING ORGANIZATIONS

Once it became clear that everyone in a firm has to work together to please internal and external customers and all other stakeholders, many changes started to happen within companies' organization. First of all, barriers between departments began to fall. Marketers formed cross-functional teams with designers, engineers, production personnel, and others in the firm to develop quality products. (See Chapters 8 to 11 for detailed treatment of this topic.)

••• MAINTAINING A PROFIT ••• ORIENTATION

Marketing must make sure that everyone in the organization understands that the purpose behind pleasing customers is to ensure a continuing and growing profit for the firm. Such profits can then be used to

- become more competitive.
- expand to create more jobs.
- satisfy other stakeholders of the firm such as shareholders, environmentalists, and the local community.

In the next section, we'll explore the marketing process in more detail so you can see how relationships are established. But first, stop and do the Critical Thinking exercise.

If she's been over breast cancer once, she's been over it a thousand times.

When Jackie Wasserman lost a breast to cancer, she didn't think she'd ever be able to get over it.

But with some help, she did. And now Jackie is dedicated to helping others get over breast cancer through the Canadian Cancer Society's Reach to Recovery Program.

Volunteers like Jackie visit women recently diagnosed with breast cancer, providing them with practical information and emotional support. And because Reach to Recovery

volunteers are cancer survivors themselves, they provide the understanding ear and helping hand women living with breast cancer often desperately need.

If you'd like to find out more, just contact us.

It's a vital program. Your contributions to the Canadian Cancer Society help keep it going.

And with volunteers like Jackie Wasserman, we're keeping more women with breast cancer going as well.

CANADIAN CANCER SOCIETY | SOCIÉTÉ CANADIENNE DU CANCER

THE FIGHT AGAINST CANCER HAS MANY FACES.

> Once you acquire marketing skills, you can use them in any organization. Nonprofit organizations, charities, and government agencies need marketers with good promotion skills.

Critical Thinking

The government is now starting to implement TQM concepts, just as business is doing. What barriers will make the process more difficult? For example, are there any signs that the post office is moving in that direction?

••• A MORE SOCIETAL CONCEPT: ••• RELATIONSHIP MARKETING

Is it enough to give individuals what they want? Don't firms have some obligation to society as well? There is some evidence today that organizations are adopting a broader **societal orientation** that includes a consumer orientation. There is much pressure on large business firms to become involved in programs designed to train the disadvantaged, improve the community, reduce the use of energy, cut back pollution, provide consumer information and consumer education, involve employees in community projects, and generally respond to the broader needs of society. A consumer orientation has become only one of the many social goals of today's progressive organizations

societal orientation
Includes a consumer orientation, but adds programs designed to improve the community, protect the environment, and satisfy other social goals.

relationship marketing
Establishing and maintaining mutually beneficial exchange relationships with internal and external customers and all the other stakeholders of the organization.

green product
A product whose production, use, and disposal don't damage the environment.

mass marketing
Developing products and promotions that are designed to please large groups of people.

and marketing managers. Balancing the wants and needs of all the firm's stakeholders is a much bigger challenge than marketing has attempted in the past. This has led to relationship marketing.

Relationship marketing is establishing and maintaining mutually beneficial exchange relationships with internal and external customers and all the other stakeholders of the organization (see Chapter 7). Organizations that adopt relationship marketing take the community's needs into consideration when designing and marketing products. For example, more products are now designed to be biodegradable so that they cause less pollution than previous products.

Many companies have responded to the environmental movement by introducing "green products" into the marketplace. A **green product** is one whose production, use, and disposal don't damage the environment.

Andora Freeman and Joy Ernst started a toy-recycling centre to teach children the importance of conservation and to make a profit for themselves. Used toys are sold at bargain prices, and the original owners keep 50 percent of the take. The store, Toy Go Round, could earn higher profits if it carried toy guns and G.I. Joe dolls, but the owners refuse because they believe war toys have a negative social impact on children who play with them.

In the next section, we'll explore the marketing process in more detail so you can see how relationships are established.

Progress Check

* What orientations did businesses have *before* the marketing concept was adopted?
* What are the five major elements of the marketing concept?
* How does the societal marketing concept differ from the traditional marketing concept?

<www.relationship marketing.com>
<www.data-driven-marketing.com/academy>

Relationship Marketing Resources Inc. is an example of a company that provides consultative/advisory services to businesses that want to enhance their customer relationships. Its Web site will give you some insight into what this field is about. The second Web site noted above is for CRM Forum Academy. It features academic papers on the topic of customer relationship management and conferencing facilities for its members to discuss them.

FROM MASS MARKETING TO RELATIONSHIP MARKETING In the world of mass production, marketers responded with mass marketing. **Mass marketing** means developing products and promotions to please large groups of people. A mass marketer tries to sell products to as many people as possible. That means using mass media such as TV, radio, and newspapers. Many marketing managers got so caught up with their products and competition that they became less responsive to the market. They began "selling to everybody and listening to nobody."[1]

Another aspect of *relationship marketing* is that it moves away from mass production toward custom-made goods. The latest in technology enables sellers to work with buyers to determine their *individual* wants and needs and to develop goods and services specifically designed for those individuals. One-way messages in mass media give way to a personal dialogue among participants.

There is a growing list of examples of such relationship marketing directed to individual consumers. Many are made possible by newer technology such as direct selling from manufacturer to consumer through the Internet. There has been explosive growth of this mode of selling and it is expected to further revolutionize how products are distributed. You will see more about this important development in the next chapter. Computer companies such as Dell and Gateway, which sell only via the Internet directly to consumers, have had phenomenal success. They package a computer, printer, and other peripherals to the exact requirements of each customer. The product is delivered directly to the customer with detailed instructions for assembly, backed up by seven-day, 24-hour service by phone or the Internet.

Certain catalogue houses like L.L. Bean and Land's End, well-known for the variety of clothing they sell now provide a special personal service via the

Reaching Beyond Our Borders

<www.qlt-pdt.com>

Canadian Cancer Drug Hits the World Market

QLT Phototherapeutics Inc., formerly Quadra Logic Technologies Inc., of Vancouver, is hitting the headlines with an unusual new cancer drug. Photofrin is a light-activated drug that treats patients who have esophageal cancer. The drug has been many years in development and has been slowly gaining approval from governments around the world. As of December 1995, Japan, Canada, and the Netherlands had approved Photofrin for treating several types of cancer.

The big battle had been to get into the U.S. market, which required approval from the U.S. Food and Drug Administration (FDA). As the FDA receives many requests for drug approval and is naturally very cautious before giving the go-ahead, it takes some time before products are approved. In the summer of 1995, QLT was finally given the green light to market Photofrin in the United States. By early 1999 a few more European countries had approved usage of Photophrin.

People who have esophageal cancer suffer from a slowly constricting throat until eventually they cannot even swallow their own saliva, let alone eat or drink. Some 13,000 Canadians and Americans die annually of this disease.

Photofrin is the first of a new type of drug that makes possible what is called *photodynamic therapy*. What happens is that the drug makes the tumour sensitive to light, and the light then kills the cancer cells. The way Photofrin works in the esophagus is quite extraordinary. First, Photofrin is injected into the patient. Some hours later, fibre-optic cables are inserted into the esophagus and a bright light is directed at the tumour. The light activates the Photofrin, which leads to the production of free radicals that kill the cancer cells. This enables patients to once again swallow on their own.

According to FDA drug chief Dr. Robert Temple, "it only makes you sick where the light hits it," which is an obvious advantage for treating cancer patients. He indicates that photodynamic therapy is also being tested for treatment against other tumours affecting the bladder and the bronchial tubes.

In 1999 QLT announced it had concluded arrangements with the Ciba Vision Corp., a subsidiary of the giant international pharmaceutical company Novartis, for the marketing of a new drug. This drug, vertoporfin, to be sold as Visudyne, was developed for the treatment of macular degeneration, a serious eye problem that is a common cause of blindness for people under 50.

This Canadian company, founded by University of British Columbia (UBC) researcher Dr. Julia Levy in the late 1980s, is aided in its research by Dr. David Dolphin, also of UBC. The company employs well over 100 researchers; many are graduates from UBC. QLT has been the recipient of important financial aid from the Natural Sciences and Engineering Research Council (NSERC). The close cooperation between NSERC, UBC, and QLT is a good example of what is required today to generate successful companies in the high-tech world. QLT is a company on the cutting edge of biotechnology, which is expected to play a very important role in the twenty-first century. QLT is developing products for global use and is organizing a marketing system that will enable it to reach well beyond Canadian boarders.

Source: Natural Sciences and Engineering Research Council Web site, <www.nserc.ca>; Canada NewsWire Web site, <www.newswire.ca>, August 18, 1999. "QLT Given Green Light to Market Cancer Drug," *Globe and Mail, Report on Business,* December 28, 1995, p. B2.

Internet. After browsing their catalogue and making tentative clothing selections, you can input your measurements and the catalogue number of the selection into your computer and see what you will look like in those clothes.

Rental-car companies, airlines, and hotels have frequent-user programs through which loyal customers can earn special services. For example, a traveller can earn free flights on Air Canada's Aeroplan, special treatment at a car rental agency (e.g., no stopping at the rental desk—just pick up a car and go),

<www.nserc.ca/seng/
success/qlt.htm>

The Natural Sciences and
Engineering Research
Council of Canada (NSERC)
comments on the develop-
ment and success of QLT at
this Web site.

A host of press releases
and announcements from
QLT are posted on the
Internet. You may wish to
check out <www.newswire.
ca/releases>.

and all kinds of special services at a hotel (e.g., faster check-in and checkout procedures, flowers in the room, free breakfasts, free exercise rooms).

Think of audio-visual electronic products custom-prepared by certain retailers or retail branches of manufacturers where you can get just the TV you want combined with the radio, cassette and CD player, and remote options of your choice. Switching to automobiles, you have always had the choice of certain options in cars that you ordered from a dealer but soon you will also be able to specify the kind of interior you want—size of seats, degree of firmness, and other customized features. Vacation packages can also be personalized by your travel agent—airline, car rental, length of stay, location, and type of hotel and accommodation are all arranged to fit your needs. You can probably come up with some additional examples of such relationship marketing.

Robert Reichheld of Bain & Company estimates that retaining 2 percent more customers has the same effect on profit as cutting costs by 10 percent.[2] Relationship marketing means establishing *and maintaining* long-term relationships with customers. Personalized service helps to ensure this.

···· ▬▬▬ ····

MARKETING MANAGEMENT AND THE MARKETING MIX

marketing mix
The four ingredients that go into
a marketing program: product,
price, place, and promotion.

It's marketing managers who are responsible for getting everyone in the firm to establish and maintain *mutually beneficial relationships* with all the stakeholders and especially with customers. *Mutually beneficial* means that when you buy, say, skis, you have no difficulty finding the kind and size of skis you want, at a satisfactory price, and the quality is very good—both you and the retailer have made a mutually beneficial exchange. You easily got the product you wanted and everything about it satisfies you, while the retailer has a satisfied customer who may return to shop there, and has made a profit on the transaction as well.

Given that goal, managing the marketing process involves four factors: (1) creating a want-satisfying product, (2) setting a price for the product, (3) getting the product to a place where people can buy it, and (4) promoting the product. These four factors (product, price, place, and promotion) have become known as the *four Ps of marketing* or the **marketing mix** because they're the ingredients that go into a marketing program. Each factor of the marketing mix will be discussed in detail in the following two chapters. Note that the marketing mix is surrounded by the marketing environment (see Figure 15.2). Note also that customers are in the middle because they are the focus. Changes in the social, economic, technological, and global environment force marketers to constantly adapt.

Raffi's autobiography,
THE LIFE OF A
CHILDREN'S TROUBADOUR
is "...full of Raffi's love
and deep understanding
of children...a fascinating
and uplifting book."
Fritjof Capra, author of
The Web of Life.

"A visionary
with a heart
as big
as the world."
Daniel Goleman, author
of *Emotional Intelligence*

This "organic"
hardcover book,
printed on
post-consumer
recycled paper,
is a rare item —
bleached entirely
chlorine-free.

RAFFI
THE LIFE OF A
CHILDREN'S TROUBADOUR

AN AUTOBIOGRAPHY

HOMELAND PRESS

Available at fine bookstores everywhere.
For more information, visit our website: www.raffiautobiography.com

Troubadour Records is committed to a child-honouring society, one that respects the Earth and all her children. Troubadour sees its choice of nontoxic bleach, inks, and glues as an investment in a healthy world. This company is enviromentally sensitive. Does this make a difference to you as a consumer?

FIGURE **15.2**

· · · ·

THE MARKETING ENVIRONMENT

Note the global and local influences on the four Ps of marketing, requiring constant adaptation to changing conditions.

Because the environment of marketing is changing faster today than ever before, marketers must make changes faster as well.

A marketing manager designs a marketing program that effectively combines these ingredients of the marketing mix (see Figure 15.3). **Marketing management**, therefore, is the process of planning and executing the conception,

marketing management
The process of planning and executing the conception, pricing, promotion, and distribution (place) of ideas, goods, and services (products) to create mutually beneficial exchanges.

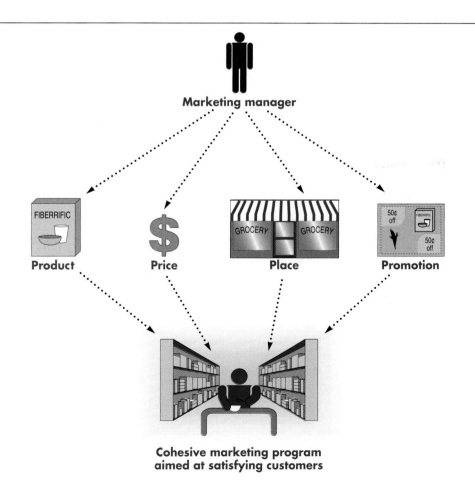

Cohesive marketing program aimed at satisfying customers

FIGURE **15.3**

· · · ·

THE FOUR PS AND THE MARKETING MANAGER'S ROLE

This figure shows the mix for Fiberrific cereal. The marketing manager chooses the proper price, promotion, and place to develop a comprehensive marketing program.

Included would be decisions about packaging, couponing, and more.

A major function of marketing is to deliver products to customers when they want and need them. Daily deliveries of items such as produce ensure customers get what they want, resulting in profits for both the purchaser and the supplier.

pricing, promotion, and distribution (place) of ideas, goods, and services (products) to create mutually beneficial exchanges.

··· LEARNING ABOUT THE MARKET ···

market
People with unsatisfied wants and needs who have both the resources and the willingness to buy.

At the beginning of the word *marketing* is the word *market*. A **market** is defined as people with unsatisfied wants and needs who have both the resources and the willingness to buy. Thus, if there are people who want a high-fibre, low-sugar cereal, like Fiberrific, and if those people have the resources and willingness to buy it, then it is said that there's a market for Fiberrific. We can learn whether there's a market for our cereal by studying consumer wants and needs. We'll look at how marketers determine customer wants and needs after the Progress Check.

Progress
Check

• What is relationship marketing? How does it differ from mass marketing?
• What are the four Ps of the marketing mix?

DETERMINING WHAT CUSTOMERS WANT

marketing research
The analysis of markets to determine opportunities and challenges.

Marketing research is the analysis of markets to determine opportunities and challenges. One goal of research is to determine exactly what customers want and need. That isn't easy because their wants and needs are constantly changing. Marketing must establish close relationships with customers. Marketing research helps determine what customers have purchased in the past, what situational changes have occurred to change what they want, and what they're likely to want in the future. In addition, marketers research business trends, the ecological impact of their decisions, international trends, and more (see Figure 15.4). Businesses need information to compete effectively, and marketing research is the activity that gathers that information.

Advertising Research

1. Motivation research
2. Copy research
3. Media research
4. Studies of ad effectiveness
5. Studies of competitive advertising

Business Economics and Corporate Research

1. Short-range forecasting (up to one year)
2. Long-range forecasting (over one year)
3. Studies of business trends
4. Pricing studies
5. Plant and warehouse location studies
6. Acquisition studies
7. Export and international studies
8. MIS (management information systems)
9. Operations research
10. Internal company employees

Corporate Responsibility Research

1. Consumers' "right-to-know" studies
2. Ecological impact studies
3. Studies of legal constraints on advertising and promotion
4. Social values and policies studies

Product Research

1. New product acceptance and potential
2. Competitive product studies
3. Testing of existing products
4. Packaging research

Sales and Market Research

1. Measurement of market potential
2. Market share analysis
3. Determination of market characteristics
4. Sales analysis
5. Establishment of sales quotas and territories
6. Distribution channel studies
7. Test markets and store audits
8. Consumer panel operations
9. Sales compensation studies
10. Promotional studies

FIGURE 15.4

• • • •

MARKETING RESEARCH TOPICS

Many organizations do research to determine market potential, to evaluate market share, and to learn more about the people in various markets. Most also do short- and long-range sales forecasting and competitor analysis.

Researchers must find out what customers have to say, but they must also pay attention to what shareholders, dealers, consumer advocates, employees, and other stakeholders have to say, too.

••• THE MARKETING RESEARCH PROCESS •••

There are four key steps in the marketing research process:

1. Define the problem and determine the present situation.
2. Collect data.
3. Analyze the research data.
4. Choose the best ethical solutions.

The following sections look at each of these steps.

DEFINE THE PROBLEM AND DETERMINE THE PRESENT SITUATION

It's as important to know what an organization does well as it is to know what it doesn't do well. Marketing research should report both sides. Marketing researchers should be given the freedom to help discover what the problems are, what the alternatives are, what information is needed, and how to go about gathering and analyzing data.

secondary data
Already-published research reports from journals, trade associations, government information services, and so forth.

primary data
Facts and figures not previously published that you have gathered on your own.

focus group
A small group of people who meet under the direction of a discussion leader to communicate their opinions about an organization, its products, or other given issues.

COLLECT DATA   Obtaining usable information is vital to the marketing research process. Nevertheless, you must first determine the scope and estimated costs of doing research. Research can become quite expensive, so some trade-off must be made between information needs and costs.

To minimize costs, it's best to explore secondary data first. **Secondary data** consist of already-published research reports from journals, trade associations, government information services, and so forth.

Usually, previously published research doesn't provide all the information necessary for important business decisions. When additional, more in-depth information is needed, marketers must do their own studies. **Primary data** are facts and figures not previously published that you gather on your own. One way to gather primary data is the observation method, in which data are collected by observing the actions of potential buyers. Can you think of a way we could use the observation method to gather the information we need to promote Fiberrific?

A more formal way to gather primary data is the survey. Telephone surveys, mail surveys, and personal interviews are the most common methods of gathering survey information. Focus groups have become a popular method of surveying individuals. A **focus group** is a small group of people (8 to 14 individuals) who meet under the direction of a discussion leader to communicate their opinions about an organization, its products, or other given issues.

Figure 15.5 lists the principal sources of both secondary and primary data.

ANALYZE THE RESEARCH DATA   Careful, honest interpretation of the data collected can help you find useful alternatives to specific marketing problems. The same data can mean different things to different people. Sometimes people become so intent on a project that they're tempted to ignore or misinterpret data. For example, if our data indicate that the market won't support another brand of cereal, we'd do well to accept the information and drop Fiberrific rather than to slant the results as we'd like to see them and go ahead with the project.

FIGURE **15.5**
. . . .

MARKETING RESEARCH DATA SOURCES

In marketing, it is best to gather as much secondary data as possible because they are relatively inexpensive to obtain. That includes internal records. Don't underestimate the value of observing people's shopping behaviour for inexpensive external data.

Sources of Secondary Data

1. Statistics, research, and reports from
   governments
   trade associations
   companies
   other organizations
2. Business journals and magazines
3. Business sections of newspapers
4. Other newspapers and magazines
5. Internal documents and reports prepared previously for other purposes

Sources of Primary Data

1. Observation
2. Surveys
3. Interviews
4. Focus groups
5. Questionnaires

Cirque du Soleil Conquers Europe

Montreal-based Cirque du Soleil started as a unique circus and has become a unique entertainment organization. Starting out in 1984, the group quickly built a reputation for highly skilled and humourous performances. There are no animals, so all concentration is on acrobats and clowns. They established their training facility to train the skilled performers they require. After attracting huge crowds in Montreal, they moved on to the United States and other parts of Canada.

With success came expansion. They soon had a huge blue-and-yellow climate-controlled tent, which cost $10 million. At the beginning, the life of a show was only three months, explains Jean Héon, director of marketing and communications for Europe. Since it now takes 18 months to develop a new show, a much larger market is required to make it a viable operation. They looked to Japan as a potential market, and with careful research they were soon able to achieve a similar success there.

However, that was still not sufficient. The first year is spent in Montreal, the second touring North America, the third in Japan, but they wanted to extend the life of these expensive shows further. That's when they decided to look to Europe, where there was a circus tradition. Again, careful marketing research was required to determine where to establish a European base and how to sell themselves. The incentives offered by Amsterdam led them to establish their headquarters there, which has now grown to 70 people.

This staff carefully plans a marketing campaign for each country. In general, their target market is the middle-income and the high-income 25- to 45-year-old age group, but each country is treated differently. In Berlin they concentrated on an extensive outdoor billboard campaign, and for the six-city German tour they spent $250,000 on a two-week TV, radio, and newspaper campaign offering free trips to Las Vegas, Nissan cars, and personal computers.

The entire carefully planned marketing effort in Europe has paid off handsomely, extending the life of the show by three years. From the start, says Héon, they were selling out most performances. They also reap substantial revenues from merchandising, food, and beverages, which together account for 11 percent of total revenue in Europe.

The Cirque du Soleil, under the guidance of joint presidents Guy Laliberté and Daniel Gauthier, has successfully expanded its operations so that there are different shows performing all over the world. You can catch *Saltimbanco* in the Asia-Pacific area until 2001; *Mystère* at Treasure Island, Las Vegas, until 2003; *Alegria* in Biloxi, Mississippi, until 2001; the European tour of *Quidam* until 2002; *O* at Bellagio, Las Vegas, until 2008; at the Walt Disney World Resort in Orlando you can see *La Nouba* until 2010. Much closer to home there's a North American tour of the new show called *Dralion* until 2001. This show was so popular at its premiere showing in Toronto July 29, 1999, that the run was extended to September 5.

The Cirque sees its mission as including social responsibility to communities all over the world, wherever it performs. It is especially concerned with disadvantaged youth, so it has a Cirque du Monde that offers workshops in various countries. At its new, imposing $25 million headquarters in Montreal, shows are put on every summer by local artists so that families can bring their children, who otherwise might not be able to see such shows. There are also open houses for young people to see the studio.

Since its start by a small group of talented, imaginative, and daring street performers in 1984, the Cirque du Soleil has blossomed into a very large, unique, complex, and successful global business. The marketing skills of its employees are constantly being honed and perfected. When Canadian astronaut Julie Payette, who loves the Cirque, was launched into space in 1999, she took along a red nose prop worn by famous clown Wayne Hronek as well as some CDs of Cirque music. Presidents Laliberté and Gauthier were invited but were unable to attend the launch. Ms. Payette brought back the nose and CDs autographed by all the astronauts.

Source: Brian Dunn, "How Quebec's Cirque du Soleil Conquered Europe," *Marketing*, March 4, 1996, p. 5; <www.cirquedusoleil.com>, August 1999; communications with the marketing department of Cirque du Soleil, August 1999.

<www.cirquedusoleil. com>

Cirque du Soleil has a colourful Web site. Check it out to learn more about this unusual but extremely successful business.

CHOOSE THE BEST SOLUTIONS   After collecting and analyzing data, market researchers determine several alternative strategies and make recommendations as to which strategy may be best and why. In today's customer-driven markets ethics is important in every aspect of marketing. Companies do what's right as well as what's profitable. This step could add greatly to the social benefits of marketing decisions.

The last steps in a research effort involve following up on the actions taken to see if the results were as expected. If not, corrective action can be taken and new research studies done in the ongoing attempt to provide consumer satisfaction in a manner that is both profitable and ethical.

In the past marketing research data were given to top managers in the firm who were then expected to make decisions based on those data. Quality-oriented organizations no longer operate that way. Instead, data are made available to customer contact people and everyone else in the organization who may benefit from the information. The most important competitive tool in the future will be an educated, trained, and informed work team. Marketing research information is critical to the success of such teams.

··· USING RESEARCH TO UNDERSTAND CONSUMERS ···

The secret to understanding consumers is to listen to them carefully. There are many techniques for doing that, such as focus groups mentioned earlier. At this point, it's important to note that effective marketing research calls for getting out of the office and getting close to customers to find out what they want and need. Laboratory research and consumer panels can never replace going into people's homes, watching them use products, and asking them what improvements they seek. Many producers are now doing this, but others still ignore this important marketing process.

In international markets, the need for marketing research is even greater. One must learn the culture of the people and talk with them directly. In Japan

This Dutch Web site is typical of Web sites available throughout the world, in many different languages. Such sites enable a company to establish a dialogue with customers and to respond quickly to their information and product needs.

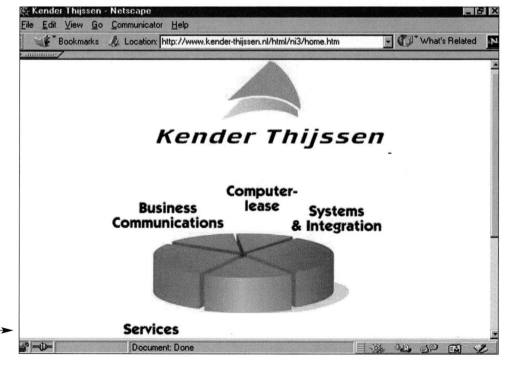

something as simple as stuffing a potential client's business card into your wallet can turn off that client. Japanese custom requires that business cards, like people, be treated with a high level of formality.[3] Furthermore, Japanese business people often exchange gifts before discussing any transactions. The goal in international business is the same as that of business in Canada: find a need and fill it. To do that, marketers must adapt to all the customs and beliefs of the people they are dealing with.

As mentioned earlier, one way to do marketing research (in both domestic and global markets) is to set up a Web site where customers can interact with the company and each other. The information exchanged in such a manner can be extremely useful in determining what customers want. Keeping that information in a database enables a company to improve its product offerings over time and to design promotions that are geared exactly to meet the needs of specific groups of consumers. Marketing majors often take courses in consumer behaviour. The following section briefly reviews what is discussed in those courses.

··· THE CONSUMER DECISION-MAKING PROCESS ···

Figure 15.6 shows the consumer decision-making process and some of the outside factors that influence it. The five steps in the process are often studied in courses on consumer behaviour. "Problem recognition" may occur, say, when your washing machine breaks down. This leads to an information search—you look for ads about washing machines and read brochures about them. You may even consult *Consumer Reports* and other information sources. And, most likely, you will seek advice from other people who have purchased washing machines. Then you evaluate alternatives and make a purchase decision. After the purchase, you may ask the people you spoke to previously how

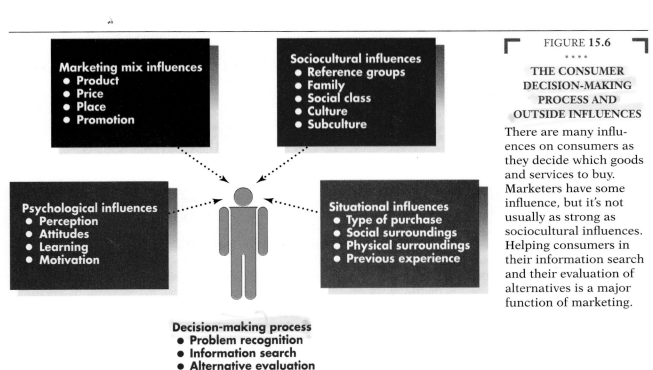

FIGURE **15.6**

· · · ·

THE CONSUMER DECISION-MAKING PROCESS AND OUTSIDE INFLUENCES

There are many influences on consumers as they decide which goods and services to buy. Marketers have some influence, but it's not usually as strong as sociocultural influences. Helping consumers in their information search and their evaluation of alternatives is a major function of marketing.

their machines perform and do other comparisons. Marketing researchers investigate consumer thought processes and behaviour at each stage to determine the best way to facilitate marketing exchanges.

Consumer behaviour researchers also study the various influences on consumer behaviour. Figure 15.6 shows that such influences include the marketing mix variables; psychological influences, such as perception and attitudes; situational influences, such as the type of purchase and the physical surroundings; and sociocultural influences such as reference groups and culture. Here are some terms whose technical definitions may be unfamiliar to you:

- *Learning* involves changes in an individual's behaviour resulting from previous experiences and information. Once you've tried a food you don't like, for example, you may never buy it again.

- *Reference group* is the group that an individual uses as a reference point in the formation of his or her beliefs, attitudes, values, or behaviour. For example, a college student who carries a briefcase instead of a backpack may see business people as his or her reference group.

- *Culture* is the set of values, attitudes, and ways of doing things that are transmitted from one generation to another in a given society. The Canadian culture, for example, emphasizes education, freedom, and diversity.

- *Subculture* is the set of values, attitudes, and ways of doing things that result from belonging to a certain ethnic group, religious group, or other group with which one closely identifies (e.g., teenagers). This group is one small part of the larger culture. Your subculture may prefer rap and hip-hop music, while your parents' subculture may prefer opera.

- **Cognitive dissonance** is a type of psychological conflict that can occur after the purchase. Consumers may have doubts about whether they got the best product at the best price. That means marketers must reassure consumers after the sale if they want to establish a long-term relationship.

cognitive dissonance
A type of psychological conflict that can occur after a purchase, when consumers may have doubts about whether they got the best product at the best price.

···· ▬▬▬ ····

RECOGNIZING DIFFERENT MARKETS: CONSUMER AND BUSINESS-TO-BUSINESS

consumer market
All individuals or households who want goods and services for personal consumption or use.

industrial market (business-to-business market)
All individuals and organizations that want goods and services to produce other goods and services or to sell, rent, or supply the goods to others.

There are two major markets in marketing: the consumer market and the industrial, or business-to-business, market. The **consumer market** consists of all the individuals or households who want goods and services for personal consumption or use. The **industrial** (or **business-to-business**) **market** consists of all the individuals and organizations that want goods and services to produce other goods and services or to sell, rent, or supply the goods to others. Oil drilling bits, cash registers, display cases, office desks, public accounting audits, and corporate legal advice are examples of such goods and services (products).

The important thing to remember is that the category of the *purchaser* determines whether a product is being sold in the industrial or consumer market. For example, a case of Fiberrific purchased by a supermarket to sell to its customers is being sold in the industrial market. But when a box from that case is bought by an individual from that supermarket for the family's breakfast, it is being sold in the consumer market.

··· THE CONSUMER MARKET ···

The consumer market consists of the approximately 30 million people in Canada and more than six billion people in world markets. Obviously, consumers vary greatly in age, education level, income, and taste. Because consumers differ so greatly, marketers must learn to select different consumer groups to develop products and services specially tailored to their needs. If a consumer group is large enough, a company may design a marketing program to serve that market.

Campbell Soup noticed that one-quarter of all households consists of single people living alone. Most of these people are busy at work. They have little time to cook, but they do have money for convenience foods. Therefore, Campbell introduced many new products to appeal to singles and married young urban professionals (yuppies). Included are Le Menu frozen dinners, French Chef frozen soups, Great Starts frozen breakfasts, and Souper Combo, a frozen, microwavable soup and sandwich combination.[4] Campbell is just one company that has had great success studying the consumer market, breaking it down into categories, and then developing products for those separate groups.

The process of dividing the total market into several groups whose members have similar characteristics is called **market segmentation**. The overall market consists of both women and men, children and adults, people in all parts of the world, and people with different wants and needs. Usually a business can't serve all of these groups; it must decide which groups to serve. **Target marketing** is marketing directed toward those groups (market segments) an organization decides it can serve profitability. For example, a shoe store may choose to sell only women's shoes, only children's shoes, or only athletic shoes.

market segmentation
The process of dividing the total market into several groups whose members have similar characteristics.

target marketing
Marketing directed toward those groups (market segments) an organization decides it can serve profitability.

SEGMENTING THE CONSUMER MARKET   There are several ways in which a firm can segment (divide) the consumer market. Let's say, for example, in trying to sell Fiberrific we begin our marketing campaign by focusing on a certain region, such as the lower B.C. mainland, where fitness is a major issue. Dividing the market by geographic area is called *geographic segmentation* (see Figure 15.7).

Alternatively, we could aim our promotions toward people aged 25 to 45 who have some college training and have high incomes—yuppies—like

VARIABLE	TYPICAL SEGMENTS
Region	British Columbia, Prairies, southwest Ontario, metropolitan Toronto, northwest Ontario, metropolitan Montreal, the rest of Quebec, Atlantic Provinces
City or county size	Under 5,000; 5,000–19,999; 20,000–49,999; 50,000–99,999; and so on
Population density	Urban, suburban, rural

FIGURE **15.7**
····

GEOGRAPHIC SEGMENTATION VARIABLES

This figure shows one way marketers divide the market. The aim of segmentation is to break the market into smaller units of homogeneous composition.

Ambico Limited is a Canadian company that produces specialized steel and wood doors and frames for niche markets. This explosion-resistant door is one of the many specialized products that Ambico produces. Other Ambico products include bullet-resistant doors, oversized steel doors, brass-clad doors, and acoustic doors.

niche marketing
The process of finding small but profitable market segments and designing custom-made products for them.

one-to-one marketing
Developing a unique mix of goods and services for each individual customer.

industrial marketing
The marketing of goods and services to manufacturers, institutions, commercial operations, and the government.

Campbell did with its Le Menu line. Segmentation by age, income, and education level is part of *demographic segmentation*.

REACHING SMALLER MARKET SEGMENTS

During the 1990s marketers became more focused on smaller market segments with large profit potential in spite of their small size. New manufacturing techniques make it possible to develop specialized products for small market groups. **Niche marketing** is the process of finding small but profitable market segments and designing custom-made products for them. For example, a small company called Evergreen makes upgraded central processing units (CPUs) for computers, a market not pursued by giants such as Intel. **One-to-one marketing** means developing a unique mix of goods and services for each individual customer. Travel agencies often develop such packages, including airline reservations, hotel reservations, rental cars, restaurants, and admission to museums and other attractions. This is relatively easy to do in industrial markets where each customer may buy in huge volume. But one-to-one marketing is now becoming possible in consumer markets as well, as discussed previously in this chapter under relationship marketing.

••• BUSINESS-TO-BUSINESS MARKETING •••

The marketing of goods and services to manufacturers, institutions (e.g., hospitals or schools), commercial operations (retail stores), and the government is called **industrial marketing**. It's also known as *business-to-business marketing*.

The basic principle of this kind of marketing is still "find a need and fill it," but the strategies are different from consumer marketing because the buyers are different. Several factors make industrial marketing different. Here are some of the important ones.

1. The market for industrial goods is a *derived* demand. Demand for consumer products such as cars creates demand for industrial goods and services including tires, batteries, glass, metal, plastics, and engines.

2. Demand for industrial goods is relatively *inelastic*. The quantity demanded doesn't always change significantly with minor changes in price. The reason is that industrial products are made up of so many parts that a price increase for one part isn't usually a significant problem.

3. The number of customers in the industrial market is relatively *low*. There are just a few construction firms or mining operations compared to the consumer market of millions of households.

4. The size of industrial customers is relatively *large*. A few large organizations account for most of the employment and production of various goods and services. Nonetheless, there are many small to medium-sized firms that together make an attractive market.

High Costs of Marketing a New Product

Haemacure Corporation, a Montreal company, sells a very specialized product: an all-fibre sealant, Hemaseel APR, that comes from human blood plasma and is used in surgery. CEO Marc Paquin is a patient man—he has had to wait almost a decade to have a product sell. The company's opportunity to market this product has a complex 10-year history involving Austrian and American companies, U.S. antitrust laws, and a long delay before the U.S. Food and Drug Administration (USFDA) was satisfied that the product was safe. Two months after the USFDA finally approved it in May 1998, Haemacure had its product on the market, on a licence from an American company. It beat out a competitor, who has a licence from the same company, by one year.

Haemacure's marketing office is located in Florida and it wages a very aggressive and costly marketing campaign. The company targets surgeons and also seeks support for its product at medical conventions and from other educational bodies. As a result of its strong

marketing campaign, its sales have been doubling every quarter, but the high marketing costs have kept the company deep in the red. Current revenues are under $2 million and Mr. Paquin is predicting that the company will turn the corner in the first quarter of 2000, when it will show its first profits.

He is counting on a new product, Hemaseel HMN, which was undergoing final clinical trials in 1999, to help achieve that goal. Haemacure has an arrangement with the manufacturing arm of the Swiss Red Cross to produce HMN after USFDA approval. It has also signed a development and supply agreement with Micromedics Inc. in the U.S. It looks as if patience, persistence, and aggressive marketing are about to pay off for Marc Paquin and his company.

Source: Eric Hamovitch, *Montreal Business Magazine*, Vol. 11 No. 3, July 1999.

5. Industrial markets tend to be *concentrated*. For example, oil and gas fields tend to be concentrated in Alberta. Consequently, marketing efforts often may be concentrated on a particular geographic area, and distribution problems are often minimized by locating warehouses near industrial centres.

6. Industrial buyers generally are more *rational* than consumers in their selection of goods and services; they use specifications and carefully weigh the "total product offer," including quality, price, and service.

7. Industrial sales tend to be *direct*. Manufacturers sell products such as tires directly to auto manufacturers, but tend to use wholesalers and retailers to sell to consumers.

Industrial markets are often more complex than consumer markets because the products are sold many times before they reach the ultimate consumer. In general, industrial firms rely more on personal selling, whereas consumer goods rely more heavily on advertising. That's because business customers tend to be large and concentrated, and it's more efficient and effective to call on them with a knowledgeable salesperson.

Relationship marketing has always been important in the business-to-business market. For example, Joe Morabito runs a small business that helps companies move from one location to another. Because the company is small,

Ethical Dilemma

REVIEW

Remember our three friends who want to do market research by secretly taping conversations? Here's what our executives have to say. Bédard is very clear in his response. "Recording a conversation without someone's knowledge is against the law" and "offensive to many people" because they "will say things that they would never say if they knew they were being taped. Other methods can be found that would produce the same data."

Reilley has an equally clear and strong opinion on this dilemma. "This procedure is unethical (and illegal in some jurisdictions). I would state this openly to Roy, Hector, and Maria. I would be very upset if anyone taped me in this manner. I might even consider legal action."

Let's look at a different scenario. Suppose the three friends went ahead with their taping, and noted who ▲ was being taped and when. After listening to the material and determining what recreational products or services these people need, they invite the friends and associates they had taped to dinner and drinks and explain what they did and why. They explain that no names were recorded or mentioned in the final conclusions and any personal or confidential information they had inadvertently recorded had been erased. They say that anyone can request a private session to listen to the tapes of their own comments. After that, the tapes would be erased, since they had served their purpose. Finally, they ask everyone to sign a release that they have no claims against Roy, Maria, and Hector as a result of the tapings. As a sweetener, everyone could be offered a token number of shares in the new company if the trio go ahead with their plan to start a company. What do you think of this alternative?

Morabito alone is not able to provide all the services companies need to have an easy, successful move. Therefore, Morabito has established a close relationship with other businesses in the area that provide the complementary services needed to make this complex process easier. The companies work closely together to provide a package of services that exceeds anything even the largest competitors can offer. This is a good example of relationship marketing in the business-to-business area.

By acting as a coordinator of many business, Morabito can provide the services of a large company while preserving the closeness and flexibility of a small company. Bob Beck, one of the people who works closely with Morabito, says, "business is moving from the transaction era to the relationship era." That is, it is more important to establish and maintain friendly and committed relationships than to simply make the sale.[5]

Critical Thinking

When businesses buy goods and services from other businesses, they usually buy in very large volume. Salespeople in the industrial field usually are paid on a commission basis; they make a certain percentage of every sale. Can you see, therefore, why industrial sales may be a more rewarding career (monetarily) than consumer sales? Industrial companies sell goods such as steel, lumber, computers, engines, parts, and supplies. Where would you find the names of such companies?

- What are the four parts of the marketing research process?
- What's the difference between primary and secondary data?
- What are some of the differences between domestic and international markets?
- Can you define *niche marketing* and *one-to-one marketing*?
- What are four key factors that make industrial markets different from consumer markets?

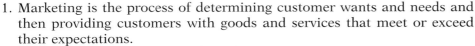

SUMMARY
. . . . . .

1. Marketing is the process of determining customer wants and needs and then providing customers with goods and services that meet or exceed their expectations.

   - ***What is the basic goal of marketing?***
   To find a need and fill it.

   - ***What kinds of organizations are involved in marketing?***
   All kinds of organizations use marketing, both profit and nonprofit organizations (including charities, churches, and nonprofit schools).

   - ***What are the basic steps in the marketing process?***
   After finding a need, the next step in the marketing process is finding a product and testing it in the marketplace. The product development process includes packaging, branding, and pricing. Marketing intermediaries often distribute the product to consumers. The final steps in the marketing process are promoting the product to consumers and building a relationship with customers.

1. Define marketing and summarize the steps involved in the marketing process.

2. The role of marketing changes as the wants and needs of consumers change.

   - ***How is the role of marketing changing?***
   Marketing is becoming more customer-oriented than ever before. Originally, marketing's goal was simply to satisfy customers. Now marketing tries to please or "delight" customers.

   - ***What are the three parts of the marketing concept?***
   The three parts of the marketing concept are: (1) a customer orientation, (2) a service orientation (this is a total and integrated organizational effort), and (3) a profit orientation (market goods and services that will earn the firm a profit and enable it to survive and expand to serve more customer wants and needs).

   - ***How has the total quality movement affected the marketing concept?***
   Total quality has led firms to have a broader orientation than customers. Marketing now is concerned with employees, customers, and other stakeholders of the firm (e.g., suppliers, dealers, and the local communities). Furthermore, marketing is establishing close relationships among firms so that the whole marketing system is customer oriented. Finally, everyone in the system must keep the profit orientation in mind.

2. Describe marketing's changing role in society and the merging of the marketing concept with total quality management.

3. The marketing process involves research, developing product ideas, branding and pricing products, distributing products to customers, and establishing long-term relationships with customers.

3. Describe how relationship marketing differs from traditional marketing.

- *What is relationship marketing?*

Relationship marketing is establishing and maintaining mutually beneficial exchange relationships with internal and external customers and all the other stakeholders of the organization. Organizations that adopt relationship marketing keep the community's needs in mind when designing and marketing products.

- *What's the difference between relationship marketing and mass marketing?*

Mass marketing means developing products and promotions that are designed to please large groups of people. That means using mass media such as TV, radio, and newspapers. Relationship marketing tends to lead away from mass production toward custom-made goods.

4. List the four Ps of marketing.

4. Marketers perform various functions that create value for customers.
- *What is the marketing mix?*

The marketing mix consists of the four Ps of marketing: product, price, place, and promotion.

5. Apply the four parts of the marketing research process to a business problem.

5. Marketing research is the first step in the "find a need and fill it" process.
- *What are the four steps in the marketing research process?*

The four steps are: (1) define the problem and determine the present situation, (2) collect data, (3) analyze the research data, and (4) choose the best solutions.

6. Differentiate between consumer and industrial markets.

6. There are two major markets: the consumer market and the business-to-business market.
- *What are the differences between the two markets?*

The consumer market is the people who buy products for their own use—people like you and me. The business-to-business market consists of all the individuals and organizations that use goods and services to produce other goods and services or to sell, rent, or supply goods to others.

- *How do businesses segment the consumer market?*

From the total market of men and women, children and adults, and other such groups, businesses choose only those groups (called market segments) that they can serve profitably. This is called target marketing.

KEY TERMS
......

brand name 474	market 482	niche marketing 490
cognitive dissonance 488	market segmentation 489	one-to-one marketing 490
consumer market 488	marketing 472	primary data 484
focus group 484	marketing concept 476	product 474
green product 478	marketing management 481	relationship marketing 478
industrial market (business-to-business market) 488	marketing mix 480	secondary data 484
industrial marketing 490	marketing research 482	societal orientation 477
	mass marketing 478	target marketing 489

DEVELOPING WORKPLACE SKILLS

1. Imagine that you are the president of a small liberal arts college. Enrollment has declined dramatically. The college is in danger of closing. Show how you might revive the college by applying the marketing concept. Develop an action plan outlining how you would implement the three

phases: (1) a customer orientation, (2) a service orientation, and (3) a profit orientation.

2. Think of a product or service that your friends want but cannot get on or near campus. Invent a product or service to fill that need. Evaluate the total market, think of a brand name and a package, develop a promotional scheme, and design a system to distribute it to students.

3. Find a company involved in business-to-business marketing. Interview a member of this firm regarding the ways business-to-business marketing differs from consumer marketing. Report your findings to the class.

4. How would you segment the market for a new, nutritious soft drink that contains no sugar and has all the vitamins required for a day? Describe a target market that you feel would be the most profitable.

5. Divide into groups of four or five students. Conduct a very basic marketing research study that identifies a problem on your campus that your group agrees needs attention. Collect information about that problem, analyze the data, and make written recommendations to the proper authority.

INTERNET CHALLENGES

1. Imagine that you are working in the marketing department of a computer company and your manager asks you to do some research into the possible consumer demand for a better type of mouse. Many users have complained of various pains and aches arising from heavy usage of the ordinary type of mouse. Your first step should be to see what research others have done, so you would commence by seeking this secondary data. How would you begin? Where would you look? You could start with searching Yahoo with the key words *computer mouse*. You may be surprised at how much you can find there.

2. Suppose your search for secondary data is not very fruitful. That is, you cannot find much information because there has been little research done or not much has been written on this topic. You then decide to do your own research and collect some primary data. Do you think you can get a focus group organized and working satisfactorily by using a real-time chat room? Can you explain exactly how that could work? Is there any other way you can use the Internet to collect primary data? Get some information on focus groups and prepare a list of questions you should ask participants. Then try to organize a couple of focus groups with 10 people in each group. Summarize your findings in a report to your class.

Practising Management Decisions

Coca-Cola and Pepsi are major competitors throughout the rest of the world as well as in North America. When it comes to Japan, however, Coke is the clear winner. Why? The sale of soft drinks in Japan began on military bases after WWII. However, the rapid growth stage didn't begin until 1957 when a Japanese business person bought a licence to manufacture Coke in Japan.

CASE 1

SELLING COCA-COLA IN JAPAN

What made Coke a success in Japan over time was its willingness to partner with local business people. Rather than simply being a multinational firm, Coke was successful in becoming a multilocal firm. That is, it found partners in various cities and worked closely with them to develop sales in those areas.

As many firms have found, it wasn't easy to break into the Japanese market. For one thing,

Coke wanted to sell directly to retailers. That simply was not—and *is* not—the tradition in Japan. The tradition is to sell through a whole series of intermediaries that control the distribution.

It is fundamentally important when trying to sell in a different country to adapt as much as possible to the local culture. Coca-Cola did that by setting up social clubs in its facilities like those in other Japanese firms. It also helped employees buy homes with low-interest loans. Every effort was made to adjust to the tastes of the local people, including the creation of a new 50 percent juice drink.

Relationship marketing is especially important in Japan where negotiations take time, and patience is truly a virtue. Consensus building is the norm, and that requires more time than North American firms are used to investing. Nonetheless, the payoff can be extraordinary. For example, Coke has some 100,000 dealers and 700,000 vending machines in Japan as a result of its patience and care in establishing local relationships.

Pepsi, on the other hand, remains a minor competitor due to its failure to invest the time necessary to establish local partners and relationships. As a consequence, Pepsi's market penetration continues to be hindered and shallow.

Decision Questions

1. What evidence can you cite showing that foreign firms have been very careful to adapt to Canadian culture when marketing their products here?
2. Many Canadian firms have had difficulty establishing relationships in Japan. Do you think that they could learn from Coke's experience and try again?
3. Talk with a local store owner or manager who sells products from various parts of the world. Ask him or her what foreign manufacturers do to establish and maintain good relationships with that store and its suppliers.

CASE 2

IMPACT OF BABY BOOMERS ON MARKETING RESEARCH

In 1996 Dr. David Foot, economist and demographer at the University of Toronto, came out with a book that became one of the all time bestsellers in Canada. On the bestseller list for two years, it sold more than 250,000 hardcover copies. There was also a French translation. The book was called *Boom Bust & Echo* and talked about the major impact that the special demographic trends of the postwar years were having on Canadian business and would continue to have for years to come. He divided Canadians born in the last half of the twentieth century into three main groups. The oldest are the large number of *boomers* born between 1947 and 1966 when the birth rate was high, about 400,000 births annually.

The 10 million boomers constitute one-third of the Canadian population and in Dr. Foot's opinion, have the largest impact of any group on the demand for various products and services. For Dr. Foot the *generation Xers* is that segment of the baby boomers born at the tail end—from 1960 to 1966. Next comes the relatively small *bust generation* born between 1967 and 1980. The last group, the large number of children of the boomers that Foot calls the *echo generation* are those born between 1980 and 1995. In 1999 Dr. Foot produced an updated paperback version of his book in which he continued to predict the likely

significant effect on Canadian business of these two groups, the baby boomers and their children, the echo boomers. He believes that the baby boomer bulge, as it moves through the population, is the most significant factor in understanding business trends. In 1992 the nine million boomers aged between 26 and 45 were the largest segment of the Canadian adult market. In 2002 they will be ages 36 to 55. The needs and lifestyles of this large segment have ruled the marketplace for many years and will continue to do so for many more years.

Foot gives examples of the economic impact of the boomers' changing demands as they move through their life cycle. When they were children, toys, schools, housing, and baby clothes were in great demand. When they became adults and had their own children, that cycle was repeated. Their lifestyle led to a boom in recreational-related products and services—sportswear and athletic equipment, health clubs, moving from cities to suburban areas.

In 1994 the baby boom peak reached age 34. "That's the average age at which Canadians buy homes," says Foot. So he predicted that demand for housing would begin to fall off after 1995. This prediction was partially confirmed by a decline in the housing market. Other changes he foresaw include "the beer and beef industries are in trouble; young people drink beer and eat beef and that market's getting older...Per capita, chicken has been rising as the baby boomers are getting older. Madonna, hockey, football, and skiing will all see declining markets for the same reason."

David Foot ends by urging businesses to look at the demographic profile, by age, of the consumers who buy their products or services. By relating this information to the baby boom bulge, they should have a good picture of what is likely to happen to their market. In 2004 the baby boom peak will be age 44.

Decision Questions

1. Can you think of what marketing research you should do to test the validity of Foot's predictions? Would you try to set up some focus groups of baby boomers? What else would you do? How about the other groups he refers to?

2. Assume that Foot is correct in his predictions. What business opportunities do you see that you might take advantage of? What additional market research would you undertake to support that business idea?

3. Suppose you own a small supermarket. Do you think that you will have to make any changes in the type of products you carry if you accept Foot's analysis? If so, what changes should you make? Would you do some market research before deciding? What exactly would you do?

4. If Foot is correct, will businesses have to continually shift the nature of their products and services to adapt to the market changes as the boomers age? Would that involve continual market research? Some products, like corn flakes, never seem to lose their popularity. How is this explained?

Sources: Radio interview series of David Foot with Peter Gzowski, host of CBC "Morningside," May 1996. *Boom Bust & Echo: How to Profit from the Coming Demographic Shift*, David K. Foot, with Daniel Stoffman (MacFarlane Walter and Ross, 1996); *Boom Bust & Echo 2000: Profiting from the Demographic Shift*, David K. Foot, with Daniel Stoffman (MacFarlane Walter and Ross, 1999); Interview of David Foot by Layth Matthews of Canadian-Investor.com, May 11, 1999, as reported on Web site <www.davidfoot.com/interview.html>.

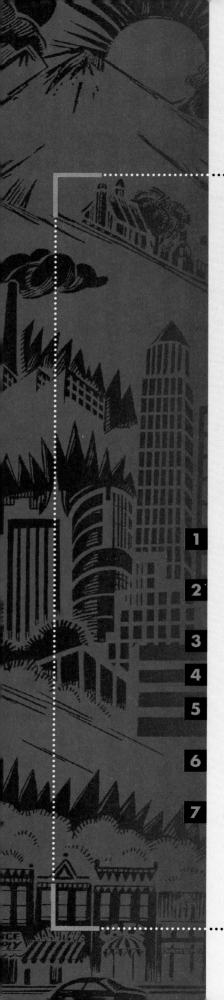

Developing and Pricing Quality Products and Services

Chapter

16

LEARNING GOALS

After you have read and studied this chapter, you should be able to

1 explain the difference between a product and a value package and between a product line and a product mix.

2 describe how businesses create product differentiation for their goods and services in both consumer and industrial markets.

3 describe the six functions of packaging.

4 give examples of a brand, a brand name, and a trademark.

5 explain the role of product managers and the five steps of the new-product development process.

6 identify and describe the stages of the product life cycle, and describe marketing strategies at each stage.

7 give examples of various pricing objectives, and describe what strategies are used to determine prices.

The wife-and-husband team of Micheline Charest and Ronald A. Weinberg founded and head the very successful CINAR Corporation headquartered in Montreal. Charest is chair and co-CEO while Weinberg is president and co-CEO. The couple met in 1976 at a New Orleans film festival organized by Weinberg and attended by Charest, who is a native of Quebec City and who studied filmmaking at university. It was love at first sight. They married, moved to New York, and set up CINAR there. Money was tight and after the birth of their son in 1984, they moved to Montreal—"cheap housing"—and slowly developed CINAR, taking the company public in 1993.

The corporate profile states that "CINAR Corporation is an integrated entertainment and education company that develops, produces, markets, and distributes high-quality, nonviolent programming and supplemental education products for children, families, and educators worldwide." By 1998, five years after becoming a public company, CINAR's sales had multiplied fivefold to $150 million and its profits sixfold to $22 million. The company has 500 full-time employees and 600 freelancers busily turning out many award-winning products. The company's Web site gives the following picture of CINAR's operations.

Over the last 20 years CINAR Entertainment has become a leading supplier of animated and live-action children's and family programming that it distributes worldwide. CINAR Entertainment's productions include the two-time Emmy-award-winning *ARTHUR*, the top-rated children's television program in the United States, *Are You Afraid of the Dark?*, and *Wimzie's House*, *Lassie*, *The Busy World of Richard Scarry*, and *The Adventures of Paddington Bear*. As of May 31, 1999, CINAR's library contained 87 titles comprising 1532 half-hours of programming. During the 1997–98 television season, three CINAR productions were among the top eight programs on television in the United States (including network, cable, and PBS), for children aged two through five.

CINAR's expansion into the supplemental education products market is a principal focus of the company's growth strategy. CINAR Education publishes and distributes approximately 2000 supplemental education products that enhance the classroom curricula and foster continued learning in the home. These products are marketed each year to more than 1.6 million teachers and 370,000 daycare providers in North America, from pre-kindergarten to grade eight.

With the acquisition of EduSoft Ltd., a developer, publisher, and distributor of multimedia education software products, CINAR Education broadens its product lines and distribution channels. EduSoft's products are distributed to consumers and schools in more than 40 countries worldwide. CINAR uses Edusoft's in-house expertise in the production of quality, interactive software in the development of new products based on CINAR's library of proprietary children's characters and programming.

CINAR and the National Head Start Association, an organization committed to helping poor children and their families in the U.S., now have an ongoing, exclusive business partnership to jointly develop, produce, and distribute a line of branded training and audio-visual products to meet the needs of the children, teachers, staff, and parents of Head Start.

Is it any wonder that *Canadian Business* magazine featured CINAR in an article titled "Move Over Mickey Mouse"?

Sources: Ian Austen, "Move Over Mickey Mouse," *Canadian Business*, May 14, 1999, p. 30; CINAR Web site, <www.cinar.com>.

PROFILE

Charest and Weinberg: The Canadian Disneys Plus

Ethical Dilemma

A "SMALL" PROBLEM OF RADIATION

This chapter introduces you to marketing research and new product development. Let's take a look at an ethical issue that can arise in the area of new product development. Suppose you are an importer of toys and games for children and that you have been having severe financial problems for the past year. You have been seeking some new products that will give your sales and profits a much-needed boost. You meet Adam, an exporter whom you know well, having dealt with him for some years. He invites you out for dinner one evening and you talk about business.

During the conversation, Adam says that he has a terrific deal for you. He has a big lot of new games and toys that he can let you have at a great price. You are all ears because it's exactly the transfusion your business needs. You are a little suspicious because the price is so low, so you ask Adam why it's such a bargain. He reluctantly tells you, because you are a valued customer, that there is a *little* problem. The material the toys and games are made of has been accidentally exposed to some radiation near a nuclear power plant. Because of that exposure, Adam was able to buy the whole lot at a ridiculous price and he is prepared to pass on this savings to you.

Adam tells you that the radiation level is very low and will not hurt children. As a matter of fact, Adam tells you, he lets his own children play with these products. He takes you up to his hotel room and shows you some of the merchandise. You are very impressed with their novelty and quality—they are just what you need to improve your business's financial health. What would you do?

<www.cinar.com>

Visit the CINAR Web site to learn more about this innovative company. Click on *Corporate Profile* to learn more about the company's history and accomplishments.

···· ▬ ····

PRODUCT DEVELOPMENT AND THE VALUE PACKAGE

International competition today is so strong that to maintain and expand markets, businesses must wage a constant battle. An important component of that battle is designing and promoting better products—meaning products perceived to have the best value—at a fair price. As we will see, whether a customer perceives a product as being better depends on many factors. To satisfy customers, marketers must learn to listen and to adapt to constantly changing market demands. Managers must also adapt to price challenges from competitors.

Learning to manage change, especially new-product changes, is critical for managers. An important part of the impression customers get about products is the price. In this chapter, we will explore two key elements of the marketing mix: product development and price.

Marketers like Micheline Charest and Ronald Weinberg of CINAR, profiled at the beginning of this chapter, know that the challenge of adapting products to markets is a continual one. An organization can't do a one-time survey of consumer wants and needs, design or acquire a line of products to meet those needs, put them in the stores, and relax. Marketers must constantly monitor customer wants and needs because consumer and business needs are constantly evolving. Here are some examples.

We have previously referred to the V-chip developed by Tim Collings of Simon Fraiser University in British Columbia. The V-chip evolved in response to parents' need to protect their children from TV violence. Two Montreal software experts founded Silanis Technologies to develop a system for creating

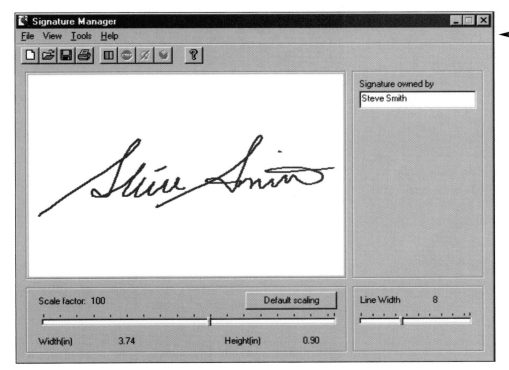

tamper-proof signatures on electronic documents to meet the needs of engineers.[1] Two Toronto men developed a successful lecture series, Unique Lives and Experiences, in which famous women speak about their lives.[2] Coca-Cola distributors have tested two different ways of wiring Coke machines, one developed by a U.S. company and the other by a New Zealand company. The machines signal the head office when they run low, fill with money, are jammed, or are being broken into. Initial results are encouraging.[3] All food companies are busily engaged in the development of low-fat or low-calorie products to meet the growing interest of consumers in healthy foods.

Note that not all product development requires an actual *new* product. Many products go through a process of incremental change or improvement with each new feature making the product more attractive to customers. This strategy is known as *product modification*. **Product modification** is the technique of extending a product's life cycle by changing the quality, features, packaging, or style to attract new market segments or to encourage continued usage by existing customers. A good example is the modern automobile—it has gone through so many incremental changes over the past five decades that new models can hardly be said to be the same vehicles (products) as those of a generation ago. Figure 16.1 shows a detailed list of some of the major improvements in areas such as safety, efficiency, environmental impact, comfort, and convenience.

Product development, then, is a key activity in any business. There's a lot more to new-product development than merely introducing new products, however. What marketers do to create excitement and demand for those products (product strategy) is as important as the products themselves.

••• DEVELOPING A VALUE PACKAGE •••

From a strategic marketing viewpoint, a value package is more than just the physical good or service. A **value package** (also known as the *total product*

Paving the way to a digital future are Silanis's Approvelt Desktop 4.0, which captures your signature using a digitizing tablet and inserts the signature into documents. Silanis was selected as one of the 75 fastest growing software vendors in North America.

<www.uniquelives.com>

Check out the *Unique Lives and Experiences* Web site. Click on *Cities & Speakers*. Do they have anyone scheduled in your town soon?

product modification
Technique used to extend the life cycle of a product by changing the quality, features, packaging, or style to attract new market segments or continued usage by existing customers.

value package
Everything that customers may evaluate before deciding to buy something.

This figure lists some of the incremental changes made to automobiles since 1950.

Performance	Safety	Convenience	Environmental
front-wheel drive	seat belts	power windows & outside mirrors	catalytic converter
higher engine HP	air bags		unleaded gas
electronic ignition	crash absorbent front & rear	day/night rear view mirror	more efficient engines
radial tires		power steering	4/5 speed transmission
4-wheel drive	power & disc brakes	computers/sensors	recyclable material
sound systems	alarm system	power seats	
long-life batteries	nonshatter windshields	remote locking	
all-season tires	limited slip differential	remote starting	
halogen lights	child safety lock	compass & satellite positioning	
fuel injection	ABS brakes	air conditioning	
ABS brakes	day running lights	sealed batteries	
lighter cars		gas cap lock	
smaller engine with fewer moving parts & reduced fuel consumption		less frequent service	
		tilt telescopic steering wheel	
		more durable paint	
		keyless entry	
		remote gas cap & trunk unlock	
		sun/moon roof	

offer) consists of everything that customers may evaluate before deciding to buy something. The basic product or service may be a washing machine, an insurance policy, or a bottle of beer, but the value package consists of

- price
- package
- store surroundings (atmospherics)
- image created by advertising
- guarantee
- reputation of the producer
- brand name
- service
- buyers' past experience
- speed of delivery
- accessibility of seller (e.g., on the Internet)

Before people buy a product, they evaluate and compare value packages on all these dimensions. A successful marketer must think like a buyer and evaluate the product offer as a total collection of impressions created by all the factors listed previously.

Let's go back and look at our highly nutritious, high-fibre, low-sugar breakfast cereal, Fiberrific, as an example. The value package as perceived by the consumer is much more than the cereal itself. Anything that affects consumer perceptions about the cereal's benefits and value may determine whether the cereal is purchased. The price certainly is an important part of the perception of product value.

Often a high price indicates exceptional quality. The store surroundings also are important. If the cereal is being sold in an exclusive health food store, it takes on many characteristics of the store (e.g., healthy and upscale). A guarantee of satisfaction can increase the product's value in the mind of consumers, as can a well-known brand name. Advertising can create an attractive image, and word of mouth can enhance the reputation. Fiberrific is more than a cereal as a value package; it's an entire bundle of impressions.

As you learned earlier one way to keep customers happy is by establishing a dialogue with them and keeping the information they provide in a database. The easiest way to do this is to establish a Web site where consumers can ask questions, get information, and chat with others. Having a close personal relationship with customers adds to the perceived benefits of products because most people would prefer to buy from someone they know and like. It can be difficult for large companies to establish such relationships, which gives an advantage to those smaller companies that can do so more easily. The box called Spotlight on Small Business discusses this issue in more depth.

<www.pg.com>

The P&G Web site is worth visiting. For example, click on *P&G Products* and then click on *Favourite Sites* to see a host of familiar products.

••• PRODUCT LINES AND THE PRODUCT MIX •••

Companies usually don't have just one product that they sell. Rather, they sell several different but complementary products. New-product lines can be added continually with the right amount of research. Figure 16.2 shows Procter & Gamble's product lines. A **product line**, as the figure shows, is a group of products that are physically similar or that are intended for a similar market. Procter & Gamble's product lines include bar soaps, detergents, and dishwashing detergents. In one product line, there may be several competing brands. Procter & Gamble has many brands of detergent in its product line, including Bold, Cheer, Tide, and Ivory Snow. All of P&G's product lines make up its product mix.

product line
A group of products that are physically similar or that are intended for a similar market.

PRODUCT LINES	BRANDS
Bar soaps	Camay, Coast, Ivory, Kirk's, Lava, Monchel, Safeguard, Zest
Detergents	Bold, Cheer, Dash, Drell, Era, Gain, Ivory Snow, Liquid Bold-3, Liquid Cheer, Liquid Tide, Oxydol, Solo, Tide
Dishwashing detergents	Cascade, Dawn, Ivory Liquid, Joy, Liquid Cascade
Cleaners and cleansers	Comet, Comet Liquid, Mr. Clean, Spic & Span, Spic & Span Pine Liquid, Top Job
Shampoos	Head & Shoulders, Ivory, Lilt, Pert Plus, Prell
Toothpastes	Crest, Denquel, Gleem
Paper tissue products	Banner, Charmin, Puffs, White Cloud
Disposable diapers	Luvs, Pampers
Shortening and cooking oils	Crisco, Crisco Oil, Crisco Corn Oil, Puritan

(The word PRODUCT MIX runs vertically down the left side of the table.)

FIGURE **16.2**
. . . .
PROCTER & GAMBLE'S PRODUCE MIX, INCLUDING ALL ITS PRODUCT LINES

Most large companies make more than one product. Here we see the various products and brands Procter & Gamble makes. Note how physically similar the products are in each product line.

You used to go to the bank. Now it comes to you. Mbanx offers completely online banking services and can be accessed by personal computer, phone, or ABM. Mbanx is just one of the products offered by the Bank of Montreal.

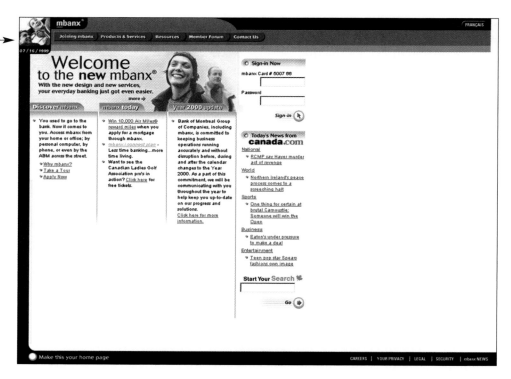

Reaching Beyond
Our Borders

<www.bce.ca>

Costly Attempts to Broaden Product Mix

During the merger and conglomerate waves that swept through Canada and the United States in the 1980s, many companies sought to broaden their product mix by acquiring companies unrelated to their core businesses. In many cases this did not work well, and a hasty retreat often turned into a rout.

For example, Lavalin, the huge international engineering group based in Quebec, went broke because of its acquisition of a petrochemical complex. BCE Inc., parent company of Bell Canada, was badly burned with its BCED venture into real estate development in the United States. Robert Campeau's attempt to become the kingpin of U.S. retailing resulted in disaster and the loss of his large real estate development company.

This trend to expand product lines by acquisition continued into the 1990s, but it is too soon to tell how ▲

many companies ran into trouble because of these acquisitions. The giant, transnational Canadian auto parts manufacturer Magna International announced in July 1999 that it had acquired Gulfstream Park Racing Association, a racetrack operation in Florida. This move was greeted with concern by investment analysts who believed Magna would suffer for this attempt to broaden product mix. The result was a drop in value of Magna's publicly traded shares. It remains to be seen whether this was a good move.

Sources: Various articles, *Globe and Mail, Report on Business,* December 29, 1990; David Hatter, "BCE Phones Home," *Canadian Business* 63, no. 8 (August 1990), p. 28; Barrie McKenna, "SNC Buys Lavalin's Prized Engineering Firm," *Globe and Mail, Report on Business,* August 13, 1991, pp. B1 and B5; Magna International Web site, <www.magnaint.com>, August 1999.

Product mix is the term used to describe the combination of product lines offered by a manufacturer. As we see in Figure 16.2, P&G's product mix consists of product lines of soap, detergents, toothpastes, shampoos, and so forth.

McCain, Canada Packers, Schneider, and Highliner have all introduced product lines of microwavable snack foods that have ben successful, including frozen microwavable milkshakes, hamburgers, french fries, and other products.[4]

Service providers have product lines and product mixes as well. For example, a bank may offer a variety of ways to deposit money, from savings accounts to money market funds. A bank's product mix may include safety deposit boxes, loans (home, car, etc.), traveller's cheques, and more. Canadian banks have expanded their product mixes by adding more product lines though acquisitions. They have acquired trust companies and stockbrokerage firms, enabling them to sell mutual funds, buy and sell shares and bonds, set up trusts, make wills, and to engage in other new activities. Companies must decide what product mix is best. The mix may include both goods and services to spread the risk among different market segments. However, companies must be careful not to diversify so widely that they lose their focus and run into other problems (see Reaching Beyond Our Borders for several examples).

product mix
The combination of product lines offered by a manufacturer.

<www.magnaint.com>

Go to the Magna Web site to learn more about this world-class Canadian manufacturer. Click on *In Brief* for a quick summary, and then check out the topics you can research by clicking on the options provided by the site.

Critical Thinking

When Armand Bombardier started his small company more than half a century ago, it manufactured his new invention, a Ski-Doo snowmobile. Three decades later, Bombardier Inc. was producing railway and subway cars for Canadian and American needs. Fifteen years later the company was making aircraft on an international scale with companies in Canada, the United States, and Ireland. What do you think prompted such major changes in its product lines? Why was Bombardier looking for other lines? Why was it expanding in these directions?

··· ▬ ····

PRODUCT DIFFERENTIATION

Product differentiation is the creation of real or perceived product differences. Often the *actual* product differences may be quite small, so marketers use a clever mix of pricing, advertising, and packaging to create a unique and attractive image. One of the more successful attempts at product differentiation was accomplished by Perrier. Perrier made its sparkling water so attractive through pricing and promotion that often people order it by brand name instead of a Coke or Pepsi. Each product requires its own marketing strategy. There is no reason why a company could not create a similar image for Fiberrific. With a high price and creative advertising, it could become the Perrier of cereals. But different products require different marketing strategies, as you will see in the next section.

product differentiation
The creation of real or perceived product differences.

convenience goods
and services
Products that the consumer wants to purchase frequently and with a minimum of effort.

<www.mbanx.com>

Banking on the Internet has grown rapidly in recent years, and all indications are that this trend will continue. The Bank of Montreal's online banking arm, mbanx, is a full-service bank in its own right. The entire array of traditional banking services is available without having to actually visit the bank's branches.

··· MARKETING DIFFERENT CLASSES OF ···
CONSUMER GOODS AND SERVICES

Several attempts have been made to classify consumer goods and services. One of the more traditional classifications has three general categories—convenience, shopping, and specialty—based on consumer shopping habits and preferences.

1. **Convenience goods and services** are products that the consumer wants to purchase frequently and with a minimum of effort (e.g.,

shopping goods and services
Products that the consumer buys only after comparing quality and price from a variety of sellers.

specialty goods and services
Products that have a special attraction for consumers who are willing to go out of their way to obtain them.

<www.shopyourmall.com>

Here's an interesting phenomenon! We visited some online malls earlier. Now, traditional malls are striving to get in on the act by introducing the concept of making a real-world visit to them quicker and easier. Try "*click on here to start your trip*" and see what you can find out.

industrial goods
Products used in the production of other products.

<www.mortonintl.com>

Visit this innovator's Web site. Click on *Morton Salt,* and try out *Fun Stuff.* Can you download the Morton Screensaver?

candy, snacks, banking). Location, brand awareness, and image are important for marketers of convenience goods and services.

2. **Shopping goods and services** are those products that the consumer buys only after comparing value, quality, and price from a variety of sellers. Shopping goods and services are sold largely through shopping centres where consumers can shop around. Because many consumers carefully compare such products, marketers can emphasize price differences, quality differences, or some combination of the two. Examples include clothes, shoes, appliances, and auto-repair services.

3. **Specialty goods and services** are products that have a special attraction for consumers who are willing to go out of their way to obtain them. Examples are fur coats, jewellery, exotic candy, cigars, and services provided by medical specialists or business consultants. These products are often marketed through specialty magazines. For example, specialty skis may be sold through ski magazines and specialty foods through gourmet magazines.

The marketing task varies depending on the kind of product; that is, convenience goods are marketed differently from specialty goods, and so forth. The best way to promote convenience goods is to make them readily available and to create the proper image. Price and quality are the best appeals for shopping goods. Specialty goods rely on reaching special market segments through advertising.

The advent in the 1990s of shopping via the Internet has had an almost revolutionary impact on specialty and shopping categories in which consumers shop around before buying. Most companies now have interactive Web sites where consumers can browse, do comparison shopping, communicate with companies, and, finally, order and pay by credit card without ever leaving their chairs. Think of the time, cost, and frustration saved by not having to drive in traffic and to look for (and sometimes to pay for) parking.

Whether a good or service falls into a particular class depends on the individual consumer. What's a shopping good for one consumer (e.g., coffee) could be a specialty good for another consumer (imported coffee). Some people shop around to compare different dry cleaners, so dry cleaning is a shopping service for them. Others go to the closest store, making it a convenience service. Marketers must carefully monitor their customer base to determine how consumers perceive their products. Can you see how Fiberrific could be either a convenience good or a shopping good?

••• MARKETING INDUSTRIAL GOODS AND SERVICES •••

Industrial goods are products used in the production of other products. Some products can be classified as both consumer goods and industrial goods. For example, personal computers could be sold to consumer markets or industrial markets. As a consumer good, the computer might be sold through computer stores or computer magazines. Most of the promotional task would be in advertising. As an industrial good, personal computers are more likely to be sold by salespeople. Advertising would be less of a factor in the promotion strategy. You can see that classifying goods by user category helps determine the proper marketing mix strategy. Figure 16.3 shows some categories of both consumer and industrial goods and services. Note the two categories of the latter: production and support goods.

- What's the difference between a product and a value package?
- What's the difference between a product line and a product mix?
- Name the three classes of consumer goods and services, and give examples of each.

PACKAGING: A MAJOR IMPACT ON THE PRODUCT

We have said that consumers evaluate many aspects of the product offer, including the package and the brand. It is surprising how important packaging can be. People once had problems with table salt because it would stick together in humid or damp weather. The Morton Salt Co. solved that problem by designing a package that kept the salt dry, thus the slogan, "When it rains, it pours." Packaging made Morton's salt more desirable than competing products, and it is one of the best-known salts in North America.

The Morton Salt Co. knew how to use packaging to improve its basic product. Other companies have used similar techniques. We have had squeezable

FIGURE **16.3**

VARIOUS CLASSES OF CONSUMER AND INDUSTRIAL GOODS AND SERVICES

Note the significance of the variety and quantity of industrial goods and services.

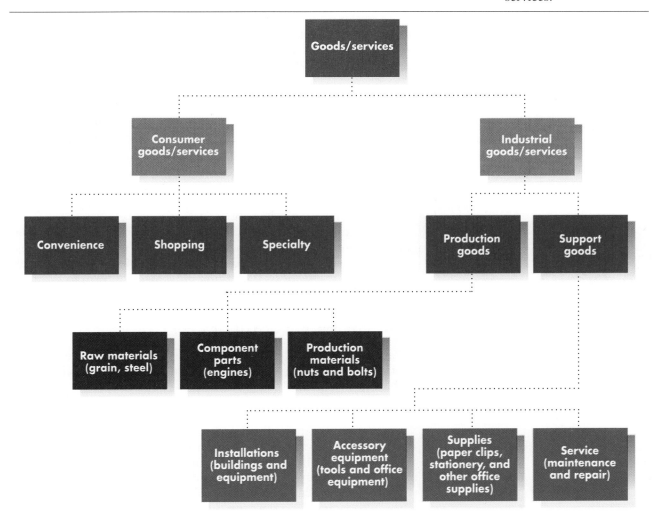

Spotlight on Small Business

Stay Close to Your Customers and Make Sure You Are Providing What they Need

One major advantage small businesses have over large ones is their ability to get closer to the customer and provide more personal and friendly service. But don't assume that a small business provides better service. Small-business managers must constantly improve their products and services. To facilitate this objective they should frequently poll their customers and employees to see what they think, using this feedback as the catalyst for change.

Small businesses shouldn't react negatively to the demands that customers place on them. Rather, they must encourage employees to give customers friendly, responsive service. Failing to do so means competitors that emphasize service will take away business.

Another good idea for small businesses is to analyze two major competitors to find weaknesses in their products or services. Then exploit those weak links, using them as a competitive edge. Smaller airlines, for example, are taking advantage of major carriers by offering service to more areas at lower prices. Smaller retailers are taking slices of the market by specializing in one or two products. You can now find stores selling just sunglasses or just kites.

Small businesses must constantly review their product mix and eliminate those products that no longer appeal to the market niche being served. That means constantly monitoring consumer trends and quickly adapting the product or service mix to meet current demands. Today, many of the greatest marketing opportunities are beyond our borders. Adapting products to successfully penetrate such markets is now and will continue to be the challenge.

Unique packaging, like potato chips in a can, helps a product to stand out in consumers' minds.

ketchup bottles, plastic bottles for oil that eliminate the need for funnels, stackable potato chips in a can, toothpaste pumps, plastic cans for tennis balls, microwavable popcorn, dinners that can be boiled in a pouch and served immediately, whipped cream in dispenser cans, vegetables in climate-controlled packages, and so forth. In each case, the package changed the product in the minds of consumers and opened large markets. Packaging can also make a product more attractive to retailers. For example, the universal product codes on many packages make it easier to control inventory and they speed up the checkout lines. Packaging changes the product by changing its visibility, usefulness, or attractiveness. Packaging must also conform to environmental regulations and to consumer attitudes on this issue.

••• THE GROWING IMPORTANCE OF PACKAGING •••

Packaging has always been an important aspect of the product offer, but today it's carrying more of the promotional burden than in the past. Many goods that were once sold by salespersons are now being sold in self-service outlets, and the package has thus been given more sales responsibility. The package must perform the following functions: (1) attract the buyer's attention, (2) describe and give information about the contents, (3) explain the benefits of the items inside, (4) provide information on warranties, warnings, and other consumer matters, (5) give some indication of price, value, and uses, and (6) protect the goods inside, stand up under handling and storage, be

Spotlight on Big Business

<www.kraftfoods.com>

Students Design a Face-Lift for Kraft Dinner

Kraft Canada Inc. decided it was time to design a new package for its popular Kraft Dinner product. One way of giving a lift to an old product is to give it a "face-lift." What makes this particular situation interesting is that Kraft chose a unique method for solving the problem. In 1994, together with the Packaging Association of Canada, The Thomas Pigeon Design Group, and Shikatani Lacroix Design Inc., Kraft sponsored a competition for Toronto students to come up with a winning design.

Ultimately, 81 students from the Ontario College of Art, George Brown College, Humber College, and Mohawk College submitted entries to their schools. The conditions they had to meet were quite demanding. The cheese had to be separated from the macaroni; the package had to be so attractive that it would "block out" other items on the shelf; students had to understand printing processes so that they didn't come up with something that could not be produced; finally, it had to be a low-cost item to manufacture since Kraft Dinner is a low-priced product.

The schools selected 17 of the 81 designs for preliminary judging by a seven-person panel. The panel chose two from each school for final judging. From this group, they selected a design by Tina Crosby, of the Ontario College of Art. She got a $1500 bursary for winning the competition.

One of the seven judges, J.P. Lacroix, president of Shikatani Lacroix Design, commended Crosby for her excellent design. She met all the requirements (listed above) with an eye-catching format that consisted of two separate boxes, one each for the cheese and macaroni, both held together by a transparent seal with the Kraft logo on it. The two boxes were illustrated with tumbling macaroni and cheese. Lacroix noted that Crosby showed excellent understanding of the printing process required. She also provided "good written documentation to back up her ideas."

Source: Paula Kulig, "Old Fave Gets a Facelift," *Globe and Mail, Report on Business*, August 29, 1995, p. B22.

---

tamperproof, and yet be easy to open and use. Clearly, packaging has become a critical part of product design. Even Perrier has added artwork to its signature green bottle to make it stand out from the crowd.

An interesting example is the problem Ault Foods faced when it sought a design for its purified, premium Lactantia milk containers. Because they developed this product through a patented filtered process, Ault wanted a special look. At first its advertising agency, Trudhope Associates, designed a high-tech silver package. However, survey groups overwhelmingly opted for a simple farm look: cows, greenery, and a country home. You can see this design today on Ault's cartons and plastic containers.[5]

LABELLING   What are the qualities that make for a successful label? Labels must be attractive and informative. They must also meet Canadian legal requirements regarding ingredients, bilingualism, grading, and expiration date (if applicable). From the marketing point of view, a good label helps to identify the product and differentiate it from competing products. We are swamped by many competing brands of everything from chocolate bars to toothpaste to soaps, so you can see why making the consumer aware of a particular product by differentiation is a major concern of marketers.

In today's world of globalized markets, many products are sold internationally. This trend makes the task of labelling more difficult as languages,

{ ⬤ }

This is where
we come in

You don't give much thought to the anti-lock brakes on your Ford, Mercury or Lincoln. You shouldn't have to. The fact is, ABS brakes interact with virtually every vehicle system to stop your car or truck safely and efficiently. They're precise components. So for brake service, or any repair, it makes sense to take your vehicle to the people who know it best. People with the training and parts your vehicle needs. See the Quality Care technicians at Ford and Lincoln-Mercury dealers. To learn more, visit us at www.qualitycareservice.com

From Ford and Lincoln-Mercury dealers
©1997 Ford Motor Company

Quality*Care*
at your service

Anti-lock brakes are largely an industrial good sold in the business-to-business market. However, consumers have to replace such items if they have their cars long enough. By encouraging consumers to shop at particular dealers, manufacturers can sell more goods to these dealers. This is called a pull strategy in marketing.

brand
A name, symbol, or design (or combination of these) that identifies the goods or services of one seller or group of sellers and distinguishes them from those of competitors.

trademark
A brand that has been given exclusive legal protection for both the brand name and the pictorial design.

private brands
Products that carry the name of a distributor or retailer instead of the manufacturer.

government regulations, and national and local traditions and practices differ. We are all familiar with multilanguage labels on packages of cookies and biscuits from Europe and multilanguage instructions accompanying electronic products. What kind of package and label would you design for Fiberrific?

•••• ▬▬▬ ••••

BRANDING

Closely related to packaging is branding. A **brand** is a name, symbol, or design (or a combination of them) that identifies the goods or services of one seller or group of sellers and distinguishes them from those of competitors. The term *brand* is sufficiently comprehensive to include practically all means of identifying a product. You will recall that a brand name consists of a logo, word, letter, or group of words or letters creating a name that differentiates the goods or services of a seller from those of competitors. Brand names you may be familiar with include Chevrolet, Sony, Del Monte, Campbell, President's Choice, Jordache, Esso, Apple, Microsoft, Michelin, Molson, and Colgate. Such brand names make it easier for consumers to remember the products.

A **trademark** is a brand that has been given exclusive legal protection for both the brand name and the pictorial design. Trademarks such as McDonald's golden arches are widely recognized. People are often impressed by certain brand names, even though they say they know there is no difference between brands in a given product category. For example, when someone who says that all aspirin are alike asks for an aspirin, put out two bottles—one with the Excedrin label and one labelled with an unknown brand. See which one that person chooses. Most people choose the brand name even when they say there is no difference.

••• BRAND CATEGORIES •••

Several categories of brands are familiar to you. *Manufacturers' brand names* are the brand names of manufacturers that distribute the product internationally. They include well-known names such as Xerox, Polaroid, Kodak, Sony, and Ford. *Knockoff brands* are illegal copies of national brand name goods such as when you see Lacoste shirts or Rolex watches being sold by street vendors. If you see an expensive brand name item for sale at a ridiculously low price, you can be pretty sure it's a knockoff.

Private brands are products that do not carry the manufacturer's name but carry the name of a distributor or retailer instead. Well-known names include Kenmore (Sears). These are also known as *house* brands or *distributor* brands. Today, some distributor brands, such as President's Choice, are as well known as manufacturers' brand names. Major supermarket chains carry their own house brands of products, which are usually manufactured by the major brand name companies. This is a growing trend that has many manufacturers worried (see the next section).

What many manufacturers also fear is having their brand names become generic names. **Generic names** are the names for product *categories*. Did you know that *aspirin* and *linoleum*, which are now generic names for products,

President's Choice is a private brand of products developed by Loblaw Company Limited. These products have been extremely successful in Canada and are now being sold in other countries.

were once brand names? So were *nylon, escalator, kerosene,* and *zipper.* All of those names became so popular, so identified with the product, that they lost their brand status and became *generic* (the name of the product category). The producers then had to come up with new names. The original *Aspirin,* for example, became *Bayer* aspirin. Companies that are working hard to protect their brand names today include Xerox (one ad reads, "Don't say 'Xerox it'; say 'Copy it'"), Styrofoam, and Rollerblades.

generic names
Names of product categories.

Generic goods are nonbranded products that usually sell at a sizeable discount from national or private brands, have very basic packaging, and are backed with little or no advertising. The quality varies considerably among generic goods. Some are copies of national brand names and may be close to the same quality, but others may be of minimum quality. There are generic tissues, cigarettes, peaches, and so forth. A label on a generic can of peaches will simply say "Peaches," with no brand name. Consumers tend to buy generic goods when they feel the quality is high enough and the price is lower than recognized brands.

generic goods
Nonbranded products that usually sell at a sizeable discount from national or private brands, have very basic packaging, and are backed with little or no advertising.

••• PRIVATE LABELS CHALLENGE NAME BRANDS •••

Since the 1980s there has been a dramatic surge in the popularity of private labels of supermarkets. In 1995 almost one-quarter of all grocery store sales in Canada were private labels and amounted to $3.8 billion. In the four western provinces, the proportion ranged from 28 percent in Alberta to 33 percent in Saskatchewan. At the annual conference of the Canadian Food Brokers' Association in St. John's, Newfoundland, in July 1999, it was reported that store brands (private labels) had continued their strong development in 1998, representing an 11 percent increase over 1997 (almost double all-commodity growth of 6 percent). Store brands are most developed in Western Canada and most prevalent in the paper and wrapping categories, frozen and refrigerated food, and dessert and snacks segments. Emphasizing private labels is one of the most common marketing initiatives among Canadian supermarkets. Elaine Pollack, director of Management Horizons in Columbus, Ohio, who shared her forecasts for the future at the Canadian Council of Grocery Distributors' 1998 Ontario Conference in Toronto, says that private label will double in growth through 2000. Supermarkets will keep growing their private label as a way to differentiate and gain greater pricing flexibility.[6]

<www.loblaw.com>

"President's Choice" is a brand name held by Loblaws. Visit the Loblaws site to see some innovative examples of how it uses the brand name. Would you like to order a *President's Choice Gift Basket?* Look at *President's Choice Financial.* If you were a senior executive at one of Canada's traditional banks, would you be alarmed?

<www.cdngrocer.com>

Visit the *Canadian Grocer* Web site. This is an online industry trade magazine. What other developments of significance to this industry can you find reported? If you were in the industry, would you visit the site regularly and frequently? Why?

brand equity
Combination of factors such as awareness, loyalty, perceived quality, feelings, images, and any other emotion people associate with a brand name.

brand loyalty
The degree to which customers are satisfied, like the brand, and are committed to further purchases.

brand awareness
How quickly a particular brand name comes to mind when a product category is mentioned.

Associating a product with a famous athletic star gives that product more recognition and acceptance, especially among young consumers. Former Toronto Argonaut quarterback Doug Flutie has his image prominently displayed on the front of this cereal box.

This popularity poses a problem for major manufacturers like Kimberly-Clark of Canada, who make Huggies diapers, and Ault Foods Ltd., whose national milk brands are Sealtest and Lactantia and Sealtest ice cream.

The production of their own brands does not require the use of all the manufacturing capacity they have. Since it is costly to have idle, unused plant capacity, they have been drawn into—guess what?—producing private-label products for supermarkets. Ault also produces about half the country's private-label ice cream products, including the very popular President's Choice product line for Loblaw's.

Doesn't it seem strange that companies produce products that compete with their own brands? Yet the economics of the situation dictate that they are better off, at least in the short run, to profit from the use of their idle capacity. There is also the pressure from supermarkets like Loblaw's to produce their private labels because they also carry the national brands.

Of course, national brands and private labels are in fierce competition. If the former could increase their market share, the companies would have less idle capacity, resulting in less pressure to produce private labels. Private labels' share has been increasing because they sell for lower prices. As the supermarkets sell more of their own labels, they reduce shelf space for national brands, resulting in still lower sales for them.

••• BUILDING BRAND EQUITY AND LOYALTY •••

A major goal of marketers in the future will be to reestablish the notion of brand equity. **Brand equity** is a combination of factors including awareness, loyalty, perceived quality, feelings, images, and any other emotion people associate with a brand name. What has happened in the past is that companies have tried to boost their short-term performance by offering coupons and price discounts to move goods quickly. This has eroded consumers' commitment to brand names. Now, companies realize the value of brand equity and are trying to measure the earning power of strong brand names.[7]

The core of brand equity is brand loyalty. **Brand loyalty** is the degree to which customers are satisfied, like the brand, and are committed to further purchases. A loyal group of customers represents substantial value to a firm, and that value can be calculated. Relationship marketing is designed to strengthen brand loyalty.

Brand awareness refers to how quickly or easily a particular brand name comes to mind when a product category is mentioned. Advertising helps build strong brand awareness. Older brands, such as Coca-Cola and Pepsi, are usually the highest in brand awareness. *Sponsorship* (e.g., Molson's Indy auto races and Chrysler Canada's sponsorship of the Canadian Olympic Team) helps improve awareness.

Perceived quality is an important part of brand equity. A product that's perceived as being of better quality than its competitors can be priced higher and thus improve profits. The key to creating a quality image is to identify what the consumer looks for in a quality product and then communicate a quality message in everything the company does. Quality cues include price, appearance, and reputation.

Today, it's so easy to copy a product's benefits that private-label products are being developed to capture the market from brand-name goods.

Brand-name manufacturers have to develop new products even faster and promote their names better to hold off the challenge of lower-priced competitors.

··· BUILDING BRAND ASSOCIATIONS ···

The name, symbol, and slogan a company uses can be great assets because they assist in brand recognition and association. **Brand association** is the linking of a brand to other favourable images. For example, you can link a brand to other product users, to a popular celebrity, to a particular geographic area, or to competitors. Note, for example, how ads for Mercedes-Benz and Cadillac associate those cars with rich people such as polo players. Note too the success of associating basketball shoes to stars such as Shaquille O'Neal and Michael Jordan, especially after his comeback. The person responsible for building brands is known as a *brand manager* or *product manager.* We'll explore that position right after the Progress Check.

brand association
The linking of a brand to other favourable images.

Progress Check

* What six functions does packaging now perform?
* What's the difference between a brand name and a trademark?
* Can you explain the difference between a manufacturers' brand, a private brand, and a generic brand?
* What are the key components of brand equity?

Critical Thinking

If you became product manager for Fiberrific, would you look for a star to advertise your product? Would you want an athlete, Nobel Prize winner, or an entertainer? Why? Do you think you could afford a big-name person?

··· ▬▬▬ ····

PRODUCT MANAGEMENT

A **product manager** has direct responsibility for one brand or one product line. This responsibility includes all the elements of the marketing mix: product, price, place, and promotion. Thus, the product manager is like a president of a one-product firm. Imagine being the product manager for Fiberrific. You'd be responsible for everything having to do with that one brand. One reason many large consumer-product companies created the position of product manager is to have greater control over new-product development and product promotion.

product manager
A manager who has direct responsibility for one brand or one product line.

Many companies are now challenging the value of product managers. As we mentioned earlier, some manufacturers' brand names have become less important to retailers, and customers' brand loyalty is declining. This gives product managers less power. The product management concept seems to be fading, and cross-functional teams and similar consumer-oriented forms of marketing are taking their place. Remaining product managers are finding that their role is expanding to include long-range planning. Brand managers now must create brand equity and turn all employees into brand ambassadors through indoctrination programs so that the brand name becomes a greater competitive advantage.[8]

··· NEW-PRODUCT SUCCESS ···

Chances that a new product will fail are overwhelmingly high, according to *The Wall Street Journal,* which reported that 86 percent of products introduced in the United States in one year failed to reach their business objectives. Products not delivering what they promise are a leading cause of new-product failure. Other reasons for failure include poor positioning, not enough differences from competitors, and poor packaging. Smaller firms may experience a lower success rate unless they do proper product planning. We'll discuss such planning next.

••• THE NEW-PRODUCT DEVELOPMENT PROCESS •••

As Figure 16.4 shows, product development for producers consists of five stages:

1. idea generation
2. screening and analysis
3. development
4. testing
5. commercialization (bringing the product to the market)

New products continue to pour into the market every year, and the profit potential looks tremendous. Think, for example, of the potential of home video conferencing, interactive TV, large-screen HDTV sets, virtual reality games and products, and other innovations. Where do these ideas come from? How are they tested? What's the life span for an innovation? The following sections look at these issues.

••• GENERATING NEW-PRODUCT IDEAS •••

Figure 16.5 gives you a good idea of where new-product ideas come from. Note that 38 percent of the new-product ideas for consumer goods come from analyzing competitors (the source of 27 percent of ideas for new industrial products). Such copying of competitors slows the introduction of new ideas.

FIGURE **16.4**

• • • •

THE NEW-PRODUCT DEVELOPMENT PROCESS

Product development is a five-stage process. Which stage do you believe to be the most important?

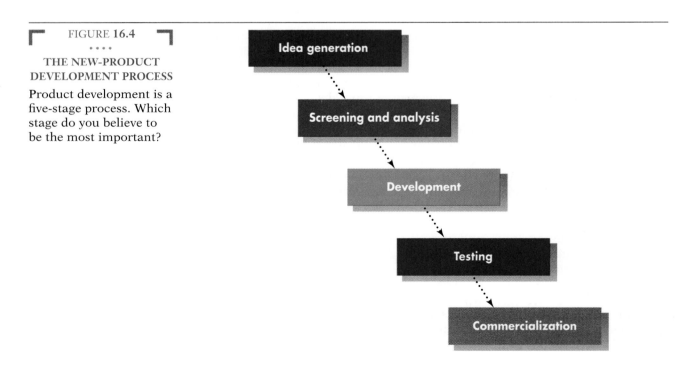

CONSUMER PRODUCTS (BASED ON A SURVEY OF 79 NEW PRODUCTS)	
Analysis of the competition	38.0%
Company sources other than research and development	31.6
Consumer research	17.7
Research and development	13.9
Consumer suggestions	12.7
Published information	11.4
Supplier suggestions	3.8
INDUSTRIAL PRODUCTS (BASED ON A SURVEY OF 152 NEW PRODUCTS)	
Company sources other than research and development	36.2
Analysis of the competition	27.0
Research and development	24.3
Product users	15.8
Supplier suggestions	12.5
Product user research	10.5
Published information	7.9

FIGURE 16.5

SOURCES OF NEW-PRODUCT IDEAS

This survey shows where ideas for new products originate. As you know, research plays an important role in the development of new products.

A strong point can be made for listening to employee suggestions for new-product ideas. The number one source of ideas for new industrial products is company sources other than research and development. They are also a major source of new consumer goods. Part of that is due to successful marketing communication systems that monitor suggestions from all sources.

Look through Figure 16.5 carefully and think about the implications. Notice that more than a third of all new-product ideas for industrial products come from users, user research, or supplier suggestions. This finding emphasizes the principle that a firm should listen to its suppliers and customers and give them what they want.

··· PRODUCT SCREENING AND ANALYSIS ···

Product screening is designed to reduce the number of new-product ideas being worked on at any one time. Criteria needed for screening include whether the product fits in well with present products, profit potential, marketability, and personnel requirements (see Figure 16.6). Each of these factors may be assigned a weight, and total scores are then computed. A new software package called Quick Insight now helps companies analyze the potential of new goods and services. By answering about 60 questions and then reviewing the answers, the user can gain an understanding of the likely problems and

product screening
A process designed to reduce the number of new-product ideas being worked on at any one time.

FIGURE 16.6

• • • •

CRITERIA FOR SCREENING NEW-PRODUCT IDEAS

Ideas for new products are carefully screened. This screening helps the company identify the areas where new products are needed and reduces the chance of a company working on too many ideas at a time.

Areas of company strengths and weaknesses	Consumer promotional considerations
Tie-ins with, or potential impact on, other company brands	Nature of competition
Production capabilities	Market segments
Consumer attitudes toward category	Distribution channels
Awareness	Trade perceptions of category
Satisfaction with existing brands	Turnover rates/optimum inventory allocations
Regional consumer differences	Seasonal characteristics
Advertising and merchandising norms, timing, and directions	Price margins

potential strengths of the new offering.[9] It takes about seven ideas to generate one commercial product.[10] *Product analysis* is done after product screening and is largely a matter of making cost estimates and sales forecasts to get a feeling for profitability. Products that don't meet the established criteria are withdrawn from consideration.

••• PRODUCT DEVELOPMENT AND TESTING •••

If a product passes the screening and analysis phase, the firm begins to develop it further. A product idea can be developed into many different product concepts (alternative product offerings based on the same product idea that have different meanings and values to consumers). For example, a firm that makes packaged meat products may develop the concept of a chicken dog—a hot dog made of chicken that tastes like an all-beef hot dog.

concept testing
Taking a product ideas to consumers to test their reactions.

Concept testing involves taking a product idea to consumers to test their reactions (see Figure 16.7). Do they see the benefits of this new product? How

FIGURE 16.7

• • • •

STEPS TO TAKE BEFORE TEST MARKETING A PRODUCT

Product development, communication development, and strategy development all are used as a company develops a new product. Extensive testing is used to indicate the likelihood of the product's success.

PRODUCT DEVELOPMENT	COMMUNICATION DEVELOPMENT	STRATEGY DEVELOPMENT
Identify unfilled need	Select a name	Set marketing goals
Preliminary profit/payout plan for each concept	Design a package and test	Establish marketing strategy
Concept test	Create a copy theme and test	Develop marketing mix (after communication developed)
Determine whether the product can be made	Develop complete ads and test	Estimate cost of marketing plan and payment (after product development)
Test the concept and product (and revise as indicated)		
Develop the product		
Run extended product use tests		

frequently would they buy it? At what price? What features do they like and dislike? What changes would they make? Different samples are tested using different packaging, branding, ingredients, and so forth until a product emerges that's desirable from both production and marketing perspectives. A good example is the testing of the package design for Ault Lactancia milk described earlier. Can you see the importance of concept testing for Fiberrific?

••• COMMERCIALIZATION •••

Even if a product tests well, it may take quite a while before it achieves success in the market. Take the introduction of the zipper, for example. It was one of the longest development efforts on record for a consumer product. Whitcomb Judson received his first patents in the early 1890s. It took more than 15 years to perfect the product, but even then consumers weren't interested. The company suffered numerous financial setbacks, name changes, and relocations before settling in Meadville, Pennsylvania. Finally, the U.S. Navy started using Judson's zippers in 1918 during World War I. Today, Talon Inc. is the leading U.S. maker of zippers, producing some 500 million of them a year.

　　This example shows that the marketing effort must include commercialization. Commercialization includes (1) promoting the product to distributors and retailers to get wide distribution and (2) developing strong advertising and sales campaigns to generate and maintain interest in the product among distributors and consumers. New products get rapid exposure on the Internet and interactive Web sites quickly give feedback about consumer reactions.

••• THE DESIGN CHALLENGE •••

Good product design has become increasingly important as a marketing tool to create product differentiation in a very crowded sea of products. To help Canadian and other companies improve the design of their existing and new products, the Toronto Design Exchange (DX) was set up in September 1994. According to DX president Howard Cohen, Europe and Japan are ahead of North America in this regard. He notes that, with few exceptions it is difficult to convince Canadian companies that it is well worth the additional investment.

<www.seiko.com>

Seiko is an innovator. Visit its Web site. Can you find any other new products, based on cutting edge technology? Click on *Seiko Instruments* to check it out.

The Design Exchange's (DX) Design Showcase celebrates innovative achievements in design in the marketplace. Designers and businesses are invited to submit innovative projects and hot new designs. Selected projects are displayed by the Trading Floor in the DX building.

Cohen hopes that educating "the public to have higher expectations of the products and services Canadian companies produce" will raise companies' awareness of sensitivity to the importance of the design component of products. DX held an exhibition to highlight some Canadian and other design success stories. The exhibit was co-sponsored by Electrohome Ltd., Spar Aerospace, and the Canadian Space Agency, who were all strong supporters of the DX.[11]

THE PRODUCT LIFE CYCLE

product life cycle
A theoretical model of what happens to sales and profits for a product class over time.

Once a product has been developed, tested, and placed on the market, it goes through a cycle consisting of four stages: introduction, growth, maturity, and decline, called the *product life cycle* (see Figure 16.8). The **product life cycle** is a theoretical model of what happens to sales and profits for a product class (e.g., all dishwasher soaps) over time. However, not all products follow the life cycle, and particular brands may act differently. For example, although frozen foods as a generic class may go through the entire cycle, one brand may never get beyond the introduction stage. Nonetheless, the product life cycle provides a basis for anticipating future market developments and for planning marketing strategies. Some products, such as microwave ovens, stay in the introductory stage for years. Other products, such as fad clothing, may go through the entire cycle in a few months.

••• EXAMPLE OF A PRODUCT LIFE CYCLE •••

You can see how the product life cycle works by looking at the introduction of instant coffee. When it was introduced, most people didn't like it as well as regular coffee, and it took several years to gain general acceptance (introduction stage). At one point, though, instant coffee grew rapidly in popularity, and many brands were introduced (growth stage). After a while, people became attached to one brand and sales levelled off (maturity stage). Sales then went

FIGURE **16.8**
••••
SALES AND PROFITS DURING THE PRODUCT LIFE CYCLE

Note that profit levels start to fall *before* sales reach their peak. When profits and sales start to decline, it's time to come out with a new product or to remodel the old one to maintain interest and profits.

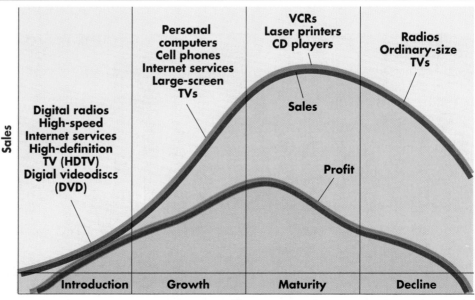

Life Cycle Stage	Marketing Mix Elements			
	Product	**Price**	**Place**	**Promotion**
Introduction	Offer market-tested product; keep product mix small	Go after innovators with high introductory price (skimming strategy) or use penetration pricing	Use wholesalers, selective distribution	Dealer promotion and heavy investment in primary demand advertising and sales promotion to get stores to carry the product and consumers to try it
Growth	Improve product; keep product mix limited	Adjust price to meet competition	Increase distribution	Heavy competitive advertising
Maturity	Differentiate product to satisfy different market segments	Further reduce price	Take over wholesaling function and intensify distribution	Emphasize brand name as well as product benefits and differences
Decline	Cut product mix; develop new-product ideas	Consider price increase	Consolidate distribution; drop some outlets	Reduce advertising to only loyal customers

FIGURE **16.9**
• • • •
SAMPLE STRATEGIES FOLLOWED DURING THE PRODUCT LIFE CYCLE

It is essential to know what stages your products are at in the life cycle to plan product strategies.

into a slight decline when freeze-dried coffees were introduced (decline stage). At present, freeze-dried coffee is at the maturity stage. It's extremely important to recognize what stage a product is in because such an analysis leads to more intelligent and efficient marketing decisions.

••• THE IMPORTANCE OF THE PRODUCT LIFE CYCLE •••

The importance of the product life cycle to marketers is this: different stages call for different strategies. Figure 16.9 outlines the marketing mix decisions that might be made. As you go through the table, you will see that each stage requires multiple marketing mix changes. (Remember, these concepts are mainly theoretical and should be used only as guidelines.)

Figures 16.8 and 16.10 show what happens to sales volume, profit and loss, and competition during the product life cycle. This information is revealing. For instance, it shows that a product at the mature stage may reach the top in sales growth while profit is decreasing. At that stage, a marketing manager may decide to create a new image for the product to start a new growth

FIGURE **16.10**
• • • •
HOW SALES, PROFITS, AND COMPETITION VARY OVER THE PRODUCT LIFE CYCLE

Many products go through these stages at various times in their life cycle. What happens to sales as a product matures?

LIFE CYCLE STAGE	SALES	PROFITS	COMPETITORS
Introduction	Low sales	Losses may occur	Few
Growth	Rapidly rising sales	Very high profits	Growing number
Maturity	Peak sales	Declining profits	Stable number, then declining
Decline	Falling sales	Profits may fall to become losses	Declining number

market modification
Technique for extending the product life cycle of mature products by finding users in new market segments.

cycle. This strategy is called *market modification*. **Market modification** is a technique used to extend the life cycle of mature products by finding users in new market segments. You may have noted, for example, that Arm & Hammer baking soda gets a new image every few years to generate sales in new markets. One year baking soda was positioned as a deodorant for refrigerators and the next year as a substitute for harsh chemicals in swimming pools. Knowing what stage in the cycle a product is in guides marketing managers as to when such strategic changes are needed. Figure 16.9 summarizes the decision making that occurs at each level of the product life cycle.

Many brands seem to go on forever. Think of Ivory Soap, Kellogg's Corn Flakes, and Coke all of which go back to the late 1800s. Life Savers, Chiclets, and Wrigley's chewing gum also go back a long way. These products have hardly changed, except for packaging, and are still leaders in their fields. Games like Monopoly—and Snakes and Ladders, which is much older—also never seem to change or die. Can you think of other products that defy the product life cycle model?

Critical Thinking

In what stage of the product life cycle are laptop computers? What does Figure 16.9 indicate firms should do at that stage? What will the next stage be? What might you do at that stage to optimize profits?

Peanut butter is in the maturity or decline stage of the product life cycle. Does that explain why Skippy introduced a reduced-fat version of its peanut butter? What other variations on older products have been introduced in the last few years?

Progress Check

- What are the five steps in the new-product development process?
- Can you draw a product life cycle and label its parts?
- Can you name one marketing strategy in product, price, place, or advertising for each stage? (See Figure 16.9.)
- Can you explain the difference between market modification and product modification, and give examples of each?

···· ▬▬▬ ····

COMPETITIVE PRICING

Pricing is so important to marketing that it has been singled out as one of the four Ps in the marketing mix, along with product, place, and promotions. Price is also a critical ingredient in consumer evaluation of the product. In this section, we'll explore price both as an ingredient of the product and as a strategic marketing tool.

···· ▬▬▬ ····

PRICING OBJECTIVES

The ultimate objective of all marketing activities of a company is long-term growth in profits. Various pricing strategies are employed to achieve that objective. When pricing Fiberrific, we may want to promote the product's image. If we price it high and use the right promotion, maybe we can make it the Perrier of cereals. We might also price it high to achieve a certain profit objective, or we could price Fiberrific lower than its competitors because low pricing may discourage competition as the profit potential is less. A low price may also help us capture a larger share of the market, which would be good in the long run. The point is, a firm may have several pricing strategies and it must have a clear goal before developing an overall pricing objective. Common strategies include:

1. *Achieving a target profit.* Ultimately, the goal of marketing is to make a profit by providing goods or services to others. Naturally, one long-run pricing objective of almost all firms is to optimize profit.

2. *Building traffic.* Supermarkets often advertise certain products at a price below cost to attract people to the store so that they will buy other products, too. These products are called *loss leaders*. The long-run objective is to make profits by following the short-run objective of building a customer base.

The exclusivity and status associated with owning a well-recognized symbol such as a Jaguar automobile justifies the application of prestige pricing.

3. *Achieving greater market share.* The Canadian auto industry was in a fierce international battle to capture and hold market share. It had lost market share to foreign producers, so it used price incentives (and quality) to win it back.

4. *Creating an image.* Certain watches, perfumes, and other socially visible products are priced high to give them an image of exclusivity and status.

Usually a target profit is set for a particular period of time. For example, for Fiberrific we might shoot for a $3 million profit over 18 months. This might be broken down into three-month (quarterly) goals:

1st quarter	$ −400,000	(loss)
2nd quarter	−100,000	(loss)
3rd quarter	200,000	
4th quarter	500,000	
5th quarter	1,000,000	
6th quarter	1,800,000	
Total	$ 3,000,000	profit

••• PRICE DETERMINATION •••

Normally, every product is sold into a market that has many competing products. In the long run, prices are determined by the interaction between many buyers and many sellers. But other considerations influence price determination.

Cost-Based Pricing   Cost does establish a level below which you cannot continue to sell your products for very long if you hope to stay alive. You normally set prices above cost. What exactly is cost? This question is much more difficult question to answer than you might imagine, especially for large companies in manufacturing and other complex activities like searching for oil and gas. How should the cost of a barrel of oil be determined when 25 wells are dry and only one is a producer in a particular area? How should a bottle of vit-amins be costed when the actual material and production cost are minimal but the cost of research and development is enormous and often produces no results? Many books and articles address this topic.

Large firms, whose products may dominate the market, sometimes adopt a below-cost strategy to drive out weaker competitors who cannot stand a long period of losses. They must be sure they are not abrogating fair competition laws and regulations that are designed to outlaw such *predatory pricing*. There have been allegations of this practice in the price wars between Air Canada and Canadian Airlines International with smaller airlines.

Producers often use cost as a primary basis for setting price. They develop elaborate cost accounting systems to measure production costs (including materials, labour, and overhead), marketing costs, add in some margin of profit, and come up with a satisfactory price. The question is whether the price will be satisfactory to the market as well. In the long run, the *market*, not the producer, determines what the price will be.

Price-Led Costing   Cost-driven pricing has been cited as the reason that the United States lost much of the consumer electronics industry. The United States had the technology and the products, but it used cost-based pricing. Prices ended up being too high. The Japanese, on the other hand, used price-led costing. That is, the Japanese determined what the market was willing to pay (price) and then designed products to fit those prices. Then, year by year, Japanese companies were able to reduce manufacturing costs until they were well below the prices originally set, thus ensuring a satisfactory profit. Eventually, the Japanese won most of the market.

••• PRICING STRATEGIES •••

Let's say a firm has just developed a new product such as high-definition TVs (HDTVs). The firm has to decide how to price the HDTVs at the introductory stage of the product life cycle. One strategy would be to price the HDTVs high to recover the costs of developing the product and take advantage of the fact that there are few competitors. A **skimming price strategy** is one in which the product is priced high to make optimum profit while there is little competition. Of course, those large profits will attract others to produce HDTVs. That is what happened with high-priced camcorders when they were first introduced.

A second strategy is to price the HDTVs low. This would attract more buyers and discourage others from making HDTVs because the profit is so low. This strategy enables the firm to penetrate or capture a large share of the market quickly. A **penetration price strategy**, therefore, is one in which a product is priced low to attract more customers and discourage competitors. The Japanese successfully used a penetration strategy with VCRs. No domestic firm could compete with the low prices the Japanese companies offered.

Ultimately, price is determined by supply and demand in the marketplace, as described in Chapter 2. For example, if we charge $2.00 for our cereal and nobody buys it at that price, we will have to lower the price until we reach a price that is acceptable to customers and to us. The price that results from the interaction of buyers and sellers in the marketplace is called the *market price*.

It is impossible to include in this textbook all of the wide range of pricing strategies and tactics that are available to and used by marketers. But you should know that it is a big topic and that many books are devoted to discussing and analyzing which strategy or tactic is best suited for certain situations. As with other issues, experts often disagree on the best course of action.

skimming price strategy
Pricing the product high to make optimum profit while there is little competition.

penetration price strategy
Pricing the product low to attract more customers and discourage competitors.

THE PRICING REVOLUTION

Discounters and warehouse merchandisers Costco, and Honest Ed's in Toronto, price based on cost, low profit margins, and high volume. They aim for a satisfactory total profit by *value pricing*. **Value pricing** means offering consumers brand-name goods and services at discount prices. In addition, these companies market their own house or private labels aggressively to increase their profits and cut into the market shares of well-known brands.

It is clear that price has become perhaps the most competitive tool in the ever-fiercer battle for the consumer dollar. Airlines, auto manufacturers, electronic and computer companies, and even retailers like The Bay, Zellers, Wal-Mart, Canadian Tire, and others are locked in competition. This battle is evidenced by endless advertisements and inserts in newspapers and magazines, and advertisements on radio and TV, as well as weekly door-to-door flyers telling consumers of the great bargains offered by pharmacies, supermarkets, fastfood franchises, and others. The mushrooming of the ubiquitous dollar stores is clear evidence that price is, perhaps, the major competitive tool.

value pricing
Offering consumers brand name goods and services at discount prices.

··· NONPRICE COMPETITION ···

In spite of the emphasis placed on price in microeconomic theory, marketers often compete on product attributes other than price. You may have noted

Ethical Dilemma

REVIEW

Do you remember the dilemma about the toys that have been exposed to radiation? Here are the answers from our executives on this one. Bédard has a detailed and clear-cut reply. "Intentionally marketing products, especially to children, that present health hazards, though minor, is highly unethical. Children are much more susceptible to developing problems when exposed to certain contaminants that would not normally affect adults. This proposition is unacceptable and the games or toys should not be bought. A company's reputation could be destroyed with such a decision."

Reilley says, "I would turn him down. Not only would it be illegal but it would [start] me on a slippery slope that could end who knows where."

It's easy to say no, but if this purchase might save your business shouldn't you, perhaps, give it a little thought? Suppose you took the sample items from Adam and had them checked out by Emiko, a scientist you know, who can verify the radiation count at her lab. You do that, and she confirms Adam's contention that there

is a very low level of harmful radiation. When you discuss this further with Emiko she tells you that most kids are exposed to just as much radiation from the atmosphere and various activities our civilization generates. However, when you ask her if she would let *her* kids play with these products she is not so sure she would.

So now what do you do? You decide to consult a medical radiation expert whom Emiko suggests you see, for another opinion. After his tests, he confirms that the risk for children is small and it probably will not have any really harmful long-term effects. He has no children but, if he did, he also is not sure if he would let them play with these toys or games. What to do? Suppose the articles Adam gave you are not really representative of the radiation levels in the whole lot? Their level could be higher or lower. You believe that you could make about $50,000 profit from the whole shipment, which would pull you out of the financial hole you are in. Adam is back in Asia and is asking you for an answer. He needs an answer so he can sell them to somebody else if you refuse. What would *you* do?

that price differences between products such as gasoline, cigarettes, candy bars, and even major products such as compact cars are often small or nonexistent. Very rarely will you see price used as a major promotional appeal on television. Instead, marketers tend to emphasize product images and consumer benefits such as comfort, style, convenience, and durability.

Many organizations promote the services that accompany basic products rather than the price. The idea is to make a relatively homogeneous product better. For example, airlines stress friendliness, promptness, more flights, better meals, and other such services. Motels stress no surprises or cable TV, swimming pools, and other extras.

Quite often, marketers emphasize nonprice differences because prices are so easy to match. It is harder to match the image of a friendly, responsive, consumer-oriented company.

Progress Check

- List two short-term and two long-term pricing objectives. Are the two kinds of objectives compatible?
- What is wrong with using a cost-based pricing strategy?
- What is price-led costing and who has used it successfully? Explain.
- What are two main pricing strategies? What is the purpose of each strategy?

Critical Thinking

Do you think price is the most important consideration when consumers decide to buy? Does it depend on the kind of product or service (a car, a tennis racquet, or rent)?

What would you do as a manufacturer of national brands to combat the inroads of private labels?

SUMMARY
· · · · ·

1. Explain the difference between a product and a value package and between a product line and a product mix.

1. Product development means developing a value package for each product and developing a product mix that will appeal to a variety of customers.
   - ***What's the difference between a product and a value package?***
   A product is any physical good, service, or idea that satisfies a want or need. A value package is much more than a physical object. A value package consists of all the tangibles and intangibles (things you can't touch) that consumers evaluate when deciding whether to buy something. A value package includes price, brand name, satisfaction in use, and more.

   - ***What's the difference between a product line and a product mix?***
   A product line is a group of physically similar products. (A product line of gum may include chewing gum, sugarless gum, bubble gum, and so on.) A product mix is a company's combination of product lines. (A manufacturer may offer lines of gum, candy bars, and hard candy.)

2. Describe how businesses create product differentiation for their goods and services in both consumer and industrial markets.

2. Product differentiation is what makes one product appear better than the competition in both consumer and industrial markets.
   - ***How do marketers create product differentiation for their goods and services?***
   Marketers use a mix of pricing, advertising, and packaging to make their products seem unique and attractive.

   - ***What are the three classifications of consumer goods and services and how are they marketed?***
   There are convenience goods and services (requiring minimum shopping effort), shopping goods and services (for which people compare price and

quality), and specialty goods and services (which consumers go out of their way to get). Convenience goods and services are best promoted by location, shopping goods and services by some price or quality appeal, and specialty goods and services by specialty magazines.

- ***What are industrial goods, and how are they marketed differently from consumer goods?***
Industrial goods are products used in the production of other products. They're sold largely through salespeople and rely less on advertising.

3. Packaging changes the product and is becoming increasingly important, taking over much of the sales function for consumer goods.
   - ***What are the six functions of packaging?***
   The six functions are (1) to attract the buyer's attention, (2) to describe the contents, (3) to explain the benefits of the product inside, (4) to provide information on warranties, warnings, and other consumer matters, (5) to indicate price, value, and uses, and (6) to protect the goods inside, stand up under handling and storage, be tamperproof, and yet be easy to open and use.

3. Describe the six functions of packaging.

4. Branding also changes a product.
   - ***Can you give examples of a brand, a brand name, and a trademark?***
   There are endless examples you could give. One example of a brand and brand name of salmon is Cloverleaf. The brand consists of the name as well as the symbol (a gold four-leaf clover). The brand name and the symbol are also trademarks, since Cloverleaf has been given legal protection for this brand.

4. Give examples of a brand, a brand name, and a trademark.

5. Product managers are like presidents of one-product firms.
   - ***What are the functions of a product manager?***
   Product managers coordinate product, place, promotion, and price decisions for a particular product. In many companies the product manager's role is gradually losing its importance as consumer brand loyalty decreases.

   - ***What are the five steps of the product development process?***
   The steps are: (1) generation of new-product ideas, (2) screening and analysis, (3) development, (4) testing, and (5) commercialization.

5. Explain the role of product managers and the five steps of the new-product development process.

6. Once a product is placed on the market, marketing strategy varies as the product goes through various stages of acceptance called the product life cycle.
   - ***What are the stages of the product life cycle?***
   They are introduction, growth, maturity, and decline.

   - ***How do marketing strategies change at the various stages?***
   See Figure 16.9.

6. Identify and describe the stages of the product life cycle, and describe marketing strategies at each stage.

7. Pricing is one of the four Ps of marketing. It can also be viewed as part of the product concept.
   - ***What are pricing objectives?***
   Objectives include achieving a target profit, building traffic, increasing market share, increasing sales, creating an image, and meeting social goals.

   - ***What strategies can marketers use to determine a product's price?***
   A skimming price strategy is one in which the product is priced high to make optimum profit while there's little competition, whereas a penetra-

7. Give examples of various pricing objectives, and describe what strategies are used to determine prices.

tion strategy is one in which a product is priced low to attract more customers and discourage competitors.

KEY TERMS
••••••

brand 510
brand association 513
brand awareness 512
brand equity 512
brand loyalty 512
concept testing 516
convenience goods
    and services 505
generic goods 511
generic names 511
industrial goods 506

market modification
    520
penetration price
    strategy 522
private brands 510
product
    differentiation 505
product life cycle 518
product line 503
product manager 513
product mix 505

product modification
    501
product screening 515
shopping goods and
    services 506
skimming price
    strategy 522
specialty goods and
    services 506
trademark 510
value package 501
value pricing 523

DEVELOPING WORKPLACE SKILLS

1. Notice the different types of shoes that students are wearing. What product qualities were they looking for when they chose those shoes? What was the importance of price, style, brand name, and colour? Describe the product offerings you would feature in a new shoe store designed to appeal to college students.

2. A product offer consists of all the tangibles and intangibles that consumers evaluate when choosing among products, including price, package, service, reputation, and so on. Compose a list of as many tangibles and intangibles as consumers might consider when evaluating the following products: a vacation resort, tennis shoes, a college, and a new car.

3. Discuss how the faculty at your college could increase student satisfaction by working more closely with students in developing new products (courses) and changing existing products (courses). Would it be a good idea for all marketers to work with their customers that way? Discuss.

4. Go to your medicine cabinet and inventory all the branded and non-branded items. Then discuss with the class the brand names they buy for the same goods. Do most students buy brand-name, private-label, or generic goods? Why?

5. Determine where in the product life cycle you would place each of the following products; then, prepare a marketing strategy for each product based on the recommendations in this chapter:
   a. Alka Seltzer
   b. Cellular phones
   c. Electric automobiles
   d. Campbell's chicken noodle soup

INTERNET CHALLENGES

1. Direct selling to consumers via the Internet has become a normal way of doing business for Canadians. One of the advantages of this method is that comparison shopping has become very easy and media reports indicate that it is a very popular activity. Select a product you normally buy, like CDs, a brand of jeans, or any other product. Do a little surfing to see

how many prices you can find for the same products. Are there any significant differences? Do you think the time and effort were worth the money you could save? Would you do this kind of comparison shopping for all your purchases?

2. The contents of supermarket shelves underwent a revolution in the 1990s because supermarket chains were locked in fierce battles for competitive edge. Check out the Web site of the *Canadian Grocer* magazine, <www. cdngrocer.com>, to see what the trends are for new food and non-food products in supermarkets' strategies to increase profitability.

Practising Management Decisions

CASE 1

THE INVASION OF THE ROBOTS

The significant advances in computer and software technology, and in particular the great strides in the power of computer chips, is bringing the era of practical, affordable, reliable robots closer than ever before. Sci-fi books, films, and videos have long used the robot as a vital part of their stories. As far back as 1968 the film *2001: A Space Odyssey* featured Hal as the scary, powerful, talking robot who ran the spaceship. Now, after years of speculation, talk, research, development, and trial and error, we are about to enter a world where robots will become as common as computers. Professor Hans Moravec of the Carnegie Mellon University in Pittsburgh believes that within the first decade of the twenty-first century, robots will be available commercially.

The Swedish firm Husqvarna expects to be selling a robotic lawnmower, *Automower*, in the U.S. in 2000 at a price between $1500 and $1800. This battery-driven mower will do the whole job, untouched by human hands. It will go around trees, flowers, and other obstacles—even your dog, if she hasn't been scared off by the noise! Automower stays within your property boundaries and when the battery is running low it will automatically find its docking station and recharge itself. No longer will parents be nagging children to mow the lawn!

Robotic vacuum cleaners and aids for people with disabilities or who are sick and at home are new products likely to hit the market sometime between 2005 and 2010. HelpMate Robotics of Connecticut now sells a product that "is an autonomous transport system that can carry meals, medical records, linens, diagnostic samples, and other loads" in hospitals and other health-care institutions. "HelpMate rides the elevators and works tirelessly 24 hours a day, seven days a week, 52 weeks a year." The unit is sold in the U.S. and Canada as well as in Europe and the Orient.

Various commentators have speculated that before long robots will be as normal and as necessary in business, in government, and in our personal lives as computers have become. In addition, they say, robots will be doing the unpleasant or difficult work such as putting out the garbage, cleaning up the basement, washing the windows, and shovelling the snow. They will also be doing the same in business by working in mines and in noisy, smelly, or dangerous jobs or locations.

Decision Questions

1. Some commentators think that the future of robots as consumer products will be similar to that of the personal computer. It will start off slowly and gradually becomes a product that is as familiar as a TV at home. Can you see that happening? What affect do you think that might have on your life?

2. If this trend becomes a reality, what will happen to the people whose jobs are lost to robots? Perhaps people will have a lot more leisure time. Can you see a market developing for more or new products or services to fill such a need? Can you think of a few possibilities?

3. The automobile killed a number of industries related to horses and carriages and created a lot of new industries besides the auto and related industries: road paving, highway and bridge construction and maintenance, shopping malls and suburbs construction, and more. Is it possible that the robot could have the same revolutionary impact on the way we live as the advent of the automobile had? Can you give some examples?

4. If you believe this scenario will unfold over the next 10 years, would you recommend to

your younger sisters or brothers that they concentrate on courses in engineering, computer science, maths, software design, and related fields of study? Why or why not?

Sources: HelpMate Robotics Web site <users.ntplx.net/~helpmate/ HM_helpmate/HM_frameset.htm>; "The Robot of the House," John M. Moran, *Hartford Courant*, as reported in the *Montreal Gazette*, August 28, 1999, p. 110.

In this chapter you learned about the importance and the process of developing new products. We live in an era when the food we eat has undergone enormous changes as a result of scientific research. One of the most important changes is the introduction of genetically modified (GM) food. This process involves inserting foreign genes into plant and animal structures so that new strains are developed that are resistant to pests or disease, harsh climates, or give higher yields. An estimated 60 percent of the food offered for sale in Canada contains GM components. Canadian and American farmers are heavily involved in producing genetically altered food. Farmers like GM food because it makes farming more profitable. The whole process is complex, involving strong control exercised by major chemical companies like Monsanto. There are currently several legal battles being waged between Canadian farmers and Monsanto. If we look at one crop, we can see how important this issue is to Canada. The production of canola by Canadian Prairie farmers constitutes 80 percent of world trade in canola and half of these farmers are growing GM canola.

The European Union does not allow the import of GM foods because they are concerned that there may be long-term dangers to human health. Many Americans and Canadians have similar objections. In the late fall of 1999 a major campaign was launched by Greenpeace, the Sierra Club, the Council of Canadians, and other organizations to alert consumers to the possible dangers of GM food. Similar concerns are being raised in many other countries in South America and Asia. At the very least, they argue, food containing GM should be so labelled so that consumers have the choice of buying these or non–GM foods. Organizations in the U.S. have announced plans to launch suits in 30 countries against major GM seed companies, complaining that they have too much control over seed supplies.

Concerns are raised because this decade has seen some important health issues arise from what we do to animals and plants. Europe had a serious scare with mad cow disease, and the bovine growth hormone (BGH), which is injected into

CASE 2

GENETICALLY MODIFIED FOOD: A FRANKENSTEIN HARVEST?

American cattle to increase milk production, is banned in the European Union. The EU will not allow dairy products from such cattle to be imported into the Union. Canadian health authorities have so far also not allowed the use of BGH in Canadian cattle, despite enormous pressure from pharmaceutical companies. Companies in North America, such as Gerber, and HJ Heinz Co., have begun phasing out GM foods from their baby-food lines. Other major companies will not accept farm products or ingredients that are not acceptable to the European Union.

Decision Questions

1. It often happens that certain products, old or new, generate a lot of controversy. Selling toy guns to children has sometimes sparked arguments. Do you think this food issue is different? Why?

2. The problem with genetically modified foods or adding hormones is that it takes a long time to find out what the long-term effects may be. For example, some researchers believe that the addition of substantial amounts of antibiotics to cattle feed is responsible for the generation of highly resistant super-bugs that are becoming a serious problem for humans now. What do you think is a good approach to solving this type of problem?

3. Farmers and their organizations point out that using genetically modified strains means that agriculture requires less pesticide and insecticide use, which is beneficial to our environment. Is it possible to evaluate whether the benefits exceed the risks? How can that be done? Who should do it?

4. Some people maintain that technology has gone too far. They contend that just because we *can* make something doesn't necessarily mean that we *must* make it. How do you feel about that? Should science and technology have limitations placed on them? Why? By whom?

Sources: Cynthia Reynolds, "Frankenstein's Harvest," *Canadian Business*, October 8, 1999, p. 65; CBC newscasts September 1999.

Promoting and Distributing Products Efficiently and Interactively

Chapter 17

LEARNING GOALS

After you have read and studied this chapter, you should be able to

1 list and describe the five elements of the promotion mix.

2 describe advantages and disadvantages of various advertising media, and explain the latest advertising techniques.

3 illustrate the seven steps of the selling process.

4 describe the functions of the public relations department and the role of publicity.

5 explain why we need marketing intermediaries and list four utilities they provide.

6 describe in detail what is involved in physical distribution management.

7 describe the two major categories of wholesale organizations in the distribution system.

8 list and explain the ways that retailers compete.

9 explain the various kinds of nonstore retailing.

In September 1999 Prime Minister Jean Chrétien led a Team Canada group of eight provincial premiers and some 300 business people and cabinet ministers on an important trade mission to Japan. The mission was one of a series to Asian countries over a two-year period, designed to establish and strengthen contacts, increase Canadian exposure to foreign markets, and increase foreign awareness of Canadian companies, products, and services to stimulate our exports.

What was unusual about this mission was that the youngest member was 19-year-old Emerson Segura, founder and CEO of Tar-get*Net* Inc., which has two major divisions: The Datacom Ad Network and AdPulse. It was the Japanese who asked that Segura be included on the team, to the surprise of the Canadian team organizers, who did not know who Segura was! The Japanese knew of him because Datacom Ad Network, whose corporate headquarters are in Toronto, has a regional office in Tokyo. Datacom also has sales representatives throughout the U.S.

The company describes its activities as follows:

AdPulse is a pioneer in the field of Targeted E-Commerce™, recently launching the Web's first successful transactional advertising campaign. This involves selling directly through ads, and not via click-throughs to an advertiser's site, in conjunction with toronto.com and indigo.ca. Datacom is an established leader as a full-service advertising network for small to medium-sized Web sites. Together these two divisions, and the company as a whole, offer unique targeted advertising and e-commerce solutions. Target*Net* will help level the playing field for those smaller players trying to survive in the midst of well-capitalized first-movers.

Nineteen-Year-Old Emerson Segura Impresses Japan

In 1997 Segura, then 17, had a vision. He foresaw tremendous growth in the use of the Internet and he envisioned the convergence of advertising and e-commerce as an interactive system of communication. Segura decided to concentrate on small and medium-sized businesses because he expected there would be rapid increase in the number of sites these businesses were creating and that specialized assistance would be required to allow them to compete against the sites of large firms. Segura believes that this is a lucrative field and that his very optimistic projections for Target*Net* Inc. over the next few years are soundly based. Segura foresees exponential increases in the number of Web sites and Internet users, Internet advertising, and e-commerce expenditures, which will result in rapid and significant growth in his company's revenues.

Emerson Segura is a good example of a person who seized an opportunity to use rapidly developing technology to provide marketing initiatives for small and medium-sized companies to promote and distribute their products more efficiently. Backed by a small group of executives from major Canadian and U.S. companies, all of whom have solid experience in marketing, finance, and communications, combined with some external management consulting support, Segura feels well prepared to cope with the rapid growth he foresees. As a result, this 19-year-old visionary expects to reap the financial benefits of his vision and effort. It is apparent that Japanese and other foreign business people like what Segura is doing. Canadians would do well to keep an eye on this entrepreneur.

Sources: Interview with Emerson Segura, September 29, 1999; communications from Target*Net* Inc; *The National* CBC TV News, September 16, 1999.

Ethical Dilemma

IS THE AD AS HONEST AS THE PRODUCT?

You are producing a high-fibre, nutritious cereal called Fiberrific and are having a modest degree of success. Research shows that your number of customers, or market segment, is a growing but is still a relatively small percentage of breakfast cereal buyers. Generally, Fiberrific appeals mostly to health-conscious people in age groups from 25 to 60. You are trying to broaden the appeal of your cereal to the under-25 and over-60 age groups. You know that Fiberrific is a tasty and healthy product that is good for customers' health. Joan, one of your managers, suggests that you should stretch the truth a bit in your advertising and publicity material so that it will attract more consumers in the age groups you are targeting. After all, your product can't hurt anybody and is actually good for them.

Joan's idea is to develop two ads each with two segments. The first segment of one ad would show a ▲

young woman on a tennis court holding a racket and talking across the net to a young man. She is complaining that she seems to tire easily. The next segment would show the same two persons, and the woman, looking lively, saying that she tried this new breakfast cereal, Fiberrific, for two weeks and she feels so energized, like a new person. A similar ad would be used to show two senior citizens walking uphill and talking. The first segment would have the man wondering why he tires so easily and the second one would show the same scene, with one man a little ahead of the other, looking lively and stating that he is amazed at the improvement in his energy and endurance after eating Fiberrific for only two weeks. Would you go along with Joan's suggestion? We'll get back to this question at the end of the chapter.

THE IMPORTANCE OF PROMOTION

trade show
An event where marketers set up displays and potential customers come to see the latest goods and services.

Promotion is the third of the four Ps of marketing. Marketers now spend more than $13 billion yearly on advertising alone trying to convince industrial and consumer buyers to choose their products. They spend even more on sales promotion efforts such as giveaways, sweepstakes, and conventions and trade shows. A **trade show** is an event where marketers set up displays and potential customers come to see the latest goods and services.

··· THE PROMOTION MIX ···

promotion
An attempt by marketers to inform people about products to persuade them to participate in an exchange.

promotion mix
The combination of tools an organization uses to promote its products or services.

Promotion is an attempt by marketers to inform people about products and to persuade them to participate in an exchange. Marketers use many different tools to promote their products and services. These tools include advertising, personal selling, sales promotion, public relations, and publicity. The combination of promotion tools an organization uses is called its **promotion mix** (see Figure 17.1). The value package is shown in the middle of the figure to illustrate that the product itself can be a promotional tool (e.g., through sampling), and that all promotional efforts are designed to sell products. We'll discuss each of these promotional tools in the first half of the chapter. Let's begin by looking at advertising.

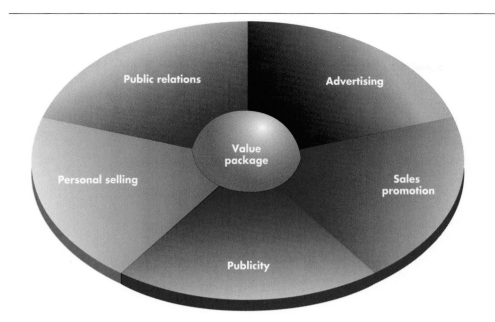

FIGURE **17.1**

····

THE PROMOTION MIX
A good promotion campaign involves all the elements shown here.

ADVERTISING

Many people equate promotion with advertising because they are not aware of the differences among promotional tools such as advertising, personal selling, publicity, and public relations. **Advertising** is paid, nonpersonal communication through various media by organizations and individuals who are in some way identified in the advertising message. Publicity is different from advertising in that publicity is a nonpaid form of advertising. Personal selling is face-to-face communication and doesn't go through a medium; therefore, it's not advertising. Public relations include a variety of activities (discussed later in the chapter) that do not involve advertising.

advertising
Paid, nonpersonal communication through various media by organizations and individuals who are in some way identified in the advertising message.

··· THE IMPORTANCE OF ADVERTISING ···

The importance of advertising in Canada is easy to document; just look at the figures. The total spent annually exceeds $13 billion. The number one advertising medium, as you would expect, is TV. More than 26 percent of total advertising expenditures was for TV time. Daily newspapers and direct mail were the second and third in dollars spent. Figure 17.2 shows the comparative analysis for all direct advertising costs for 1997 and 1992. To this must be added the heavy production costs and the cost of in-house advertising departments, which bring the total to more than $13 billion.

Direct mail (the use of mailing lists to reach an organization's most likely customers) is an informative shopping aid for consumers. Each day, consumers receive mini-catalogues in their newspapers or in the mail that tell them what's on sale, where, at what price, for how long, and more.

Advertising not only informs us about products; it also provides us with free TV and radio programs because advertisers pay for the program costs. Advertising also covers the major costs of producing newspapers and magazines. When we buy a magazine, we pay mostly for mailing or promotional costs. Figure 17.3 discusses advantages and disadvantages of various advertising media to the advertiser. Newspaper, radio, and Yellow Pages ads are especially attractive to local advertisers.

These figures include
advertising by govern-
ments and commercial
companies. The figures
are based on direct costs
only—amounts paid to
the various media. They
do not include production
costs and costs of main-
taining in-house advertising departments. These
additional costs would
bring the 1997 total to
more than $13 billion.

The most effective media
are often very expensive.
The inexpensive media
may not reach your
market. The goal is to
use the most efficient
medium that can reach
your desired market.

| MEDIUM | (in millions of dollars) | | | |
	1997		1992	
	$	%	$	%
Television	2,100	26	1,732	25
Daily Newspapers	1,545	19	1,376	20
Direct Mail	1,168	14	949	14
Radio	849	11	749	10
Yellow Pages	894	11	862	12
Community and Weekly Newspapers	634	8	570	8
Consumer Magazines	347	4	340	5
Trade Publications	252	3	243	3
Outdoor and Transit	220	3	116	2
Other Print	48	1	50	1
TOTALS	$8,057	100%	$6,987	100%

Source: *Marketing*, Media Digest 1999–2000, September 13, 1999, p. 12.

Medium	Advantages	Disadvantages
Newspapers	Good coverage of local markets; ads can be placed quickly; high consumer acceptance; ads can be clipped and saved.	Ads compete with other features in paper; poor colour; ads get thrown away with paper (short life span).
Television	Uses sight, sound, and motion; reaches all audiences; high attention with no competition from other material.	High cost; short exposure time; takes time to prepare ads.
Radio	Low cost; can target specific audiences; very flexible; good for local marketing.	People may not listen to ad; depends on one sense (listening); short exposure time; audience can't keep ad.
Magazines	Can target specific audiences; good use of colour; long life of ad; ads can be clipped and saved.	Inflexible; ads often must be placed weeks before publication; cost is relatively high.
Outdoor	High visibility and repeat exposures; low cost; local market focus.	Limited message; low selectivity of audience.
Direct mail	Best for targeting specific markets; very flexible; ad can be saved.	High cost; consumers may reject ad as "junk mail"; must conform to post office regulations.
Yellow Pages advertising	Great coverage of local markets; widely used by consumers; available at point of purchase.	Competition with other ads; cost may be too high for very small businesses.
Internet	Inexpensive: global coverage; always avalaible; interactive.	Only available to relatively small audience of computer owners with Internet access.

SUPER BOWL	YEAR	COST OF "60 SPOT"
I	1967	$ 80,000
IV	1970	200,000
VIII	1974	214,000
XIII	1979	444,000
XVII	1983	800,000
XXII	1988	1,300,000
XXVI	1992	1,700,000
XXIX	1995	2,000,000
XXXIII	1999	1,600,000* (30-second spot)

*Now commercials are sold in 30-second spots; the first six Super Bowls had only 60-second spots.

FIGURE **17.4**

• • • •

THE COST OF
SUPER BOWL ADS

The growth of America's premier sporting event is reflected in the rising cost of a TV commercial over the years. One minute of advertising during the 1995 Super Bowl cost US$2 million. A 30-second spot cost up to US$1.6 million in 1999.

TV provides many advantages to national advertisers, but it's expensive. Figure 17.4 shows how the cost of one minute of advertising during the Super Bowl telecast leaped to two million U.S. dollars in 1995, and $1.6 million for 30 seconds in 1999. The cost of a 30-second commercial for the 1999 Grey Cup Game was $41,000, but to get that spot the advertiser had to have bought four 30-second ads in the preceding playoff games at a cost of $11,800 per ad. These costs are for TV time only; the even higher costs of shooting and producing the actual commercial must also be taken into consideration. How many bottles of beer or bags of dog food must a company sell to pay for such a commercial? Is it any wonder that companies are now buying 15-second commercials to save money and that they're thinking of alternative ways to reach the public? Figure 17.5 lists various forms of advertising.

Few other media besides television allow advertisers to reach so many people with such impact. Marketers must choose which media and which programs can best be used to reach the audience they desire.

FIGURE **17.5**

• • • •

MAJOR CATEGORIES
OF ADVERTISING

Different kinds of advertising are used by various organizations to reach different target markets. These are the major categories.

- Retail advertising—advertising to consumers by various retail stores such as supermarkets and shoe stores.
- Trade advertising—advertising to wholesalers and retailers by manufacturers to encourage them to carry their products.
- Industrial advertising—advertising by manufacturers to other manufacturers. A firm selling motors to auto companies would use industrial advertising.
- Institutional advertising—advertising designed to create an attractive image for an organization rather than for a product. Sprint's "the most for the least" is an example. "Beautiful British Columbia," "Ontario—Yours to Discover" are two provincial government campaigns.
- Product advertising—advertising for a good or service to create interest among consumer, commercial, and industrial buyers.

- Advocacy advertising—advertising that supports a particular view of an issue (for example, an ad in support of gun control or against nuclear power plants). Such advertising is also known as cause advertising.
- Comparison advertising—advertising that compares competitive products. For example, an ad that compares cold care products' speed and benefits is a comparative ad.
- Interactive advertising—customer-oriented communication that enables customers to choose the information they receive, such as interactive video catalogues that let customers select which items to view.
- Online advertising—advertising messages that are available by computer when customers want to receive them. Customers can also select what they want to view.

Spotlight on Small Business

<www.eagle.ca/bluecat/>
<www.carmax.com>

The Internet Revolution

In the past small businesses have felt that it was their responsibility to advertise to buyers to persuade them to buy. However, as a buyer, you know that there are products you're interested in buying, but what often prevents you from making a decision to purchase is information. The question then becomes: How can small businesses make more information available at an affordable cost so that buyers can obtain it whenever they want? The answer today is the Internet.

In 1995 there was an explosion in the awareness of and use of the Internet as a promotional medium for business. According to one article, by early 1996 as many as 265,000 individuals and companies in North America alone had established Web sites to promote themselves. By 1999 the number of Web sites had soared. The Profile of Emerson Segura shows how significant this way of reaching markets has become, especially for small businesses. E-commerce, or sales via a company Web site, is one of the fastest-growing sales phenomena. One magazine reports that in 1999 a survey revealed that 10 percent of Canadians had made a purchase on the Internet in the previous six months. The figure jumped to 21 percent for Canadians who had access to the Net at home or at work. Because the cost is low and the exposure high, that number is growing at an incredible rate. This growth has given rise to a whole new industry of Web site designers. One such person is ▲

Christine Rowland, who runs Blue Cat Design out of her home-based office in Port Hope, Ontario.

Comments such as "advertisers drool over soaring Internet population" and "electronic retailing is heating up" can be seen in the business press. It seems as if hardly a week goes by without another TV program on this new phenomenon or without a new use being found by businesses and consumers for this new method of advertising and promotion. People are searching for homes to buy and looking for jobs by surfing the Internet. Companies are also finding skilled employees that way. One enterprising car dealer in Atlanta, Georgia, advertises and sells cars that way. Interested buyers e-mail Car Max and get a phone call the same or the next day from a Car Max salesperson.

Of course, large companies have been quick to exploit this new medium as well. It is just about impossible to find any large company today that does not have an active (and interactive) Web site.

Sources: "Purchasing Via the Net," *Montreal Business Magazine*, September 1999, p. 42; *Marketing, Media Digest 1999–2000*, September 13, 1999, p. 51. Randy Ray, *"Surf the Net for a New Home," Globe and Mail, Report on Business*, October 14, 1995, p. B21; Susan Bourette, "Sites for Sore Eyes from Web Pioneer," *Globe and Mail, ROB*, February 27, 1996, p. C8; Mary Gooderham, "Advertisers Drool over Soaring Internet Population," *Globe and Mail, ROB*, February 27, 1996, p. C8; and Geoffrey Rowan, "Online Interest Rising Rapidly," *Globe and Mail, ROB*, December 4, 1995, p. B11.

Some retailers may find it less expensive to run advertisements if they get co-op advertising funds from manufacturers. This arrangement means that manufacturers will often pay half of the cost or more of advertisements if a retailer has sold enough of its products.

Some products, such as personal development seminars or work-out tapes, are hard to sell without showing people testimonials and a sample of how they work. Infomercials have sold such services so well that major companies are now trying to buy time for their own infomercials.[1] (See the section on Infomercials.)

••• TECHNOLOGY IN ADVERTISING •••

The technology revolution is having a major impact on advertising. For example, promoters are using interactive TV to carry on dialogues with customers instead of merely sending them messages, and they're using **CD-ROM** technology to provide more information.

This online ad for Indigo illustrates many advantages of advertising in cyberspace. An advertiser can use sight, sound, and interactivity to show information and respond to individual consumer inquiries. This gives consumers more control and makes it possible for advertisers to provide vast amounts of information.

Customers can now request information via e-mail and can reach service people from almost any location using cellular phone technology and pagers. In short, the information revolution has greatly affected advertising in a positive way for both seller and buyer.

Next, let's look at some specific ways marketers are using technology in advertising.

USING ONLINE COMPUTER SERVICES IN ADVERTISING   Online services, such as Prodigy, America Online, and CompuServe, are computer services that provide information on a variety of subjects such as business, entertainment, financial, and sports news. Online services are expanding at an explosive rate. Recently, marketers have been devising ways to provide marketing information to users via such services. The future is promising as individuals by the millions are tapping into this medium, locally, nationally, and internationally.

Online services and the Internet can provide massive amounts of product information when customers want it (see the Spotlight on Small Business). For example, a flower shop can list and display all the floral arrangements available for Mother's Day. A busy person can scan the selection quickly, make a choice, and send in an order with a credit card number, and the flowers can be sent anywhere in Canada or the United States the same day. The entire transaction can be accomplished in a matter of minutes. Compare that to having to physically visit a flower shop, see the arrangements, wait if the store is busy, conclude all the details of ordering and payment, and return to your home or office.

Once potential customers see what information is available, they can go online with sellers (directly contact them by computer) and get additional information immediately. The potential for two-way communication between buyers and sellers is almost endless. Any data that can be put into a computer can be accessed by others. The challenge is to make online searches easy for consumers and profitable for companies.

··· INFOMERCIALS ···

infomercials
TV programs that are devoted exclusively to promoting goods and services.

One of the faster-growing forms of advertising is the use of infomercials. **Infomercials** are TV programs devoted exclusively to promoting goods and services. They're so successful because they show the product in great detail. A great product can sell itself if there's some means to how the public how it works. Infomercials provide that opportunity. People have said that a half-hour infomercial is the equivalent of sending your very best salespeople to a person's home where they can use everything in their power to make the sale: drama, demonstration, testimonials, graphics, and more.

··· CUSTOMIZED ADVERTISING VERSUS ··· GLOBAL ADVERTISING

Harvard professor Theodore Levitt is a big proponent of global marketing and advertising. His idea is to develop a product and promotional strategy that can be implemented worldwide. Certainly that would save money in research costs and advertising design. That strategy is being used by major companies like Compaq, IBM, and Intel. However, other experts think that promotion targeted at specific countries may be much more successful since each country has its own culture, language, and buying habits.

The evidence supports the theory that promotional efforts specifically designed for individual countries work best.[2] For example, commercials for Camay soap that showed men complimenting women on their appearance were jarring in cultures where men don't express themselves that way. A different campaign is needed in such countries.

People in Brazil rarely eat breakfast and treat Kellogg's Corn Flakes as a dry snack like potato chips. Kellogg is trying a promotional strategy of showing people in Brazil how to eat cereal—with cold milk in the morning. Many more situations could be cited to show that international advertising calls for researching the wants, needs, and culture of each specific country and then designing appropriate ads and testing them.

Even in Canada we have regional differences that are important enough to constitute separate market segments. Each province has its own history and culture and different populations, and Quebec has a different language. The large metropolitan areas like Toronto, Montreal, Vancouver, Edmonton, Calgary, Winnipeg, Ottawa, and Quebec City are different from the rest of the provinces in which they are located. All require their own promotions and advertising.

At the same time it is clear that ads can be prepared in one country for another country. For example, the advertising agency for IKEA Canada prepared a very successful ad for IKEA Germany.[3]

mass customization
The design of custom-made products and promotions, including advertising.

Mass customization is the term used to describe the design of custom-made products and promotions, including advertising.[4] For example, Coke made more than two dozen Coke Classic commercials for 20 different TV networks. For Much Music the ads are a bit strange to traditional viewers, cutting quickly from one shot to another; the Coke Classic ads are more wholesome and heart-tugging on adult shows like "Murder, She Wrote." Marketers in other large companies do the same thing.

Progress Check

- What are the five elements of the promotion mix?
- What are the advantages and disadvantages of TV, magazine, and radio advertising?
- Can you list three new avenues of marketing made available by modern technology?

···· ▬ ····

PERSONAL SELLING

Personal selling is the face-to-face presentation and promotion of products and services. It also involves the search for new prospects and follow-up service after the sale. Effective selling isn't simply a matter of persuading others to buy (see Figure 17.6). It's more accurately described today as helping others to satisfy their wants and needs. Sales people are using hand-held computers to place orders and to help customers design custom-made products. The average cost of a single sales call to a potential industrial buyer is about $400. Any firm incurring such costs would not send out anyone but a highly skilled professional salesperson. Many thousands of people are engaged in this work in Canada. You might think of this as a possible interesting career for yourself. Let's take a closer look at what's involved in the process of selling.

··· STEPS IN THE SELLING PROCESS ···

The best way to get a feel for personal selling is to go through the selling process for a particular product and see what's involved. One product that you are familiar with is textbooks, like the one you are now reading. A college textbook salesperson has the job of showing faculty members the advantages of using a particular book and the teaching aids that go with it. Let's go through the selling process in this case to see what the job entails.

1. *Prospect and qualify*. The first step in the selling process is prospecting. **Prospecting** involves researching potential buyers and choosing those most likely to buy. That selection process is called *qualifying*. To qualify people means to make sure they have a need for the product, the authority to buy, the ability to pay, and the willingness to listen to a sales message.[4] People who meet these criteria are called *prospects*. You find prospects by asking schools which faculty members are teaching the courses that might assign the book or books you are selling.

2. *Preapproach*. Before making a sales call, the sales representative must do further research. Robert E. Keller, author of *Negotiating Skills That*

---

personal selling
Face-to-face presentation and promotion of products and services, and searching out prospects and providing follow-up service.

prospecting
Researching potential buyers and choosing those most likely to buy.

<www.mcgrawhill.ca>

Visit the McGraw-Hill Ryerson Web site yourself. Notice that the site presents several different elements of interest to different people. These elements include an introduction to the company, information on its businesses and products, and information on how to place orders.

You may already be familiar with the *Web community* offered for this course. The publisher of this textbook has provided a service to instructors all across the country that allows them to exchange ideas about material and topics for the course.

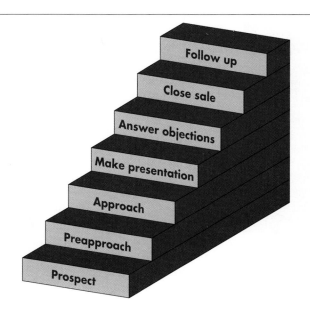

FIGURE **17.6**
····

STEPS IN THE SELLING PROCESS
Selling is a highly organized procedure requiring a series of steps as indicated.

Sell, says that 50 percent of a sales negotiation's outcome is determined before you meet the customer face-to-face.[5] As much as possible should be learned about customers and their wants and needs.

3. *Approach.* "You don't have a second chance to make a good first impression." That's why the approach is so important. When you call on a faculty member for the first time, your opening comments are important. The idea is to give an impression of friendly professionalism, to create rapport, and to build credibility. The objective of the initial sales call probably won't be to make a sale that day. Rather, the goal may be to set the faculty member at ease.

4. *Make presentation.* In the actual presentation of the text and the materials that come with it, the idea is to match the benefits of your value package to the client's needs. The presentation may involve audiovisual aids, such as a Powerpoint presentation on the computer.

5. *Answer objections.* A salesperson should anticipate potential objections clients may raise and determine proper responses. Questions should be viewed as opportunities for creating better relationships, not as a challenge to what you're saying. Customers have legitimate doubts, and salespeople are there to resolve those doubts.

6. *Close sale.* You have to ask for the sale to finalize the sale process. A salesperson has limited time and can't spend forever with one client answering questions and objections. Closing techniques include getting a series of small commitments and then asking for the order and showing the client where to sign. Salespeople are taught to remember their ABCs—Always Be Closing.

7. *Follow up.* The selling process isn't over until the order is approved and the customer is happy. Customer service is as important to the sale as the product itself. Many faculty members today want to maintain a semiconstant dialogue with textbook authors and other faculty. Most publishers have established Web sites for various texts where information may be obtained and discussions may take place. McGraw-Hill Ryerson, publishers of this text, keep their Web site current by updating it weekly.

The selling process varies somewhat among different goods and services, but the general idea is the same. Your goals as a salesperson are to help the buyer buy and to make sure that the buyer is satisfied after the sale.

••• BUSINESS-TO-BUSINESS SELLING •••

Salespeople who sell to commercial accounts (wholesalers and retailers), institutional accounts (hospitals and schools), and industrial accounts (manufacturers and service providers) often make more money and have a more challenging experience than those selling to consumers. The customers tend to buy in larger quantities, and as a result the salesperson often makes a larger commission.

Customers are often easier to find because the government classifies business customers using

This ad for an HP Palmtop PC shows the power and benefits of such new high-tech sales tools. Information about the company and the various members of the buying team can be stored in such computers so they are accessible at any time.

You know Starbucks for its more than 2100 stores around the world. But did you know Starbucks also has many business accounts that contribute 15 percent to the company's revenues?

<www.starbucks.com>

By 1999 the number of Starbucks stores had risen to 2100. The Starbucks Web site provides, among other things, an interesting retelling of the history of the company, from its first store opening in Seattle in 1971. Starbucks pioneered a new approach to marketing coffee: the coffee bar. The phenomenal success of the concept and the company itself demonstrate the value of good marketing.

standard industrial classification codes (SIC). Using those codes, once a salesperson has found one customer in an industry, he or she can easily find other customers with the same SIC code. Industrial salespeople are often called *marketing consultants* because they help their business customers become more effective at marketing.

Sales force automation also helps business-to-business salespeople. Using laptop computers, e-mail, fax software, and scanners, salespeople can get specifications by e-mail, get product announcements from the company and then e-mail them to customers, scan documents and fax them to customers, find information in databases and use that data in sales presentations, and more. With such high-tech backing, salespeople have become the eyes and ears of all businesses.

Critical Thinking

What kind of products do you think you would enjoy selling? Think of the customers for that product. Can you imagine yourself going through the seven-step selling process with them? Which steps would be hardest? Which would be easiest? Which step could you avoid by selling in a retail store? Can you picture yourself going through the sales process on the phone (telemarketing)?

···· ▬▬▬ ····

SALES PROMOTION

Sales promotion is the promotional tool that stimulates consumer purchasing and dealer interest by means of short-term activities (such things as displays, shows and exhibitions, and contests). Figure 17.7 lists some sales promotion techniques.

Those free samples of products that people get in the mail, the cents-off coupons that they clip from newspapers, the contests that retail stores sponsor, and those premiums you find in cereal boxes are examples of sales promotion activities. Sales promotion programs are designed to supplement personal selling, advertising, and public relations efforts by creating enthusiasm for the overall promotional program.

sales promotion
The promotional tool that stimulates consumer purchasing and dealer interest by means of short-term activities (displays, shows and exhibitions, contests, and so forth).

FIGURE 17.7
• • • •
SALES PROMOTION
TECHNIQUES

FIGURE 17.7
• • • •

SALES PROMOTION
TECHNIQUES

Spend some time with this list. Most students aren't familiar with all the activities involved in sales promotion. This is the time to learn them.

Displays (store displays)
Contests ("You may have won $1 million!")
Samples (toothpaste, soap)
Coupons (25 cents off)
Premiums (free glass when you buy a meal)
Shows (fashion shows)
Deals (price reductions)
Trade shows
Bonuses (buy one, get one free)
Incentives (the prize in a cereal box)

Rebates (refunds from producers)
Lotteries
Audiovisual aids
Catalogues
Demonstrations
Special events
Exhibits
Portfolios for salespeople
Conventions
Sweepstakes

Sales promotion can be both internal (within the company) and external (outside the company). It's just as important to get employees enthusiastic about a sale as it is to attract potential customers.

After enthusiasm is generated internally, it's important to get distributors and dealers involved so that they too are enthusiastic about helping to promote

Reaching Beyond Our Borders

<www.hasc.ca/~holtz/>
<www.eagle.ca/bluecat/>

Canadians Shine in the Borderless World of the Internet

Tabatha Holtz is Canada's self-proclaimed *Web queen*. That's what her business card says. Her college training was as a visual artist and after a variety of jobs she was introduced to the Internet in 1993 and "fell in love" with it. Holtz taught herself to understand the Internet and to appreciate the art of attractive Web sites. Her specialty now is designing such sites, and it was her personal Web site that drew the attention of her then employer, Medus Communications Inc., who offered her a job. She has prepared a variety of award winning "cool Web sites" and has designed a site for the Boston Restaurant Guide. (Holtz is currently employed by Hutchison Avenue Software in Montreal.)

Christine Rowland is a graphics designer who runs her Blue Cat Design company out of her home in Port Hope, Ontario. She also specializes in designing Web sites and has done work for leading Canadian companies. In addition to two employees, she regularly uses freelancers from all over the map—from Dallas, Texas, to Italy. Her services are in demand across the globe. That is no surprise as her own Web site was voted the coolest Canadian site by her peers.

Both of these talented Canadian women continue to expand their operations beyond our borders. Check their interesting Web sites and you will see the kind of work they do, who their customers are and the kind of flexible sites they design. In 1999, Blue Cat reported that they have clients in the U.S., Mexico, Australia and the Caribbean.

Why are companies so interested in a "cool" Web site? With hundreds of thousands of companies competing to attract customers on the Internet, it is obviously important to make a quick and strong impact as potential consumers surf the Net. The Internet's growing importance as an international marketing tool increases the value of having a site that will hold people's attention. We are fortunate to have in Canada many talented designers and graphic artists who can do this kind of work.

Sources: Both Web sites as shown above; Janet McFarland, "Tabatha's World Is a Cool Site," *Globe and Mail, Report on Business,* February 16, 1995, p. B9; and Susan Bourette, "Sites for Sore Eyes from Web Pioneer," *Globe and Mail, ROB,* February 27, 1996, p. C8.

the product. Trade shows are an important sales promotion tool because marketing intermediaries are able to see products from many different sellers and make comparisons among them. Today, virtual trade shows—trade shows on the Internet—enable buyers to see many products without leaving the office. Furthermore, the information is available 24 hours a day, seven days a week.

After the company's employees and intermediaries have been motivated with sales promotion efforts, the next step is to promote to final consumers using samples, coupons, cents-off deals, displays, store demonstrations, premiums, and other incentives such as contests, trading stamps, and rebates. Sales promotion is an ongoing effort to maintain enthusiasm, so different strategies are used over time to keep the ideas fresh.

One popular sales promotion tool is *sampling*. Often consumers won't buy a new product unless they've had a chance to try it. As a consequence, stores often have people standing in the aisles handing out samples of food and beverage products. Sampling is a quick and effective way of demonstrating a product's superiority at the time when consumers are making a purchase decision. Can you see the importance of allowing faculty to "sample" textbooks?

···· ▬▬▬ ····

PUBLIC RELATIONS AND PUBLICITY

Public relations (PR) are all activities designed to give an organization or its products or services a better image among all stakeholders, including existing and potential customers, employees, shareholders, governments, the local community, and the whole country.

PR departments aim to give their company or organization the best public image possible. When there is good news, like a plant expansion, a major contract, or removal of an environmental hazard, the job of the PR department is to give that news the widest possible distribution. On the other hand, when there is bad news—pollution or other violations of laws or regulations—the PR people do their best to limit the damage to the company's reputation.

It is the responsibility of the public relations department to maintain close ties with the media, community leaders, government officials, and other

public relations (PR)
Activities designed to give an organization or its products or services a better image among all stakeholders, including existing and potential customers, employees, shareholders, governments, the local community, and the whole country.

This print ad for New Brunswick is designed to create a favourable impression of the province and encourage tourists to visit there. An integrated marketing program would link such ads with a publicity campaign, a personal selling campaign, and a direct marketing campaign (direct mail) to create a unified campaign.

corporate stakeholders. The idea is to establish and maintain a dialogue with those stakeholders so that the company can respond to inquiries, complaints, and suggestions quickly. It is not enough for a company to have programs that support the community, such as donations of computers to schools or "volunteer days"—the company also needs to publicize that involvement. We'll explore the subject of publicity next.

publicity
Any information about an individual, a product, or an organization that is distributed to the public through the media and is not paid for or controlled by the sponsor.

Publicity is any information about an individual, a product, or an organization that is distributed to the public through the media and is not paid for or controlled by the sponsor.

The best thing about publicity is that the various media will publish publicity stories free if the material is interesting or newsworthy. The idea, then, is to write publicity that meets these criteria.

In addition to being free, publicity has several advantages over other promotional tools such as advertising. Publicity may reach people who would not read an ad. It may be placed on the front page of a newspaper or in some other very prominent position. Perhaps the greatest advantage of publicity is its believability. When a newspaper or magazine publishes a story as news, the reader treats that story as news, and news is more likely to be believed than advertising, which we know is paid for by the advertiser.

There are several disadvantages to publicity as well. The media does not have to publish a publicity release, and most are thrown away. Furthermore, the story may be edited in a fashion that changes its original purpose, goal, or meaning.

Publicity may also be generated by news stories published or broadcast by the media. This may be favourable ("Air Canada reduces fares") or unfavourable ("CPR conductor ejects passenger with disabilities"). Once a story has appeared, it is not likely to be run again unless it is a major news item that is followed up.

Advertising, on the other hand, can be repeated as often as needed. One way to see that the media handle publicity well is to establish a friendly relationship with media representatives, cooperating with them when they seek information. Then, when you want their support, they are more likely to cooperate with you.

···· ▬▬▬ ····

PREPARING THE PROMOTION MIX

Each target group calls for a separate promotion mix. For example, large, homogeneous groups of consumers are usually most efficiently reached through advertising. Large organizations are best reached through personal selling. To motivate people to buy now rather than later, sales promotion efforts such as coupons, discounts, special displays, premiums, and so on may be used. Publicity adds support to the other efforts and can create a good impression among all consumers. What combination of promotional tools would you use if you were the product manager for Fiberrific? Why?

··· PROMOTIONAL STRATEGIES ···

push strategy
Use of promotional tools to convince wholesalers and retailers to stock and sell merchandise.

There are three ways to promote products' movement from producers to consumers. The first is called a *push strategy*. In a **push strategy**, the producer uses advertising, personal selling, sales promotion, and all other promotional tools to convince wholesalers and retailers to stock and sell merchandise. If it works, consumers will then walk into the store, see the product, and buy it. The idea is to push the product down the distribution system to the stores.

One example of a push strategy is to offer dealers one free case for every dozen cases they purchase.

A second strategy is called a *pull strategy*. In a **pull strategy**, heavy advertising and sales promotion efforts are directed toward consumers so that they'll request the products from retailers. If it works, consumers will go to the store and order the products. Seeing the demand for the products, the store owner will then order them from the wholesaler. The wholesaler, in turn, will order them from the producer. Products are thus pulled down through the distribution system. Tripledge wipers reached retail stores through a pull strategy generated by TV advertising to the consumer. Of course, a company could use both push and pull strategies at the same time in a major promotional effort.

The latest in push and pull strategies is being conducted on the Internet with companies sending messages to both consumers and businesses.

The third way to move goods from producer to consumer is to make promotion part of a total systems approach to marketing. That is, promotion would be part of supply-chain management. In such cases, retailers work with producers and distributors to make the supply chain as efficient as possible. Then a promotional plan is developed for the whole system. The idea is to develop a value package that will appeal to everyone: manufacturers, distributors, retailers, and consumers. The trend today is toward everyday low pricing because that results in the greatest profit for sellers and good bargains for consumers. The best deal for consumers is to take advantage of coupons and other money-saving promotions, but those have proven less profitable for sellers and thus may be unsustainable in the long run.

pull strategy
Use of promotional tools to motivate consumers to request products from stores.

···· ▬ ····

INTEGRATED MARKETING COMMUNICATION (IMC)

An **integrated marketing communication (IMC)** system is a formal mechanism for uniting all the promotional efforts in an organization to make them more consistent and responsive to that organization's customers and other stakeholders. In the past, advertising was created by ad agencies, public relations was created by PR firms, and so forth. There was little coordination of promotional efforts. Today that system is changing in many companies. To implement an IMC system, you start by gathering data about customers and stakeholders and their information needs. Gathering such data and making them accessible to everyone in the channel of distribution is a key to future marketing success. All messages reaching customers, potential customers, and other stakeholders must be consistent and coordinated.

Effective marketing communication demands a complete restructuring of the communication function. Let's explore the three steps in developing an interactive marketing communication system. An **interactive marketing communication system** is one in which consumers can access company information on their own and supply information about themselves in an ongoing dialogue. Here are the basic steps.

integrated marketing communication (IMC)
A formal mechanism for uniting all the promotional efforts in an organization to make them more consistent and more responsive to that organization's customers and other stakeholders.

interactive marketing communication system
A system in which consumers can access company information on their own and supply information about themselves in an ongoing dialogue.

1. Gather data constantly about the groups affected by the organization (including customers, potential customers, and other stakeholders) and keep that information in a database. Make the data available to everyone in the organization. An up-to-date information database is critical to any successful program. Today, a company can gather data from sales transactions, letters, e-mail, and faxes. It may also turn to a company that specializes in gathering such data.

2. Respond quickly to customer and other stakeholder information by adjusting company policies and practices and by designing wanted products and services for target markets. A responsive firm adapts to changing wants and needs quickly and captures the market from other, less responsive firms. That's why information is so vital to organizations today and why so much money is spent on computers and information systems. One reason why small firms are capturing markets from large firms is that small firms tend to be better listeners, to have fewer layers of management in which information gets lost, and to be more responsive to changes in the market.

3. Make it possible for customers and potential customers to obtain the information they need to make a purchase. Then make it easy for people to buy your products in stores or from the company directly by placing an order through e-mail, fax, phone, or other means.

••• INTERACTIVE MARKETING ON THE INTERNET •••

The key to marketing success in the future is interactivity: maintaining a dialogue with consumers.[7] Eventually, such open communication will lead marketers from today's emphasis on mass marketing to a greater emphasis on one-to-one marketing or mass customization. The advantages of interactive marketing on the Internet include the following.[8]

1. Customers can access information anytime they want, 24 hours a day. From the company's perspective, product information can reach markets anywhere in the world inexpensively.

2. Electronic advertisements and catalogues can be updated continually and do not have to be printed, stored, or shipped. Traditional promotional materials, on the other hand, are relatively costly and are difficult to change.

TD Waterhouse Investor Services is a leading provider of online financial services and the world's second-largest discount broker. Their Web site at <www.tdwaterhouse.ca> shows that TD Waterhouse has listened to the needs of today's consumer by designing a homepage that is easy-to-use, uncomplicated and creates a fluid, interactive online experience.

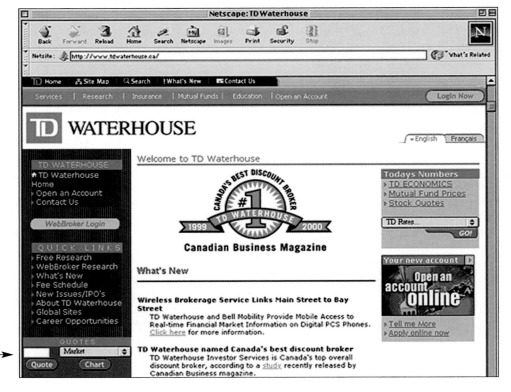

3. Small companies can reach consumers as easily as large firms can, especially if those large firms fail to adjust to the new technologies and market realities.

4. Buyers and sellers can engage in a dialogue over time so that both feel they are getting the best deal. Transactions become interactions.

Integrated marketing communication blends with interactive communications when phone, fax, e-mail, television, and radio are all combined in one promotion. A radio station, for example, may promote a TV show by allowing listeners to participate in a contest in which they answer a series of questions by e-mail, fax, or phone. If participants are required to give their name, address, and phone number, the promoter can build a great database of potential customers. This enables the TV show to get sponsors.

With the Internet, a whole new world of interactivity develops. Chat rooms can be established where consumers talk with other consumers about products. They can also chat with people from different departments in the company.

The net result of the new technology is that companies will have to rethink how marketing and promotion is done. There is likely to be a big dropoff in TV and other mass advertising, although such advertising will still be needed to establish name recognition and to introduce new products. There is expected to be a huge increase in the use of the Internet as a promotional and marketing tool. The same is true of e-mail, fax, and other communication tools. Students who learn how to communicate interactively with customers—that is, in a dialogue—will rise to the top of marketing firms quickly. Many jobs will be created in the management of databases. Salespeople will be intimately linked to the system through laptop computers, fax machines, and e-mail.

Soon there may be as many Internet malls as there are regional malls. Shoppers will be able to request information from multiple firms, compare prices, and make purchases from their homes. What effect will this have on traditional retailers? What will they have to do to encourage customers to keep coming into their stores? Retail location on the Internet will be as important as retail location in cities. How many retailers are prepared for such a shift?

The greatest form of advertising is still word of mouth.

Word of mouth is not really a form of advertising because advertising by definition goes through a medium such as newspapers and magazines. Word of mouth *is* one of the most potent forms of promotion. What customers say about a product is often more powerful than what marketers say in their ads. By putting word of mouth messages into their ads, Jaguar has the best of both worlds.

WORD OF MOUTH

Sometimes word of mouth is referred to as another tool of promotional activities alongside advertising, publicity, public relations, personal selling, and sales promotion. These activities all have one thing in common: they involve actions initiated by a company or organization. This is the major difference between these promotional activities and word of mouth. Word of mouth is initiated by customers or potential customers *in reaction to* the quality or value of a particular product or service. Of course, good promotion of such a product or service helps to bring attention to that item.

If a company has done something that impresses customers in a very favourable or unusual way, they will generate positive word-of-mouth promotion. Similarly, a negative impression will generate negative word-of-mouth promotion. Think of a good or bad film you saw and then publicized among your friends. Or a terrific car, or a lemon, which led you to similar action.

Critical Thinking

What kinds of problems can emerge if a firm doesn't communicate with environmentalists, the news media, and the local community? In your area have you seen examples of firms that aren't responsive to the community? What were the consequences?

Progress Check

- What are the seven steps in the selling process?
- Promoters spend more money on sales promotion than on advertising. Figure 17.7 lists 20 different sales promotion techniques. Do you remember most of them?
- Could you describe how to implement a push strategy for Fiberrific cereal? A pull strategy?

···· ▬▬▬ ····

THE ROLE OF DISTRIBUTION IN BUSINESS

Thus far, we've looked at three of the four Ps of the marketing mix: product, price, and promotion. We'll now look at the fourth element: place. Products have to be physically moved from where they're produced to a convenient place where consumer and industrial buyers can see and purchase them. **Physical distribution (logistics)** is the movement of goods from producers to industrial and consumer users. It involves activities such as transportation, purchasing, receiving, moving them through the premises, inventorying them, storing them, and shipping finished goods to final users (including all the warehousing, reshipping, and physical movements involved). How efficiently those tasks are performed often makes the difference between success and failure of the whole system. Such a system is made up of a series of marketing organizations called *marketing intermediaries*.

Marketing intermediaries are organizations that assist in moving goods and services from producer to industrial and consumer users. They're called *intermediaries* because they're organizations in the middle of a whole series of organizations that join together to help distribute goods from producers to consumers. You can see why these organizations as a group are known as a *channel of distribution*. A **channel of distribution** consists of marketing intermediaries such as wholesalers and retailers who join together to transport and store goods in their path (channel, if you will) from producers to consumers. A **wholesaler** is a marketing intermediary that sells to organizations and individuals, but not final consumers. A **retailer** is an intermediary that sells to ultimate consumers. Figure 17.8 presents channels of distribution for both consumer and industrial goods and services.

Channels of distribution ensure that the right quantity and assortment of goods will be available when and where needed.

Few people are aware of how many different wholesale institutions there are, and the careers available in them. Competition for jobs in physical distribution often isn't as stiff as it is in other areas of business. There are many career opportunities in logistics, and the number of students majoring in that

physical distribution (logistics)
The movement of goods and services from producers to industrial and consumer users.

marketing intermediaries
Organizations that assist in the movement of goods and services from producer to industrial and consumer users.

channel of distribution
Marketing intermediaries such as wholesalers and retailers who join together to transport and store goods in their path (channel) from producers to consumers.

wholesaler
A marketing intermediary that sells to organizations and individuals, but not to final consumers.

retailer
A marketing intermediary that sells to consumers.

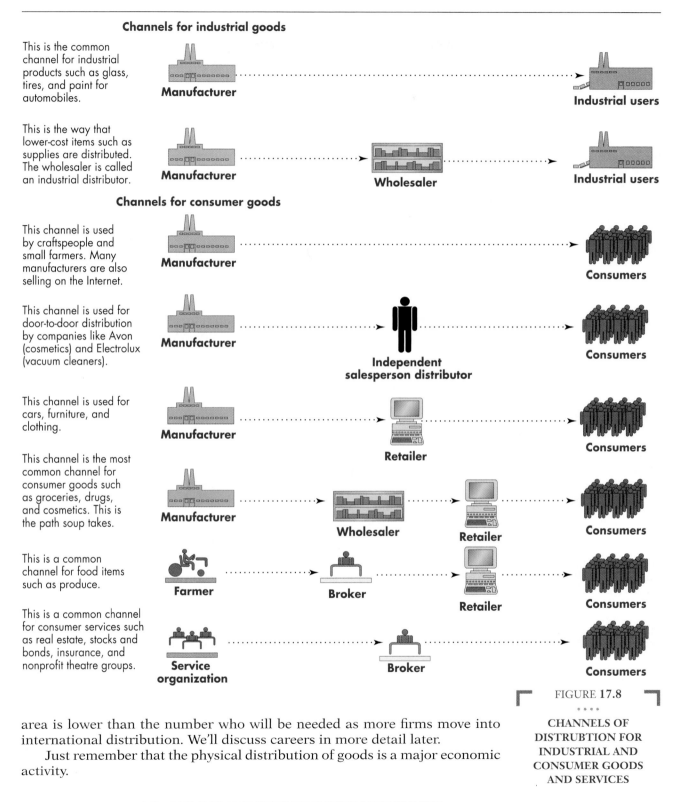

Channels for industrial goods

This is the common channel for industrial products such as glass, tires, and paint for automobiles.

Manufacturer → Industrial users

This is the way that lower-cost items such as supplies are distributed. The wholesaler is called an industrial distributor.

Manufacturer → Wholesaler → Industrial users

Channels for consumer goods

This channel is used by craftspeople and small farmers. Many manufacturers are also selling on the Internet.

Manufacturer → Consumers

This channel is used for door-to-door distribution by companies like Avon (cosmetics) and Electrolux (vacuum cleaners).

Manufacturer → Independent salesperson distributor → Consumers

This channel is used for cars, furniture, and clothing.

Manufacturer → Retailer → Consumers

This channel is the most common channel for consumer goods such as groceries, drugs, and cosmetics. This is the path soup takes.

Manufacturer → Wholesaler → Retailer → Consumers

This is a common channel for food items such as produce.

Farmer → Broker → Retailer → Consumers

This is a common channel for consumer services such as real estate, stocks and bonds, insurance, and nonprofit theatre groups.

Service organization → Broker → Consumers

FIGURE **17.8**

· · · ·

CHANNELS OF DISTRUBTION FOR INDUSTRIAL AND CONSUMER GOODS AND SERVICES

area is lower than the number who will be needed as more firms move into international distribution. We'll discuss careers in more detail later.

Just remember that the physical distribution of goods is a major economic activity.

··· WHY DISTRIBUTION REQUIRES INTERMEDIARIES ···

Manufacturers do not always need intermediaries to sell their goods to consumer and industrial markets. Figure 17.8 shows manufacturers that sell directly to buyers. So why have intermediaries at all? The answer is that intermediaries perform certain marketing functions such as transportation, storage, selling, and advertising more effectively and efficiently than could be done by most manufacturers. A simple analogy is this: You could deliver your own packages to people anywhere in the world, but usually you do not. Why not? Because it is usually cheaper and faster to have them delivered by the post office or some private agency such as Purolator, Loomis, or Air Canada.

Similarly, you could sell your own home, but most people do not. Why? Again, because there are specialists called *brokers* who make the process more efficient and easier. **Brokers** are marketing intermediaries who bring buyers and sellers together and assist in negotiating an exchange but do not take title to the goods. Usually they do not carry inventory, provide credit, or assume risk. The examples with which you are probably most familiar include insurance brokers, real estate brokers, and stockbrokers. Figure 17.8 shows that brokers act as intermediaries in other situations as well. Food brokers, for example, sell commodities such as wheat, corn, and potatoes. Brokerage is an activity with many interesting career opportunities.

HOW INTERMEDIARIES CREATE EXCHANGE EFFICIENCY   The benefits of marketing intermediaries can be illustrated rather easily. Suppose that five manufacturers of various food products tried to sell directly to five retailers. The number of exchange relationships that would have to be established is 5 times 5, or 25. But picture what happens when a wholesaler enters the system. The five manufacturers would contact one wholesaler to establish five exchange relationships. The wholesaler would have to establish contact with the five

brokers
Marketing intermediaries who bring buyers and sellers together and assist in negotiating an exchange.

FIGURE **17.9**
· · · ·

HOW INTERMEDIARIES CREATE EXCHANGE EFFICIENCY

Adding a wholesaler to the channel of distribution cuts the number of contacts from 25 to 10. This makes distribution more efficient.

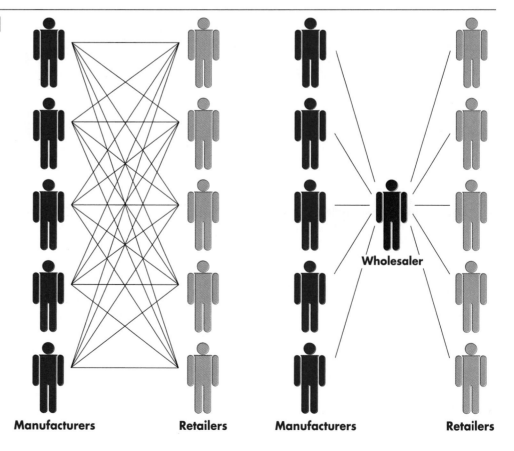

Manufacturers   Retailers   Manufacturers   Retailers

retailers. That would mean another five exchange relationships. Note that the addition of a wholesaler reduces the number of exchanges from 25 to only 10 (see Figure 17.9).

In the past, intermediaries conducted exchanges not only more efficiently than manufacturers or retailers but more effectively as well. Recently, however, technology has made it possible for manufacturers to reach consumers much more efficiently than in the past. For example, some manufacturers reach consumers directly on the Internet. Companies such as Dell Computers are famous for their direct-selling capability. They then outsource their delivery function to a marketing intermediary (a logistics firm). Note, however, that there is no wholesaler or retailer in the middle and no need for local storage facilities.

Similarly, retailers are now so closely linked with manufacturers that they can get delivery as often as once or twice a day. Again, that means that there is often no need for a wholesaler to perform functions such as storage and delivery. Does that mean that wholesalers are obsolete? The answer is *not yet*, but wholesalers need to change their functions to remain viable in today's rapidly changing distribution systems. In this next section, we shall explore the value that intermediaries can provide.

Marketing intermediaries provide invaluable assistance to manufacturers. This advertisement for the electronics industry highlights the reliable, fully tracked delivery service available from UPS.

THE VALUE CREATED BY INTERMEDIARIES   The public has always viewed marketing intermediaries with some suspicion. Surveys have shown that about half the costs of the things we buy are marketing costs that go largely to pay for the work of intermediaries. People reason that if we could only get rid of intermediaries, we could greatly reduce the cost of everything we buy. Sounds good, but is the solution really that simple?

Let's take as an example a box of cereal such as Fiberrific, which sells for $4. How could we, as consumers, get the cereal for less? Well, we could all drive to Saskatchewan, where some of the cereal is produced, and save some shipping costs. But would that be practical? Can you imagine millions of people getting into their cars and driving to Saskatchewan just to get some cereal? No, it doesn't make sense. It is much cheaper to have intermediaries bring the cereal to the cities. That involves transportation and warehousing by wholesalers. But these steps add cost, don't they? Yes, but they add value as well, the value of not having to drive to Saskatchewan.

The cereal is now somewhere on the outskirts of the city. We could all drive down to the wholesaler's outlet store and pick up the cereal; some people do just that. But that is not really the most economical way to buy cereal. If we figure in the cost of gas and time, the cereal would be rather expensive. Instead, we prefer to have someone move cereal from the warehouse to another truck, drive it to the supermarket, unload it, unpack it, stamp it with a price, put it on the shelf, and wait for us to come in to buy it. To make it even more convenient, the supermarket may stay open 24 hours a day, seven days a week. Think of the *costs*. Think also of the *value*. For $4, we can get a box of cereal when we want it, where we want it, and with little effort on our part.

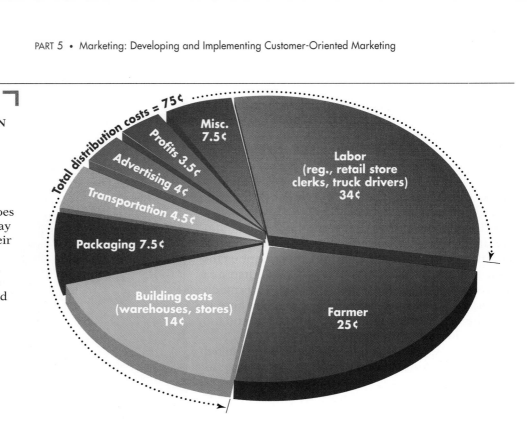

FIGURE 17.10
. . . .
HOW DISTRIBUTION AFFECTS YOUR FOOD DOLLAR

Note that the farmer gets only 25 cents of your food dollar. The bulk of your money goes to intermediaries to pay distribution costs. Their biggest cost is labour (truck drivers, clerks). The next biggest costs are for warehouses and storage.

Figure 17.10 shows where food money goes in the distribution process. Notice that the largest percentage of your food dollar goes to people who drive trucks and work in the warehouse and retail organizations that serve your needs. Only 3.5 cents goes to profit.

Three basic points about intermediaries are the following:

- Marketing intermediaries can be eliminated, but their activities cannot be eliminated. That is, you can get rid of retailers, but then consumers or someone else would have to perform the retailer's tasks, including transportation, storage, finding suppliers, and establishing communication with suppliers.
- Intermediary organizations survive because they perform marketing functions more effectively and efficiently than others can.
- Intermediaries add costs to products, but these costs are usually more than offset by the values they create.

Critical Thinking

Imagine that we did get rid of intermediaries and you had to go shopping for groceries and shoes. How would you find out where the shoes and groceries were? How far would you have to travel to get them? How much money do you think you would save for your time and effort? Which intermediary do you think is most important and why?

utility
Value- or want-satisfying ability that intermediaries add to products by making them more useful or accessible to consumers.

HOW INTERMEDIARIES ADD UTILITY TO GOODS **Utility** is an economic term that refers to the value- or want-satisfying ability that intermediaries add to goods or services. They achieve utility by making products more useful or accessible to buyers. Four utilities are mentioned in economic literature: time, place, possession, and service.

BUILDING COOPERATION IN DISTRIBUTION SYSTEMS

How can manufacturers get wholesalers and retailers to cooperate to form an efficient distribution system? One answer is to link the firms together somehow in a formal relationship. Three systems have emerged to tie firms together: corporate systems, contractual systems, and administered systems.

··· CORPORATE DISTRIBUTION SYSTEMS ···

A *corporate distribution system* is one in which all the organizations in the channel are owned by one firm. If the manufacturer owns the retail firm, clearly it can exert much greater control over its operations. Au Coton, for example, owns its own retail stores and thus coordinates everything: display, pricing, promotion, inventory control, and so. Other companies that have tried corporate systems include Goodyear and Firestone, manufacturers that had their own retail outlets. Paramount Pictures in the United States owns Canadian Famous Players' chain of cinemas across Canada.

Au Coton builds cooperation in its distribution through its use of a corporate distribution system.

··· CONTRACTUAL DISTRIBUTION SYSTEMS ···

If a manufacturer cannot buy or set up retail stores, it can try to get the retailers to sign a contract to cooperate. A *contractual distribution system* is one in which members are bound to cooperate through contractual agreements. There are three forms of contractual systems. First, there are franchise systems such as McDonald's, Delta Hotels, Baskin-Robbins, and Speedy Muffler. The franchisee agrees to all the rules, regulations, and procedures established by the franchisor. This results in the consistent quality and level of service you find in most franchised organizations.

Second, there are wholesaler-sponsored chains such as IGA food stores. Each store signs an agreement to use the same name, participate in chain promotions, and cooperate as a unified system of stores, even though each store is independently owned and managed.

A third form of contractual system is a retail cooperative. This arrangement is much like a wholesaler-sponsored chain except it is initiated by smaller retailers. They form a central buying organization to gain substantial clout. The same cooperation is agreed to, and the stores remain independent. Sometimes they set up or buy a wholesale organization.

··· ADMINISTERED DISTRIBUTION SYSTEMS ···

What does a producer do if it has no retail outlets or cannot get retailers to sign an agreement to cooperate? The best thing to do is to manage all the marketing functions itself, including display, inventory, control, pricing, and promotion. The management by producers of all the marketing functions at the retail level is called an *administered distribution system*. Kraft does that for its cheeses. Retailers cooperate with producers in such systems because they get so much help for free. Large retail companies exert powerful pressure on manufacturers to build, staff, and maintain their own selling space in stores

<www.cmisltd.com>

Go to this site, click on *Electronic Data Interchange,* and then click on *History of EDI.* Callero Management Information Services is in the EDI business. Its Web site traces the early beginnings of EDI.

electronic data interchange (EDI)
Software that enables the computers of producers, wholesalers, and retailers to communicate with each other.

and keep the shelves stocked, if they want to distribute their products there. All the retailer has to do is provide the space and ring up the sale.

••• SUPPLY CHAIN MANAGEMENT •••

Most firms in a channel of distribution are forced to carry higher levels of inventory than absolutely necessary to assure that goods will be available when needed. Much lower levels of inventory could be carried if those firms had better communication links with and faster response times from their suppliers. That is exactly what is happening today. *Supply chain management (SCM)* is the overall process of minimizing inventory and moving goods through the channel faster by using computers to improve communications among the channel members.[9]

Electronic Data Interchange (EDI) enables the computers of producers, wholesalers, and retailers to communicate with each other.[10] EDI makes it possible for a retailer to be directly linked with a supplier electronically. As a result, the supplier can ship new goods as soon as the retail sale is made. EDI is a critical part of an effective supply chain management system.

Total cost reductions using supply chain management have been 30 percent or more. Similar reductions in inventory have also been achieved. Bergin Brunswig, a major distributor of pharmaceuticals and health-care products, has cut the amount of time between when an order is placed and when it is delivered to just 12 hours.[11]

Progress Check

- What is the relationship among intermediaries, channels of distribution, and physical distribution? Why do we need intermediaries?
- Can you illustrate how intermediaries create exchange efficiency? How would you defend intermediaries to someone who said that if we got rid of them we would save millions of dollars?
- Can you illustrate how computers make distribution and retailing more efficient and less costly?

PHYSICAL DISTRIBUTION— (LOGISTICS) MANAGEMENT

Historically, intermediaries helped perform the physical distribution function; that is, they helped move goods from the farm to consumer markets or move raw materials to factories and so forth. Distribution involved the movement of goods by truck, train, and other modes, and the storage of goods in warehouses along the way. (*Modes,* in the language of distribution, are the various means used to transport goods such as trucks, trains, planes, ships, and pipeline.) Today, logistics systems involve more than simply moving products from place to place. They involve all kinds of activities such as processing orders and taking inventory of products. In other words, logistics systems involve whatever it takes to see that the right products are sent to the right place quickly and efficiently.

••• TRANSPORTATION MODES •••

In Canada we have always had a particular economic problem regarding the transportation component of operating costs. We are a very large country with

Spotlight on Big Business

<www.homegrocer.com>

Another Canadian Success Story in the U.S.

In 1997 Terry Drayton and two other Vancouver friends, Ken Deering and Mike Donald, had the idea of starting their own Internet supermarket. Unable to get venture capital financing in Canada, the trio moved down the coast to Seattle and quickly got their financing in the U.S. They raised US$75 million from individuals who had previously backed big winners like Amazon.com, Federal Express, and Netscape. In no time Home-Grocer.com was in business and by the end of 1999 was serving 35,000 homes in Seattle and Portland, Oregon. The company is planning to expand into heavily populated Southern California, and are preparing for this expansion by ordering 1400 trucks. Drayton notes that estimates of online grocery shopping have severely underestimated how quickly this market is growing. He believes the amount spent will reach US$15 billion by 2002 and he is aiming to get a good slice of that business.

Running an Internet supermarket requires a complex, sophisticated organization. Here's a brief outline of how it works. Customers submit orders through the 24-hour Web site where they are automatically routed to the nearest warehouse. Pickers load the orders on conveyor belts that bring the orders to the door where the trucks are loaded. As the orders leave the warehouse, the customers' credit cards are charged. Groceries are delivered the day after orders are received and the

driver get the customers' signature electronically. Since the drivers are the only human contact the customers have with the company, HomeGrocer.com goes to great lengths to ensure that its drivers make a good impression on customers. The company's Web site has bios of their drivers and they try to convey the idea that their drivers are like the old friendly milkmen who used to deliver milk daily to your grandparents.

To set up and operate this system the company has a staff of 1500. The company currently employs more than 100 software specialists and programmers. Warehouses and custom-built trucks are equipped to handle perishable goods and a satellite-based global positioning system tracks the trucks.

The company is valued at US$125 million and Drayton expects another US$100 million injection soon to cover the cost of the additional 1400 trucks mentioned above. Not bad progress for Vancouver boys Drayton and Donald (Deering left to pursue other interests). HomeGrocer.com is a good example of how a company can combine modern technology with excellent distribution, showing again how traditional retail business has changed.

Source: Ric Mazareeuw, "One Foot In The Door.Com," *Canadian Business*, October 8, 1999, p. 101.

a very low population density. None of our main business competitors face this problem. Our main competitor, the United States, as well as Japan and European countries, have high population densities and relatively short distances to their main domestic markets. The transportation factor makes unit costs in Canada higher, which makes us less competitive.

This Canadian situation makes the job of distribution managers particularly important. They select transportation modes that minimize cost while maintaining the required level of service—speed and reliability. Since the inception of substantial railroad service in the middle of the nineteenth century, this mode has carried the overwhelming bulk of goods in Canada where water transport was not available. With the establishment of a wide network of paved highways in the middle of the twentieth century, trucking became an important mode of transportation.

SOME THINGS ARE WORTH THE WAIT.
YOUR DELIVERY ISN'T ONE OF THEM.

Whoever said "good things come to those who wait" never worked in the transportation business.

We're Epic Express, a new freight transportation company that's dedicated to total customer satisfaction, and eliminating the word "wait" from your business vocabulary.

This dedication to shippers in Ontario and Quebec is why we offer time-definite deliveries, where you set the delivery times yourself.

It's why we provide a superior tracking and tracing system, so you'll never have to wait for shipment information at any point in transit. And it's why we've assembled an experienced, customer-focused staff, ready to provide expedient solutions to your transportation needs.

At Epic Express, we're driven by ideas that will help your business become more competitive and more profitable. Don't wait. Call us today at 1-800-387-6759.

EPIC EXPRESS
A NEW ROAD IN TRANSPORTATION
For more information circle No. 20

This ad places emphasis on consistent on-time delivery and customer service. Advanced computer technology and industry cooperation are revolutionizing the distribution industry and reducing stress enormously.

piggybacking
Shipping the cargo-carrying part of a truck on a railroad car or ship over long distances for greater efficiency.

In the early 1980s freight tonnage carried by trucks surpassed rail tonnage for the first time. By the end of the decade, truck tonnage exceeded rail tonnage by some 30 percent.[12] Of course, the progress of modern technology in transportation is making it increasingly difficult to make clear distinctions between these and other modes.

We are all familiar with the huge trailer trucks that dominate our highways with their detachable trailers and containers. These containers usually complete their journey in a different mode, so the process is called **piggybacking**, shipping the cargo-carrying part of a truck on a railroad car or ship over long distances. This makes the total trip as efficient as possible and blurs the lines between the different modes of transport. Sealed container transport has become a major form of transportation all over the world. (See the section on containerization.)

In Canada we have a unique waterway that stretches from the Atlantic Ocean through the St. Lawrence River and the Great Lakes to the heart of the continent—Thunder Bay in western Ontario and Detroit and Chicago in the United States. This major transportation artery carries a huge volume of tonnage through the St. Lawrence Seaway channel (which is closed for the three winter months). The locks at Sault Ste. Marie and the Welland Canal are among the busiest in the world. This system has made Quebec City, Montreal, and Toronto into significant ports. Our ports on the Atlantic and Pacific oceans are busy all year long receiving and shipping vast amounts of cargo.

Whereas trucks and railway cars carry similar products, ships are most useful for very large bulky objects. Airplanes, which have the obvious advantage of speed, have the disadvantage of size limitations and high costs. Airplanes are an economic mode for high-cost, small items like jewellery or replacement parts for downed equipment that is delaying huge projects or important manufacturing processes. They are also ideal for the daily transport of parcels and envelopes that form the bulk of the rapid delivery required by business. Thus, we have companies like Canada Post, Purolator, Federal Express, and Air Canada guaranteeing overnight delivery to any part of Canada or the United States. (It takes a little longer for delivery to other parts of the world.)

Pipelines are a form of transportation used mostly for oil and natural gas. They crisscross the North American continent carrying these natural resources long distances, 24 hours a day, 365 days a year, immune from weather and other hazards. They also carry coal and other products, in small pieces, in water, or *slurry*. The water is removed at the end of the journey.

The job of the distribution manager is to find the most efficient combination of these forms of transportation. Figure 17.11 shows the advantages and disadvantages of each mode.

••• CRITERIA FOR CHOOSING LOGISTIC SYSTEMS •••

Two criteria dominate thinking in physical distribution planning. One is *customer service*. Customer wants and needs come first. In Japan, the goal is to serve all a firm's customers' needs with 100 percent reliability. North

Mode	Cost	Speed	On-time Dependability	Flexibility Handling Products	Frequency of Shipments	Reach
Railroad	Medium	Slow	Medium	High	Low	High
Trucks	High	Fast	High	Medium	High	Most
Pipeline	Low	Medium	Highest	Lowest	Highest	Lowest
Ships (water)	Lowest	Slowest	Lowest	Highest	Lowest	Low
Airplanes	Highest	Fastest	Low	Low	Medium	Medium

FIGURE **17.11**

· · · ·

COMPARING TRANSPORTATION MODES

Combining trucks with railroads lowers costs and increases the number of locations reached. The same is true when combining trucks with ships. Combining trucks with airlines speeds goods long distances and gets them to almost any location.

American distribution managers strive for an 85 to 95 percent level of customer satisfaction.

The other criterion is *cost*. Marketing systems are designed to accomplish mutually satisfying exchanges. This means that the buyer *and* the seller must be satisfied. The objective of distribution is to provide a certain standard of customer service at the lowest cost that will result in a profit for the seller.

Transportation modes vary from relatively slow carriers, such as barges, to high-speed jet airplanes. Generally speaking, the faster the mode, the higher the cost. Marketers must select those transportation modes that deliver goods at a reasonable price and maintain an acceptable level of customer service. You can see in Figure 17.11 the value of combining railroading with trucking to get less expensive transportation by railroad and more flexible distribution with trucks.

··· CONTAINERIZATION ···

You can imagine the problem of moving many small items from place to place in large trucks, railroad cars, or other forms of transportation. There is the danger of damage, theft, and loss. An effective answer is to pack and seal groups of items in one large container that can be easily moved and stored. The process of packing and sealing a number of items into one unit that is easily moved and shipped is called **containerization**. More and more companies are using this technique so that shipping has become more efficient and goods flow more smoothly. Containerization is the most common method of packaging international shipments.

containerization
The process of packing and sealing a number of items into one unit that is easily moved and shipped.

··· THE STORAGE FUNCTION ···

About 25 to 30 percent of the total cost of physical distribution is storage. This includes the cost of buying and operating warehouses, and movement of goods within the warehouses. There are two kinds of warehouses: storage and distribution. A *storage warehouse* stores products for a relatively long time. Seasonal goods such as lawnmowers would be stored in such a warehouse.

Distribution warehouses are facilities used to gather and redistribute products. You can picture a distribution warehouse for Canada Post, Federal Express, or United Parcel Service handling vast numbers of packages for a very short time.

GE built a combination storage and distribution facility in San Gabriel Valley, California, that will give you a feel for how large such buildings can be. This distribution centre is 660 m long and 142 m wide. It is big enough to hold three Statues of Liberty, two *Queen Mary* ships, *and* one CN Tower.

··· MATERIALS HANDLING ···

materials handling
The movement of goods within a warehouse, factory, or store.

Materials handling is the movement of goods within a warehouse, factory, or store. It is instructive to go to a warehouse and watch the operations for a while. You may see forklift trucks picking up stacks of merchandise and moving them around. In more modern warehouses, computerized vehicles and robots move the materials. It is important to note that the combination of two developments has greatly reduced the amount of storage and materials handling for many manufacturing and retail companies. Just-in-time inventory control (discussed in Chapter 10) reduces the amount of inventory that is required and the Internet makes possible direct shipment from manufacturers to consumers, doing away with intermediaries altogether. These developments eliminate a lot of handling and storage, significantly reducing costs. Warehouse management could be an interesting career possibility for business students.

Progress Check

- What are some of the activities involved in physical distribution?
- Which of the transportation modes is fastest? Cheapest? Most flexible? Which modes can be combined to improve the distribution process?
- What are the two criteria for selecting a distribution system?
- What percentage of the distribution costs comes from storage?

···· ▬▬▬ ····

WHOLESALE INTERMEDIARIES

Now that we have talked about channels of distribution and logistics, we can talk about the organizations that make up the channel. Let's begin with wholesalers. Remember that one goal of this discussion, and similar discussions throughout the text, is to introduce you to the variety of careers in this area. Most college students know little or nothing about wholesaling, yet the rapid growth of warehouse clubs offers many career possibilities.

There's much confusion about the difference between wholesalers and retailers. It's helpful to distinguish wholesaling from retailing and to clearly define the functions performed so that more effective systems of distribution can be designed. Some producers won't sell directly to retailers but will deal with wholesalers. Some producers give wholesalers a bigger discount than retailers. What confuses the issue is that some organizations sell much of their merchandise to other intermediaries (a wholesale sale) but also sell to ultimate consumers (a retail sale). Warehouse clubs are a good example.

Warehouse clubs and wholesalers such as Costco operate in many Canadian cities. They provide a special type of cash-and-carry service to members.

The issue is really rather simple: A *retail sale* is the sale of goods and services to consumers for their own use. A *wholesale sale* is the sale of goods and services to businesses and institutions (e.g., hospitals) for use in the business or to wholesalers or retailers for resale.

What difference does it make whether an organization is called a wholesaler or a retailer? One difference is that all provinces, except Alberta, impose a sales tax on retail sales. To charge such a tax, the province must know which sales are retail and which are not. Retailers are sometimes subject to other rules and regulations that do not apply to wholesalers.

••• MERCHANT WHOLESALERS •••

Merchant wholesalers are independently owned firms that take title to goods they handle. About 80 percent of wholesalers fall into this category. There are two types of merchant wholesalers: full-service wholesalers and limited-function wholesalers. **Full-service wholesalers** perform all necessary distribution functions, including transportation, storage, risk bearing, credit, and market information (see figure 17.12). Risk bearing includes buying merchandise that you may not be able to sell or may have to sell at a loss. It also includes selling on credit to retailers and risking that the retailer may not be able to pay for the goods. **Limited-function wholesalers** perform only selected functions but do them especially well. These wholesalers include rack jobbers, cash-and-carry wholesalers, and drop shippers.

Smaller manufacturers or marketers that don't ship enough products to fill a railcar or truck can get good rates and service by using a freight forwarder. A **freight forwarder** puts many small shipments together to create a single large shipment that can be transported cost-effectively.

Perhaps the most useful marketing intermediaries as far as you are concerned are retailers. They are the ones who bring goods and services to your neighbourhood and make them available day and night. We look at retailers next.

full-service wholesalers
Merchant wholesalers that perform all eight distribution functions.

limited-function wholesalers
Merchant wholesalers that perform only selected distribution functions.

freight forwarder
An organization that puts many smaller shipments together to create a single large shipment that can be transported cost-effectively.

RETAIL INTERMEDIARIES

Next time you go to a giant store, stop for a minute and look at the tremendous variety of products. Think of how many marketing exchanges were involved to bring you the 15,000 or so items that you see. Some products may have been imported from halfway around the world. Others have been processed and frozen so you can eat them out of season, such as strawberries.

The categories of stores is truly astounding. Supermarkets, discounters, factory outlets, giant warehouse stores, department stores, specialty stores, hypermarkets, convenience stores, chain stores, catalogue stores, and the list goes on and on.

Then there is the megamall, the West Edmonton Mall in Edmonton. The mall has 800 stores and shops, including two McDonald's. There are 19 movie

1. **Provide a sales force** to sell the goods to retailers and other buyers.
2. **Communicate** manufacturers' advertising deals and plans.
3. **Maintain inventory**, thus reducing the level of the inventory suppliers have to carry.
4. Arrange or undertake **transportation**.
5. **Provide capital** by paying cash or quick payments for goods.
6. Provide suppliers with **market information** they cannot afford or are unable to obtain themselves.
7. Undertake **credit risk** by granting credit to customers and absorbing any bad debts, thus relieving the supplier of this burden.
8. **Assume the risk** for the product by taking title.

FIGURE **17.12**
• • • •
FUNCTIONS OF A FULL-SERVICE WHOLESALER
Full-service wholesalers typically provide the eight services listed here.

Source: Thomas C. Kinnear and Kenneth L. Bernhardt, *Principles of Marketing*, 2nd ed. (Glenview, IL: Scott, Foresman, 1986), p. 369.

theatres, a miniature golf course, an indoor water park with 20 water slides, an indoor amusement park with 28 rides, a lake with submarines, and a skating rink where the Edmonton Oilers sometimes practise.

All of these retailers are marketing intermediaries that sell mainly to consumers. In Canada there are approximately 230,000 retailers, selling everything from soup to automobiles. Retail organizations employ more than a million people. They are a major employer of marketing graduates and many careers are available in retailing in all kinds of firms.

Despite this vast variety and number of stores, a rapidly growing and significant market share is being grabbed by the nonstore retailing sector, which we look at shortly.

··· HOW RETAILERS BENCHMARK: STRATEGIES ··· FOR COMPETING AGAINST THE BEST

Retailers use five major strategies to compete for the consumer's dollar: price, service, location, selection, and total quality. Since consumers are constantly comparing retailers on price, service, and variety, it is important for retailers to benchmark. This means comparing themselves to the best in the field to make sure that they meet or exceed those standards. The following sections describe the five major ways of competing.

PRICE COMPETITION   Competing on the basis of price is not new. Honest Ed's in Toronto and similar stores across Canada became famous for their ads loudly proclaiming the lowest prices in town. Today, however, most stores have taken up this cry and giant stores, pharmacy, and other chains, supermarkets, discounters, department stores, warehouse clubs, and more are all competing fiercely based on price. Old companies like The Bay, Zellers, Sears, Canadian Tire, Safeway, Loblaw's, and Metro are now fighting it out with the new or revitalized kids on the block: Wal-Mart, Home Depot\Réno-Dépôt, Real Canadian Superstores, Costco, Ikea, Staples\Bureau En Gros, Big Box, Shoppers Drug Mart\Pharmaprix, London Drugs, and Jean Coutu. Endless ads in all media, newspaper inserts, junk mail, door-to-door weekly handouts, and so on stress sales and special prices for every conceivable type of product. Retailers who do not adapt to this changed environment run into trouble, evi-

Canadian Tire is an example of a retailer that started as a specialty store but now sells a wide variety of different product lines.

denced by the disappearance of such stalwarts as Woodward's out west, the Robert Simpson department stores, and the collapse of the once-prestigious, national department store giant, the T. Eaton Co. Ltd.

SERVICE COMPETITION   This competitive strategy means putting the customer first. That requires that all staff are courteous and accommodating. Here again the *biggies* mentioned previously are going all out so that customers are not *lost* in the cavernous stores when they are confronted by so many thousands of items. Wal-Mart and Réno-Dépôt have greeters at the door who welcome customers and direct them to whatever they want to buy. Smaller stores have a chance to star in this category because they can give personal service. Department stores, having trimmed personnel to stay in the black, have been criticized for the lack of staff when customers need service. Keeping customers waiting long on the telephone or at cash counters is a sign of inadequate service. For companies that provide services rather than goods, such as banks, couriers, dry cleaners, and Internet service providers, excellent service is obviously a key competitive strategy.

LOCATION COMPETITION   In the retail business there is an old saying that the three requirements for success are location, location, location. Convenient or strategic locations are obviously important for retailers. One of the features that led to Ikea's success early on was their location in the then new shopping malls on the outskirts of cities, because the malls provided free and easily accessible parking. For the same reason, malls are still popular with consumers. The banks' ABMs are conveniently found in many locations. If you are in the mood for a pizza or other food from a fastfood outlet, you don't want to wait long for delivery so these stores need to be everywhere to ensure fast service. Location is so important for certain retailers that they pay as much as double the rental rates for a high traffic spot in a mall as they would for another location in that mall.[13]

SELECTION COMPETITION   This form of competition involves offering a wide variety of products as well as a very good selection in a particular product category. Toys "R" Us carries some 18,000 toys. A similar situation exists in the superstores mentioned previously. Smaller stores can only compete by specializing in a particular category. Some innovations in this area have been coffee shops, like Second Cup and Starbucks, which carry a very wide variety of coffees not usually found elsewhere.

TOTAL QUALITY   Any retailer that offers a combination of great pricing, location, selection, and service is offering the customer total quality. These retailers seek to provide the best of everything so that the consumer is completely satisfied and will return again and again to the same stores. This is what total quality management (mentioned several times in previous chapters) is all about.

••• RETAIL DISTRIBUTION STRATEGY •••

A major decision manufacturers must make is to select retailers to sell their products. Different products call for different retail distribution strategies. There are three categories of retail distribution: intensive distribution, selective distribution, and exclusive distribution.

Intensive distribution puts products into as many retail outlets as possible, including vending machines. Products that need intensive distribution include candy, cigarettes, gum, and popular magazines (convenience goods).

Selective distribution is the use of only a preferred group of the available retailers in an area. Such selection helps to assure producers of quality sales and service. Manufacturers of appliances, furniture, and clothing (shopping goods) usually use selective distribution.

Exclusive distribution is the use of only one retail outlet in a given geographic area. Because the retailer has exclusive rights to sell the product, it is more likely to carry more inventory, give better service, and pay more attention to this brand than others. Auto manufacturers usually use exclusive distribution, as do producers of specialty goods.

···· ▬▬▬ ····

NONSTORE RETAILING

During the past decade both the volume and percentage of nonstore retail sales have been rising steadily. There is a wide variety of modes in this category and because of its increasing importance, we will end this chapter with a review of this aspect of retailing or quasi-retailing.

··· THE INTERNET ···

<www.shopnow.com>
<www.shopatthemall.com>
<www.springfield-mall.com>
<www.baystatemall.com>

There are a large number of virtual malls on the Internet, offering every type of product imaginable. These are just four examples. Visit their sites to see what that offers. Do some surfing to find other virtual malls and research what they offer.

In the past few years there has been a phenomenal leap in the volume of direct sales to consumers, mostly because of the Internet. As more people get on the Net, more companies set up Web sites and do business directly with consumers and other businesses. Hundreds of millions of people now constitute a market that is easily accessible as people sit in the comfort of their home or office. You can browse or shop without budging from your chair. There are virtual malls and all kinds of displays to help purchasers make a decision to buy, using their credit cards or toll-free telephone lines. This captive audience is growing, globally, by the millions every month. Mentioned in previous chapters were two very successful computer companies, Gateway and Dell, who sell only online. These companies customize the equipment to the exact requirement of the customer.

The best example of this revolutionary mode of selling is bookseller *Amazon.com* in the U.S. In late 1998 and early 1999, this company, because of its rapid success, attracted a lot of attention from the global business world. The company's stock shot up to unbelievable numbers before it showed any earnings at all. *Business Week* noted that "Amazon offers an easily searchable trove of 3.1 million titles—15 times more than any bookstore on the planet and without the costly overhead of multimillion-dollar buildings and scads of stores clerks." The report drives home the point that Amazon's 1600 employees *each* generate triple the amount of business that the 27,000 employees of giant U.S. bookseller Barnes and Noble generate.[14]

··· TELEMARKETING ···

Telemarketing is the sale of goods and services by telephone. Thousands of companies use telemarketing to supplement or replace in-store selling. You have probably had your dinner interrupted by one of these telemarketers selling subscriptions to magazines and newspapers, "investment opportunities," home cleaning, home heating equipment, and so on. Perhaps you have done such work to earn a few extra dollars. This is a fast-growing area in marketing.

Carts and kiosks, often found in malls and along streets, have much lower overheads than stores. They will often offer reduced prices on merchandise.

••• DIRECT PERSONAL SELLING •••

Direct personal selling involves selling to consumers in their homes or where they work. Major users of this category include cosmetics producers (Avon) and vacuum cleaner manufacturers (Electrolux). The newest trend is to sell lingerie, artwork, plants, and other goods at house parties sponsored by sellers. No doubt you've heard of Tupperware parties. One of the real veterans of direct selling to consumers in their homes, Encyclopedia Britannica, announced in 1996 that it was abandoning this route and opting for the Internet.

••• VENDING MACHINES, KIOSKS, AND CARTS •••

A vending machine dispenses convenience goods when customers deposit sufficient money in the machine. The benefit of vending machines is the convenient location in airports, office buildings, schools, service stations, and other high-traffic areas. Vending machines in Japan sell everything from bandages and face cloths to salads and spiced seafood. This type of vending has not yet taken hold in Canada or the U.S.

Carts and kiosks have lower overhead costs than stores do, so they can offer lower prices on items such as T-shirts and umbrellas. You often see vending carts outside stores on the sidewalk or along walkways in malls. Mall owners often use them because they're colourful and create a marketplace atmosphere. Kiosk workers dispense coupons and provide all kinds of helpful information to consumers, who seem to enjoy this interaction.

••• SELLING BY CATALOGUE •••

Finally, there is the important area of selling by sending catalogues to customers and having them order by toll-free telephone or by e-mail using their credit cards. Catalogue sales are still expanding rapidly because it is a convenient way to buy. Two very popular American catalogue sellers are Land's End and L.L. Bean, who ship to Canada as well. Their telephone lines are open 24 hours a day, all year. Many companies maintain a catalogue at a Web site online to make products easily accessible. For example, a college professor

Ethical Dilemma

REVIEW

Now that you have worked your way through the chapter, how do you feel about the ethical question posed at the beginning of the chapter? Here's the response of our two business people.

Bérdard says that "False advertising is illegal." Reilley is of the opinion that "stretching the truth can lead to questions being raised by Health Canada and other agencies. Also, your competitors might publicly attack your claims, which could harm your business. My answer would be no. Rather, I would attempt to make our ads more attractive, increase our marketing efforts, and overhaul production and distribution to increase business."

Some of you might say, "What's the big deal? Lots of ads exaggerate." Others might be concerned about how ethical it is to use such an ad. Does the answer depend on what your personal values are and how strongly you feel about them? We are often confronted with decisions that are more or less ethical and sometimes it may seem as if a particular issue is not too important. Is it okay to cheat when writing exams? If a cashier omits punching in an item would you tell him?

We may tell little white lies to make life more convenient. For example, if you want to avoid going out with someone, you might say you are too busy or that you have a bad headache. How often have you used a phony alibi when you didn't do your homework, you came home late, or didn't do some household chore? Is there any significant difference between any of these scenarios and the ad problem? The decision about using or not using that ad will finally depend upon your ▲ own set of ethical standards.

searching for a textbook can access the site of the publishers of this book, McGraw-Hill Ryerson, scan the catalogue, direct an inquiry, or make a selection and order by e-mail.

Critical Thinking

Given the rise in importance of direct marketing methods (particularly the Internet, but also catalogues and direct personal selling), do you see a declining role for marketing intermediaries? What intermediaries do you think will survive and why? Consider all the kinds of intermediaries discussed in the chapter.

Progress Check

- What are the five major ways retailers compete with each other?
- What advantages and disadvantages do you see to having an intensive distribution strategy versus an exclusive one?
- Give some examples of direct marketing.

SUMMARY
· · · · ·

1. List and describe the five elements of the promotion mix.

1. Promotion is an attempt by marketers to persuade others to participate in exchanges with them.
   - ***What are the five promotional tools that make up the promotion mix?***
   The five promotional tools are advertising, personal selling, sales promotion, public relations, and publicity.

2. Describe advantages and disadvantages of various advertising media, and explain the latest advertising techniques.

2. Many people mistake other promotional tools for advertising.
   - ***How does advertising differ from the other promotional tools?***

Advertising is limited to paid, nonpersonal communication through various media by organizations and individuals who are in some way identified in the advertising message.

- ***What are the advantages of using the various media?***
You can review the advantages and disadvantages of the various advertising media in Figure 17.3.

- ***How's technology used in advertising?***
Rather than passively *receive* programming (news, entertainment, and commercials), consumers using interactive TV can actively *control* what they receive and can conduct a dialogue with advertisers. They can eliminate commercials from shows or watch the commercials and respond electronically, including placing orders. Some online computer services will offer advertising—and nothing but advertising—on demand. There will be databases for "considered purchases," offering consumers in-depth information (via text, pictures, and sound) about cars, travel, consumer electronics, and other high-priced items.

3. Personal selling is the face-to-face presentation and promotion of products and services. It also involves the search for new prospects and follow-up service after the sale.
   - ***What are the seven steps of the selling process?***
   The steps of the selling process are (1) prospect and qualify, (2) preapproach, (3) approach, (4) make presentation, (5) answer objections, (6) close sale, and (7) follow up.

3. Illustrate the seven steps of the selling process.

4. Public relations (PR) are all activities designed to give an organization or its products/services a better public image.
   - ***What does a PR program actually consist of?***
   PR departments keep a close eye on all news that relates to their organization. They try to emphasize all the positive news or developments by giving them wide distribution through interviews and press releases. At the same time they try to limit the damage to a company's reputation by playing down unfavourable news. They keep senior managers informed of stakeholders reaction to company activties.

   - ***What is publicity?***
   Publicity is information distributed by the media that's not paid for, or controlled by, the sponsor. It's an effective way to reach the public. Publicity's greatest advantage is its believability.

4. Describe the functions of the public relations department and the role of publicity.

5. Marketing intermediaries are organizations that assist in moving goods and services from producer to industrial and consumer users.
   - ***Why do we need marketing intermediaries?***
   We need intermediaries because they perform marketing functions more effectively and efficiently than others can. Marketing intermediaries can be eliminated, but their activities can't. Intermediaries add costs to products, but these costs are usually more than offset by the values they create.
   Utility is an economic term that refers to the value or want-satisfying ability that's added to goods or services by intermediaries because the products are made more useful or accessible to consumers.

   - ***What different types of utilities do intermediaries add?***
   Normally, marketing intermediaries perform the following utilities: time, place, possession, and service.

5. Explain why we need marketing intermediaries, and list four utilities they provide.

6. Describe in detail what is involved in physical distribution management.

6. Physical distribution can be a complex process because it involves all the activities needed to get products from producers to consumers as quickly and efficiently as possible.
   - ***What's involved in physical distribution management?***
   A primary concern of distribution managers is the selection of a transportation mode that will minimize costs and ensure a certain level of service. Logistics managers must also keep down storage costs. That's why supply chain management has become so popular. Furthermore, logistics managers are responsible for materials handling, moving goods within the warehouse and from the warehouse to the production or selling floor. Less inventory means less materials handling.

7. Describe the two major categories of wholesale organizations in the distribution system.

7. A wholesaler is a marketing intermediary that sells to organizations and individuals, but not to final consumers.
   - ***What are the two major categories of wholesalers that assist in the movement of goods from manufacturers to consumers?***
   Full-service wholesalers perform all necessary distribution functions including transportation, storage, risk bearing, credit, and market information. A variety of limited-function wholesalers perform only selected functions but do them especially well.

8. List and explain the ways that retailers compete.

8. A retailer is an organization that sells to ultimate consumers.
   - ***How do retailers compete in today's market?***
   There are five different ways of competing for the consumer's dollar today: price, service, location, selection, and total quality, which is a combination of the first four.

9. Explain the various kinds of nonstore retailing.

9. A growing number of consumers are ordering goods and services by mail, by phone, and by the Internet.
   - ***What are the various kinds of nonstore retailing?***
   Nonstore retailing includes telemarketing; selling goods in vending machines, kiosks, and carts; and other direct marketing including the Internet and catalogues.

KEY TERMS
......

advertising 533
brokers 550
channel of
    distribution 548
containerization 557
electronic data inter-
    change (EDI) 554
freight forwarder 559
full-service
    wholesalers 559
infomercials 538
integrated marketing
    communication
    (IMC) 545

integrated marketing
    communication
    system 545
limited-function
    wholesalers 559
marketing
    intermediaries 548
mass customization
    538
materials handling 558
personal selling 539
physical distribution
    (logistics) 548
piggybacking 556

promotion 532
promotion mix 532
prospecting 539
public relations (PR)
    543
publicity 544
pull strategy 545
push strategy 544
retailer 548
sales promotion 541
trade show 532
utility 552
wholesaler 548

DEVELOPING WORKPLACE SKILLS

1. The four utilities of marketing are time, place, possession, and service. Give examples of organizations in your area specifically designed to perform each of these functions.

2. The emergence of the Internet has changed the face of retailing forever. Try shopping for a good or service on the Internet to find the best price.

You might begin with Consumer World at <www.consumerworld.org>. This site lists all kinds of places where you can shop for cars, gifts, computer equipment, and more. Be prepared to discuss your findings in class.

3. This text describes five kinds of retail competition: price, service, location, selection, and total quality. Give a five-minute report on your experience as a consumer with each type of competition. Do you prefer one over the others? Why?

4. Visit the newest stores in your community. Compare their prices, products, and services with the older stores. What are the trends in retailing that seem most significant to you?

5. Recall some of the experiences you have had with telemarketers. How could they change their approach so you would be more responsive and positive about their calls? You might practise such approaches on your classmates to see if they really work.

INTERNET CHALLENGES

1. Access this site <auctions.yahoo.com> and look at the choices of categories of items you can buy or sell directly through the Internet. How many broad categories do you see? Look at the number of types in each category. How many different types of items are available? Click on *Full Category Index*. How many subcategories do you see? Would you make use of this vehicle to do any buying or selling? Why?

2. Do a little surfing to find various booksellers or retailers. See if you can find any of the texts that you are using this year. Compare the prices offered (including postage, handling, and so on) with what you paid. Did you find any lower prices? Don't forget to try <www.amazon.com>. What do you conclude from your search.

Practising Management Decisions

CASE 1

TIM HORTON'S— FROM PUCKS TO DONUTS: THE HOLE TRUTH

Tim Horton, born Miles Gilbert Horton, in Cochrane, Ontario, was the Maple Leafs' hockey star who crashed his car and died in 1974 at age 44. His old Toronto coach, Punch Imlach, had moved to Buffalo to coach the Sabres and he had prevailed upon Horton to come out of retirement for one year to beef up the Sabres' defence. The car Horton crashed was the signing bonus Imlach had given him. Horton had needed the money to finance the fledgling donut enterprise he had started in Hamilton with partner Ron Joyce, a retired police officer. In those days hockey stars did not make a fraction of the multimillion dollar salaries they now earn. In 25 years, under Ron Joyce's leadership, the little donut shop has grown into Tim Horton's Donuts, a super chain of more than 1700 franchises in Canada and 100 in the U.S.

Tim Horton's Donuts became so popular because their products filled a widely felt Canadian need. There are franchise units from Whitehorse in the Yukon to Cape Breton in Nova Scotia. A lot of people are unable to pass a day without some time spent at a Tim Horton's hangout, enjoying their favourite donut and coffee. Students, executives, computer engineers, construction workers, salespeople, and secretaries can all be found at Tim Horton's Donut shops.

The result is a company that sells about three million donuts daily, with expected sales of $1.4 billion in 1999. If you want to buy a new franchise unit, it will cost you up to $400,000 just for the licence fee. In 1995 Joyce, who was the sole owner, sold out to Wendy's International for a 13 percent stake in Wendy's where he is the largest single shareholder and sits on the board of directors. Joyce remains senior chairperson of Tim Horton's.

If Horton were alive he would have been 70 years old in 2000, the same age as Joyce. Too bad he didn't live to see the great success that his partner made of his original idea. In 1999 Joyce's management abilities were recognized when he was named Canada's Entrepreneur of the Year by Ernst & Young.

Decision Questions

1. Are you surprised that something as simple as a doughnut and coffee can be the basis of such a success story in Canada? What does it tell us about the importance of finding a product that fills consumers' needs if you want to be successful?
2. Can you think of other products or services that have had a similar success from simple beginnings? Think of clothes, computer games, software, or Internet service providers.

3. Do you think that the popularity of Tim Horton's doughnuts will continue for a long time? Would you be prepared to try to raise the kind of big money needed to set up one of their franchise units? Remember also that they are open 24 hours daily, seven days a week. That's a heavy workload.
4. Have you ever thought of a product or service that is needed, that you think is not being provided now, or inadequately provided, that could be a winner? How would you test your ideas to see if there is a real consumer or industrial market for it?

Sources: Elizabeth Church, "Doughnut Entrepreneur Takes the Cake," *The Globe and Mail*, October 27, 1999, p. M1; Joan Skogan, "Once upon a Tim," *Saturday Night*, September 1999, p. 69.

In 1995, after a big, noisy party at his Toronto home, Wolfgang Spegg was busy picking up all the CDs strewn all over the place and refiling them. It wasn't the first time he had had to do that clean-up job and he started thinking about how to avoid that problem. He began to wonder if it would be possible to have all his CDs on a database so that they could be accessed directly. This early idea eventually led to the creation of musicmusicmusic inc. in 1997. Through the company's RadioMoi service, radio-moi.com, anyone can access the company's database of 30,000 songs. By Fall 1999 there were 80,000 subscribers.

This reach is what interests advertisers, whose payments for ads keeps the service free to subscribers. Advertisers who want to sell to music lovers know this site is a great way to reach that market. But Spegg is not satisfied to rest at the current level of subscribers. He's planning to spend $9 million on ads so that he can boost that 80,000 to much higher levels. The greater the number of subscribers the more he can charge for advertising and the greater the interest of potential advertisers in reaching such a large music-focused market segment.

Spegg is developing a network of global affiliates and plans to pipe music into restaurants, malls, office buildings, and even record shops and radio stations. By 2002 Spegg expects the company to have a revenue of $45 million, but it will just be breaking even, losing an estimated $24 million by that date. Even a great idea takes money to start and requires deep pockets to cover losses in the early years. Spegg plans to go

CASE 2
••••••
THE INTERNET IS MUSIC TO WOLFGANG SPEGG'S EARS
••••••

public and have his shares trade on the large Frankfurt Stock Exchange in Germany. By 2002 he believes the company's shares could be worth $2 billion. Wolfgang Spegg is joining the ranks of other Canadian entrepreneurial dreamers who dream big, and many of whom succeeded.

The case highlights the two major trends that have been stressed in this book—how technology and globalization are driving business today.

Decision Questions

1. Here we see another example of how the Internet is being used to reach customers—both the service provider and the advertiser rely on this method to reach their markets. Can you see yourself as a potential user of this service? Would you use it often?
2. Do you think this is a service that is filling a need that many consumers have? What is your evidence? Do you think Mr. Spegg is too optimistic? Why?
3. Is this another example of the growth of non-retailing methods of reaching customers? What kind of advertisers use such a service? Does direct selling to consumers or general advertising get you to go to stores to buy the product?
4. Access <www.radiomoi.com> and see if it works well for you. Do you think it's a good service? Does the company have any competitors now? How does their service differ from RadioMoi? Have they kept up to date?

Source: George Koch, "canadians.com," *Profit*, September 1999, p. 29.

Part 6

Accounting Information and Financial Activities

Accounting
Fundamentals

Chapter

18

I n 1926, young McGill graduates, chartered accountants Bill Richter and Cecil Usher, established their accounting and auditing firm, Richter, Usher & Co. Seventy years later, Richter, Usher & Vineberg threw a big party to celebrate the achievements and foresight of both founders, now deceased. As senior partners Howard Gilmour and Marvin Corber noted, the firm now has more than 500 employees, with offices in Montreal, Toronto, Halifax, and New York, encompassing a wide variety of activities.

The Firm has continued to evolve with changing market demands and has expanded beyond the traditional audit and tax practice. Richter now offers professional services in the areas of corporate finance, financial reorganization, business valuations, forensic accounting, management consulting, government assistance, research and development, estates and trusts, and wealth management.

Longtime practitioners Gilmour and Corber have witnessed the transition to a computer-dominated method of practising, which has revolutionized operations. They have participated in the development of the other services indicated above, which were a natural outgrowth of their clients' needs. They have also had to cope with a host of major new issues that all accounting firms must contend with.

For example, they now counsel clients not to undertake any mergers or acquisitions or any purchase of land or buildings without an environmental audit. Such an audit would reveal any potential environmental liabilities stemming from previous activities. Similarly, the real value of many companies cannot be determined simply by examining their financial statements and accounting records. A highly skilled workforce or valuable know-how and patents might be a company's most important asset. These assets may yield high profits in the future without showing up at all or at true value on a company's current balance sheet.

Senior partners Gilmour and Corber see accounting and the profession as being in a constant state of evolution. As society, the economy, and business continue evolving, so must practitioners modify their thinking and practices to meet the new challenges constantly being generated.

Sources: Interviews with Howard Gilmour and Marvin Corber, September 9, 1999, and June 25, 1996; and company documents.

PROFILE

Richter, Usher & Vineberg After 75 Years

Ethical Dilemma

DEVELOPING "MAGIC" NUMBERS

You are the only accountant employed by a small company, and you have full charge of the books. The company's financial position is weak because of a downturn in the economy. You know that your employer is going to ask the bank for an additional loan so that the company can continue to pay its bills. Unfortunately, the financial statements for the year just ended will not be very strong. You are convinced that no bank will approve a loan increase based on those figures.

Your boss approaches you before you close the books for the year and makes some suggestions for showing higher profits so that he will have a better chance of getting the loan approved. He even suggests ▲ that you should find some way of covering your tracks so that the auditors who must approve the statements will not be aware of the "adjustments." You know that both the scheme and the cover-up are against the professional practice rules of your profession and that it would probably be fraudulent. You try to get him to change his mind but he tells you that if the company does not get the loan, it will be forced to close down and you will lose your job. You know that this is true. Your job pays well and your employer is a good boss. What should you do?

Think about this problem as you study this chapter and we will get back to it when you reach the end of the chapter.

THE IMPORTANCE OF ACCOUNTING

Many small-business owners discover the importance of accounting when problems arise. Take Sharon and Brian Rowan, for example. They learned the hard way that you'd better keep track of the figures, even if your company seems to be doing well. After receiving a large inheritance, the Rowans opened an electric appliance store and advertised aggressively. Six months later they were doing $75,000 business monthly, so they believed things were going great.

Soon after, Sharon said to Brian that perhaps they ought to engage an accounting firm to deal with income taxes and see if they were handling the GST properly. That's when they got the bad news: they were really incurring losses. It was hard to believe because they were always able to pay their bills. Yet, as Brian said, "We found out that we were spending $60 to make $50."

Brian and Sharon knew how to sell appliances, but they knew almost nothing about accounting. Neither of them had ever seen an income statement. They couldn't understand how their sales could be increasing and they could pay their bills on time and still have losses instead of profits. We will explain at the end of the chapter what their accountants told them. Where they went wrong was in not getting advice *before* they started. Howard Gilmour and Marvin Corber could easily have assigned one of their staff members to provide the necessary services.

••• ACCOUNTING: A KEY COMPONENT ••• OF BUSINESS MANAGEMENT

Brian and Sharon Rowan's story is repeated often throughout the country. Small businesses often fail because they do not know where they are going or what is really happening. Accounting is different from marketing, production, and human resource management. We have all had some experience with marketing or production. We have observed management in practice, understand management concepts, and seem to grasp human resource procedures quite readily. But we do not know enough about accounting from experience. What is it? What do accountants do? Is it interesting?

The truth is that many people, including some business majors, are not interested in accounting at all. There are thousands of business people who are highly skilled in most areas of business but relatively ignorant when it comes to accounting. The result? Like the Rowans, they plunge into the world of trade and seem to be doing well for a while. Sales go up, they appear to have enough cash, but in reality they are losing money. Soon their losses catch up with them. The net result is business failure. Others are operating profitably but because they are short of cash and cannot pay their bills, they think they are incurring losses. This chapter will explain how both of these situations can occur.

The fact is that you must know something about accounting if you really want to understand business; accounting is not that hard. You will have to learn a few terms; that is mandatory. Then you have to understand bookkeeping and how accounts are kept. That is not too difficult, either. From the figures accountants gather and record, they prepare reports called *financial statements*. These reports tell a business person how healthy the business is. It is almost impossible to run a business effectively without being able to read, understand, and analyze accounting reports and financial statements. These statements are as revealing of the health of a business as pulse rate and blood pressure are in revealing the health of a person. It is up to *you*, however, to make sure your accountants give you the information you need in the form you need it. That means you must know something about accounting, too.

This chapter helps to introduce you to basic accounting principles. By the end of it, you should have a good idea of what accounting is, how it works, and why it is important. Spend some time learning the terms and reviewing the accounting statements. A few hours invested in learning this material will pay off repeatedly as you become more involved in business or investing, or simply in understanding what's going on out there in the world of business and finance.

WHAT IS ACCOUNTING?

Accounting is the recording, classifying, summarizing, and interpreting of financial transactions to provide management and other interested parties with the information they need. Transactions include buying and selling goods and services, acquiring equipment, using supplies, and receiving and paying cash. Transactions may be recorded by hand or in a computer system. Most businesses use computers because the process is repetitive and complex, and computers greatly simplify the task. Computers can handle large amounts of data more quickly and more accurately than manual systems.

> **accounting**
> The recording, classifying, summarizing, and interpreting of financial transactions to provide management and other interested parties with the information they need.

After transactions have been recorded, they are usually classified into groups that have common characteristics. For example, all purchases are grouped together, as are all sales transactions. The business is thus able to obtain needed information about purchases, sales, and other transactions that occur over a given period of time. The methods used to record and summarize accounting data are called an **accounting system** (see Figure 18.1). Computers enable an organization to get financial reports daily if desired. One purpose of accounting is to help managers evaluate the financial condition and the operating performance of the firm. They compare results to those forecast and are better able to make decisions for the future. Another purpose is to

> **accounting system**
> The methods used to record and summarize accounting data.

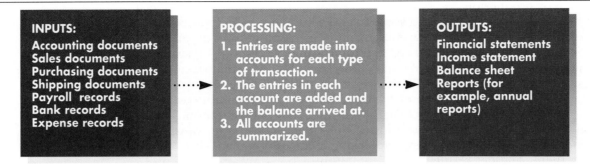

FIGURE **18.1**

· · · ·

THE ACCOUNTING SYSTEM

The inputs to an accounting system include documents arising from sales, cash, purchases, and other transactons. The data are recorded, classified, and summarized. They are then put into summary financial statements such as an income statement and a balance sheet.

managerial accounting
Providing information and analyses to managers within the organization to assist them in decision making.

report financial information to people outside the firm such as shareholders, lenders, suppliers, and the government (for tax purposes).

··· ACCOUNTING IS USER ORIENTED ···

In more basic terms, accounting is the measuring and reporting to various users (inside and outside the organization) of financial information regarding the economic activities of the firm (see Figure 18.2). Accounting has been called the language of business, but it is also the language used to report financial information about nonprofit organizations such as religious and community organizations, schools, hospitals, and governmental units. Accounting can be divided into two major categories: managerial accounting and financial accounting.

Managerial accounting is used to provide information and analyses to managers within the organization to assist them in decision making. Managerial accounting is concerned with measuring and reporting costs of production, marketing, and other functions (cost accounting); preparing budgets (planning); checking whether or not departments are staying within their budgets or meeting sales and other targets (controlling); and designing strategies to minimize taxes (tax accounting).

Simple analysis of corporate figures can disclose important information. For example, a slight month-to-month increase in payroll costs may not appear significant. But multiply that increase by 12 months and the increase

FIGURE **18.2**

· · · ·

USERS OF ACCOUNTING INFORMATION AND THE REQUIRED REPORTS

Many different types of organizations use accounting information to make decisions. The kinds of reports these users need vary according to the information they require. An accountant, then, needs to prepare the appropriate reports.

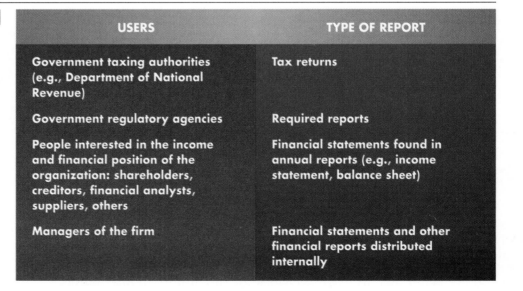

USERS	TYPE OF REPORT
Government taxing authorities (e.g., Department of National Revenue)	Tax returns
Government regulatory agencies	Required reports
People interested in the income and financial position of the organization: shareholders, creditors, financial analysts, suppliers, others	Financial statements found in annual reports (e.g., income statement, balance sheet)
Managers of the firm	Financial statements and other financial reports distributed internally

in costs can be important. Monitoring profit margins, unit sales, travel expenses, cash flow, inventory turnover, and other such data is critical to the success of a firm. Management decision making is based on such data.

Some of the questions that managerial accounting reports are designed to answer include:

- What goods and services are selling the most and what promotional tools are working best?
- How quickly is the firm selling what it buys, and how does that compare with other firms in the same industry?
- How much profit is the firm making, and does that compare favourably with other firms? If not, why not?
- What are the firm's major expenses, and are they in line with what other firms spend?
- How much money does the firm make on the owners' investment in the business, and does that compare favourably with other firms in the same industry? If not, why not?
- How much tax is the firm paying, and how can it minimize that amount?
- Will the firm have enough cash to pay its bills? If not, has it made arrangements to borrow that money?
- Are the firms' costs of doing business in line with the costs of other firms in the industry? If not, why not?

In all cases, results are compared with budgets to see if the results are achieving the targets set for the current year. When they do not, management must figure out how performance can be improved.

You can see how important such information is. That is why accounting is a good subject to learn in school.

Financial accounting includes the preparation of financial statements for people inside and outside the firm (for example investors). Financial accounting differs from managerial accounting in that the information and analyses it provides are also needed by people outside of the organization. This information goes to owners and prospective owners (new shareholders), creditors and lenders, employee unions, customers, government units, and the general public. The external users are interested in the organization's profits, its ability to pay its bills, and other financial information. Much of the information is contained in the annual report, a yearly statement of the financial condition and progress of the firm. Various quarterly (every three months) reports keep the users more current. These reports are required by law for the shareholders of all public companies (those whose shares trade on the stock exchange).

Financial accounting reports answer such questions as

- Has the company's income been satisfactory? Should we invest in this company?
- Should we lend money to this company? Will it be able to pay it back?
- Are our costs getting out of control?
- Is the company financially strong enough to stay in business to honour product warranties?
- Should we sell to this company? Will it be able to pay its bills?

We hope you are getting the idea that accounting is critical to business and to anyone who wants to understand business. You may want to know

financial accounting
The preparation of financial statements for people inside and outside of the firm (for example, investors).

private accountants
Employees who carry out managerial and financial accounting functions for their employers.

public accountants
Independent firms that provide accounting, auditing, and other professional services for clients on a fee basis.

<www.cica.ca>

The Canadian Institute of Chartered Accountants (CICA) is organized provincially, but admission to the profession requires passing a standard set of national tests. Prior to taking the tests, candidates must hold a university degree and successfully complete a period of indentureship and courses while working for a firm of chartered accountants. The CICA Web site provides more information about the organization and its program. The site also provides a number of other services to CAs and others who are interested in issues associated with the accounting profession.

One purpose of accounting is to report financial information to people outside the company. Investors (owners) and potential investors need all kinds of information, such as sales, profits, and debts. The annual report is an excellent vehicle for communicating financial information.

more about accounting firms, the people who prepare these reports, and how you can be sure that they know what they are doing. Accounting data can be compiled by accountants who work for the firm or by independent accounting firms.

⋯ PRIVATE AND PUBLIC ACCOUNTANTS ⋯

Private accountants are employees who carry out managerial and financial accounting functions for their employer. Many have degrees in accounting and are qualified professionals. Very small companies often cannot afford or do not require accounting employees, so they hire independent public accounting firms.

Public accountants are independent firms that provide accounting, auditing, and other professional services for different clients on a fee basis. These firms employ qualified accountants and auditors, apprentices, and other types of personnel. The most prestigious professional accounting degree in Canada is that of chartered accountant (CA). This degree is granted by a provincial Institute of Chartered Accountants (L'Ordre des comptables agréés in Quebec) that supervises the training, education, and practice of chartered accountants in that province. The final examinations are very rigorous to ensure that only qualified candidates will earn the degree of CA.

All provincial institutes together have organized the Canadian Institute of Chartered Accountants, which sets accounting and auditing standards across the country. The CICA also prepares the uniform final exams (UFE), which are given every September over a four-day period in many cities across Canada.

There are chartered accountants or their equivalents in all industrialized countries. All the national organizations coordinate their work and theories by membership in international accounting associations.

There are two other important associations of professional accountants in Canada. Certified General Accountants (CGA) and the Society of Manage-

1998 ANNUAL REPORT

The Scotiabank Group

Committed to customers, shareholders, employees and the communities where we work.

Scotiabank™

Scotiabank

Putting people first.

ment Accountants (CMA) also train and certify accountants. Large companies, governments, and nonprofit bodies employ many accountants; some do financial accounting, others managerial accounting. Many financial accountants have a CA degree, whereas managerial accountants generally opt for a CMA degree. Many CGAs are employed by governments; others are in public practice.

Public accounting firms have other important functions. Their most important activity for businesses and other organizations—and their largest income producer—is performing independent audits (examinations) of the books and financial statements of companies. An **independent audit** gives the public, governments, and shareholders (owners) an outside opinion of the fairness of financial statements. This audit is required by law for all public corporations in Canada.

Public accounting firms also provide consulting services to management, give tax advice to companies and individuals, and prepare their income tax returns. Large accounting and auditing firms operate internationally to serve large transnational companies.

As you can see, a variety of interesting challenges are part of the daily fare of professional accountants. Many successful executives in senior management positions started their careers as public accountants. Think carefully about a career for yourself in this field. Accounting is a continually expanding area with many specialties. Yes, it is difficult, but what worthwhile professional career is not?

ACCOUNTING AND BOOKKEEPING

Bookkeeping involves the recording of transactions. It is a rather mechanical process that does not demand much creativity. Bookkeeping is part of accounting, but accounting goes far beyond the mere recording of data. Accountants *classify* and *summarize* the data. They *analyze* and *interpret* the data and *report* them to management. They also *suggest strategies* for improving the financial condition and progress of the firm. Accountants are especially valuable for providing income tax advice and preparing tax returns.

Now that you understand what accountants do and whom they do it for, we can get down to the fundamental aspects of bookkeeping and accounting.

At the end of this chapter, you should have a better idea of what accountants do and how they do it. You should also be able to read and understand financial statements and discuss accounting intelligently with an accountant and others in the world of business. The goal is not to learn how to be an accountant, but to learn some terms and concepts. So let's start at the beginning.

Bookkeepers record all the transactions of a company, which usually include

- sales documents (sales slips, cash register receipts, and invoices)
- purchasing documents
- shipping documents
- payroll records
- bank documents (cheques, deposit slips)
- various expense documents.

<www.cma-ontario.org>
<www.cma-canada.org>

The Society of Management Accountants of Canada (CMA-Canada), which awards the designation of chartered management accountant (CMA) to those who satisfy the requirements for admission, is, like the CICA, an amalgam of provincial organizations with uniform national standards and examinations. CMA-Canada, too, requires a university degree. The CMA-Canada Web site includes information about the organization and its members, together with a useful summary of the distinctions among the three professional accounting bodies and their members.

<www.cga-canada.org/general>

Members of the Certified General Accountants' Association of Canada who have successfully completed its program of studies hold the designation of CGA. The CGA-Canada Web site provides a history of the organization, as well as useful information for its members, prospective students, and others interested in the profession's activities.

independent audit
Examination of a company's books by public accountants to give the public, governments, and shareholders an outside opinion of the fairness of financial statements.

bookkeeping
The recording of transactions.

Progress Check

- Can you explain the difference between managerial and financial accounting?
- Could you define accounting to a friend so that he or she would clearly understand what is involved?
- What is the difference between a private and a public accountant? What professional degrees do accountants have?
- What is the difference between accounting and bookkeeping?
- Can you name five original transaction documents that bookkeepers use to keep records?

Critical Thinking

In business hundreds of documents are received or created every day. So you can appreciate the valuable role a bookkeeper plays. Can you see why most businesses have to hire people to do this work? Would it be worth the owners' time to do all the paperwork? Can you understand why most bookeepers find it easier to do this work on a computer?

assets
Things of value owned by a business.

liquid
How quickly an asset can be turned into cash.

A bookkeeper gathers accounting documents such as sales slips, bills, cheques, payroll, and travel records, and records them in journals and ledgers. These are the first steps in the accounting system, which provides managers and interested parties with the information they need regarding the financial progress and condition of the firm.

THE ACCOUNTS OF ACCOUNTING

When bookkeepers record transactions they use six major categories of accounts to accumulate useful information. These accounts are a basic part of the accounting system. These categories are:

1. *Assets:* things of value owned by the firm (cash, inventory, buildings)
2. *Liabilities:* debts owed by the firm to others.
3. *Owners' (or Shareholders') Equity:* the amount owners (or shareholders) invest in the business *plus* accumulated profits *less* dividends or other withdrawals of profits
4. *Revenues:* sales of goods or services rendered.
5. *Cost of Goods Sold:* cost of goods sold and recorded as revenues.
6. *Expenses:* costs incurred in operating the business (rent, wages, insurance, taxes)

The next few sections will fill in the details concerning these categories of accounts.

••• ASSET ACCOUNTS •••

Assets are things of value owned by the business. Assets include the following: cash on hand or in the bank, accounts receivable (money owed by customers), inventory, investments, buildings, trucks and cars, patents, and copyrights.

Assets are listed according to how liquid they are. **Liquid** refers to how quickly an asset can be turned into cash. When inventory is sold and the customer pays, this asset becomes cash. Because this normally happens in a few months, inventory and accounts receivable are said to be liquid assets. Assets are divided into three main categories, listed in order of liquidity (see Figure 18.3 and 18.4).

1. **Current assets.** Items that are normally converted into cash within one year.
2. **Fixed assets.** Items that are acquired to produce services or products for a business. They are not bought to be sold. These assets include equipment, buildings, trucks, and the like.
3. **Other assets.** Items that are not included in the first two categories. This catchall group includes items such as copyrights and patents, which have no physical form.

You can see why one of the key words in accounting is *assets*. Take a few minutes to go through the list, visualizing the assets. Notice that they are things of value.

The valuation of assets can be a complex matter beyond the scope of this book. All assets are normally recorded at the cost of acquisition. When you look at a balance sheet (see Figure 18.6 later in this chapter), you see assets listed at their original cost. The real values are often different from their *book values*. In other words, the market value—what would be realized if the asset were sold—is normally different from the value as shown on the books.

The long, steady period of inflation we have witnessed since the 1960s has resulted in most book values being substantially below market value. For example, a building purchased in 1960 for $1 million could have a market value of perhaps 30 times that amount today. Nevertheless, it remains on the books at original cost. This asset, and therefore total assets, are grossly understated.

Obviously, this is not a satisfactory state of affairs. The accounting profession and other interested parties have been struggling with alternatives for many years. It's a problem awaiting a creative solution that will not cause more problems than it solves. Perhaps one of you will take up the challenge and come up with the answer.

current assets
Cash and assets that are normally converted into cash within one year.

fixed assets
Items that are acquired to produce services or products for a business. They are not bought to be sold.

other assets
Assets that are not current or fixed. This catchall group includes items such as copyrights and patents, which have no physical form.

Companies invest large amounts in fixed assets, such as trucks and equipment, that are used to produce and distribute goods and to provide services to customers. Accounting provides information about the costs of obtaining, maintaining, and using these assets.

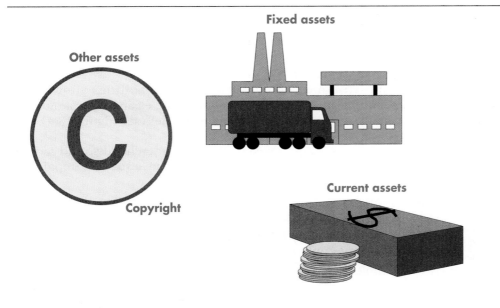

Other assets

Copyright

Fixed assets

Current assets

FIGURE **18.3**
• • • •
CLASSIFICATIONS OF ASSETS

Assets are classified by what normally happens to them. Cash and those assets that usually turn into cash (inventory and accounts receivable) are considered to be liquid. They are called *current assets*. Those assets that are bought to run the business (e.g., equipment, trucks) are not bought to be sold, so they are called *fixed assets*. Patents and copyrights are listed in a third class called *other assets*.

Spotlight on Small Business

Keep Your Banker Happy with a Steady Flow of Information

As you learned in Chapter 7, positive or negative relations with your banker can often be predictors of success or failure for a small business. Entrepreneurs learn fast that keeping their banker happy can pay off, particularly if the company finds itself in a financial crunch. How do you keep your bank happy? That question occupies a good deal of the entrepreneur's time. One answer is accounting information. Few entrepreneurs realize that financial ratios (see Appendix D after Chapter 18) are important numbers to bankers and often form the basis of the decisions bankers make concerning financing requests.

Financial ratios not only can help the entrepreneur manage his or her business more efficiently, but they also can make your banker a more reliable business partner. Bankers see ratios as useful measurements for comparing a company's financial position to that of competing companies. Also, bankers see ratios as an effective guide for evaluating the firm's performance compared to industry standards or trends that are occurring in the market. What are some of the more important ratios at which the banker looks closely?

Bankers believe that a firm's ability to repay bank loans and make timely interest payments is important for evaluating financial requests. Liquidity ratios such as the current ratio (current assets divided by current liabilities) are important in determining the firm's short-term financial ▲ strength. Is it best for a firm to always maintain a high current ratio? Not necessarily! If a company has too high a current ratio, bankers may feel it is making poor use of resources. If your current ratio is falling, you must be prepared to explain why this is happening. Staying on top of the situation may mean receiving continued financial support from your bank. Keeping track of inventory and the debt position of the firm will also impress your banker. Low turnover of inventory could suggest to bankers that trouble is ahead. Excess inventory can boost interest rates and possibly lower profits. Ratios such as inventory turnover can offer valuable insights into how to prevent these problems and keep the bank on your side. Debt is a potential source of worry for both the business person and the bank. Therefore, debt to equity and total debt to total assets are ratios of major concern.

What should small-business managers do to build a working relationship with their bankers? Working closely with their accountant, they should prepare and regularly update a report binder that contains key financial ratios as well as cash-flow forecasts and projections. The entrepreneurs should discuss with the banker what ratios are most relevant to their businesses and then keep track of them on a regular basis. With such diligence, you not only build a good working relationship with your banker, but you also build a partnership with an informed partner.

••• LIABILITIES ACCOUNTS •••

liabilities
Amounts owed by the organization to others.

Another important term in accounting is *liabilities*. **Liabilities** are what the business *owes* to others. As with assets, you will more easily understand what liabilities are when you review a list of some examples (see Figure 18.4):

- *Accounts payable.* Money owed to others for merchandise and services purchased on credit but not yet paid. If you have such an unpaid bill, you have an account payable.
- *Accrued expenses payable.* Expenses the firm owes but that have not been billed by the end of the month, when financial statements are prepared (e.g., utilities bills, credit card statements).
- *Bonds payable.* Long-term loans to the business.
- *Notes payable.* Usually shorter-term loans from banks.
- *Taxes payable.* Sales taxes and GST collected, and income tax payable.

Accounting for New Kinds of Assets and Liabilities

Technology is not the only thing that is changing today. A host of new issues in accounting are causing the profession some giant headaches. One area of problems relates to environmental issues.

There are four aspects to this area. One is the production process that harms the environment. Smoke emission containing harmful gases and liquid emission into rivers and lakes into the ground are two common problems. Then there are solid wastes that are accumulated or dumped into rivers and lakes. Third, there is the problem of acquiring a site that a previous user or owner has polluted, unbeknown to the new owner. Finally, there is the issue of accidents—nuclear, oil spills, PCB and tire dump fires, and many others. All of these have occurred in Canada and elsewhere in the world.

In all of these cases, liability for past damage or cost of future cleanup arises. The difficulty lies in assessing the dollar amount and determining who is liable. The issue is further complicated by the fact that different environmental laws came into force at different times in different provinces and countries. It is a nightmare scenario from the accounting point of view, because the amounts involved can be extremely large.

A different topic relates to the fact that in today's high-tech world, knowledge is a major asset. Indeed, some people argue that it may be more important than all the physical assets of companies. How does a company evaluate the education, skills, and experience of its workforce? These assets are called *off-balance sheet* assets because they do not show up there and yet they may be the crucial assets for many important companies. In Canada we have hundreds of software companies whose real assets are the brains of their owners and employees.

These problems are obviously not easy to solve, but they must be dealt with if financial statements are to reflect reality. These challenges and many more await the next generation of accountants and auditors. They make this profession a lot more interesting than the image that is commonly portrayed.

Sources: Nelson Luscombe, "A Learning Experience," *CA Magazine*, February 1993, p. 3: "Sustainable Decision Making," ibid., p. 19; Robert Walker, "In Search of Relevance," ibid., p. 26; Michael Stanleigh, "Accounting for Quality," *CA Magazine*, October 1992, p. 40; interviews with three CAs, May 1999.

All liabilities that are due within one year from the balance sheet date are classified as *current liabilities*. Those amounts due later are called *long-term liabilities*. You can see these categories later in Figure 18.6.

••• OWNERS' EQUITY ACCOUNTS •••

The **owners' equity** in a company consists of all that the owners have invested in the company *plus* all the profits that have accumulated since the business commenced but that have not yet been paid out to them. This figure *always* equals the book value of the assets minus the liabilities of the company, as you will see later on. Why this is so will be discussed shortly.

owners' equity
Owners' investments in the company plus all net accumulated profits.

In a partnership, owners' equity is called *partners' equity* or *capital*. In a sole proprietorship, it is called owner's or *proprietor's equity* or capital. In a corporation, it is called *shareholders' equity* and is shown in two separate accounts. The amount the owners (shareholders) invest is shown in one account, called *common stock;* the accumulated profit that remains after dividends have been paid to shareholders is shown in an account called *retained earnings.* You can see this later in Figure 18.6.

••• REVENUE ACCOUNTS •••

Revenue accounts are where income from all sources is recorded. That includes sales, rentals, commissions, royalties, and other sources of income. These amounts are shown in the income statement. (A sample income statement is shown later in Figure 18.5. See also Figure 18.4.)

••• COST OF GOODS SOLD ACCOUNTS •••

Cost of goods sold accounts are used when a company sells products. The account shows all the costs of selling products that were recorded in the sales (revenues) account. These costs include transportation, storage, packaging and purchases of goods for resale. These amounts appear on the income statement. The cost of goods sold will be discussed further in the section on financial statements.

••• EXPENSE ACCOUNTS •••

Expense accounts are where the expenses of running a business are recorded. These are the costs incurred in operating the business such as rent, insurance, salaries, utilities, and advertising. They are also shown on the income statement. Figure 18.4 lists many of the usual expense accounts.

••• DOUBLE-ENTRY ACCOUNTING SYSTEM •••

The method of recording transactions that is practised throughout the world is called the *double-entry* accounting system. As the name implies, two entries are made for each transaction: a debit and a credit. For example, when a non-cash sale is made on credit for $100, the accounts receivable account is debited for $100 and the sales account is credited with $100. When the customer pays for this sale, the cash account is debited and the accounts receivable account is credited.

This ingenious method, reputed to have been invented in Northern Italy about 600 years ago, has an important feature. When you make a monthly summary, listing all balances in the accounts (a *trial balance*), the sum of all the debits must equal the sum of all the credits. If it doesn't, you know you have made some errors. You must find them and redo your trial balance to see if the debits now equal the credits. Computers eliminate the need for a

```
┌     FIGURE 18.4     ┐
       ••••
   SAMPLE OF SPECIFIC
    ACCOUNT TITLES
```
Each account accumulates data relating to a specific activity.

For the Balance Sheet			For the Income Statement		
Assets	**Liabilities**	**Owner's Equity**	**Revenues**	**Expenses and Costs**	
Cash	Accounts payable	Capital stock	Sales	Wages	Interest
Accounts receivable	Notes payable	Retained earnings (accumulated profits not paid out)	Rentals	Rent	Donations
Inventory	Bonds payable		Commissions	Repairs	Licences
Investments	Taxes payable		Royalties	Travel	Professional fees
Equipment	Accrued expenses payable			Insurance	Supplies
Land				Utilities	Advertising
Buildings				Entertainment	Taxes
Motor vehicles				Storage	Purchases
Goodwill					

trial balance because they do not make the kind of errors that humans can and do make.

- Name the six classes of accounts that are used in accounting, and give two examples of items that go into those accounts.
- Can you list various assets by degree of liquidity?
- What goes into the category called liabilities?
- What is the formula for owners' equity?

···· ▬▬▬ ····

FINANCIAL STATEMENTS

The accounting process consists of two major functions: (1) recording data from transactions and (2) preparing financial statements from that data. **Financial statements** report the operations and condition of a firm. The two most important financial statements are the income statement and the balance sheet.

1. The **income statement** shows revenues, expenses, and profit or loss resulting from operations *during* a specific period of time.
2. The **balance sheet**, which consists of assets, liabilities, and owners' equity, shows the financial position of a firm at the *end* of that period.

Think of a balance sheet as a snapshot or freeze-frame of a company *at* a certain point in time. The income statement shows the company in action and the results of activities for a period *ending* on the same date as the balance sheet.

Financial statements are an important indication of the health of a firm. That is why they are of interest to the managers, owners (shareholders), banks, suppliers, and future investors. (There is another important financial statement, *statement of changes in financial position,* but it is more complex and beyond the scope of this introductory text.)

To understand accounting, you must be able to read and understand both income statements and balance sheets as well as understand cash flow. In the following sections, we shall explore financial statements and cash flow. Once you learn the concepts, you will know more about accounting than many small-business managers.

financial statements
Report the operations and position (condition) of a firm; they include the income statement and the balance sheet.

income statement
Reports revenues, expenses, and profit or loss during a specific period of time.

balance sheet
Reports the financial position of a firm at the end of a specific period of time. Balance sheets consist of assets, liabilities, and owners' equity.

··· THE INCOME STATEMENT ···

The financial statement that shows the bottom line, that is, profit after expenses and taxes, is the *income statement* or *profit and loss statement* (see Figure 18.5). The income statement summarizes all the resources that come into the firm from operating activities (called *revenue*), resources that are used up (*cost of goods sold* and *expenses*), and what resources are left after all costs and expenses are incurred (*net income* or *net loss*). The income statement reports the results of operations over a period of time. The income statement may be summarized by the following formulas:

Beginning inventory + Purchases – Ending inventory = Cost of goods sold

Revenue – Cost of goods sold = Gross margin (Profit)

Gross margin – Operating expenses = Net income before taxes

Net income before taxes – Income taxes = Net income

Gross margin is calculated by subtracting the cost of goods sold from net sales (revenue). The revenue from the sale of products can be quite high. But so can the cost of all the matierials needed to make the products. You will know how much gross profit (margin) you make by subtracting the cost of goods sold from the sales revenue. When you subtract other expenses, you get the net profit (income) from operations.

REVENUES   For a company selling products, sometimes revenues come only from sales of its products. In that case revenues and sales are equal and refer to the same thing. However, in many cases, there are additional sources of revenue such as rent, interest, fees, and royalties. In those instances total revenue is greater than sales and the two terms are *not* synonymous. It is also important not to confuse *revenue* with *income*. In accounting terminology *income* or *net income* refers to what's left after costs and expenses are deducted from revenue. Net income is sometimes called the *bottom line* because it is the last line at the bottom of an income statement (see Figure 18.5).

Be careful not to confuse the terms *revenue* and *income*. Revenues are at the top of the income statement and income is at the bottom; net income is revenue *minus* costs and expenses.

COST OF GOODS SOLD   To calculate how much money a business earned by selling merchandise, subtract how much it cost to buy that merchandise. That cost includes the purchase price plus any freight charges paid to bring in the goods plus the costs associated with storing the goods. In other words, all the costs of buying and keeping merchandise for sale, including packaging, are included in the **cost of goods sold**. Of course you must take into account how much stock or inventory you had at the beginning and end of the period.

When you subtract the cost of goods sold from net sales, you get what is called gross margin or *gross profit*. **Gross margin**, then, is how much the firm earned by buying and selling merchandise before the expenses of operations are deducted.

In a service firm, there may be no cost of goods sold because the firm is not buying and selling goods; therefore, net sales equals gross margin. Whether you're selling goods or services, the gross margin or gross profit figure doesn't tell you enough. What you are really interested in is net profit or net income. To get that, you must subtract expenses.

cost of goods sold
A particular type of expense measured by the total cost of merchandise sold, including costs associated with the acquisition, storage, transportation, and packaging of goods.

gross margin (profit)
Net sales minus cost of goods sold before expenses are deducted.

operating expenses
Various expenses of a business incurred in the course of earning revenue.

OPERATING EXPENSES   Every business incurs expenses in the course of its operations. **Operating expenses** are the various expenses a business has,

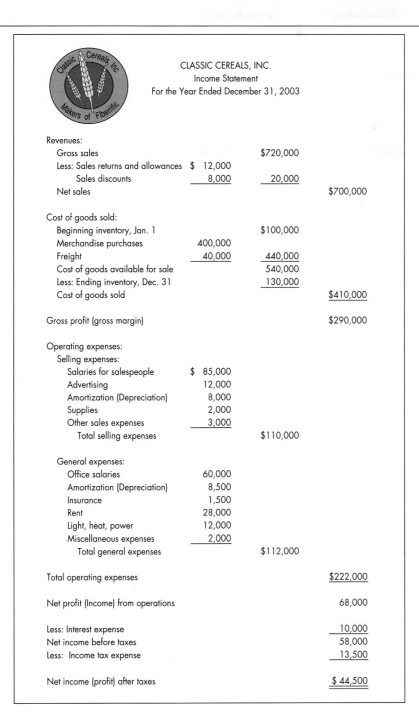

CLASSIC CEREALS, INC.
Income Statement
For the Year Ended December 31, 2003

Revenues:			
Gross sales		$720,000	
Less: Sales returns and allowances	$ 12,000		
Sales discounts	8,000	20,000	
Net sales			$700,000
Cost of goods sold:			
Beginning inventory, Jan. 1		$100,000	
Merchandise purchases	400,000		
Freight	40,000	440,000	
Cost of goods available for sale		540,000	
Less: Ending inventory, Dec. 31		130,000	
Cost of goods sold			$410,000
Gross profit (gross margin)			$290,000
Operating expenses:			
Selling expenses:			
Salaries for salespeople	$ 85,000		
Advertising	12,000		
Amortization (Depreciation)	8,000		
Supplies	2,000		
Other sales expenses	3,000		
Total selling expenses		$110,000	
General expenses:			
Office salaries	60,000		
Amortization (Depreciation)	8,500		
Insurance	1,500		
Rent	28,000		
Light, heat, power	12,000		
Miscellaneous expenses	2,000		
Total general expenses		$112,000	
Total operating expenses			$222,000
Net profit (Income) from operations			68,000
Less: Interest expense			10,000
Net income before taxes			58,000
Less: Income tax expense			13,500
Net income (profit) after taxes			$ 44,500

FIGURE **18.5**
• • • •
**CLASSIC CEREALS
INCOME STATEMENT**
Note that revenues are at the top of the income statement and income is at the bottom. A simple formula for the income statement is revenue minus costs and expenses equals income.

such as taxes, utilities, communication, travel, salaries, and so on, incurred in the course of earning its revenue. After cost of goods sold and operating expenses are deducted from revenue, we arrive at net profit or net income. Pause here and review the income statement in Figure 18.5 until you feel you understand it.

Remember that the *bottom line*, the **net income** for a particular year, is the revenue minus the costs and expenses of that year. The net income is then added to the accumulated profits from previous years (recorded in an account called *retained earnings*). When the company decides it wants to pay out some

net income
Revenue minus costs and expenses.

retained earnings
Accumulated profits less dividends to shareholders.

of the retained earnings to shareholders in the form of dividends, this amount is deducted from the retained earnings account. So we see that **retained earnings** consists of accumulated profits less dividends to shareholders.

••• THE BALANCE SHEET •••

A balance sheet is the financial statement that reports the financial position of a firm at a *specific date*. The balance sheet is composed of assets, liabilities, and owners' equity. Note that the income statement reports on changes *over a period* and the balance sheet reports conditions *at the end of that period*.

The term *balance sheet* implies that the statement shows a balance, an equality between two figures. That is, the balance sheet shows a balance: assets equal liabilities plus owners' equity. If you look at Figure 18.6, you will see this.

fundamental
accounting equation
Assets = liabilities + owners' equity; it is the basis for the balance sheet.

THE FUNDAMENTAL ACCOUNTING EQUATION   Suppose a company doesn't owe anybody any money. That is, it has no liabilities. Then the assets it has (cash and so forth) are equal to what it owns (equity). The **fundamental accounting** equation is rather obvious. If a firm has no debts, then

Assets = Owners' equity

This means that the owners of a firm own everything. If a firm has debts, the owners own everything except the amount due others, or

Assets – Liabilities = Owners' equity

Another way of stating this is:

Assets = Liabilities + Owners' equity

If you look at the balance sheet in Figure 18.6, you will note that total assets (in the middle of the page) equal the combined total of liabilities and shareholders' equity, in this case $801,000. This basic accounting equation derives from the double-entry accounting system mentioned earlier. You will recall that because transactions are entered in this way, the numbers on both sides—debits and credits—have to be in balance.

Let us analyze this equation in a little more depth. Where does a firm get its assets? If you think about it for a moment, you will see that there are only three sources:

1. The money the owners invested	→	shares issued to shareholders (common stock)
	plus	plus
2. Profits the company generates	→	retained earnings
		= shareholders' equity
	plus	plus
3. Creditors who have not been paid	→	liabilities
= Total sources of assets	→	= Total assets

The balance sheet shows that assets are divided into three categories: (1) current assets such as cash or accounts receivable, (2) fixed assets, and (3) other assets, such as patents and copyrights.

FIGURE **18.6**
• • • •
**CLASSIC CEREALS
BALANCE SHEET**

Assets = Liabilities + Shareholders Equity. In this case, each side totals $801,000.

CLASSIC CEREALS, INC.
Balance Sheet
Dec. 31, 2003

Assets

Current assets		
Cash	$115,000	
Accounts receivable	200,000	
Notes receivable	50,000	
Inventory	130,000	
Total current assets		$495,000
Fixed assets		
Land	$ 40,000	
Buildings and improvements	200,000	
Equipment and vehicles	120,000	
Furniture and fixtures	26,000	
Less: Accumulated depreciation	(180,000)	
Total fixed assets		$206,000
Other assets		
Goodwill	$ 20,000	
Patents and copyrights	80,000	
Total other assets		$100,000
Total assets		**$801,000**

Liabilities and Shareholders' Equity

Current liabilities		
Accounts payable	$ 40,000	
Notes payable	8,000	
Accrued taxes	150,000	
Accrued salaries	15,000	
Employees' Pension fund	75,000	
Total current liabilities		$288,000
Long-term liabilities		
Notes payable	$ 30,000	
Bonds	190,000	
Total long-term liabilities		$220,000
Total liabilities		$508,000
Shareholders' equity		
Common stock *	$ 100,000	
Retained earnings **	193,000	
Total shareholders' equity		$293,000
Total liabilities and shareholders' equity		**$801,000**

* Invested by owners/shareholders
** Accumulated profits after paying dividends

Liabilities are divided into two categories: (1) current liabilities such as accounts payable and (2) long-term liabilities such as bonds. Shareholders' equity consists of common stock (investment in the company) and retained earnings (earnings not distributed to owners). For businesses that are not corporations, these terms are different. The retained earnings account is the link

Reaching Beyond Our Borders

<www.ifac.org>

Accounting Problems When Going International

As you have made your way through this book, you have seen many examples of Canadian companies that have developed important ties beyond our borders. As part of the globalization of business, Canadian companies look to joint ventures and alliances with other companies in the Pacific Rim, Europe, Mexico, and elsewhere. For example, McDonald's Canada Ltd. formed a joint venture with a Russian agency to operate the largest McDonald's unit in the world, in Moscow. Sometimes Canadian businesses buy out other companies. Bombardier bought the national Mexican railway car construction company in 1992. Smaller companies are also getting involved in this process.

One problem that often arises is how to determine the real value of the foreign company. The starting point

is an examination of its financial statements. Have they been prepared on the basis of the same generally accepted accounting principles (GAAP) that are applied in Canada and the United States? (The two are very similar.) Often there are major differences that make it difficult to determine the real value of the company. Obviously, this is very important, especially if you are trying to establish how much you should offer to buy the company or you want to be sure that the assets being contributed to a joint venture have the value your partner claims.

Accounting bodies all over the world have been working for many years toward establishing a common set of GAAP through organizations like the International Federation of Accountants. It is a major task that is slowly being achieved.

between the income statement and the balance sheet. The net income (profit) shown at the bottom of the income statement is transferred to the retained earning account each year.

If you go back to the beginning of this chapter and reread the sections on the accounts of accounting (asset accounts, liabilities accounts, and so on),

Home Depot maintains an enormous inventory. That's why it depends heavily on financial ratios to make certain it is effectively managing its resources compared to the competition.

you will see that the asset, liabilities, and owners' equity accounts are all part of the preparation of the balance sheet. Review the lists of items in these accounts to learn more about what is behind the figures on the balance sheet.

··· RATIO ANALYSIS ···

Now that we have the financial statements, how do we interpret these results? One of the most common and useful methods of analyzing financial statements is called **ratio analysis**. This is done by comparing the current year's results with those of

- the previous year
- the budget or plan for the year
- competing firms

ratio analysis
A way to analyze financial statements by comparing results with the previous year's, the budget, and competing firms' results.

Many ratios are used to better understand a company's operations and position. Some of the important ones are reviewed in Appendix D, which follows this chapter.

···· ▬▬▬ ····

ACCOUNTING COMPLEXITY

If accounting were nothing more than the repetitive function of gathering and recording transactions and preparing financial statements, the major functions could be assigned to computers. In fact, most firms have done just that. The truth is that there is much more involved.

Take depreciation, for example. **Amortization (depreciation)** is based on the fact that assets such as machinery have a certain life span. Therefore, part of the cost of the machinery is calculated as an expense each year over its useful life. Subject to certain technical rules that are beyond the scope of this chapter, a firm may use one of several techniques for calculating depreciation. However, once a method is chosen, it is difficult to change. Each technique results in a different bottom line, a different net income. Net incomes can change dramatically based on the specific accounting procedure that is used. Accountants can recommend ways of handling this problem as well as other issues such as insurance, valuing inventory and investments, and other accounts that will also affect the bottom line.

amortization (depreciation)
Since assets such as machinery lose value over time, part of their cost is calculated as an expense each year over their useful life.

Accountants have to make many judgments and decisions regarding the recording of certain types of transactions. Say, for example, that when you started your business your sister gave you a computer and printer as a gift to help you on your way. You know that all assets are supposed to be recorded at cost, but how do you record something that has no cost because it was a gift? Or suppose you bought two machines for your factory; one proved useless and ended up quietly gathering dust in a corner. You normally amortize the cost of a machine (apportioned over its useful life) by charging a portion annually as an expense (depreciation). What do you do about the unused machine that contributes nothing to the annual profit but still has a cost?

\<handbook.cica.ca\>

The CICA Handbook is the primary authority on accounting principles and practices in Canada. The Handbook is on the Internet, but is available only to members and others who have arranged for access. In addition to the Handbook itself, the Web site also provides related information and articles on current issues regarding the application of these principles.

··· GENERALLY ACCEPTED ACCOUNTING PRINCIPLES ···

These and many more complicated transactions require certain guidelines that help accountants to make proper and consistent decisions. These guidelines are called *generally accepted accounting principles (GAAP)*. They are published in the handbook of the Canadian Institute of Chartered Accountants, along with many other important guidelines. This handbook is the bible of the accounting profession. Bankers, financial analysts, and others also refer to it. From time to time (and after much discussion) it is updated.

There are about a dozen important accounting principles. Every audited set of financial statements includes a series of notes explaining how these principles have been applied, as well as a report by the auditors that GAAP have been used. This makes it possible for financial statements to be compared from one year to the next as well as from one company to another. Accountants all over the world are working to harmonize GAAP (see the box Reaching Beyond our Borders).

cash flow
The difference between cash receipts and cash disbursements.

Critical Thinking

Take a look at the table of contents in this book and think about how many of the chapters involve calculation, measurement, recording, and analysis of data. Do you think there are any chapters in which the material discussed does not involve accounting? Does this make accounting a critical skill for effective business operations? How about nonprofit organizations? Is accounting of equal importance in hospitals, school systems, universities, museums, and government?

If you ask small businesses for a wish list of items that would make their lives easier, one request that's sure to be close to the top is a simple way to handle the firm's financial information. Peachtree software is one of several companies that offer software packages that address the specific accounting needs of small businesses.

•••• ▬▬▬ ••••

CASH-FLOW PROBLEMS

Cash flow is the difference between cash receipts and cash disbursements. One of the greatest problems confronting business is ensuring that there will always be enough cash to meet payments as they fall due. This is a constant challenge for businesses of all sizes. Sometimes very large companies are forced to sell off one or more of their good subsidiaries to raise cash because of recession or other unexpected developments. This is the problem that caused huge Olympia & York Developments to go bankrupt in 1992. Sometimes, as in the case of Campeau Corp. in the early 1990s, a company is practically destroyed by cash-flow problems.

The problem is most severe with small companies because they often have very few resources to fall back on. We can all understand a company having a cash shortage when it is suffering loses, but what about companies that are doing well? Why should they run short of cash?

There are several reasons profitable companies have this problem. If they are growing very rapidly, their profits may not be sufficient to finance the greater inventories and accounts receivable they are forced to carry because of increased sales. Or they may be buying a lot of new equipment to increase production to keep up with the increased demand. Growing slowly gives companies the chance to avoid this problem.

The two companies mentioned above expanded very rapidly, using extensive borrowed capital, and then ran into trouble. When a series of unexpected events hit them, they did not have enough cash flow to meet their heavy debt repayments, leading to a collapse of their empires.

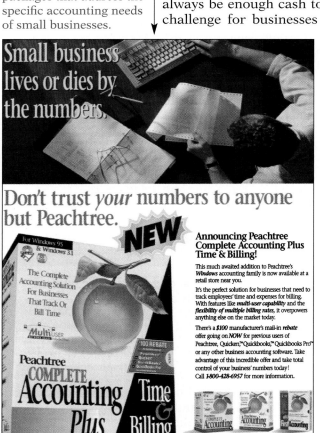

Small business lives or dies by the numbers.

Don't trust *your* numbers to anyone but Peachtree.

NEW

For Windows 95 & Windows 3.1

The Complete Accounting Solution For Businesses That Track Or Bill Time

MultiUser

Peachtree
COMPLETE
Accounting
Plus

Time & Billing

Announcing Peachtree Complete Accounting Plus Time & Billing!

This much awaited addition to Peachtree's *Windows* accounting family is now available at a retail store near you.

It's the perfect solution for businesses that need to track employees' time and expenses for billing. With features like *multi-user capability* and the *flexibility of multiple billing rates*, it overpowers anything else on the market today.

There's a *$100* manufacturer's mail-in *rebate* offer going on *NOW* for previous users of Peachtree, Quicken,™ Quickbooks,™ Quickbooks Pro™ or any other business accounting software. Take advantage of this incredible offer and take total control of your business' numbers today! Call *1-800-428-6957* for more information.

©1997 Peachtree Software, Inc. All rights reserved. Peachtree, Peachtree Complete and the peach device are registered trademarks and Peachtree Complete Plus is a trademark of Peachtree Software, Inc. All other brands are trademarks of their respective companies.

Sometimes a company that is not well managed will tie up too much cash in inventory or let customers delay payments too long. This obviously will put pressure on the cash balance. If you hire an accounting firm before you start a business, it will prepare (with your help) a cash-flow forecast. This is a schedule for one year that shows clearly what the cash situation will be every month, based on your estimate of monthly sales, expenses, terms of credit, and other data. The cash flow can be prepared in three versions: optimistic, pessimistic, and most likely. This equips you to anticipate any scenario, so you can act in accordance with whichever one unfolds and avoid crises. Cash flow will be discussed in more detail in the next chapter.

••• SHARON AND BRIAN ROWAN'S SURPRISE •••

The Rowans (remember them from the beginning of the chapter?) had a different problem. They had no cash-flow problems, so they were surprised when their accountants told them they were incurring losses. How could they feel no cash pressure, a rare occurence in a new business, while they were losing money? There are several possibilities. Since they started with their large inheritance they may simply have been eating into their original investment. Their bank balance was declining and eventually they would have run into trouble.

Another possibility is that as a retail store they did not extend any credit, so they were getting paid cash for their sales. At the same time they were getting credit from their suppliers. That gave them a cushion of a month or two of cash income before they had to start paying creditors. This would have caught up with them in a short while.

Finally, they may have stocked up heavily at the start and were now depleting their inventory. This was providing them the cash to pay their bills. Again, they soon would have had to start building up stock and that would have created additional cash pressures.

So we see how business people may be deceived by either cash shortages or surpluses into thinking that their businesses are doing well or not doing well. A proper accounting system and an understanding of the information it yields are essential for a reliable assessment of how a business is performing.

The Canadian Institute of Chartered Accountants represents a membership of more than 65,000 professional accountants and 8500 students. The CICA conducts research into current business issues and sets accounting and auditing standards for business, nonprofit organizations, and governments.

•••• ▬▬ ••••

SOME CONCERNS OF THE ACCOUNTING PROFESSION

The Spotlight on Big Business box and the Profile highlight a growing concern of accountants about some difficult issues. The new knowledge-based industries and environmental problems have created whole new sets of issues that must be considered if financial statements are to truly reflect the financial position of companies. The troubling questions relate to how to evaluate certain significant intangible (nonphysical) assets and some potentially huge liabilities.

As the Spotlight notes, how can brainpower, skills, and abilities be valued in dollars? Yet these

assets are becoming increasingly important in today's high-tech world. Similarly, the problem with buying or selling polluted or toxic materials, land, buildings, or other assets, or hazards arising from production processes is that potential buyers, consumers, affected persons, or governments may launch major damage suits. How are such potential liabilities to be evaluated?

A balance sheet is supposed to show all the assets and liabilities of a company at a given date. If important assets and liabilities are omitted, does the balance sheet reflect reality? These are the current concerns of the accounting profession.

···· ▬▬▬ ····

CAREERS IN ACCOUNTING

Would accounting be a good career for you? Certain aptitudes are important for anyone who wants to be an accountant:

- an appreciation of accuracy
- a feel for figures
- an analytical mind
- an ability to handle masses of detail without losing perspective
- a sense of order

If you have not done well in math in school and don't particularly enjoy working with figures, you probably would not enjoy accounting. A good accountant must also be able to spot inaccuracies and work creatively with numbers, because he or she often works with figures prepared by others. If that sounds interesting to you, you might find accounting a rewarding career.

You should also be aware that obtaining an accounting degree is often the first step to wider opportunities in business consulting or in senior management positions. Many accountants, after extensive experience in the business world, have gone on to lead companies as chief executive officers (CEO). To give one well-known example, the former CEO of Bombardier, Laurent

Ethical Dilemma

REVIEW

Do you recall the ethical question at the start of the chapter that involved "cooking" the books? Our executives agree on the answer to this one. Bédard is very clear in his response. "You must respect the law. As chief financial officer you have an obligation to disclose all important information in the financial statements. This information appears to be material and should be disclosed."

Reilley is equally clear. "I would take no part in fudging the books. Rather, the company should present the situation openly to the bank, complete with sound business and restructuring plans for improving the situation."

You should be aware that there are two serious risks involved if you go along with the suggestion made by your boss: losing your professional licence and being found guilty of fraud. You don't want to threaten your career and perhaps your whole life. Difficult as the situation may be, you really have no choice. If your boss does not agree with the suggestions of our two executives, you will have to refuse your employer's request and find a new job.

Beaudoin, is a highly regarded chartered accountant (CA) who successfully led his company for many years. The Canadian author of this book, who is a CA, has had an interesting career in different fields that have taken him to many countries around the world.

Progress Check

- What four formulas make up the income statement? What is the difference between revenue and income on that statement?
- What is the fundamental accounting equation used to make up the balance sheet? What is balanced on the balance sheet?
- What is the connection or link between the income statement and the balance sheet?
- What is cash flow? How can a small business protect itself against cash-flow problems before they occur?

SUMMARY
· · · · · ·

1. Accounting is the recording, classifying, summarizing, and interpreting of financial transactions that affect the organization. The methods used to record and summarize accounting data into reports are called an accounting system.

   - ***How does managerial accounting differ from financial accounting?*** Managerial accounting provides information and analyses to managers within the firm to assist them in decision making. Financial accounting provides information and analyses to managers and to external users of data such as creditors and lenders.

   - ***What is the difference between a private and public accountant?*** Public accountants are independent firms that provide services for a fee to a variety of companies; private accountants are employees of a company. Only public accountants perform independent audits.

1. Define accounting and explain the differences between (a) managerial accounting and financial accounting and (b) private and public accountants.

2. Many people confuse bookkeeping and accounting.
   - ***What is the difference between bookkeeping and accounting?*** Bookkeeping is part of accounting, but only the mechanical part of recording data. Accounting also includes classifying, summarizing, interpreting, and reporting data to management.

2. Compare accounting and bookkeeping.

3. There are six major classes of accounts in accounting: assets, liabilities, owners' equity, revenues, cost of goods sold, and expenses.
   - ***What are assets?*** Assets are economic resources owned by the firm, such as buildings and machinery. Current assets are converted to cash within a year; fixed assets are relatively permanent and are used to operate the business. Liquidity refers to how fast an asset normally becomes cash. Current assets are thus more liquid than fixed assets.

   - ***What are liabilities?*** Liabilities are debts owed by the organization to others (for example, creditors, bond holders).

   - ***What is owners' equity?*** It is the sum of owners' investments plus profits to date not yet paid out to owners.

   - ***What are revenues?*** Revenues are what are received from the sale of goods or services rendered.

3. Identify and describe the major accounts used to prepare financial statements.

> • *What are cost of goods sold?*
> They are a particular type of expense measured by the total cost of merchandise sold.

> • *What are expenses?*
> Expenses are incurred in operating the business to earn the revenues. They include salaries, rent, and utilities.

4. Understand simple income statements and balance sheets, and explain their functions.

4. The primary financial statements provided by accountants are income statements and balance sheets.
   > • *What is an income statement?*
   > An income statement reports revenues, costs, and expenses for a specific period of time. The basic formula is revenue minus costs and expenses equals income. (Note that income and profit mean the same thing.)

   > • *What is a balance sheet?*
   > A balance sheet reports the financial position of a firm at a specific date. The fundamental accounting equation used to prepare the balance sheet is assets = liabilities + owners' equity.

5. Describe the role of computers in accounting.

5. Most business people realize the value of using computers to help them with their accounting activities.
   > • *How can computers help accountants?*
   > Computers can easily record and analyze data and quickly provide financial reports. Software is available that can continual analyze and test accounting systems to be sure they are functioning correctly. This software makes regular reporting very easy. Computers can help in decision making by providing appropriate information, but they cannot make good financial decisions independently. Management creativity is still a human trait.

6. Explain the concept of cash flow.

6. Cash flow is the difference between cash in and cash out.
   > • *Why is cash flow so important?*
   > Having enough cash at all times to be able to pay bills, salaries, loans, and the like is the first requirement for a business if it is to stay alive. Making a profit is not enough. Many small businesses do not estimate cash flow in advance, and it is one of the main reasons why they fail.

7. Explain how a business can be making profits and still be short of cash.

7. Profits and cash are not the same thing.
   > • *What happens to profits?*
   > Cash and profits are not the same thing (except for street vendors who have no inventory and no expenses and sell for cash only). Usually when companies sell goods, profits get tied up in additional inventory, accounts receivable, or equipment and are not available to pay bills. This usually happens when companies are growing rapidly. Slow, steady growth allows profits to show up in stronger cash positions.

8. Understand the new concerns of accounting.

8. Important assets and liabilities are not being accounted for in financial statements.
   > • *What are these assets and liabilities, and why are they not stated on balance sheets?*
   > Major assets are the skills and education of the employees. Another one is the combined technological knowledge of a company. All these intangible assets may be more important than a company's tangible assets. Similarly, liability for environmental damage has emerged as a major potential liability for many companies. The problem is that there is no recognized method for evaluating these assets and liabilities.

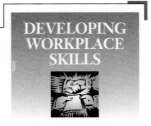

DEVELOPING WORKPLACE SKILLS

1. Why are college and university students, even business majors, so hesitant to take accounting courses? Would a different approach by colleges and universities be more successful? What should that be?

2. Take a sheet of paper. On every fourth line, write one of the following headings: assets, liabilities, owners' equity, expenses, and revenues. Then list as many items as you can under each heading. When you are finished, look up the lists in the text and add to your own. Keep the lists for your notes. As you complete the lists, create a mental picture of each account so that you can understand the concepts behind accounts and accounting.

3. Prepare an income statement for your own imaginary company. See how far you can get without looking back to Figure 18.5. Then check the text to see what you have forgotten, if anything.

4. Now prepare the balance sheet. Remember the simple formula: *Assets = Liabilities + Owners' equity.* Go back and check your balance sheet against Figure 18.6.

5. Write your own explanation of how small businesses get into trouble with cash flow by expanding too rapidly. Think of several ways a business could expand rapidly and still avoid such problems. Discuss your thoughts with the class.

INTERNET CHALLENGES

1. Check out the Web sites of the three large professional accounting organizations in Canada:

   a. Canadian Institute of Chartered Accountants (CA), <www.cica.ca>

   b. Chartered Management Accountants of Canada (CMA Canada), <www.cma-canada.org>

   c. Certified General Accountants' Association of Canada (CGA), <www.cga-canada.org>

   and follow the links to careers and other information that might interest you. Note that there are links to specific provinces so that you can click on your province to get relevant information.

2. Using the search engines with which you are familiar, find the Web sites for some large public Canadian companies. From their most recent annual report, examine their financial statements. Scrutinize the income statement and the balance sheet. Do they look like the ones shown in Figures 18.5 and 18.6? If not what are the differences? What are the similarities? Discuss in class.

Practising Management Decisions

Stuart Jenkins started Neighbourhood Landscaping Service when he was in high school. As the business grew, Stu hired several of his friends. He is doing well and is now in a position to begin keeping better records. After six months, Stu has written down some of his figures, but he doesn't know how to interpret them. He wants to take out a loan and needs to prepare a balance sheet to calculate his financial position. These are his figures:

CASE 1
CONSTRUCTING AN INCOME STATEMENT AND A BALANCE SHEET

Assets

Cash	$ 5,350
Truck	13,500
Accounts receivable	2,400
Equipment	6,300
Office furniture	945
Supplies	550
Total assets	$29,045

Liabilities

Money owed bank	$7,500
Money owed supplier	545
Money owed for equipment	500
Total liabilities	$8,545

Some other figures Stu hastily put together in no consistent order are:

Income from work done	$64,000
Expenses incurred for trees, shrubs, etc.	15,000
Salaries of helpers (2)	16,000
Advertising	1,350
Insurance	2,000
Office costs (phone, heat, rent, etc.)	8,400
Depreciation on truck and equipment	4,000

Stu paid $1250 for other supplies such as gravel, sand, and slate used for walkways.

Decision Questions

1. How much did Stu earn? Prepare an income statement to show Stu how you calculated his profit for six months.
2. Make a balance sheet. What is Stu's equity? Can you figure out his initial investment?
3. Use the balance sheet to determine if Stu is in a good financial position. Can he pay his debts?

Katherine Potter knew a good thing when she saw it. At least, it seemed so at first. She was travelling in Italy when she spotted pottery shops that made beautiful products ranging from ashtrays to lamps. Some of the pottery design was stunning.

Katherine began importing the products to Canada, and sales took off. Customers immediately realized the quality of the items and were willing to pay top price. Katherine decided to keep prices moderate to expand rapidly, and she did. Sales in the second three months were double

CASE 2
WHERE DID KATHERINE GO WRONG?

those of the first few months. Sales continued to grow during the rest of the first year.

Every few months, Katherine had to run to the bank to borrow more money. She had no problems getting larger loans, because she always paid promptly. To save on the cost of buying goods, Katherine always took cash discounts. That is, she paid all bills within 10 days to save the 2 percent offered by her suppliers for paying so quickly.

More customers bought Katherine's products on credit. They would buy a couple of lamps and a pot and Katherine would allow them to pay over time. Some were very slow in paying her, taking three months or more.

Toward the end of the year, Katherine noticed a small drop in her business. The local economy was not doing well because many people were being laid off from their jobs. Nonetheless, Katherine's business stayed level. One day the bank called Katherine and told her she was late in her payments. She had been so busy that she hadn't noticed that. The problem was that Katherine had no cash available to pay the bank. She frantically called several customers for payment, but that raised very little cash as only one person was able to pay immediately. Katherine was in a classic cash-flow bind.

She decided to raise prices and refused to make any sales on credit. She started delaying payment on her bills, thus losing the discounts. Then she engaged an accounting firm to review her financial condition.

Their examination showed that she had made nice profits and her overall position was good. Her cash problems were due to the fact she had allowed customers to run behind in payments and she had built up a lot of inventory that she had paid in full. They prepared financial statements and a cash-flow projection, which showed a good picture.

Based on this information, the bank increased her loan. But it urged her to get after her late-paying customers and reduce her inventory, both of which actions would considerably improve her cash flow. Her accountants had told her the same thing.

Decision Questions

1. Do you see how it was possible to have high sales and profits and still run out of cash? How could Katherine have avoided the problem?
2. Do you think it was wise of Katherine to raise prices and refuse to sell on credit? Will it hurt future business?
3. Was she right to get an accountant at this point? Should she have done so earlier? How would that have prevented her from having a cash squeeze?

Financial Ratios: Evaluating a Company's Operations and Financial Health

Appendix D

Everyone interested in finance needs to understand basic accounting. What is especially helpful to financial analysis is the use of ratios to measure a company's health. You are familiar with ratios. They are used all the time to measure the success of sports teams. For example, in basketball, the ratio of shots made from the foul line versus attempts is measured. TV announcers say, "Jones is shooting 85 percent of his foul shots, so he is not the one to foul in the final minutes." We judge basketball players by such ratios: 80 percent is good for foul shots, 65 percent is not good. We calculate similar ratios for baseball ("He's batting .300," or 30 percent), football ("He's completed 50 percent of his passes"), and so on. So ratios are not hard to understand or compute, and they give a lot of information about the relative performance of athletes or of business. Now let's look at some key ratios that business people use. All the data are obtained from the balance sheet or the income statement.

···· ▬▬ ····

HANDLING CASH-FLOW PROBLEMS: AVERAGE COLLECTION PERIOD OF RECEIVABLES

We have already noted that a major financial problem of small business is poor liquidity or cash flow. In many cases, poor cash flow is caused by not collecting accounts receivable fast enough. Many customers do not pay their bills until they are reminded or pressured to pay. Incentives such as discounts for paying early are often helpful for minimizing collection time. To determine whether or not a business is collecting its receivables as it is supposed to or in a reasonable period of time, an analyst calculates the average collection period. Unlike the other financial analysis calculations, this one takes two steps. The first step is to divide the annual credit sales by 365 to obtain the average daily credit sales. The second step is to divide accounts receivable by the average daily credit sales (the first step) to get the average collection period in days. For example:

1. Average daily credit sales = $\dfrac{\text{Total annual credit sales}}{365 \text{ days}}$

2. Collection period in days = $\dfrac{\text{Accounts receivable}}{\text{Average daily credit sales}}$

If total annual credit sales were \$365,000, then the average daily credit sales would be \$1,000:

$$\text{Average daily credit sales} = \dfrac{\$365,000}{365} = \$1,000$$

If the accounts receivable today were \$60,000, then the collection period would be 60 days:

$$\text{Average collection period of receivables} = \dfrac{\$60,000}{\$1,000} = 60 \text{ days}$$

If your terms of sale were 30 days, then this would show that, on average, your customers are taking twice as long as they should to pay their bills.

···· ■■■ ····

INVENTORY TURNOVER

A business supply store once asked a consultant why its inventory turnover ratio was so low. The consultant walked through the warehouse and found box after box filled with computer software. These obsolete items were being carried on the books as inventory and lowering the turnover ratio. What signalled the problem was that the owner compared his turnover ratio to the average industry ratio.

A lower than average ratio indicates obsolete merchandise or poor buying practices. A higher than average ratio may indicate an understocked condition, where sales are lost because of inadequate stock, or a very good buyer of merchandise. The faster merchandise moves out, the greater the inventory turnover. The result is greater profit without investing more money in increased inventory. The aim is to have the smallest inventory that can produce the greatest amount of sales.

Calculate the ratio to determine inventory turnover by dividing the cost of goods sold by the average inventory for the period. For example, if the cost of goods sold were \$160,000 and the average inventory were \$20,000, the turnover ratio would be 8. That means 8 times during one year or every 1.5 months. This figure by itself is rather meaningless. It has to be compared to industry figures to tell a company how it is doing in relation to competitors. It must also be analyzed to see if it makes sense for that particular type of business. The calculation looks like this:

$$\text{Turnover} = \dfrac{\text{Cost of goods sold}}{\text{Average inventory}} = \dfrac{\text{Cost of goods sold}}{(\text{Beginning} + \text{Ending inventories})/2}$$

$$= \dfrac{\$160,000}{(\$23,000 + \$17,000)/2} = \dfrac{\$160,000}{\$20,000} = 8 \text{ times annually}$$

If you are operating a high-fashion women's clothing store, your inventory changes with every season. If you carry clothes for four seasons, then you try to sell everything by the end of each season, which is why you always see end-of-season sales. For example, you don't want to carry this fall's line over to next fall because styles will change and very few women will want to buy the previous year's styles. So, if you have four seasons' merchandise and clear them out each season, your inventory turnover ratio should be four. If it is more than four, it means you are not selling out each season's stock and are carrying more inventory than you should, and one that's losing value. If your ratio is less than four, it means that you are an excellent buyer and able to generate sales with minimal inventory, replacing fast-moving items often.

In general, with just-in-time (JIT) inventory systems and electronic data interchange (EDI) among all members of the supply chain (mentioned in previous chapters), becoming more and more common, many companies are able to operate with minimal inventories, thus tying up less money. This ability should be reflected in inventory turns going up in companies that are following these procedures.

···· ▬▬▬ ····

GROSS MARGIN (OR PROFIT)

A major concern for all retail merchandising companies is the rate of profit earned on the merchandise sold. If you buy sweaters for $50 and sell them for $120, your markup is $70. That means you have added $70 to your cost to arrive at your selling price. This markup, or gross margin (or gross profit), is usually expressed as a percentage of the selling price.

$$\text{Gross margin rate} = \frac{\text{Gross margin}}{\text{Sales}} = \frac{\$70}{\$120} = .58, \text{ or } 58\%$$

You know the average gross margin rate of your sales from prior years, so you can apply that to the sales in any period, say one month, and get a rough approximation of your total gross profit for that period. Then, subtracting your estimated monthly expenses from monthly gross margin immediately tells you what profit or loss you have made that month.

Similarly, it is easy to calculate your break-even point—how much sales you must do just to cover your expenses. The procedure is a little more complicated for a manufacturing company.

···· ▬▬▬ ····

RETURN ON SALES (ROS)

Each industry has a different rate of return on sales. That is, the percentage of profit your sales generate. Such figures are well known in the industry. Therefore, a firm can determine whether or not it is doing as well as other businesses by calculating the return-on-sales ratio. This involves dividing net income by net sales. If net income were $10,000 and net sales were $200,000, the return-on-sales ratio would be 5 percent:

$$\text{Return on sales} = \frac{\text{Net income}}{\text{Net sales}} = \frac{\$10,000}{\$200,000} = .05, \text{ or } 5\%$$

Investors pay attention to the return-on-sales ratio. One way to increase the ratio is to increase prices, but a competitive market usually keeps prices low. Another way is to reduce costs. Shareholders compute return on sales when evaluating a firm (or look up the ratio in business reports). Another ratio they look for is return on investment.

···· ▬▬ ····

RETURN ON INVESTMENT (ROI)

Shareholders invest in a business expecting to make a greater return on their money than if they made a low-risk investment, like depositing it in a bank or buying government bonds. You can calculate the return on equity (current book value of your investment) in a firm by dividing net income by the owners' equity. You are more likely to hear this formula referred to as *ROI*, or *return on investment*. If net income were \$10,000 and shareholder's equity (investment) were \$100,000, the return on investment would be 10 percent:

$$\text{ROI} = \frac{\text{Net income}}{\text{Owners' equity}} = \frac{\$10,000}{\$100,000} = 10\%$$

···· ▬▬ ····

EARNINGS PER SHARE (EPS)

Earnings per share (EPS) measures the profit a company earns for each share of common stock it has outstanding. As you probably guessed, this is a crucial ratio for corporations since earnings stimulate growth in the company and pay for stockholders' dividends. Earnings per share is calculated as follows:

$$\text{Earnings per share} = \frac{\text{Net income}}{\substack{\text{Number of} \\ \text{common shares} \\ \text{outstanding}}} = \frac{\$120,000}{100,000} = \$1.20 \text{ earnings per share}$$

Earnings per share is an excellent indicator of a firm's current performance and growth on a year-by-year basis. Continued earnings growth is well received by both investors and lenders.

···· ▬▬ ····

DEBT/EQUITY RATIO

The debt/equity ratio tells you how much money the company has borrowed compared to the shareholders' (owners') equity. A high ratio triggers caution among investors. But high or low is meaningful only as compared to the average of the same industry.

If total liabilities were \$150,000 and owners' equity were \$150,000, the debt/equity ratio would be 1:

$$\text{Debt/equity ratio} = \frac{\text{Total liabilities}}{\text{Owners' equity}} = \frac{\$150,000}{\$150,000} = 1$$

Most consultants feel a ratio greater than 1 is not good, but again that varies by industry. Sometimes more debt is a good sign if it means the company is trying to optimize the return to shareholders by assuming more risk. Industry Canada reported that the primary reason for banks turning down loan applications is an unsatisfactory debt/equity ratio.*

---

*George Haines and Alan Riding, Carleton University, *Access to Credit: Lending Priorities and SMEs*, submitted to Industry Canada, August 17, 1994.

LIQUIDITY: CAN PAYMENT COMMITMENTS BE MET?

Analysts are also interested in certain other ratios. One important calculation analysts make is the current ratio:

$$\text{Current ratio} = \frac{\text{Current assets}}{\text{Current liabilities}}$$

This ratio measures a company's ability to pay its short-term debts. A ratio of 1.5 or higher is usually desired. Anything more than 1 indicates the firm's ability to pay all its debts. Less than 1 means that its current liabilities exceed its current assets, so the company cannot pay all its bills.

If we leave inventories out of the above equation, we get a more accurate feel for whether or not a business could quickly pay its current liabilities. Thus, another test is called the *quick ratio* or *acid-test ratio*. This is the supposed acid test of whether a firm is on solid ground, short term or not. The formula is:

$$\text{Quick ratio} = \frac{\text{Current assets} - \text{Inventory}}{\text{Liabilities}}$$

If the result is 1 or more, it means that the company can easily pay its bills, which indicates a sound current financial condition. These two ratios measure a company's liquidity; the more liquid a company is, the more easily it can pay its bills.

WHO IS INTERESTED IN RATIOS?

There are three groups that pay close attention to ratios: managers, shareholders, and outside parties. The latter include lenders, creditors, and potential investors. Managers want to watch out for problem areas and to improve performance. Shareholders are interested in seeing if the company is being well run. If they feel there are long-standing problems, they may ask for a change in management. Everybody pays attention to the trend over a period of years. Are the ratios improving, getting worse, or remaining unchanged? These are the important questions.

Professionals use several other ratios to learn more about the condition and performance of a business, but this appendix gives you an idea of what ratios are and how they are used. The point is that financial analysis begins where accounting reports end. Ratios represent the link between accounting and finance.

Managing Financial Resources

Chapter 19

LEARNING GOALS

After you have read and studied this chapter, you should be able to

1 explain the role and importance of finance and the responsibilities of financial managers.

2 outline the steps in financial planning by explaining how to forecast financial needs, develop budgets, and establish financial controls.

3 recognize the financial needs that must be met with available funds.

4 distinguish between short-term and long-term financing and between debt capital and equity capital.

5 identify and describe several sources of short-term capital.

6 identify and describe several sources of long-term capital.

7 compare the advantages and disadvantages of issuing bonds, and identify the classes and features of bonds.

8 compare the advantages and disadvantages of issuing stock, and outline the differences between common and preferred stock.

Greig Clark is an entrepreneur and a veteran in the struggles to overcome cash squeezes. On a rafting trip with three others in British Columbia, the rugged camp owner tells Clark that what they're facing is not Class 1 or Class 2 rapids, which are for "Eastern wimps." Ahead are Class 3, which are dangerous. "Class 4 could kill you and Class 5 probably will." Similarly, Clark believes that you are not a real entrepreneur unless you have faced and overcome "the top three classes of cash crunches." He knows what he is talking about after 20 years of experience running companies.

Clark quotes the well-known American Harold Geneen, former CEO of ITT, who has written extensively on managing companies. Geneen said, "Keep your eyes on your cash, because if you run out of cash they take you out of the game." For 18 years Clark owned and ran College Pro with a unique financing system peculiar to that type of business. Every spring Clark would pledge all his personal assets to the bank to support a $1 to $2 million line of credit, which he needed to meet his weekly payrolls. It wasn't until late summer that the business was generating enough cash to operate without a bank loan.

In subsequent businesses Clark continued to learn the hard lesson that cash is king. Once, while on a ski trip in Whistler with his brothers, he got a call from his chief financial officer advising him that the bank had called in their loan (demanded payment in full). Clark had to drop everything, get on the phone and round up the necessary funds. Clark has been through the fire many times. He has weathered his Class 3, 4, and 5 cash crises. Now he operates the Horatio Enterprise Fund out of Toronto.

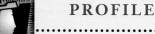

PROFILE

Coping with and Surviving Cash Crises

Source: Greig Clark, "Show Me the Money," *Profit*, October 1999, p. 31.

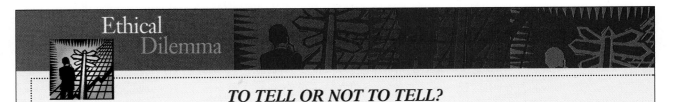

Ethical Dilemma

TO TELL OR NOT TO TELL?

You are the chief financial officer of Proto Corp. and have just completed all the preparations for a $60 million bond issue. The president of Proto has had extensive discussions with the president of Petra Trust Co., which manages some large pension funds, and Petra has agreed to buy the entire issue. You are not confident about the future of Proto because of some deep-rooted problems that are not yet public knowledge. These problems could have a serious impact on Proto's financial position and even threaten its existence.

A few days later you are having lunch with Karina, a good friend of yours, who is a manager of one of the pension funds overseen by Petra Trust. She tells you that her fund will be buying $20 million of the bond issue, and she seems quite pleased with this investment decision. You are somewhat uneasy because of your concerns about the long-term viability of Proto.

You are torn between your responsibility to your company and your friendship with Karina and the possible risk to her pension fund. You know that if it were your own money, or that of a pension fund you were managing, you would not make this investment. What should you do? What would be the result of your decision? Let's return to this question at the end of the chapter.

FINDING FINANCING: A CRUCIAL ISSUE

The story of Greig Clark's efforts to obtain financing illustrates how vital financing is both to a new and an existing business. Because this is one of the toughest problems facing small, medium, and large businesses, this chapter explores the different avenues available for obtaining finances.

THE ROLE OF FINANCE

An accountant in a company may be compared to a skilled laboratory technician who takes blood samples and other measures of a person's health and writes the findings on a health report (financial statements). A financial manager in a business is the doctor who interprets those reports and makes recommendations to the patient regarding changes that would improve health. Financial managers use the data prepared by the accountants and make recommendations to top management regarding strategies for improving the health (financial strength) of the firm.

A manager cannot be optimally effective at finance without understanding accounting. Similarly, a good accountant needs to understand finance.

Venture magazine ran an article citing the mistakes companies make in this area: "Sources for this story couldn't emphasize enough that many companies' financial and money-raising woes come down to inaccurate financial reporting. Young, growing companies need to live and die by the numbers, they say."[1] The message could not be clearer—good finance begins with good accounting.

As you may remember from Chapter 7, and as you can see from the Profile of Greig Clark, financing a *small* business is a difficult but critical function if a firm expects to survive, especially during the first two years. The simple reality is that the need for careful financial management is an essential, ongoing challenge for a business of any size throughout its entire life. Financial problems can arise in any organization.

··· CAUSES AND EFFECTS OF FINANCIAL PROBLEMS ···

The most common causes of financial problems are:

1. *Undercapitalization*. This means not enough funds to start or to continue operations. Many small businesses fall into this trap. Starting on a shoestring and a prayer is a good formula for failure.
2. *Inadequate expense control*. This leads to constant unpleasant surprises.
3. *Credit terms*. Consistently giving your customers more time (long terms) to pay their accounts than you get from your suppliers will reduce your cash flow and squeeze you financially.

In addition, events occur over which firms have no control. These are generally changes in the macroenvironment, the world outside the company, and are beyond normal business relationships. New government policies on taxes, interest rates, or imports; fluctuations in Canadian dollar exchange rates with the U.S. dollar; inflation or deflation; recession; cross-border shopping; technological developments; and new competitors can all play havoc with the best-laid plans. In Part 1 these issues were discussed in more detail.

Three very large Canadian companies ran into serious trouble in the past decade because of a big drop in their cash flows. Robert Campeau of Campeau Corp. and the Reichman brothers of Olympia & York have both been mentioned in previous chapters as examples of when extreme cash-flow problems caused the collapse of their empires.

A third member of this triumvirate was the giant Edper conglomerate of hundreds of companies, reputed at the time to be the largest such grouping in Canada, controlled by Peter and Edward Bronfman. Severe cash-flow problems had them selling off companies and adopting other drastic measures to survive.

In all three cases, the companies were in trouble because they had huge debts acquired in various expansions and they were counting on continual inflation and prosperity to provide enough cash to meet their crushing interest and capital repayment requirements. The recession in the United States, Canada, and England and the collapse of the real estate market upset their plans.

One does not have to pursue finance as a career to be interested in finance. Financial understanding is important to anyone who wants to invest in stocks and bonds or plan a retirement fund. In short, finance is something everyone should be concerned with. Let us take a look at what finance is all about.

··· WHAT IS FINANCE? ···

Finance is the business function that is responsible for the acquisition and disbursement of funds. Figure 19.1 outlines the responsibilities of financial managers. The major preoccupation of finance managers is developing a financial plan for the amount of funds required and how to obtain them. Without a carefully calculated financial plan, a firm has little chance for survival regardless of its product or marketing effectiveness. Managing finances is the crucial link that makes both production and marketing effective.

You are probably somewhat familiar with several finance functions—for example, the idea of buying merchandise on credit and collecting payment

finance
The business function that is responsible for the acquisition and disbursement of funds.

FIGURE **19.1**

· · · ·

WHAT FINANCIAL MANAGERS DO

Many of these functions depend on the information provided by the accounting statements discussed in Chapter 18.

- Planning
- Budgeting
- Obtaining funds
- Controlling funds (funds management)

- Collecting funds (credit management)
- Internal auditing
- Managing taxes
- Advising top management on financial matters

from companies that buy the firm's merchandise or services. Both *credit* and *collections* are important responsibilities of financial managers. The finance manager must be sure that the company does not lose too much money because of bad debts (people or firms that don't pay). Naturally, this means that the finance department is further responsible for collecting overdue payments. These functions are critical to all types of businesses but particularly important to small and medium-sized businesses, which typically have smaller cash or credit cushions than large corporations.

Tax payments represent an outflow of cash from the business. Therefore, they too fall under finance. As tax laws and tax liabilities have changed, finance people have taken on the increasingly important responsibility of tax management. Tax management is the analysis of the tax implications of various managerial decisions in an attempt to minimize taxes paid by the business. Businesses of all sizes must concern themselves with managing taxes.

Finally, the finance department has an internal audit division. The internal auditor makes sure company assets are properly controlled and secured, company accounting and financial procedures are carried out, and all transactions are properly recorded. In smaller companies, the internal auditing role is divided between the owners and the external auditors.

Without internal audits, accounting statements would be much less reliable. Regular internal audits offer the firm assurance that financial planning will be effective. We turn next to how financial planning is carried out.

Relationships with banks are invaluable to businesses. Bankers can assist with financial planning, financial management, and of course, needed funds.

FINANCIAL PLANNING

Planning has been a continual theme throughout this book. We have empha-sized the importance of planning as a managerial function and offered insights into planning your career. Financial planning involves analyzing the short- and long-term money flows to and from the firm. The overall objective of financial planning is to optimize profits by making the best use of money. It's probably safe to assume that we all could use better financial planning in our lives.

Financial planning involves three steps: (1) forecasting financial needs, both short and long term, (2) developing budgets to meet those needs, and (3) establishing financial control to ensure the company is following the financial plans. Let's look at the important role each step plays in the financial health of an organization.

••• FORECASTING FINANCIAL NEEDS •••

Forecasting is an important component of financial planning (see Figure 19.2). A **short-term forecast** is a prediction of revenues, costs, and expenses usually for one year. This forecast is the foundation for most other annual financial plans, so, its accuracy is critical. Part of the short-term forecast may be a **cash-flow forecast**, which projects the expected cash inflows and out-flows. Naturally, the inflows and outflows recorded in the cash-flow forecast are based on expected sales revenues and on various costs and expenses incurred and when they'll come due. A firm often uses past financial state-ments as a basis for these forecasts.

short-term forecast
A prediction of revenues, costs, and expenses for of one year.

cash-flow forecast
A projection of expected cash inflows and outflows in the coming year.

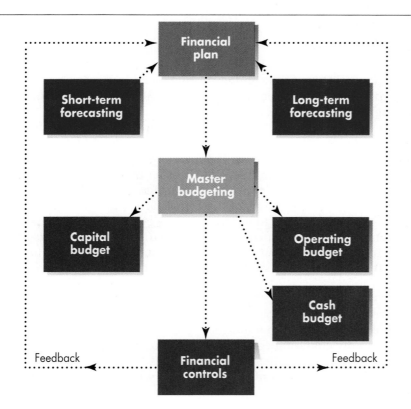

FIGURE **19.2**
••••
FINANCIAL PLANNING
Note the close link between financial plan-ning and budgeting.

long-term forecast
A prediction of revenues, costs, and expenses for more than 1 year, sometimes extending 5 or 10 years into the future.

A **long-term forecast** is a prediction of revenues, costs, and expenses for more than 1 year, sometimes as far as 5 or 10 years into the future. This forecast plays a crucial part in the company's long-term strategic plan. The strategic plan asks questions such as: What business are we in, and should we be in it five years from now? How much money should we invest in automation and new equipment over the next decade? Will there be cash available to meet long-term obligations? If not, what is the best way to obtain these funds?

The long-term financial forecast gives top management and operations managers some sense of the income or profit potential possible of different strategic plans. Additionally, long-term projections assist financial managers with the preparation of company budgets.

••• DEVELOPING BUDGETS •••

A budget is itself a financial plan. Specifically, a budget sets forth management's expectations for revenues and, based on those financial expectations, allocates the use of specific resources throughout the firm. You may live on a carefully constructed budget of your own. A business operates in the same way. A budget becomes the primary basis and justification for financial operations in the firm.

Most firms compile yearly budgets from short- and long-term financial forecasts. This leads to a master budget that has three components (see Figure 19.2):

- an operating budget
- a capital budget
- a cash budget

operating budget
The plan of the various costs and expenses needed to operate the business, based on the short-term forecast.

An **operating budget** is the plan of the various costs and expenses needed to operate the business, based on the short-term forecast. How much the firm will spend on supplies, travel, rent, advertising, salaries, and so on is planned in the operating budget.

capital budget
The spending plan for the acquisition of capital assets that involve large sums of money.

A **capital budget** highlights the firm's spending plans for the acquisition of capital assets. The capital budget primarily concerns itself with the purchase of such capital or fixed assets as land, buildings, and equipment that involve large sums of money.

cash budget
The projected use of cash during a given period (e.g., monthly, quarterly, or annually).

A **cash budget** is based on the cash-flow forecast and projects the use of cash over a given period (e.g., monthly, quarterly, or annually). Cash budgets can be important guidelines that assist managers in anticipating borrowing, debt repayment, operating expenditures, and short-term investment expectations.

At this point, it should be obvious to you that financial managers play an important role in the operations of the firm. These managers often determine what long-term investments to make, when specific funds will be needed, and how the funds will be generated. Once a company has projected its short- and long-term financial needs and established budgets to show how funds will be allocated, the final step in financial planning is to establish financial controls.

 Critical Thinking

Budgets are designed to keep strict controls on spending. An important theme of this book is the need for managers to be flexible so that they can adapt quickly to rapidly changing conditions. This often means modifying previous plans. Do you see any conflict between budgets and such flexibility? How do managers stay within the confines of budgets when they must shift gears to accommodate a rapidly changing world? Which forecasts are more affected by these problems, short term or long term? Why?

··· ESTABLISHING FINANCIAL CONTROL ···

Financial control means that the actual revenues, costs, and expenses are periodically reviewed and compared with projections. Deviations can thus be determined and corrective action taken. Such controls provide feedback to help reveal which accounts, which departments, and which people are varying from the financial plans. Such deviations may or may not be justified. In either case, some financial adjustments to the plan may be made. You will recall reading in Chapter 8 that an important function of managers is controlling. Financial control is one major aspect of this function. After the Progress Check we will explore specific reasons why firms need to have funds readily available.

Progress Check

- Name three finance functions important to the firm's overall operations and performance.
- In what ways do short-term and long-term financial forecasts differ?
- What is the organization's purpose in preparing budgets? Can you identify at least three different types of budgets?

THE NEED TO HAVE FUNDS AVAILABLE

Sound financial management is essential to businesses because the need for operating funds never seems to cease. Also, like our personal financial needs, the capital needs of a business change over time. For example, as a small business grows, its financial requirements shift considerably. The same is true with large corporations such as Bell Canada and Canadian Tire. As they venture into new product areas or markets, their capital needs intensify. It's safe to say that different firms need available funds for a variety of reasons. However, in virtually all organizations, funds must be available to finance specific operational needs. Let's take a look at the financial needs that affect the operations of both the smallest and the largest business enterprises.

··· FINANCING DAILY OPERATIONS ···

If employees are scheduled to be paid on Friday, they don't expect to have to wait until Monday for their paycheques. If tax payments are due on the 15th of the month, the government anticipates the money will be there on time. If the interest payment on a business loan is due on the 30th, the lender doesn't mean the 1st of next month. If you habitually pay late, you may be subject to interest and penalties or refusal of future loans. As you can see, funds have to be available to meet the daily operational costs of the business. The challenge of sound financial management is to see that funds are available to meet these daily cash expenditures without compromising the investment potential of the firm's money.

David Berch, the president of Cognetics, Inc., has this to say about cash flow:

> *Cash flow is a constant issue if you don't go for large outside financing, which we've chosen not to do. You've got a fixed payroll. Everything on the expense side is fixed, and everything on the revenue side is variable. Somebody gets sick and doesn't pay on his receivable, or a salesperson*

Credit cards serve multiple purposes for business. Like you and me, however, businesses must be careful about spending too freely. Financial budgeting helps managers control spending.

gets lazy and doesn't sell for a couple of months. All of a sudden your cash flow goes to [pot]. You find yourself constantly managing cash flow. It's a major issue.[2]

As you may know, money has a time value. In other words, if someone offered to give you $200 today or $200 one year from today, you should take the $200 today. Why? A very simple reason. You could start collecting interest on the $200 you receive today and over a year's time your money would grow. In business, the income gained on the firm's investments is important in maximizing its profit. For this reason, financial managers often try to have receipts at a maximum and keep cash expenditures at a minimum to free funds for investment. It's not unusual for finance managers to suggest that the firm pay bills as late as possible (unless a cash discount is available) and set up collection procedures to ensure that the firm gets what's owed to it as fast as possible. This way finance managers maximize the investment potential of the firm's funds. As you might expect, efficient cash management is particularly important to small firms in conducting their daily operations.

••• FINANCING ACCOUNTS RECEIVABLE •••

Every business knows that availability of credit helps to keep current customers happy and entices other buyers to do business with the firm. In today's highly competitive business environment, it's important to keep customers happy.

The major problem that arises with credit sales is that as much as 25 percent of the firm's assets can be tied up in accounts receivable. [To refresh your memory, accounts receivable is money owed to a business from customers who bought goods or services on credit. If you refer back to Figure 18.6, you will see that accounts receivable are 25 percent of total assets ($200,000/$801,000 = 25%).] This means the firm needs to spend its own funds to pay for the goods or services already provided to customers who bought on credit. This outflow of funds causes financial managers to focus a good part of their attention on efficient collection procedures. For example, a firm often provides cash discounts to purchasers who pay their account quickly. Also, finance managers scrutinize old and new credit customers to see if they have a history of meeting their credit obligations on time. In essence, the credit policy of the firm reflects its financial position and its financial policy. Of course, the desire to expand into new markets may also affect the firm's credit policy.

In recent years numerous airlines have struggled with severe financial difficulties. Onex Corporation of Toronto announced in August 1999 a comprehensive plan to revitalize Canada's troubled airline industry by creating a new air carrier through the acquisition and merger of Air Canada and Canadian Airlines.

••• FINANCING THE PURCHASE OF INVENTORY •••

As we noted earlier, the marketing concept implies a clear consumer orientation. One implication of this concept is that service and availability of goods are vital if a firm expects to prosper in today's markets. To satisfy customers, businesses are forced to maintain inventories that involve a sizeable expenditure of funds. Although it's true the firm expects to recapture its investment in inventory through sales to customers, a carefully constructed inventory policy assists in managing the use of the firm's available funds and maximizing profitability. For example, an owner of a neighbourhood ice-cream parlour ties up more funds in inventory (ice cream) in the summer months than in winter, since demand for ice cream goes up in the summer. As you may recall from

Chapter 10, innovations such as just-in-time inventory reduce the funds the firm has tied up in inventory. Ratio analysis of inventory turnover (see Chapter 18, Appendix D) also helps to prevent inventory from getting too high or having too much slow-moving or unsaleable goods.

••• FINANCING MAJOR CAPITAL EXPENDITURES •••

In many organizations, it is essential to purchase major assets such as land for future expansion, plants to increase production capabilities, new research facilities, and equipment to maintain or exceed current levels of output or to reduce costs by modernizing. As you might imagine, these purchases require a large expenditure of the organization's funds. It's critical that the firm weigh all the possible options before it commits what may be a large portion of its available resources. (As you may remember, these purchases are referred to as long-term or fixed assets.) Financial managers and analysts are called in to provide important insights into the appropriateness of such purchases.

Let's look at an example. Suppose a firm needs to expand its production capabilities because of increases in demand. One option is to buy land and build a new plant from scratch. Other options are to purchase an existing plant, rent a building, or contract out some part of the work. Can you think of financial and accounting considerations that would come into play in this decision?

It's evident the firm's need for available funds raises several questions that need to be considered. How does the firm obtain funds to finance operations and other business necessities? How long will specific funds be needed? Will funds have to be repaid at a later date? What will the needed funds cost? How much profit will the expansion yield? These questions will be addressed in the next section.

Progress Check

- Money is said to have a time value. What exactly does this mean?
- Why are accounts receivable a financial concern to the firm?
- Is an efficient account collection plan more important to a small firm or a large corporation? Why?
- What is the major reason organizations spend a good deal of their available funds on inventory?

•••• ▬▬▬ ••••

ALTERNATIVE SOURCES OF FUNDS

Earlier in the chapter, you learned that finance is the function in a business that is responsible for acquiring funds for the firm. The amount of money needed for various periods and the most appropriate sources of these funds are fundamental questions in sound financial management. We will look at the different methods and sources of acquiring funds next, but first let's highlight some key distinctions involved in funding the firm's operations.

Large corporations regularly encounter short- and long-term financing needs. Short-term financing refers to the need for capital that will be repaid within one year and that helps finance current operations. Long-term financing refers to capital needs for major purchases that will be repaid over a specific period longer than one year. We will explore sources of both short- and long-term financing in the next section.

A firm can seek to raise capital through debt or equity sources. **Debt capital** refers to funds raised through various forms of borrowing that must be

debt capital
Funds raised by borrowing that must be repaid.

equity capital
Funds raised from selling shares in the firm.

repaid (debt). **Equity capital** is money raised through the sale of shares (equity) in the firm. Again, we will discuss these two financing alternatives in depth later.

SHORT-TERM FINANCING

The bulk of a finance manager's time is not spent obtaining long-term funds. The nitty-gritty, day-to-day operation of the firm takes up most of the manager's time and calls for the careful management of short-term financial needs. Cash may be needed for additional inventory or some emergency that may arise unexpectedly. As with your personal finances, a business sometimes needs to obtain short-term funds when other funds run out. This is particularly true of small businesses. It's rare that small businesses even attempt to find funding for long-term needs. They are more concerned with just staying afloat until they are able to build capital and creditworthiness. Short-term financing can be obtained in a variety of ways, and we look at some of these next.

··· TRADE CREDIT ···

trade credit
The practice of buying goods now and paying for them in the future.

The most widely used source of short-term funding is called **trade credit**. This means that a business is able to buy goods today and pay for them sometime in the future. When a firm buys merchandise, it receives an invoice (bill).

Spotlight on Big Business

<www.cdnair.ca>
<www.aircanada.ca/home>

Canada's Airlines: A Case of Financial Crash

One of the major stories that dominated Canadian headlines in the 1990s was the financial mess of Canada's two largest airlines. Both Air Canada and Canadian Airlines International suffered enormous losses in 1991, 1992, and into 1993. The airlines' very existences were in question, and each sought deliverance through alliances with U.S. airlines. How did they get into such a terrible state?

There were many problems, but the basic cause was the deep, long recession; revenues slid steeply, resulting in huge losses. Both of these companies had large debts from airplane acquisition and big operating expenses, so when cash flow dried up because revenues collapsed, they found themselves in serious trouble. It's the classic problem that hits most businesses from time to time: shortage of cash to pay their bills.

How did they cope? Well, they could not get funds by loans or bond issues because nobody would lend them money then. It was too risky. They were unable to raise equity capital because nobody would buy their shares. So they resorted to the only methods left: they reduced operational expenses by laying off employees and cutting other costs. They also delayed paying their creditors or didn't pay them at all, as Canadian Airlines did for a few months in late 1992 and early 1993.

Canadian companies were not the only ones hurting. Airline companies all over the world were having problems. Some well-known American companies, like Eastern Airlines and PanAmerican Airlines went under or were taken over by other airlines.

By 1999 Air Canada was in good shape again but Canadian Airlines was still in serious financial trouble. At the time this book was being written it looked quite certain that Canadian would be taken over by another company.

Every purchase is made under certain credit terms. The invoice will indicate that payment is due in 30 or 60 days or whatever arrangements have been made. Sometimes terms may read "2/10, net 30," which means that if payment is made within 10 days, a 2 percent discount will be deducted. Otherwise, payment is due in full in 30 days. Figure 19.3 shows when it pays to take discounts.

Sometimes companies that are strapped for cash offer larger discounts, 5 or 10 percent for immediate payment. These discounts clearly mean a big reduction in cost to the purchaser who has the cash to take advantage of such offers.

The decision to take or not to take discounts is often not based on financial considerations alone. If a firm deals with certain suppliers on a regular basis and has a reputation for paying bills promptly, it will be a favoured customer. This status could be very useful whenever it needs a special order, a rush delivery, or merchandise that is in short supply. Of course, if it is short of cash, it may not be able to take advantage of discounts.

••• FAMILY AND FRIENDS •••

A second source of short-term funds for most smaller firms is money lent by family and friends. Because short-term funds are needed for periods of less than a year, often friends are willing to help. Such loans can be dangerous if the firm does not understand cash flow and cannot repay them when promised. As we discussed earlier, the firm may suddenly need funds and have no other sources. It is better not to borrow from friends, but instead go to a commercial bank that understands the risk and can help analyze future financial needs.

If the firm does borrow from family or friends, it is best to be very professional about the deal and (1) agree on terms at the beginning, (2) write an agreement, and (3) pay them back the same way it would a bank loan. If the firm is lucky, the family members or friends who lend the money might say, "Pay me back whenever you can."

••• COMMERCIAL BANKS •••

Banks are in the business of loaning but they are often reluctant to loan money to small businesses. Nonetheless, the most promising and best-organized ventures can usually get bank loans. If they're able to get such a loan, small to medium-sized businesses should have the person in charge of the finance function keep in close contact with the bank. It's wise to see your banker periodically (as often as once a month) and send the banker all financial statements so that the bank continues to supply funds when needed.

Where terms of payment are 2/10, N30, 60, or 90, there can be quite a difference between taking the 2 percent discount versus paying in full in 30 or 60 or 90 days.

		Approximate gain
2% for 20 days (10 instead of 30)	=	36% per annum
2% for 50 days (10 instead of 60)	=	15%
2% for 80 days (10 instead of 90)	=	9%

If a company is borrowing from the bank at 15 percent per annum, there is no advantage in earning 15 percent, a loss in earning 9 percent, and a big gain in earning 36 percent. If a company is borrowing at 8 percent, it pays to take the discount in all cases.

FIGURE **19.3**

••••

CREDIT TERMS

Discounts can yield major savings on cost of merchandise purchases.

Farmers often go to the bank to borrow money for seed, fertilizer, and equipment. Careful financial management is critical when farm profits are low and expenses are rising. Bankers can help with finances if given the right information.

<www.cba.ca/eng/ index.cfm>

The Canadian Bankers Association's Web site provides a wealth of information about the activities of Canada's banks. The site includes a breakdown of the number of branches by province, interest rates on mortgages the number of credit cards in circulation, the number of bank accounts, the dollar volume of activities, the number of automatic banking machines and transactions they are used for, the level of small-business lending, and much more. The site even includes information on the status of the GDP and the national debt. Be sure to visit this Web site to get the latest information!

Try to imagine different kinds of business people going to the bank for a loan, and you'll get a better feel for the role of the financial manager. Picture, for example, a farmer going to the bank to borrow funds for seed, fertilizer, equipment, and other needs. Such supplies may be bought in the spring and paid for when the fall harvest comes in. Now picture a local toy store buying merchandise for Christmas. The money for such purchases might be borrowed in October and November and paid back after Christmas. A restaurant may borrow funds at the beginning of the month and pay by the end of the month. Can you see that how much a business borrows and for how long depends on the kind of business it is and how quickly the merchandise purchased with a bank loan can be resold or used to generate funds?

Obviously, if the firm and its accountant have carefully prepared a cash-flow forecast, there will be fewer surprises. No cash-flow forecast can prevent a drop in sales or the sudden bankruptcy of a major customer. But it does help to alert the firm to the size of the problem immediately. Sometimes a business gets so far into debt, so far behind in its payments, that the bank refuses to lend it more. Suddenly the business can't pay its bills. More often than not, this results in bankruptcy or business failure, and you can chalk up another business failure to cash-flow problems.

Can you see why it's important for a business person to keep friendly and close relations with his or her banker? The banker may spot cash-flow problems early and point out the danger. Or the banker may be more willing to lend money in a crisis if the business person has established a strong, friendly relationship built on openness and trust. It's always important to remember that the banker wants the firm to succeed almost as much as the firm does. Bankers can be an invaluable support—especially to small, growing businesses.

In the past, there has been much criticism of Canadian banks for their apparent reluctance to make loans to small companies. Many small business owners voiced their complaints about the banks. The banks have reacted to the criticism with a whole range of measures to improve the situation (see Chapter 7). Data from the seven largest banks, compiled by the Canadian Bankers Association, show that as of March 31, 1998, 754,000 business customers had loans of less than $1 million each, totalling $70 billion. Of this group 556,000 customers had loans of less than $100,000 each, totalling $15 billion. There were also 36,000 business customers with authorized loans of more than $1 million each, totalling $467 billion.[3]

Banks have initiated a wide variety of direct and indirect ways and many policies to help small business. These are outlined in publications such as *Serving the Needs of Small Business* and *Small Business Annual Reports*.[4]

Because the six largest banks (see Figure 19.4) are responsible for an estimated 80 percent of all loans to small firms, these policies have a major impact on the ability of small businesses to obtain financing. The banks point out that research has shown that venture capital angels refuse 97 percent of requests for funding and venture capital firms reject 95 percent of them.[5] They also note that Statistics Canada has determined that friends and relatives only refuse 12 percent, banks 19 percent, and other financial institutions 16 percent of all applicants for funding.[6]

DIFFERENT FORMS OF BANK LOANS   The most difficult kind of loan to get from a bank or other financial institution is an unsecured loan, a loan not backed by any collateral. Normally, only highly regarded customers of the bank receive unsecured loans. A **secured loan** is one backed by collateral, something valuable such as property. If the borrower fails to pay the loan, the lender may take possession of the collateral. That takes some of the risk out of lending money. **Pledging** is the term for using accounts receivable, inventory, or other assets as security. Other property can also be used as collateral, including buildings, machinery, and other things of value, for example, company-owned stocks and bonds.

If your business is sound and you develop a good relationship with a bank, it will open a **line of credit** for you, meaning it will agree to lend the business up to a given amount. The purpose of a line of credit is to speed the borrowing process so that a firm does not have to go through the hassle of applying for a new loan every time it needs funds. The funds are available as long as the credit ceiling is not exceeded. As businesses mature and become more financially secure, the amount of credit is often increased. A line of credit is a particularly good way to obtain funds for future or unexpected cash needs.

THE PRIME RATE   Periodically you will read that the prime rate has been raised or lowered. For most people, that report has little meaning. But for a financial manager, the level of the prime rate is very important. The *prime rate*

secured loan
Loan backed by something valuable, such as property.

pledging
Using accounts receivable, inventory, or other assets as security for a loan.

line of credit
The maximum amount a bank will agree to lend a borrower.

	ASSETS	LOANS	NET INCOME FOR YEAR
	(IN BILLIONS OF DOLLARS)		
CIBC	281.43	152.26	1.06
Royal Bank of Canada	274.40	165.25	1.82
Scotiabank	233.59	148.26	1.39
Bank of Montreal	222.59	129.69	1.35
Toronto Dominion Bank	181.83	97.22	1.12
National Bank of Canada	70.66	46.38	0.32
Total	1,264.50	739.06	7.06

FIGURE **19.4**

• • • •

DATA OF CANADA'S SIX LARGEST BANKS

These data are for banks at October 31, 1998. These banks account for 90 percent of all banking assets and loans in Canada.

Source: Used by permission of the Canadian Bankers Association, <www.cba.ca>.

is the short-term interest rate that banks charge their preferred (creditworthy) customers. Most firms pay more than the prime rate for a loan, but some very good credit risks can negotiate loans at prime. In either case, the prime rate is the base from which many loan rates are calculated.

··· GOVERNMENT PROGRAMS ···

Elaborate programs of government financing for specific purposes are available. These programs were discussed in detail in Chapter 4 and Appendix A.

··· FACTORING ···

One relatively expensive source of short-term funds for a firm is called *factoring*. It works like this: as we know, a firm sells many of its products on credit to other businesses. Some of these buyers are slow in paying their bills. The company may thus have a large amount of money due in accounts receivable. A *factor* buys the accounts receivable from the firm at a discount (usually advancing 50 to 70 percent of the value of the accounts receivable) for cash. The factor then collects and deducts the amount that was advanced plus its charges and remits the balance to the company.

factoring
Selling accounts receivable for cash.

   Factoring, then, is the process of selling accounts receivable for cash. How much this costs the firm depends on the age and the quality of accounts receivable, the nature of the business, the general interest rate level, and the conditions of the economy. Factoring is the most expensive form of financing. It is more common in industries where businesses are undercapitalized and have no other source of funds.

··· COMMERCIAL PAPER ···

commercial paper
A short-term corporate equivalent of an IOU that is sold in the marketplace by a firm. It matures in 270 days or less.

Sometimes a large corporation needs funds for a few months and wants to get lower rates than those charged by banks. One strategy is to sell **commercial paper**, which consists of promissory notes, in amounts starting at $25,000, that mature in 270 days or less. A promissory note shows the fixed amount of money the business agrees to repay the lender on a specific date. The interest rate is identified on the face of the promissory note, and the accumulated interest is payable on the date the note matures. Commercial paper is unsecured, so only large and financially stable firms can sell it. Since most commercial paper comes due in 30 to 90 days, it is also an investment opportunity. Buyers, often companies with surplus funds, can put cash into commercial paper for short periods to earn some interest.

Progress Check

- If you received terms of 3/10, net 25, what would this mean?
- What is the difference between trade credit and a line of credit at a bank?
- What is meant by factoring? What are some of the considerations for establishing a discount rate in factoring?
- How does commercial paper work? What is the main advantage of issuing commercial paper?

···· ▬ ····

LONG-TERM FINANCING

Financial planning and forecasting help the firm develop a financial plan. This plan specifies the amount of funding that the firm will need over various periods and the most appropriate sources of those funds. In setting long-term financing objectives, the firm generally asks itself three major questions:

- What are the long-term goals and objectives of the organization?
- What are the financial requirements needed to achieve these long-term goals and objectives?
- What sources of long-term capital are available and which will best fit our needs?

In business, long-term capital is used to buy fixed (capital) assets such as a plant or equipment and to finance any expansion of the organization. The revenue generated from these assets is expected to continue over many years, so it will finance the repayment of the cost of these assets. In major corporations, decisions concerning long-term financing normally involve the board of directors and top management, as well as finance and accounting managers. Sometimes an expert investment banker is included in the decision-making group. In smaller businesses, the owners are always actively involved in seeking all forms of financing.

Initial long-term financing usually comes from three sources: surplus funds, debt capital, and equity capital, shown in detail in Figure 19.5. The role of government in financing, especially for small business, is highlighted in the Spotlight on Small Business.

··· SURPLUS CASH FUNDS ···

Successful businesses often generate surplus cash over and above their normal operating requirements. All or part of these funds may be available for investment in fixed (capital) assets that the company requires. The finance

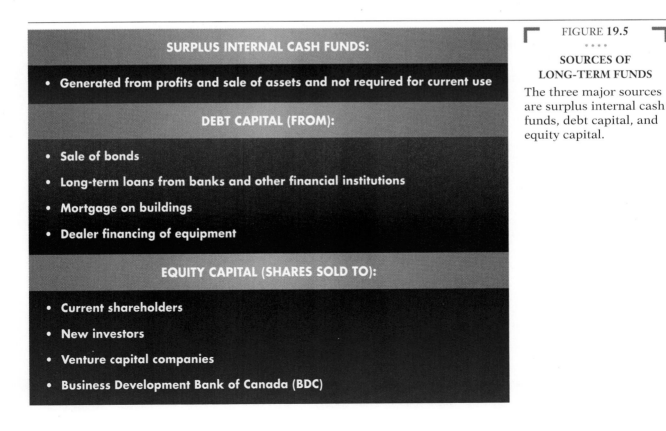

SURPLUS INTERNAL CASH FUNDS:

- Generated from profits and sale of assets and not required for current use

DEBT CAPITAL (FROM):

- Sale of bonds
- Long-term loans from banks and other financial institutions
- Mortgage on buildings
- Dealer financing of equipment

EQUITY CAPITAL (SHARES SOLD TO):

- Current shareholders
- New investors
- Venture capital companies
- Business Development Bank of Canada (BDC)

FIGURE **19.5**

····

SOURCES OF LONG-TERM FUNDS

The three major sources are surplus internal cash funds, debt capital, and equity capital.

managers will compare how much interest these funds are earning to how much interest will have to be paid for loans. Usually the loan costs will exceed the revenue from the investments made with the surplus funds, so the decision is not too difficult. If you are earning 6 percent and have to pay 9 percent to borrow, you save money by using your own funds for new equipment rather than borrowed monies. Sometimes there are other considerations that will lead a company to borrow despite the extra cost.

··· DEBT FINANCING ···

A business can meet long-term financing needs through debt capital. Debt capital is funds the firm borrows from lending institutions or acquires from selling bonds (explained later in the chapter). With debt financing, the company has a legal obligation to repay the amount borrowed plus regular interest at fixed rates.

Once a firm is established and has developed a rapport with a bank, it can often secure a long-term loan. (For small businesses, the Business Development Bank of Canada [BDC], a crown corporation, is often a good source of such loans—see Spotlight on Small Business.) Long-term loans are usually repaid within three to seven years but may go even longer. For such loans, a business must sign a term-loan agreement, which is a promissory note that requires the borrower to repay the loan plus interest in specified installments, usually monthly.

A mortgage on land and buildings is a long-term loan that is secured by the property. If the firm does not pay installments as they come due the property may be seized by the mortgagor and sold to repay the amount owing. Any excess amount is returned to the borrower. Most long-term loans require some form of collateral, perhaps real estate, machinery, or stock. The interest rate for such loans is based on factors such as whether there is adequate collateral, the firm's credit rating, and the general level of market interest rates. The rates are usually higher than for short-term loans because of the longer period.

If an organization cannot meet its long-term financing needs from a lending institution, it may decide to issue bonds. Businesses compete with governments to sell bonds. Bonds sold by the federal or provincial governments

<www.bdc.ca>

This is the Web site of the Business Development Bank of Canada. The site is well designed and has a lot of useful information and links explaining what the Bank does and how to contact them in every province.

The Business Development Bank of Canada (BDC) is a small-business bank that helps create and develop Canadian small and medium-sized businesses. The BDC plays an important role in delivering financial and management services, with a particular focus on the emerging and exporting sectors of the economy.

Spotlight on Small Business

<www.orchid.com>

The Vital Role of the Business Development Bank of Canada

Since 1945, the federal Business Development Bank of Canada (BDC) has been an important source of financing for small- and medium-sized businesses in Canada. The BDC has gradually widened its activities to embrace a whole range of financing and management aids to new and existing businesses. At December 31, 1995, it had more than $3 billion in loans, investments, and guarantees outstanding to some 14,400 businesses across the country. A good example is the Orchid company.

In 1988, Grant Bibby, president of Orchid Automation Group Inc. of Cambridge, got a $900,000 loan from the BDC. He actually asked for $400,000, but the BDC's examination showed that the company really needed more than that to function satisfactorily. It isn't every 29-year-old who can command enough confidence to secure a $900,000 loan, of course. But Bibby had a hot product.

Orchid had devised computerized equipment that could change the dies on big metal-stamping machines, used by titans like Chrysler, in three minutes flat instead of the traditional seven days. In 1990, two years after its launch, Orchid boasted sales of $1.1 million. By 1992 the figure was $5.2 million, and Bibby was predicting that would rise to $30 million within five years. (In fact, the company did much better.)

In planning for expansion, Bibby tried to avoid the cash shortages that traditionally plagued and sometimes killed fast-growing small firms. It wasn't easy. Like many businesses, Orchid was started on a shoestring. Bibby's customers, who usually doled out from $100,000 to $1 million for each machine, paid only on delivery. And that came several months after Orchid had laid out money for materials, engineering, and labour.

In 1991 Bibby recognized that further help from traditional lenders was a nonstarter, since they liked their loans to be secured by tangibles such as buildings or machinery. Orchid was leasing its factory space and had already put its existing machines on the line to secure a modest term loan.

Bibby heard he might qualify for a new pilot project called the *Venture Loan* program, which had been launched by the federal government's BDC in 1991 and which was aimed at businesses three to five years' old that were profitable and ripe for expansion. Venture loans mix elements of a bank loan with techniques used by venture capitalists and, most crucial to Bibby, don't ▲

require any collateral. Instead, the BDC bets on the future earnings of the borrower. "They came in, analyzed our operations, did a 100-page report, and concluded that we would hit our sales and profit goals," said Bibby.

He was even more pleased when the BDC didn't demand an ownership stake in Orchid, something most venture capitalists would insist upon. "Entrepreneurs hate to give up ownership of their companies," says Francois Beaudoin, president and CEO of BDC. "They've slaved for years to build what they've got and they don't want to dilute the ownership." Under the deal he struck with BDC, Bibby agreed repay the Venture Loan over five years, with a 20 percent annual return on the investment for the bank. The payback is a combination of an interest payment and a royalty that's based on the company's revenues.

The BDC justifies its return on the grounds that its government mandate requires it to be self-financing. And although 20 percent is much higher than a standard bank loan (typically the prime rate plus 1 or 2 percent), it's far lower than the 35 to 45 percent expected by traditional venture capitalists. What's more, with the BDC's $900,000 in its coffers, Orchid was able to obtain an additional $600,000 from banks at just over the prime rate.

Recently the BDC has become a lot more aggressive in publicizing its existence and funding capabilities. The Bank has sharply increased the number of its ads on TV and in print media and has changed the tone of these ads. The BDC has more funding and a wider scope, and its successful Venture Loan program has had a steady increase in funding. The program started with $6.5 million in 1991, reached $22.5 million in 1995, and $67 million in 1998, which was the second consecutive year that funding had doubled.

Most of the money is going to high-tech firms with growing workforces and significant exports. That makes BDC it one of the biggest venture-financing operations with a national focus in Canada. "We believe the economic recovery will be based on these small companies," said Beaudoin, "and we want to play a key role."

Sources: BDC Web site, <www.bdc.ca>, July 1998; *Together We Make It Happen*, annual report 1995, Federal Business Development Bank; Jerry Zeidenberg, "Shaking the Money Tree," *Globe and Mail, Report on Business*, June 1993, pp. 73–74.

are risk free because they are backed by the taxing power of governments, which makes them attractive. Bonds may be issued for 5, 10, or even 20 or 30 years. If a firm cannot secure a long-term loan from a lender or issue bonds, it often turns to equity capital. Sometimes there are good reasons to turn to equity capital first.

··· EQUITY FINANCING ···

Basically, equity financing refers to issuing (selling) shares or stock of the company. The new owners of shares in the company acquire a piece of the ownership or equity. The firm may offer shares to

1. Existing owners by asking them to buy additional stock. If the company is doing well, existing owners may be pleased to do so.
2. The public in general through stockbrokers who handle such transactions. This arrangement will be necessary if more shares have to be sold than existing shareholders are willing to buy. (This option is not available to private companies; see next section.)
3. Venture capital companies. (These were discussed in Chapter 7.)
4. The Business Development Bank of Canada (discussed previously).

Bonds and shares are discussed in detail in the rest of the chapter.

 Progress Check

- What is the difference between long-term and short-term capital? Do firms actually need both types of funding?
- What are the two major forms of debt financing available to a firm?
- How does debt financing differ from equity financing?
- What are four sources of equity financing?

···· ▬ ····

SECURITIES MARKETS

The importance of obtaining long-term funding cannot be overemphasized, because the most common problem facing new companies is starting without sufficient capital. Adequate long-term funding allows a firm to concentrate on operations instead of always looking for funds. It gives company managers a stable base from which to operate.

You will remember from Chapter 6 that public companies can obtain financing by selling bonds and shares (securities) to the public at large. This selling is made possible by the existence of markets—*stock exchanges*—through which stockbrokers buy and sell these securities on behalf of clients. **Stock exchanges** are markets where the securities of public companies are traded and they are efficient places for carrying out these transactions. Pension funds, insurance companies, banks and other companies, and individuals with funds to invest (domestic or foreign) constitute a market with a huge appetite for quality securities.

Companies that issue securities to raise funds obtain them only when the securities are first sold. All subsequent trading is between buyers and sellers and has nothing to do with the issuing company. This trading constitutes the bulk of trading on stock exchanges and is called *secondary trading*.

stock exchange
Markets where the securities of public companies are traded.

DEBT FINANCING THROUGH SELLING BONDS

To put it simply, a bond is a certificate (see Figure 19.6) indicating that the owner has lent money to the issuer of the bond. The company (or government) has a legal obligation to make regular (annual or semi-annual) interest payments and to repay the principal, all on the dates indicated on the certificate. Bonds come in a wide variety, with a terminology to match.

••• THE TERMINOLOGY OF BONDS •••

A **bond** is a contract of indebtedness issued by a corporation or government unit that promises payment of a principal amount at a specific future time plus annual or semi-annual interest at a specified or variable rate. As you may suspect, the interest rate paid varies depending on many factors, such as the general level of interest rates, the reputation of the company, and the rate being paid for government bonds. Generally, once an interest rate is set for specific bonds, it cannot be changed. **Principal** refers to the *face value* of the bond (common bonds are almost always issued in multiples of $1000).

The borrower is legally bound to repay the bond principal in full to the bondholder on the bond's **maturity date**. For example, if you purchase a $1000 bond with an interest rate of 9 percent and a maturity date of July 1, 2010, the firm undertakes to pay you $90 interest annually. This is done in two semi-annual installments on January 1 and July 1 each year until July 1, 2010, when it must repay the full $1000.

bond
A contract of indebtedness issued by a corporation or government unit that promises payment of a principal amount at a specified future time plus annual or semi-annual interest at a specified or variable rate.

principal
The face value of a bond.

maturity date
The date on which a borrower must legally repay the bond principal to the bondholder.

FIGURE 19.6

A SAMPLE BOND CERTIFICATE FROM IBM

This is an unsecured and convertible bond (debenture) paying 7 7/8 percent interest. The bond matures November 21, 2004, when the principal amount (or face value) of the bond must be repaid.

··· ADVANTAGES AND DISADVANTAGES OF ISSUING BONDS ···

As a source of long-term capital, bonds offer advantages to an organization. The decision to issue bonds is often based on careful evaluation of all of the following advantages and disadvantages:

- Bondholders have no vote on corporate affairs, so management maintains control over the firm's operations. Remember, bondholders are creditors of the firm, not owners as shareholders are.
- The interest paid on bonds is a deductible expense to the firm's operations, which reduces income taxes.
- Bonds are a temporary source of funding for a firm. They are eventually repaid and the debt obligation eliminated.

However, bonds also have some significant drawbacks.

- Bonds are an increase in *debt* (liabilities) and may adversely affect the market's valuation of the firm.
- Interest on bonds is a legal obligation. It must be paid even when the company is incurring losses or is short of cash. If interest is not paid when due, bondholders can take legal action to force payment and seize any assets securing the bond.
- The face value of the bonds must be repaid on the maturity date. This could cause a possible cash shortage for the firm on that date.

··· DIFFERENT CLASSES OF BONDS ···

unsecured bonds
Bonds that are not backed by any collateral.

An organization can choose between two different classes of corporate bonds. The first class is **unsecured bonds**, sometimes called *debentures* or *debenture bonds*. These bonds are not supported by any special type of collateral on the part of the issuing firm. In other words, the primary security the bondholder has is the reputation and credit rating of the company. Unsecured bonds are issued only by well-respected firms with excellent credit ratings. Such bonds do have the backing of all corporate assets not otherwise pledged, but other creditors have an equal claim on those assets.

secured bonds
Bonds backed by some tangible asset that is pledged to the bondholder to guarantee payment of principal and interest.

The second class of bonds is **secured bonds**. These are bonds backed by some tangible asset that is pledged to the bondholder. If interest or principal is not paid when due, the assets may be seized. There are several kinds of secured bonds.

- *First mortgage bonds* are backed by the company's real assets such as land and buildings. They are the most common of secured bonds and among the most desirable.
- *Collateral trust bonds* are backed by the stock that the company owns and that is held in trust by a financial institution (thus the word *trust* in the title).
- *Equipment trust bonds* are backed by the equipment the company owns. This may include trucks, aircraft, and other equipment that is widely used in industry. A trustee often holds title to the equipment pledged until the bondholders are paid.

Secured bonds are obviously quite a safe investment, while unsecured bonds are less safe but still less risky than investment in shares. Bond interest rates are closely related to the degree of risk—the higher the risk the higher the interest rate. Some bonds have a variable interest rate. The market price of bonds is usually quite stable with none of the wide price swings often seen with shares. Bonds have a wide range of other features that we look at next.

Considering the disadvantages and advantages of different forms of raising funds, which method would you adopt if you had to make that decision in your company? How would your decision be affected in a high-interest year? If your company did well? What would you do for short-term financing? For long-term financing? How would you justify your choices?

··· SPECIAL BOND FEATURES ···

One special feature of a bond issue is a call provision, which lets the issuer pay off a bond prior to its maturity date by *calling* in the bond. Call provisions must be clearly indicated in the original bond issue so that investors are aware of this clause.

This feature is useful for the issuer; if interest rates fall, the issuer can recall the bonds and pay them off with a new issue at a lower interest rate. Normally this right cannot be exercised until several years after the original issue date, as shown on the bond certificate.

There is often a *redemption* feature that gives the bondholder the right to redeem the bond. That means the right to be repaid prior to date of maturity. The bondholder would exercise this right if interest rates had risen and higher interest could be obtained elsewhere.

A last feature that can be included in bonds is convertibility. A **convertible bond** is one that can be converted into shares of common stock in the issuing company. This feature can be an inducement for an investor to buy the bond because common stock has the potential to grow in value over time. When we discuss common stock this advantage will become evident to you.

convertible bond
A bond that can be converted into shares of common stock.

··· BONDS AS INVESTMENTS ···

As investments, bonds are safer than shares. But two questions often bother first-time investors in corporate bonds. One question is: "If I purchase a corporate bond, do I have to hold it to the maturity date?" No! You do not have to hold a bond until maturity, because bonds are bought and sold daily on securities markets. However, if you sell your bond to another investor, it's unlikely you will get the face value (usually $1000), since prices fluctuate, usually in a narrow range. You would get a higher or lower amount.

The second question on investors' minds is, "How do I know how risky an investment a *particular* bond issue is?" Fortunately, four companies, Dominion Bond Rating Service, Canadian Bond Rating Service, Standard & Poor's, and Moody's Investor Service (the first two are Canadian, the last two are American), rate various corporate and government bonds' degree of risk to investors. Naturally, the higher the risk associated with the bond issue, the higher the interest rate the organization must offer investors. Investors will not assume high levels of risk if they don't feel the potential return is worth it.

Dominion Bond Rating Service (DBRS) is one of four companies that rates various corporate and government bonds' degrees of risk to investors.

Bonds provide an excellent source of long-term financing for firms and good investment vehicles for investors. They are a form of debt financing as opposed to equity financing. Let's explore the most common form of equity financing, the issuing of corporate stock (shares).

Progress Check

<tse.com/market>
<tse.com/investor>

The Toronto Stock Exchange (TSE) Web site provides information on stock market conditions in general, as well as specific information of interest to investors. The site includes a useful glossary of terms used by the industry. Check it out, and learn the jargon of this exciting business.

stock certificate
Tangible evidence of stock ownership.

dividends
Part of the firm's profits that are distributed to shareholders.

- Why are bonds considered a form of debt financing?
- What is meant if a firm states it is issuing a 7 percent debenture bond due October 1, 2010?
- Explain the difference between an unsecured and a secured bond.
- Why do issuing companies typically like to include call provisions in their bonds?
- What role do the bond rating services play in the bond market?

···· ▬▬▬ ····

EQUITY FINANCING THROUGH ISSUING STOCK

As noted earlier, equity financing is another form of long-term funding. *Equity financing* is the obtaining of funds through the sale of shares of ownership in the corporation. There are two different classes of equity instruments: preferred and common stock. We will discuss each after a brief look at the terminology of stock and the advantages and disadvantages of issuing stock as a financing alternative.

··· THE TERMINOLOGY OF STOCK ···

Stocks are shares of ownership in a company. A **stock certificate** is tangible evidence of stock ownership. It is usually a piece of paper that specifies the name of the company, the number of shares it represents, and the type of stock it is. **Dividends** are the part of a firm's profits that are distributed to shareholders. Dividends can be distributed in the form of cash or more shares of stock.

··· ADVANTAGES AND DISADVANTAGES OF ISSUING STOCK ···

There are some advantages to raising long-term funds via equity financing.

- Because shareholders are owners of the business, their investment never has to be repaid. These funds are therefore available for acquisition of fixed (capital) and other assets.
- There is no legal obligation to pay dividends to shareholders. Note that dividends are payable only when the board of directors declares a dividend out of accumulated profits. In practice, most stable firms declare dividends regularly to keep their shares attractive for investors. New companies normally retain the profits for additional investment and growth for a few years before they begin to pay dividends.
- Selling shares rather than bonds can actually improve the company's financial position because it does not increase the company's debt.

Nevertheless, as the saying goes, there's no such thing as a free lunch. As you might suspect, there are disadvantages to equity financing as well.

- As owners of the firm, shareholders have the right to vote for the board of directors. As you remember from Chapter 6, the board of directors decides who will manage the firm and what its policies will be. Hence the direction of the firm can be altered through a significant sale of shares. In reality this rarely happens, because most issues add only a small percentage of shares to the total amount outstanding.

- Dividends are not a deduction for tax purposes, but interest on bonds is.
- Management decision making is often tempered by the need to keep shareholders happy. This often forces managers to use short-term tactics to keep earnings up rather than strategies to keep the firm profitable in the long run. The true cost of equity financing may be much higher than is shown on the books of the company.

Figure 19.9 summarizes some important features of equity and debt financing. Let's see how bonds, preferred stock, and common stock differ. See Figures 19.7 and 19.9 for further information on these differences.

••• ISSUING PREFERRED STOCK •••

Preferred stock gives its owners preference over common shareholders in the payment of dividends and in a claim on assets if the company is liquidated. However, it normally does not include voting rights in the firm. Preferred stock is frequently referred to as a *hybrid investment* in that it has characteristics of both bonds and stock. (This can be seen in Figure 19.8.) To illustrate, consider the treatment of preferred stock dividends.

Preferred stock dividends differ from common stock dividends in several ways. Preferred stock is generally issued with a par value, which becomes the basis for the dividend the firm is willing to pay. For example, if a par value of $100 is attached to a share of preferred stock and a dividend rate of 8 percent is attached to the same issue, the firm is committing to an $8 dividend for each share of preferred stock the investor owns (8 percent of $100 = $8). If you

preferred stock
Stock that gives owners preference over common shareholders in the payment of dividends and in a claim on assets if the business is liquidated; it does not include voting rights.

PREFERRED STOCK FEATURE	DESCRIPTION
Convertible	The shares may be exchanged after a stated number of years for common shares at a preset rate, at the option of the shareholder.
Cumulative	If the dividend is not paid in full in any year, the balance is carried forward (accumulates). The cumulative unpaid balance must be paid before any dividends are paid to common shareholders.
Callable	The company that issued the shares has the right after a stated number of years to call them back by repaying the shareholders their original investment.*
Redeemable	After a stated number of years, the investor may return the stock and ask for repayment of his or her investment.*

*If the shares are also cumulative, all dividend arrears must be paid as well.

FIGURE **19.7**
• • • •
OPTIONAL FEATURES AVAILABLE WITH PREFERRED STOCK
Each feature holds some attraction for the potential investor.

FIGURE **19.8**

• • • •

COMPARISON OF BONDS,
PREFERRED STOCK,
AND COMMON STOCK
OF PUBLIC COMPANIES

The different features
help both the issuer
and the investor decide
which vehicle is right
for each of them at a
particular time.

	Bonds	Preferred Shares	Common Shares
Interest or Dividends			
Must be paid	Yes	No	No
Pays a fixed rate	Yes	Yes	No
Deductible from payor's income tax	Yes	No	No
Canadian payee is taxed		(if payor company is Canadian)	
at reduced rate	No	Yes	Yes
Stock or bond			
Has voting rights	No	Not normally	Yes
May be traded on the stock exchange	Yes	Yes	Yes
Can be held indefinitely	No	Usually	Yes
Is convertible to common stock	Maybe	Maybe	Not applicable

own 100 shares of this preferred stock, your yearly dividend should be $800. Furthermore, this dividend is *fixed*, meaning it does not change each year. Also, if any dividends are paid, the dividends on preferred stock *must* be paid in full before any common stock dividends can be distributed. Common dividend may then be whatever rate the board of directors wants to pay out. Preferred stockholders normally lose their voting rights in the firm in exchange for this preferred dividend treatment.

As you can see, a similarity exists between preferred stock and bonds in that both have a face (or par) value and both have a fixed rate of return. Why not just refer to preferred stock as a form of bond? Remember, bondholders *must* receive interest and be *repaid* the face value of the bond on a maturity date. Preferred stock dividends do not legally *have* to be paid unless the stock is redeemed or called. Nor are the shares usually repurchased. Both bonds and preferred stock can fluctuate in market price.

cumulative preferred stock
Preferred stock that accumulates unpaid dividends.

One of the more important features of preferred stock is that it is often cumulative. **Cumulative preferred stock** guarantees an investor that if one or more dividends are not paid or only partially paid, the missed dividends will be accumulated. All the dividends, including the back dividends, must be paid in full before any common stock dividends can be paid. For example, as producers of Fiberrific, we may decide not to pay our preferred shareholders the full 8 percent dividend this period to retain funds for further research and development. The preferred shareholders must be paid the missing amount the following period before we can pay any dividends to common shareholders. If preferred stock is noncumulative, any dividends missed are lost to the shareholder. Figure 19.9 illustrates how this process works.

Figures 19.7 and 19.8 show some of the features available with preferred stock. If preferred stock does not meet the objectives of the firm or an individual investor, the firm can issue or the individual can invest in common stock. Let's look at this interesting alternative.

••• ISSUING COMMON STOCK •••

common stock
Represents ownership of a firm and the rights to vote and to receive all of the firm's profits (after preferred shareholders are paid), in the form of dividends declared by the board of directors.

Common stock represents ownership of a firm and gives shareholders the rights to vote and to receive all of the firm's profits after preferred shareholders are paid. As long as the company exists, these profits can be received only

Dividends Paid

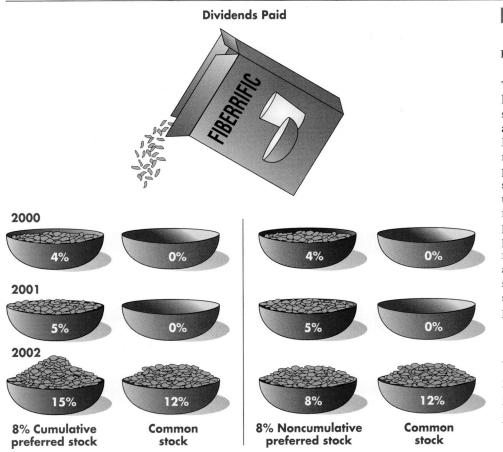

2000
8% Cumulative preferred stock
Common stock
8% Noncumulative preferred stock
Common stock

FIGURE **19.9**
· · · ·

A COMPARISON OF DIVIDENDS FOR VARIOUS TYPES OF SHARES

This figure shows what happens to different stock when dividends are missed or paid later. Note that if a dividend is not paid or only partially paid for noncumulative stock, it is never made up. Common stock cannot be paid anything if preferred is not first paid, and cumulative must be paid in full for all arrears. The schedule shows the year by year situation for cumulative preferred stock

8% CUMULATIVE PREFERRED

Year	Due	Paid	Owing
2000	8%	4%	4%
2001	12%	5%	7%
2002	15%	15%	0%

in the form of dividends declared by the board of directors. Shareholders influence corporate policy by electing the board of directors, which selects the management and makes major policy decisions.

Common stock is considered more risky and speculative than either bonds or preferred stock. Remember, common shareholders receive dividends only after both bondholders and preferred shareholders receive their interest and dividends. Also, if a company is forced to cease operations and money remains after creditors are paid, common shareholders share the funds only *after* bondholders and preferred shareholders recover their loans and investments.

Why, then, would investors select common stock as an investment alternative? Because the risk is often accompanied by higher returns. Several investment opportunities are available. For example, an investor may select a growth stock, a stock of a corporation whose earnings are expected to grow faster than other stocks or the overall economy. High-technology companies fall into this category. Rapid growth stocks are often quite speculative and pay rather low dividends, but the potential for growth is strong. Income stocks offer investors a rather high dividend yield on their investment. Care must be taken to ensure that these are good stocks, referred to as *blue chip*. **Blue chip stocks** are those of high-quality companies. Canadian banks, Bell Canada, and Microsoft are some examples.

Investors can even invest in a type of stock called a *penny stock*, which sells for less than $1 per share. Such stocks frequently represent ownership in mining companies and are usually highly speculative. The Vancouver Stock Exchange has many such offerings.

blue chip stocks
Stocks of high-quality companies.

It's important to remember that the value of common stock is very dependent on the performance of the corporation. Common stock is often referred to as participating stock because shareholders participate in the success or failure of the firm. Common stock offers great opportunities but is subject to a high degree of risk, as was evidenced by the major stock market crash of 1987, and the great volatility in share prices in 1998 and 1999.

Progress Check

- Name at least two advantages and two disadvantages of issuing stock as a form of equity financing.
- What are the major differences between preferred stock and common stock?
- In what ways are preferred stock and bonds similar? In what ways are they different?
- How does an investor benefit by owning cumulative preferred stock as opposed to noncumulative preferred?
- What is the difference between blue chip stocks and penny stocks?

TRADING IN BONDS AND STOCKS

Bonds and shares of public companies are bought and sold by investors through stockbrokers, who charge a commission on all sales and purchases. These brokers have representatives on the floor of the stock exchanges, where actual trading occurs. That is where a broker's agent with a security for sale on behalf of a client who has given the broker a sell order finds a broker's agent with a similar order to buy.

If you look at the financial pages, where the shares traded are listed daily, you will see that a vast number of shares of many different securities are traded regularly. For example, the Toronto Stock Exchange was trading about 100 million shares daily in October 1999. See Figure 19.10 for an excerpt of a daily listing.

Several major stock exchanges around the world dominate securities trading. New York, Tokyo, Frankfurt, and London are such major markets where billions of shares are traded daily. Five Canadian cities have local stock exchanges: Toronto, Montreal, Vancouver, Calgary, and Winnipeg. There are specialized exchanges in major financial centres where trading in commodities, futures, and other activities is carried on. These are complex fields where expert knowledge is required.

In the late 1990s a new phenomenon in security trading emerged. The Internet, whose impact we have seen throughout this book, has also made its presence known in this area. Many financial institutions and brokerage firms offer discount rates for trading via the Internet. Using your computer and a connection to one of these companies, you can easily buy and sell securities at very low cost. A good example is TDWaterhouse (see margin Web address).

<www.tdwaterhouse.ca>

This is the online trading system used by Green Line, the discount brokerage arm of the Toronto-Dominion Bank (TD). Although TD is one of the smaller banks in Canada and very small by global standards, its acquisition of the U.S. discount giant Waterhouse resulted in TDWaterhouse ranking among the largest discount brokerage firms in the world. Investors who want to trade directly online can do so via the Internet.

••• BUYING SECURITIES ON MARGIN •••

buying on margin
Purchasing securities by borrowing some of the cost from the broker.

Buying on margin means you purchase securities by borrowing some of the cost from your broker, who holds them as collateral security until you pay the balance due. In effect the broker lends you the money and charges you interest. Provincial regulatory agencies, such as the Ontario Securities Commission, control all aspects of this industry, including what minimum percentage of the

A	B	C	D	E	F	G	H	I	J	K	L
365-day									Vol.		P/E
high	low	Stock	Sym	Div	High	Low	Close	Chg	(100s)	Yield	ratio
1.00	0.33	ABL Cda	ABL		0.45	0.45	0.45		30		
9.20	7.70	ADF Group	DRX		8.95	8.95	8.95	+0.50	10		10.2
28.10	15.55	AGF Ma	AGF.B	0.32	21.00	20.00	20.55	−0.75	263	1.6	14.3
25.50	18.95	AJC Divers	ADC		19.25	19.25	19.25	−1.25	6		
25.00	23.25	AIC	ADC.PR.A	1.50	23.85	23.40	23.40	−0.45	61	6.4	
1.75	0.30	AIT Advanc	AIV		0.70	0.65	0.65		23		
16.50	3.40	♣ ALI Tech	ALT		3.70	3.60	3.65	+0.05	358		14.6
3.15	1.75	AMR Tech	AMR		2.00	2.00	2.00	−0.30	13		
11.05	4.50	AT Plastics	ATP	0.18	4.90	4.65	4.75	+0.10	177	3.8	13.6
49.00	41.87	AT&T Cd	TEL.B		49.00	48.25	48.60	+0.20	183		37.4
27.90	11.20	♣ ATI Tech	ATY		17.10	16.10	16.90	−0.60	28208		18.4
23.50	9.50	ATS Autom	ATA		13.50	13.25	13.35	−0.30	123		20.2
6.50	4.80	Aastra Tec	AAH		6.00	5.45	5.90	+0.40	1307	13.4	
0.88	0.19	Abacan	ABC		0.23	0.20	0.21	+.005	2692		
16.10	6.80	Aber Res	ABZ		8.25	7.90	8.25	+0.30	871		
20.55	11.65	Abitibi Cons	A	0.40	18.00	17.00	17.90	+0.65	11245	2.2	
6.50	5.25	Acanthus	ACR	0.48	6.00	6.00	6.00		50	8.0	9.7
6.60	1.90	Acetex	ATX		6.00	6.00	6.00	+0.25	21		
14.25	11.15	Acktion	ACK		12.00	12.00	12.00	−0.70	10		12.5
5.50	4.80	Ad Opt Tec	AOP		5.00	5.00	5.00	+0.10	1	31.2	
0.55	0.22	Adrian Res	ADL		0.26	0.25	0.25	−0.01	204		
0.59	0.15	Advantex	ADX		0.52	0.44	0.50	−0.02	545		
14.25	5.60	Agnico-Ea	AGE	0.03	12.35	11.40	11.80	−0.55	2529	0.2	
11.75	7.95	♣ Agra	AGR	0.16	11.00	10.35	11.00	−0.15	109	1.4	14.3
17.25	11.85	Agrium	AGU	.163	14.20	13.95	14.15	−0.15	708	1.1	12.4
15.00	7.00	Armglobal	AGT		9.40	8.55	8.60	−9.65	18		
12.85	2.60	Ainsworth L	ANS		6.90	6.45	6.45	−0.05	253		5.9
11.20	5.70	Air Canada	AC		10.15	9.65	10.15	+0.40	7729		
10.50	4.60	Air Canad	AC.A		9.70	9.10	9.70	+0.45	2589		
5.50	2.45	AirBoss	BOS		4.47	4.45	4.45	+0.05	48		14.3
11.45	6.10	Akita	AKT.A	0.28	9.40	9.25	9.25	−0.15	25	3.0	14.7
1.18	0.70	Alarmforce	AF		1.00	1.00	1.00		10		14.3
48.90	30.75	♣ Alta Ener	AEC	0.40	43.40	42.70	43.20	+0.30	2936	0.9	
26.00	24.55	AltaE	AEC.PR.A	2.125	25.40	25.30	25.40	+0.10	155	8.4	
54.90	34.15	♣ Alcan	AL	.892	49.70	48.80	49.40	+0.20	6016	1.8	21.0
26.10	25.00	♣ Alcan	AL.PR.E	1.681	25.55	25.50	25.50	+0.05	31	6.6	
24.10	22.40	♣ Alcan	AL.PR.F	1.172	23.00	23.00	23.00	2	5.1		
1.73	0.22	Alexa Vent	AXA		1.35	1.30	1.35	−0.01	255		
3.48	1.63	Altoma Stl	ALG		2.15	2.08	2.10	+0.02	867		
5.45	3.00	Algonquin	AM	0.40	4.60	4.60	4.60	−0.10	1	8.7	
25.75	21.50	Aliant	AIT	0.90	22.70	22.15	22.50		431	4.0	18.0
38.40	21.50	Allbanc	ABK		26.75	25.75	26.50	+0.25	96		21.9
26.25	24.50	Allba	ABK.PR.A	1.385	25.00	24.50	24.55	−0.45	203	5.6	
6.35	2.00	♣ Allelix	AXB		2.45	2.45	2.45	+0.20	8		
29.50	17.25	AlincAti	AAC.A		20.00	20.00	20.00		10		
29.50	12.50	AincAt	AAC.B		14.00	14.00	14.00	+0.25	120		14.6
20.75	13.85	♣ AllianceFo	ALP		17.50	17.00	17.25	+0.20	6337		

This is a small segment of the list of stocks traded on the Toronto Stock Exchange (TSE), October 21, 1999, as reported the following day in *The Globe and Mail*.

Here is an explanation of what the column headings mean:

A & B: highest and lowest price in the last year

C: abbreviated name of the company

D: the symbol used to identify the company for trading purposes

E: annual dividend per share

F, G, & H: highest, lowest, and closing price for *that* day

I: change in closing price from the previous day

J: number of shares traded that day in hundreds (e.g., first line is 3000 shares)

K: *yield* refers to estimated percent income your investment would yield if you bought at closing price and kept the stock for a year. It is the ratio of annual dividend to closing price. There is no yield for those companies that show no dividend paid.

L: *P/E ratio* refers to ratio of closing price to estimated earnings per share (which is not shown but is known). Where no ratio is shown it means either that the company is not making any profits or no estimate of earnings is available.

purchase price must be paid in cash. For example, if the current rate is 50 percent for shares and 10 percent for bonds, you would have to invest a minimum of $4 to buy an $8 share (plus commissions to the broker), and $97 to buy a bond selling for $970.

If the stock or bond drops in price, you will get a *margin call* from your broker. This means that you will have to make a payment to your broker to

E*TRADE Canada is an online service that allows Canadians to trade Canadian and U.S. stocks and options and Canadian mutual funds.

maintain the margin of collateral protection that the broker is obligated to observe. In this case, the loan cannot exceed 50 percent of the stock value or 90 percent of the bond value.

PERSONAL SITUATIONS OF INVESTORS   Any type of investing carries some amount of *risk* with it. Some investments are riskier than others. The personal situation and temperament of an investor dictates the type of investment he or she will choose. Important considerations are the age, income, wealth, and philosophy of the investor. A young person with a good income and a daring outlook will be likely to take a higher risk when investing. A retired person will be less interested in risk and more concerned about the security of the investment, a reliable, steady flow of income, particularly if he or she has limited funds.

The existence of such a widely diversified market of potential investors lets public companies create varying kinds of securities to raise the funds they need by satisfying a wide spectrum of investor needs. However, the largest buyers of securities are not individuals. They are pension funds, mutual funds (discussed below), banks, insurance and trust companies, stock brokerage firms, and large corporations with surplus funds not immediately required for operations.

DIVERSIFYING INVESTMENTS   A prudent policy for investors is to avoid having all their eggs in one basket. If you place all your money in one stock you have a great deal of confidence in, you are exposing yourself to high risk should you be wrong. Diversify your investment by buying a variety of stocks and bonds that give you a mix of income, security, and growth.

One way to achieve this goal when your money is limited is to invest in mutual funds. A **mutual fund** buys a variety of securities and then sells units of ownership in the fund to the public. It has expert analysts who constantly watch the market.

mutual fund
A fund that buys a variety of securities and then sells units of ownership in the fund to the public.

Reaching Beyond Our Borders

<www.sleeman.com>

Hands Across the Border

John Sleeman's family had been in the brewery business for three generations before they closed down in the 1930s. In 1984 Sleeman decided to rebuild the family brewery, armed with the family recipe book and a 20 percent U.S. partner, Stroh Brewing Co. But in August 1988, a month away from bottling the cream ale aging in its casks, Sleeman hit a $3 million snag.

After agreeing to finance the brewery with a $3 million loan, Sleeman's bank abruptly decided it wanted its money back—within 30 days. The bank had had second thoughts, doubting that the venture could succeed. They couldn't see how Sleeman hoped to compete against Molson and Labatt, "when Molson was spending more just to advertise the launch of Molson Dry in Ontario" than Sleeman was spending for his entire operation.

But John Sleeman isn't the kind of man who will allow his business to fail. His attitude is, "if you want it bad enough, you find a way to fund it and keep it going." So he spent the first 15 days soliciting other Canadian banks, which, he says, treated him "like a leper." Then Sleeman looked south and the first U.S. bank he approached, The National Bank of Detroit, agreed to finance the company. Sleeman's U.S. partner Stroh's 20 percent interest in the company helped swing the deal.

Sleeman's is now Canada's third-largest brewer and Sleeman holds no grudges. In 1996, when he felt that the company had outgrown its Detroit bankers, Sleeman turned to Canadian banks again and this time, not surprisingly, he had no problems. Sleeman is very satisfied with the support his bank gives him now. Still, he says, "if I had given up when the Canadian bank said 'game's over,' I wouldn't be having this conversation." Sleeman's sells $76 million of beer annually and employs 500 people. His advice is that if you "have a good idea and you've done your homework, don't give up on it."

▲ Source: Rick Kang, "Banks for Nothing," *Profit,* October 1999, p. 9.

Mutual funds let even the smallest investor diversify a portfolio. A wide assortment of mutual funds specialize in acquiring certain types of domestic and foreign securities. This can satisfy the needs of all investors. *The Globe and Mail* daily mutual funds report of October 22, 1999, lists some 1800 Canadian mutual funds. There are thousands in the U.S.

At the same time, by enlarging the market for securities, mutual funds make it easier for public companies to obtain financing for their operations and expansion.

Critical Thinking

What form of investment seems most appropriate to your needs now? Do you suspect your objectives and needs will change over time?

Would investing other people's money be an interesting career to pursue? What are some of the problems stockbrokers or mutual fund managers might face in the course of their jobs?

Does it make sense for investors to diversify their investments or would it be more logical to put all their eggs in one basket?

STOCK INDEXES

Stock indexes measure the trend of different stock and commodity exchanges. Every country with stock exchanges has such indexes. In Canada there are several thousand companies listed on various exchanges, and the prices of their shares fluctuate constantly. Some may be rising over a certain period and others may be falling. Some may seesaw up and down. Various indexes have been developed to give interested parties useful information about significant trends.

In Canada a commonly used index is the TSE 300, which consists of the weighted average of 300 of the most important stocks listed on the Toronto Stock Exchange. In the United States, the major (and oldest) index is the Dow Jones Industrial Average, the *Dow*, as it is commonly called. The Dow measures the movements of the shares of 30 of the largest companies in the United States that are listed on the New York Stock Exchange. It is an important index that receives worldwide attention.

Both of these averages have been carefully designed to give a realistic picture of the results of all trading in their respective stock exchanges each day. They do not work perfectly, but usually give a fair picture. You can find these and other indexes in the financial pages of your daily newspaper or in the financial papers.

•••• ▬▬ ••••

CYCLES IN THE STOCK MARKET AND INTEREST RATES

There are many reasons why the prices of shares listed on stock exchanges fluctuate. A popular stock in strong demand will rise because of that demand. A company that is doing well or that is rumoured to be on the verge of being taken over will usually see its stock go up. Certain industries are favoured or out of favour at certain times because they are expected to do well or poorly.

On the other hand, rumours of financial troubles or scandals will drive a stock down. Some industries, like pulp and paper, are said to be cyclical. That is, they have a few good years followed by some poorer years. Naturally, their stock prices fluctuate in such periods.

Another major cause of stock price fluctuation is that the capitalist economic system undergoes periodic cycles of recession and recovery. These ups and downs are reflected in the general movement of price levels of stocks. The stock market does not move in tandem with the level of economic activity; it does not exactly parallel but rather is thought to predict the cyclical movement of the economy in a particular country.

With the globalization of business, volatility in international economies now has a marked affect on every domestic economy, including Canada's. When the Russian economy and many Asian economies took a big tumble in 1998, their stock exchanges and currencies practically collapsed, and the effect was felt globally. Of course, our exchanges and currency were not immune from the "Asian flu," so we suffered too.

The level of interest rates in a country also fluctuates, and this has a marked effect on the stock market. In Canada in the 1980s, interest rates climbed to historic highs. Banks were charging ordinary businesses 22 percent for commercial loans in 1980. In mid-1999, this rate was down to 7.5 percent. The reasons for such fluctuations are complex. If you are interested in following up on this important topic, consider taking courses in economics.

These fluctuations have a major impact on bond prices and on the interest rates of new bond issues. Preferred share prices are also affected, as are the dividend rates on new issues. If you are going into the market for funding, you must plan carefully to avoid getting caught in a long-term commitment to high dividends and interest costs. That is one reason there is such a variety of vehicles that enable businesses to make flexible financing arrangements.

REVIEW

It's time now to try to cope with the dilemma discussed at the beginning of the chapter. Our two executives have somewhat different answers to this question. Bédard has this response: "A chief financial officer of a company has an obligation to make public all material information on the viability of the company. I believe that it should be disclosed."

Reilley feels that "this is a hard question because Proto's problems could be overcome with no one being the wiser and with everyone winning. I would suggest to Karina, in a neutral fashion, that, in spite of our friendship and as good business practice, I would expect her to undertake extensive due-diligence before she acted."

Since you have some serious concerns about the financial health of the company, you have probably been thinking about looking for another position in a stronger company where security and the chances of promotion are much better. Since you may be leaving

Proto in the near future, why not drop a hint to Karina that she should reconsider her pension fund's plan to buy Proto's ordinary debenture bonds. However you should tell her that you will only share information if she agrees not to ask for explanations or discussions and to keep your suggestion confidential. Remember that if you are licensed by a professional organization, it most likely requires that you do not divulge confidential information that you have obtained through your work.

You have another option and that is to get the message to her via a third party she trusts and who would keep you name out of it, preferably someone Karina does not know is your acquaintance. As far as Proto Corp. is concerned, it may very well sell the bond issue to other buyers so no harm would have been done to the company and you would have protected Karina from recommending a risky investment for her pension fund.

CAREER OPPORTUNITIES

As you can see the financial world offers a choice of careers. You can work in the finance division of any company or in a financial institution like a bank, insurance, trust, or brokerage company, any one of which has a large number of positions. You can also, as many of the authors' students do, get one of the many jobs available with investment bankers or business consulting firms. Concentrating on the areas of finance and international business would be a good way to find interesting, global careers in finance.

Progress Check

- What does buying on margin mean? How does it work?
- What exactly are mutual funds? How do they benefit small investors?
- What is a stock index? What is its purpose? Can you name a Canadian index? A U.S. index?

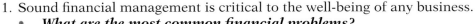

SUMMARY

1. Sound financial management is critical to the well-being of any business.
   - ***What are the most common financial problems?***
   The most common financial problems are (1) undercapitalization, (2) poor cash flow, and (3) planning and control weaknesses. Finance is that function in a business responsible for acquiring funds for the firm and managing funds within the firm by, for example, preparing budgets, ana-

1. Explain the role and importance of finance and the responsibilities of financial managers.

lyzing cash flow, and planning for the expenditure of funds on various assets.

- ● *What do finance managers do?*
  Finance managers plan, budget, control funds, obtain funds, collect funds, audit, manage taxes, and advise top management on financial matters.

2. Outline the steps in financial planning by explaining how to forecast financial needs, develop budgets, and establish financial controls.

2. Financial planning involves short- and long-term forecasting, budgeting, and financial controls.
- ● *What are the three budgets of finance?*
  The operating budget is the projection of dollar allocations to various costs and expenses, given various revenues. The capital budget is the spending plan for capital or fixed assets. The cash budget is the detailed cash-flow forecast for the period.

3. Recognize the financial needs that must be met with available funds.

3. During the course of a business's life, its financial needs shift considerably.
- ● *What are the areas of financial needs?*
  Businesses have financial needs in four major areas: (1) daily operations, (2) credit services, (3) inventory purchases, and (4) major assets purchases.

4. Distinguish between short-term and long-term financing and between debt capital and equity capital.

4. Businesses often have needs for short- and long-term financing and for debt capital and equity capital.
- ● *What is the difference between short- and long-term financing?*
  Short-term financing refers to funds that will be repaid in less than one year; long-term financing is money that will be repaid over a longer period.

- ● *What is the difference between debt capital and equity capital?*
  Debt capital refers to funds raised by borrowing (going into debt). Equity capital is raised by selling ownership (stock) in the company.

5. Identify and describe several sources of short-term capital.

5. There are many sources for short-term financing, including trade credit, family and friends, commercial banks, government programs, factoring, and commercial paper.
- ● *Why should businesses use trade credit?*
  Because it is financing without cost.

- ● *What is a line of credit?*
  It is an advance agreement by a bank to loan up to a specified amount of money to the business whenever the business requires it.

- ● *What is the difference between a secured loan and an unsecured loan?*
  An unsecured loan has no collateral backing it. A secured loan is backed by accounts receivable (called *pledging*), inventory, or other property of value.

- ● *Is factoring a form of secured loan?*
  No, factoring means selling accounts receivable for a fee.

- ● *What is commercial paper?*
  Commercial paper is a promissory note maturing in 270 days or less.

6. Identify and describe several sources of long-term capital.

6. An important function of a finance manager is to obtain long-term capital.
- ● *What are the three major sources of long-term capital?*
  Major sources of long-term capital are surplus cash funds, debt capital (including dealer financing), and equity capital. See Figure 19.5 for full details.

7. Compare the advantages and disadvantages of issuing bonds, and identify the classes and features of bonds.

7. Companies can raise capital by debt financing, which involves issuing bonds.
- ● *What are the advantages and disadvantages of issuing bonds?*

The advantages of issuing bonds include (1) management retains control since bondholders cannot vote, (2) interest paid on bonds is tax deductible, and (3) bonds are only a temporary source of finance. The disadvantages of bonds include (1) because bonds are an increased debt, they may adversely affect the market's valuation of the company; (2) interest must be paid on bonds; and (3) the face value must be repaid on the maturity date.

- *Are there different types of bonds?*

Yes. There are unsecured (debenture) and secured bonds. Unsecured bonds are not supported by collateral. Secured bonds are backed by tangible assets such as mortgages, stock, and equipment. They all have different features.

8. Companies can also raise capital by equity financing, which involves selling stock.

- *What are the advantages and disadvantages of issuing stock?*

The advantages of issuing stock include (1) the stock never has to be repaid since shareholders are owners in the company, (2) there is no legal obligation to pay dividends, and (3) no debt is incurred, so the company is financially stronger. The disadvantages include (1) shareholders are owners of the firm and can affect its management through election of the board of directors, (2) it is more costly to pay dividends since they are paid after taxes, and (3) managers may be tempted to make shareholders happy in the short term rather than plan for long-term needs.

- *What are the differences between common and preferred stock?*

Holders of common stock have voting rights in the company. Holders of preferred stock have no voting rights. In exchange for the loss of voting privileges, preferred stocks offer a *fixed* dividend that must be paid in full before holders of common stock receive a dividend. Preferred stock has other various features.

8. Compare the advantages and disadvantages of issuing stock, and outline the differences between common and preferred stock.

KEY TERMS

blue chip stocks 629	**debt capital** 613	**pledging** 617
bond 623	**dividends** 626	**preferred stock** 627
buying on margin 630	**equity capital** 614	**principal** 623
capital budget 610	**factoring** 618	**secured bonds** 624
cash budget 610	**finance** 607	**secured loan** 617
cash-flow forecast 609	**line of credit** 617	**short-term forecast** 609
commercial paper 618	**long-term forecast** 610	**stock certificate** 626
common stock 628	**maturity date** 623	**stock exchange** 622
convertible bond 625	**mutual fund** 632	**trade credit** 614
cumulative preferred stock 628	**operating budget** 610	**unsecured bonds** 624

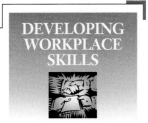

DEVELOPING WORKPLACE SKILLS

1. Obtain annual reports from three major corporations. Study the balance sheets. Which assets are fixed and what is their value? How much have the companies borrowed? (Look under liabilities.) Which one is in the best financial condition? Why?

2. Visit a local bank lending officer. Ask what the current interest rate is and what rate small businesses pay for short- and long-term loans. Ask for blank forms that borrowers use to apply for loans. Share these forms with your class, and explain the types of information they ask for.

3. Use information from the Canadian and Dominion Bond Rating Services to find their evaluation of the bonds of three large Canadian companies. Ask the librarian what similar references are available. Report what you find to the class.

4. The banking crisis of the early 1990s made banks even more reluctant to lend money to small businesses. Assume you are a small-business consultant. Draft a memo to your clients advising them regarding the best sources for financing.

5. Analyze the risks and opportunities of investing today in stocks, bonds, and mutual funds. Assume your Great Aunt Hildi just left you $10,000. Since you and your parents already saved enough money to cover your college bills, you decide to invest the money so that you can start your own business after you graduate. How will you invest your money? Why? Name specific investments.

INTERNET CHALLENGES

1. Check out the Web sites of the Canadian Bankers Association <www.cba.ca> to see if you can find information on the trend in lending to small business. Are more companies receiving loans? What was the rate of refusal of loans to small businesses during the last few years? Is the refusal rate rising, declining, or unchanged?

2. Look through the Web site of the Business Development Bank of Canada (BDC) at <www.bdc.ca> to see how helpful it is. If you were starting a small business, would the information lead you to apply for a loan with the BDC? Is there anything you were looking for that you cannot find? Is there much information for those wanting to start an Internet-based company?

Practising Management Decisions

CASE 1

VANCITY ENTERS SMALL-BUSINESS VENTURE CAPITAL MARKET

Vancouver City Savings Credit Union is a well-known credit union that has expanded into various banking activities in the Vancouver area. VanCity decided to add providing venture capital loans to small businesses to its activities by setting up VanCity Capital Corp. in January 1999. President and CEO Dave Mowat, who had 20 years of experience with the Business Development Bank of Canada, says that they are not going after any "elephants" and that they will settle for loans of less than $1 million. There won't be much glamour but neither will there be massive write-offs of bad loans. By October 1999 VanCity had invested in 18 companies and the average loan was $270,000.

VanCity cooperates with other local organizations in helping to finance local companies. It has joined Working Opportunity Fund in a $1.75 million venture capital loan to Soft Tracks Enterprises Inc., "a Vancouver company that makes software for wireless point-of-sale transactions." VanCity has a reputation for stressing ethical investments and this venture appears to be in line with this policy. Included in the 18 companies are Co-operative Auto Network, a co-op that runs a fleet of cars for its members, and the Victorian Order of Nurses, a well-known non-profit agency "that will use its loan to expand its contract nursing services."

Mowat plans invest about $25 million over the next three to five years. The company will also consider investments beyond the Vancouver area once the company is well established. VanCity is Canada's largest credit union and "makes a good profit for its members," but it likes to give back to the community because "the healthier the community, the healthier the service providers in the community."

Decision Questions

1. Do you think that this new venture shows that the market for small business financing is continuing to expand? Or does it indicate that current sources of financing are not doing

enough for small business? Look at the chapter carefully and see if its possible that both of these statements are correct.

2. Do you think VanCity's policy of financing co-ops and nonprofit organizations is a good idea? Do you think they are riskier than loans made to new small businesses? Why?

3. Have you seen any reports in the media or on the Net mentioning difficulties that small businesses are having getting financing? Have you seen any referring to companies in your city or region? Do you think there is a need for a *VanCity* in your area? Explain.

4. VanCity Savings Credit Union has been operating profitably for its members for some years. It has been able to do so despite the limitation of investing only in what it deems are ethical companies. Do you find it encouraging that this is the case? Would you like to work for such a company? Even if the salary structure or promotion possibilities are not as good as elsewhere? Discuss.

Source: Wendy Stueck, "VanCity Capital Settles on Boring But Profitable," *Globe and Mail, Report on Business,* October 11, 1999. p. B5.

CASE 2
BONDS OR STOCK? THAT IS THE QUESTION

In 1963, Carlos Galendez had dreams but very little money. He spent more than 10 years working as a dishwasher and then cook for a major restaurant. His dream was to save enough money to start his own Mexican restaurant. In 1965 his dream finally came true. With a small business bank loan, he opened his first Casa de Carlos restaurant. His old family recipes and appealing decor helped the business gain immediate success. Galendez repaid his loan within 14 months and immediately opened a second, then a third, location. By 1975 Casa de Carlos was the largest Mexican restaurant chain in the nation.

In 1976 the company decided to go public. Galendez believed continued growth was beneficial to the company, and he felt offering ownership was the way to bring in loyal investors. Nevertheless, he made certain his family maintained controlling interest in the firm's stock: in its initial public offering, Casa de Carlos offered to sell only 40 percent of the available shares in the company to investors. The Galendez family kept control of 60 percent of the stock.

As the public's craving for Mexican food grew, so did the fortunes of Casa de Carlos, Inc. Heading into the 1980s, the company enjoyed the position of being light on debt and heavy on cash. But in 1983, the firm's debt position changed when it bought out Captain Al's Seafood Restaurants. Three years later, it expanded into full-service wholesale distributor of seafood products with the purchase of Mariner Wholesalers. The firm's debt increased, but the price of its stock was up and demand at all three operations was booming.

In 1995 Galendez died. His oldest child, Maria, was selected to take control as chief executive officer. Maria had learned the business from her father. He taught her to keep an eye out for opportunities that seemed fiscally responsible. Unfortunately, in 1998 the fortunes of the firm began to shift. Two major competitors were taking market share from Casa de Carlos, and the seafood venture began to flounder. The recession in the 1990s didn't help either. Consumers spent less, causing some severe cash problems. Maria Galendez had to decide how to get the funds the firm needed for improvements and other expenses. Banks wouldn't extend the firm's credit line. She considered a bond or stock offering to raise capital.

Decision Questions

1. What advantages and disadvantages of offering bonds to investors should Maria consider?

2. What would be the advantages and disadvantages to the company of offering new stock to investors?

3. Are any other options available to Maria Galendez?

4. If you were Maria, what choice would you make? Why?

Chapter Endnotes

Chapter 1

1. "From World Trade to World Investment," *The Wall Street Journal*, May 26, 1987.

2. Robert Reich, "Who Is Us?" *Harvard Business Review*, January–February 1990, p. 53.

3. Statistics Canada, CANSIM, Matrix 3685, Series D399443-8, May 1999.

4. George Dufour, Chief, Trade Statistics, Canada, <www.bcstats.gov.bc.ca>, 1999.

5. Sources for the entire section are Wendy Dobson, "Canada Missing Business Opportunities in East Asia," *Financial Post*, September 23, 1995, p. 25; *Globe and Mail* series, "The Changing West," January 1996.

6. Timothy Pritchard, "Chrysler Changes Tone to Woo Customers," *Globe and Mail, Report on Business*, July 1, 1992, p. B1.

7. Interview with Walter McCall, February 20, 1996.

8. Greg Keenan, "$500-million Overhaul Slated for Bramalea Plant," *Globe and Mail, ROB*, February 16, 1996, p. B1; interview with Walter McCall, November 17, 1999.

9. Compiled from a variety of sources including reports and internet sites of Industry Canada, Business Development Bank of Canada, Statistics Canada, Export Development Corp., Royal Bank, and articles in *Profit* and *Canadian Business* magazines, *The Globe and Mail, ROB*, and the *Montreal Gazette*.

10. Bill Taylor, "The Next Millennium," *Montreal Gazette*, January 10, 1966, p. C1.

11. Interview with Judith Aston, February 15, 1996.

12. Shirley Won, "Homing in on New Careers," *Globe and Mail, ROB*, April 25, 1992, p. B1.

13. Cleta Moyer, "Sending Your Employees Home," *Profit*, October–November 1995, p. 9.

14. Some of the data in this section is from *Manufacturing Our Future*, Canadian Manufacturers Association (CMA), 1995, and four articles by Susan Noakes in the *Financial Post*, December 17–21, 1990.

15. Bruce Little, "Manufacturing Keeps Economy on Growth Target," *Globe and Mail, ROB* June 1, 1999, C1. Michael Valpy, "Fate of Manufacturing, a Make-or-Break Crisis," *Globe and Mail*, May 8, 1989, p. A8; Madeleine Drohan, "Service Becoming Canada's New Backbone," *Globe and Mail, ROB*, April 16, 1990, p. B1; *Manufacturing Our Future*, CMA.

16. Nuala Beck, *Shifting Gears: Thriving in the New Economy* (Toronto: Harper & Collins, 1992), as reported by Crawford Kilian, the *Province* (Vancouver), reprinted in the *Montreal Gazette*, December 19, 1992, p. B6.

17. All the data in this section comes from Ronald Logan, "Immigration During the 1980s," and Gordon Priest, "The Demographic Future," *Canadian Social Trends*, Spring 1991, Statistics Canada, Cat. No. 11-008E. Also Statistics Canada, 1996 data, the Internet.

18. David Schindler, interviewed on "Quirks and Quarks," CBC, February 24, 1996.

19. *Daily* Archives, Statistics Canada, <www.statcan.ca>, February 29, 1996.

20. *Montreal Gazette*, March 2, 1996, pp. B4–5; "Cross-Country Checkup," CBC, March 3, 1996.

21. Statistics Canada, <www.statcan.ca>, May 1999.

22. *Daily* Archives, Statistics Canada, <www.statcan.ca>, May 1999.

23. Interview with Paul Swinwood, "Daybreak," CBM Montreal, CBC, February 23, 1996; interview with Paul Swinwood, April 16, 1999.

24. *Manufacturing Our Future*, CMA.

25. John Holusha, "First College, then the Mill," *New York times*, as reported in *The Globe and Mail, ROB*, August 29, 1995, p. B10.

Chapter 2

1. *Time*, February 15, 1999, 36.

2. "Lessons from the Brink," *Business Week*, September 21, 1998, p. 146.

3. *Daily* Archives, Statistics Canada, <www.statcan.ca>, May 1999.

4. Bruce Little, "Manufacturing Keeps Economy on Growth Tract," *Globe and Mail, ROB*, June 1, 1999, B1.

5. Eric Beauchesne, "OECD Admits Error," *Montreal Gazette*, May 21, 1999, C1.

6. Compiled from various reports: Bank of Canada, Statistics Canada, and 1999 federal budget documents.

7. Sandra Cordon, "Strong Growth Forecast," *Montreal Gazette*, May 20, 1999, A1; "Sheltered from the Global Storm," *Scotia Plus*, Spring/Summer 1999, p. 5.

Chapter 3

1. *Daily* Archives, Statistics Canada, <www.statcan.ca>, May 1999.

2. Ibid.

3. Madelaine Drohan, *Globe and Mail, ROB*, March 28, 1996, p. B3.

4. "A Musical Ride to the Cash Register," *MacLean's*, March 11, 1996, p. 10.

5. "Free Trade Closer for Canada and Chile," *Financial Post*, March 23, 1996, p. 10.

6. Bartlett & Ghoshall, *Transnational Management*, Irwin, 1995, 176–182.

7. Donald N. Thompson, "Porter on Canadian Competitiveness," *Business Quarterly*, Winter 1992, p. 55.

8. This section is based on three sources: Alan Freeman, "Manufacturing Exports on a Roll," *Globe and Mail*, April 25, 1992, p. G1; Harvey Enchin, "Competitiveness Not New to Canadians," *Globe and Mail*, ROB, May 7, 1992, p. B1; *Manufacturing Our Future*, 1995.

9. Eric Beauchesne, "OECD Admits Error," *Montreal Gazette*, May 21, 1999, C1.

Chapter 4

1. CBC News, December 4, 1998.

2. Various titles of the *Globe and Mail*, ROB, December 1995, and January and February 1996.

3. Joe Bryan, "Delegates Will Week Way to Untangle Barriers to Interprovincial Trade," *Montreal Gazette*, February 1, 1992, p. B1.

4. "Ottawa Mulls $150 Million Aid for Aerospace Industry," *Financial Post*, January 25, 1996, p. 4.

5. Oliver Bertin, "Spar's Radarstat Succeeds in Sending Clear Image," *Globe and Mail*, ROB, December 15, 1995, p. B9.

6. Barrie McKenna, "$200-Million Aerospace Project Threatened," *Globe and Mail*, ROB, January 19, 1996, p. B1.

7. Anne-Marie Tobin, "Algoma Steel Rescued by Employee Takeover," *Montreal Gazette*, February 29, 1992, p. D3.

8. CBC News, January 27, 1999.

9. John Partridge, "Bank Machine Revolution Near," *Globe and Mail*, ROB, September 11, 1995, p. B1.

10. Barrie McKenna, "Neilsen Data Monopoly Cancelled," *Globe and Mail*, ROB, August 31, 1995, p. B1.

11. Rod Macdonell, "Proposed Takeover of Maple Leaf Mills Raises Fears of Concentration of Flour Power," *Montreal Gazette*, April 6, 1996, p. D1.

12. Lawrence Surtees, "CRTC Orders Cut in Overseas Phone Rates," *Globe and Mail*, ROB, February 3, 1996, p. B1.

13. *Annual Reports*, National Research Council; and other NRC publications, 1991–1998.

14. "U.S. Agricultural Policy Facing Radical Changes," *Globe and Mail*, ROB, September 11, 1995, p. B10.

15. Interview with agricultural economist Dr. Garth Coffin, Associate dean, MacDonald College, McGill University, April 6, 1996, and October 10, 1998.

16. For example, see *Globe and Mail*, ROB, September 21, 1995, p. B14 and February 13, 1996, p. B9.

17. *Montreal Gazette*, October 25, 1998, D7.

18. John Godfrey, "Big League Trade," Report on the Nation, *Financial Post*, Winter 1989, p. 26.

19. Headlines such as "Slash-and-Burn Equals Civil Strife," "Rethinking Employment," "Budget Cutters Thinking Twice," and "Watching Government Shrink," can be found throughout many media in January, February, and March 1996, and these articles express varying degrees of concern about or disagreement with current policies. Important radio and TV business programs in Canada and the United States expressed similar opinions.

20. "Politics This Week," *The Economist*, April 6, 1996, p. 4.

21. *Montreal Gazette*, October 25, 1998, D7.

22. CBC News, June 18, 1999.

23. *Civilization*, June/July 1999, pp. 86 and 87.

Chapter 5

1. Madelaine Drohan, "Capitalism Must Develop a Hart, Executives Told," *Globe and Mail*, ROB, February 2, 1996, p. B7.

2. John Neinzel, "Ethics Sell, Consumers Say," *Globe and Mail*, ROB, December 1, 1995, p. B15.

3. Douglas Goold, "Sharp Words on Corporate Ethics," *Globe and Mail*, ROB, December 1, 1995, p. B15.

4. Shirley Won, "Clean Environment Turns in Polished Performance," *Globe and Mail*, ROB, February 8, 1996, p. B18.

5. Linda Hossie, "UN Stymied on Stopping Weapons Sales," *Globe and Mail*, ROB, May 29, 1993, p. A7.

6. "Canada Praised for Land-Mine Stand but Efforts at Moratorium Fall Short," *Montreal Gazette*, January 20, 1996, p. H10; "60 Minutes," CBS, August 4, 1996; Hossie, "UN Stymied on Stopping Weapons Sales."

7. Interview on CBC Radio, CBM Montreal, with Paul Hannon December 2, 1998.

8. Dean Jobb, "A Legal Minefield," *Elm Street*, November 1998, p. 71.

9. *Globe and Mail*, March 7, 1992, p. A3.

10. *Financial Times*, March 16, 1992, p. 2.

11. Ibid.

12. "Gas-Cartel Fines Should be a Lesson to Others," *Financial Times*, September 23, 1991, p. 34.

13. *Canadian Business*.

14. Michael Lane, "Improving American Business Ethics in Three Steps," *CPA Journal*, February 1, 1991; Susan Sonnesyn, "A Question of Ethics," *Training and Development Journal*, March 1, 1991.

15. John Stackhouse, "Canadian on Mission to Save the Planet," *Globe and Mail*, May 2, 1992, p. A1.

16. Keith Bradsher, "Trade Official Assails Europe over Ecology," *New York Times*, October 31, 1991, p. D2.

17. "Kyoto Planners Pessimistic about Pact," *Globe and Mail*, June 17, 1999, A11.

18. "Trade and the Environment," *New York Times*, March 11, 1992, p. D1.

19. *Montreal Gazette*, September 21, 1991, p. K6.

21. Interview with David Church, October 29, 1998; Canadian Pulp and Paper Association charts and publications, 1998; *Globe and Mail*, ROB, May 4, 1992, B2.

22. Report prepared by Kathy Abusow, Abusow International Ltd., 1997.

22. "Morningside," CBC, March 8, 1992.

23. Claire Bernstein, "Heavy Legal Artillery Now Turned against Environment Offenders," *Toronto Star*, December 16, 1991, p. B3.

24. Douglas Goold, "Laidlaw Is a 'Green Jungle' Risk," *Globe and Mail*, *ROB*, March 14, 1992, p. B25.

25. Interview with A. Delisle, Radio-Canada's chief heating engineer, June 8, 1993.

26. Kathy Sawyer, "Satellite Findings Show Harmful Radiation Has Increased while Ozone Layer Thinned," *Washington Post*, as reported in the *Montreal Gazette*, August 2, 1996, p. B1.

27. *Globe and Mail*, *ROB*, March 16, 1992, p. B18.

28. Robert Williamson, "B.C. Passes Regulations for Less-Polluting Vehicles," *Globe and Mail*, *ROB*, December 8, 1995, p. B4.

29. Jim Dawson, "A Gem of an Idea," *Montreal Gazette*, March 7, 1992, p. J8.

30. David Suzuki, "Only in This Century Has Growth Become Part of Life," *Montreal Gazette*, July 20, 1991, p. J8.

31. "Living on Borrowed Time," *Montreal Gazette*, May 9, 1992, p. K6.

32. Charles Hampden-Turner, "the Boundaries of Business: The Cross-Cultural Quagmire," *Harvard Business Review*, September–October 1991, p. 94.

33. John Stackhouse, "Toronto Engineering Firm Sees Profit in Bombay Sewage," *Globe and Mail*, *ROB*, January 4, 1996, p. B9.

34. Newsletter, David Suzuki Foundation, Jun 7, 1999.

35. Oliver Bertin, "Spar to Build Canadarm for Toxic, Nuclear Waste Cleanup," *Globe and Mail*, *ROB*, December 5, 1995, p. B5.

36. "Zenon wins Pact with Egypt," *Globe and Mail*, *ROB*, December 7, 1995, p. B12.

37. Kim Honey, "These Little Piggies are a Scientific Marvel," *Globe and Mail*, June 23, 1999, p. A1.

38. *Annual Report, 1998–1999*, Institute for Sustainable Development.

39. *Sustainable Consumption*, Brochure UNEP, Division of United Nations, 1999.

40. CBC News Report, CBM Radio Montreal, June 13, 1999.

41. Paul Hawken, "A Declaration of Sustainability," *Utne Reader*, Sept./Oct. 1993, 54–61.

Chapter 6

1. D. Gray and N. Friend, *So You Want To Buy a Franchise*, McGraw-Hill Ryerson, 1998, <www.francom.com/franchise_facts.htm>. Interview with Sue McSherry, Canadian Franchisors' Association, May 2, 1996.

2. *Annual Report, 1998*, Cara Ltd.; interview with Ms. Jennifer Quinn, June 30, 1999.

3. Meg Whitmore, "Franchising Options for Opportunity," *Forbes*, August 24, 1987, pp. 83–87.

4. Allan Freeman, "Trade Surplus Biggest Since 1991," *Globe and Mail*, *ROB*, March 19, 1993, p. B9.

Chapter 7

1. Statistics Canada, CANSIM, Matrix3451, Series D986059, 986061, May 1999.

2. *Starting a New Business in Canada: A Guide for New Canadians*, Federal Business Development Bank, 1990.

3. *Business Report*, Royal Bank, Fall 1995; *Financing a Small Business: A Guide for Women Entrepreneurs*, Federal Business Development Bank, 1992; Statistics Canada, <www.statcan.com>, August 1995 and May 1999.

4. Statistics Canada, ibid.

5. Douglas R. Sease, "Entrepreneurship 101," *The Wall Street Journal*, May 15, 1987, pp. D32–35.

6. "Royal Bank, Ottawa, Offering Shortcut for Small Business," *Globe and Mail*, *ROB*, March 3, 1996, p. B2.

7. *Globe and Mail*, Internet Web site, April 5, 1996.

8. "B of M Offers Small-Business Incentive," *Globe and Mail*, *ROB*, January 13, 1996, p. B5.

9. *Small Business*, October 1990, p. 9.

10. Web site of National Association of Home-Based Businesses (NAHBB), <usahomebusiness.com>, July 2, 1999.

11. Diane Luckow, "The Hottest Home-Based Businesses," *Globe and Mail*, *ROB*, January 6, 1996, p. B19.

12. *Annual Report, 1998*, Export Development Corp.

Chapter 8

1. Janet McFarland, "How a Business Fad Went Wrong," *Globe and Mail*, *ROB*, January 31, 1996, p. B13.

2. *Montreal Gazette*, February 19, 1991, p. D3.

3. Shona McKay, "The New Breed," *Financial Post Magazine*, December 1991, pp. 65–67.

4. "Message to Managers: Get Out of Your Offices," *Montreal Gazette*, February 19, 1991, p. D3.

5. Michael H. Jordan, "The Role of Top Management," *Harvard Business Review*, January–February 1995, pp. 142–144.

6. "Molson Breweries Decentralizes," *Globe and Mail*, *ROB*, December 20, 1995, p. B13.

7. Rahul Jacob, "How to Retread Customers," *Fortune*, Autumn–Winter 1993, pp. 23–24.

8. John A. Byrne, "Borderless Management," *Business Week*, May 23, 1994, pp. 24–26.

9. Andrew Campbell, Michael Gould, and Marcus Alexander, "Corporate Strategy: The Quest for Parenting Advantage," *Harvard Business Review*, March–April 1995, pp. 120–132.

10. Dori Jones Yang, "When the Going Gets Tough, Boeing Gets Touchy-Feely," *Business Week*, January 17, 1994, pp. 65–67.

11. Joy Riggs, "Empowering Workers by Setting Goals," *Nation's Business*, January 1995, p. 6.

12. Michael Elliot, "Take Me to Your Leader," *Newsweek*, April 25, 1994, p. 6.

13. Walter Kiechell III, "A Manager's Career in the New Economy," *Fortune*, April 4, 1994, pp. 68–72.

14. B. G. Yovovich, "Convergence Creates New Executive Breed," *Business Marketing*, January 1995, p. 5.

15. Sunita Wadekar Bhargava and Fred F. Jespersen, "Portrait of a CEO," *Business Week*, October 11, 1993, pp. 64–65.

Chapter 9

1. R.K. Lester, M.J. Piore and K.M. Malek, "Interpretive Management: What General Managers Can Learn From Design," *Harvard Business Review*, March–April 1998, pp. 86–96.

2. Gene Koretz, "Will Downsizing Ever Let Up?" *Business Week*, February 16, 1998, p. 26.

3. Gene Koretz, "The Downside of Downsizing," *business Week*, April 28, 1997, p. 26.

4. James Donnelly, Jr., James L. Gibson, and John M. Ivancevich, *Fundamentals of Management* (Burr Ridge: IL, Irwin, 1995), p. 382.

5. As quoted in John Raymond's column, "Worth Repeating," *Globe and Mail, ROB*, August 13, 1992, p. B2.

6. Bruce Little, "How to Make a Small Smart Factory," *Globe and Mail, ROB*, February 2, 1993, p. B24.

7. Major Rick Charlebois, "A Trial in Decentralized Decision-Making," *CMA Magazine*, June 1992, p. 8.

8. Cathryn Motherwell, "From the Oilfield to the Boardroom," *Globe and Mail*, classroom edition, December 1992, p. 14.

9. Jim Clemmer, "How to Make Empowerment Work," *Globe and Mail*, classroom edition, April 1993, p. 17.

10. Little, "How to Make a Small Smart Factory."

11. Ibid.

12. Jessica Lipnack and Jeffrey Stamps, *The TeamNet Factor* (Essex Junction, VT: Oliver Write Publications, 1993).

13. Gene Koprowski, "Only Connect," *Marketing Tools*, Jan/Feb 1998, pp. 30–34.

14. Gene Koprowski, "Intranets: Broader Applications Require New Skills," *Washington Post*, June 15, 1997, p. M19.

15. Mary J. Cronin, "Intranets Reach the Factory Floor," *Fortune*, August 18, 1997, p. 208.

16. Lori Ioannu, "The Journey Toward Empowerment," *International Business*, January 1995, p. 74.

17. D.B. Scott, "Lean Machine," *Globe and Mail, ROB*, November 1992, p. 90.

18. Motherewll, "From Oilfield to Boardroom."

19. Michael Hammer and James Champy, *Reengineering the Corporation* (New York: Harper Collins, 1993).

20. Stanley A. Brown, *What Customers Value Most: How to Achieve Business Transformation by Focusing on Processes That Touch Your Customers* (John Wiley & Sons Canada Ltd., Etobicoke, Ontario, 1996), as reviewed in *CA Magazine*, May 1996, p. 14.

21. *Better Change* (Burr Ridge: IL, Irwin, 1995).

22. Canadian Industry Statistics (CIS), Classic 1, 2, and 3: SIC-E 1052, 1131, 2713, 3361, 3511, 3994; Bob Besaari, Alliance of Manufacturers and Exporters Canada, <besaari@the-alliance.com>.

23. C.A. Bartlett and S. Ghoshal, *Transnational Management* (New York: Times Mirror, 1995).

24. Michael Rothchild, "Coming Soon: Internal Markets," *Forbes*, ASAP, June 7, 1993, pp. 19–21.

Chapter 10

1. John Holusha, "First College, then the Mill," *Globe and Mail, ROB*, August 29, 1995, p. B10.

2. World Economic Forum Web site: <weforum.org/Publications/GCR/99rankings.asp>, July 31, 1999.

3. *Daily* Archives, Statistics Canada, <www.statcan.ca>, May 1999.

4. Jay Bryan, "Shrinking Manufacturing Labour Force Isn't Necessarily Bad News," *Montreal Gazette*, March 18, 1993, p. C1; *Manufacturing Our Future*, Canadian Manufacturers Association, 1995.

5. Andrew S. Grove, *High Output Management* (New York: Random House, 1995).

6. Allan Fishman, "Managing Inventory Is Difficult," *St. Louis Post Dispatch*, March 4, 1991, p. 10BP.

7. Michael Schrage, "The Pursuit of Efficiency Can Be an Illusion," *Washington Post*, March 20, 1992, p. F3.

8. "New Software = Faster Factories," *ASAP*, October 10, 1994, pp. 36–41.

9. Robert J. Samuelson, "The Assembly Line," *Newsweek*, special issue, 1997.

10. Patricia Lush, "Just-in-Time Pays Off for the Auto Sector," *Globe and Mail, ROB*, February 21, 1990, pp. B1 and B4.

11. C.M. Seifert, "Pratt & Whitney Goes High-Tech at Halifax Plant," *Materials Management and Distribution* 34, no. 3 (March 1989), p. 22.

12. Sam Lightman, "Cradle-to-Grave," *Materials Management and Distribution* 34, no. 2 (February 1989), pp. 27–28.

13. William H. Davidow and Michael S. Malone, *The Virtual Corporation* (New York: HarperCollins, 1992).

14. James B. Treece, "Motown's Struggle to Shift on the Fly," *Business Week*, July 11, 1994, pp. 111, 112.

15. Reported by Jayson Myers, chief economist, Canadian Manufacturers Association, interviewed July 15, 1996.

16. Davidow and Malone, *The Virtual Corporation*.

17. Peter M. Senge, *The Fifth Discipline* (New York: Doubleday, 1990).

18. "Custom Made," *Success*, October 1994, p. 28.

19. Walter S. Mossberg, "Personal Technology," *The Wall Street Journal*, October 27, 1994, p. B1.

20. Chris Woodward, "Virtual Tailors Fashion Apparel," *USA Today*, February 16, 1998, 3B

21. Tom Hout and George Stalk, Jr., *Competing Against Time* (New York: Free Press, 1990).

22. Damon Darlin, "Automating the Automators," *Forbes*, February 14, 1994, pp. 156–60.

23. CBC Radio News, May 13, 1999.

24. Janet McFarland, "Factories-for-Hire Feed High-Tech Assembly Boom," *Globe and Mail, ROB*, February 8, 1996, p. B12.

25. Donna Brown, "Ten Ways to Boost Quality," *Management Review*, January 1991.

26. The comments are from James L. Riggs, *Production Systems* (New York: Free Press, 1987), pp. 614–615; Riggs's description of Deming's process is from W. Edwards Dem-

ing, *Quality, Productivity and Competitive Position* (Cambridge, MA: MIT University Press, 1982).

27. Louis S. Richman, "Why the Economic Data Mislead Us," *Fortune*, March 8, 1993, pp. 108–13.

28. "The Big Payoff from Computers," *Fortune*, March 7, 1994, p. 28.

29. Roland T. Rust, "The Dawn of Computer Behaviour," *Marketing Management*, Fall 1997, 31–33.

Chapter 11

1. James Coates, "Classroom in a Box," *Chicago Tribune*, January 5, 1998, section 4, p. 1.

2. Nuala Moran, "Knowledge Management," *Financial Times*, October 1, 1997, p. 8; Jeff Angus, "Knowledge Management: Great Concept ... But What Is It?," *Information Week*, March 16, 1998, p. 38.

3. Dave Ulrich, "Intellectual Capital = Competence × Commitment," *Sloan Management Review*, Winter 1998, pp. 15–21.

4. Vanessa Houlder, "The High Price of Know How," *Financial Times*, July 14, 1997, p. 10; Carol Levin, "Business Class Net," *PC Magazine*, February 24, 1998, p. 28.

5. "Intranets Yield Returns for Most User firms, According to Survey," *The Wall Street Journal*, June 19, 1997; Joe Mullich, "Enjoying the Intranet Ride," *PC Week*, March 9, 1998, p. 31.

6. George Black, "Growth of the Intranet," *Financial Times*, September 10, 1997, p. 9.

7. John Gilroy, "Ask the Computer Guy," *The Washington Post*, September 1, 1997, p. F19.

8. George Melloan, "Where Is the Information Technology Payoff?" *The Wall Street Journal*, August 11, 1997, p. A15.

9. Tamara E. Holmes, "Choosing a Database of Contact Manager; Getting to Know Bots," *USA Today*, August 28, 1997, p. 5D; Bob Wallace, "Extranet Service Helps Users Tailor Info Access," *Computer World*, March 9, 1998, p. 4.

10. Jeff Moad, "Forging Flexible Links," *PC Week*, September 15, 1997, p. 74; Daniel Grebler, "Survey Points Out Growing Internet Use by Small Businesses," *St. Louis Post-Dispatch*, February 6, 1998, p. BP14.

11. Philip Manchester, "Impact of the Internet," *Financial Times*, October 1, 1997, p. 4.

12. Joia Shillingford, "Enterprise Networks," *Financial Times*, June 4, 1997, p. 6.

13. Matt Kelley, "Scientists and Supercompanies Turn to vBNS for High Speed," *The Wall Street Journal Interactive Edition*, February 3, 1997.

14. Reva Basch, "The Next Net," *Computer Life*, September 1997, pp. 48–49; Cary Lu, "Make Room for Data," *Inc. Technology*, March 18, 1997, p. 33; Jeff Caruso, "Cisco Weaves Faster Fabric—Frames, Not Cells, Will Dominate Gigabit Enterprise Networking," *Internet Week*, February 9, 1998, p. 1.

15. Geoffrey Nairn, "Office Communications," *Financial Times*, October 1, 1997, p. 9.

16. Geoffrey Wheelwright, "Information Overload," *Financial Times*, October 1, 1997, p. 9.

17. Walter S. Mossberg, "Average Home Users May Find Push Services Slow, Irritating," *The Wall Street Journal Interactive Edition*, October 16, 1997.

18. Louise Kehoe, "A Block on the Old Chip," *Financial Times*, October 3, 1997, p. 19.

19. Philip Albinus, "the Shape of Things to Come," *Home Office Computing*, November 1997, pp. 70–76.

20. N. MacDonald and C. Goodhue, "What Is a Networked Computing Devices?" *the Wall Street Journal Interactive Edition*, July 21, 1997; "Boise Cascade Office Products: Intelligent Technology," *Selling Power*, January/February 1998, p. 78.

21. Virginia Baldwin Hick, "Shareware is Now More Than a Hobby," *St. OLouis Post-Dispatch*," January 12, 1998, pp. BP1, 14.

22. Carol Venezia, "PIM Improvements," *PC Magazine*, March 24, 1998, p. 80; and Dan Gillmor, "Old Technology Keeps Coming Back in Smaller, Practical Uses," *St. Louis Post-Dispatch*, March 16, 1998, p. BP16.

23. Charles H. Gajeway, "Message Centers," *Home Office Computing*, November 1997, p. 103.

24. Carla Lazzareschi, "Telecommuters Still Feel Pull of Office," *Loss Angeles Times*, September 13, 1997, p. D1.

25. Jerri Stroud, "Home Suite ... Office" *St. Louis Post-Dispatch*, October 19, 1997, p. 1E; Carol Kleiman, "Many Would Take a Home Office Over a Corner Office," *St. Louis Post-Dispatch*, March 12, 1998, p. C8.

26. Joia Shillingford, "Teleworking," *Financial Times*, September 10, 1997, p. 13.

27. "Advances Let Disabled into Computer World," *St. Louis Post-Dispatch*, January 14, 1998, p. C7.

28. Michelle V. Rafter, "Too Much Time on the Net Can Leave You Stressed Out," *St. Louis Post-Dispatch*, January 17, 1998, p. C7.

29. Richard Behar, "who's Reading Your E-Mail?" *Fortune*, February 3, 1997, pp. 57–70.

30. "The Privacy Debate," *The Wall Street Journal Interactive Edition*, October 16, 1997.

31. "Internet-based Commerce Needs Better Security," *USA Today*, October 1, 1997, p. 12A; Heather Newman, "Cookies are Good For You," *Home Office Computing*, March 1998, p. 16.

32. Thomas E. Weber, "Concerned Web Users Ask: Is Public Data Too Public?" *The Wall Street Journal Interactive Edition*, June 19, 1997; "Cookie Managers," *PC Magazine*, March 24, 1998, p. 182.

33. Michele Weldon, "High-Tech Skills Ease the Gender Gap," *Chicago Tribune*, June 8, 1997, p. 3.

34. Reid Goldsborough, "Computers Scare You Bitless?" *MSNBC*, March 17, 1997.

35. Sherwood Ross, "The Internet Generation Will Shake Corporations, Author Says," *St. Louis Post-Dispatch*, February 23, 1998, p. BP4.

Chapter 12

1. Richard L. Daft, *Management* (Hinsdale, IL: Dryden Press, 1988), p. 39.

2. Alan Farnham, "the Man who Changed Work Forever," *fortune*, July 21, 1997, p. 114.

3. Ibid.

4. Douglas A. Blackmon, "Shippers Pitch Power of Gizmos and Gadgets," *The Wall Street Journal*, June 2, 1997, p. B1.

5. Abraham H. Maslow, *Motivation and Personality* (New York: Harper & Brothers, 1954).

6. David Kirkpatrick, "Intel's Amazing Profit Machine," *Fortune*, February 17, 1997, pp. 60–72.

7. Andrea Gabor, "Hard Work and Common Sense," *Los Angeles Times*, February 8, 1998, p. 5.

8. Jim Collins, "The Human Side of Enterprise," *Inc.*, December 1996, p. 55.

9. "First Discipline Then Empowerment," *The Wall Street Journal*, February 20, 1998, p. A19.

10. Robert Maynard, "How to Motivate Low-Wage Workers," *Nation's Business*, May 1997, pp. 35–39.

11. *Globe and Mail*, "Delta Promotes Empowerment," May 31, 1999, p. C5.

12. William G. Ouchi, *Theory Z: How American Business Can Meet the Japanese Challenge* (Menlo Park, CA: Addison-Wesley, 1981).

13. Harold Geneen, *Managing* (New York: Avon Books, 1984), p. 17.

14. Frederick Herzberg, *Work and the Nature of Man* (New York: World Publishers, 1966).

15. Virginia Baldwin Hick, "What Works at Work: Kind Word from Boss," *St. Louis Post-Dispatch*, January 3, 1994, p. 1C.

16. "Loyalty Surprise," *Boardroom Reports*, April 15, 1994, p. 15.

17. Jim Barlow, "Company Loyalty: The Feeling Is Mutual," *Washington Times*, April 18, 1994, p. E13.

18. Meg Carter, "What to Ask the Workers," *Financial Times*, February 18, 1998, p. 23: Bob Nelson, "Dump the Cash, Load on the Praise," *personnel Journal*, July 1996; p. 65; Sherwood Ross, "Employees Prize Career Development When Deciding to Change Jobs," *St. Louis Post-Dispatch*, February 2, 1998, p. BP4.

19. Herman Cain, "Leadership Is Common Sense," *Success*, February 1997, pp. 41–48.

20. Theodore H. Poister and Gregory Streib, "MBO in Municipal Government: Variations on a Traditional Management Tool," *Public Administration Review*, January–February 1995, pp. 48–56.

21. Victor H. Vroom, *Work and Motivation* (New York: John Wiley & Sons, 1967).

22. David Nadler and Edward Lawler, "Motivation—a Diagnostic Approach," in *Perspectives on Behavior in Organizations*, ed. Richard Hackman, Edward Lawler, and Lyman Porter (New York: McGraw-Hill, 1977).

23. Ron Frank, "The Inspiration of Experience: Six Bestselling Leadership Principles You won't Find in a Business Bestseller," *Management Review*, January 1997, pp. 33–38.

24. Joseph B. White and Oscar Suris, "New Pony: How a 'Skunk Works' Kept the Mustang Alive—on a Tight Budget," *The Wall Street Journal*, September 21, 1993; Anita Lienert, "A Special Delivery From Ford," *Chicago Tribune*, February 12, 1998, p. 11.

25. Barrie McKenna, "Reborn in Rimouski," *Globe and Mail, ROB*, July 20, 1993, p. B20.

26. High McBride, "A Corporate Obsession Pays Off," *Globe and Mail, ROB*, July 13, 1993, p. B22.

27. "Open the Books," *Globe and Mail, ROB*, December 19, 1995, p. B9.

28. Diane Summers, "Generation X Comes of Age," *Financial Times*, February 16, 1998, p. 16

29. Sam Walton, "In His Own Words," *Fortune*, June 29, 1992, pp. 98–106.

30. Sylvia Odenwald, "Global Work Teams," *Training and Development*, February 1996, pp. 54–60; Vijay Govindarajan and Anil Gupta, "Success is All in the Mindset," *Financial Times*, February 27, 1998, p. 2.

31. Vincent Alonzo, "Recognition? Who Needs It?" *Sales & Marketing Management*, February 1997, p. 26.

32. Linda Grant, "Happy Workers, High Returns," *Fortune*, January 12, 1998.

33. Morey Stettner, "Five Painless Steps to Motivate Colleagues," *Investor's Business Daily*, February 5, 1998, p. A1.

Chapter 13

1. Campbell Clark, "National Sets Up Banking School," *Montreal Gazette*, February 7, 1996, p. D8.

2 E. Innes, J. Lyons, and J. Harris, *The Financial Post 100 Best Companies to Work for in Canada* (Toronto: HarperCollins, 1990).

3. Salem Alaton, "The Learning Organization," *Globe and Mail, ROB*, December 19, 1995, p. B26.

4. David Shoalts, "HR Adopts Virtual Concept," *Globe and Mail, ROB*, December 19, 1995, p. B24.

5. Interview with Toronto-Dominion HRM manager S. Churchin, May 17, 1996; *Canadian Business*, August 1989, p. 9; Hewitt Associates, "Benefits by the Year 2000," *Benefits Canada*, February 1991, p. 11; *Financial Post*, January 8, 1990, p. 3.

6. Christopher Caggiano, "How You Gonna Keep 'em Down on the Firm," *Inc. Online*, January 7, 1998.

7. Nina Colwill, "Understanding the Aspects of Networking,," *Women in Management*, National Centre for Management Research and Developments' Women in Management Program, Western Business School, August-September 1994, p. 6.

8. Rosabeth Moss Canter, "Wired Rewards," *A World of Networks*, a Northern Telecom publication, as reported in *Globe and Mail, ROB*, December 19, 1995, p. B9.

9. Debra Black, "Canadian Women Get Short Shrift, UN Says," *Montreal Gazette*, July 5, 1993, p. C1.

10. *Labour Force Survey*, Statistics Canada, Cat. No. 71F0004XCB, 1999.

11. Perry Pascarella, "Compensating Teams," *Across the Board*, February 1997, p. 16–23.

12. Interviews with Norma Tombari, May 19, 1996 and December 15, 1998; various publications of Royal Bank.

13. Robert Maynard, "The Growing Appeal of Telecommuting," *Naton's Business*, August 1994, pp. 61–62.

14. Virginia Baldqwin Hick, "Virtual Office Means More Home Work," *St. Louis Post-Dispatch*, March 21, 1994, pp. B1 and 2.

15. Bob Weinstein, "New Frontiers," *Entrepreneur*, May 1995, pp. 158–65.

16. "Sunday Morning," CBC Radio, May 19, 1996.

17. Margot Gibb-Clark, "Sex Harassment Case Sent to Labour Board," *Globe and Mail, ROB*, February 26, 1996, p. B10.

Chapter 14

1. Yahoo Internet site, <www.dailynews.yahoo.com>, December 31, 1998.

2. *Directory of Labour Organizations in Canada*, Human Resources and Development, Canada, 1998.

3. Mike King, "Lost Work-Days Could Hit Record Level in '99," *Montreal Gazette*, August 16, 1999, p. A5.

4. Sheila McGovern, "Wage-Discrimination Settlement Could Cost $1.5 Billion," *Montreal Gazette*, February 17, 1996, p. G2.

5. Margot Gibb-Clark, "CUPE to Appeal Same-Sex Spouse Ruling," *Globe and Mail, ROB,* September 20, 1995, p. B4.

6. Oliver Bertin, "Air Canada Beefs Up Staff," *Globe and Mail, ROB*, March 1, 1996, p. B4.

7. Ian McGugan, "A Crapshoot Called Compensation," *Canadian Business*, July 1995, p. 67.

8. Margot Gibb-Clark, "Court Restores Award to Lark Employees." *Globe and Mail, ROB*, December 12, 1995, p. B4; Alan Freeman, "Ex-STN Directors Ordered to Pay $567,000 to Workers," *Globe and Mail, ROB*, September 20, 1995, p. B1.

9. Mike Brennan, "GM Suing VW Executives for Espionage," *Knight-Ridder Newspapers*, as reported in *Montreal Gazette*, March 9, 1996, p. E2.

10. Gayle MacDonald, "Who's Minding the Parents?" *Globe and Mail, ROB*, January 30, 1996, p. B12.

Chapter 15

1. This quote is from one of the first and best books on relationship marketing: Regis McKenna, *Relationship Marketing* (Reading, MA: Addison-Wesley, 1991).

2. William H. Davidow and Michael S. Malone, *The Virtual Corporation* (New York: HarperBusiness, 1992), p. 153.

3. Paul Ruine and Cheryl Stuart Ruine, "Being a Global Winner," *Nation's Business*, December 1997, p. 6.

4. *Canadian Grocer*, 104, no. 6 (June 1990), pp. 59–60.

5. Thomas Petzinger, Jr., "Joe Morabito Beats the Competition with Cooperation," *The Wall Street Journal*, February 7, 1997, p. B1; Frequent Shopper Review, *Supermarket Strategic Alert*, December 1996, p. 4.

Chapter 16

1. Mathew Friedman, "Two Guys in the Paperless Office," *Montreal Gazette*, January 29, 1996, p. F6.

2. Michael Grange, "Unique Formula Speaks to Working Women," *Globe and Mail, ROB*, February 20, 1996, p. B11.

3. Carolyn Leitch, "Coke Machines Signal When It's Time for a Refill," *Globe and Mail, ROB*, August 30, 1995, p. B20.

4. *Canadian Grocer*, 104, no. 6 (June 1990), pp. 59–60.

5. Salem Alaton, "Design Solutions from Candies to Countries," *Globe and Mail, ROB*, August 29, 1995, p. B22.

6. *Canadian Grocer* Web site <www.cdngrocer.com>, August 1999.

7. Jack Edmonston, "Taxing ad Spending to Reflect Equity," *Business Marketing*, January 1995, p. 20.

8. Alan J. Bergstrom, "Brand Management Poised for Change," *Marketing News*, May 7, 1997, p. 5.

9. "Instant Market Analysis," *Success*, February 1996, p. 10.

10. "Got a Good Idea for a New Product?" *The Wall Street Journal*, May 1, 1997, p. 1

11. Ann Kerr, "Design Exchange Has a Tough Sell," *Globe and Mail, ROB*, August 29, 1995, p. B23.

Chapter 17

1. Yvonne Nava, "Apple's First Infomercial," *Business Marketing*, February 1995, p. A7.

2. Gary Levin, "Global PR Efforts on the Wane," *Advertising Age*, May 16, 1994, p. 28.

3. John Heinzl, "IKEA Ads Made in Canada? Wunderbar!" January 27, 1999, p. B30.

4. Kristin Dunlap Godsey, "Back on Tract," *Success*, May 1997, p. 52.

5. Kristin Dunlap Godsey, "Critical Steps in the Sales Process," *Success*, May 1997, pp. 24–25.

6. Minna Levine, "Consistency Counts in Sealing Interactive Brand Identity," *Marketing News*, January 19, 1998, p. 8.

7. Thomas R. Schori and Michael L. Garee, "Capitalize on the Interactive Nature of the Internet," *Marketing News*, January 19, 1998, p. 12.

8. Regina Brady, Edward Forrest and Richard Mizerski, *Cybermarketing* (Lincolnwood, IL: NTC Business Books, 1997).

9. Interview with IBM's marketing department, 1992.

10. "EDI in Action," *Business Week*, March 30, 1992, pp. 85–92.

11. Alfred J. Battaglia and Gene Tyndall, "Implementing World Class Management," a paper given to the authors, February 1992.

12. *Rail in Canada*, Statistics Canada, Cat. No. 52-216, 1990, p. 174.

13. Confidential interview with a senior executive at a leading Canadian shoe company chain, February 3, 1999.

14. Amazon.com, "The Wild World of E-Commerce," *Business Week*, December 14, 1998, p. 106.

Chapter 19

1. Eileen Davis, "The Root of All Evil," *Venture*, December 1988, pp. 77–78.

2. "David L. Berch," *Inc.*, April 1989, pp. 38–39.

3. Canadian Bankers Association, <wwwcba.ca/eng/statistics_results.cfm>, May 1999.

4. *Serving the Needs of Small Business*, Canadian Bankers Association, May 28, 1996; *Small Business Annual Report 1995*, Canadian Bankers Association, p. 21.

5. Ibid.

6. Ibid.

Glossary

accounting: The recording, classifying, summarizing, and interpreting of financial transactions to provide management and other interested parties with the information they need.

accounting system: The methods used to record and summarize accounting data.

acquisition: One company buys another company.

advertising: Paid, nonpersonal communication through various media by organizations and individuals who are in some way identified in the advertising message.

affirmative action (employment equity): Employment activities designed to right past wrongs endured by females and minorities by giving them preference in employment.

agency shop (Rand Formula): Workplace in which a new employee is not required to join the union but must pay union dues. Judge Rand devised this historic formula.

amortization (depreciation): Since assets such as machinery lose value over time, part of their cost is calculated as an expense each year over their useful life.

analytic system: Manufacturing system that breaks down raw materials into components to extract other products.

apprentice programs: Training programs involving a period during which a learner works alongside an experienced employee to master the skills and procedures of a craft.

arbitration: The process of resolving all disputes, not only grievances, through an outside, impartial third party.

articles of incorporation: The legal documents, obtained from the federal or provincial governments, authorizing a company to operate as a corporation.

assembly process: Production process that puts together components.

assets: Things of value owned by a business.

autocratic leadership: Leadership style that involves making decisions without consulting others and implies power over others.

balance of trade: The relationship of exports to imports.

balance sheet: Reports the financial position of a firm at the end of a specific period. Balance sheets consist of assets, liabilities, and owners' equity.

bartering: The exchange of goods or services for goods or services.

bid rigging: Secret agreement among competitors to make artificially high bids.

blue chip stocks: Stocks of high-quality companies.

bond: A contract of indebtedness issued by a corporation or government unit that promises payment of a principal amount at a specified future time plus annual or semi-annual interest at a specified or variable rate.

bookkeeping: The recording of transactions.

boycott: Urging union members and the public at large not to buy a particular company's products or services.

brand: A name, symbol, or design (or combination of these) that identifies the goods or services of one seller or group of sellers and distinguishes them from those of competitors.

brand association: The linking of a brand to other favourable images.

brand awareness: How quickly a particular brand name comes to mind when a product category is mentioned.

brand equity: Combination of factors such as awareness, loyalty, perceived quality, feelings, images, and any emotion people associate with a brand name.

brand loyalty: The degree to which customers are satisfied, like the brand, and are committed to further purchases.

brand name: A word, letter, or group of words or letters that differentiates your product from those of your competitors.

brokers: Marketing intermediaries who bring buyers and sellers together and assist in negotiating an exchange.

bureaucracy: An organization with many layers of managers who set rules and regulations and oversee all decisions.

business: An organization that manufactures or sells goods or services in an attempt to generate profit.

business plan: A detailed written statement that describes the nature of the business, the target market, the advantages the business will have over competitors, the resources and qualifications of the owners, and much more.

buying on margin: Purchasing securities by borrowing some of the cost from the broker.

cafeteria-style benefits: Benefit plans that allow employees to choose which benefits they want up to a certain dollar amount.

capital budget: The spending plan for the acquisition of capital assets that involve large sums of money.

capitalism: An economic system with free markets and private ownership of companies operated for profit.

cash budget: The projected use of cash during a given period (e.g., monthly, quarterly, or annually).

cash flow: The difference between cash receipts and cash disbursements.

cash-flow forecast: A projection of expected cash inflows and outflows in the coming year.

centralized authority: Maintaining decision-making authority at the top level of management.

channel of distribution: Marketing intermediaries such as wholesalers and retailers who join together to transport and store goods in their path (channel) from producers to consumers.

check-off: Contract clause requiring the employer to deduct union dues from employees' pay and remit them to the union.

closed shop: Workplace in which all new hires must already be union members.

cognitive dissonance: A type of psychological conflict that can occur after a purchase when consumers may have doubts about whether they got the best product at the best price.

collective bargaining: The process by which a union represents employees in relations with their employer.

commercial paper: A short-term corporate equivalent of an IOU that is sold in the marketplace by a firm. It matures in 270 days or less.

common market: A regional group of countries that aim to remove all internal tariffs and nontariff barriers to trade, investment, and employment. (An important example is the European Union.)

common stock: Represents ownership of a firm and the rights to vote and to receive all of the firm's profits (after preferred shareholders are paid) in the form of dividends declared by the board of directors.

communications software: Computer programs that make it possible for different brands of computers to transfer data to each other.

comparative advantage theory: Theory that a country should produce and sell to other countries those products that it produces most efficiently and effectively and should buy from other countries those products it cannot produce as effectively or efficiently.

competitive benchmarking: Rating an organization's practices, processes, and products against the world's best.

compressed workweek: Work schedule made up of four 10-hour days.

computer-aided design (CAD): The use of computers in the design of products.

computer-aided manufacturing (CAM): The use of computers in the production process.

conceptual skills: Ability to picture the organization as a whole and the relationship between the various parts.

consortium: A temporary association of two or more companies to bid jointly on a large project.

consumer market: All individuals or households who want goods and services for personal consumption or use.

consumer price index (CPI): Measures monthly changes in the price of a basket of goods and services that and average family would buy.

containerization: The process of packing and sealing a number of items into one unit that is easily moved and shipped.

contingent workers: Workers who do not have the expectations of regular, full-time employment.

contingency planning: Preparation of alternative courses of action that may be used if the primary plans do not achieve the objectives of the organization.

continuous improvement (CI): Constantly improving the way the organization does things so that customer needs can be better satisfied.

controlling: Management function that involves checking to determine whether an organization is progressing toward its goals and objectives, and taking corrective action if it is not.

convenience goods and services: Products that the consumer wants to purchase frequently and with a minimum of effort.

convertible bond: A bond that can be converted into shares of common stock.

cookies: Pieces of information, such as registration data or user preferences, sent by a Web site over the Internet to a Web browser that the browser software is expected to save and send back to the server whenever the user returns to that Web site.

co-operative: An organization that is owned by members who pay an annual membership fee and share in any profits.

core competencies: Functions that the organization can do as well as or better than any other company in the world.

core time: The period when all employees must be present in a flextime system.

corporate social responsibility: The recognition by corporations that their actions must take into account the needs and ethical standards of society.

corporation: A legal entity with an existence separate from its owners.

cost of goods sold: A particular type of expense measured by the total cost of merchandise sold, including costs associated with the acquisition, storage, transportation, and packaging of goods.

countertrading: Bartering among several countries.

critical path: The sequence of tasks that takes the longest time to complete.

cross-functional teams: Groups of employees from different departments who work together on a semipermanent basis (as opposed to the temporary teams established in matrix-style organizations).

cumulative preferred stock: Preferred stock that accumulates unpaid dividends.

current assets: Cash and assets that are normally converted into cash within one year.

customer-driven: Customer satisfaction becomes the driving force of the company.

cyclical unemployment: Unemployment caused by a recession or a similar downturn in the business cycle.

database program: Computer program that allows users to work with information that is normally kept in lists: names, addresses, schedules, inventories, and so forth.

data processing (DP): Technology that supported an existing business; primarily used to improve the flow of financial information.

debt capital: Funds raised by borrowing that must be repaid.

decentralized: Decision making is spread downward from the top of an organization.

decentralized authority: Delegating decision-making authority to lower-level managers, who are more familiar with local conditions.

decision making: Choosing among two or more alternatives.

deficit: An excess of expenditures over revenues.

deflation: A general decline in the price level of goods and services.

delegating: Assigning authority and accountability to others while retaining responsibility for results.

demand: The quantity of particular products or services that buyers are willing to buy at certain prices and at certain locations.

democratic leadership: Leadership style that consists of managers and employees working together to make decisions.

departmentalization: Dividing an organization's structure into separate homogeneous units.

directing: Management function that involves guiding and motivating others to achieve the goals and objectives of the organization.

dividends: Part of the firm's profits that are distributed to shareholders.

economics: The study of how society chooses to employ resources to produce goods and services and distribute them for consumption among various competing groups and individuals.

economies of scale: The cost savings that result from large-scale production.

electronic data interchange (EDI): Software that enables the computers of producers, wholesalers, and retailers to communicate with each other.

embargo: A complete ban on all trade with or investment in a country.

employee orientation: The activity that introduces new employees to the organization; to fellow employees; to their immediate supervisors; and to the policies, practices, and objectives of the firm.

employment equity (affirmative action): Employment activities designed to right past wrongs endured by females and minorities by giving them preference in employment.

empowerment: The leaders of organizations give workers the freedom, incentive, and training to be decision makers and creative contributors to the organization; they give employees the authority to respond quickly to customer requests.

enterprise resource planning (ERP): Computer-based production and operations system that links multiple firms into one integrated production unit.

entrepreneur: A person who organizes, manages, and assumes the risks of starting and operating a business to make a profit.

entrepreneurship: Having the skills and determination to start and operate a business and to accept the calculated risks that are part of such an undertaking.

equity capital: Funds raised from selling shares in the firm.

equity theory: Theory that employees try to maintain equity between inputs and outputs compared to others in similar positions.

exchange rate: The value of one currency relative to the currencies of other countries.

expectancy theory: Victor Vroom's theory that the effort employees exert on specific tasks depends on their expectations of the outcomes.

exponential function: The mathematical description of anything that changes steadily in one direction over a given period.

external customers: Dealers who buy products to sell to others, and ultimate customers who buy products for their own use.

extranet: An extension of the Internet that connects suppliers, customers, and other organizations via secure Web sites; a semiprivate network that uses Internet technology and allows more than one company to access the same information or allows people on different servers to collaborate.

extrinsic rewards: Something given to you by someone else as recognition for good work; extrinsic rewards include pay increases, praise, and promotions.

factoring: Selling accounts receivable for cash.

finance: The business function that is responsible for the acquisition and disbursement of funds.

financial accounting: The preparation of financial statements for people inside and outside the firm (for example, investors).

financial statements: Report the operations and position (condition) of a firm; they include the income statement and the balance sheet.

fiscal policy: The use of taxation to stimulate or restrain various aspects of the economy or the economy as a whole.

fixed assets: Items that are acquired to produce services or products for a business. They are not bought to be sold.

flexible manufacturing: Designing and using individual machines that can do multiple tasks so that each can produce a variety of products.

flextime plans: Work schedules that give employees some freedom to adjust when they work, within limits, as long as they work the required number of hours.

focus group: A small group of people who meet under the direction of a discussion leader to communicate their opinions about an organization, its products, or other important issues.

foreign subsidiary: A company owned by another (parent) company in a foreign country.

formal organization: The official system that details responsibility, authority, and position; it is the structure that is shown on the organization chart.

form utility: The value added to inputs by the creation of outputs.

franchise: The right to use a specific business's name and sell its products or services in a given territory.

franchise agreement: An arrangement whereby someone with a good idea for a business sells the rights to use the business name and sell its products or services to others in a given territory.

franchisee: A person who buys a franchise.

franchising: A method of distributing a product or service, or both, to achieve a maximum market impact with a minimum amount of investment.

franchisor: A company that develops a product concept and sells others the rights to make and sell the products.

freight forwarder: An organization that puts many smaller shipments together to create a single large shipment that can be transported cost-effectively.

full-service wholesalers: Merchant wholesalers that perform all eight distribution functions.

functional structure: Grouping of workers into departments based on similar skills, expertise, or resource use.

fundamental accounting equation: Assets = liabilities + owners' equity; it is the basis for the balance sheet.

Gantt chart: Bar graph that shows managers what projects are being worked on and what stage they are in on a daily basis.

General Agreement on Tariffs and Trade (GATT): Agreement among trading countries that provides a forum for negotiating mutual reductions in trade restrictions.

general partner: An owner (partner) who has unlimited liability and is active in managing the firm.

generic goods: Nonbranded products that usually sell at a sizeable discount from national or private brands, have very basic packaging, and are backed with little or no advertising.

generic names: Names of product categories.

globalization: A globally integrated system of production, marketing, finance, and management.

goals: Broad, long-term accomplishments an organization wants to attain.

goal-setting theory: Theory that setting specific ambitious goals can motivate workers and improve performance if the goals are accepted, accompanied by feedback, and facilitated by organizational conditions.

goods-producing sector: The sector that produces tangible products, things that can be seen or touched.

green product: A product whose production, use, and disposal don't damage the environment.

grievance: A formal protest by an individual employee or a union when they believe a particular management decision breaches the union contract.

gross domestic product (GDP): The total value of a country's output of goods and services in a given year.

gross margin (profit): Net sales minus cost of goods sold before expenses are deducted.

groupware: Software that allows people to work collaboratively and share ideas.

Hawthorne effect: The tendency for people to behave differently when they know they are being studied.

hierarchy: A system in which one person is at the top of the organization and many levels of managers are responsible to that person.

horizontal merger: Joins two firms in the same or similar industries to allow them to diversify or to expand their products.

human relations skills: Ability to lead, communicate, motivate, coach, build morale, train, support, and delegate.

human resource management: The process of evaluating human resource needs, finding people to fill those needs, and motivating employees to get the best work from each one by providing the right incentives and job environment, all with the goal of meeting the organization's objectives.

hygiene factors: Factors that cause dissatisfaction but do not motivate if they are removed.

import quota: A limit on the number or value of products in certain categories that can be imported.

income statement: Reports revenues, expenses, and profit or loss during a specific period.

independent audit: Examination of a company's books by public accountants to give the public, governments, and shareholders an outside opinion of the fairness of financial statements.

industrial goods: Products used in the production of other products.

industrial market (business-to-business market): All individuals and organizations that want goods and services to produce other goods and services or to sell, rent, or supply the goods to others.

industrial marketing: The marketing of goods and services to manufacturers, institutions, commercial operations, and the government.

industrial park: A planned area where land, shipping facilities, and waste disposal outlets are readily available so businesses are attracted to the area to build a manufacturing plant or storage facility.

industrial policy: A comprehensive coordinated government plan to revitalize and guide the economy.

inflation: A general rise in the prices of goods and services over time.

infomercials: TV programs that are devoted exclusively to promoting goods and services.

informal organization: The system of relationships and lines of authority that develop spontaneously outside the formal organization; it is the human side of the organization and does not appear on any organization charts.

information age: An era in which information is a crucial factor in the operation of organizations.

information systems (IS): Technology that helps companies do business; includes such tools as automated bank machines (ABMs) and voice mail.

information technology (IT): Technology that helps companies change business by using new technology on new methods.

injunction: An order from a judge requiring strikers to limit or cease picketing or stop some threatening activity.

integrated marketing communication (IMC): A formal mechanism for uniting all the promotional efforts in an organization to make them more consistent and responsive to that organization's customers and other stakeholders.

integrated software package (suite): A computer program that offers two or more applications in one package.

interactive marketing communication system: A system in which consumers can access company information on their own and supply information about themselves in an ongoing dialogue.

internal customers: Units within the firm that receive services from other units.

international joint venture (JV): A partnership in which companies from two or more countries join to undertake a major project or to form a new company.

International Monetary Fund (IMF): An international bank that makes short-term loans to countries experiencing problems with their balance of trade.

Internet 2: The new Internet system that will link government supercomputer centres and a select group of universities; it will run 100 to 1000 times faster than today's public infrastructure and will support heavy-duty applications.

intranet: A set of communication links in a company that travels over the Internet; a companywide network, closed to public access, that uses Internet technology.

intrapreneur: A person with entrepreneurial skills who is employed in a corporation to launch new products and who takes hands-on responsibility for innovation in an organization.

intrinsic reward: The good feeling you have when you have done a job well.

inverted organization: Organization method that has contact people at the top and a chief executive officer at the bottom.

ISO 9000: Quality management and assurance standards published by the International Standards Organization (ISO).

job analysis: A study of what is done by the employees who hold various job titles.

job description: A summary of the objectives of a job, the type of work to be done, the responsibilities and duties, the working conditions, and the relationship of the job to other functions.

job enlargement: Job enrichment strategy involving combining a series of tasks into one assignment that is more challenging and interesting.

job enrichment: A motivational strategy that emphasizes motivating the worker through the job itself.

job rotation: Job enrichment strategy involving moving employees from one job to another.

job sharing: An arrangement whereby two part-time employees share one full-time job.

job simplification: Process of producing task efficiency by breaking down the job into simple steps and assigning people to each of those steps.

job simulation: The use of equipment that duplicates job conditions and tasks so that trainees can learn skills before attempting them on the job.

job specifications: A written summary of the qualifications required of workers to do a particular job.

just-in-time (JIT) inventory control: The delivery of the smallest possible quantities at the latest possible time, to keep inventory as low as possible.

knowledge technology (KT): Technology that adds a layer of intelligence to filter appropriate information and deliver it when it is needed.

Labour Relations Board (LRB): A quasi-judicial body consisting of representatives of government, labour, and business. It functions more informally than a court but has the full force of law. It administers labour codes in each jurisdiction, federal or provincial.

laissez-faire capitalism: The theory that if left alone, unhindered by government, the free market, in pursuit of economic efficiency, would provide an abundance of goods at the lowest prices, improving everyone's life.

laissez-faire (free-rein) leadership: Leadership style that involves managers setting objectives and employees being relatively free to do whatever it takes to accomplish those objectives.

leadership: Creating a vision for others to follow, establishing corporate values and ethics, and transforming the way the organization does business so it is more effective and efficient.

lean manufacturing: The production of goods using less of everything compared to mass production.

liabilities: Amounts owed by the organization to others.

licensing: An agreement in which a producer allows a foreign company to produce its product in exchange for royalties.

limited-function wholesalers: Merchant wholesalers that perform only selected distribution functions.

limited liability: The responsibility of a business's owners for losses only up to the amount they invest; limited partners have limited liability.

limited partner: Owner who invests money in the business but does not have any management responsibility or liability for losses beyond the investment.

line of credit: The maximum amount a bank will agree to lend a borrower.

line personnel: Employees who perform functions that contribute directly to the primary goals of the organization.

liquid: How quickly an asset can be turned into cash.

lockout: A drastic negotiating strategy in which the employer locks the premises against the employees.

long-term forecast: A prediction of revenues, costs, and expenses for more than one year, sometimes extending five or ten years into the future.

management: The process used to accomplish organizational goals through planning, organizing, directing, and controlling organizational resources.

management by objectives (MBO): A system of goal setting and implementation that involves a cycle of discussion, review, and evaluation of objectives among top and middle-level managers, supervisors, and employees.

management by walking around: Managers get out of their offices and personally interact with employees and customers.

management development: The process of training and educating employees to become good managers and then developing their managerial skills over time.

managerial accounting: Providing information and analyses to managers within the organization to assist them in decision making.

managing diversity: Building systems and a culture that unite different people in a common pursuit without undermining their diversity.

manufacturing: An important part of production, it means people producing goods using materials, machinery, robots, and computers.

market: People with unsatisfied wants and needs who have both the resources and the willingness to buy.

marketing: The process of determining customer wants and needs and then profitably providing customers with goods and services that meet or exceed their expectations.

marketing boards: Organizations that control the supply or pricing of certain agricultural products in Canada.

marketing concept: A three-part business philosophy: (1) a customer orientation, (2) training of all employees in customer service, and (3) a profit orientation.

marketing intermediaries: Organizations that assist in the movement of goods and services from producer to industrial and consumer users.

marketing mix: The ingredients that go into a marketing program: product, price, place, and promotion.

marketing research: The analysis of markets to determine opportunities and challenges.

market modification: Technique for extending the product life cycle of mature products by finding users in new market segments.

market segmentation: The process of dividing the total market into several groups whose members have similar characteristics.

Maslow's hierarchy of needs: Theory of motivation that places different types of human needs in order of importance, from basic physiological needs to safety, social, and esteem needs, to self-actualization needs.

mass customization: Tailoring products to meet the needs of individual customers; the design of custom-made products and promotions, including advertising.

mass marketing: Developing products and promotions that are designed to please large groups of people.

materials handling: The movement of goods within a warehouse, factory, or store.

materials requirement planning (MRP): A computer-based production and operations management system that uses sales forecasts to make sure needed parts and materials are available at the right place and time.

matrix organization: Organization in which specialists from different parts of the organization are brought together to work on specific projects but still remain part of a line and staff structure.

maturity date: The date on which a borrower must legally repay the bond principal to the bondholder.

mediation: The use of a third party to attempt to bring disputing parties to a resolution by modifying their positions.

mentor: An experienced employee who supervises, coaches, and guides lower-level employees by introducing them to the right people and generally being their organizational sponsor.

mercantilism: The economic principle advocating the selling of more goods to other nations than were bought from them.

merger: Two firms unite to form one company.

message centre software: A new generation of computer programs that uses fax or voice modems to receive, sort, and deliver phone calls, e-mail, and faxes.

middle management: Level of management that includes plant managers and department heads who are responsible for tactical plans.

mission statement: An outline of the fundamental purposes of the organization.

mixed economies: Economies with varying degrees of state ownership or control of the means of production or both.

monetary policy: The Bank of Canada's exercise of control of the supply of money and the level of interest rates in the country.

motivators: Factors that provide satisfaction and motivate people to work.

MNC or TNC (multinational or transnational corporation): An organization that has investments, plants, and sales in many different countries; it has international stock ownership and multinational management.

mutual fund: A fund that buys a variety of securities and then sells units of ownership in the fund to the public.

national debt: The accumulated amount owed by the Canadian government from its past borrowings.

National Policy: Federal government policy imposing high tariffs on imports from the United States to protect Canadian manufacturing.

net income: Revenue minus costs and expenses.

networking: Using communications technology and other means to link organizations and allow them to work together on common objectives; the process of establishing and maintaining contacts with key managers in your own organization and other organizations and using those contacts to weave strong relationships that serve as an informal development system.

network computing system (client/server computing): Computer systems that allow personal computers (clients) to obtain needed information from huge databases controlled by a network server.

niche marketing: The process of finding small but profitable market segments and designing custom-made products for them.

NIMBY: Not in my backyard, meaning that people don't want waste disposal facilities in their town, though they agree that such facilities are needed somewhere.

objectives: Specific, short-term statements detailing how to achieve an organization's goals.

off-the-job training: Training that occurs away from the workplace and consists of internal or external programs to develop any of a variety of skills or to foster personal development.

one-to-one marketing: Developing a unique mix of goods and services for each individual customer.

on-the-job training: Training program in which the employee immediately begins his or her tasks and learns by doing, or watches others for a while and then imitates them, right at the workplace.

open shop: Workplace in which employees are free to join or not join the union and to pay or not pay union dues.

operating budget: The plan of the various costs and expenses needed to operate the business, based on the short-term forecast.

operating expenses: Various expenses incurred in the course of earning revenue.

organic farming: Farming that is done without chemicals.

organizational culture: Widely shared values within an organization that provide coherence and cooperation to achieve common goals.

organizational design: The structuring of workers so that they can best accomplish the firm's goals.

organizing: Management function that involves designing the organizational structure, attracting people to the organization (staffing), and creating conditions and systems that ensure that everyone and everything work together to achieve the objectives of the organization.

other assets: Assets that are not current or fixed. This catchall group includes items such as copyrights and patents, which have no physical form.

outsourcing: Assigning various functions, such as accounting and legal work, to outside organizations.

owners' equity: Owners' investments in the company plus all net accumulated profits.

partnership: A legal form of business with two or more owners.

partnership agreement: Legal document that specifies the rights and responsibilities of each partner.

penetration price strategy: Pricing a product low to attract more customers and discourage competitors.

performance appraisal: An evaluation in which the performance level of employees is measured against established standards to make decisions about promotions, compensation, additional training, or firing.

personal selling: Face-to-face presentation and promotion of products and services, and searching out prospects and providing follow-up service.

PERT (program evaluation and review technique): A method for analyzing the tasks involved in completing a given project, estimating the time needed to complete each task, and identifying the minimum time needed to complete the total project.

physical distribution (logistics): The movement of goods and services from producers to industrial and consumer users.

picketing: The process whereby strikers carrying picket signs walk back and forth across entrances to their places of employment to publicize the strike and discourage or prevent people, vehicles, materials, and products from going in or out.

piggybacking: Shipping the cargo-carrying part of a truck on a railroad car or ship over long distances for greater efficiency.

planning: Management function that involves anticipating future trends and determining the best strategies and tactics to achieve organizational objectives.

pledging: Using accounts receivable, inventory, or other assets as security for a loan.

preferred stock: Stock that gives owners preference over common shareholders in the payment of dividends and in a claim on assets if the business is liquidated; it does not include voting rights.

primary data: Facts and figures not previously published that you have gathered on your own.

principal: The face value of a bond.

principal of motion economy: Theory that every job can be broken down into a series of elementary motions.

private accountants: Employees who carry out managerial and financial accounting functions for their employers.

private brands: Products that carry the name of a distributor or retailer instead of the manufacturer.

private corporation: Corporation that is not allowed to issue stock to the public, so its shares are not listed on stock exchanges and it is limited to 50 or fewer shareholders.

privatization: The process of governments selling crown corporations.

process manufacturing: Production process that physically or chemically changes materials.

producers' cartels: Organizations of commodity-producing countries that are formed to stabilize or increase prices to optimize overall profits in the long run. (An example is OPEC, the Organization of Petroleum Exporting Countries.)

product: Any physical good, service, or idea that satisfies a want or need.

product differentiation: The creation of real and perceived product differences.

production: The creation of goods and services using the factors of production: land, labour, capital, entrepreneurship, and information.

production and operations management: All the activities of managers to create goods and services.

productivity: The total output of goods and services in a given period of time divided by work hours (output per work hour).

product life cycle: A theoretical model of what happens to sales and profits for a product class over time.

product line: A group of products that are physically similar or are intended for a similar market.

product manager: A manager who has direct responsibility for one brand or one product line.

product mix: The combination of product lines offered by a manufacturer.

product modification: Technique used to extend the life cycle of a product by changing the quality, features, packaging, or style to attract new market segments or continued usage by present users.

product screening: A process designed to reduce the number of new-product ideas being worked on at any one time.

program evaluation and review technique (PERT): A method for analyzing the tasks involved in completing a given project, estimating the time needed to complete each task, and identifying the minimum time needed to complete the total project.

promotion: An attempt by marketers to inform people about products to persuade them to participate in an exchange.

promotion mix: The combination of tools an organization uses to promote its products or services.

prospecting: Researching potential buyers and choosing those most likely to buy.

prospectus: A document, which must be prepared by every public company seeking financing through issue of shares or bonds, that gives the public certain information about the company. A prospectus must be approved by the securities commission of the province where these securities will be offered for sale.

public accountants: Independent firms that provide accounting, auditing, and other professional services for clients on a fee basis.

public corporation: Corporation that has the right to issue shares to the public, so its shares may be listed on the stock exchanges.

public domain software: Software that is free for the taking.

publicity: Any information about an individual, a product, or an organization that is distributed to the public through the media and is not paid for, or controlled, by the sponsor.

public relations (PR): Activities designed to give an organization or its products or services a better image among all stakeholders, including existing and potential customers, employers, shareholders, governments, the local community, and the whole country.

pull strategy: Use of promotional tools to motivate consumers to request products from stores.

push strategy: Use of promotional tools to convince wholesalers and retailers to stock and sell merchandise.

push technology: Software that delivers information tailored to a previously defined user profile; it pushes the information to users so that they don't have to pull it out.

quality control: The measurement of products and services against set standards.

ratio analysis: A way to analyze financial statements by comparing results with the previous year's, the budget, and competing firms' results.

recruitment: The set of activities used to obtain a sufficient number of the right people at the right time and to select those who best meet the needs of the organization.

reengineering: The rethinking and radical redesign of organizational processes to achieve dramatic improvements in critical measures of performance.

reinforcement theory: Positive and negative reinforcers will motivate a desired behaviour.

relationship marketing: Establishing and maintaining mutually beneficial exchange relationships with internal and external customers and all the other stakeholders of the organization.

replacement workers: Management's name for strikebreakers.

restructuring: The process of reorganizing the structure of companies to make them more efficient.

retailer: A marketing intermediary that sells to consumers.

retained earnings: Accumulated profits less dividends to shareholders.

reverse discrimination: The unfairness unprotected groups may perceive when protected groups receive preference in hiring and promoting.

robber barons: Capitalists of the nineteenth century whose wealth came in part through shady if not criminal acts.

robot: A computer-controlled machine capable of performing many tasks.

rule of 72: Divide the rate of increase of any activity into 72 to get the number of years it takes for the result of that activity to double.

sales promotion: The promotional tool that stimulates consumer purchasing and dealer interest by means of short-term activities (displays, shows, exhibitions, and contests, and so forth).

scabs: Unions' name for strikebreakers.

scientific management: The study of workers to find the most efficient way of doing things and then teaching people those techniques.

seasonal unemployment: Unemployment that occurs when the demand for labour varies over the year.

secondary data: Already-published research reports from journals, trade associations, government information services, and so forth.

secured bonds: Bonds backed by some tangible asset that is pledged to the bondholder to guarantee payment of principal and interest.

secured loan: Loan backed by something valuable, such as property.

securities commission: The official body set up by a province to regulate its stock exchange and to approve all new issues of securities in that province.

selection: The process of gathering information to decide who should be hired, under legal guidelines, for the best interests of the organization and the individual.

service sector: The sector that produces services, not goods. Examples are banking, insurance, communications, and transportation.

shareware: Software that is copyrighted but distributed to potential customers free of charge.

shopping goods and services: Products that consumers buy only after comparing quality and price from a variety of sellers.

short-term forecast: A prediction of revenues, costs, and expenses for a period of one year.

skimming price strategy: Pricing the product high to make optimum profit while there is little competition.

skunkworks: Highly innovative, fast-moving entrepreneurial units operating at the fringes of a corporation.

small business: Business that is independently owned and operated, not dominant in its field, and meets certain standards of size in terms of employees or annual receipts.

social audit: A systematic evaluation of an organization's progress toward implementing programs that are socially responsible and responsive.

societal orientation: Includes a consumer orientation, but adds programs designed to improve the community, protect the environment, and satisfy other social goals.

sole proprietorship: A business that is owned directly, and usually managed, by one person.

span of control: The number of subordinates a manager supervises.

specialty goods and services: Products that have a special attraction for consumers who are willing to go out of their way to obtain them.

spreadsheet program: The electronic equivalent of an accountant's worksheet, plus such features as mathematical function libraries, statistical data analysis, and charts.

staff personnel: Employees who perform functions that assist line personnel in achieving their goals.

stakeholders: Those people who can affect or are affected by the achievement of an organization's objectives; they include shareholders, employees, customers, suppliers, distributors, competitors, and the general public.

stock certificate: Tangible evidence of stock ownership.

stock exchange: Market through which the securities (shares and bonds) of public companies are traded.

strategic alliances or joint ventures: Arrangements whereby two or more companies cooperate for a special or limited purpose.

strategic (long-range) planning: Process of determining the major goals of the organization and the policies and strategies for obtaining and using resources to achieve those goals.

structural unemployment: Unemployment caused by people losing their jobs because their occupation is no longer part of the main structure of the economy.

supervisory (first-line) management: First level of management above workers; includes people directly responsible for supervising employees and evaluating their daily performance.

supply: The quantity of particular products or services that suppliers are willing to sell at certain prices and at certain locations.

sustainable development: Economic development that meets the needs of the present without endangering the external environment of future generations.

SWOT analysis: An analysis of an organization's strengths, weaknesses, opportunities, and threats.

synthetic system: Production process that either changes raw materials into other products or combines raw materials or parts into finished products.

tactical (short-range) planning: Process of developing detailed, short-term strategies about what is to be done, who is to do it, and how it is to be done.

target marketing: Marketing directed toward those groups (market segments) an organization decides it can serve profitably.

technical skills: Ability to perform tasks of a specific department (such as selling or bookkeeping).

telecommuting: Working from home via computer and modem.

time–motion studies: Studies of the tasks performed to complete a job and the time needed to do each task.

top management: Highest level of management, consisting of the president and other key company executives who develop strategic plans.

total quality management (TQM): Striving for maximum customer satisfaction by ensuring quality from all departments.

trade credit: The practice of buying goods now and paying for them in the future.

trade deficit: Buying more goods from other nations than are sold to them.

trademark: A brand that has been given exclusive legal protection for both the brand name and the pictorial design.

trade protectionism: The use of government regulations to limit the import of goods and services, based on the theory that domestic producers should be protected from competition so that they can survive and grow, producing more jobs.

trade show: An event in which marketers set up displays and potential customers come to see the latest goods and services.

training and development: All attempts to improve productivity by increasing an employee's ability to perform.

TNC or MNC (multinational or transnational corporation): An organization that has investments, plants, and sales in many different countries; it has international stock ownership and multinational management.

union shop: Workplace in which the employer is free to hire anybody, but the recruit must then join the union within a short period, perhaps a month.

unlimited liability: The responsibility of a business owner for all of the debts of the business, making the personal assets of the owner vulnerable to claims against the business.

unsecured bonds: Bonds that are not backed by any collateral.

utility: Value- or want-satisfying ability that intermediaries add to products by making them more useful or accessible to buyers.

value package: Everything that customers may evaluate when deciding to buy something.

value pricing: Offering consumers brand-name goods and services at discount prices.

venture capitalist: Individuals or organizations that invest in new businesses in exchange for partial ownership.

vertical merger: The joining of two firms involved in different stages of related businesses.

vestibule training: Training done in schools where employees are taught on equipment similar to that used on the job.

virtualization: Accessibility through technology that allows business to be conducted independent of location.

virus: A piece of programming code inserted into other programming to cause some unexpected and, for the victim, usually undesirable event.

vision: A sense of why the organization exists and where it's heading.

white-collar crime: A crime, usually theft, committed by an executive or other white-collar office worker.

wholesaler: A marketing intermediary who sells to organizations and individuals, but not to final consumers.

World Bank: An autonomous United Nations agency that borrows money from the more prosperous countries and lends it at favourable rates to less-developed countries to develop their infrastructures.

Credits

Chapter 1

P. 3, Courtesy Robin King; p. 7, Stephen Ward/Canadian Press CP; p. 8, Todd Korol/Canadian Press MACLEANS; p. 9, Louisa Buller/AP; p. 11, Terry Sammon, Air Photo 85; p. 12, Courtesy Corel Corporation; p. 14, Rene Johnston/Canapress Photo Service; p. 17, Photodisc; p. 19, Courtesy of Avid Technology; p. 22, Corel; p. 25, Photodisc; p. 27, Courtesy Gallatin Steel Co. Photo by Rich Nugent.

Chapter 2

P. 35, Bettman; p. 37, Bettman; p. 37, Courtesy Chateau Whistler; p. 39, Jose Goitia/Canadian Press CP; p. 44, Courtesy Ford Motor Company; p. 46, Michael Polselli; p. 50, Photodisc; p. 51, Nick Procaylo/Canadian Press CP.

Chapter 3

P. 59, Courtesy BioChem Pharma Inc.; p. 62, Courtesy Nortel Networks; p. 63, Photodisc; p. 69, Courtesy Coca-Cola Ltd.; p. 69, Courtesy McDonald's; p. 75, Tel Korol/Canapress and MacLean's; p. 79, Richard Sobol Ho/Canapress; p. 80, Photodisc; p. 85, Photodisc.

Chapter 4

P. 93, Courtesy Frank McKenna; p. 96, Courtesy The St. Lawrence Seaway Management Corporation; p. 97, OgilvyOne Worldwide; p. 97, Darren Price; p. 100, Courtesy Department of National Defense; p. 103, Courtesy Algoma Steel; p. 106, W.P. McElligott; p. 107, Photodisc; p. 113, Courtesy of Canadian Egg Marketing Agency.

Chapter 5

P. 127, Courtesy of Jed Goldberg; p. 131, Courtesy Palliser Furniture Ltd.; p. 132, Used with permission of Ben & Jerry's Homemade Holdings, Inc. 1999; p. 133, Fred Chartrand/Canadian Press CP; p. 138, John Lehman/Canadian Press CP; p. 141, Tom Hanson/Canapress; p. 144, Corel; p. 148, Courtesy MacMillan Bloedel Ltd.; p. 149, Ryan Remiorz/Canapress; p. 152, Photodisc; p. 152, Dale Atkins/CP; p. 156, Courtesy International Institute for Sustainable Development.

Chapter 6

P. 167, Courtesy Bombardier Inc.; p. 170, Photodisc; p. 174, Michael Polselli; p. 177, Courtesy NOVA Chemicals Corporation; p. 180, Corel; p. 184, Courtesy Crown Plaza Hotels and Resorts, Edinburgh; p. 188, John Ulan/Canadian Press.

Chapter 7

P. 197, Courtesy Jim Carroll – jcarroll@jimcarroll.com, & www.jimcarroll.ca; p. 199, Copyright © 3M IPC 1999. This material is reproduced by courtesy of 3M. No further reproduction is permitted without 3M's prior written consent; p. 202, Photodisc; p. 204, Nancy Mathis, PhD., P.Eng.; p. 205, Michael Polselli; p. 209, Courtesy Business Development Bank of Canada; p. 213, Michael Polselli; p. 215, Photodisc; p. 218, Photodisc.

Chapter 8

P. 229, Joan C. Tonn/Unwich Management Centre; p. 231, Photodisc; p. 231, Courtesy McGill University; p. 232, Photodisc; p. 234, Photodisc; p. 240, Courtesy Beoing Company; p. 243, Photodisc; p. 244, Barry Gossage/NBA Photos; p. 253, Paul Henry/Canapress Photo Service.

Chapter 9

P. 261, The HP information, logo and copyrighted information contained within this textbook is reproduced with the permission of Hewlett-Packard (Canada) Ltd. Hewlett-Packard expressly reserves its copyright interest in all Hewlett-Packard reproduced material in this textbook and is not to be reproduced without the expressed written consent of Hewlett-Packard (Canada) Ltd.; p. 264, Michael Polselli; p. 265, Courtesy Bombardier Inc.; p. 267, German Information Centre, NYC; p. 270, Photodisc; p. 272, Photodisc; p. 275, Emerito Daluz; p. 280, Bruce Ayres/Tony Stone Images; p. 283, Courtesy Adeo Communications Corporation; p. 286, © 1999 Hertz System, Inc. Hertz is a registered service mark and trademark of Hertz System, Inc.

Chapter 10

P. 297, Courtesy Erik Brinkman; p. 300, Courtesy Nortel Networks; p. 305, Photodisc; p. 307, National Quality Institute, Webmaster Azeem Amir; p. 309, Copyright © Cognos Incorporated. Cognos and Power-House are registered trademarks of Cognos Incorporated in the United States and/or other countries; p. 311, BARBIE and MY DESIGN are trademarks of Mattel, Inc. © 1998 Mattel, Inc. All rights reserved. Used with permission. MY DESIGN Patent Pending; p. 312, Michael Rosenfeld/Tony Stone Images; p. 314, Courtesy of Celestica; p. 317, Courtesy Pintendre Autos, Inc.; p. 323, Courtesy RDS Data Group Inc.

Chapter 11

P. 333, Photodisc; p. 335, Photodisc; p. 337, © DMC Inc.; p. 338, Courtesy Room Linx; p. 340, Photodisc; p. 341, The materials have been reproduced by McGraw-Hill Ryerson Limited with the permission of Cisco Systems, Inc. Copyright © 1999 Cisco Systems, Inc. All Rights Reserved; p. 342, The materials have been reproduced by McGraw-Hill Ryerson Limited with the permission of Cisco Systems, Inc. Copyright © 1999 Cisco Systems, Inc. All Rights Reserved; p. 351, Photodisc.

Chapter 12

P. 361, Courtesy Dr. David S. Weiss; p. 363, John Lehmann/Canadian Press; p. 365, Property of AT&T Archives. Reprinted with permission of AT&T; p. 369, Darren Price; p. 370, The HP information, logo and copyrighted information contained within this textbook is reproduced with the permission of Hewlett-Packard (Canada) Ltd. Hewlett-Packard expressly reserves its copyright interest in all Hewlett-Packard reproduced material in this textbook and is not to be reproduced wihout the expressed written consent of Hewlett-Packard (Canada) Ltd.; p. 374, Ray Dykes, PR Plus Communications; p. 374, Courtesy Harley-Davidson Inc.; p. 377, Ron Turenne/NBA Photos; p. 382, Courtesy of J. Walter Thompson; p. 387, Darren Price.

Chapter 13

P. 395, Courtesy MacMillan Bloedel Ltd.; p. 398, Courtesy BC TEL. TELUS Learning Services; p. 402, Courtesy Jobs Canada; p. 406, Phill Snel/Canapress; p. 407, Michael Rosenfeld/Tony Stone Images; p. 407, Courtesy Video Arts; p. 409, Photodisc; p. 411, Photodisc; p. 417, Canapress; p. 418, Courtesy Royal Bank; p. 420, Photodisc.

Chapter 14

P. 443, Courtesy Alan B. Gold; p. 445, David Hartman, Photography Toronto; p. 447, Courtesy of Rockwell; p. 453, Ryan Remiorz/Canadian Press CP; p. 455, Ryan Remiorz/Canadian Press CP; p. 458, Steve McKinley/Canapress; p. 459, Paul Chaisson/Canadian Press CP; p. 463, Courtesy Marriott International Inc.

Chapter 15

P. 471, Courtesy Raman Agarwal; p. 473, © Mastermind Educational Technologies Inc.; p. 475, Courtesy of Lifestyles; p. 476, Courtesy In-Touch Survey Systems; p. 477, Reprinted with the permission of the Canadian Cancer Society; p. 480, Courtesy Troubadour Records Ltd.; p. 482, Corel.

Chapter 16

P. 501, Courtesy Silanis Technologies Inc.; p. 504, Courtesy mbanx; p. 508, Emerito Daluz; p. 510, Courtesy of Ford Motor Corporation; p. 511, Darren Price; p. 512, David Lucas/Canadian Press CP; p. 517, Canadian Design Icons Exhibition; p. 521, Courtesy Jaguar Cars.

Chapter 17

P. 531, Courtesy Emerson Segura; p. 537, Courtesy of www.indigo.ca; p. 540, The HP information, logo and copyrighted information contained within this textbook is reproduced with the permission of Hewlett-Packard (Canada) Ltd. Hewlett-Packard expressly reserves its copyright interest in all Hewlett-Packard reproduced material in this textbook and is not to be reproduced without the expressed written consent of Hewlett-Packard (Canada) Ltd.; p. 541, © 1999 Starbucks Coffee Company. All rights reserved; p. 543, Courtesy Department of Economic Development and Tourism; p. 546, TD Waterhouse Investor Services (Canada) Inc. ("TD Waterhouse") is a subsidiary of TD Waterhouse Group, Inc., a subsidiary of TD Bank. TD Waterhouse-Member CIPF; p. 547, Courtesy Jaguar Cars; p. 551, Courtesy UPS; p. 553, Courtesy Au Coton; p. 558, Darren Price; p. 560, Michael Polselli; p. 563, Darren Price.

Chapter 18

P. 571, Courtesy of Richter & Usher; p. 576, Courtesy Scotiabank; p. 578, Photodisc; p. 579, Darren Price; p. 584, Photodisc; p. 588, Courtesy Home Depot; p. 590, Courtesy of Peachtree Software Inc.; p. 591, Reproduced with permission of the Canadian Institutue of Chartered Accountants.

Chapter 19

P. 605, Courtesy Greig Clark; p. 608, Phill Snel/Canapress; p. 611, Photodisc; p. 612, Nick Procaylo/Canadian Press CP; p. 616, Michael Polselli; p. 620, Courtesy Business Development Bank of Canada; p. 625, Courtesy Dominion Bond Rating Service; p. 632, E*Trade Canada is a trademark of E*Trade Securities, Inc. and is used with their permission.

Name and Organization Index

Subject Index

URL Index